# Students with Emotional and Behavioral Disorders

## An Introduction for Teachers and Other Helping Professionals

SECOND EDITION

**Douglas Cullinan**
North Carolina State University

Upper Saddle River, New Jersey
Columbus, Ohio

**Library of Congress Cataloging in Publication Data**

Cullinan, Douglas.
    Students with emotional and behavioral disorder / Douglas Cullinan.
      p. cm.
    Includes bibilographical references (p. ) and indexes.
    ISBN 0-13-118182-3
    1. Problem children—Education. 2. Mentally ill children—Education. 3. Emotional problems of children. 4. Behavior disorders in children. I. Title

LC4801.C78 2007
371.94—dc21
                                                        2006036232

**Vice President and Executive Publisher:** Jeffery W. Johnston
**Senior Editor:** Ann Castel Davis
**Editorial Assistant:** Penny Burleson
**Production Editor:** Sheryl Glicker Langner
**Production Coordination:** GGS Book Services
**Design Coordinator:** Diane C. Lorenzo
**Cover Design:** Terry Rohrbach
**Cover Image:** Artville Royalty Free CD
**Photo Coordinator:** Lori Whitley
**Production Manager:** Laura Messerly
**Director of Marketing:** David Gesell
**Marketing Manager:** Autumn Purdy
**Marketing Coordinator:** Brian Mounts

**Photo Credits:** Tom Watson/Merrill, p. 2; Richard Hutchings/PhotoEdit, Inc., pp. 11, 106; Major Morris/PH College, p. 24; Orlando/Getty Images, Inc.–Hulton Archive Photos, p. 34; Lambert/Getty Images, Inc.–Hulton Archive Photos, p. 46; Barbara Schwartz/Merrill, pp. 54, 62; Scott Cunningham/Merrill, pp. 66, 160, 328, 334, 356, 383; Larry Hamill/Merrill, p. 85; Shirley Zeiberg/PH College, p. 128; Michael Provest/Silver Burdett Ginn, p. 135; © Royalty-Free/Corbis, p. 148; Irene Springer/PH College, p. 170; Howard Grey/Getty Images, Inc.–Stone Allstock, p. 184; PH College, p. 199; © David Katzenstein/Corbis, p. 212; Teri Stratford/PH College, p. 218; Valerie Schultz/Merrill, p. 223; Anne Vega/Merrill, pp. 230, 284; Anthony Magnacca/Merrill, pp. 258, 277, 393; Eugene Gordon/PH College, p. 304; Charles Gatewood/PH College, p. 340; David Young-Wolff/PhotoEdit, Inc., p. 350; Marc Anderson/PH College, p. 374; Richard Hutchings/Photo Researchers, Inc., p. 408; Spencer Grant/PhotoEdit, Inc., p. 413; Laima E. Druskis Photography, p. 428

**Copyright © 2007, 2002 by Pearson Education, Inc., Upper Saddle River, New Jersey 07458.**
Pearson Prentice Hall. All rights reserved. Printed in the United States of America. This publication is protected by Copyright and permission should be obtained from the publisher prior to any prohibited reproduction, storage in a retrieval system, or transmission in any form or by any means, electronic, mechanical, photocopying, recording, or likewise. For information regarding permission(s), write to: Rights and Permissions Department.

**Pearson Prentice Hall**™ is a trademark of Pearson Education, Inc.
**Pearson**® is a registered trademark of Pearson plc
**Prentice Hall**® is a registered trademark of Pearson Education, Inc.
**Merrill**® is a registered trademark of Pearson Education, Inc.

Pearson Education Ltd.                                   Pearson Education Australia Pty. Limited
Pearson Education Singapore Pte. Ltd.            Pearson Education North Asia Ltd.
Pearson Education Canada, Ltd.                   Pearson Educación de Mexico, S.A. de C.V.
Pearson Education–Japan                           Pearson Education Malaysia Pte. Ltd.

ISBN: 0-13-118182-3

# *Preface*

In recent years, remarkable changes have occurred in professional perspectives on emotional and behavior disorders of children and adolescents. Advances in measurement and classification have pointed to needed modifications in our views of these disorders. Discoveries about biological and psychosocial influences on child development have required us to adjust existing theories that seek to explain how emotions, behaviors, and cognitions develop normally or become deviant. As professionals in various disciplines have applied, evaluated, and disseminated a range of new practices and programs, they have expanded intervention options in schools and other places of service. In addition, there are changes that have affected education and/or other disciplines in general, and including education of children and adolescents with emotional and behavior disorders. Examples include greater emphasis on teaching and assessing reading, mathematics, and other student academic performance, larger numbers of young people who speak little or no English, and increased stress on scientific evidence for the value of interventions.

The role of educators in serving students with emotional and behavior disorders has been prominent for several decades, but it must be strengthened, expanded, and linked with other service efforts for these young people. To achieve this, educators must remain informed about significant changes. To provide up-to-date, interesting, and comprehensive introductory coverage of such changes is a main purpose of this text.

*Students with Emotional and Behavior Disorders* is intended as the text for a course that introduces key concepts of emotional and behavior disorders of children and adolescents, including students in preschool, elementary, and secondary school situations. Ideas from special education, school and clinical psychology, counseling, and several other relevant fields are presented and integrated. At the same time, the material in this book does not assume that the reader is already well acquainted with those fields.

Coverage is broad in scope, in order to present a substantial proportion of the many topics that contribute to a proper context for understanding emotional and behavior disorders of students. Therefore this text addresses a wide variety of concepts that are essential in undergraduate and graduate courses that prepare knowledgeable teachers, as well as school psychologists, counselors, and other helping professionals. However, I have been careful to adjust topic detail so that depth of coverage is appropriate for an introduction to the field. Extensive references and other resources are provided to enable and motivate students to further explore topics of special interest to them.

Chapters 1 and 2 (Part I) provide context for conceptualizing and studying emotional and behavior disorders of children. Chapter 1 introduces some of the variety of forms that emotional and behavior disorders can take, along with various definitions and their implications. Also addressed are key social contexts of emotional and behavior problems of young people. Chapter 2 considers historical developments that continue to affect today's ideas about, and efforts to serve, students with emotional and behavior disorders.

Part II addresses measurement and characteristics of emotional and behavior disorders of students. Chapter 3 examines methods and purposes of assessing problems of emotion, behavior, and cognition, as well as ways to classify the wide variety of such problems. Assessment and classification are prerequisites for understanding the major patterns of emotional and behavior disorders of students, detailed in Chapter 4. Chapter 5 presents some extreme forms of emotional and behavior disorders that are only partially encompassed by the patterns covered in Chapter 4.

Part III (Chapters 6–10) discusses causes of emotional and behavior disorders of children from several viewpoints. Chapter 6 examines the concepts of causation and risk, then looks at biological, psychological, and sociocultural influences that seem to create and sustain emotional and behavior disorders. These influences are given different emphases in the various models (theories about causes and interventions) of emotional and behavior disorders of children. Chapters 7, 8, and 9 are concerned, respectively, with psychodynamic, behavioral, and cognitive models, while Chapter 10 briefly addresses sociological, ecological, and values-based/spiritual models.

Chapters 11 and 12 (Part IV) describe services and interventions for students with emotional and behavior disorders that are delivered in a variety of settings. Chapter 11 discusses interventions designed to prevent and improve emotional and behavior disorders of students in school environments. Chapter 12 describes interventions delivered by child service systems other than education.

## Developmental Perspective

The developmental psychopathology perspective examines emotional and behavior disorders in relation to biological, psychological, social, and cultural processes, from conception to maturity. This perspective is presented in brief, simplified form herein. It helps the reader to contextualize young people's adaptive and maladaptive emotions, behaviors, and cognitions in terms of age and other indicators of developmental level.

## Focus on Prevention

Long a significant concept in children's emotional and behavior disorders, prevention has rapidly expanded in importance and interest in the 21st century. Several chapters consider prevention and related concepts such as risk, along with their effects on intervention efforts in school and other systems of child service.

## Tools for Learning

Terms listed in each chapter briefly identify concepts that the reader is encouraged to keep in mind while reading, and to define once the chapter is completed. Chapter objectives and summaries are likewise designed to help the reader focus on key points. Chapters 7–10 contain summary tables of the theoretical models, including a concise description of theory, who receives and delivers intervention, the intervention's rationale, selected strategies, and other related points. Many displays (figures and tables) present listings, graphs, and diagrams that clarify explanations found in the text. The use of vignettes and photographs keeps the reader focused on real-life challenges that confront children and adolescents with emotional and behavior disorders and those who educate them.

## UP-TO-DATE INFORMATION

This text presents current information, integrated with traditional perspectives and issues that continue to challenge the field. Most references first appeared after 2000. In each chapter, recent information and perspectives have been retrieved from professional journals, government reports, and other appropriate sources. Some issues in our field are variations on traditional controversies about human nature (such as the relative importance of biological and cultural influences on children's functioning, or conflicts between what may be best for the individual and what may be best for the group). Recent developments in societal, scientific, educational, legal, and other realms can refresh these controversies and underscore their relevance for teaching students with emotional and behavior disorders.

Faculty members using this text in their courses have access to an instructor's manual, which includes (1) ideas and materials for taking advantage of the book's features to enhance instructional effectiveness, (2) suggested class meeting activities and assignments, and (3) sample test items. Contact your Merrill Prentice Hall representative or call Faculty Services at 1-800-526-0485 to request your complimentary copy.

Earlier versions of this book have been used as a text in courses I teach about students with emotional and behavior disorders. Present and future special educators, regular educators, school psychologists, counselors, and other professionals have given me ideas on content, coverage, and enrichment activities, as well as critiques. Likewise, faculty members from other universities who adopted the first edition generously offered their suggestions for improvement. I appreciate all their feedback, and I am eager to receive additional comments on this second edition (Douglas_Cullinan@ncsu.edu).

## ACKNOWLEDGMENTS

This book is dedicated to my Mom and Pop, Jean Ford Cullinan and Douglas R. Cullinan, as a small acknowledgment of their lifelong encouragement and support. I appreciate the expertise and patience of Allyson Sharp and the editorial staff at Merrill/Prentice Hall.

Thank you to the following reviewers for their thoughtful comments: Amelia Blyden, The College of New Jersey; E. Paula Crowley, Illinois State University; Janice A. Grskovic, Indiana University Northwest; Elizabeth D. Heins, Stetson University; Martha J. Meyer, Butler University; and Ruth Nash Thompson, Edinboro University of Pennsylvania.

# *Discover the Merrill Resources for Special Education Website*

Technology is a constantly growing and changing aspect of our field that is creating a need for new content and resources. To address this emerging need, Merrill Education has developed an online learning environment for students, teachers, and professors alike to complement our products—the *Merrill Resources for Special Education* Website. This content-rich website provides additional resources specific to this book's topic and will help you—professors, classroom teachers, and students—augment your teaching, learning, and professional development.

Our goal with this initiative is to build on and enhance what our products already offer. For this reason, the content for our user-friendly website is organized by topic and provides teachers, professors, and students with a variety of meaningful resources all in one location. With this website, we bring together the best of what Merrill has to offer: text resources, video clips, web links, tutorials, and a wide variety of information on topics of interest to general and special educators alike. Rich content, applications, and competencies further enhance the learning process.

The *Merrill Resources for Special Education* Website includes:

- Video clips specific to each topic, with questions to help you evaluate the content and make crucial theory-to-practice connections.
- Thought-provoking critical analysis questions that students can answer and turn in for evaluation or that can serve as basis for class discussions and lectures.
- Access to a wide variety of resources related to classroom strategies and methods, including lesson planning and classroom management.
- Information on all the most current relevant topics related to special and general education, including CEC and Praxis™ standards, IEPs, portfolios, and professional development.
- Extensive web resources and overviews on each topic addressed on the website.
- A search feature to help access specific information quickly.

To take advantage of these and other resources, please visit the *Merrill Resources for Special Education* Website at
**http://www.prenhall.com/cullinan**

# Teacher Preparation Classroom

See a demo at
**www.prenhall.com/teacherprep/demo**

## Your Class. Their Careers. Our Future. Will your students be prepared?

We invite you to explore our new, innovative and engaging website and all that it has to offer you, your course, and tomorrow's educators! Organized around the major courses pre-service teachers take, the Teacher Preparation site provides media, student/teacher artifacts, strategies, research articles, and other resources to equip your students with the quality tools needed to excel in their courses and prepare them for their first classroom.

This ultimate on-line education resource is available at no cost, when packaged with a Merrill text, and will provide you and your students access to:

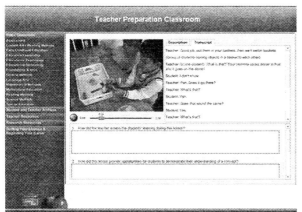

**Online Video Library.** More than 150 video clips—each tied to a course topic and framed by learning goals and Praxis-type questions—capture real teachers and students working in real classrooms, as well as in-depth interviews with both students and educators.

**Student and Teacher Artifacts.** More than 200 student and teacher classroom artifacts—each tied to a course topic and framed by learning goals and application questions—provide a wealth of materials and experiences to help make your study to become a professional teacher more concrete and hands-on.

**Research Articles.** Over 500 articles from ASCD's renowned journal *Educational Leadership*. The site also includes Research Navigator, a searchable database of additional educational journals.

**Teaching Strategies.** Over 500 strategies and lesson plans for you to use when you become a practicing professional.

**Licensure and Career Tools.** Resources devoted to helping you pass your licensure exam; learn standards, law, and public policies; plan a teaching portfolio; and succeed in your first year of teaching.

---

**How to ORDER *Teacher Prep* for you and your students:**

For students to receive a *Teacher Prep* Access Code with this text, instructors **must** provide a special value pack ISBN number on their textbook order form. To receive this special ISBN, please email **Merrill.marketing @ pearsoned.com** and provide the following information:

- Name and Affiliation
- Author/Title/Edition of Merrill text

Upon ordering *Teacher Prep* for their students, instructors will be given a lifetime *Teacher Prep* Access Code.

# Brief Contents

## Part I: Social, Legal, and Historical Context  1

Chapter 1  Emotional and Behavior Disorder in Society and School  2
Chapter 2  Roots of Current Perspectives  34

## Part II: Assessment and Characteristics  61

Chapter 3  Assessment and Classification  62
Chapter 4  Patterns of Emotional and Behavior Disorder  106
Chapter 5  Extreme Emotional and Behavior Disorder  148

## Part III: Causes and Models  183

Chapter 6  Biological and Psychosocial Influences  184
Chapter 7  Psychodynamic Model  218
Chapter 8  Behavioral Model  258
Chapter 9  Cognitive Model  304
Chapter 10  Sociological, Ecological, and Values-Based/Spiritual Models  340

## Part IV: Prevention and Intervention  373

Chapter 11  Intervention in the Education System  374
Chapter 12  Intervention in Other Systems  408

# Contents

## PART I: Social, Legal, and Historical Context     1

**CHAPTER 1**    **Emotional and Behavior Disorder in Society and School**    2
Needed: Resourceful and Knowledgeable Teachers    5
Defining E&B Disorder    6
    *Authoritative Definitions*    7
    *Administrative Definitions*    7
    *Some Common Ground*    10
Prevalence    13
    *Prevalence of Mental Disorders*    14
    *Prevalence of ED*    14
Why Serve These Children?    17
    *To Help the Children*    18
    *To Help Society*    19
    *To Meet Lawful Obligations*    29
Who Serves These Children?    29
Responding to the Challenge    30
Chapter Summary    30

**CHAPTER 2**    **Roots of Current Perspectives**    34
Before the Twentieth Century    36
    *Prehistoric Viewpoints*    36
    *Early Western Civilization*    36
    *The Middle Ages*    37
    *Renaissance Thinking*    38
    *The Late 18th and 19th Centuries*    39
The 20th Century and Beyond    41
    *Scientific Study of Children*    41
    *Child Mental Health*    44
    *The Profession of Special Education*    45
    *Legal Developments*    46
    *Criticism of Society's Responses to Children with E&B Disorder*    48
Psychological Models    52
    *Psychodynamic Model*    52
    *Behavioral Model*    55
Chapter Summary    58

## PART II: ASSESSMENT AND CHARACTERISTICS    61

**CHAPTER 3    Assessment and Classification    62**
Basic Concepts of Measurement    64
   *Operational Definitions*    64
   *Reliability*    65
   *Validity*    65
   *Norms*    66
   *Measurement and the Practice of Special Education*    67
Measurement Methods    67
   *Reported Functioning*    68
   *Actual Functioning*    74
   *Multifaceted Measurement Systems*    78
   *Measurement of Environments*    80
Purposes of Assessment    82
   *Selecting Candidates*    82
   *Deciding Eligibility for ED*    84
   *Determining Services*    86
   *Monitoring Outcomes*    87
   *Program Evaluation and Research*    91
Classification    91
   *Purposes of Classification*    93
   *Existing Classification Systems*    94
   *Evaluating Classification*    100
Chapter Summary    103

**CHAPTER 4    Patterns of Emotional and Behavior Disorder    106**
Determining Patterns    107
Key Information    109
   *Description*    109
   *Relation of Classification and Definition*    109
   *Measurement*    110
   *Prevalence*    110
   *Course*    111
   *Other Considerations*    112
Patterns of E&B Disorder    112
   *Aggression*    112
   *Anxiety*    116
   *Depression*    121
   *Impulsiveness*    124
   *Relationship Problem*    128
Linkages Between and Among Patterns of E&B Disorder    131
Connected Problems    133
   *Law-Breaking Behavior*    133
   *Learning Difficulty*    137

  *Substance Misuse*    138
  *Suicidality*    141
 Chapter Summary    144

**CHAPTER 5**    **Extreme Emotional and Behavior Disorder**    **148**
 Background    150
  *One-Disorder Perspectives*    151
  *Two-Disorder Perspective*    151
  *Children's Extreme E&B Disorder*    152
  *Extreme E&B Disorder and Education*    152
 Key Information    153
 Mood Disorders    153
  *Description*    153
  *Relation to Classification and Definition*    157
  *Prevalence*    157
  *Course*    158
  *Interventions*    159
 Psychotic Disorders    161
  *Description*    161
  *Relation to Classification and Definition*    169
  *Prevalence*    169
  *Course*    169
  *Interventions*    171
 Pervasive Developmental Disorders    171
  *Description*    171
 Observations on Extreme E&B Disorder    177
  *Classification Uncertainty*    177
  *Education*    177
  *Modifying the Prognosis*    179
 Chapter Summary    179

## PART III: CAUSES AND MODELS    183

**CHAPTER 6**    **Biological and Psychosocial Influences**    **184**
 Some Basic Concepts in Child Development    185
  *Developmental Pathways*    186
  *Risk Factors*    187
  *Protective Factors*    188
 Biological Influences    188
  *The Brain*    189
  *Brain Disorder and its Relation to E&B Disorder*    190
  *Causes of Brain Disorder*    193
 Psychosocial Influences    201
  *Family Socialization*    201

*Beyond the Family* 208
*Stress* 211
Interaction of Biological and Psychological Influences 212
*Diathesis-Stress* 212
*Temperament* 213
Comment on Biological and Psychosocial Influences 214
Chapter Summary 215

**CHAPTER 7  Psychodynamic Model  218**
Psychoanalysis 219
*Theory* 219
*Psychodynamic Intervention* 226
Psychodynamic Approaches for School 228
*Social Discipline Approach* 228
*Person-Centered Approach* 231
*Reality Therapy Approach* 237
*Psychoeducational Approach* 242
*Psychodynamic Programs and Curricula* 252
Chapter Summary 256

**CHAPTER 8  Behavioral Model  258**
Behavioral Theory 261
*Respondents* 261
*Operants* 262
Behavioral Interventions 271
*Applied Behavior Analysis* 271
*Behavior Modification* 274
*Package Interventions* 288
Behavior Modification Programs 296
*Regular Education* 296
Chapter Summary 301

**CHAPTER 9  Cognitive Model  304**
Modeling and Social Cognitive Theory 307
*Modeling* 307
*From Modeling to Social Cognitive Theory* 309
*Social Cognitive Theory and E&B Disorder* 310
*Other Cognitive Explanations of E&B Disorder* 311
Cognitive Intervention 316
*Modeling* 316
*Intervention for Cognitive Deficits* 316
*Interventions for Cognitive Distortions* 327
*Cognitive Interventions for Particular E&B Disorders* 332

*Separate School Program: Aggression Replacement Training* 335
*Comment on Cognitive Intervention* 337
Chapter Summary 337

**CHAPTER 10 Sociological, Ecological, and Values-Based/Spiritual Models 340**
Sociological Perspective 341
*Theory* 341
*Intervention* 346
Ecological Perspective 349
*Theory* 349
*Assessment and Intervention* 351
Values and Spiritual Perspectives 358
*Teaching Morality, Character, and Values* 359
Chapter Summary 369

# PART IV PREVENTION AND INTERVENTION 373

**CHAPTER 11 Intervention in the Education System 374**
Forms of Prevention 377
*Universal Prevention* 380
*Selective Prevention* 386
*Indicated Prevention* 388
*Comment on Prevention* 394
Intervention 395
*Regular Class* 397
*Resource Room* 398
*Separate Classroom* 398
*More Restrictive Education Settings* 404
Chapter Summary 405

**CHAPTER 12 Intervention in Other Service Systems 408**
Prevention 410
Mental Health System 412
*Outpatient Treatment* 412
*Day Treatment* 413
*Residential Settings* 414
*Psychotropic Drug Therapy* 416
Child and Family Welfare System 422
Juvenile Justice System 425
*Juvenile Justice Process* 425
*Diversion* 426

*Residential Placement*   427
*Delinquency and E&B Disorder*   428
New Directions in Intervention Systems   428
*Need for Reform*   428
*System of Care*   429
*Other Reforms in Service to Children with E&B Disorder*   437
Chapter Summary   439

**References   443**

**Name Index   481**

**Subject Index   495**

Note: Every effort has been made to provide accurate and current Internet information in this book. However, the Internet and information posted on it are constantly changing, and it is inevitable that some of the Internet addresses listed in this textbook will change.

PART I

# Social, Legal, and Historical Context

CHAPTER 1  *Emotional and Behavior Disorder in Society and School*

CHAPTER 2  *Roots of Current Perspectives*

Chapter **One**

# *Emotional and Behavior Disorder in Society and School*

## CHAPTER OBJECTIVES

**After reading this chapter, you should be able to:**
- State the purposes of authoritative and administrative definitions.
- List the five characteristics of emotional disturbance found in the federal definition.
- Describe two ways in which children's functioning is impaired by emotional and behavior disorders.
- State the percent prevalence of emotional disturbance.
- Explain why the Other Health Impairments category is of special interest.
- Identify the education environment that serves the largest percentage of students with emotional disturbance.

## CAN YOU DEFINE THESE 10 TERMS?

administrative definition of E&B disorder
emotional disturbance (ED)
National Mental Health and Special Education Coalition
mental disorder
prevalence
Other Health Impairments (OHI)
rule of one third
continuum of education environments
regular class education environment
Individuals With Disabilities Education Improvement Act (IDEA)

When children and adolescents behave in ways that create significant discomforts or hindrances for themselves or other people, they may be experiencing an emotional and behavior disorder (E&B disorder). This term, like many others that are used to describe such problems, is not very specific. Many different emotions, behaviors, and thoughts can create discomforts and hindrances of varying severity. Young people with E&B disorder can be disruptive, unhappy, distracted, violent, self-doubting, disorganized, dependent, antisocial, fearful, or destructive, and they may show various other problems. Consider the situations of Robert, Vince, Shaune, and Jeaneen in Display 1-1; they have little in common except that each may be experiencing an E&B disorder.

A large proportion of the children and adolescents with E&B disorders attend school. The quality of any student's schooling can strongly influence his or her well-being in the present and future; for children with an E&B disorder, educational

**Display 1-1** Sample students with E&B disorders

> The psychologist described Robert as intelligent and sensitive, but acting out his anxieties about his place in the family; the neurologist diagnosed minimal brain dysfunction. Many of his peers and teachers cannot help but recognize Robert as a nuisance. He often fails to pay attention to his third-grade teacher or work on his assignments. He remains seated no more than 10 minutes at a time, often less, and disturbs the class by inappropriate talking. When the teacher attempts to correct him or penalize him for breaking the rules, Robert's response is often to cry, yell at the teacher, or verbally and physically attack a classmate immediately or soon thereafter. He has been suspended twice in the first 2 months of school, and a student services team has begun to consider what steps to take.
>
> Tall, thin 12-year-old Vince is no pleasure to teach, even though he is proficient in his academic work, obeys the teacher, and shows considerable drawing and painting skill. However, the teacher agrees with the boy's parents that the content of much of his art is disturbingly gory: skillfully drawn bloody attacks, injuries, and dismemberments. Vince is a perfectionist. Often after a minor mistake in his assignments or artwork, he rips or balls up his paper; sometimes this is accompanied by a raging tantrum. Vince is terrified of dogs, pictures of dogs, and small animals. He refuses to go near or even look at the hamsters being raised in a cage by his classmates. Vince often cries for no apparent reason; picks, chews at, and writes on his skin; and talks about his sleepiness, stomachaches, and "growing pains."
>
> Shaune is a 16-year-old on probation after receiving 3 months of detention and counseling, having admitted to juvenile court authorities that he beat and robbed a teacher as she walked to her car one evening. Shaune attends a different school as a condition of probation, and his academic functioning is average. Shaune's defiance, aggression, destructiveness, and poor school attendance have been known to school, legal, and mental health agencies since he was about 8 years old. He has set fires in the school, community, and home. Shaune has been in special classes, a special day school, and a residential treatment center. His mother has a history of alcohol abuse and depression, and she has never been able to provide for or control her children adequately. She says that Shaune's father is in prison for robbery.
>
> Jeaneen, the 7-year-old foster daughter and only child of a professional couple, is highly disruptive in her first-grade class. She does not usually follow the teacher's instructions, and some of her most common statements are "No," "Leave me alone," "'Cause I don't wanna," and some obscenities. Jeaneen has no friends; usually she does not even get along with peers in group activities in the classroom or elsewhere at school. She sometimes pushes or hits other students and steals things from them. In meetings with the teacher and other school staff, her parents acknowledge that the pattern is much the same at home. Jeaneen has been prescribed a behavior-controlling drug, and the family is seeing a psychotherapist. Within the past 2 months, Jeaneen has broken a car window near home and used a screwdriver to mar several thousand dollars' worth of furnishings in her home.

experiences may be particularly crucial. E&B disorders can be aggravated or perpetuated by what a teacher does or fails to do. On the other hand, fortunately, educators can play a key role—sometimes, *the* key role—in reducing or eliminating a student's E&B disorder.

## NEEDED: RESOURCEFUL AND KNOWLEDGEABLE TEACHERS

The challenge of providing appropriate, effective education to these students can best be met by resourceful and knowledgeable teachers. Resourceful teachers of students with E&B disorder possess a range of teaching and other skills. They are open to working with others and confident about their own skills and decisions. Resourceful teachers carefully consider the ideas of parents, teaching colleagues, counselors, psychologists, and other support personnel, as well as authorities such as course instructors and textbook authors. At the same time, resourceful teachers recognize that they are ultimately responsible for implementing educational practices skillfully and effectively. After selecting particular intervention practices, resourceful teachers persevere until either desired results occur or it becomes apparent that different practices are needed.

To maximize the value of resourcefulness, the teacher must be knowledgeable about E&B disorder and intervention options that can help students with E&B disorder (Guetzloe, 2004). This knowledge arises from diverse sources, including education, psychology, medicine, and other helping professions. Education for students with E&B disorder also continues to be shaped by personal and cultural influences such as philosophy, science, religion, law, and politics, which have contributed to a variety of professional and informal viewpoints on E&B disorder.

One consequence of this variety is that many of the important questions about E&B disorder have several answers, and some of these answers conflict with one another. Such conflict is good, because when different viewpoints provide conflicting answers to a particular question, we may be able to devise a scientific test to determine which answer best matches observed facts. On the other hand, different viewpoints sometimes disagree as to what the important *questions* are. That kind of disagreement among viewpoints makes it difficult to devise research that might produce results that support one hypothesis, theory, or viewpoint over another.

For example, consider Vince: (1) Do his perfectionism and physical complaints reflect subtle brain chemistry abnormalities? (2) Do his bloody art and skin defacements betray a deep, unrecognized motivation to hurt, as he must have been hurt recently or early in life? (3) The boy's teacher and classmates cannot help but pay attention to his unusual artwork and complaints and usually give in to his strongest tantrums; do their attention and giving in unintentionally support Vince's maladaptive actions? (4) Are his teachers, fellow students, and other people in different social situations so intolerant of differences in behavior and personal characteristics that they emphasize and magnify Vince's? Are they making him the scapegoat for problems that arise, and leaving him little choice but to accept the role of "outsider" and behave ever more deviantly? Are there other explanations for Vince's situation?

Display 1-2 lists some questions about E&B disorder of children and adolescents. There are others, and I invite you to strengthen this list by adding additional interesting questions.

To address some of the important questions about young people with E&B disorder, this book presents several viewpoints, explores differences among the viewpoints, and considers implications of these differences. Such an approach generally does not offer

**Display 1-2** Questions about E&B disorder of children and adolescents

- How can we define E&B disorder of children and adolescents?
- How can we discriminate E&B disorder from everyday emotional and behavior problems?
- How widespread is E&B disorder among children and adolescents?
- How can we assess emotional, behavior, and other relevant problems of students?
- Should we be talking about "E&B disorders" rather than "E&B disorder"? That is, are there different kinds of E&B disorder?
- Is E&B disorder caused by biological factors, such as heredity or brain functioning? By psychological factors, such as interactions with parents or other adults and children? By sociological factors, such as the neighborhood where one lives or race-ethnic discrimination?
- Is E&B disorder linked to alarming or tragic personal experiences of children, such as suicide, substance abuse, school violence, and ineffective education? To other disturbing aspects of society, such as poverty, explicitly violent or sexual entertainment, corruption among the powerful, spiritual disconnection, or child abuse?
- If biological, psychological, sociological, and other factors do cause E&B disorder, how does this happen? What are some theories or models of E&B disorder of children, which factors does each model emphasize, and how are the factors said to operate to cause E&B disorder?
- What implications for school and other intervention are provided by psychodynamic, behavioral, cognitive, sociological, and other models of E&B disorder of children?
- What can be done in schools and other child intervention systems to prevent E&B disorder or reduce its unfortunate outcomes?

simple answers to complex questions and issues, but it can help the reader expand her or his knowledge. Just as important, exploring background issues, complications, and divergent ideas in this field, including the many yet-unsolved puzzles, is a big part of the appeal of studying E&B disorder of children and adolescents.

## Defining E&B Disorder

Who are children and adolescents with E&B disorder? Part of the answer lies in how E&B disorder is defined. It may be surprising to learn that experts disagree about something so fundamental as how to define the phenomenon that we are trying to understand and improve. Even though examining definitions is frustrating, it is a good way to begin studying E&B disorder because doing so illustrates how different perspectives on a significant question can yield different answers. Clearly, definitions are important in both theory and practice.

For one thing, a definition often reflects how an expert, professional group, or government agency views E&B disorder. Therefore, definitions may influence how a special educational program is communicated to the students, parents, school district authorities, the community asked to support the program, and other interested people.

Second, many definitions describe which students are eligible to receive certain services. As a result, definitions can be an important basis for identifying individual students with E&B disorder, as well as counting the number or proportion of students with E&B disorder in a school district, state, or nation. Of course, financial, personnel, and other support for serving children with E&B disorder are based in part on such data.

Support for services is only one kind of decision by legislators, administrators, and advocacy groups that may be shaped by the prevailing definition of E&B disorder. Consequently, a definition may affect activities as diverse as how teachers are prepared, how local school programs provide services, and how intervention effectiveness is evaluated.

In addition, definitions are critical in the continuing effort to understand E&B disorder through scientific research. For example, communication of potentially important study findings among researchers requires a definition of E&B disorder that is "reliable" (has the same meaning for all; see Chapter 3). An unreliable definition of E&B disorder makes it uncertain whether findings from a particular study also apply to other children and adolescents with E&B disorder.

## Authoritative Definitions

One kind of definition is an authoritative definition—one that reflects the professional training, practical experience, and personal philosophies of its author(s). Authoritative definitions are usually intended either to structure a discussion of E&B disorder (as in a textbook or position paper) or to put forward a perspective or position to provoke analysis, research, or even controversy.

Display 1-3 presents a few authoritative definitions. The first five illustrate some of the different theoretical perspectives on E&B disorder, which will be elaborated in later chapters. The last definition was contributed by a pioneer in identifying and serving young students with early indicators of E&B disorder. This definition was the basis for another kind of definition, discussed next. Each authoritative definition represents a viewpoint worth considering as you attempt to understand E&B disorder more fully.

## Administrative Definitions

Perhaps even more influential are administrative definitions, found in official statements of government and other organizations. For example, state education agencies have administrative definitions intended to guide identification of students with E&B disorder and delivery of services to them. The wording of different administrative definitions can vary widely. By describing the emotional, behavior, cognitive, and other characteristics of eligible students, administrative definitions help determine whether a particular student will receive services.

One especially important **administrative definition of E&B disorder** is the "federal" (U.S. Department of Education; [USD Education]) definition of **emotional disturbance (ED)**. Emotional disturbance is the term for E&B disorder of students that is used in federal laws and regulations pertaining to special education.

**Display 1-3** Selected authoritative definitions of E&B disorder

**Biological Perspective**
"A biogenic mental disorder is a severe behavior disorder that results solely from the effects of biological factors, including both gene action and the effects of the physical-chemical environment" (Rimland, 1969, p. 706).

**Psychodynamic Perspective**
"A child suffers emotional conflict whenever anything interferes with the satisfaction of his instinctual drives and his frustration produces a state of tension" (Lippman, 1962, p. 3).

**Behavioral Perspective**
"Psychological disorder is said to be present when a child emits behavior that deviates from an arbitrary and relative social norm in that it occurs with a frequency or intensity that authoritative adults in the child's environment judge, under the circumstances, to be either too high or too low" (Ross, 1980, p. 9).

**Cognitive Perspective**
"Man is . . . a uniquely irrational animal; . . . his emotional or psychological disturbances are largely a result of his thinking illogically or irrationally" (Ellis, 1962, p. 36).

**Ecological Perspective**
"Emotional disturbance [is] a reciprocal condition which exists when intense coping responses are released within a human microcommunity by a community member's atypical behavior and responses. The triggering stimulus, the rejoinder of the microcommunity, and the ensuing transaction are all involved in emotional disturbance" (Rhodes, 1970, p. 311).

**Perspective of a Pioneer in Early Identification and Education**
"Emotionally handicapped children . . . demonstrate one or more of the following characteristics to a marked extent and over a period of time:
1. An inability to learn which cannot be explained by intellectual, sensory, or health factors . . .
2. An inability to build or maintain satisfactory interpersonal relationships with peers and teachers . . .
3. Inappropriate types of behavior or feelings under normal conditions . . .
4. A general, pervasive mood of unhappiness or depression . . .
5. A tendency to develop physical symptoms, pains, or fears associated with personal or school problems" (Bower, 1969, pp. 22–23).

To qualify for a federal subsidy that partially defrays the excess cost of educating students with education disabilities, state and local agencies must declare that students qualify under one of 13 defined education disability conditions, including ED. The federal definition of ED (Display 1-4) is very similar to that of Bower (see Display 1-3), a main difference being that the federal version specifically excludes students who are socially maladjusted, "unless . . . they have an emotional disturbance."

The federal definition says that to qualify under the ED disability, a student must exhibit at least one of the characteristics (A) to (E) enduringly, intensively, and in a way that adversely affects his or her educational performance. Whether the student has schizophrenia or is socially maladjusted is irrelevant, as long as he

**Display 1-4** Federal administrative definition of emotional disturbance (ED)

---

(i) The term means a condition exhibiting one or more of the following characteristics over a long period of time and to a marked degree that adversely affects a child's educational performance:
  (A) An inability to learn that cannot be explained by intellectual, sensory, or health factors.
  (B) An inability to build or maintain satisfactory interpersonal relationships with peers and teachers.
  (C) Inappropriate types of behavior or feelings under normal circumstances.
  (D) A general pervasive mood of unhappiness or depression.
  (E) A tendency to develop physical symptoms or fears associated with personal or school problems.
(ii) The term includes schizophrenia. The term does not apply to children who are socially maladjusted, unless it is determined that they have an emotional disturbance.

---

*Source:* USD Education, 1998, p. II-46.

or she qualifies as ED. Schizophrenia and social maladjustment are discussed in later chapters.

The federal definition has been vigorously criticized (e.g., Forness & Kavale, 2000; Kauffman, 2001; Tankersley, Landrum, & Cook, 2004), especially on the following grounds:

1. The five characteristics under which students may qualify for ED were arbitrarily selected, are stated vaguely, and lack research support. Other characteristics not in the ED definition, by contrast, do have some research support.
2. The wording of the federal definition makes it easy for schools to ignore or overlook many children and adolescents with E&B disorder. Unjustly, such students are not considered for special education.
3. The exclusion of "socially maladjusted" as a characteristic that can qualify a student for ED is especially illogical, particularly in light of characteristic (B) (see Display 1-4). This exclusion can eliminate some of the youths who most need special education.

Dissatisfaction with the federal definition of ED brought together numerous special education, mental health, and other professional and advocacy groups concerned with E&B disorder of children to create an alternative definition. Operating as the **National Mental Health and Special Education Coalition**, the group petitioned Congress to substitute its proposed alternative (Display 1-5) for the existing official definition.

To date, this alternative definition has not been adopted as the federal definition of ED. Critics may have overstated some of the problems in the existing definition or insufficiently considered possible shortcomings of the proposed alternative (Cullinan, 2004). Perhaps the main outcomes of the Coalition's valuable work were encouraging widespread contemplation of the federal definition of ED and raising professional awareness of the importance of administrative definitions in general.

**Display 1-5** National Mental Health and Special Education Coalition proposed definition of "emotional or behavioral disorder"

---

(i) The term emotional or behavioral disorder means a disability characterized by behavioral or emotional responses in school programs so different from appropriate age, cultural, or ethnic norms that they adversely affect educational performance, including academic, social, vocational or personal skills, and which;
  (A) is more than a temporary, expected response to stressful events in the environment;
  (B) is consistently exhibited in two different settings, at least one of which is school-related; and
  (C) persists despite individualized interventions within the education program, unless, in the judgment of the team, the child's or youth's history indicates that such interventions would not be effective.
Emotional or behavioral disorders can co-exist with other disabilities.
(ii) This category may include children or youth with schizophrenic disorders, affective disorders, anxiety disorders, or other sustained disturbances of conduct or adjustment when they adversely affect educational performance in accordance with Section 1.

---

*Source:* Forness & Knitzer, 1992, p. 13.

## Some Common Ground

Authoritative and administrative definitions presented so far show considerable variations, and many others could be listed to increase the diversity. However, two broad points of concern are found in many definitions:

> Children and adolescents with *E&B disorder* exhibit *behavioral, emotional,* and *cognitive characteristics* that (1) *deviate from standards* or expectations for behavior, and (2) *impair the functioning* of themselves and/or others.

Consider the italicized material in this statement.

### E&B Disorder

Many terms are used to describe this problem. As noted earlier, *emotional disturbance* (ED) is the term used by the USD Education to describe the education disability involving E&B disorder that qualifies a student for "free appropriate education" under the Individuals With Disabilities Education Improvement Act (a federal special education law discussed later). **Mental disorder** is a term for an E&B disorder that meets established criteria for a psychiatric or clinical diagnosis (see Chapter 3). Some additional terms include behavioral disorders, behaviorally–emotionally disabled, emotional impairment, emotionally maladjusted, mental illness, social-affective disorders, socially–emotionally disturbed, and social-personal handicaps. Although some of these terms may have unique meanings for certain agencies, advocacy groups, or professions, they often seem to be used interchangeably. Emotional and behavior disorder is a generally acceptable term that is not aligned with any particular purpose or theory.

### Behavior, Emotional, and Cognitive Characteristics

Educators are concerned with a student's behavior characteristics and the effects of those behaviors on people in the environment and on the student. They are also concerned about the student's emotional characteristics, such as aspects of fearfulness,

A student may express feelings of depression through body language.

anger, self-doubt, hopelessness, and other emotions that, unlike behavior, they cannot directly observe. Emotional characteristics are of particular interest insofar as they involve behavior. Ordinarily the student expresses emotional problems through behavior—that is, by what he does, says, and shows through facial expressions and body language.

Furthermore, teachers are concerned about a student's cognitive characteristics that are important for school achievement or are involved in problem behaviors and emotions. For example, maladaptive fearfulness may involve not only avoidant behavior and extreme emotional tension, but uncontrolled, repetitive, racing thoughts of failure. A child's maladaptive aggression might involve not only assaultive behavior and feelings of anger, but thoughts that the victim is personally despicable and probably was planning to attack first.

For educators of students with an E&B disorder, these concerns with emotion, behavior, and cognition characteristics have practical implications. Resourceful teachers informally observe a student's characteristics by paying attention to her behaviors, including actions, statements, and physiological responses (e.g., tears, muscle tenseness). Resourceful teachers also observe the effects of those behaviors on people in the student's environment. In addition to such informal observations, educators should conceptualize important patterns of E&B disorder in terms of emotional, behavioral, and cognitive characteristics that can be formally assessed (see Chapters 3 and 4).

### *Deviate from Standards*

Each student exhibits a range of behavior, which differs from student to student. Each teacher has expectations or standards for student behavior, expectations that may vary across time (different days of the week, or September versus May), from student to student, and perhaps in other ways. Further, among teachers such standards often vary. Despite all the variations, however, each teacher has limits beyond which a student's behavior is said to deviate from standards and expectations. Its frequency may be too high or too low, its duration may be too long or too short, its intensity may be too strong or too weak, or it may deviate in some other dimension. The teacher becomes aware that this behavior is deviant.

Therefore, does E&B disorder involve extraordinary behaviors, emotions, or thoughts? Do young people qualify for the ED education disability because their behaviors, emotions, and cognitions are different in kind from those of most children? Generally, no. In most cases, an E&B disorder involves ordinary behaviors that are deviant in frequency, duration, or intensity or in some other way. But some authorities conceptualize a few problems of behavior, emotion, or cognition as deviant in kind rather than deviant in degree. That is, they are not experienced at all by children without E&B disorder. Recurrent hallucinations (see Chapter 5) might be one example of a problem that is deviant in kind.

### *Impair the Functioning*

Some E&B disorders involve emotions, behaviors, and thoughts that impair the student's own functioning. Examples include anxieties that limit socially adaptive behavior, intrusive or disgusting actions that repel peers, excessive dependence on the teacher, a lack of friend-making skills, self-derogatory thoughts or statements, or an incapacity to feel joyful. These emotions, behaviors, and thoughts show that the young person is substantially distressed and/or seriously challenged in personal and educational development. Other E&B disorders greatly interfere with the functioning of other people, including individual peers (bullying, extorting food), task-oriented student groups (destruction of the group's project), teachers (disruptive movement and statements), or the school in general (theft, vandalism).

It is possible that emotions, behaviors, and cognitions that deviate from educators' standards of normality will not impair anyone's functioning, or that such impairment may not be noticed. But when deviance is noted and judged to impair the functioning of the student or others, the student is likely to be considered a candidate for special attention, perhaps including identification and service as a student with ED.

Of course, these two types of impairment (self and others) are often interrelated. Impairments to a student's own functioning tend to concern and otherwise disturb parents, teachers, and others (even peers) eventually (Farmer, Quinn, Hussey, & Holahan, 2001). Conversely, a student whose behavior significantly impairs others will probably eventually experience substantial social and personal disadvantages.

## PREVALENCE

**Prevalence** usually refers to the number of cases in, or the percentage of, a specified population showing some phenomenon within a particular period of time (U.S. Department of Health and Human Services [USDHHS], 1999; Wicks-Nelson & Israel, 2006). The phenomenon of interest may be E&B disorder in general or a specific kind of E&B disorder. For example, to estimate the prevalence of anxiety-related disorders, we might determine the proportion of children aged 6 to 17 living in large cities who were referred to mental health clinics for extreme fears and worries in 2006.

Prevalence data are not important to everyday educational practice because whether there is 1 case or 100,000 cases, each student with ED is to receive an individualized program of education and services (Friend, 2005; Turnbull, Huerta, & Stowe, 2006). However, prevalence data are important in decisions about funding, need for teachers and other resources, and many other issues in educating students with E&B disorder.

Prevalence can also influence our ideas about causes and interventions (Offord & Bennett, 2002). Prevalence studies might show us variations in the prevalence of E&B disorder according to age, gender, race-ethnic status, geographic area, socioeconomic status, or other variable. Suppose a study found that the prevalence of "Z," a specific form of E&B disorder, is the same among children from families of low, medium, and high wealth. This finding would weaken a hypothesis that poverty causes Z.

Unfortunately, there is considerable uncertainty about the prevalence of E&B disorder. One reason is disagreements over defining E&B disorder and classifying particular forms of E&B disorder. A second cause of uncertainty is variations in how E&B disorder is assessed, because different ways of assessing the same phenomenon may produce different results (Kazdin, 2003; Wicks-Nelson & Israel, 2006). For example, prevalence estimates of extremely sad or angry mood might be based on teacher observations or on student self-report. These two ways of assessment could produce different data because students may know something about their own sadness or anger that teachers do not (and, perhaps, vice versa).

A third reason involves applicability of study results to children in general. Few studies examine all children; instead, they usually examine a sample of young people, then generalize resulting prevalence data to the larger population of interest. Naturally, the accuracy and confidence of generalizing from a particular sample to a larger population depend on how well the sample represents the population (Van Acker, Yell, Bradley, & Drasgow, 2004). For example, suppose we have prevalence data on E&B disorder based on a large sample of 8-, 9-, and 10-year-old boys attending school in two large cities in the western part of the United States. How confident are we that results also represent 8-, 9-, and 10-year-old girls? Students who are 16 and 17 years old? Second-graders in rural areas of the northeastern United States? In fact, many prevalence data are based on samples of uncertain generalizability and must usually be viewed with this caution in mind.

Of course, researchers are aware of definition, assessment, generalization, and other possibilities for misleading results. They design prevalence studies so as to reduce such problems when feasible. Chapters 3, 4, and 5 give prevalence information on particular forms of E&B disorder and note a few prevalence issues.

## Prevalence of Mental Disorders

There are quite a few prevalence studies of E&B disorder of children and adolescents. These studies often define E&B disorder in terms of mental disorders (problems that meet criteria for a psychiatric diagnosis). Resulting prevalence estimates for E&B disorder have varied a great deal, from less than 1 percent to more than 30 percent of young people. These differences are due mainly to the definition, assessment, and sample issues noted previously. Despite the variations, such prevalence studies are valuable; for one thing, different studies can be compared and combined in various ways to produce a most-likely estimate of prevalence. The better studies indicate that between 5 and 20 percent of children and adolescents have some kind of mental disorder (Frick & Silverthorn, 2001; Kauffman, Brigham, & Mock, 2004; Offord & Bennett, 2002; Wicks-Nelson & Israel, 2006).

The prevalence of mental disorders is related to the prevalence of ED in schools, but the connection is not clear. Diagnosable mental disorders often overlap with ED (Mattison, 2004). However, not every mental disorder qualifies as an ED and not every student with ED has a mental disorder. ED is an education-specific disability. For instance, to qualify under the federal definition (see Display 1-4), the student's problems have to adversely affect educational performance. Suppose an adolescent's problems of behavior, emotion, and cognition meet clinical diagnostic criteria for a depressive mental disorder (discussed in Chapters 4 and 5), but he has average grades, is an elected officer of a school club, and has a few peers with whom he interacts each day at school. Should this student be identified as ED?

## Prevalence of ED

### *Student Counts*

Because federal law requires yearly accounting of the number of students served in each category of education disability, we have a highly accurate record of prevalence of ED—that is, if we can overlook reservations about the federal definition of ED. Data for a recent school year reveal that 483,926 U.S. students aged 3 to 21 were identified as having ED (USD Education, 2005). During that school year there were about 47.2 million U.S. public school students in prekindergarten through grade 12 (National Center for Education Statistics [NCES], 2003a). (An additional 5 to 6 million attended private schools or received home schooling.) Therefore, students with ED constitute approximately 1.0 percent of U.S. public school students.

### *Prevalence Discrepancies*

In light of the much higher percentages found in prevalence studies of children's mental disorders (as noted, 5 to 20 percent), many experts view the 1 percent prevalence of ED as a gross underestimate of the actual proportion of students who should be identified with ED (Forness & Kavale, 2000; Kauffman et al., 2004). It has been suggested that because federal and state special education laws require services to all students identified with any education disability, many school districts identify as ED only as many students as can be served within personnel, budget, and other resource limitations (Kauffman, 2001).

## *Increasing Numbers*

The number of students with ED aged 6 to 21 increased 18 percent from 1992 to 2002 (USD Education, 2002). The rapid growth in two other education disability categories, Other Health Impairments (OHI) and autism, also has implications for educators of students with ED. During the 1992 to 2002 period, OHI increased 400 percent and Autism increased 1,350 percent. Prevalence changes in ED, OHI, and Autism are shown in Display 1-6.

**Other Health Impairments (OHI)** is a miscellaneous category for students with health problems that impair strength or alertness in ways that adversely affect their education. Asthma, diabetes, and epilepsy may qualify for the OHI category, and so may the mental disorder attention deficit/hyperactivity disorder (ADHD). The steep

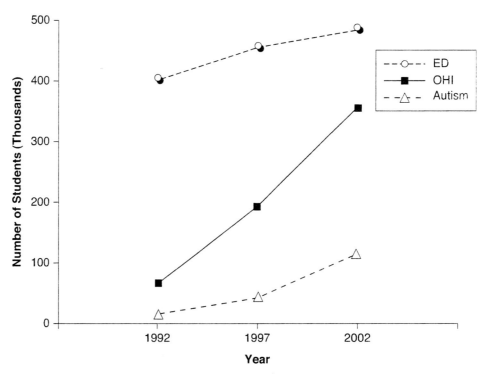

**Display 1-6** Number of students identified with ED,[1] OHI, and Autism in three recent school years
[1]ED = emotional disturbance; OHI = Other Health Impairments.
*Sources:* USD Education, 1994, 1999, 2005.

rise in the OHI category is due in part to increased identification and educational services to students with ADHD (Forness, 2004; USD Education, 2002). Many children with ADHD show very disruptive behavior and other problems (Barkley, 2005; Hechtman, 2005), and about one in seven students with ADHD in special education is identified as ED (USD Education, 2005). Thus teachers of students with ED can expect to teach some students with OHI as well.

Educational, psychological, and psychiatric concepts of autism as a disorder of children have changed considerably in the past half century (Volkmar, Lord, Bailey, Schultz & Klin, 2004; see Chapter 5). For instance, in the original (1975) federal special education law, autism was included within the ED category. In 1980 it was reclassified as a variety of OHI, and in 1990 Autism became a separate category of education disability. Many students in this category have severe social, language, intellectual, and other disabilities. Some students with autism, especially those with less severe language and intellectual problems, may be educated by teachers of students with ED.

### *Multiple Problems*

Prevalence studies show that many children experience more than one mental disorder or other form of E&B disorder at the same time, a phenomenon termed comorbidity or co-occurrence (Kauffman et al., 2004; Wicks-Nelson & Israel, 2006). Similarly, many students with ED simultaneously exhibit more than one of the five characteristics in the federal definition (see Display 1-4). Comorbidity of characteristics of ED might have important implications for individualizing education and other services for such students (Cullinan & Epstein, 2001; Forness, 2004). Suppose both Andrew and Kevin have extreme difficulties on ED characteristic (B) "relationship problems," but Kevin additionally has extreme difficulties on ED charactistic (E) "physical symptoms or fears." The additional ED characteristic may require school intervention for Kevin's relationship problems to be very different from the intervention for Andrew.

The patterns of comorbidity among the five federal definition characteristics seem to vary depending on the student's level in school. For example, different proportions of elementary, middle, and high school students with ED experience comorbidity involving ED characteristic (E). The three bars at the far right of Display 1-7 show that 28 percent of elementary school students but only 17 percent of middle and 13 percent of high school students exhibit characteristic (E) plus at least one other characteristic.

Many students identified with ED also experience other significant education problems (Forness, 2004). For instance, an estimated 25 to 35 percent of students with ED could qualify for the Specific Learning Disabilities education disability category as well (USD Education, 2000).

Despite some unresolved issues about definitions, assessment, and study samples, the evidence does indicate that there are many more students with E&B disorder than there are students identified with ED. Cullinan and Epstein (1995), in consideration of individual studies and literature reviews of prevalence, proposed that E&B disorder among students may approximately follow a **"rule of one third:"**

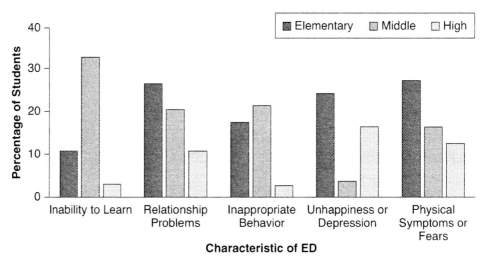

**Display 1-7** Percentage of elementary, middle, and high school students with ED showing more than one characteristic of ED, by characteristic
*Source:* Cullinan & Epstein, 2001.

1. In any school year, about one third of all students exhibit emotional and behavior problems that concern their teachers.
2. Around one third of this group (roughly 10 percent of students) show a greater degree of problems, so intense or persistent that changes from the usual educational procedures are required to serve them.
3. In approximately one third of this group (3 to 4 percent of students), E&B disorder is serious enough to justify referral for special education or other specialized intervention services.

## WHY SERVE THESE CHILDREN?

To many, the question "Why serve these children?" may appear trivial; the typical answer might be something like, "Because they need the help we can give them." Most religions and many philosophies emphasize helping people, and our society is accustomed to the idea of offering a helping hand to those who need it, especially children.

It may not be that simple, however. This charitable attitude is not characteristic of all people, organizations, societies, places, or times. Approaches to people with E&B disorder have changed over the years (see Chapter 2) and may do so again. Further, endorsing the idea of helping these youngsters is not the same as actually providing needed help. It might be necessary to use personnel and other resources in different ways, requiring changes that some people will resist. The resources of individuals, organizations, and governments are finite, and services for youths with

E&B disorder compete with other priorities. For these and many other reasons, we all know that splendid ideas do not inevitably become beneficial realities.

Also, why should *schools* be heavily involved in dealing with E&B disorder? Some citizens believe that the goal of education should be to transmit knowledge and students whose behavior impedes this goal must shape up or ship out. So it is important to consider why there should be special education for children and adolescents with E&B disorder.

One of the rewards of studying E&B disorder of children is that so many topics raise fundamental questions about human existence and purpose. You are invited to perform a brief philosophy check by reflecting on the following questions:

1. What is your philosophy of life?
2. What is your philosophy about helping people who need help?
3. What is your philosophy of education?
4. What is your philosophy of educating children and adolescents with ED?

What key points and issues should you consider? You may find it worthwhile to keep a record of your responses and, after some time, answer these questions again.

## To Help the Children

For educators of students with ED, the most important reason to help may be to fulfill a personal and professional need to reduce the suffering and maladaptive functioning of the students they teach. E&B disorder interferes with the well-being of young people and their families. Take a moment to remember a time when you felt, thought, or acted on intense anger; constant, grinding tension; deep sadness, perhaps even hopelessness; confusion about what to do next; or heart-pounding fear. What might have brought about such emotions, thoughts, and behaviors? Threats to your safety or situation? Loss of someone or something you had come to rely on? Strong pressure from others or yourself to complete a difficult activity? Neglect or rejection by people you loved or valued? Many students with E&B disorder experience, again and again, personal disappointment, misery, disparagement, and loss of opportunities, as well as a general low quality of life. To what extent are educators obliged to address these problems?

This question involves, among other things, the goals of education, which depend in part on a society's priorities. In an earlier era, schooling was mainly for teaching academic and classical topics and religious values to selected youngsters; gradually, it has taken on a wider range of goals and students. Our society now generally acknowledges the right of every child to equal educational opportunity. Today's educator serves a population of students with more diverse needs than before (Smith, 2004).

Teachers give students with ED the prospect of present and future help when they provide appropriate education to them. To help in the present, the teacher must understand and reduce the young person's current socially and personally maladaptive emotions, behaviors, and cognitions, especially within the school setting. She usually must identify and strengthen the student's assets as well. If this effort is successful, the teacher may be increasing the young person's chances for a better future. E&B disorders of children and adolescents do not invariably foreshadow adult maladaptation, but in many cases they do (see Wicks-Nelson & Israel, 2006). Thus, appropriate education, alone or together with other help, can improve present and future life functioning.

## To Help Society

There are many good things about our society and our children's education in it, and at the same time there are many problems that we would like to reduce or eliminate. Most teachers, as citizens and professionals, recognize their opportunities and duties to help improve education and society. Let's look briefly at selected aspects of education and society related to young people in general and with relevance for students with ED.

### *Educational Concerns*
***Personal and Schooling Characteristics.*** Early in the 21st century, approximately 48 million students were served by 3 million teachers in 93,000 U.S. public schools (NCES, 2003a, 2003b, 2004a, 2004b). (Nearly 6 million students were enrolled in private schools or home schooled.) There were 4.2 million students in prekindergarten and kindergarten, 18.5 million in grades 1 to 5, 11.2 million in grades 6 to 8, and 13.7 million in grades 9 to 12. Almost 50 percent of students were female. The approximate race-ethnic breakdown was as follows: 1 percent American Indian/Alaskan Native, 4 percent Asian or Pacific Islander, 17 percent Black, 17 percent Hispanic, and 60 percent White.

The number of students with ED varies by age (see Display 1-8). Overall the percent prevalence of ED is 1%; however, it differs across school levels (USD

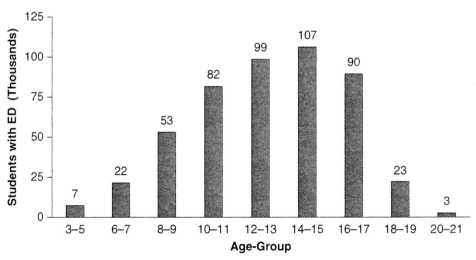

**Display 1-8** Number of students with ED, by age-groups
*Source:* USD Education, 2005.

Education, 2005). About 161,000 students with ED were 6 to 11 years old; dividing by the number of U.S. elementary school students yields a percent prevalence of 0.9%. Likewise, the 148,000 students with ED aged 12 to 14 years made up 1.3% of middle school students, and the 157,000 students with ED aged 15 to 18 years were 1.2% of high school students. (Meaningful percent prevalence rates are difficult to derive for (a) the 8,500 students with ED aged 3 to 5 years, because educators tend to use Developmental Delay, a nonspecific federal education disability category, when identifying preschoolers who show troubling behavior; and (b) the 7,800 students with ED aged 19 to 21 years, because most people in this age range have left high school.)

The USD Education provides few data on prevalence of ED by sex. Various studies indicate that a little more than 20 percent of students with ED are females (Bradley, Henderson, & Monfore, 2004; Coutinho & Oswald, 2005; Trout, Nordness, Pierce, & Epstein, 2003). Thus males are said to be "overrepresented" (the group's proportion of the ED student population is greater than its proportion of the public school population).

About 1 percent of students with ED are American Indian/Alaskan Native, 1 percent Asian or Pacific Islander, 28 percent Black, 9 percent Hispanic, and 60 percent White (USD Education, 2005). This means that two race-ethnic groups, American Indian/Alaskan Native and White, are proportionately represented among students with ED, two groups (Asian or Pacific Islander and Hispanic) are disproportionately underrepresented, while Black students are disproportionately overrepresented among students with ED (Display 1-9). Many professionals are concerned about the large

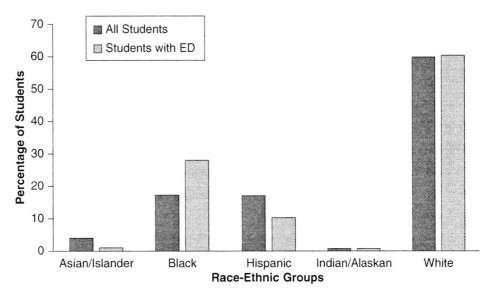

**Display 1-9** Race-ethnic status proportions of all public school students and those with ED "Asian/Islander" = Asian/Pacific Islander; "Indian/Alaskan" = American Indian/Alaskan Native.
*Sources:* USD Education, 2005; NCES, 2004.

overrepresentation of Black students with ED (e.g., Osher, Cartledge, Oswald, Sutherland, Artiles, & Coutinho, 2004; Webb-Johnson, 2003).

Like other students with education disabilities, students with ED are educated within a **continuum of education environments** (placements), which involve diverse locations, arrangements, and instruction methods. Education environments can be categorized in order of most to least physically integrated with nondisabled students (Display 1-10). We must keep in mind that although this categorization is a "quick-and-dirty" aid to communication and accounting, it greatly understates the diversity of placements and provisions for students with ED. To illustrate, suppose

**Display 1-10** Continuum of education environments for students with ED

| Education Environment | Description[1] | Percent of ED[2] |
|---|---|---|
| Regular class | Students receive the majority of their education program in a regular classroom and receive special education and related services outside the regular classroom for less than 21 percent of the school day. It includes children placed in a regular class and receiving special education within the regular class, as well as children placed in a regular class and receiving special education outside the regular class. | 27 |
| Resource room | Students receive special education and related services outside the regular classroom for at least 21 percent but not more than 60 percent of the school day. This may include students placed in resource rooms with part-time instruction in a regular class. | 23 |
| Separate class | Students receive special education and related services outside the regular classroom for more than 60 percent of the school day. Students may be placed in self-contained special classrooms with part-time instruction in regular classes or placed in self-contained classes full-time on a regular school campus. | 32 |
| Separate school | Students receive special education and related services in separate day schools for students with disabilities for more than 50 percent of the school day. | 13 |
| Residential facility | Students receive education in a public or private residential facility, at public expense, for more than 50 percent of the school day. | 4 |
| Homebound/hospital | Students receive special education in hospital or homebound programs. | 1 |

[1]USD Education, 1995, pp 13–14.
[2]USD Education, 2005 (children with ED ages 6–21).

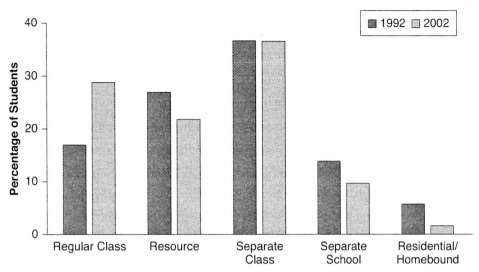

**Display 1-11** Percentage of students with ED served in each of five education environments,[1] in two school years
[1]Residential (public and private) and Hospital/Homebound categories combined as Residential/Homebound.
*Sources:* USD Education, 1995, 2005.

Luis spends half his day at a separate school for intensive treatment and the other half in regular classes at his neighborhood school (e.g., Jacobs, Randall, Vernberg, Roberts, & Nyre, 2005); Trina leaves her regular classes for 90 minutes per day of academic remediation and social skills practice. The education environment of both students would be considered "resource room" (away from a regular classroom 21 to 60 percent of the time) but these two placements are very different.

The low proportion of students with ED served in the "least restrictive" placement (outside the **regular class education environment** no more than 20 percent of the time; see Display 1-10) continues to be a concern (USD Education, 2005). This proportion has increased in the past decade (Landrum, Katsiyannis, & Archwamety, 2004). Concurrently, the proportion in separate class placements has remained the same, while proportions served in resource environments, separate special education schools, and residential institutions have declined (Display 1-11).

***Learning Performance.*** Academic outcomes of U.S. education are mediocre. In the last three decades, U.S. students on average have improved a little in mathematics, science, and writing, while remaining stable in reading (NCES, 2003b, 2004a). U.S. students rank in the middle among nations in comparisons of student performance.

Of special concern are low-achieving students—those who do not have the fundamental knowledge and skills required for success in their schooling (NCES, 2003a). More than one third of 9-year-old students and 8% of 13-year-olds have too little reading proficiency to understand simple passages and make correct inferences from them. About 70% of 9-year-olds and 21% of 13-year-olds cannot perform basic numerical operations and simple problem-solving in mathematics. Twenty-two percent of 17-year-olds do not achieve basic proficiency in writing.

Among students with ED, a large majority are low-achieving (Trout et al., 2003) and the problems extend to all major areas of academics (Reid, Gonzalez, Nordness, Trout, & Epstein, 2004). This often results in grade retention for academic failure (Wagner, Kutash, WD Duchnowski, Epstein, & Sumi, 2005).

***Completing School.*** In recent years about 87 percent of American older adolescents and young adults have completed high school by graduation or an equivalency certificate (NCES, 2003b). High school completion varies by family income level: high income, 97 percent completion; low income, 75 percent (Snyder & Sickmund, 1999). Recent high school dropouts are 1½ to 3 times as likely to be unemployed as are graduates (NCES, 2003a).

Of adolescent students with ED who leave school, only about 40 percent graduate with a diploma; 6 percent receive a completion certificate, and more than half drop out (USD Education, 2002). A national study revealed that 3 to 5 years after leaving high school, about half of the former students with ED are unemployed and those with employment earn a low wage (Cheney & Bullis, 2004; Wagner, 1995). Most have been arrested (three fourths of the dropouts); most do not live independently, and about 15 percent live in a correction or mental health facility.

***Behavior Problems at School.*** Data collected in the first years of the 21st century (see DeVoe et al., 2003, 2004; NCES, 2003a, 2003b) show that since the mid-1990s, school behavior problems in the U.S. have declined substantially from historically high levels around 1990. However, they remain disturbingly great.

Large proportions of public school teachers and administrators are very concerned about the extent of student nonattendance, disrespect, apathy, unpreparedness to learn, disruptive behavior, bullying, substance abuse, and pregnancy, as well as lack of support from parents. Annually, 9 percent of teachers report being threatened with injury by a student and teachers are victims of about 95,000 violent crimes at school.

Each year there are about 0.75 million incidents of violent crime—simple, aggravated, or sexual assault; rape; robbery—against adolescents at school (includes going to and from school) and about the same number away from school. Nonviolent (mainly theft) victimization of students occurs considerably more often at school than away, however. About 3 percent of girls and 10 percent of boys in high school report carrying a gun, knife, or club at school. Surprisingly, in light of these data, homicide of a student at school is rare (yearly average, about 23).

Twenty percent of adolescent students report that there are street gangs at their schools. Six percent fear for their safety at school, and 5 percent avoid certain locations (e.g., particular hallways). Such fear and avoidance disproportionately characterize younger adolescent students, Black and Hispanic students, and students in urban schools (DeVoe et al., 2003).

Nearly half of high school students acknowledge having used alcohol and one quarter having used marijuana within the prior month. Such widespread substance use inevitably affects schooling: 29 percent of high school students had been offered, sold, or given an illegal drug at school; 5 percent had used alcohol and 6 percent marijuana, at school, within the prior month.

Students with ED, of course, show a variety of serious behavior problems at school, and experience distressing, debilitating emotions and thoughts that interfere with school and life success (see Chapters 4 and 5). However, comparable national data are not available on the involvement of students with ED in particular behavior problems, violence, crimes, and substance use at school.

***Removal from School.*** In a recent year, more than half of U.S. public schools disciplined students by removing them from school (DeVoe et al., 2003). Reasons for removal of a student included firearm use (2 percent of schools) or possession (4 percent), other weapon use (5 percent) or possession (19 percent), substance distribution (10 percent) or possession (20 percent), physical attacks and fights (35 percent), threatening someone (22 percent), and insubordination (18 percent). There were about 1.2 million instances of disciplinary school removal (the number

Most students with E & BD have learning problems and are far below grade level in academic achievement.

of students was not reported); 83 percent were suspensions for at least 5 days, 11 percent were expulsions, and 7 percent were transfers to special schools.

Students with ED are at least six times as likely to engage in serious school misconduct than students with no disability (USD Education, 2002). Among students with disabilities, those with ED are by far the most likely to be disciplined by removal from school: annually, 31 percent suspended, 3 percent expelled. Next most likely are students with OHI (12 percent suspended annually). Disciplinary school removal is of special interest regarding students with ED (Zhang, Katsiyannis, & Herbst, 2004) because excessive use of such discipline triggers legal protections for students with an education disability (Yell, 2006), as described later.

***Teacher Supply.*** The 3 million U.S. teachers in public elementary and secondary schools average more than 15 years of teaching experience (NCES, 2003a, 2004a). There are shortages of teachers in some subjects, locations, and other specifics.

For students with ED, the supply of teachers has rarely satisfied demand. Projecting data from past studies (e.g., USD Education, 1995) suggests that in 2005 there were roughly 39,000 teachers of students with ED, but 6,000 more were needed. Hiring uncertified teachers is one way to address this shortage, and among students with disabilities, those with ED are most likely to be taught by an uncertified teacher (USD Education, 2002). In general, uncertified teachers pursue needed knowledge, skills, and certification while they teach, which often amounts to a heavy burden of extra responsibilities while filling a very challenging role for which one is incompletely prepared. This may help explain why there is high turnover among teachers of students with ED. At the same time, there are many highly skilled, caring, and effective teachers of students with ED who continue to enjoy great satisfaction from their successful, long careers.

***Education Expenditures.*** The U.S. has about the highest cost of educating a public school student in the world. Currently this averages more than $8,000 annually (NCES, 2004a). Education for a student with ED costs about twice that (USD Education, 2002). These expenditures are mostly state and local; the federal government covers around 7 percent.

### Societal Concerns

As citizens, teachers of students with ED have concerns about societal problems, perhaps especially those closely related to the functioning of their students. A few are mentioned here; later chapters explore in detail these and other variables that appear to be significantly linked to the development of E&B disorder of children.

***Poverty.*** About 16 percent of all Americans under age 18, more than 11 million young people, live in poverty (NCES, 2004a). Poverty is five times as high among children of mothers without husbands (around 40 percent in poverty) than married-couple families (7 percent). Some of the possible links between poverty and behavior problems of children are poor health care or substance abuse during pregnancy, parental substance abuse or mental disorder, ineffective parenting, child maltreatment, exposure to destructive community influences, and inadequate education and intervention services.

About one third of students with ED live in poverty. At least one third live with a single parent, a high percentage of their parents are unemployed, and on average their household income is low (USD Education, 2002; Wagner et al., 2005).

***Violence and Crime.*** Despite sharp declines since about 1995, children and adolescents continue to be frequent victims and perpetrators of crime (DeVoe et al., 2003, 2004). Adolescents aged 12 to 17 are more likely than any other age range to be victimized by a violent crime. About 2,100 U.S. persons age 5 to 19 annually die by homicide (only 1 percent while at school). Victims are mainly older adolescent boys.

At the same time, 12- to 17-year-olds perpetrate more than 20 percent of all violent crimes committed by a lone offender and half of the violent crimes by multiple offenders. Much of the latter is due to youth gangs (Miller, 2001). A large proportion of violent offenses by juveniles is accounted for by a relatively few "serious, violent, and chronic" offenders, who perform numerous violent crimes and dozens of other offenses per year (Huizinga, Loeber, Thornberry, & Cothern, 2000).

Several hundred thousand juvenile offenders are confined for some time each year, most of them briefly. At any one time there are about 100,000 in juvenile detention facilities and perhaps 15,000 more in adult detention facilities (Sickmund, 2002; Snyder & Sickmund, 1999). Many—estimates range from 20 to 80 percent—have an E&B disorder (e.g., Cauffman, 2004; Nelson, Leone, & Rutherford, 2004; Teplin, Abram, McClelland, Dulcan, & Mericle, 2002). A similarly large proportion use or abuse alcohol and drugs.

Many young people who become juvenile offenders already have been identified by schools as having ED. Persons who have prepared themselves to educate students with ED may teach these and other offenders in detention centers. Among any group of middle and high school students with ED, it is probable that some have been adjudicated as delinquents.

***Treatment for E&B Disorder.*** Each year 5 to 10 percent of U.S. children and adolescents participate in "psychosocial intervention" (psychotherapy or other nonmedical treatment) of various kinds, for diverse problems of personal and social adjustment (Landolf, 2005; USDHHS, 1999). Many of these cases involve family conflict or other problems that are not E&B disorder. The wide variety of kinds and locations of treatment (see Chapter 12) make it difficult to specify the extent to which U.S. young people receive psychosocial treatment for E&B disorder. Also unknown is the proportion of students with ED who participate in psychosocial intervention outside school.

The aforementioned societal problems, among other issues involving E&B disorder of children and adolescents, will be revisited in later chapters. It is safe to conclude that such problems result in vast personal, social, and financial costs to individual children, their families, the community, and society in general. There

**Display 1-12** Summary of IDEA 2004

The Individuals With Disabilities Education Improvement Act of 2004 (IDEA 2004) is a U.S. federal law that guarantees the right to an appropriate education for all children and youth with an education disability. In IDEA 2004, appropriate education (or special education) is defined as specially designed education that appropriately addresses the particular needs of a student with an education disability. The law identifies 13 varieties of education disability, one of which is emotional disturbance (ED).

IDEA 2004 has complex aspects and implications, but straightforward objectives. It is meant to ensure that each student with a disability obtains:
1. a free appropriate public education
2. delivered in the least restrictive environment (LRE), which includes
3. appropriate assessment and evaluation,
4. an individualized education program (IEP),
5. parent and student participation, and
6. due process and procedural safeguards.

**Free Appropriate Public Education**

IDEA 2004 legislates that states identify and evaluate children with education disabilities, from birth to age 21. States must provide an appropriate education, at no cost to the parents, to students with disabilities aged 6 to 17 years. If the state educates students without disabilities before age 6 or after age 17, like-age students with disabilities must also be educated. Appropriate education means not only special education but "related services," which might include psychological counseling, certain health services, and other rehabilitation and support.

**Least Restrictive Environment**

Students with disabilities must receive their education with nondisabled students "to the maximum extent appropriate." Placement decisions must be based on the student's educational needs, not administrative convenience or a lack of the appropriate LRE.

Students with disabilities must be educated with nondisabled peers unless it is clear that the student will not progress under these circumstances. It is generally considered best practice to provide a continuum of possible education environments, including regular classrooms, resource rooms, separate special classes, special schools, and out-of-school education placements. Students may be assigned to one or more environments in this continuum.

**Appropriate Assessment**

All students with disabilities must be identified and offered special education. To determine the presence and nature of disabilities, assessment must be nondiscriminatory. Procedures must be designed and validated for the education disabilities at issue and administered appropriately by properly trained personnel in the student's native language or communication mode (such as Braille). Educational placement cannot be determined based on results from just one assessment procedure, but must be based on a variety of sources of information. Assessments must be made by a multidisciplinary team that includes a specialist in the suspected disability area.

Before a student's evaluation that may result in identification with a disability, parents must give informed consent. The assessment results and other reasons for a decision to identify the student must be explained to the parents. A parent who is unsatisfied with the evaluation can receive another, independent evaluation that must be considered in subsequent decisions about the student. Students with disabilities must be included in districtwide or statewide assessments of achievement, with accommodations or alternative forms of assessment as appropriate.

*(continued)*

**Display 1-12 (Continued)**

### Individualized Education Program

IDEA 2004 requires that an individualized education program (IEP) be provided for each child in need of special education. Although IEP formats differ from locality to locality, all IEPs must include the following:
1. Specific information as to the student's present level of educational performance
2. Measurable annual goals, with regular monitoring and reports to parents
3. Criteria for evaluating whether instructional objectives are being met, and a schedule (at least once per year) for performing this evaluation
4. What special education and related services are to be provided, including the extent to which the student will not participate in the regular education program with nondisabled peers
5. When services will begin, their anticipated duration, and where they are located
6. Accommodations for the student's participation in districtwide or statewide assessments

The IEP results from one or more planning conferences. Participants should include the student's general education and special education teacher(s), other professionals as needed, a representative of the local education agency, the student's parent or parent surrogate, and (when appropriate) the student.

In addition, by no later than age 16, special education students must receive individualized planning for transition that describes goals, services, and activities supporting movement from student to adult citizen status. This should include work and independent-living considerations and should link the student to appropriate agencies outside school. For young children receiving early intervention services under IDEA 2004, an individualized family service plan (a document similar to the IEP) describes support for family involvement in early intervention and prevention.

### Parent and Student Participation

Parents, guardians, and surrogate parents have a variety of rights under IDEA 2004. In identification, assessment, placement, IEP, and other matters, schools must notify parents and, in many cases, receive their consent to proceed. As members of the IEP team, parents may choose to be involved in many appropriate education decisions. The law provides that parents may appeal school decisions through various specified mechanisms, including mediations and hearings.

### Due Process

The U.S. Constitution requires that government entities must treat all citizens equally unless there are compelling reasons for doing otherwise. Due process refers to the rights of citizens to take exception to unequal treatment and to force government to prove the necessity for it. In the IDEA 2004, due process safeguards are involved in many of the rights of notification, participation, and appeal available to parents. Parents can inspect all educational and related records and evaluations on their child.

Of particular relevance to students with ED, IDEA 2004 requires special consideration of serious discipline violations of students with disabilities. Disciplinary consequences involving suspension, expulsion, or other change of placement are restricted and may be influenced by a "manifestation determination" (a decision by the IEP team as to whether or not the violation is a manifestation of the student's ED or other disability).

Violations that involve weapons, drugs, or injurious assault at school are special cases. Students with such violations may be removed to an "interim alternative education setting" for up to 45 school days, regardless of any manifestation determination. They must continue to receive appropriate education as described in the IEP. These special cases and certain other discipline violations require the IEP team to perform a functional behavioral assessment (examination of the environmental contexts and purposes of the behavior; see Chapters 3 and 8), leading to a behavior intervention plan. IDEA 2004 does not prevent schools from addressing law violations by a student with disabilities through the legal system.

*Sources:* Heward, 2006; Yell, 2006.

is little doubt that effective teaching for students with ED has the power not only to help the young people but to reduce tragic, alarming, and expensive problems for the school and the society.

## To Meet Lawful Obligations

Over the past four decades, court cases and laws have established a legal foundation that promotes and supports changes in societal attitudes toward equal educational opportunity, including opportunity for students with disabilities. Early legal developments eliminated local practices that kept children with ED and other education disabilities from attending public schools and specified actions required to provide "appropriate education" for such students. These legal developments led to the 1975 passage of the Education of All Handicapped Children Act (Public Law 94-142), a landmark federal law designed to ensure that students with disabilities receive free education appropriate to their needs. This law has been amended several times since, including in 2004, when Congress renamed it **Individuals With Disabilities Education Improvement Act** (Turnbull et al., 2006; USD Education, 2005). Also called IDEA 2004, it is briefly described in Display 1-12.

IDEA and related federal regulations have established a strong federal role in ensuring educational opportunity for students with ED. Additionally, many state and local laws and educational policies are compatible with the federal mandates. There is, in summary, considerable legal support and direction for our profession's commitment to appropriate education for children and adolescents identified with ED.

## WHO SERVES THESE CHILDREN?

Teachers, school psychologists, and other education personnel are not the only professionals concerned with children having an E&B disorder. Interventions for these young people can be provided by professionals associated with the mental health, child and family welfare, juvenile justice, and other service systems. Services may be delivered in mental health and psychotherapy clinics, day or residential treatment centers, the child's home or community, juvenile detention institutions, therapeutic foster placements, and numerous other settings (Wicks-Nelson & Israel, 2006).

Other professionals who provide service differ in several ways, including the amounts and kinds of training they receive, their responsibilities toward children and their families, and the situations in which they interact with young people. As a result, members of different professions tend to develop different viewpoints on E&B disorder. Although this is to be expected, we must consider the danger that several professionals dealing with a student could cooperate ineffectively or actually work against each other. Educators who understand the language and assumptions of members of other helping professions are better able to communicate and work cooperatively with other professionals. The roles and perspectives of some professions and service agencies with which educators often cooperate are described in Chapter 12.

## Responding to the Challenge

There are compelling reasons to effectively educate children and adolescents with E&B disorder. People who are determined to lead the way in such education begin with recognizing the need to improve the well-being of individual students, to reduce costs of E&B disorder to society, and to follow and support legal mandates for providing appropriate education. To help you prepare for teaching and other education roles, this book provides a comprehensive introduction to E&B disorder of children and adolescents.

Comprehensive means that core topics (assessment; varieties of E&B disorder; models of causes and treatments of E&B disorder; and intervention principles, methods, and programs) are supplemented by information that places such topics in proper context. To be knowledgeable at a professional level requires an appreciation, for example, of formative historical developments, selected theory and research from other disciplines, areas of uncertainty or dispute that have implications for educating students with ED, and other issues related to providing special services. Proper context also requires considering scientific evidence and other information useful in evaluating the merits of ideas and practices in this field. Where feasible, this book takes note of classic as well as recent research and ideas. Comprehensive coverage of the broad scope of events, ideas, practices, and directions in this field is essential to the kind of informed understanding desired by those pursuing professional growth.

At the same time, introductory coverage requires limits on the amount and kind of material presented. Obviously, most of the discussion must be allocated to core topics. References to sources that examine topics in greater detail are provided to encourage you to satisfy your professional curiosity and achieve fuller understanding of discussion points. Descriptions of interventions will familiarize you with practices and programs and show how they exemplify models or other principles of intervention; sources are provided so you can find original material and learn implementation details.

Responding to the E&B disorders of children and adolescents often involves more than education, but education must play a major part in any effective response to this challenge. The school is the site for much of a young person's socialization and learning, and to a large extent E&B disorders are socialization and learning problems. Educators want to serve children and adolescents with E&B disorder, and legal developments require that the services be provided. But the possibilities and promises of appropriate education can be realized best by those who are prepared, by virtue of their resourcefulness and knowledge, to serve students with ED.

## Chapter Summary

Children and adolescents with E&B disorder show a great variety of emotional, behavior, and cognitive problems. As students, they need the help of teachers who are resourceful and knowledgeable.

- Many definitions of E&B disorder can be classified as either authoritative or administrative.
- Authoritative definitions are available that represent different psychological models of normal and abnormal functioning, including E&B disorders of young people. Some of these definitions represent the following:
  — Psychodynamic model
  — Behavioral model
  — Cognitive model
  — Ecological model
- The U.S. Department of Education administratively defines ED as one of several official education disabilities. ED is delimited in this federal definition primarily by five characteristics or emotional, behavioral, or cognitive problems, briefly:
  — Unexplained inability to learn
  — Relationship problems
  — Inappropriate behavior
  — Sadness or depression
  — Physical symptoms or fears
- Many critics are dissatisfied with the federal definition, but have not convincingly shown that alternatives improve upon it.
- Prevalence of E&B disorder is important for large-scale decisions and for insights into causes and interventions. Obstacles to good prevalence data include problems with definitions, assessment, and applicability of sample data to populations.
- Prevalence studies suggest that 5 to 20 percent of U.S. children and adolescents experience E&B disorder. However, only 1 percent of students are identified with ED.
- Prevalence of ED shows interesting variations by age, gender, race-ethnic status, and comorbidity.
- Among the reasons people serve as educators of students with ED are:
  — To help children with E&B disorder
  — To help society
  — To help schools follow the IDEA
- Educators of students with ED work with other professionals to meet the large challenges such students present.

## IDEAS FOR CONSIDERATION AND DISCUSSION

1. Remember some class or school mates in elementary, middle, or high school who showed, to some degree, emotional and behavior problems. Without giving any identifying information, describe one or two to the group in terms of the following considerations:
   a. What were some things these young people did to show that their behaviors, emotions, or thoughts deviated from standards?

b. What standards did they deviate from?
c. What behaviors, emotions, or thoughts impaired the functioning of other people or themselves?
d. In what ways did they impair the functioning of peers? Of teachers? In what ways did they impair their own functioning?
e. What were the reactions of teachers and administrators to these emotional and behavior problems? What were reactions of peers? What were the reactions of the young people who were showing these problems?
f. What became of these former class or school mates of yours?
2. Describe four ways in which a definition of E&BD can be important.
3. Consider Robert, Shaune, and Jeaneen in Display 1-1. For each child, create two questions that might produce additional information contributing to a fuller understanding of their E&BD.
4. Describe ways in which prevalence data are influential.
5. Why are teachers of students with ED likely to teach students with OHI as well?
6. Examine Displays 1-6, 1-7, 1-8, and 1-9.
   a. For each, what does the vertical axis display? What does the horizontal axis display?
   b. Prepare a concise statement of 25 words or fewer that summarizes the message of each display. In case someone doubts that your statement is correct, be ready to substantiate it with information from the display.

## Resources for Further Study

**www.ed.gov/about/reports/annual/osep/2003/execsumm.html** 25th Annual Report to Congress on the Implementation of IDEA
**www.bazelon.org/** Bazelon Center for Mental Health Law
**www.cdc.gov/ncipc/dvp/bestpractices.htm** Best Practices of Youth Violence Prevention
**www.air.org/cecp/** Center for Effective Collaboration and Practice
**www.nimh.nih.gov/healthinformation/childmenu.cfm** Child and Adolescent Mental Health (NIMH)
**ericec.org/** Educational Resources Information Center on Disabilities
**www.safeyouth.org/scripts/faq/ganginvolve.asp** Gang Involvement Warning Signs
**thomas.loc.gov/cgi-bin/query/z?c108:h.1350.enr:** IDEA 2004
**www.surgeongeneral.gov/library/mentalhealth/home.html** Mental Health: A Report of the Surgeon General
**www.nasponline.org/** National Association of School Psychologists
**http://nces.ed.gov/programs/crimeindicators/** NCES School Crime and Safety reports
**http://nces.ed.gov/programs/youthindicators/** NCES Youth Indicators
**www.specialedcareers.org/** National Clearinghouse for Professions in Special Education
**www.nichcy.org/** National Information Center for Children and Youth With Disabilities
**www.specialedconnection.com/LrpSecStoryTool/splash.jsp** Special education legal information
**http://www.ed.gov/policy/speced/guid/idea/idea2004.html** USD Education Topic Briefs on IDEA 2004

**ojjdp.ncjrs.org/** U.S. Office of Juvenile Justice and Delinquency Prevention
**http://oas.samhsa.gov/** U.S. Substance Abuse and Mental Health Services Administration data reports
**http://www.wrightslaw.com/idea/** Wrightslaw IDEA 2004 analysis
**www.surgeongeneral.gov/library/youthviolence/** Youth Violence: A Report of the Surgeon General
**www.cdc.gov/healthyyouth/yrbs/** YRBSS: Youth Risk Behavior Surveillance System

Chapter **Two**

# Roots of Current Perspectives

## CHAPTER OBJECTIVES

**After reading this chapter, you should be able to:**
- State a prehistoric, early Western civilization, and Middle Ages perspective on E&B disorder.
- List three events that shaped today's special education for children with E&B disorder.
- Name two contributions by the National Committee for Mental Hygiene.
- Describe two 20th-century reports on children with E&B disorder.
- Explain how the psychoeducational approach is a modification of the psychodynamic model.
- Identify two people who made early contributions to the behavioral model.

## CAN YOU DEFINE THESE 10 TERMS?

trephining
humors
moral treatment
empirical
mental hygiene movement

litigation-legislation-litigation cycle
Council for Children With Behavior Disorders (CCBD)
National Agenda
therapeutic milieu
operant conditioning

Special education for children and adolescents with E&B disorder has emerged as a profession mainly within the last five decades (Whelan & Kauffman, 1999), but it is based on perspectives and events of earlier times—much earlier in some cases. For instance, quite a few current ideas about causes of and interventions for E&B disorder among young people are not entirely new, but instead are extensions of earlier ideas. Also, education for students with E&B disorder is linked to developments in other disciplines and helping professions, including psychology, medicine, and sociology, and our field continues to be influenced by these linkages.

A consideration of selected historical roots has several benefits. By indicating successful advances, costly setbacks, and diverse perspectives of the past, history can broaden present understanding and guide future efforts (Sarason & Sarason, 2005; Silk, Nath, Siegel, & Kendall, 2000). To illustrate, history shows that attitudes toward and treatment of deviant (different from ordinary) behavior have changed over time. These changes are tied to larger societal forces such as the prevailing beliefs of a culture (Roccatagliata, 1986). Special educators in the 21st century should not ignore this lesson.

In addition, the brief historical overview that follows gives needed context for material found in later chapters. Of course, brief overviews necessarily call for generalizations that disregard subtle but important complications, counter-trends, and nuances. For fascinating detailed accounts, see Achenbach (1982); Colp (2005); Donohue, Hersen, and Ammerman (2000); Grob (1994); Kauffman (1976); Kauffman and Landrum (2006); Roccatagliata (1986); Silk et al. (2000); and Zilboorg and Henry (1941).

# Before the Twentieth Century

## Prehistoric Viewpoints

Several lines of evidence from the study of prehistory, early history, and anthropology (Sarason & Sarason, 1982; Kakar, 2005) indicate that people have long been concerned with deviant and disordered behavior. For example, prehistoric human skulls have been found whose former residents had undergone **trephining** (a procedure in which a hole is made in the skull) and lived. Was the purpose to remove brain tissue? To free evil spirits? Some other reason? Moreover, ancient writings of various religions label as deviant those who, for example, abuse alcohol, cannot control their tempers, are filthy, commit suicide, or experience delusions (Parrinder, 1983). Additionally, the people of early cultures, like those in many societies today, no doubt ingested various plant and fungus materials that change thinking, emotions, and behavior dramatically. Other obvious physical reasons for human deviance, such as behavior, emotion, and thought changes following illness or head injury, were no doubt familiar to our ancestors as well.

Probably, however, the earliest explanations of and treatments for behavioral deviance were mainly framed in terms of the supernatural (beyond natural or scientific explanation). To explain various aspects of life that were unpredictable or difficult to understand, many primitive societies presumably relied heavily on systems of belief involving the activities of spiritual powers (Butcher, Mineka, & Hooley, 2004; Kakar, 1982; Parrinder, 1983; Roccatagliata, 1986). Such powers must have been mediated through societally approved experts (magicians, elders, priests, wise ones, shamans) who played major roles in key aspects of life, including the interpretation and treatment of deviant emotions, behaviors, and cognitions (such as dreams). Many forms of E&B disorder probably were interpreted as evidence of possession by spirits—sometimes to be honored; sometimes exorcised through incantations, potions, or sacrifices; and sometimes resisted by expelling, confining, abusing, or killing the possessed person.

## Early Western Civilization

Among the many remarkable achievements of the classical Greek era were early medical explanations of deviant behavior (Green & Groff, 2003; Roccatagliata, 1986). Hippocrates, the "Father of Medicine," was a careful observer of human biology and behavior who proposed natural causes of physical and mental disorders, rejecting supernatural interpretations. He applied an earlier theory—that physical illnesses are caused by imbalances among four basic body **humors** (blood, phlegm, yellow bile, and black bile)—to explain normal and deviant emotions, behaviors, and thoughts. For instance, an excess of black bile was thought to cause melancholia (depression). The important legacies of this perspective are its insistence on finding natural causes of maladies and its suggestion of physiological causes of E&B disorder. These legacies foreshadow some modern biological perspectives, even though their specifics are basically inaccurate. Classical Greek perspectives remained influential in Europe and the Middle East for at least 15 centuries (Dols, 1992; Segal & Coolidge, 2001; Zilboorg & Henry, 1941).

More than 20 centuries ago, philosophers and physicians of the Roman era emphasized the importance of temperament and emotions in producing E&B disorder, suggesting that E&B disorders were just extremes of normal personality. Dreams and their interpretation continued to interest ancient philosophers and therapists, who also advocated discussion and reasoning as therapy for mental disorders, anticipating modern talking psychotherapies. Some authorities recommended comforting treatments for people with E&B disorder, such as special diets, body massage, therapeutic baths, mood-changing music, exercise, and pleasant environments for recovery (Colp, 2005; Roccatagliata, 1986).

On the other hand, like many past and present societies, Roman and Greek civilizations viewed children as property and thus absolutely subject to the will of parents or the government. Children with physical or mental disabilities were greatly devalued, and it was acceptable to abandon or kill them (Donohue et al., 2000).

## The Middle Ages

As the extended era of Roman civilization and its domination of the Western world declined, the Christian church grew in influence. From about 500 to 1300 AD, the church was the primary institution that stored historical, literary, and other elements of knowledge from early Western civilization. Church and state interests often overlapped, giving strong governmental power to religious leaders.

During this time, the church paid great attention to the influences of good and evil supernatural forces. Satan and his human intermediaries—magicians, sorcerers, witches, and others—were officially believed to cause many deviant behaviors, emotions, and thoughts. Such Satanic manifestations might be exorcised through the use of holy objects, potions, and prayers, especially if the person were involuntarily "possessed." Alternatively, if the deviant individual were viewed as voluntarily serving Satan, priests could best protect the populace and salvage that person's soul by imprisoning, torturing, or killing the carrier of evil. The latter option (e.g., the Inquisition) became widespread from about 1450 to 1600 over large areas of Europe.

Simultaneously, however, church leaders recognized biological and other non-Satanic causes of deviance. Thus they offered—in addition to religious support—counseling, consolation, other kind treatment, and asylum in monasteries and elsewhere (Foskett, 1996). Also, asylums built in the late medieval era by Islamic rulers in Spain may have prompted Christian European rulers to do the same (Colp, 2005).

## Renaissance Thinking

As the Middle Ages slowly came to a close in Europe, the influence of the church declined and competing ideas surfaced about many things. The view that a person should do little else but serve God and the church while preparing for the afterlife slowly gave way to a view that put more emphasis on the individual person's rights, achievements, and potential while in the present life. World-changing inventions and events such as timepieces, lenses that made small and distant objects visible, printing, and expeditions to faraway lands challenged long-standing perspectives on the place of humankind in the world (Borstin, 1983). Special value came to be placed on observation and reason—carefully observing events, drawing conclusions based on those observations, and defending such conclusions even if they challenged established beliefs. This change in emphasis is linked to the rise of science as a way of understanding the world, as well as expansions in literature, technology, exploration, music, and art—in other words, the Renaissance.

Starting about 1300, various Renaissance thinkers championed reason and appreciation for the individual person. Their challenges to traditional ideas set the stage for greatly changed conceptions of human physical, emotional, behavioral, and cognitive functioning. Based on reason and observation they opposed the official view that evil supernatural spirits are at the root of much human misery and deviance. So their challenges to prevailing ideas set the stage for very different conceptions of emotion, behavior, and thinking that contributed to modern psychological models of E&B disorder (Butcher et al., 2004).

Although these Renaissance thinkers helped revise our culture's ideas about normal and abnormal functioning, they had little immediate impact on treatment of people with E&B disorder, who might still be tortured or confined with little hope of release. This seems to have been especially so for children with E&B disorder (Mash & Dozois, 2003). Many of the asylums that had begun in charity to provide refuge and kind treatment came to be known for their deplorable conditions. For instance, in London, the monastery of Saint Mary of Bethlehem (pronounced "Bedlam") was a place where mentally ill people were kept; in Paris, they were kept at Bicêtre Hospital. "Kept," but often not cared for: "From the standpoint of the care and treatment of the mentally ill, Bedlam and Bicêtre were no more hospitals than a trench on a battlefield is a retreat and shelter of safety" (Zilboorg & Henry, 1941, p. 313). Treatment could be cruel; inmates, with heads shaven, were put in straitjackets and chains, isolated in dark cells, and forgotten except for occasions on which citizens could pay a small fee to the keepers for the privilege of observing these unfortunate children and adults displaying their deviant behavior (Zilboorg & Henry, 1941).

## The Late 18th and 19th Centuries

The emergence of humane treatment for people with E&B disorder is often traced to the appointment of Philippe Pinel as head of Bicêtre Hospital in 1792. Pinel argued for and received permission to reduce restraints and restrictions on the patients, maintaining that they were "intractable only because they are deprived of fresh air and of their liberty" (Zilboorg & Henry, 1941, p. 322). Under the more humane conditions, many patients showed improvement, indicating that confinement or inhumane treatment could contribute to or maintain E&B disorder. Pinel also strongly opposed some common medical therapies of those times, such as bloodletting, "ducking" in water, and administering potions and drugs indiscriminately. Instead, he advocated treating people with E&B disorder with kindness and respect (Segal & Coolidge, 2001).

Independent of Pinel, similar efforts at humane treatment were begun elsewhere (Colp, 2005), often motivated by religious or spiritual considerations. In England, William Tuke established the York Retreat to care for people with E&B disorder. In naming the facility a "retreat," Tuke hoped to avoid the stigma associated with the conventional term "asylum." York Retreat provided a family-like setting in which the residents could work, live, and exercise within a supportive environment. In the United States, the innovations of Pinel and Tuke were reflected in the efforts of Benjamin Rush, a signer of the Declaration of Independence, energetic social reformer, and founder of psychiatry in the United States. Rush fought for and achieved more humane conditions for people with E&B disorder (Achenbach, 1982; Kauffman, 1976).

The work of Pinel, Tuke, Rush, and others is generally referred to as **moral treatment**. Practitioners of moral treatment tried to improve the social, psychological, and physical well-being of their patients by providing recreational, athletic, educational, vocational, and other productive activities. The moral therapist used kindness and patience to treat people with E&B disorder, but also persistent firmness in emphasizing that they were expected to behave and think more acceptably (Bockoven, 1963; Colp, 2005).

In the early 1800s, American proponents of moral treatment established several facilities patterned after the York Retreat. They seemed to be effective but were generally reserved for clients who could afford the considerable cost. A crusade for extension of moral treatment and medical therapy to the poor, through the development of publicly funded institutions, was led by Dorothea Dix (Display 2-1). Her appeals to citizens in general, wealthy and influential people, and state legislatures led to the establishment of about 30 new facilities and the enlargement of existing ones. Their control was placed in the hands of physicians specializing in the new medical discipline of psychiatry, which tended to favor biological explanations of E&B disorder. Guided by this perspective, these facilities soon became "mental hospitals."

Unfortunately the public mental hospitals did not capture the essence of moral treatment, for various reasons (Achenbach, 1982). Legislatures failed to provide adequate financial support, the institutions rapidly became overcrowded, and

**Display 2-1** Dorothea Dix profile

> Dorothea Dix (1802–1887) was a humanitarian who, beginning in her teenage years, started and operated schools in New England for nearly two decades, until illness forced her to stop. While offering religious services in a Massachusetts jail, she became deeply troubled over the confinement there of adults with emotional and behavioral problems along with the criminals. After determining that this was a widespread practice, she issued a report describing the inhumane conditions she found. Dix persuaded the Massachusetts legislature to provide separate and improved facilities for people with E&B disorder.
>
> For four decades Dix crusaded in many states for similar improvements. Through her persuasive public speaking, published writings, and private appeals to key citizens, she obtained in numerous states publicly financed residential facilities for poor people with E&B disorder and improved living and treatment conditions for them. She carried her campaign of reform to several European countries as well.
>
> Among her many other humanitarian accomplishments were prison reform and advocacy for deaf-blind-mute people. During the Civil War, Dorothea Dix organized and administered nursing services for the U.S. Army.

*Sources:* Kazdin, 2000; Zilboorg & Henry, 1941.

crucial features of moral treatment (e.g., kind, individualized treatment) were neglected. Mental hospitals became mainly custodial, and conditions often were as bad as in the jails, streets, and poorhouses where many of their residents were formerly found.

### *Growth of Education*

Developments outlined so far relate to people with E&B disorder, not particularly to children with E&B disorder. In the late 18th and 19th centuries, other events helped shape contemporary special education for children with E&B disorder.

***Compulsory Schooling.*** Early in our nation's history, even very young children commonly contributed to family survival by helping their parents in farming or businesses. With the expansion of the Industrial Revolution, children could still help the family by working in factories or elsewhere, but they were widely victimized by unhealthy working conditions and the loss of educational opportunities. Laws restricting child labor and requiring school attendance contributed to the growth of the public school system.

Public schools also played a major role in socializing the children of millions of culturally and ethnically diverse immigrants to the United States in the latter half of the 19th century. Thus the role of schools changed from that of a relatively minor social institution primarily for the middle and upper classes to one intended to deal with all children: "Compulsory school attendance marked a new era in the history of American education. . . . Thousands of recalcitrants and incorrigibles who in former times might have dropped out of school now became public charges" (Cremin, 1961, p. 127).

***Education for Special Groups.*** Because of the educational problems of an increasing number of children who could not adapt to regular school programs, educational alternatives—special classes, ungraded programs, tutorial sessions, truancy classes, and disciplinary classes—began to appear (Richardson, 1999). Such alternatives were established first in large cities (Osgood, 2000), but by the early 1900s nearly 200 cities had programs for difficult students (Sarason & Doris, 1979). Social critics of the time noted that the labels assigned to students in the special education classes were stigmatizing, that the poor and race-ethnic minorities were disproportionately represented, and that such programs often isolated rather than educated the children. Of course, these same issues and criticisms confront special educators today.

***Special Teaching Techniques.*** The origin of specialized teaching methods for people with disabilities is often traced to the work of Jean-Marc-Gaspard Itard, a French physician and student of Pinel. In 1799, Itard began his work with Victor, a 12-year-old "wild boy" who had been found by hunters after apparently being abandoned at age 2 or 3. Victor had been diagnosed as profoundly retarded, and Itard's description indicated extreme behavior and emotional problems as well (Kauffman, 1976). Using a systematic, structured education plan featuring sensory stimulation and rewards for appropriate behavior, Itard taught Victor to spell simple words, follow easy instructions, identify a number of objects, and perform personal hygiene skills. Itard's work is an important legacy to special education because of the optimism he inspired, the successes he achieved, and the systematic teaching procedures he described.

## THE 20TH CENTURY AND BEYOND

Several developments of the 20th century were especially important in shaping special education and other treatments for children with E&B disorder (Mash & Dozois, 2003; Musto, 2002; Silk et al., 2000; Wicks-Nelson & Israel, 2006). These include a growth in scientific study of children's psychological development; organized efforts to promote children's welfare and psychological adjustment; the rise of a profession of special education; court decisions and laws that required and encouraged the provision of appropriate education to children and adolescents with education disabilities, including emotional disturbance (ED); an increase in critical analysis of how our society serves children with E&B disorder; and the emergence of psychological models for understanding and treating E&B disorder, along with adaptations of the models for students with ED.

### Scientific Study of Children

Until the very end of the 19th century, there had been little systematic study of normal or abnormal child development. Children were generally perceived as miniature versions of adults, so when E&B disorder of children was considered at all, it tended to be seen as an early-occurring form of adult disorder. Progress in understanding the psychology of child development would reveal that this is not always true.

One of the first scholars to carefully examine what children and adolescents think and know at various points in their development was G. Stanley Hall. Hall was a founder of the discipline of psychology, an early proponent of scientifically studying young people's development (Musto, 2002), and the author of books and other publications that described how young people develop in and adapt to their environments. Hall believed his scientific approach to child study would revolutionize child-rearing, education, and even U.S. society (Borstin, 1974). Beginning in the early 1900s, several of Hall's students elaborated his work on child study and related issues. For instance, Arnold Gesell intensively observed many children over several years, concluding that child psychological development is largely a biologically conditioned "unfolding" process characterized by definite stages. In 1921, Lewis Terman began a longitudinal study of a large number of children that lasted five decades. Its purpose was to measure physical, emotional, behavioral, and cognitive characteristics to obtain objective information on how these characteristics typically change or remain stable throughout development.

From such beginnings the scientific study of emotional, behavior, and cognitive development has grown steadily in magnitude and taken many different directions (Berk, 2006; Bukatko & Daehler, 2004; Shaffer, 2002). Research into biological influences on development has made steady progress in revealing how some psychological characteristics are inherited and how brain functioning can play a role in normal and abnormal emotions, behaviors, and thoughts. Other significant research has examined psychosocial (psychological, social, and cultural) determinants of young people's emotions, behaviors, and thoughts. For example, studies of psychosocial conditions of children that are associated with a heightened chance of later E&B disorder have identified a variety of risk factors (see Chapter 6) and clarified our understanding of how E&B disorders are caused.

Another interesting and promising area of child study has been empirical classification, in which statistical techniques are used to establish categories of E&B disorder (see Chapter 3). In the 1960s, Herbert Quay and others applied statistical techniques to data collected on the emotional and behavior problems of large numbers of children and adolescents, to find which problems tend to occur together. Studying young people of various ages and situations (Quay, Morse, & Cutler, 1966; Quay & Peterson, 1996), Quay consistently found several co-occurring collections of problems. He considered each collection to be one category in an **empirical** (based on observation and experience) system for classifying E&B disorders. More recently, Thomas Achenbach and associates (Achenbach & Rescorla, 2001) have further developed empirical classification of children's E&B disorder through advanced measurement and analysis techniques.

Results from the scientific study of child development are important not only for understanding E&B disorder of children but for treating them (Mash & Dozois, 2003; Tankersley et al., 2004). For one thing, objective information on emotions, behaviors, and cognition at various points during development tells us what is typical (normal). This helps teachers and other professionals judge the nature and extent of deviance in a particular child. Second, a major purpose of intervention for children with E&B disorder is to restore their development to a more normal course.

Research that better specifies what constitutes "a normal course" can help us select goals of intervention. Third, by learning which early behaviors and other characteristics predict later maladjustment, we may be able to identify the children who are most likely to benefit from preventive services.

Within the past three decades the amount, diversity, and significance of this biological and psychosocial research has generated a new multidisciplinary field: *developmental psychopathology.* It is concerned with how biological and psychosocial forces interact in normal and deviant human development, including children's E&B disorders (Mash & Dozois, 2003; Rutter, 2002; Wicks-Nelson & Israel, 2006). Research on disorders of emotion, behavior, and cognition encountered during development is usually reported in professional journals, of which Display 2-2 lists a selection.

**Display 2-2** Selected professional periodicals publishing research on E&B disorder of children and adolescents

---

*American Journal of Orthopsychiatry*
*Behavior Modification*
*Behavioral Disorders*
*Beyond Behavior*
*Child Abuse & Neglect*
*Child and Family Behavior Therapy*
*Clinical Child and Family Psychology Review*
*Crime and Delinquency*
*Development and Psychopathology*
*Education and Treatment of Children*
*Intervention in School and Clinic*
*Journal of Abnormal Child Psychology*
*Journal of the American Academy of Child and Adolescent Psychiatry*
*Journal of Applied Behavior Analysis*
*Journal of Child and Family Studies*
*Journal of Clinical Child Psychology*
*Journal of Emotional and Behavioral Disorders*
*Journal of Positive Behavior Interventions*
*Journal of School Psychology*
*Journal of Special Education*
*Journal of the American Academy of Child and Adolescent Psychiatry*
*Reclaiming Children and Youth*
*Remedial and Special Education*
*School Psychology Quarterly*
*School Psychology Review*

## Child Mental Health

With increased interest in children's psychological development came an increased concern for their physical and psychological well-being (Lourie, 2003; Musto, 2002). In 1896, the first psychological clinic for children in the United States was opened at the University of Pennsylvania by Lightner Witmer, who adapted principles of psychology to help children with learning and behavior problems. Another early clinic was the Juvenile Psychopathic Institute, established by William Healy in 1909 for the treatment of delinquent adolescents. About this time, psychiatrist Adolph Meyer emphasized the importance of unfortunate childhood experiences as causes of E&B disorder and insisted that adult maladjustment could be prevented during childhood.

### *Mental Hygiene*

A book published in 1908 led to increased public understanding of E&B disorder and a reform movement. In *A Mind That Found Itself,* Clifford Beers described his institutionalization for and recovery from a depressive mental disorder. Beers exposed inhumane conditions and inadequate treatment often found in mental hospitals and suggested needed reforms in mental health care. Beers, together with Meyer and other professionals, helped establish the National Committee for Mental Hygiene in 1909. This event signaled the start of the **mental hygiene movement** in the U.S.

Mental hygiene involves advancing social and personal conditions that support good emotional and behavioral functioning, prevent E&B disorder, and restore good functioning to people with E&B disorder (Colp, 2005). Among the Committee's purposes were educating the public about mental health and mental illness, encouraging prevention and early identification of mental illness, and improving services—especially reforming mental hospitals. In accord with its purposes, the Committee encouraged research on and innovative services to young people with E&B disorder.

For example, the Committee supported and conducted surveys of children's mental health, finding that (a) behavior and emotional problems among children were surprisingly extensive and (b) most E&B disorders of children were not hopeless or permanent, but (c) existing services were grossly inadequate. Later, it advocated legislation that created the National Institute of Mental Health, a U.S. government agency that supports research and service related to E&B disorder.

The Committee also helped establish child guidance clinics that developed a multidisciplinary team approach to treatment. Psychologists tested and interviewed children, social workers contacted parents, and psychiatrists provided treatment (Achenbach, 1982). This approach spread and evolved in the decades following its beginning in 1921 in Boston. For example, child guidance clinics made cooperative arrangements with the schools and juvenile courts. In 1950, the Committee merged with other groups, and continues its work as the National Mental Health Association.

### *Drug Treatment*

For several decades, psychotropic (psychologically active) medication has been an important form of treatment for E&B disorder of children (Birmaher & Axelson, 2005; Gershon, 2002; Heyman & Santosh, 2002; Scahill & Martin, 2002). Sedatives and various other drugs prepared from plants and other natural sources have long been used in treatment of adults, and perhaps children, with E&B disorder. A large variety of modern psychotropics are not from natural sources but are chemically synthesized. Bradley (1937) reported learning and behavior benefits of using amphetamine with children in residential treatment for E&B disorder. Since then the variety of therapeutic drugs has greatly increased (Konopasek & Forness, 2004; see Chapter 12), as have the number of children receiving them and the degree to which such intervention is controversial, at least with the general public.

The growth of multidisciplinary child guidance clinics foreshadowed the development of contemporary community-based, multidisciplinary approaches to serving children and adolescents with E&B disorder (Eber & Keenan, 2004; Lourie & Hernandez, 2003). The mental hygiene and child mental health movements increased professional and public concern about E&B disorder of young people, and provided directions for concrete efforts in these areas. One important direction has been special education for children with E&B disorder.

## The Profession of Special Education

Along with compulsory school attendance laws, the growth of education in residential institutions for people with disabilities helped set the stage for the emergence of special education as a profession. In the late 1800s and early 1900s, preparation to work with children having physical, sensory, and intellectual disabilities generally took place within institutions where many of them lived. Training was provided primarily for employees, but public school teachers occasionally participated as well. Around 1900, a few U.S. colleges began to offer courses on children with disabilities, and by the 1920s some states had certification requirements for special education teachers. From 1910 to the mid-1940s, there was slow, geographically uneven, but steady growth in special education for students with various disabilities, including E&B disorder. Counselors, psychologists, and social workers worked with educators in meeting students' emotional and social needs.

Many U.S. servicemen returned from World War II with physical, sensory, and psychological disabilities, which generated strongly supportive attitudes and policies about people with disabilities. In these postwar years, parents and advocacy organizations worked for and demanded more and better professional services, including special education, for children with disabilities. By this time most states had enacted laws providing for the education of children with some kinds of disabilities; state and federal financial support was increasing; and universities were accelerating their efforts to prepare special education teachers.

During the 1950s, special education for children with E&B disorder became more widespread in public schools as well as residential institutions and special schools

Educators and other professionals concerned with the well-being of students with E&B disorders founded CCBD, which is nearing its 50th anniversary.

(Smith & Wood, 1986), as recognition grew that education is often an indispensable part of the overall therapy. In a status report on U.S. school programs for students with E&B disorder, Morse, Cutler, and Fink (1964) found that such programs were no longer rare, but were often plagued by poor administration and inappropriate teacher preparation—or none at all.

In New York in 1922, Elizabeth Farrell, a special education teacher and instructor at Columbia University, and others interested in the welfare of exceptional children created an organization that was to become the Council for Exceptional Children (CEC) (Kode, 2002). As the chief professional association for special educators, CEC advocates legal and other changes, publishes journals and instruction materials, organizes conferences and other professional development opportunities, and sponsors professional subgroups (divisions) for specialized concerns. On of CEC's specialized interest divisions, the **Council for Children with Behavioral Disorders (CCBD)**, was created in 1964 (Display 2-3).

## Legal Developments

U.S. laws and agencies have become much more prominent in education of students with E&B disorder since the mid-20th century. In 1950, Congress enacted a law that financed college preparation of teachers of students with mental retardation and later, teachers of students with E&B disorder. In 1966, a federal bureau (now called the Office of Special Education Programs within the U.S. Department of Education) was formed to encourage teacher training, research, and other programs related to education of students with disabilities. Federal financial support for special education

**Display 2-3** Council for Children With Behavioral Disorders

The work of many dedicated people and organizations, especially a pioneering Michigan organization for teachers of students with E&B disorder, culminated in the approval in 1964 of a national professional organization for educators and others concerned for students with ED: the Council for Children With Behavioral Disorders (CCBD). The general purposes of CCBD are to promote the education and general welfare of children and youth with E&B disorder and to promote professional growth and research as a means to better assist these young people. With approximately 8,000 members, CCBD pursues its purposes through the following:
1. Advocacy in work with government agencies and other organizations
2. Sponsorship of conferences, workshops, materials, and other professional development activities
3. Support for the work of regional CCBD groups
4. Publications addressing research and practice
5. Opportunities for social networking and mutual support among CCBD members

CCBD keeps abreast of and works to affect government policies on education of children with E&B disorder. It operates with other organizations to pursue common goals. Its position papers present CCBD viewpoints on selected issues in education of children with E&B disorder, including terminology and definitions of emotional and behavioral disabilities, punishment, school discipline, cultural diversity, and assessment. The organization sponsors conferences and training events on current topics.

Branches of CCBD have been established in nearly all U.S. states and Canadian provinces. They influence the parent organization's policies and actions and are supported in their pursuit of local issues. Among its publications are CCBD's journal of research and policy, *Behavioral Disorders*, and *Beyond Behavior*, which emphasizes teaching practices and the experiences of practitioners.

*Sources:* Bullock & Menendez, 1999; Wood, 1999.

in the United States has risen steadily from less than $1 million in 1960 to about $50 billion per year in recent years (USD Education, 2002).

Until the middle of the 20th century it was widely assumed that attendance at public school was not an unrevokable right but a privilege that need not be extended to every child and that could be withdrawn under certain conditions. Children and adolescents showing physical, sensory, or learning problems were sometimes excluded; those with severe misbehavior or E&B disorders very often were.

During the period 1950 to 1975, the conditions under which young people could be excluded or unserved by public education became more and more limited. This was largely due to the advocacy of parents, professionals, and organizations, including outcomes of lawsuits, which produced changes in local and state laws. In 1975, the landmark federal special education law, Education for All Handicapped Children Act, made it illegal for public education agencies to avoid providing education to a student with any education disability (Friend, 2005; Heward, 2006), including ED.

The nature of special education for children with E&B disorder has been shaped by various legal developments that clarified and extended the educational and related rights of students with disabilities (Kauffman & Landrum, 2006). Their access to appropriate public education has been pursued through a **litigation-legislation-litigation cycle**, similar to that used to establish other civil rights. This process begins with court cases in which specific complaints are heard. After several court decisions establish a trend of legal precedents, the principles decided in court are put into laws. In the third step, concerned parties begin additional court cases to clarify details and limits of the new laws and to ensure compliance with them.

### *Background Litigation*
The right-to-education movement for students with disabilities is often traced to the famous civil rights case of *Brown v. Board of Education* in 1954, in which the U.S. Supreme Court ruled that racially segregated public education was a violation of the rights of Black children to equal treatment under the law. This decision's general implication was that one child may not be educated differently from others without very good legal reasons.

Later court decisions directly addressed educational rights for students with disabilities. For example, in the 1972 case of *Pennsylvania Association for Retarded Children v. Commonwealth of Pennsylvania*, the court ruled that because Pennsylvania provided a free public education to its children, it could not deny this to a child with mental retardation, even severe retardation. Other court decisions soon broadened this ruling to include other disabilities and U.S. regions. Still other cases dealt with various special education practices, including student eligibility, assessment, "related services" (those that support education), and discipline (Turnbull, Huerta, & Stowe, 2006; Yell, 2006). Together the court cases defined several basic rights for students with education disabilities that became codified into federal legislation affecting special education, as well as similar state laws and regulations.

### *Legislation*
The Education for All Handicapped Children Act of 1975, hailed as a "Bill of Rights" for students with disabilities, has been amended several times and renamed IDEA 2004 (see Chapter 1). It requires school systems to ensure a free, appropriate education for every qualifying student with an education disability, including ED. Additionally, states have similar laws that reiterate and in some cases expand provisions and protections for students with disabilities.

### *Follow-Up Litigation*
The federal special education law contains ambiguities. Quite a few lawsuits have been filed over the years to resolve disputes about the meaning of many of its features. Some of the decisions, out-of-court settlements, and other results of these lawsuits have produced important changes in assessment, identification, teaching, and other matters involving students with disabilities (Turnbull et al., 2006; Yell, 2006). Follow-up litigation will continue to determine the meaning of IDEA 2004.

## Criticism of Society's Responses to Children with E&B Disorder

Over the years, concerned people have pointed out desperate needs of children with E&B disorder and critical shortcomings in the services for them. In the last hundred years, many investigations and reports have been sponsored by government

**Display 2-4** Selected reports addressing young people with E&B disorder

*Crisis in Child Mental Health* (Joint Commission on the Mental Health of Children, 1969) was the report of experts empaneled by President Lyndon Johnson. It found that mental health treatment was generally unavailable except to the most disturbed and disruptive children, and then most often in highly restrictive settings such as mental hospitals. This report recommended prevention of E&B disorder through family support and health services, increased child advocacy to obtain and coordinate services for children with E&B disorder and their families, and basing those services primarily in communities and schools instead of institutions.

*A System of Care for Children and Youth with Severe Emotional Disturbance* (Stroul & Friedman, 1986) described problems related to children's E&B disorder and proposed sweeping changes in mental health services for them. As in earlier reports, the main problems were that such services were (a) generally unavailable, (b) especially to race-ethnically diverse children. If available, they were often (c) poorly coordinated and (d) located in restrictive, faraway placements and (e) they excluded families in planning and delivery. To correct the problems, Beth Stroul and Robert Friedman advocated a reformed "system of care" (see Chapter 12) that would encourage state and other agencies and organizations to work together, deliver services locally, treat family members as a main resource for intervention, and make special efforts to serve race-ethnically diverse young people.

*At the Schoolhouse Door* (Knitzer, Steinberg, & Fleisch, 1990) evaluated special education for students with ED by considering professional literature, interviews of practitioners and parents, and visits to selected programs. This report found major problems involving identification, placement, instruction, and supportive services. Students with ED often were bored with unchallenging content, waited a long time for instruction or help, and got little recess or physical education. Many of their teachers were poorly prepared, emphasized order over learning, and instructed mainly via teacher-centered lecturing. The result was quiet but uninspiring classrooms of socially isolated students who had few opportunities to develop self-control. Supportive mental health services were rarely available. Knitzer's report called for changes in teacher preparation and placement of mental health workers in school programs for ED.

The *Peacock Hill Paper* (Peacock Hill Working Group, 1991), by James Kauffman and others, was a response to *At the Schoolhouse Door* and other strong criticisms of special education for students with ED. It reviewed significant problems, then surveyed effective practices and programs at preschool, elementary, and secondary levels. Peacock Hill rejected radical changes that could "throw out the baby with the bathwater." It argued for continued scientific development of favorable practices and emphasized that practices and programs of known effectiveness must become widely used.

*Mental Health: A Report of the Surgeon General* (USDHHS, 1999) resulted from collaboration of U.S. agencies heavily involved in research and services related to mental health and E&B disorder, along with many experts. This report examined research and services across the life span, with substantial attention to children and adolescents. The surgeon general's report emphasized scientific breakthroughs in understanding and treating E&B disorder, and the growth of advocacy movements to eliminate stigma attached to mental illness and to push for extensive family involvement in deciding intervention services for a child's E&B disorder. This document stressed that because mental health is a fundamental aspect of overall health, E&B disorders should be viewed primarily as health conditions. It concluded that there are effective interventions for a variety of E&B disorders.

agencies, professional organizations, charitable foundations, advocacy groups, and other concerned parties. As long ago as 1915, the National Committee for Mental Hygiene presented data that showed how great were the problems of children with E&B disorder and how limited the services available to them. This report was one basis for dramatic increases in child mental health services in the first half of the 20th century.

Since 1960, recognition of mental health and related needs of children and adolescents—and perhaps the needs themselves—have greatly increased. It is clear that the number and severity of these needs are far beyond existing service capacities (Mash & Dozois, 2003; USDHHS, 1999). Over these same years there have been changes in American life that put more young people at risk for E&B disorder (see Chapter 6), such as sharp increases in children of single parents and children who are immigrants, together with continued poverty (Zigler, Finn-Stevenson, & Tanner, 2002). These problems and some recommended solutions have been presented in numerous influential reports. Selections are abstracted in Display 2-4.

One person who stands out in this regard is Jane Knitzer, who has examined mental health, education, early childhood care, and other services for children with E&B disorder, exposed them as deficient, and recommended corrective actions (Knitzer, 1982; Knitzer, Steinberg, & Fleisch, 1990; Yoshikawa & Knitzer, 1997; Display 2-5). Her report, *Unclaimed Children* (Knitzer, 1982), revealed huge problems in the policies and treatments for children with E&B disorder. This report caused widespread professional soul searching and sparked new initiatives to correct these problems.

Such an initiative was the Child and Adolescent Service System Program (CASSP), a federal effort to foster innovation and improvement in states' mental health services to children. CASSP encouraged states to make children's mental health a top priority, ensure collaboration among mental health and other agencies that serve children,

**Display 2-5** Jane Knitzer

> Jane Knitzer's advocacy for children with emotional and behavior challenges and their families has greatly influenced state and federal policies affecting them. Knitzer received her doctoral degree in school psychology in 1968 at Harvard University and has experience in school, clinical, and community settings. Early work with low-income families taught her that professionals can be inadvertently disrespectful to people who are poor or culturally diverse. This insight led Knitzer away from clinical practice and toward efforts for larger scale changes.
>
> At the Children's Defense Fund, a national child advocacy organization, Knitzer analyzed policy and practice in the child welfare system. The resulting report, *Children Without Homes* (brief title) affected federal child welfare legislation. Knitzer became committed to training professionals in various service disciplines, emphasizing a family perspective in policies to help children, and using research to improve such policies. These commitments were evident in later reports such as *Unclaimed Children* and *At the Schoolhouse Door*. Knitzer has been honored in various ways, including the Nicholas Hobbs Award for child advocacy from the American Psychological Association, the Marion F. Langer Award from the American Association of Orthopsychiatry, and the Outstanding Contribution to Leadership in Behavioral Disorders Award from the Midwest Symposium on Behavior Disorders. She has served as president of Division 37 (Children, Family and Youth Services) of the American Psychological Association and president of the American Association of Orthopsychiatry. Presently Knitzer is Director, National Center for Children in Poverty, Columbia University.

increase availability of local, "community-based" services, help families advocate for their children with E&B disorder, and better accommodate the needs of race-ethnic and language minority children and families.

The use of these and related CASSP principles creates what is called a *system of care* (Stroul & Friedman, 1986; see Chapter 12). System-of-care concepts and practices are revolutionizing mental health, juvenile justice, and other child service systems, as well as influencing special education for students with ED (Eber & Keenan, 2004; Stroul, 2003).

Several years later, Knitzer turned her attention to special education for students with ED in *At the Schoolhouse Door* (Knitzer et al., 1990; Steinberg & Knitzer, 1992). She found serious problems in many areas, most alarmingly in deficient instruction and curriculum, overemphasis on control of behavior, and uncoordinated mental health and other needed services. As with her earlier exposé of mental health services, Knitzer's recommendations for educational improvements have been influential. In recognition of such problems with education for students with ED (e.g., Knitzer et al., 1990; Peacock Hill Working Group, 1991), the U.S. Department of Education in the early 1990s sponsored the development of a **National Agenda** of actions needed to enable more success for students with ED (USD Education, 1995) (Display 2-6).

**Display 2-6** Summary of National Agenda targets for improving services and outcomes for children and youth with ED

---

**Target 1:** *Expand Positive Learning Opportunities and Results:* Provide engaging, useful, and positive learning opportunities to students with ED.

**Target 2:** *Strengthen School and Community Capacity:* Strengthen the capacity of schools and communities to serve students with ED in the least restrictive environments appropriate.

**Target 3:** *Value and Address Diversity:* Encourage culturally competent collaborations among families, professionals, students, and communities, including services that are responsive to issues of race, culture, gender, and social and economic status.

**Target 4:** *Collaborate With Families:* Include family members on the team of service providers that implements family focused services that are school-and community-based.

**Target 5:** *Promote Appropriate Assessment:* Ensure that culturally appropriate, ethical, and functional practices are integral to the identification, design, and delivery of services.

**Target 6:** *Provide Ongoing Skill Development and Support:* Strengthening the knowledge, understanding, and sensitivity of families, teachers, service providers, and other stakeholders to collaborate, persevere, and improve outcomes for children and youth with ED.

**Target 7:** *Create Comprehensive and Collaborative Systems:* Promote family-centered, community-based, and appropriately funded services built around the individual needs of children and youth with and at risk of developing ED.

---

*Source:* USD Education, 1995.

# Psychological Models

Humans have probably always had various ideas and philosophies about the emotions, behaviors, and thoughts involved in conflict and distress, but the development of extensive psychological models (theories about the nature, causes, and treatments) of E&B disorder began in earnest in the 20th century. The influence of psychological models has been and remains so pervasive that there may be a tendency to overlook it. Yet it is difficult to imagine the shape of contemporary special education for students with ED—in fact, most interventions for children and adults with E&B disorder—without these models.

One could identify dozens of models or just a handful (Corsini & Wedding, 2005; Friedman & Schustack, 2005; Schultz & Schultz, 2005; Wicks-Nelson & Israel, 2006), depending on whether modest theory differences are taken to represent separate models or variations in the same one. Two models—the psychodynamic and behavioral models—are briefly described here because of their special historical impact on the education of students with ED. Chapters 7 through 10 present concepts and practical applications of psychodynamic, behavioral, cognitive, and other models in more detail.

## Psychodynamic Model

In the psychodynamic model, a combination of biological forces and social relationships, especially between child and parent, create and activate intrapsychic processes (special mental structures and forces) that develop beginning in early life. Interactions among these intrapsychic processes, although often unconscious (beyond the person's awareness), create needs and other motivations that cause various emotions, behaviors, and cognitions. It is unconscious disturbances involving these intrapsychic processes that cause a person to experience or exhibit maladaptive or distressing emotions, behaviors, and thoughts. In other words, just as fever, nausea, and other ills are symptoms of a disease, E&B disorders are symptoms of intrapsychic disturbance.

Psychodynamic interventions generally do not attempt to change maladaptive emotions, behaviors, and thoughts directly. This is because reducing or eliminating such symptoms does not correct the intrapsychic disturbance that caused them. The intrapsychic disturbance remains to generate other symptoms, perhaps more serious than the original. Instead, the general goal of psychodynamic intervention is to help the person achieve insight (deep understanding) into the nature and origins of his intrapsychic disturbance. Thus he will become able to improve his own maladaptive emotions, thoughts, and behaviors.

### *The Psychodynamic Model and Children.*

Sigmund Freud's *psychoanalysis* (see Display 2-7) is the starting point for all psychodynamic perspectives (Marans & Cohen, 2002; Meissner, 2005). Although Freud performed psychoanalysis almost entirely with adults, many of his disciples applied psychoanalytic treatment to children in clinics and other settings.

**Display 2-7** Sigmund Freud profile

---

Sigmund Freud (1856–1939) studied medicine, was particularly interested in neurology, and spent 8 years researching neurology in the laboratory. He then began a clinical practice in neurology, but was dissatisfied with conventional treatments, which seemed insufficient to remedy the psychological problems of many of his patients. In the latter half of the 19th century, most mental disorders were thought to have biological causes, but Freud doubted that all of his patients' problems were biological in origin.

Freud knew that hypnotized persons could be made to behave as if they could not see, hear, move, or remember. Based on this and other considerations Freud concluded that there must be a largely unknown part of the mind—the unconscious—that strongly influences behaviors, emotions, and thoughts. The unconscious seemed to make sense of the previously illogical symptoms of his patients.

Freud then began work on the theory of psychoanalysis that was to consume nearly half a century of hypothesizing, exploring how his ideas applied to patients that he treated, and revising his theory as needed. Freudian psychoanalysis is a theory of normal personality development, an explanation of the origins of E&B disorder, and a method of treating persons experiencing E&B disorder or dissatisfaction with their lives. It not only altered the course of psychology, it has widely influenced many human-service professions, including education for children with E&B disorder. Psychoanalysis also continues to influence art, literature, and the general public's ideas about psychological functioning and malfunctioning.

---

*Sources:* Corsini & Wedding, 2005; Friedman & Schustack, 2005; Schultz & Schultz, 2005.

In the 1920s, August Aichhorn, a disciple of Freud, applied the psychodynamic model in a residential program for antisocial boys (Aichhorn, 1965; Brendtro & Long, 1998). Aichhorn interpreted their aggressive and delinquent behavior as symptoms of unconscious intrapsychic disturbances caused by a lack of parental warmth and love in their early formative years. Aichhorn's program provided a friendly, permissive atmosphere, fostered relationships between students and staff, and encouraged frequent individual discussion opportunities, but did not pressure a boy to reform. In this environment, the boys were free to act out their disturbances through misbehavior, which the staff explained to them in psychoanalytic terms so as to help them understand the unconscious causes of their misbehavior. Aichhorn reported that although antisocial acts temporarily increased, after therapeutic bonds developed between student and staff the antisocial symptoms typically diminished.

Similar psychodynamic principles have been applied within classrooms. Pearl Berkowitz and Esther Rothman (Berkowitz, 1974; Berkowitz & Rothman, 1960), teachers at New York's Bellevue Hospital school in the 1950s, described teaching practices for students with E&B disorder that were basically classroom extensions of psychodynamic therapy. The role of the teacher was to accept and understand the student's behavior no matter how deviant it might be, thus building the student's capabilities to understand and accept herself.

Such permissive practices are now rare. One reason is that they are incompatible with educating students with ED in most schools. Much more common are adaptations of the psychodynamic model that can be more readily accommodated by schools (see Chapter 7).

For example, in 1946, Fritz Redl and David Wineman opened Pioneer House, a residential treatment center for severely aggressive preadolescent boys—the "children

On-the-spot therapeutic discussions are intended to help a young person gain insight into his or her problems.

who hate," who very soon become the "children nobody wants" (Redl & Wineman, 1951). The psychodynamic treatment at Pioneer House involved a **therapeutic milieu** (environment designed to encourage improvement) based on three main premises. First, the staff created a nurturing climate by tolerating misbehavior up to a point and providing friendly affection regardless of misbehavior. Second, the boys' time was filled with nonaggressive recreation and other activities carefully chosen to provide success in order to develop feelings of competence and self-control. Third, incidents of emotional distress and behavioral conflict were selected as occasions for *life space interviews*. These were on-the-spot therapeutic discussions about such incidents intended to help the young people recognize their problems, understand the unconscious and other causes of them, and solve them (Brendtro, 2001; Morse, 2001).

Importantly, however, Redl made it clear to the children that "we like you, we take you the way you are, but of course in the long range we'd like you to change" (Redl & Wineman, 1952, p. 59). Thus Redl broke with other applications of the psychodynamic model by not only providing therapy when and where behavior incidents occur (instead of at a scheduled time and place) but rejecting total permissiveness about misbehavior. By adapting psychodynamic concepts to the realities of intervention with groups of children, Redl established a *psychoeducational* (psychodynamic-educational) approach that has continued to influence educators of students with ED (Long, 1974; Long & Morse, 1996; Long, Wood, & Fecser, 2001; Wood, Brendtro, Fecser, & Nichols, 1999).

Nicholas Long (Display 2-8), who worked with Redl, advanced the psychoeducational approach by developing the *Conflict Cycle* (Long, 1974), a simplified psychodynamic interpretation of E&B disorder as a self-sustaining cycle of stress and reaction

**Display 2-8** Nicholas Long profile

> Nicholas J. Long has served with distinction in various professional roles. In 1953, he worked at an early psychoeducational program for young people with emotional and behavior problems, the University of Michigan Fresh-Air camp. After receiving his doctorate in child development and educational psychology from University of Michigan (1956), he directed the Children's Residential Treatment Center at the National Institute of Mental Health, under the leadership of Fritz Redl.
>
> These experiences deepened Long's understanding of group interaction, the therapeutic role of social relationships, and the influence of daily life events on children's emotions and behaviors. He realized that to foster emotional growth and self-esteem, one must help the child overcome stressful situations rather than eliminate the stress itself. He also saw that the treatment principles espoused by Redl needed to be applied in public schools serving students with E&B disorder.
>
> During the 1960s and 1970s, Long expanded applications of the psychoeducational approach in education situations. He formulated the Conflict Cycle and developed strategies for altering or stopping the Conflict Cycle so that teachers could both manage inappropriate school behavior and teach students to overcome stressful crises on their own.
>
> In addition to direct work with children having E&B disorder and director of programs serving such young people, Long has been a distinguished teacher trainer. He has served on the faculty at American University and other institutions and is well known for innovative, field-based teacher training programs built around the psychoeducational approach. Long is coeditor of *Conflict in the Classroom*, a widely used text for teachers of students with E&B disorder since 1965, now in its fifth edition. He has edited professional periodicals (e.g., *Reclaiming Children and Youth*) and authored influential journal articles. Nicholas Long has received many professional and service awards, including the Outstanding Teacher Educator Award (1993) from the Teacher Education Division, Council for Exceptional Children.

*Source:* Long, 1974.

to stress. The conflict cycle (see Chapter 7) helps teachers visualize and understand a student's problems and decide how to intervene. Another Long contribution was clarifying Redl's life space interview and expanding it into *life space crisis intervention* (Long et al., 2001), a major intervention strategy of psychoeducationists.

## Behavioral Model

The behavioral model can be traced to the work of early 20th-century psychologist John Watson. He argued that psychologists should stop philosophizing about subjective aspects of human existence such as feelings, consciousness, and other mental phenomena that are difficult to study scientifically because they are unobservable. Instead, as "a purely objective experimental branch of natural science [striving to achieve] the prediction and control of behavior" (Watson, 1913, p. 158), psychology must be concerned with observable and measurable behaviors, stimuli in the environment, and the relationships between behaviors and stimuli (Tryon, 2001).

### *Operant Conditioning*

For several decades, behaviorism had strong appeal to researchers but little influence on treatment or education of children with E&B disorder. In 1953, behavioral scientist B. F. Skinner (Display 2-9) published *Science and Human Behavior*, which extended

**Display 2-9** B. F. Skinner profile

> B. F. Skinner (1904–1990) abandoned an attempted career in literature to study psychology and animal behavior research. Skinner took seriously admonitions from John Watson and other early behaviorists that psychology should be a science of observable behavior and stimuli.
>
> Beginning in the 1930s, Skinner advocated a scientific psychology perspective that until you can predict or control a phenomenon, you have not explained it. The role of psychology was to explain various behaviors by demonstrating through experiments that they are under the control of particular environmental stimuli. This perspective rejected "intervening variables" such as intrapsychic processes, consciousness, motivation, cognition, willpower, and other common psychological concepts because they are unobservable and they divert researchers from the requirement to demonstrate that they can analyze and control the relationships between actual behaviors and environmental stimuli (that is, change behaviors by manipulating those stimuli).
>
> In 1938, Skinner published *The Behavior of Organisms*, a book describing principles of operant conditioning derived from his laboratory research. It had enormous influence on psychologists and others interested in the experimental analysis of behavior. Although Skinner's early work was based on experiments involving simple responses of animals, he maintained that the basic principles of operant conditioning apply to complex behaviors of humans as well. *Science and Human Behavior* (1953) was a general introduction to how operant conditioning applies to human functioning. Later publications described how it applies to language (Skinner, 1957), education (Skinner, 1968), and other areas. Skinner's work established the foundation for behavioral perspectives on normal and abnormal child development, leading to behavior modification approaches to changing maladaptive behaviors of children, such as behavioral modification in delivering special education for students with ED.

*Source:* Hawkins, 1990.

his extensive laboratory research on animal learning to human psychological and social issues. Human behavior in various areas, including education (Skinner, 1968), was explained in terms of operant conditioning, Skinner's conceptualization of the essential principles of learning. He criticized the psychodynamic model and offered **operant conditioning** as an alternative for the treatment of E&B disorder.

Briefly, operant conditioning involves scientifically demonstrated principles that describe relationships between behaviors and the environmental stimuli that affect them (Lewis, Lewis-Palmer, Newcomer, & Stichter, 2004). For example, the principle of reinforcement describes how a behavior's effects on environmental stimuli strengthen the behavior (make it occur more frequently in the future). To use the reinforcement principle therapeutically, a behaviorist might first determine that some aspect of a child's E&B disorder involves an important adaptive behavior that the child performs so infrequently that people see her or him as abnormal. Then the behaviorist reinforces this adaptive behavior to increase its frequency to a normal level.

### *Behavior Modification in Schools*

Of course, for a very long time teachers have used techniques for motivating and managing behavior and developing new skills that are similar to contemporary behavioral teaching procedures (e.g., Kazdin, 1978). But the application of operant conditioning to help students with disabilities can be traced to the work of Skinner's student Sidney

Bijou and his associates in the late 1950s and early 1960s, in their classrooms for students with mental retardation. Bijou found that carefully structured academic material together with consistent reinforcement of behavior improvement could help these children's learning and behavior performance (Birnbrauer, Bijou, Wolf, & Kidder, 1965). Others used operant conditioning to dramatically improve the behavior of children with extreme disorders of behavior, emotion, and thought (Ferster & DeMyer, 1962; Lovaas, 1966; Wolf, Risley, & Mees, 1964). Soon, operant conditioning research on more ordinary behavior problems in school began to appear (Allen, Hart, Buell, Harris, & Wolf, 1964; Becker, Madsen, Arnold, & Thomas, 1967; Patterson, 1965). The favorable results of these practical research efforts helped set the stage for widespread adoption of behavioristic procedures in special education.

In the 1960s, Frank M. Hewett (Display 2-10) applied operant conditioning principles to the education of students with E&B disorder. He designed the Engineered Classroom, which pioneered the use and evaluation of a system of tokens (money-like rewards) and teacher praise to reinforce task accomplishment within a carefully structured separate classroom environment (Hewett, 1968). Later, Hewett adapted the Engineered Classroom to help in the gradual integration of students with learning and behavior disabilities into resource and general education classrooms (Hewett & Taylor, 1980).

**Display 2-10** Frank Hewett profile

---

Frank M. Hewett (1927–1994) was for several years a teacher of children and adolescents with learning and behavior disabilities. This experience taught him the importance of structure and planning, the interdependence of learning and behavior problems, and the need to optimize the use of educational time. After completing his doctorate in clinical psychology in 1961, Hewett became principal at the Neuropsychiatric Institute School, a new inpatient educational program at University of California, Los Angeles (UCLA) for children with severe E&B disorder.

Hewett recognized a major weakness in educating students with E&B disorder: "No distinctly educational conceptual model for describing our students' problems and our goals and objectives for them" (Hewett, 1974, p. 127). So Hewett created the Developmental Sequence of Educational Goals, a hierarchy of life skills to which learning and teaching should be directed. This was a key feature of the Engineered Classroom.

Among Hewett's most valuable contributions were demonstrations that his ideas could be useful in public schools. He developed the first behavior modification classroom for public school students with E&B disorder. His Santa Monica Project and Madison School Plan showed the value of the Engineered Classroom in educating pupils with behavior and learning disorders in separate and mainstream education environments.

Hewett was a faculty member at UCLA for more than 30 years, serving as chair of special education much of that time. He belonged to organizations serving students with disabilities, wrote books and scholarly journal articles, served on the editorial boards of professional journals, and received numerous awards in recognition of his distinguished service.

---

*Sources:* Forness, 1995; Hewett, 1974.

Many have built on these early behavioral interventions, none better than Hill Walker, who developed advanced programs of assessment and intervention for students with emotional, behavior, and learning problems. With colleagues, Walker created behavioral intervention programs for schools to improve disruptive classroom behaviors, poor academic skills, social withdrawal, and aggressive play; methods to screen students at risk for future ED; and programs to prevent and intervene with school violence (Walker, Hops, & Greenwood, 1984; Walker, Kavanagh, Stiller, Golly, Severson, & Feil, 1997; Walker, Ramsey, & Gresham, 2004). Walker's programs are appreciated for the scientific rigor with which they are developed, as well as the practical value they offer to practitioners.

After the mid-1960s, behaviorism became a dominant influence on special education for students with ED (Smith & Wood, 1986) and contributed to a significant expansion of it. Why? Compared to psychodynamic or even psychoeducational interventions, 1960s-era behavioral techniques seemed to be more like typical teaching activities (such as encouraging adaptive behaviors while discouraging maladaptive behaviors). Behavioristic principles were also more compatible with existing programs for students with E&B disorder that featured highly structured behavior management and curriculum (e.g., Haring & Phillips, 1962) and therefore more efficiently incorporated into special educator preparation. They were also more scientifically supported.

Early applications of the behavioral model tended to be practical demonstrations rather than scientific evaluations. In 1968, the *Journal of Applied Behavior Analysis* was instituted to publish scientific evaluations of behavioristic methods for improving important human behaviors in real-life situations, including E&B disorder of students in schools. Together with other journals, this encouraged an expansion of scientific evaluations, eventually yielding research evidence in support of quite a few behavioristic teaching practices for a range of behavior and learning problems (Alberto & Troutman, 2006; Kazdin, 2001; Lewis, Lewis-Palmer, Newcomer, & Stichter, 2004). Thus, many professionals became convinced that the behavioral model has considerable value for teaching students with ED.

## CHAPTER SUMMARY

Perspectives on disorders of emotion, behavior, and thought have changed dramatically over time. Still, some historical developments involved ideas or events that bear some similarity to issues and challenges of today.

- People of prehistoric cultures linked E&B disorder with physical disorders, as well as spiritual and supernatural causes.
- Thinkers of the classical Greek and Roman era proposed that human biological functions affect emotions, behaviors, and thoughts, including E&B disorder.
- Spiritual views were dominant in the Middle Ages in Europe. Many cases of E&B disorder were seen as manifestations of Satan.
- Renaissance philosophers emphasized natural causes over supernatural ones to explain various phenomena, including E&B disorder.

- The trend toward humane treatment of people with E&B disorder is symbolized by Pinel's releasing of patients at Bicêtre and the establishment of public asylums for people with E&B disorder.
- During the 1800s in the United States schooling become more accessible to all children, including immigrants and the poor. Special teaching practices were developed for use with hard-to-educate students.
- Over the course of the 20th century, contemporary practices for children and adolescents with E&B disorder gradually took shape in the United States.
- At the beginning of the 20th century, early U.S. psychologists began scientifically studying children over time and in depth.
- The mental hygiene reform movement early in the 20th century had many benefits. The National Committee for Mental Hygiene:
  — educated the public about E&B disorder
  — encouraged prevention of E&B disorder
  — supported research
  — promoted child guidance clinics
- Since the early years of the 20th century, many individuals and organizations have called for reforms in how children with E&B disorder are treated.
- One powerful reform was IDEA 2004, a federal law that changed how students with ED are served by schools.
- Another significant influence was psychological models of E&B disorder, especially the psychodynamic and behavioral models and the effects they had on ways of providing educational interventions for students with ED.

## IDEAS FOR CONSIDERATION AND DISCUSSION

1. How can results of studies of the emotional, behavior, and cognitive characteristics of large numbers of children affect special education for students with ED?
2. Obtain information on state and local branches of CCBD, including meeting and conference dates. If feasible, attend a meeting or conference. Report to the class about the meeting and anticipated activities of this group.
   Identify specific evidence to illustrate what CCBD has done recently
   a. to advocate for children with E&BD and students with ED
   b. to sponsor professional development activities
   c. to support regional CCBD groups in your area
   d. to publish material about research and practice.
3. Discuss how each of the National Agenda targets might affect education for students with ED.
4. Identify one problem, issue, or other historical development noted in the Chapter 2 that has relevance to E&BD of children in the present. Demonstrate its relevance by specifying a current or recent event (local or national) that makes the identified development still relevant.

5. Describe how compulsory schooling in the U.S. affected education for children with E&BD.
6. Think of examples of how the psychodynamic model has affected U.S. culture (e.g., literature, popular media) and U.S. education. What are examples of how the behavioral model has affected U.S. culture and education?

## Resources for Further Study

**www.bfskinner.org/media.asp** B.F. Skinner images and audio
**www.ccbd.net** Council for Children with Behavioral Disorders (CCBD)
**www.webster.edu/~woolflm/dorotheadix.html** Dorothea Dix
**www.freud.org.uk/** Freud Museum, London
**www.psy.pdx.edu/PsiCafe/KeyTheorists/Hall.htm** G. S. Hall
**ancienthistory.about.com/cs/hippocrates/a/hippocraticmeds.htm** Hippocrates' four humors concepts
**http://www.nlm.nih.gov/hmd/emotions/balance.html** Historical perspectives on the nature and problems of emotions
**http://www.cec.sped.org/ab/history.html** History of Council for Exceptional Children
**http://www.nmha.org/about/history.cfm** History of National Mental Health Association
**http://hpy.sagepub.com/archive/** History of Psychiatry journal archives
**http://www.surgeongeneral.gov/library/mentalhealth/home.html** Mental health: A report of the Surgeon General
**www.mentalhealthcommission.gov/** President's New Freedom Commission on Mental Health
**http://rtckids.fmhi.usf.edu/soc_toc.html** *A system of care for children and youth with severe emotional disturbances*
**www.ed.gov/about/offices/list/om/fs_po/osers/special.html** U.S. Office of Special Education Programs

PART II

# Assessment and Characteristics

CHAPTER 3    *Assessment and Classification*
CHAPTER 4    *Patterns of Emotional and Behavior Disorder*
CHAPTER 5    *Extreme Emotional and Behavior Disorders*

Chapter **Three**

# *Assessment and Classification*

## OBJECTIVES

**After reading this chapter, you should be able to:**
- List five or more variations of reported functioning.
- State two differences between low-structure and high-structure measurement interviews.
- Differentiate frequency and partial-interval target-behavior recording.
- Describe four purposes of measurement for special education.
- State the general procedure for completing a functional behavioral assessment.
- Name two kinds of classification for children's E&B disorder and an example of each.

## CAN YOU DEFINE THESE 10 TERMS?

| | |
|---|---|
| operational definition | behavior rating scale |
| reliability | projective personality assessment |
| validity | screening |
| norms | functional behavioral assessment |
| sociometric | co-occurrence |

Assessment is the process in which information about a situation is gathered and combined. The situation of special interest here includes determining whether the student has an E&B disorder, specifying important strengths and weaknesses of the student, and evaluating the student's response to intervention efforts (Huberty, 2003; Taylor, 2006). These important tasks rarely could be completed without assessment. Assessment is so fundamental to special education that it is addressed in some detail in IDEA 2004, especially its use in creating and using the Individualized Education Program (IEP).

A main aspect of assessment is measurement, through which information is collected in a formal and relatively objective way. Assessment of students with E&B disorder involves planning for measurement, performing the measurement, and using results of measurement to make important education decisions (McLoughlin & Lewis, 2005; Reynolds, Livingston, & Willson, 2006). In practice these three steps often affect each other and so are usually recycled several times for each student. For instance, unexpected results of measurement may call for further measurement. Measurement may show student improvement in primary areas of concern, signaling a need for measurement of and intervention for other student problems. Alternatively, results may show lack of improvement, requiring changes in intervention.

This chapter considers some measurement methods used in assessment, as well as several key purposes of assessment. One purpose of assessment can be to help classify E&B disorder of children, so classification is considered after assessment. First, let us look briefly at some basic measurement concepts.

## Basic Concepts of Measurement

Measurement is the process of assigning a number to a variable so that the number stands for the variable. A variable might be anything that can change. In studying and teaching children with E&B disorder, we are especially interested in variables such as forms of E&B disorder (depressive behaviors and feelings, angry thoughts, etc.), possible causes of E&B disorder (e.g., biological disorders, family circumstances, school situations), students' educational strengths and weaknesses (such as academic achievement or vocational skills), and intervention practices (degree of classroom structure, self-controlled versus teacher-controlled rewards, number of counseling sessions, or the like).

Depending on the methods of measurement used, a variable may be measured as either (a) totally absent versus totally present, in which case the measured variable is assigned only the number 0 or 1; or (b) present in different degrees, including not at all, and thus assigned a number from 0 up to some maximum. For instance, the variable "cruelty to peers" could be measured by asking the teacher whether the student's status on this variable is best represented by 0 (does not show cruelty to peers) or 1 (does show cruelty to peers). Alternatively, the variable could be measured by counting instances of cruelty to peers during the school day. This method would produce a number ranging from 0 up.

Measurement results obviously do not equal the variable. For example, no number can truly portray all the subtle, complex aspects of cruelty to peers or any other aspect of E&B disorder. Yet by measuring variables we obtain important advantages (Gunter & Denny, 2004). Unlike informal descriptions or unmeasured perceptions, numbers can be added, averaged, and arithmetically combined in other ways. Measuring variables helps us objectively describe characteristics of young people, trace changes in a variable over time, and compare individuals or groups on educationally important characteristics. In turn, these advantages clarify communication among practitioners, researchers, and others concerned with E&B disorder of children and adolescents.

### Operational Definitions

To be measured a variable must be given an **operational definition**, which means defining the variable in terms of the method by which it is measured. Operational definitions are necessary because most variables can be measured in a variety of ways, yet different ways of measuring the same variable may not produce the same results. For example, the data resulting from measurement of cruelty to peers might turn out quite differently depending on whether the operational definition of that variable calls for teacher judgments about a student's cruelty, a count of observed instances of cruelty, the student's score on a scale of self-reported cruelty to peers, a private poll of all students asking which classmate shows the most cruelty to peers, or some other measurement method.

When a variable has a suitable operational definition, we can better understand what was meant by that variable. Everyone may not agree that a particular operational definition is a good way to measure the variable, but the operational definition enables them to judge its logic and usefulness, and use it themselves if they choose. Operational definitions of a variety of emotional and behavior problems are presented later in this chapter.

## Reliability

**Reliability** is the extent to which two independent measurements, using the same operational definition, produce the same result. There are several kinds of reliability and several methods for estimating reliability (Murphy & Davidshofer, 2005; Salvia & Ysseldyke, 2004; Taylor, 2006). For instance, when a variable is measured at one point in time by two independent users of the operational definition (such as raters of emotional problems, recorders of classroom behavior, or scorers of a test), and their results closely agree, there is high scorer reliability. When a variable is measured at two points in time and those measurements closely agree, the variable shows high stability reliability.

On the other hand, an operational definition has low reliability if independent observers make substantially different judgments about a behavior, or if measurements separated by a brief period of time yield very different results. If an operational definition of any variable can be measured with only low reliability, it is of little use. In fact, high measurement reliability is needed for practical educational decisions.

## Validity

The **validity** of an operational definition is the degree to which measurement results based on that operational definition accurately represent the variable of interest. There are various kinds of validity and methods for estimating validity (Salvia & Ysseldyke, 2004; Taylor, 2006), and their details are beyond the scope of this book. To give one brief example (predictive validity), consider a measurement procedure for depressed mood that is administered to many elementary school students. This procedure would have predictive validity to the extent that scores on it allow us to identify which individuals are most likely to be diagnosed with a depressive disorder at some later time, such as by age 18.

Information about the validity of many standardized measurement procedures is published in their manuals and other references (see Spies & Plake, 2005). Validity information can aid the teacher or other assessor in choosing a measurement method and interpreting its results.

Students can provide valuable assessment information.

## Norms

Measuring a child's status on some variable results in a score. But what does this score mean? Is it low, medium, or high? In many cases a score's meaning is clarified by comparing it to **norms**, a collection of scores that provides context for understanding how low or high a particular score is (McLoughlin & Lewis, 2005; Murphy & Davidshofer, 2005).

One way to use norms involves the concept of percentile, defined as the percentage of scores in the norms that fall below a particular score. Suppose a boy is measured on cruelty to peers and scores 27. Also suppose that norms have been created by measuring 600 other young people on this same variable and arranging their scores from lowest to highest. There are 534 scores in the norms that are lower than a score of 27, so this boy's percentile is calculated as 534/600 = .89, or 89th percentile. That is, his cruelty to peers was measured as higher than 89 percent of the norms. This is clearly a high score, because a score at the 50th percentile is average. Norms provide valuable context for a score, but norms alone cannot determine whether the score is so extreme as to indicate an E&B disorder. Subjective decisions must still be made (e.g., at what percentile does extreme begin?).

A norm group should be representative of the population to which a particular child will be compared (McLoughlin & Lewis, 2005; Salvia & Ysseldyke, 2004). The norm group should be similar to that population in regard to age, sex, race-ethnic status, geographic region, or other important variables. Usually the population of interest consists of typical children (without E&B disorder), but at times other populations, such as students with E&B disorder, may be needed for comparison. Assessors should carefully evaluate norms and norm group characteristics for appropriate usage.

## Measurement and the Practice of Special Education

It is difficult to overstate the importance of measurement to educational efforts for students with E&B disorder. People who try to lose weight, reduce smoking, or use their time more efficiently ordinarily keep track of what they are trying to change, but some educators of students with E&B disorder pay insufficient attention to measurement (Kauffman, 2001). Of course it is impossible for a teacher to measure all facets of a student's education situation, but measuring selected aspects of a student's E&B disorder is good practice and likely to justify the time and effort spent.

## MEASUREMENT METHODS

The methods by which professionals measure variables resemble the ways people get information about other things in life. Mainly, they seek reports from individuals who have observed variables of interest, and they observe those variables for themselves. Regarding students with ED, the variables of interest include (a) a student's behaviors, emotions, thoughts, and learning and (b) important physical and social aspects of the education environment, such as school and class schedules, structure, rules, groupings, and instruction practices. Many other variables are also of interest.

In measuring *reported functioning* of students, the information seeker may be a teacher, school psychologist, or other assessor. The reporter of information (or informant) may be the student, a teacher, a parent, a classmate, or anyone else in a position to know the information. Usually the report is oral or written. Reported functioning may include stored information such as the student's school records (Mattison, 2004).

Measuring *actual functioning* calls for systematic observation of variables in "natural" (ordinary, everyday) situations. These methods are often used to measure student behavior in classrooms. Important behaviors of the young person who needs or may need help are operationally defined, observed, and recorded over a period of time (Alberto & Troutman, 2006; Maag, 2003). In some cases it is important to record those same behaviors as performed by classmates, to get a clearer idea of how different the selected student's behavior is from that of his peers.

When it is not feasible to observe in natural situations, stimulated ones can be created. For instance, many standardized tests simulate natural situations in which a person's knowledge, reasoning, or other capabilities must be demonstrated. During assessment interviews, a child's behaviors, emotions, and other characteristics are often observed and noted (Angold & Costello, 2002; McConaughy, 2003), under the assumption that the child's functioning during interviews may represent her functioning under everyday circumstances.

## Reported Functioning

### Nomination by Teacher

The special education process often begins with the referral of a student whom a teacher perceives as troubling or troubled. Referral signals that the student needs further assessment and perhaps intervention. The teacher has begun the assessment process by nominating (naming) the student as filling the role, "may need intervention." Nomination by teacher is the first of three steps in using the *Systematic Screening for Behavior Disorders* (SSBD; Walker & Severson, 1992), an important measurement system described later in this chapter.

### Nomination by Peers

In another measurement method, students nominate their peers as filling various roles. For example, every student in a class may be asked to name privately one peer whom he most likes (or admires, respects) and one he most dislikes. The assessor can then tabulate all positive and negative nominations to reveal social information about the group (Haager & Klingner, 2005; Rubin, Burgess, Kennedy, & Stewart, 2003). This process may identify students who are:

1. Liked by many peers and disliked by few ("popular")
2. Disliked by many and liked by few ("rejected")
3. Liked and disliked by many ("controversial")
4. Rarely named as either liked or disliked ("neglected")

This is a simple **sociometric**, a procedure that measures a group's social preferences, then combines this information to obtain various kinds of social information about individuals or subgroups (Farmer, Goforth, Leung, Clemmer, & Thompson, 2004). Measurement methods other than peer nomination also can be used in sociometric assessment.

Some forms of peer nomination get more specific than overall social preferences ("like"). To illustrate, each student in a class could privately write the name of classmates who fit various roles, such as "often looks angry" and "doesn't have many friends." Tabulation of such information can be used to help identify students at risk for E&B disorder or establish groups for prevention of or intervention with problems of anger or relationships.

Although sociometric measurement generally has adequate reliability and validity, many educators are reluctant to use it. They worry that peer-completed items might encourage students to single out and perhaps discriminate against each other (Merrell, 2003).

### Ratings by Others

A **behavior rating scale** (also called a checklist or questionnaire) is a standard group of items each of which describes an emotional, behavior, or other characteristic (Elliott & Busse, 2004; Verhulst & Van der Ende, 2002). Usually each characteristic is a fairly specific problem. Some rating scales have items describing positive attributes, also called strengths or assets (e.g., has self-confidence, has good friends; see Epstein, 2004; Masten & Coatsworth, 1998).

A teacher, parent, caseworker, other adult, or peer rates the young person on each of the items. The rater marks each item according to a scale that contains two or more "points" (ordered choices) indicating different degrees to which the student shows the stated characteristic. Depending on the scale, a rater may judge each problem's frequency (e.g., "never" = 0, "rarely" = 1, "once per week" = 2, "once per day" = 3, "several times per day" = 4), its significance (e.g., "no problem," "mild problem," "severe problem,"), or some other aspect.

***Rating One Characteristic.*** For rating a single problem of a particular student and particular situation, the educator can create an individually tailored rating scale (ITRS) (Finch, Deardorf, & Montgomery, 1974). The four steps for creating an ITRS are as follows:

1. Write down examples of what the student says and does that constitute the problem. Other adults who know the student's problem, and the student himself, may add good examples.
2. Make sure that the problem examples illustrate a single characteristic (e.g., all examples indicate ways this child shows sadness).
3. Arrange the examples in order of seriousness (least to most or vice versa). Be sure to have at least one example of the problem at its worst, and one description of acceptable behavior.
4. To the worst examples of the problem assign a rating of 5; to the acceptable behavior assign a rating of 1. Then establish a 3 rating to represent examples of the problem as exhibited roughly halfway between the extremes. Finally, fill in 2 and 4 ratings with examples of appropriate seriousness.

Display 3-1 presents an ITRS created according to these steps. The teacher marked this ITRS at the end of each day to help evaluate the effectiveness of an intervention for the student's sexual misconduct.

***Rating Multiple Characteristics.*** Most rating scales cover more than one problem characteristic. For example, on the *Teacher's Report Form* (TRF) (Achenbach & McConaughy, 2003a; Achenbach & Rescorla, 2001), the teacher rates each of approximately 120 emotional and behavior problem items (Display 3-2) as either 0 ("not true [of this child]"), 1 ("somewhat or sometimes true"), or 2 ("very true or often true"). Different groups of these items contribute to eight subscores, each representing a different kind of E&B disorder. For example, there is an Anxious/Depressed subscore based on 14 items, including "feels persecuted," "lonely," "feels too guilty," and "feels worthless."

The TRF can be used alone but was designed to be one of several parts of an assessment and classification system called *Achenbach System of Empirically Based Assessment (ASEBA;* Achenbach & Rescorla, 2001; Breen, 2003). This classification system is described later in the chapter.

**Display 3-1** Individually Tailored Rating Scale for "inappropriate sexual behavior"

---

*Inappropriate Sexual Behavior*

Today's date: _____   Rater: _____

Directions to rater: At about 2:45 each day, recall Justin's behavior for the day in regard to inappropriate sexual behavior. Circle the rating below corresponding to Justin's worst instance of behavior today. If no rating corresponds exactly, select the rating that most closely corresponds.

| Rating | Content |
|---|---|
| 5 | <u>Physical sexual behavior</u>. Examples:<br>• Justin sneaks up behind a peer and grabs peer's crotch, or sexually thrusts his pelvis next to his or her rear.<br>• Justin grabs or feels female peer's breast.<br>• Justin publically fondles himself in crotch area while talking or making noise.<br>• Justin makes noise while he repeatedly thrusts his pelvis standing up or lying on the floor. |
| 4 | <u>Verbal sexual abuse to staff</u>. Examples:<br>• Justin grabs or points to groin and tells teacher or other staff person, "s*** this."<br>• Justin says "f*** you" to teacher or other staff person or about staff person's loved ones. |
| 3 | <u>Verbal sexual abuse to peers</u>. Examples:<br>• Justin grabs or points to groin and tells peer, "suck this" or "eat this."<br>• Justin says "f*** you" to peer.<br>• Justin tells classmate that he would like to perform sex act with him or her, or states that he would like to do so with a named classmate. |
| 2 | <u>Undirected sexual talk</u>. Examples:<br>• Justin says a word or phrase describing a sex organ or sex act, not directed at any person.<br>• Justin states that he would like to perform sex act, but does not name or otherwise direct the comment to a peer or staff person. |
| 1 | <u>Sexual appropriateness</u>.<br>• No physical sex behavior detected from Justin.<br>• No sexual language detected from Justin. |

---

**Display 3-2** Illustrative items from the Teacher Rating Form

| Ratings | | | Item Number and Name | |
|---|---|---|---|---|
| 0 | 1 | 2 | 2. | Hums or makes other odd noises in class |
| 0 | 1 | 2 | 23. | Disobedient at school |
| 0 | 1 | 2 | 30. | Fears going to school |
| 0 | 1 | 2 | 76. | Explosive and unpredictable behavior |
| 0 | 1 | 2 | 111. | Withdrawn, doesn't get involved with others |

Adapted from Achenbach & Rescorla, 2001.
0 = Not True   1 = Somewhat or Sometimes True   2 = Very True or Often True

There are many multiple-characteristic rating scales for emotional and behavior problems that can be completed by teachers (e.g., Breen, 2003; Eckert, DuPaul, & Carson, 2003; Verhulst & Van der Ende, 2002). Some scales stand alone, while others are part of a larger "multifaceted" assessment package or system that brings together information based on different sources and methods of measurement. Rating scale information is often used to assist decisions about a child's emotional and behavior problems (e.g., *ASEBA*, Achenbach & Rescorla, 2001; *Behavior Assessment System for Children*, Reynolds & Kamphaus, 1992, 2002; *Social Skills Rating System*, Gresham & Elliott, 1990), or specifically about a student's ED disability (e.g., *Behavior Evaluation Scale—2*, McCarney & Leigh, 1990; *Scale for Assessing Emotional Disturbance*, Epstein & Cullinan, 1998).

A behavior rating scale also can be completed by peers, whose experiences and observations about a classmate's problems may differ from those of teachers and other adults. For example, each student in a classroom might rate every other student on one or more characteristics. Pooling these data can yield sociometric information about each student's relationships to classmates, as well as other aspects of emotional and behavioral functioning from the perspective of peers. Peer rating information has important similarities to, as well as key differences from, sociometric data obtained by the peer nomination method, discussed earlier.

### *Ratings by Self*

Self-report on a rating scale involves many of the considerations involved in ratings by others. Some self-ratings focus on a narrow aspect of emotion or behavior such as anxiety (*Revised Children's Manifest Anxiety Scale;* Reynolds & Richmond, 1985) or self-concept (*Piers-Harris Children's Self-Concept Scale;* Piers, 1984).

Other self-ratings address multiple characteristics (Breen, 2003; Eckert et al., 2003). The *Self-Report of Personality* (SRP) is a checklist of items that describes many thoughts, feelings, and actions that a child may have, some adaptive, others maladaptive (Reynolds & Kamphaus, 1992). The child marks each item as true or false. Different combinations of SRP items (Display 3-3) yield information on personal characteristics such as anxiety, school maladjustment, and attitude toward school. The SRP can be used alone but is meant to be part of a multifaceted assessment system, *Behavior Assessment System for Children* (BASC). Among other multiple-characteristic self-rating instruments for children and adolescents are the *Minnesota Multiphasic Personality Inventory-Adolescent* (Butcher et al., 1992), the *Conners-Wells Adolescent Self-Report Scale* (Conners & Wells, 1997), and the *Youth Self-Report* (Achenbach & Rescorla, 2001).

### *Interviews*

***People Interviewed.*** In a measurement interview, a skilled interviewer prompts the parent, teacher, child, or other informant to report information about variables of interest (Angold, 2002; McConaughy, 2003). Interviews of parents often seek background information about their child, such as health history, developmental

**Display 3-3** Illustrative items from Self Report of Personality

| Mark each item as true or false about yourself | | |
|---|---|---|
| 1. I am good at making new friends. | T | F |
| 38. I just don't care anymore. | T | F |
| 103. My parents are often proud of me. | T | F |
| 108. My stomach gets upset more than most people. | T | F |
| 179. I still have fits of temper. | T | F |

Adapted from Reynolds & Kamphaus, 1992.

milestones (timing of significant events in early development such as vocalizing, walking, and socializing), how the family functions, the child's activities outside school, and her emotional, learning, and behavior problems and strengths.

Interviews of teachers typically seek information about the student's education history, present emotional or behavior problems, social and physical aspects of the classroom or other situations in which the problem occurs, and what remedies the teacher has attempted. Forms that help structure teacher reporting of such information (Walker, Block-Pedigo, Todis, & Severson, 1991) provide results that can be a starting point for follow-up with an interview.

An interview of the child or adolescent also usually seeks some background information such as relationships with family, friends, school functioning, other interests, and personal information (such as the student's concerns, predominant emotions and moods, understanding of why she is being interviewed). Beyond this, the kind of information sought often varies according to the interviewer's theory preferences. For instance, psychodynamic interviewers may explore possible early causes of emotional conflicts ("How did you feel when your mother left you at school that day?"), while behaviorist interviewers may identify reinforcers for appropriate behavior ("If you had 30 minutes to do whatever you want, what would that be?").

***Degree of Structure.*** Interviews also differ in structure. In a high-structure interview (e.g., Shaffer, Fisher, Lucas, Dulcan, & Schwab-Stone, 2000), the interviewer might ask a standard sequence of questions, record the informant's responses, and perhaps compare responses to norms. Interviewer expertise is not a major consideration, and interviewers need only moderate training. In fact, computerized administration may be feasible.

On the other hand, in a low-structure interview the interviewer typically brings up topics that appear relevant to the child's situation, such as fears, conflict with peers, or poor grades. The interviewer asks questions, shows pictures, or otherwise prompts the young person to talk about such topics. Alternatively, the interviewer may encourage the child to use toys or puppets to enact a scenario about the topics.

However prompted, the child's responses are then interpreted for clues as to how the E&B disorder may have originated, how it might be corrected, and so on. Such interpretations, obviously, are based to some extent on interviewer theory preferences. They are often interesting, but critics of low-structure interviews point out drawbacks such as poor reliability. For example, other interviewers with different expertise or theory preferences may interpret the child's reported information very differently (Angold & Costello, 2002).

Other interview formats involve intermediate levels of structure. The Semistructured Clinical Interview for Children and Adolescents (SCICA) (McConaughy & Achenbach, 2001) specifies areas to be explored, including school and out-of-school activities, peer social issues, relations within the family, goals and wishes, private thoughts and feelings, and particular problems identified before the interview. The SCICA includes directions on how to verbally explore these areas, but the interviewer must adapt specific wording, order of questions, and other interview features to the situation (McConaughy, 2003). For instance, if the young person states that he hates school, the interviewer might say, "What are the classes at school that you dislike the most?," following with "What is it about social studies class that you do not like?," then perhaps "What do Thomas and Sonya do that hassles you?" Other interview instruments with an intermediate level of structure are described by Angold & Costello (2002).

### *Personality Measurement*

The term *personality* refers to a person's enduring tendencies to behave, feel, and think in consistent ways, even across very different situations. The existence, nature, and relevance of human personality are controversial and complex issues (Friedman & Schustack, 2005; Schultz & Schultz, 2005); regardless, personality measurement is common. Personality measurement methods (Adams & Culbertson, 2005) are similar to some already described (such as interview, ratings by others, and ratings by self), but there may be differences in how the instrument was developed (e.g., based on a particular theory) and how its results are interpreted.

***Objective Personality Measurement.*** In objective personality measurement, items are presented in a standard way, scores are determined objectively (no subjective judgment required), and results are compared to norms to help determine how much the child's measured personality characteristics vary from instrument norms. For instance, the Minnesota Multiphasic Personality Inventory-Adolescent is an objective instrument that measures a range of personality characteristics based on a student's self-report (Rowe, 2003). The Personality Inventory for Children (Lachar & Gruber, 2003) objectively measures numerous personality characteristics based on, for example, a mother's report about her child.

***Projective Personality Assessment.*** **Projective personality assessment** is a controversial idea based on the following assumptions of the psychodynamic model.

1. E&B disorder is produced mainly by unconscious intrapsychic conflict, that is, mental discord of which the person is not even aware (see Chapters 2 and 7).

2. An expert interpreter can understand such conflicts by getting the person being assessed to reveal important clues about them.
3. Unconscious conflicts are best revealed by obtaining responses to ambiguous stimuli, in reaction to which the person will "project" (say and do things because of) unconscious conflict.

Typically, projective assessment is obtained during a low-structure interview.

Various kinds of ambiguous stimuli have been used for projective measurement (Chandler, 2003; Moss & Racusin, 2002). For instance, a child may be asked to explain ambiguous drawings, create artistic expressions and then talk about them, complete unfinished sentences or stories, or play with dolls or puppets.

The *Rorschach Inkblot* method includes a set of 10 symmetrical inkblots. As each is presented, the child is asked to tell what he sees in them. Verbal responses, facial expressions, delays in answering, and other reactions are interpreted according to the assessor's training and experience, sometimes using a system for scoring and norms to aid interpretation (Allen & Hollifield, 2003). Such a system might emphasize location (what parts of the inkblot does the child talk about?), content (what people, animals, or objects are reported?), and themes (especially sexual, aggressive, and other emotional themes).

In the *House-Tree-Person* method, the child is asked to draw these three items on separate sheets of paper. The assessor asks questions about the completed drawings, such as: "What is behind that door?" "If the tree were to be cut down, what should be done with the wood?" "How does that person feel? Why?" As with the Rorschach, drawings and verbal responses are interpreted according to the assessor's training, experience, and sometimes a scoring system.

## Actual Functioning

Many important aspects of E&B disorder involve things that students ordinarily say and do in their "natural" environments of home, community, and school (e.g., classrooms, halls, playgrounds). To accurately represent such behaviors, measurement is carried out in these natural environments (Alberto & Troutman, 2006; Kazdin, 2001). The assessor takes care to minimize any effect of her presence and actions on the words and deeds being measured. Two variations of this kind of measurement are recording of target behaviors and behavior products.

### *Target-Behavior Recording*

To use a target behavior recording procedure, the measurer must first decide exactly what is the target behavior (specific behavior of most concern). One or more target behaviors are then each given an operational definition designed to produce highly reliable results. Display 3-4 illustrates target behavior definitions that could be used in recording classroom disruption.

For each target behavior, a recording strategy is selected that will produce valid results (accurately representing the extent to which the behavior of concern occurs). Further, the strategy must be practical to use in the educational setting

**Display 3-4** Target behaviors suited for recording some classroom aspects of disruption

| Target Behavior | Description | Recording Method and Results |
|---|---|---|
| Motor Disruption | (a) Leaving desk without teacher's permission. Moving or tipping the desk. Showing objects to another child in or out of desk. **Note:** Mark no matter how briefly these occur. | Frequency. During the 30-minute language arts period, make one tally for each instance. If two or more kinds of motor disruption simultaneously occur, tally only once. |
| | (or) | |
| | (b) While in desk, rocking or other repetitive, disruptive body movement, or turning trunk of body away from staight ahead (e.g., toward side or back). **Note:** Mark only if such a behavior lasts at least 4 seconds. | Result of measurement is the sum of tally marks for today's language arts period. |
| Noise Disruption | (a) Answering or making comments to teacher without being called on. Giving irrelevant response, even if called on. Unpermitted talking to other students. Calling teacher's name to get her attention. Crying, screaming, singing, whistling, laughing loudly, coughing loudly. | Partial interval. Divide the 30-minute language arts period into 15 intervals of 2 minutes each. If one or more noise disruptions occur at any time during an interval, mark the interval. |
| | (or) | |
| | (b) Tapping pencil or other objects; clapping; tapping feet; rattling or tearing paper. Mark only if you can hear noise with your eyes closed. Do not mark noise from accidentally dropped object or noise ordinarily or reasonably made as a student performs appropriate tasks. | Result of measurement is the sum of marked intervals for today's language arts period. |

(Gunter & Denny, 2004). Various target behavior recording strategies have been described (see Maag, 2003; Windsor, 2003). Each is meant to be used daily or very regularly, for periods ranging from 5 or 10 minutes up to several hours, to produce an ongoing record of the target behavior. For example, to use the frequency recording strategy, the teacher or other recorder tallies each occurrence of the target behavior, then totals the tallies at the end of the recording session (such as a school day, reading period, or recess). Results from several sessions are then compared to see if there is a pattern, such as a similar number of tallies each session, or a trend of increasing or decreasing target behaviors.

Another target behavior recording strategy, the partial-interval strategy, represents how the target behavior is distributed within a recording session. The session is subdivided into a number of intervals of time. The recorder decides, separately for each interval, whether the target behavior did or did not occur at any time during that interval. For example, the teacher may choose to subdivide lunch, which lasts 28 minutes, into 14 two-minute intervals for recording. The teacher will decide at the end of each interval whether or not the target behavior occurred (14 separate yes-or-no decisions). The number of "yes" intervals in which it did occur is the measurement result for that session.

Target behavior measurement results are often graphed to aid interpretation, especially as results describe the child's functioning before and during intervention. Display 3-5 shows graphs of the hyperactivity-related target behaviors of Display 3-4. Chapter 8 discusses using target behavior measurement results to evaluate the power of interventions to produce behavior improvements.

### *Behavior-Products Recording*

Many behaviors generate some kind of tangible change in the environment ("product"). Because behavior products endure for some time after the behaviors that produced them, behavior-product recording can take place well after the behaviors have occurred. This method allows the teacher to measure behavior that happens when he is intensively instructing or otherwise cannot record. Additionally, it usually yields high reliability.

Behavior-product recording is widely used in measuring academics because many academic responses leave a behavior product (e.g., writing). Some school behaviors related to emotional and behavior problems are also suitable for behavior-products recording. For example, "neatness" might be measured by observing the arrangement of books, materials, and desks in the classroom (such as percentage stacked or lined up appropriately), rather than the many different behaviors that can produce a neat arrangement. Torn or balled-up assignments might be used to measure a student's self-doubt; counting new gouges, marks, and other damage to a desk might be used to measure vandalism. Of course, many important behaviors related to E&B disorder do not create a product suited for this recording strategy.

### *Actual Functioning in a Simulated Situation*

Another form of measurement involves observing the performance of a student in an arranged or simulated situation. The student is given a standard collection of tasks that are judged to represent performance requirements found in natural situations. The logic of this kind of measurement is evident in ability and achievement tests, in which items are tasks believed to represent challenging situations encountered in schools and other real-life situations.

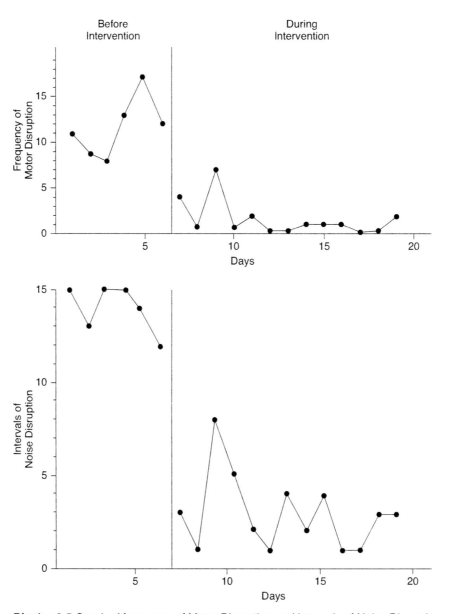

**Display 3-5** Graphed frequency of Motor Disruption and intervals of Noise Disruption, measured as specified in Display 3-4, in a 30-minute period each school day for 19 days (6 before and 13 during intervention).

This method also may be used to measure emotional and behavior problems that may be difficult to measure in natural situations, because the natural situations occur so unpredictably. Bornstein, Bellack, and Hersen (1977) constructed the Behavioral Assertiveness Test for Children to measure children's "assertiveness deficits" (lack of social skills required to effectively communicate one's thoughts and feelings). This instrument consists of a series of role-play situations in which some hypothetical peer is violating the rights of the child. How the child responds to each role-play determines her or his assertiveness score.

Another application of this method occurs in clinical psychological interviews of children and adolescents, in which it is general practice for the clinician to observe and note various physical, behavior, emotional, cognitive, and social characteristics of the young person as the interview proceeds (Lewis & King, 2002; Sergeant & Taylor, 2002). Although the interview is a simulated situation, not a natural one, it is hoped that observation of the child's movements, attention span, mood or emotions, social skills, communication, appearance, reasoning, and other characteristics during the interview may represent and reveal her functioning outside the interview.

## Multifaceted Measurement Systems

For some assessment purposes it is recommended or even required practice to use multiple measurement methods, multiple sources of information, and data collected from multiple settings (Huberty, 2003; Merrell, 2003; Reynolds et al., 2006). Assessors can achieve this by (a) selecting several appropriate measurement procedures, then integrating the results, or (b) using one of the multifaceted measurement systems such as ASEBA (Achenbach & Rescorla, 2001), *Behavior Assessment System for Children* (Reynolds & Kamphaus, 1992), or *Systematic Screening for Behavior Disorders* (Walker & Severson, 1992).

### *Achenbach System of Empirically Based Assessment*
The ASEBA is widely acknowledged as an excellent clinical system for assessing E&B disorder of children and adolescents (Breen, 2003). It assesses five "axes" (sources of information) using various measurement methods covering several locations or situations.

> *Axis I: Parent Reports* uses ratings by and clinical interviews of the child's parents.
>
> *Axis II: Teacher Reports* is based on information from teacher-completed rating scales (TRF, described earlier), interviews with teachers, and school records.
>
> *Axis III: Cognitive Assessment* depends on tests of general and specific cognitive abilities and educational achievement.
>
> *Axis IV: Physical Assessment* involves general medical and neurological evaluation.
>
> *Axis V: Direct Assessment* of Child uses information from clinical and classroom observations of the young person, interviews (SCICA, described earlier), a child-completed rating scale, and objective personality tests.

Additional measurement procedures can be added, and not all forms of assessment are necessarily used with every child.

ASEBA assessment information is examined in different ways depending on particular circumstances (Achenbach & McConaughy, 2003b; Achenbach & Rescorla,

2001). This information yields subscores representing eight different kinds of emotional and behavior problems. Each subscore is compared to norms in order to indicate how deviant it is. A subscore is considered "clinical" (of great concern) if it is more extreme than 97 percent of the norm group and "borderline" (of concern) if it is more extreme than 93 to 97 percent of the norm group. The assessor can use a profile graph to show how the child's eight subscores compare to the norms, as shown in Display 3-6.

As noted, ASEBA collects information from various sources about the same problems of the young person. ASEBA users are especially interested in areas of agreement and disagreement between parents, teachers, and the child. For example, what might it mean when a mother and father perceive their child to show very different kinds of problems? When three teachers' ratings drastically disagree? When the child and teacher report many serious problems but the parents perceive only a few minor ones?

Although the ASEBA was developed primarily for use by child mental health clinicians, teachers of students with ED are likely to encounter psychological reports involving this system. Achenbach and McConaughy (2003a) suggested how to use ASEBA results to identify ED among students.

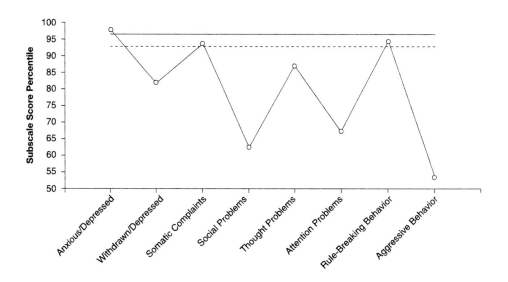

**Subscales of Emotional and Behavior Problem**

**Display 3-6** Profile of ASEBA assessment results for a hypothetical student

**Note:** Solid horizontal line in graph indicates percentile cutoff for a "clinical" subscore (above, Anxious/Depressed). Dashed horizontal line indicates percentile cutoff for "borderline" subscore (above, Somatic Complaints and Rule-Breaking Behavior).

For details on ASEBA, see Achenbach and Rescorla, 2001.

### *Behavior Assessment System for Children*

The Behavior Assessment System for Children (BASC; Reynolds & Kamphaus, 1992, 2002) is another widely used, multifaceted measurement system. It features rating scales for problem and adaptive behaviors, completed by the parents, the teacher, and the student (SRP, described earlier). There is also a procedure for in-school observations of school problem behaviors. BASC measurement information is integrated to facilitate decisions about the student's emotional, behavior, and learning problems from clinical and educational perspectives.

### *Systematic Screening for Behavior Disorders*

The Systematic Screening for Behavior Disorders (SSBD) is a three-step procedure to screen elementary school students at risk for ED, using teacher nomination, teacher rating, and target-behavior recording (Severson & Walker, 2002). The SSBD conserves school resources by applying its successively more complex and expensive steps to successively fewer students. It has been adapted for early identification of preschool children at risk for E+B disorder (Beard & Sugai, 2004; Conroy & Brown, 2004).

First, the regular class teacher nominates two lists of students in the class: those who show aggression, disruption, and other forms of conflict with adults and peers ("externalizing" profile), and those who show depression, anxiety, social isolation, or other personal distress ("internalizing" profile). Students nominated on each list are ranked.

In step two, the teacher completes rating scales on the three highest ranked externalizing and the three highest ranked internalizing students. She rates how frequently each student exhibits common adaptive and maladaptive behaviors at school (e.g., "expresses anger appropriately," "refuses to participate at recess"). In addition, the teacher notes whether the student recently has exhibited uncommon but important problems ("sets fires," "suicidal statements").

Students whose ratings in step two are extreme compared to norms move to step three, which involves target-behavior recording of two key indicators of school success: academic engagement in class (working on an assigned learning task without inattentiveness or rule breaking) and peer interaction at recess (appropriate verbal or nonverbal interaction with one or more peers). Students whose target-behavior data are extreme compared to norms can then receive prereferral intervention (see Chapter 11), additional assessment to determine ED eligibility, or other action.

## Measurement of Environments

In addition to measurement of emotions, behaviors, thoughts, and learning, some aspects of the child's physical and social environment can be of strong interest. Classroom and school environments are measured most often through reports by the teacher and direct observation by various assessors. Exactly what is measured differs greatly from instrument to instrument mainly because of the huge variation in what different educators view as critical components of education. Display 3-7 presents several aspects of education environments that may be important to measure when assessing a student with ED (see also Smith, Polloway, Patton, & Dowdy, 2006; Ysseldyke & Christenson, 2002).

**Display 3-7** Areas to consider in measuring education environments

| Areas | Specifics |
|---|---|
| Classroom Physical | • Number of students<br>• Seating and other space arrangements<br>• Work areas, desks, tables, partitions, other furnishings<br>• Bulletin and chalkboards<br>• Noise<br>• Lighting |
| Schoolwide Physical | • Security<br>• Classroom location in relation to restrooms, lunchroom, gym and recreation areas, school office, school bus area, exits |
| Other Personnel | • Nature of assistants<br>• Teacher use of assistants and volunteers<br>• Access to and interaction with related services professionals |
| Student Social | • Attitude toward schooling and this particular school<br>• Acceptance of new students<br>• Disruptiveness, aggressiveness among students<br>• Sex, race, age considerations<br>• Relations with school staff |
| Teacher Social | • Attitude toward schooling<br>• Communication with group<br>• Communication with individual students<br>• Communication with students' families<br>• Acceptance of new students<br>• Competence<br>• Expectations for student success<br>• Toleration for behavior incidents |
| Scheduling | • Learning and other activities for school day<br>• Learning and other activities for class period<br>• Allocation and use of instruction time<br>• Transitions between activities |
| Grouping | • Individual, small group, cooperative learning groups<br>• Students participate in multiple learning groups |
| Instruction | • Planning and organization for the day's lesson<br>• Planning and organization for the instructional unit<br>• Directiveness<br>• Student participation in lessons<br>• Lesson presentation skills<br>• Homework policies and practices<br>• Computer usage<br>• Evaluation of and feedback for student work<br>• Lesson adaptations for unsuccessful learners<br>• Persistence in reteaching unsuccessful learners |

(*continued*)

**Display 3-7 (Continued)**

| | |
|---|---|
| Behavior Management | • Rules posted, reviewed, enforced<br>• Classroom procedures (e.g., using restroom) are clear to students and reviewed<br>• School regulations (e.g., hall travel) are clear to students and reviewed<br>• Management style: structured, permissive, etc. (e.g., degree of activity or undirected talking tolerated)<br>• Management practices: behavioristic versus humanistic, etc.<br>• Reaction to blowups and crises<br>• Motivational practices |

Such aspects of an education environment can be measured by teacher reports on a checklist or in an interview, target-behavior recording, and in other ways. Results could be useful in decisions about intervention, preparing for the student's inclusion into general education classes, or functional behavioral assessment (discussed later).

##  PURPOSES OF ASSESSMENT

Assessment serves several purposes in the special education process for students with ED, particularly the appropriate assessment and IEP provisions of IDEA 2004. Assessment helps educators (a) select candidates for possible ED eligibility; (b) decide whether or not a candidate should be identified with ED; (c) determine appropriate education and related services; and (d) monitor outcomes of such services (Display 3-8).

### Selecting Candidates

When a student in a regular classroom is showing an emotional and behavior problem, a good teacher usually attempts to help him and minimize disruption by making changes in some ordinary classroom practices. In addition to adapting instruction and classroom management, she may contact parents about the problem and seek advice from colleagues, as well as drawing on her own experience and training. If the problem continues despite such informal adaptations, the teacher will probably consider referring this student for possible identification as ED.

Before referral, however, a period of *prereferral intervention* is usually recommended. A prereferral intervention is similar to an informal adaptation except that advice, training, and other support is usually available from a specialized consultant (special education teacher, case manager, or school psychologist) or a team of experienced educators who collaborate with the teacher to develop additional and perhaps more intensive management and instruction modifications (Friend & Bursuck,

**Display 3-8** Special education service process as related to measurement

| What's the issue? | What to do? |
|---|---|
| A student in general education class is showing an emotional and behavioral problem. | **Make Informal Adaptations**<br>• General teacher contacts parents about the problem<br>• Teacher draws on own experience and seeks advice from colleagues for correcting the problem<br>• Teacher implements adaptations in regular education |
| The teacher's informal adaptations have not solved the emotional and behavioral problem. | **Make Prereferral Interventions**<br>• General teacher contacts parents about the problem<br>• Teacher works with specialized consultant (e.g., special education teacher, case manager, school psychologist) to develop greater adaptations to ordinary management and instruction practices<br>• Teacher implements adaptations in regular education |
| Prereferral interventions have not solved the emotional and behavioral problem. | **Decide Eligibility for ED**<br>• Plan measurement that will yield information relevant to the particular situation<br>• Perform measurement<br>• Consider measurement results and other information in the context of the definition of ED |
| The decision team has classified the student as ED. | **Determine Services**<br>• Supplement existing data with measurement that will obtain information needed to design and monitor appropriate education and related services for behavior, emotional, learning, and other problems and needs of the student<br>• Determine goals related to behavior, emotional, learning, and other problems and needs<br>• Establish measurement practices that will monitor goals and services<br>• Create IEP |
| The student's program and functioning must be evaluated. | **Monitor Outcomes**<br>• Measure implementation of education and related services<br>• Measure behavior, emotional, learning, and other problems and needs identified in prior step, both frequently and annually<br>• Modify intervention as needed based on measurement results<br>• Perform functional assessment leading to behavior intervention plan |

2006; Hammill & Bartel, 2004; Meese, 2001; Smith, et al., 2006). Prereferral intervention and related concepts are discussed in Chapter 11.

If the emotional or behavior problem remains even after reasonable informal adaptations and prereferral interventions have been tried, it is probably appropriate to refer the student. The majority of candidates for identification as having ED arise through referral.

Other candidates arise through screening. One form of screening seeks students who should qualify as ED but are unlikely to be referred. For instance, teachers tend to notice disruptive behavior more readily than social isolation, constant tension, and hopeless thoughts and feelings. They may view such personal impairments as more properly child or family responsibilities than educational ones (Severson & Walker, 2002). The SSBD, as noted, and other measurement procedures can help in **screening**.

## Deciding Eligibility for ED

Whether a candidate is eligible under IDEA 2004 to receive special education as ED is supposed to hinge on whether the student meets criteria in the federal definition. In brief, a student must show any one or more of the five characteristics in Display 1-4 over a long period of time and to a marked degree; and such characteristic(s) must adversely affect the student's educational performance. States and localities can make eligible and serve students who do not fit the federal definition of ED, but legally they cannot receive federal IDEA 2004 money to support such services.

IDEA 2004 has several requirements related to deciding eligibility (Fiedler, 2003; Yell, 2006), as follows:

1. Parental consent must be obtained prior to ED assessment.
2. Measurement procedures should be valid and free of cultural, racial, and language bias.
3. Eligibility for ED must not be based on a single measurement procedure.
4. Eligibility must be decided by a team that includes the student's teacher(s), school administrator, parents, and other professionals as appropriate.

The team should first determine what additional information is needed to decide eligibility and what measurements will produce that information. Once sufficient measurement information is obtained, the team assesses whether the student fits the criteria well enough to be identified and served as ED.

What is "sufficient" measurement for this decision? Certain procedures may be required by state or local regulations (such as individually administered intelligence tests, psychiatric examinations, or neurological testing). Also, measurement procedures vary according to the candidate's particular problems, his or her age, the theoretical preferences of the team, the expertise of assessors, local resources, and other factors. However, there are often some similarities across cases as to variables measured and methods of measurement. Typically, extensive multidisciplinary

A team considers assessment data.

assessments address medical, social, and learning variables, as well as behavior and emotional variables (Shapiro & Kratochwill, 2000).

### *Medical, Social, and Learning Variables*
Close attention may be given to assessing the possibility that medical conditions, especially brain disorders or dysfunctioning, might contribute to the student's problems (Eisler, 2002; Lewis & King, 2002; Schroeder & Gordon, 2002; Schultz et al., 2002). The student's current (and, sometimes, past) social relationships with adults and children at home and at school can be relevant in planning educational interventions and related services. Many students with ED have prominent learning problems. Measuring learning abilities and levels of academic skills and knowledge broadly indicates the student's educational potential and present status (Hyatt & Howell, 2004; Taylor, 2006), although broad learning assessment rarely provides enough detail to plan specific academic interventions. Other learning areas to assess may include communication, vocational skills, and independent living.

### *Behavior and Emotional Variables*
Behavior and emotional problems on which referral was based, obviously, should be assessed thoroughly. Additionally, a referral problem could be linked to other problems in various ways. For instance, it may be necessary to resolve unnoticed or seemingly minor problems in order to adequately tackle the problem for which referral was made. Thus, successful intervention may require assessing multiple emotional and behavior problems. Yet measuring every possible emotional and behavior problem that each referred student might experience would quickly exhaust available resources.

One solution is to proceed in steps, perhaps starting with a rating scale that measures multiple characteristics, such as the TRF or the *Scale for Assessing*

*Emotional Disturbance* (discussed next). Results should indicate which problem areas need to be assessed in further detail. The SSBD uses similar logic, but different measurement methods. Alternatively, assessors could use a multifaceted measurement system such as ASEBA or BASC.

**Measurement Linked to the Federal Definition.** The IDEA 2004 definition of ED (Display 1-4) includes five characteristics, at least one of which a student must exhibit extremely, persistently, and with adverse results on his or her education, in order to be eligible. A few instruments directly address this definition (Epstein & Cullinan, 1998; McCarney & Leigh, 1990).

The *Scale for Assessing Emotional Disturbance* (SAED) is a standardized, norm-referenced instrument completed by teachers to help make identification and other decisions (Epstein & Cullinan, 1998; Epstein, Cullinan, Ryser, Pearson, 2002). SAED measures the five federal definition characteristics (A) to (E), plus socially maladjusted, by means of 45 rated emotional and behavior problem items. They are organized into the following six subscales: (A) Inability to Learn measures a student's problems with educational tasks; (B) Relationship Problems addresses difficulties in establishing and maintaining relationships with other students and teachers; (C) Inappropriate Behavior assesses disruptive and aggressive behaviors; (D) Unhappiness or Depression measures negative emotional response, cognition, and mood; (E) Physical Symptoms or Fears measures anxiety and physical discomfort; and Socially Maladjusted assesses the student's involvement in out-of-school antisocial behaviors. The federal definition states that a student who is socially maladjusted must show one or more of the characteristics (A) to (E) to be eligible for identification as ED (in other words, socially maladjusted alone is not enough).

A student's scores on the subscales may be compared to the SAED's national norms to give the assessor a better understanding of how extreme the student's problems are. SAED also assesses how much the student's problems "adversely affect" educational performance. It has additional features not required in the federal definition, including a subscale measuring important social and personal assets of the student (e.g., family support for school), and open-ended items to obtain information that may help in planning appropriate education.

A graph of SAED results for a 12-year-old boy being considered for special education is presented in Display 3-9. It shows that emotional and behavior problems are present to a high degree, compared to other students of his age level and sex—specifically on the characteristics (B) Relationship Problems, (C) Inappropriate Behavior, and (D) Unhappiness or Depression. These problems adversely affect his educational performance to a severe extent.

## Determining Services

Results of measurement for referral, screening, and deciding eligibility can produce extensive information about the student's situation. Some of this information may help determine what interventions are needed, but unfortunately these measurement

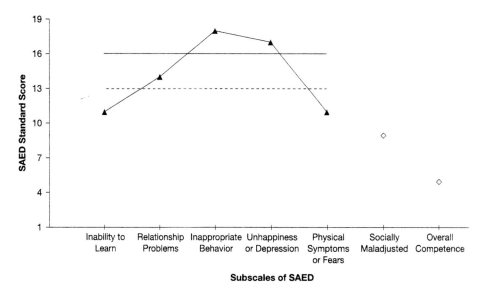

**Display 3-9** SAED results profile for a 12-year-old student

**Note:** On the five characteristics of ED subscales, a score higher than 16 (solid horizontal line) is "very likely" to qualify for the ED disability (here, Inappropriate Behavior and Unhappiness or Depression). A score higher than 13 (dashed line) is "likely" to qualify (here, Relationship Problems).

results are not always directly relevant to the teacher(s) who must plan and implement an intervention program.

To determine more specifically what the student with ED does and does not do, feel, think, and know, and what services are needed, the assessor (often, the teacher) must measure these areas more specifically. To do so she may use some of the methods described earlier in this chapter. For instance, to measure specific problems in emotions and behaviors, the teacher could use an ITRS and target-behavior recording. To measure specific problems and improvements in academic, study, transition, and other learning skills, the teacher could use academic skill probes and curriculum-based assessment (Hyatt & Howell, 2004). Measuring specifics of a student's functioning clarifies his status on each measured variable and is useful for planning an intervention program, completing the IEP, and monitoring student outcomes (McLoughlin & Lewis, 2005; Salvia & Ysseldyke, 2004).

## Monitoring Outcomes

Monitoring outcomes primarily means evaluating a student's progress or lack of progress. Evaluation typically occurs after a period of receiving education and related services that were agreed to in the IEP. Additionally, monitoring outcomes can mean evaluating whether and perhaps how well these services are actually provided.

### *Student Progress*
The teacher can monitor progress in the short-term by continuing to measure specific functioning regularly, employing the methods used for determining services. Such results provide feedback to help the teacher judge whether a teaching method, behavior management system, curriculum, or other aspect of the IEP or overall intervention plan should be continued or changed.

The peer comparison procedure (Kazdin, 2003) may be helpful in monitoring short-term progress. It uses target-behavior recording to evaluate the status of a student's problem relative to that of peers. A particular behavior problem is recorded for both the student with ED and a comparison classmate who has not shown this problem to any great extent. Target-behavior data for the comparison student are assumed to indicate an acceptable level of this behavior problem (Simpson, 2004). Progress, at least in one area, is suggested if data for the ED student are approaching the acceptable level.

IDEA 2004, as well as state and local regulations and good educational practice, calls for regular reevaluations of student progress toward IEP goals (Yell, 2006). Required frequency of reevaluations varies across locations and circumstances. A variety of measurement procedures can be appropriate. Suppose a student with ED has IEP goals for disruptive behavior and unpopularity with peers, as well as reading and math deficits. One year after the start of the IEP this student may be reevaluated, and may show improvements in disruptive target behavior, sociometric status, and achievement test performance. Depending on the size of the improvements and many other considerations, the IEP team will make decisions about changes in goals and other aspects of the IEP (McLoughlin & Lewis, 2005; Reynolds et al., 2006).

### *Functional Behavioral Assessment*
Especially unfavorable outcomes may call for extraordinary assessment and intervention. IDEA 2004 indicates that under certain circumstances the IEP team should (a) perform a **functional behavioral assessment** (FBA; also called functional assessment) of the education situation, and (b) use FBA results to create a new or revised "behavior intervention plan." A main circumstance for the FBA is school discipline involving extensive exclusion from school, or other change of the student's IEP-specified placement.

The FBA examines physical or social environment variables that precede and/or follow the behavior receiving disciplinary action. The object is to identify a "function" (effect on the environment; Barnhill, 2005; Scott, McIntyre, Liaupsin, Nelson, & Conroy, 2004) or purpose (Frey & Wilhite, 2005) accomplished by the student's inappropriate behavior. The IEP team then develops a behavior intervention plan based on this hypothesized function (Fischer, 2003; Fox & Gable, 2004; Kerr & Nelson, 2006). Often the plan helps the student accomplish the same function via acceptable behavior.

Variables that *precede* the inappropriate behavior and might influence it include (a) general aspects of the education setting (such as time of day, school or class rules, seating arrangements, particular peers or teachers present, extent of activity's structure), (b) types of activity (lecture, small group, one-on-one tutoring, independent work, activity transition), and (c) specifics of the curriculum (particular subject or skill taught, level of difficulty). Variables that *follow* the unacceptable behavior and might influence it include changes in the behavior of teachers (withdrawing schoolwork assignment or requirements to follow a rule) or of peers (showing approval or other obvious reaction). In FBA, such preceding or following variables are measured by means of interviewing the teacher and the misbehaving student, recording student and teacher target behaviors, completing checklists that address environment variables noted above and in Display 3-7, and in other ways (see Fischer, 2003; Scott et al., 2004).

To illustrate, suppose William, a student with ED, is being considered for a change of placement because of vigorous tantrums in class—shouting, making disrespectful remarks, throwing books and chairs, and threatening the teacher and peers. To begin an FBA, the teacher might first record the occurrence of tantrums by time of day, revealing that tantrums occurred mainly following transitions into the classroom (from art, library, music, lunch, and recess). Next, using a simple form constructed by the IEP team (Display 3-10), the teacher or another observer could record some details of transitions over several days to identify more specific environmental variables associated with tantrums.

Depending on assessment results, the team may be able to formulate a hypothesized function of William's tantrums and create a behavior intervention plan based on this hypothesis. For example, suppose results revealed a pattern: tantrums were most likely to occur (a) when students did not return to their desks immediately upon reentering the classroom but instead "milled about" for half a minute or more; and (b) when the teacher instructed the students to begin working independently on a worksheet to practice academic skills taught earlier in the day. Also, results showed that after the beginning of a tantrum, the teacher sometimes reduced the length of William's assignment, offered a different activity, or had the teacher assistant escort him out of the room.

Next, the IEP team might hypothesize that William's tantrums were prompted by the unstructured environment upon classroom reentry, and/or functioned as a way for him to escape worksheet and similar assignments, perhaps because he lacks or believes he lacks the skills needed. The team could then create a behavior intervention plan that addresses part or all of this hypothesis. For example, the teacher could (a) give rule reminders before, and greater structure during, classroom reentry; (b) increase the amount of William's instruction in the academic skills each day; and (c) reduce the value of escape by requiring William to complete the assignment before receiving access to a desired activity.

*Positive behavior support* (PBS) builds on the FBA and behavior intervention plan to provide a system of prevention and intervention for individual, classroom-wide, or schoolwide inappropriate behavior (Kerr & Nelson, 2006; Sugai, Sprague, Horner, & Walker, 2000). In PBS as a schoolwide strategy, FBA identifies physical and social variables common to many classrooms or to the school as a whole that, hypothetically, prompt or facilitate inappropriate behavior. The school gets a behavior intervention plan in which those variables are modified to create a school environment that encourages appropriate behavior (Liaupsin, Jolivette, & Scott, 2004). Many PBS advocates also see little need for, and counsel against, punishing consequences for inappropriate behavior.

| | |
|---|---|
| Date and Time: | Observer: |

Kind of transition: Music, art, library/Lunch/Recess

### Transition events before reentering classroom

| | |
|---|---|
| William's behavior | Talked loudly with peers. Pushed several peers, mostly in jest. |
| Peer behavior | Several talked loudly with William, pushed him back (not in anger). |
| Teacher behavior | Requested that all students keep hands to themselves, stop shouting. |
| Other events | Vice principal approached us, told the group to quiet down, gave me a dirty look. |

### Transition events after reentering classroom

| | |
|---|---|
| William's behavior | Continued loud talking and pushing. Refused to sit down, but did so after multiple requests. |
| Peer behavior | Sat at desks within about 10 seconds of my instruction. |
| Teacher behavior | Instructed all students to sit at desks, begin work on worksheet. Reminded students that this is practice on the skill I taught them during earlier math time. Requested and instructed William to sit in his desk. |
| Other events | |

### Events during or after the tantrum

| | |
|---|---|
| William's behavior | Called me an ugly bitch, said he won't do this goddamn math. Tore up the worksheet and threw it into the air. Grabbed the worksheet of Jermane (sitting beside William), balled it, threw it at me. |
| Peer behavior | Several laughed, made comments about tantrum, watched William but ignored their work sheets. |
| Teacher behavior | Requested William to quiet down and I would help him do the work sheet. When this did not work, asked the assistant to take William to the office. |
| Other events | |

**Display 3-10** Observation form suitable for functional assessment

## Program Evaluation and Research

Aside from the special education process, measurement is important in at least two other areas: evaluation and research (Sasso, 2004). To develop more valuable approaches to students with ED, we must evaluate the implementation, effectiveness, cost, and other aspects of existing intervention programs. Scientific research based on sound measurement extends our understanding of ED (Stichter & Conroy, 2004) and, more generally, E&B disorder of young people. This is the main way we will learn more about assessment, characteristics, causes, interventions, outcomes, and—as described next—classification of E&B disorder.

Obviously, the main role of a teacher or other practitioner is not to evaluate programs or perform research on children and adolescents with E&B disorders. However, to be informed consumers of evaluation and research, special educators must stay abreast of developments as reported in professional periodicals and elsewhere.

## CLASSIFICATION

What is different about young people with E&B disorder? The answer partly depends on the level at which human characteristics are analyzed. At a very general level, all children appear much more alike than different. Children and adolescents with E&B disorder experience the emotions, thoughts, and behaviors that all young humans do. They have personal and social successes, failures, strengths, and shortcomings.

At the same time, experience and research have shown that children with E&B disorder are not all alike and they do differ from children without E&B disorder in key ways. Many of these differences involve excesses or deficiencies in various behaviors, emotions, and thoughts, to an extent that interferes with the functioning of that child and/or other people. In other words, emotional, behavioral, and cognitive differences create problems that are an important basis for deciding whether a particular child has E&B disorder or has ED.

Display 3-11 lists 50 such problems as reported by teachers, parents, mental health professionals, children and adolescents identified with E&B disorder, and their peers. This is by no means an exhaustive list. An early survey of approximately 2,500 referrals to child guidance clinics (Gilbert, 1957) identified hundreds of problems for which the young people were referred. Of course, no student exhibits all of these problems, but sooner or later a teacher of students with ED will probably encounter most of the problem characteristics listed in Display 3-11.

Although it is interesting to consider many different problems, including rare ones and highly specific variations of a general problem, there is a drawback to this. The more problem characteristics we consider, the more difficult it becomes to conceptualize possible linkages among multiple characteristics, as well as relationships between characteristics and their causes or between characteristics and treatments. Therefore, it would be handy to organize the large number of problems into a smaller, manageable number of categories of problems. The basis for such categories might be a convincing theory of E&B disorder, similarities and differences among the

**Display 3-11** Selected emotional and behavior problems of children with E&B disorder

| | |
|---|---|
| Abuses drugs or alcohol | Has been in trouble with the law |
| Afraid of unlikely dangers to self or others | Has feelings of worthlessness |
| Angers readily; explosive temper | Has few or no friends |
| Anxious, worried, tense | Lacks self-confidence |
| Assaults kids or adults | Lacks skills to be friendly and sociable |
| Associates with older companions | Lies to peers or adults |
| Bowel, bladder control problems (e.g., enuresis, encopresis) | Little or no motivation for school learning |
| Cruel to peers | Misbehaves due to peer pressure |
| Defiant of school authorities | Nervous habits (e.g., twitching, nail-biting, hair-twisting) |
| Destroys or ruins things | Not flexible when faced with new social activities |
| Disruptive, loud, rowdy | Obscene, profane, or sexually oriented language |
| Does not follow instructions, rules | Overly sensitive feelings and emotions |
| Does not independently complete assigned work | Participates in illegal or antisocial gang activities |
| Does not work well in group activities | Precocious sexual behavior |
| Dreads school or particular aspects of school (e.g., recess, tests, bullying) | Produces messy, sloppy schoolwork |
| Eating problems or appetite problems | Rejected or avoided by peers |
| Excessively active; fidgety | Reports stomach aches or discomfort |
| Experiences headaches | Sad much of the time; does not smile |
| Experiences little pleasure or joy | Sexually harrasses or molests peers or teachers |
| Expresses hopelessness | Shows no guilt about misbehaviors |
| Fails to anticipate outcomes of own behaviors | Steals |
| Feels excessive guilt | Talks about suicide or own death |
| Feels persecuted | Threatens peers or adults |
| Harms own body (e.g., picks self, cuts self, writes on self) | Tries to avoid interacting with people |
| | Verbally abuses, teases, taunts people |
| | Violates major home rules |

problems, or some other organizing principle. Finding categories of problems is one main purpose of efforts at classification of E&B disorder.

Classification is the process of grouping information on the basis of similarities and differences. People tend to classify information about all sorts of important things in life and thereafter to compare new events to familiar ones. The new event is not usually treated as if it were totally unprecedented and unique. Instead, its important similarities to and differences from familiar things are emphasized, while less relevant characteristics are disregarded.

Likewise, to classify the problems of a particular child, we assess important variables such as behavior, emotional, and cognitive problems, medical status, and personal history. We then use this information to compare the child's functioning on the measured variables to the categories of an established classification system for E&B disorders (Cullinan, 2004). If enough similarities are detected, the child's problems may be classified.

## Purposes of Classification

A good classification system can serve several important purposes (Adams, Luscher, & Bernat, 2001; Quay, 1986; Scotti & Morris, 2000; Wicks-Nelson & Israel, 2006). Important among them are communication, organization, and intervention selection.

### *Communication*

Classification eases communication among practitioners, researchers, policy makers, and others concerned with E&B disorder by giving some consistency to terms and concepts. This makes it more likely that information shared about E&B disorder will be reliable, even among professionals of different disciplines and points of view.

### *Organization*

Good classification makes it easier to organize and get access to a wide range of potentially significant information about E&B disorder(s). Such information includes prevalence, biological and psychosocial risk factors for E&B disorder, and course (expected changes in the E&B disorder over time and its eventual outcome). Classification can help researchers look for linkages among prevalence, risk factors, course, and other variables that may be clues to causes and interventions. For instance, suppose it is discovered that the prevalence of one category of E&B disorder, but not other categories, is much higher among children whose parents use a particular discipline style. What might be some implications of this discovery for causes and interventions?

### *Intervention Selection*

If we assume that no single intervention is best for all instances of E&B disorder, how will we decide which ones to apply to which children? Research on the success of different interventions for various categories of E&B disorder may show which intervention produces the most improvement for a particular category of E&B disorder. This holds the promise of enabling practitioners to select the best intervention for each category of E&B disorder.

To illustrate, suppose there were an ideal classification system that consisted of three categories of E&B disorder. Research tells us that children and adolescents with characteristics of Category I always return to normal functioning within a few months whether or not they receive intervention. Young people with characteristics of Category II continue to show E&B disorder unless they receive highly structured behavior management and academic tutoring; however, those who get these treatments show steady improvement. Children and adolescents with characteristics of Category III continue to show E&B disorder unless both youth and parents receive intensive psychotherapy. The value of this hypothetical ideal system is obvious:

1. Any child with emotional and behavior problems is assessed on relevant characteristics.
2. Based on these results, the case is assigned to one of the three categories.
3. The category determines what form of treatment, if any, is needed to bring about normalization.

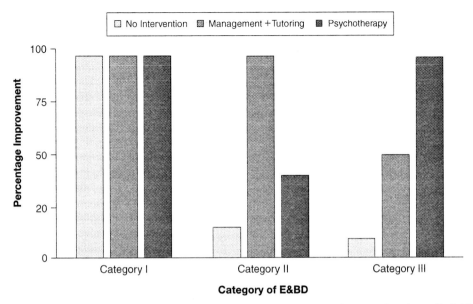

**Display 3-12** Ideal classification (category of E&BD prescribes intervention that will yield most improvement)

This ideal classification system (see Display 3-12) identifies *prognosis* (expected future functioning) and clarifies treatment decisions.

## Existing Classification Systems

Like many ideals, the ideal classification system for E&B disorder of young people does not presently exist. Our imaginary ideal system shows the potential value of classification and suggests why great interest in classification continues. There have been many diverse and innovative attempts to create and improve classification systems (e.g., Achenbach, 1995; Adams et al., 2001; Quay, 1986; Reynolds & Kamphaus, 2002; Zimmerman & Spitzer, 2005). Today's most influential systems are of two kinds, *nosological* and *dimensional*. They are based on different perspectives about the nature of E&B disorder, how to establish categories, and what the categories are.

### *Nosological Classification*

In the nosological ("disease-oriented;" alternatively termed clinical) perspective, an E&B disorder is a collection of maladaptive and distressing behaviors, emotions, and thoughts that is different in kind from normality. Just as a person either does or does not have a particular disease, he either does or does not have a particular E&B disorder. Among the classification systems based on this perspective is the most influential one in North America, the *Diagnostic and Statistical Manual of Mental Disorders* (DSM).

DSM is considered the official classification system by many mental health agencies, government bureaus, insurance companies, medical service organizations, and other powerful forces that shape our society's perspectives on and services to E&B disorder of young people (Zimmerman & Spitzer, 2005). DSM diagnoses and related information may be presented to school multidisciplinary teams making decisions about a student or may be found in a student's school records. Thus educators of students with ED should have some knowledge of DSM.

DSM was created in the mid-20th century, mainly by psychiatric authorities for fellow psychiatrists (American Psychiatric Association, 1952), as an adaptation of classification systems for medical diseases. The creators of DSM saw important parallels between E&B disorders and diseases, and they were strongly influenced by psychodynamic theories about E&B disorder. Some of the E&B disorders (called "mental disorders" in the DSM system) had known or suspected biological causes, whereas others were seen as caused by unconscious disturbances involving intrapsychic processes.

In medicine, classification and diagnosis rely heavily on *symptoms* (subjective indicators such as feelings or other complaints) and *signs* (observable indicators such as behaviors, physical damage, or laboratory tests) of an underlying health problem. Symptoms and signs that often occur together can constitute a disease *syndrome*. By analogy in DSM, maladaptive and distressing emotions, cognitions, and behaviors are considered symptoms and signs of an underlying mental disorder. A syndrome of these symptoms and signs suggests the existence of a particular category of mental disorder (Sadock, 2005).

DSM remains influenced by the concepts that (a) E&B disorder is similar to a medical disease and (b) intrapsychic disturbances are important causes of some E&B disorders. However, recent revisions to DSM have incorporated changes in theories, feedback from clinicians, results of scientific research, input from fields other than psychiatry, and other influences (Adams et al., 2001; Scotti & Morris, 2000; Zimmerman & Spitzer, 2005). The current version, *DSM-IV-TR* ("DSM four TR") is used by a range of mental health professionals and covers a large number of E&B disorders of children and adolescents (American Psychiatric Association, 2000).

***DSM-IV-TR.*** To use DSM-IV the assessor makes judgments about five kinds of information, called axes. On Axis I and/or Axis II the assessor identifies one or more of about 400 categories of mental disorder and other phenomena related to E&B disorder (e.g., a V-code ["vee code"] condition that, although it does not qualify as a mental disorder, is a important problem needing intervention). Display 3-13 presents two groups of Axis I and Axis II categories. The first lists mental disorders reserved for children and adolescents; the second is a selection of other mental disorders that are not specifically for children and adolescents but still may be applied to them. Note that many problems not generally considered to be E&B disorders (e.g., mental retardation) do fall within the DSM concept of mental disorder.

On Axis III the assessor indicates medical problems that may have caused or resulted from the mental disorder or may affect its treatment. Axis IV is for psychosocial and environmental stressors (e.g., economic, educational, social support

**Display 3-13** Selected DSM-IV categories used with children and adolescents

### *Disorders Usually First Diagnosed in Infancy, Childhood, or Adolescence*

MENTAL RETARDATION
  Subcategories include Mild, Moderate, Severe, and Profound

LEARNING DISORDERS
  Subcategories include Reading, Mathematics, Written Expression, and Not Otherwise Specified (NOS)

COMMUNICATION DISORDERS
  Subcategories include Communication, Expressive Language, Mixed Receptive-Expressive Language, and NOS

PERVASIVE DEVELOPMENTAL DISORDERS
  Subcategories include Autistic Disorder, Rett's Disorder, Childhood Disintegrative Disorder, Asperger's Disorder, and NOS

ATTENTION-DEFICIT AND DISRUPTIVE BEHAVIOR DISORDERS
  Subcategories
    Attention-Deficit/Hyperactivity Disorder (sub-subcategories: Predominantly Inattentive, Predominantly Hyperactive-Impulsive, Combined, and NOS)
    Conduct Disorder
    Oppositional Defiant Disorder
    NOS

FEEDING AND EATING DISORDERS OF INFANCY OR EARLY CHILDHOOD
  Subcategories include Pica

TIC DISORDERS
  Subcategories include Tourette's Disorder

ELIMINATION DISORDERS
  Subcategories include Encopresis, Enuresis not due to medical condition

OTHER DISORDERS OF INFANCY, CHILDHOOD, OR ADOLESCENCE
  Subcategories include Separation Anxiety Disorder, Selective Mutism, Reactive Attachment Disorder of Infancy or Early Childhood, and NOS

### *Other Disorders That May Be Diagnosed Among Children and Adolescents*

SUBSTANCE USE DISORDERS
  Subcategories include Substance Dependence, Substance Abuse, Substance-Induced Disorders

COGNITIVE DISORDERS
  Subcategories include Delirium due to Head Trauma

PSYCHOTIC DISORDERS
  Subcategories include Schizophrenia, Schizophreniform Disorder, Schizoaffective Disorder, Delusional Disorder

MOOD DISORDERS
  Subcategories include Depressive Disorders (includes Major Depressive Disorder, Dysthymic Disorder), Bipolar Disorders (includes Bipolar I Disorder, Bipolar II Disorder, Cyclothymic Disorder), Other Mood Disorders

> EATING DISORDERS
>   <u>Subcategories</u> include Anorexia Nervosa, Bulimia Nervosa
> ANXIETY DISORDERS
>   <u>Subcategories</u> include Social Phobia, Posttraumatic Stress Disorder, Specific Phobia, Obsessive-Compulsive Disorder, Panic Disorder
> GENDER IDENTITY DISORDER
> ADJUSTMENT DISORDER
>   <u>Subcategories</u> include Adjustment Disorder with Depressed Mood, with Anxiety, with Disturbance of Conduct, with Mixed Disturbance of Emotions and Conduct
> V-CODES
>   <u>Subcategories</u> include Relational Problems (e.g., parent–child), Child Abuse, Child or Adolescent Antisocial Behavior, Identity Problem

*Source:* Adapted from American Psychiatric Association, 2000.

problems) that may have contributed to the mental disorder. On Axis V, the assessor judges the quality of the client's current functioning. This suggests, among other things, the degree of impairment associated with the mental disorder.

Proponents of DSM-IV are optimistic that it corrects major problems with earlier DSMs and is a highly useful classification system. Proponents and critics alike have identified important problems remaining in DSM, as well as problems for any nosological classification system (Achenbach, 2000; Adams et al., 2001; Rounsaville et al., 2002; Scotti & Morris, 2000; Segal & Coolidge, 2001; Zimmerman & Spitzer, 2005). Planning and research are underway for DSM-V, anticipated in about 2010 (Kupfer, First, & Regier, 2002).

### *Dimensional Classification*

While the nosological perspective views E&B disorder as an extraordinary phenomenon, the dimensional (also called "empirical") perspective assumes that an E&B disorder consists of problems involving ordinary behaviors, emotions, and thoughts. These are problems that all of us experience to some extent, but a person experiencing them to an extreme extent probably has an E&B disorder. "Extreme extent" means unusually high or low frequency, duration, intensity, perceived seriousness, or other measurable aspect of problems.

In the dimensional perspective, a category of E&B disorder is a collection of behavior, emotional, and/or cognitive problems that belong together because they "co-occur." To understand **co-occurrence**, consider two problems, A and B, measured on a group of adolescents. Assume that for nearly all these adolescents, when the score of A is low, B is low too; when A is high, B is high. Problems A and B can be said to co-occur.

To expand this illustration, suppose an investigator measures each adolescent on Problems K, L, M, N, O, P, Q, and R, then examines the resulting data. Also suppose she finds that young people who have a high score on Problem K nearly always have high scores on Problems L, M, and N as well. However, they may have low, medium, or high scores on Problems O, P, Q, and R. This investigator has discovered a co-occurring collection of problems consisting of K, L, M, and N. The other problems do not belong to that collection. A dimensional category of E&B disorder is a collection of problems that, as measured, tend to be similar to every other problem within the collection, but do not tend to be similar to additional problems outside the collection.

Creating a classification system consisting of dimensional categories involves activities like those described above, but on a larger scale. Typically an investigator studies many dozens of problems measured on hundreds or thousands of young people who have already been identified as experiencing E&B disorder. With such numbers, finding collections of co-occurring problems would be nearly impossible without the use of a computer and multivariate statistics such as factor analysis. Each collection of co-occurring problems found in this way is called a factor (alternatively, a dimension). Ordinarily, factor analysis finds at least two dimensions.

Each dimension represents something in common among the individual problems in that one collection—some quality the problems share with each other but do not share with problems outside that collection. It is logical to consider this "something in common" to be the essence of a category of E&B disorder. The dimension is usually named so as to summarize this essence. For instance, suppose a dimension consists of the four problems, "publicly refuses to follow teacher's directions," "does the opposite of what school personnel ask," "attempts to persuade peers not to cooperate with adults," and "calls the teacher insulting names." This dimensional category might be named "Oppositional" or some similar term.

Once a dimensional system is developed, using it to classify E&B disorder is straightforward (Cullinan, 2004). First, the child whose emotional and behavior problems are to be classified is measured on a standard set of problem items (mainly those on which the dimensions are based). This produces a score for each of the problem items.

Second, the assessor calculates a dimension score for the first dimension by combining (e.g., adding) the scores of all problem items that make up the first dimension.

Third, a dimension score for every other dimension is calculated similarly, by combining the scores of all individual items in that particular dimension. At this point the child will have a dimension score on each of the dimensions in the classification system.

Fourth, the assessor needs to determine how extreme this child's dimension scores are. To do so, the assessor consults the classification system's norms. The norms might show, for example, that the child's score on the third dimension is at the 95th percentile, that is, more extreme than 95 percent of the norming group's scores.

Finally, the assessor must answer the question, are the child's dimension scores extreme enough to indicate the presence of E&B disorder? To help answer this question, the dimensional system may have a "cutoff"—a percentile beyond which a dimension score is too extreme to ignore. A dimension score beyond cutoff calls for further assessment, special help, or other action and supports a decision that the child shows E&B disorder.

It should be noted that as yet there is not much scientific basis for selecting cutoffs. Recommended cutoffs are informed opinion; in some circumstances an assessor may arbitrarily choose a different cutoff. In any case, an extreme dimension score cannot determine whether or not a student has an E&B disorder, because identification decisions must be based on more than one assessment procedure.

There are several dimensional classification systems for E&B disorders of young people (Breen, 2003). The ASEBA (Achenbach & Rescorla, 2001) is in widest use and has generated the most research.

***ASEBA.*** The ASEBA first appeared in the early 1980s and was based on earlier work by Achenbach and others. Its development and revision have been guided by scientific research and clinical experience (Achenbach, 1995; Achenbach & McConaughy, 2003b). In a review of dimensional classification studies of E&B disorders of children and adolescents, Achenbach and Edelbrock (1978) identified about 20 different dimensions. Many seemed to apply primarily to a specific age level of child, sex of child, or "informant perspective" (i.e., whether it was the teacher, parent, or child herself who provided data on child problems). Achenbach and his colleagues saw the need for a system in which dimensions of E&B disorder apply across ages, sexes, and informant perspectives (Achenbach & McConaughy, 2003b).

The investigators developed assessment procedures to obtain the teacher's perspective, one or both parent perspectives, and the young person's perspective (Achenbach & Rescorla, 2001). After collecting data from the different informant perspectives on many children, Achenbach identified eight dimensions of E&B disorder, which he terms *cross-informant syndromes* (Display 3-14).

Achenbach and colleagues established norms for these cross-informant syndromes and grouped them by use of statistical and other methods. Anxious/Depressed, Withdrawn/Depressed, and Somatic Complaints syndromes came together into a group of dimensions termed *Internalizing*. Rule-Breaking Behavior and Aggressive Behavior came together into a group referred to as *Externalizing*. The remaining syndromes—Social Problems, Thought Problems, and Attention Problems—were not grouped because they did not show statistical alignment with either Externalizing or Internalizing or with each other (Achenbach & Rescorla, 2001).

To use the ASEBA to classify problems of a particular child, an assessor obtains the teacher perspective by using the ASEBA instruments *Teacher Report Form;* the parent perspective by using the *Child Behavior Checklist*, and the young person's perspective with *Youth Self-Report* and *Semistructured Clinical Interview for Children and Adolescents* procedures (Achenbach & Rescorla, 2001; McConaughy & Achenbach, 2001). ASEBA also makes use of other instruments and forms of measurement.

From data thus obtained, the assessor calculates the child's score on each of the eight cross-informant syndromes, then compares these scores to ASEBA norms. A syndrome score below the 93rd percentile of the norm group is considered normal. A score above the 93rd percentile but below the 97th percentile is in the "borderline range" (of some concern); a score above the 97th percentile is in "clinical range" (of

**Display 3-14** Illustrative emotional and behavior problem items of ASEBA Cross-Informant Syndromes

**INTERNALIZING SYNDROMES**

| Anxious/Depressed | Withdrawn/Depressed | Somatic Complaints |
|---|---|---|
| Cries a lot | Enjoys very little | Dizzy |
| Feels worthless | Keeps things to self | Headaches |
| Talks about killing self | Unhappy, sad, depressed | Nausea |
| Too fearful or anxious | Withdrawn, not involved | Overly tired |

**EXTERNALIZING SYNDROMES**

| Rule-Breaking Behavior | Aggressive Behavior |
|---|---|
| Bad companions | Destroys others' property |
| Lacks guilt for misbehavior | Disobedient at school |
| Lying, cheating | Fights |
| Steals outside home | Threatens people |

**NEITHER INTERNALIZING NOR EXTERNALIZING**

| Social Problems | Thought Problems | Attention Problems |
|---|---|---|
| Complains of loneliness | Can't get mind off thoughts | Can't concentrate |
| Feels others mistreat her/him | Hears things | Can't sit still |
| Jealous of peers | Strange behavior | Impulsive |
| Not liked by peers | Strange ideas | Poor school work |

**Note:** Items listed suggest the essence of ASEBA items concisely. For full wording of items and listings of all problem items by syndrome, see Achenbach & Rescorla, 2001.

strong concern) (see Display 3-6). A syndrome score of clinical or even borderline range, if supported by other assessment evidence, may indicate that the child should be identified with an E&B disorder and receive intervention and other services. The ASEBA can be used to help decide whether a student's emotional and behavior problems should qualify him for special education as ED (Achenbach & McConaughy, 2003a).

## Evaluating Classification

As stated earlier, no existing system is close to ideal. So is there any merit in classifying E&B disorder? Evaluating classification involves some thought-provoking, complex issues (see, e.g., Achenbach, 1995; Adams et al., 2001; Cullinan, 2004; Mash & Wolfe, 2002; Scotti & Morris, 2000; Segal & Coolidge, 2001; Taylor & Rutter, 2002; Zimmerman & Spitzer, 2005). A few issues involving the philosophy of classifying E&B disorder, and technical problems in classification, are very briefly noted below.

### Philosophical Issues

***Questionable Logic.*** The search for a good classification system might be an impossible, illogical quest because there really are no such things as categories of E&B disorder (see Lamiell, 1997; Rogers, 1951). Perhaps each instance of what we call E&B disorder is actually that person's unique "problem of living" (Szasz, 1960). Therefore one might say that there are billions of categories of E&B disorder, with one unique case per category. Or maybe the opposite is true: there is really only one category—one form—of E&B disorder. What appear to be different categories are actually variations of the same disorder, differing from one another mainly in degree of severity and personal life circumstances (Menninger, 1963).

Such reservations, whether correct or not, remind us that each child has important individual circumstances. To classify, one must overlook individual circumstances to emphasize important similarities across many children. However, appropriate assessment and intervention require the practitioner to remain mindful of the child's distinctive circumstances (Doucette, 2002).

***Detrimental Effects.*** By defining and classifying E&B disorder we may at the same time "label" the young person involved, which may lead to various undesired effects (Scotti & Morris, 2000; Wicks-Nelson & Israel, 2006; see Chapter 10). First, many students identified as having E&B disorder do not like that label and may suffer lowered self-esteem and popularity. Second, if a label reduces the expectations of teachers and others, the labeled student may detect this and behave according to these lowered expectations, producing a self-fulfilling prophecy of failure, deviance, and irresponsibility.

Third, labels meant to be temporary identifiers of a problem can become permanent, prejudicing the impressions and efforts of teachers and others on a long-term basis. Finally, some believe that classification is just another way to justify isolation and oppression of people whose behavior displeases or threatens powerful interests in society (Cockerham, 2006; Szasz, 1960).

### Technical Issues

***Characteristics.*** Problems of behavior, emotion, and cognition are the main basis for classification decisions. Obviously, these variables and others used in classification must be measured with high reliability and validity for a classification system to have much value.

***Categories.*** The categories in a classification system also should have high reliability and validity. Categories have low reliability if, for example, various practitioners who have the same information about a particular case assign that case to different categories. Categories have low validity if, for instance, E&B disorders in different categories improve about the same amount when a particular intervention is applied (i.e., the opposite of what was illustrated in Display 3-12).

***Usability.*** A classification system is more readily usable if it has enough categories to include all significant forms of E&B disorder, yet not so many categories that it is confusing or cumbersome. It is also more usable if it can be implemented without extensive training and if the assessor can easily communicate classification procedures and results.

## *Conclusions*

Many unresolved questions remain about classification, but on balance the evidence suggests that there is value in discriminating different kinds of E&B disorder of children. Current classification systems have various strengths and weaknesses. A system that is best for one purpose may not be best for other purposes (Adams et al., 2001; Cullinan, 2004).

We must always be concerned about potentially detrimental effects of labeling, particularly as long as strong benefits of classifying E&B disorder remain unproven. Yet we do not know the extent and severity of harmful labeling effects, and exaggerating dangers of labeling could hinder needed services such as prevention and early intervention (Kaufman, Brigham, & Mock, 2004). Many education and other services must be focused on a particular student, even though doing so may, in effect, label him. Besides, labeling occurs unofficially as well as officially: if formal definitions and classifications of E&B disorder were abolished, practitioners and researchers alike would probably adopt informal categories and names in an effort to organize and communicate their ideas about young people with E&B disorder. Classmates would label peers with E&B disorder, as well.

The best dimensional systems generally have better reliability and validity than nosological systems. Nosological systems typically include infrequent disorders that dimensional systems cannot. Technical aspects of nosological and dimensional classification of E&B disorder of children and adolescents have advanced recently (Achenbach, 1995; Adams et al., 2001; Taylor & Rutter, 2002). Even so, much more work is needed to develop reliable, valid, and usable classification. Very unfortunately, available systems have limited validity for the most important purpose of classification: helping specify interventions that will lead to the best improvement for a particular category of E&B disorder.

The prospects and problems of classification suggest the following directions. First, educators should understand pros and cons of the process of classification. Second, they should be familiar with major current classification systems. This is an ongoing task because the systems are occasionally revised. However, it is worth the trouble because new knowledge in this field is often framed in terms of categories in one of the classification systems. Third, in hope that more effective classification systems will help us provide better education and other intervention to students with E&B disorder, researchers must continue to improve reliability, validity, usability, and other aspects of classification.

At present there is little evidence that knowing a student's category of E&B disorder helps a teacher select the proper intervention. Thus special educators should not make too much of the fact that a student has been classified as showing a particular kind of E&B disorder. For now it is more productive to identify, measure, and remediate specific problems of behavior, emotion, thought, and learning that interfere with the student's school and life adjustment. When and if research clearly shows how classification can significantly aid special education, teachers can modify their practices accordingly.

## Chapter Summary

Assessment is critical to understanding and serving students with ED. Important measurement concepts include variable, operational definition, reliability, validity, and norms. The main methods of measurement can be subdivided into reported or actual functioning.

- Reported functioning is measured via:
  — Nomination by teachers or peers
  — Ratings by the student herself or others (teacher, other adult, peer)
  — Interviewing the student, parent, or teacher
  — Objective or projective personality measurement
- Actual functioning is measured via:
  — Target-behavior recording (e.g., frequency or partial interval)
  — Behavior-product recording
- Multiple methods and sources of measurement information are built into multifaceted systems such as ASEBA and SSBD.
- Measurement serves six main purposes in education for students with ED, helping to:
  — Select candidates for possible ED eligibility
  — Make the decision as to whether the candidate should be identified with ED
  — Determine appropriate education and related services for the student
  — Monitor results of those services
  — Evaluate the strengths and weaknesses of a special education program
  — Enable research into ED of students and E&B disorder of children

    Classification of E&B disorder organizes a large number of specific problems into a more manageable number of categories of problem.

- Ideal classification would enable matching a category of E&B disorder to a well-suited intervention.

- Two forms of classification, nosological and dimensional, are based on very different assumptions and methods of classifying.
  — DSM-IV is an influential system illustrating nosological classification.
  — ASEBA is an important system illustrating dimensional classification.
- Interesting and important issues, both philosophical and technical, remain to be resolved.

## IDEAS FOR CONSIDERATION AND DISCUSSION

1. Describe the value of norms for understanding results of measurement of emotional and behavior problems.
2. A student's fearfulness was measured in two ways, self-rating and partial-interval recording. Self-rating results indicated a low degree of fearfulness. Partial-interval recording results indicated a high degree of fearfulness. What implications does this situation have for
   a. understanding fearfulness?
   b. providing appropriate assessment of this student?
   c. providing appropriate education to the student?
3. Create a table similar to Display 3-4. Under a *Recording Method and Results* column, use both frequency and partial interval methods to record the following problems:
   a. poor self-concept
   b. disrespectful attitude toward teacher
   c. inadequate social participation
   d. refusal to accept responsibility for misconduct
   e. persistent hopelessness
4. From each of the "Areas" in Display 3-7, choose one of the "Specifics."
   a. How might each of your chosen Specifics interfere with or hamper education for students with ED?
   b. How might each Specific facilitate or help education for students with ED?
   c. For each of your Specifics, say how an educator could use measured information to improve the school functioning of a student with ED.
5. Suppose a student's emotional and behavior problem is very specific (e.g., aggressive threats and behaviors toward teachers and peers) and exhibited to a severe extent.
   a. Describe and justify assessment activities focused on aggression.
   b. Describe and justify other assessment activities that are focused on characteristics other than aggression.
6. In 100 words or fewer, explain what Display 3-12 shows.

## RESOURCES FOR FURTHER STUDY

**www.aseba.org/** Achenbach System of Empirically Based Assessment
**www.agsnet.com/** American Guidance Services (publisher of assessment material)
**www.agsnet.com/Group.asp?nGroupInfoID=a30000** Behavior Assessment System for Children
**www.appi.org/dsm.cfx** DSM information
**http://cecp.air.org/fba/problembehavior/main.htm** Functional behavioral assessment
**http://www.psychoeducational.com/** Journal of Psychoeducational Assessment
**http://www.unl.edu/buros/bimm/html/catalog.html#mmy** Mental Measurements Yearbooks

**www.proedinc.com/** PRO·ED (publisher of assessment material)
**www.parinc.com/** Psychological Assessment Resources
**www.guidetopsychology.com/testing.htm** Psychological testing
**www.sopriswest.com/** Sopris West (publisher of assessment material)
**www.apa.org/science/standards.html#overview** Standards for Educational and Psychological Testing

Chapter **Four**

# *Patterns of Emotional and Behavior Disorder*

## OBJECTIVES

**After reading this chapter, you should be able to:**
- Name the five patterns of E&B disorder.
- Describe behavior, emotional, and cognitive aspects of (a) *Aggression*, (b) *Anxiety*, (c) *Depression*, (d) *Impulsiveness*, and (e) *Relationship Problem*.
- Describe a student self-rating scale item to measure each of the five patterns of E&B disorder.
- Propose a target behavior definition to measure each of the five patterns of E&B disorder.
- For each pattern of E&B disorder, state how prevalence varies according to the age level of the young person.
- Name the four connected problems associated with E&B disorder.

## CAN YOU DEFINE THESE 10 TERMS?

| | |
|---|---|
| prevalence | gang |
| course | club drug |
| prognosis | substance tolerance |
| relational aggression | lethality |
| concurrent comorbidity | precipitating risk factors |

The main purpose of this chapter is to present key information about five important patterns of E&B disorder of students. A "pattern of E&B disorder" is a combination of intense and continuing problems involving behavior, emotions, and thoughts—a combination that significantly impairs the functioning of the child and/or other people. The key information includes a brief description of each pattern, its relation to classification and definition, how the pattern can be measured, its prevalence, and its course. The chapter also discusses four other serious adjustment problems that are closely connected to these patterns of E&B disorder.

## DETERMINING PATTERNS

As Display 3-11 shows, children in general and those with E&B disorder may experience many different problem characteristics. How, then, can one choose a few important patterns of E&B disorder on which to focus? One major consideration is information about classification. Chapter 3 presented two main ways of classifying E&B disorder of children and adolescents: nosological (e.g., *Diagnostic and Statistical Manual of Mental Disorders* [DSM-IV]) and dimensional (e.g., *Achenbach System of Empirically Based Assessment* [ASEBA]). That chapter showed how classification enables us to condense many problem characteristics into a few categories.

However, despite important similarities, DSM-IV, ASEBA, and other classification systems also have substantial points of difference—even some outright contradictions. Scientific research is pursuing but has not yet resolved some of the key classification issues (Adams, Luscher, & Bernat, 2001; Cullinan, 2004; Mash & Dozois, 2003; Segal & Coolidge, 2001; Zimmerman & Spitzer, 2005).

Until such issues are resolved, one must make a few subjective decisions to determine which possibilities to emphasize. Evidence indicates that children and adolescents experience five main patterns of E&B disorder: *Aggression, Anxiety, Depression, Impulsiveness,* and *Relationship Problem*. Because of their nature and severity, these patterns of E&B disorder greatly impair the functioning and adjustment of the young person and of others. A few of the many possible impairments to the young person include restricted access to desirable places, limited friendships and peer interactions, decreased opportunities for participation in positive activities, and high levels of stressful discord with parents, teachers, and other authorities. Among the impairments to others are intense and repeated negative emotions (e.g., embarrassment, disappointment, alarm) experienced by parents, teachers, and others who care about the young person, and disruptions to effective operation of a peer learning or work group.

Besides creating personal disturbances and environmental conflicts in the present, *Aggression, Anxiety, Depression, Impulsiveness,* and *Relationship Problem* have repercussions for future adjustment. To varying degrees, each predicts an increased chance that the individual will continue to experience E&B disorder, as well as undesirable involvement with legal and social agencies, and various other manifestations of poor functioning in schooling, work, family life, and other areas of life.

Children and adolescents have serious emotional, behavioral, and cognitive problems aside from E&B disorder. Four of these are discussed in this chapter: *Law-Breaking Behavior, Learning Difficulty, Substance Misuse,* and *Suicidality*. Even though these are not patterns of E&B disorder, they are strongly connected in that many young people with E&B disorder also experience these problems in a significant way.

Finally, there are three other important, fascinating kinds of E&B disorder that can be understood only partially in terms of this chapter's five patterns. Instead, they are more fully understandable with reference to their DSM-IV categories: Mood Disorders, Psychotic Disorders, and Pervasive Developmental Disorders. These "extreme E&B disorders" are considered in Chapter 5.

## KEY INFORMATION

### Description

Each of the patterns of E&B disorder resembles the emotions, behaviors, and cognitions that most young people experience to some degree at one time or another during development. Yet these patterns are not the same as ordinary problems. In some cases they may differ entirely in the extent (e.g., frequency, duration, intensity) to which the problem is exhibited. For example, sobbing and crying may be just an ordinary problem at a frequency of 2 per day, but strongly suggestive of E&B disorder at a frequency of 8 per day. But in other cases a difference in the extent of the problem does not fully explain a pattern of E&B disorder. Instead, additional considerations such as the child's age when the problem first appeared, the extent of impairment caused by the problem, or some other variables must be taken into account to better explain the E&B disorder (Mash & Dozois, 2003).

Of course, significant issues about how to identify E&B disorder remain unresolved. These include how to decide that certain emotional, behavioral, cognitive, and other problems experienced by a young person qualify, or do not qualify, as an E&B disorder (see Chapters 1 and 3). Fortunately, researchers have not put off conducting scientific studies of E&B disorder just because these issues are difficult and unsettled. Research involving children and adolescents identified with E&B disorder is the basis of much of the information presented in this chapter.

A young person would seldom be identified with E&B disorder based on a single problem of emotion, behavior, or thinking, regardless of how different from ordinary that problem was. It is for this reason that the patterns of E&B disorder are described in terms of multiple problems involved.

Each description of a pattern contains generalizations that apply to many or most young people with that pattern, but certainly not all. As research on classification, measurement, prevalence, course, and other aspects of E&B disorder continues to provide clarification, we can expect fewer exceptions and other improvements in the accuracy of such generalizations.

Please keep in mind that patterns of E&B disorder are not types of child. Instead, they are forms of disorder that a child with E&B disorder exhibits and experiences to a greater extent, and with more maladaptive repercussions, than other children.

### Relation to Classification and Definition

Much of this chapter's information about each pattern is based on studies of young people whose E&B disorder was established according to DSM, ASEBA, or other classification criteria. Therefore the patterns of E&B disorder are compared to DSM-IV categories and ASEBA dimensions. Patterns are also compared to the federal definition of ED. Although there are important similarities, none of the five patterns of E&B disorder is identical to any DSM category, ASEBA dimension, or ED characteristic.

## Measurement

Each pattern involves emotional, behavior, and cognitive characteristics that can be measured by a variety of methods. For each pattern, selected methods are described based on common or best practices.

An interesting complication is that different measurement methods sometimes point to diverse conclusions about a pattern. For example, Lewin, Davis, and Hops (1999) found that the elementary school adjustment problem that best predicted high school antisocial behavior differed, depending on whether antisocial behavior was self-reported by the students or measured by another method.

## Prevalence

**Prevalence** usually refers to the proportion of a population of interest that shows a certain E&B disorder or other phenomenon. The population of interest, for most purposes, involves young people who have not been identified as showing an E&B disorder. This is termed an "unselected" or "community" sample. Prevalence data obtained on this basis tell us how common an E&B disorder is among young people in general.

Ideally, prevalence would be revealed in a grand study that defined the pattern of E&B disorder truly, measured it in a perfectly reliable and valid way, and applied it to a perfectly representative sample of children and adolescents. In reality, several prevalence studies are available for each pattern, and they differ in ways that introduce some uncertainty about prevalence (Fombonne, 2002; Mash & Dozois, 2003; Mezzich & Ustun, 2005; Offord & Bennett, 2002).

For example, studies may have used different operational definitions of a particular pattern of E&B disorder (e.g., diagnosis with a particular DSM mental disorder, very high score on one of the ASEBA cross-informant syndromes, or an extreme result from recording a target behavior in classrooms). The samples of children in different studies may differ as to age and other demographic variables (e.g., just elementary school age male children or females and males age 6 to 18 years). Further, some studies examine a fairly specific E&B disorder (e.g., one of the DSM categories), whereas others measure more general phenomena (e.g., any form of E&B disorder). Taking into account the variations in study methods and results, we should conclude that the better prevalence studies yield a range of estimates within which the true prevalence probably falls.

This chapter presents overall prevalence estimates, along with a few remarks about prevalence variations by age and sex. Age and sex differences in prevalence probably have important—but at present, poorly understood—implications for understanding E&B disorder (Frick & Silverthorn, 2001; Mash & Dozois, 2003). Prevalence of some patterns may also vary by other variables, such as socio-economic and race-ethnic status, on which there is less research. Socioeconomic and race-ethnic status are addressed in Chapters 6 and 10.

It is possible for prevalence data to change over the years. To illustrate, suicide deaths among U. S. adolescents increased during the 1970s, then leveled off, and, more recently, declined somewhat (Pfeffer, 2002). However, a sharp change in prevalence within a short time is unusual. Most changes are gradual, requiring several years to clearly show a different trend.

Finally, as professionals we should be alert for potentially misleading claims about prevalence changes of E&B disorder and related phenomena. For example, suppose that from one year to the next, a particular state's arrest rate of adolescents changed from 3.75 to 3.73 per 100 adolescents. Popular media sources or incumbent politicians might proclaim, "juvenile crime is down," which would be correct but probably not meaningful.

## Course

The **course** of a pattern of E&B disorder is studied by measuring, over some period of time, many young people who show the pattern. This can reveal consistent developmental changes in important aspects of the pattern and can inform us about the probable short-term and long-term outcome(s).

Developmental changes refer to aspects of a pattern of E&B disorder that change from childhood through adolescence and into young adulthood. Some behaviors, emotions, or cognitions are important components of a pattern at one stage of development but decline in significance over the years. Conversely, other problems may arise, becoming important components of the pattern only some years after the child was first identified with E&B disorder.

Probable outcome of an E&B disorder is also called **prognosis**. Many children with E&B disorder at present will become adults who no longer function maladaptively (i.e., no more so than most of us). Other children with E&B disorder at present will continue to function maladaptively in adulthood. They may experience (a) the same or a very similar form of E&B disorder in adulthood that they did in childhood, (b) a different form of E&B disorder in adulthood, or (c) no pattern of E&B disorder but other serious impairments in personal and social functioning (e.g., imprisonment, addiction). Prognosis varies across the different patterns of E&B disorder, by severity, sometimes by age and sex of the child, and by other variables.

Outcome and prognosis are relative terms. The fact is that some children with no E&B disorder at present will come to have poor adjustment in adulthood (E&B disorder or other problems). Suppose outcome research tells us that 23% of children with E&B disorder have a poor adult adjustment. To understand what this means we must know the proportion of children without E&B disorder who also have a poor adult adjustment. In general, poor outcome or poor prognosis means that a higher proportion of young people with E&B disorder than without E&B disorder will experience maladaptive functioning in the future. Poor outcome does not mean that all—often not even most—young people with E&B disorder will remain maladapted.

## Other Considerations

The five patterns of E&B disorder suggest many interesting educational, philosophical, scientific, and other implications. For each pattern I suggest a few for consideration. I heartily invite the reader to think of others.

One aspect of the patterns that is not presented under *Key Information* is causes of E&B disorder. Causes can be broadly subdivided into biological and psychosocial influences. Scientific evidence demonstrates or suggests some role for both kinds of influence in most if not all E&B disorders. This is discussed in Chapter 6. Also, there are various interpretations of how the biological or psychosocial influences operate over time to create and maintain E&B disorders, as well as to reduce or eliminate them via interventions. These interpretations are the core of different "models" of E&B disorder, as discussed in Chapters 7 through 10.

Finally, many young people with E&B disorder show two or more of the patterns. This is termed *comorbidity* or *co-occurrence* (Wicks-Nelson & Israel, 2006). It has important implications for understanding the patterns and other aspects of E&B disorder (Angold, Costello, & Erkanli, 1999; Cullinan, 2004). Some points involving comorbidity are discussed briefly after the patterns of E&B disorder.

# Patterns of E&B Disorder

## Aggression

### Description

Aggression is displayed in a wide variety of conduct meant to inflict injury, harm, or pain on others and to negate others' rights. This could include intense and chronic forms of disobeying and disrespecting teachers, harrassing peers, tantrumming, destroying property, arguing, disrupting group activities, stealing, lying or charmingly misleading people, threatening, bullying, fighting, assaulting, performing cruelties, acting vengefully, and inducing others to perform antisocial behavior (Connor, 2002; Furlong, Morrison, & Jimerson, 2004; Hinshaw & Lee, 2003; McConville & Cornell, 2003; Steiner & Karnik, 2005). Students with *Aggression* often show no guilt about, and take no responsibility for, the results of their actions. Display 4-1 sketches a young person with the *Aggression* pattern of E&B disorder.

### Relation to Classification and Definition

If a child with the *Aggression* pattern has a DSM-IV diagnosis, it may be a mental disorder such as Conduct Disorder or Oppositional Defiant Disorder (Thomas, 2005). Alternatively, the diagnosis could be a V-code problem such as Child or Adolescent Aggression. In ASEBA classification, Aggressive Behavior cross-informant syndrome would probably apply.

The federal Education Department definition of ED does not address *Aggression* in words denoting fighting, defying, arguing, or something similar. However, research

**Display 4-1** One manifestation of the *Aggression* pattern

> Mike is an 8-year-old boy from a family well known to the city's legal, social service, and education agencies. His father has an arrest record for drunkenness, disorderly conduct, and multiple traffic offenses. An older brother and sister were adjudicated delinquent and assigned to detention centers for several months, following many complaints and several court appearances regarding petty theft, violence to other youngsters, setting fires in the neighborhood, nighttime roaming, and generally being beyond parental control. In the first grade, Mike disobeyed the teacher; threw tantrums; bullied peers on the playground; used coarse language; and stole money, lunches, and other things from classmates. This pattern continued, and after several attempts to address these problems failed, he was referred for possible special education services early in his second year of school.
>
> Assessment indicated a normal IQ score (94), no substantial evidence of brain disorder, and academic achievement similar to that of a beginning first-grader. The diagnostician noted that in interviews Mike seemed a little nervous but friendly and eager to do well. Mike's parents emphasized that he was a good boy most of the time but did sometimes get into trouble at school and around the neighborhood. They also doubted that they could control him but supported whatever the school decided to do. His mother offered to "whip this boy's rear end" whenever requested by a teacher; this offer was declined because she had been reported to have severely beaten the children on several occasions.
>
> The IEP team's decision involved providing academic tutoring in a structured resource room for part of the school day, plus consultation with the boy's regular class teacher about managing his behavior. But Mike's academic and social performance deteriorated, and by the end of the year he was identified as ED and assigned to a separate special class in a nearby school. Mike remains enrolled in that class, where he is slowly learning to read and do simple arithmetic. On some days his behavior is tolerable, but arguments with classmates or the teacher are not uncommon. About once a week he is involved in a serious incident of fighting with or terrorizing another pupil before, during, or after school.

evidence and logic (Cullinan, 2004; Cullinan, Harniss, Epstein, & Ryser, 2002) suggest that a pattern of *Aggression* should be inferred in ED definition characteristic (C), "inappropriate types of behavior or feelings under normal circumstances." Students with ED show *Aggression* to a much greater extent than students without disabilities (e.g., Cullinan, Evans, Epstein, & Ryser, 2003; Cullinan, Osborne, & Epstein, 2004; Cullinan & Sabornie, 2004).

Display 4-2 summarizes how *Aggression* is related to DSM-IV and ASEBA classification systems and the federal ED definition. It does so, too, for the other patterns of E&B disorder.

### *Measurement*

Nearly all published rating scales of multiple emotional and behavior problems, such as those described in Chapter 3, contain many items about *Aggression* (e.g. "disobeys the teacher" or "threatens to hurt peers"). Usually there is at least one subscale that measures *Aggression*. Other rating scales focus specific aspects, such as anger (Connor, 2002).

Gable, Hendrickson, and Sealander (1997) used the following target-behavior definition for "aggressive/disruptive": "using verbal or physical behavior that may

**Display 4-2** Similarities of the five patterns of E&B disorder of children and adolescents to DSM-IV and ASEBA classification and the federal definition of emotional disturbance (ED)

| E&B Disorder Pattern | DSM-IV Categories | ASEBA Dimensions | ED Definition Characteristics |
|---|---|---|---|
| Aggression | • Conduct Disorder<br>• Oppositional Defiant Disorder<br>• Child or Adolescent Antisocial Behavior (V-code) | • Aggressive Behavior | • Not directly addressed; probably characteristic (C) Inappropriate types of behavior or feelings under normal circumstances |
| Anxiety | • Social Phobia<br>• Generalized Anxiety Disorder<br>• Panic Disorder<br>• Post-Traumatic Stress Disorder | • Anxious/Depressed<br>• Somatic Complaints | • (E) Physical symptoms or fears |
| Depression | • Depressive Disorders<br>• Bipolar Disorders | • Anxious/Depressed | • (D) Unhappiness or depression |
| Impulsivity | • Attention-Deficit/Hyperactivity Disorder (except Predominantly Inattentive Type) | • Attention Problems | • Not directly addressed |
| Relationship Problem | • No disorder in particular, but a part of many disorders | • Withdrawn/Depressed<br>• Social Problems | • (B) Poor relationships with peers and teachers |

cause harm to person or property or that is commonly acknowledged as unacceptable for school, such as threatening to do harm, intentional kicking and hitting with or without an object, biting, hair pulling, and so on" (p. 26). They recorded the proportion of time a student exhibited this behavior. *Aggression* target behaviors have been recorded in various locations in school, home, community, and other settings.

A permanent product, the number of times a student receives a discipline referral to the school office, can be a useful indicator of the extent of a student's *Aggression* (Walker, Ramsey, & Gresham, 2004). Other procedures for measuring *Aggression* include classmate-completed ratings of aggressive and disruptive behavior; peer nomination of classmates who fill specified aggressive roles (e.g., "Which classmate acts like a bully?"); student self-report inventories of anger; and interviews of the child that explore his or her aggressive behaviors, feelings, and thoughts.

### *Prevalence*

Studies of DSM Conduct Disorder or Oppositional Defiant Disorder, together with studies using other definitions of *Aggression*, indicate that 3 to 5 percent of U.S. children and adolescents exhibit this pattern of E&B disorder (Connor, 2002; Hinshaw &

Lee, 2003; Lahey, Miller, Gordon, & Riley, 1999). It accounts for at least 30 percent of referrals of children to treatment clinics, and is a prominent pattern among young people receiving psychiatric treatment (Frick & Silverthorn, 2001).

The prevalence of *Aggression*, as defined here, does not vary greatly by child age. Many children with *Aggression* at an early age desist from this pattern during adolescence; conversely, other cases do not first appear until adolescence. Note that this book treats *Aggression* and juvenile delinquency as separate phenomena; delinquency is addressed as a connected problem called *Law-Breaking Behavior*. However, many discussions assume that *Aggression* and juvenile delinquency are essentially similar (Connor, 2002). The combined prevalence of *Aggression* and delinquency is higher among adolescents than younger children.

Males exceed females on *Aggression* by a ratio of about 3:1 (Foster, 2005; Hinshaw & Lee, 2003). The gender difference is greater than this among young children, less among older adolescents (Connor, 2002). A particular form of aggressive behavior, **relational aggression** (Display 4-3), is found more commonly among females.

## *Course*

Follow-up research shows a poor prognosis for the *Aggression* pattern (Connor, 2002; Frick & Loney, 1999; Furlong et al., 2004; Hinshaw & Lee, 2003; Patterson & Yoerger, 2002; Thomas, 2005). Severely aggressive children are at high risk not only for continued antisocial behavior in later childhood and adolescence, but for diverse adjustment problems in adolescence and adulthood such as educational and vocational failure, marital and social problems, substance abuse, and a variety of psychiatric disorders.

Prognosis is especially poor for a subgroup that manifests *Aggression* to a severe extent by about age 6 years and continues to do so into adolescence (Hinshaw & Lee, 2003). This distinct prognosis is one basis for proposals to discriminate early-onset versus adolescent-onset subtypes (see Display 4-3), and to begin interventions in early childhood (see Chapter 11).

## *Other Considerations*

Aggression is a very broad class of behaviors that has been subdivided in various ways (Connor, 2002; Graczyk & Tolan, 2005; Hinshaw & Lee, 2003). Selected "subtypes" of *Aggression* with some degree of scientific support are listed in Display 4-3.

There are circumstances in which vigorous aggressive behavior, verbal or physical, has obvious adaptive advantages for the individual aggressor (Rodkin, Farmer, Pearl, & Van Acker, 2000) or the society that he or she may represent. Further, engaging in aggressive and defiant behavior while opposing injustice and standing up for one's rights is widely admired and encouraged. Just as obviously, students who intensively and persistently defy, destroy, and behave aggressively toward school personnel and peers will seriously impair the functioning of other students and, almost certainly, themselves.

Discriminating adaptive from maladaptive aggression (Connor, 2002) may have implications for intervention. Among the challenging tasks for any teacher is balancing students' needs for developing assertive citizenship and self-reliance and, at the same time, cooperation, kindness, and respect for others' person and property.

**Display 4-3** Selected subtypes of the *Aggression* pattern of E&B disorder

| Subcategories | Distinctions |
|---|---|
| Early-onset versus adolescent-onset | • Early-onset aggression involves intense defiance and aggression first evident by age 8, typically persisting into and becoming more severely antisocial in adolescence and adulthood.<br>• Adolescent-onset aggression involves antisocial behavior first evident in the early to middle teen years, typically desisting by early adulthood. |
| Direct versus relational | • Direct aggression involves physical attacks, threats, and other acts intended to obtain resources or dominate others through direct confrontation.<br>• Relational aggression involves manipulating a group to exclude a peer, spreading gossip, informing on a peer, retracting one's friendship, and other acts intended to emotionally hurt, reduce the social status of, or similarly victimize a peer. |
| Undersocialized versus socialized | • Undersocialized aggression is performed alone, by young people with social relationship deficits and, typically, little remorse.<br>• Socialized aggression is performed in and with support from deviant social groups. |
| Proactive versus reactive | • Proactive aggression involves planful use of force, threats, or alliances with peers to dominate or harm others.<br>• Reactive aggression is a response to a real or misperceived provocation, consisting of emotional, defensive attacks. |
| Overt versus covert | • Overt aggression includes arguing, being defiant and stubborn, swearing, disobeying, blaming others, threatening, fighting, and other openly confrontational behaviors.<br>• Covert aggression includes lying, cheating, stealing, vandalizing, setting fires, using substances, and other concealed antisocial behavior. |

*Sources:* Foster, 2005; Hinshaw & Lee, 2003; O'Connor, 2002.

## Anxiety

### Description

Anxiety consists of distressingly unpleasant and maladaptive feelings, thoughts, behaviors, and physical reactions (Albano, Chorpita, & Barlow, 2003; Albano & Krain, 2005; Fonseca & Perrin, 2001; Ollendick, King, & Muris, 2002). Young people with the *Anxiety* pattern often feel scared, guilty, tense, and inadequate. They think a great deal about being threatened, losing control of their thoughts and actions, being criticized or harrassed by peers, suffering the loss of loved ones through death or otherwise, and performing incompetently or mistakenly. They may vividly imagine danger and humiliation and have difficulty paying attention, remembering, and thinking things through (Freeman, Garcia, & Leonard, 2002).

These children behave in various ways to avoid or escape from anxiety-provoking situations. They also may cry, sigh, exhibit voice changes, or show other indicators of strong negative emotion; talk a great deal about their worries; and engage in diverse rituals that have no obvious function, such as pacing, twitching, grimacing, stammering, or fidgeting with their hands, arms, or legs.

Finally, children with the *Anxiety* pattern of E&B disorder can experience unpleasant, alarming physical responses such as excessive heart rate, profuse sweating, fast breathing, headache, stomach pain, nausea, bowel problems, muscle tension or shaking, and chills (Albano et al., 2003; Egger, Costello, Erkanli, & Angold, 1999; Nishina, Juvonen, & Witkow, 2005). Display 4-4 presents an illustration of *Anxiety*.

*Anxiety* is often associated with actual places, events, and separations from or loss of a loved one. However, in many cases the pattern is activated by cognitions alone, such as imagined events, an inability to stop having certain distressing thoughts, or disturbing impulses to act based on such thoughts (Klein & Pine, 2002).

Students who exhibit this pattern of E&B disorder may experience problems with peers (Frick & Silverthorn, 2001). Classmates may avoid associating with them, devalue them in conversations with others, or taunt them directly.

### *Relation to Classification and Definition*

Various DSM-IV diagnoses share *Anxiety* as a main feature but involve diverse other problems as well (Albano et al., 2003; Charney, 2005; Shelton, Williford, & Woods, 2003). These include Separation Anxiety Disorder (*Anxiety* about separation from

**Display 4-4** One manifestation of the *Anxiety* pattern

---

Nine-year-old Pamela is being considered for homebound education because of her repeated episodes of school absenteeism. There had been five situations since kindergarten in which she did not come to school for periods varying from 2 to 8 weeks. Also, she was very frequently absent for several days at a time.

When in school, Pamela usually performed suitably in individual assignments but would not answer questions, read, or otherwise respond aloud in the presence of peers. If she was asked to do so, her eyes teared, her voice trembled, her head became bowed, and sometimes she would sob or run from the room. She had adequate social relations and often played with peers, but avoided group games.

Pamela often complained to her teachers of headaches, dizziness, stomach pains and upset, and general body weakness. This often predicted her absence the next day. When these complaints occurred in the morning before school she was often permitted to stay home, but she usually recovered by midmorning. When her parents tried to make her go to school, she often sobbed, threw tantrums, and begged; sometimes she vomited or fainted. Her parents had consulted with several physicians, who could find no physical disorders to explain these complaints. To her parents and a mental health clinician who briefly treated her, Pamela admitted being afraid of other kids' making fun of her, doing poorly in schoolwork, and being sent to an orphanage. Only the second fear had much substance. Although testing confirmed her teachers' judgments that Pamela was quite capable of learning, it also showed that her levels of academic achievement were very low for a third-grader even though she had been retained in the third grade because of missing so much material the first time through.

people or places to which the child is attached), Social Phobia (*Anxiety* about public performance failure), Specific Phobia (*Anxiety* about a particular phenomenon), Generalized Anxiety Disorder (no apparent source of *Anxiety*), Obsessive-Compulsive Disorder (repetitive thoughts or behaviors that greatly distress), Panic Disorder (unpredictable bouts of *Anxiety* along with strong physical reactions such as pounding heartbeat, and thoughts of dying), and Post-Traumatic Stress Disorder (described below).

In the ASEBA classification, *Anxiety* is addressed by Anxious/Depressed and, to a lesser extent, Somatic Problems (see Display 4-2). The federal definition of ED approximates the *Anxiety* pattern in its characteristic (E), "physical symptoms or fears." Students with ED have this characteristic to a greater extent than students with no disabilities (e.g., Cullinan et al., 2003, 2004; Cullinan & Sabornie, 2004; Newcomer, Barenbaum, & Pearson, 1995).

## *Measurement*

Items and subscales of many parent- and teacher-completed rating scales address *Anxiety* (Klein & Pine, 2002). Moreover, children and adolescents may rate themselves on items involving thoughts ("Thinking about my future worries me"), feelings ("I feel mentally tense and nervous"), and physiological perceptions ("My heart pounds and races"). Some self-report scales also explore the degree to which *Anxiety* is associated with different sorts of stressful events, such as personal failure, danger and injury, or loss of a loved one.

Interviews allow exploration of the child's thoughts, feelings, and perceptions related to fears and anxieties (Angold & Costello, 2002; Fonseca & Perrin, 2001). Although many interviews are oriented to clinical diagnosis and treatment, some reflect school-based concerns (McConaughy, 2003).

Because personal distress and unhappiness are especially significant in *Anxiety*, information the child reveals through self-rating scales, interviews, self-recording of thoughts and feelings, and other self-report measurement methods is particularly valuable (Albano et al., 2003; Fonseca & Perrin, 2001; Merikangas, 2005). Like all measurement methods, however, self-report has potential disadvantages. For instance, some self-reported information is uncheckable, raising possible questions of reliability and validity. Use of self-report often assumes a level of verbal ability and self-understanding that many younger or learning-impaired children do not possess.

Target-behavior recording focuses on anxious behaviors such as talking about a need for perfection or particular fears or worries, leaving the location of a feared situation, trembling, facial expressions reflecting distress, or crying. If social interaction problems accompany *Anxiety*, additional target behaviors could include participating in groups, speaking up in class, starting conversations, responding to social initiations of others, or showing proper assertiveness.

Another important facet of this pattern of E&B disorder concerns physiological responses. Measuring changes in blood flow, sweating, muscle tension, and breathing rate associated with *Anxiety* may indicate needed targets of intervention and help monitor treatment progress. Technology for direct measurement of physiological responses is feasible in treatment clinics but generally not in schools and other natural settings. But in some interventions teachers are advised to observe physiological responses, including the student's breathing, muscle tension, or flushed face.

## *Prevalence*

Prevalence estimates of the several DSM disorders involving *Anxiety*, as well as other pervasive or intense fears that impair adjustment, range as high as 20 percent of children and adolescents (Albano et al., 2003; Freeman et al., 2002; Klein & Pine, 2002; Merikangas, 2005; Ollendick et al., 2002). The most relevant studies indicate that 6 to 12 percent of young people show the *Anxiety* pattern of E&B disorder.

In *Anxiety*, age must be considered (Freeman et al., 2002; Verhulst, 2001). In the first place, what is feared varies by age. Younger children tend to fear animals, monsters, parental conflict, or intense natural events (such as thunder or tornadoes), whereas older children tend to fear illness, injury, and school or personal inadequacy. Both age-groups fear peer rejection. Violence and bullying by peers are significant causes of students' worries and avoidance behaviors, including school nonattendance (DeVoe et al., 2003). In addition, prevalence varies by age for some of the DSM disorders involving *Anxiety*. For example, younger children are more likely to have Separation Anxiety Disorder and adolescents are more likely to have Social Phobia (Albano et al., 2003; Verhulst, 2001). Overall, higher proportions of adolescents than children experience the *Anxiety* pattern.

More males than females seem to experience Obsessive-Compulsive Disorder and perhaps a few other kinds of DSM disorders involving Anxiety. However, overall females are more likely than males to experience *Anxiety*, especially during adolescence (Verhulst, 2001).

## *Course*

Anxiety can be persistent over the years (Klein & Pine, 2002; Ost & Treffers, 2001; Wicks-Nelson & Israel, 2006). Many adults with *Anxiety* recall that their problems began in adolescence or childhood. Also, children with *Anxiety* may eventually show other patterns of E&B disorder in adolescence or adulthood, especially *Depression*, or other serious problems such as misusing substances. Some of the DSM subcategories (e.g., Separation Anxiety Disorder, Generalized Anxiety Disorder) seem to have very different outcomes (Freeman et al., 2002); this complicates understanding the course (courses?) of *Anxiety*.

In general, young people with *Anxiety* have a long-term prognosis that is worse than for children with no E&B disorder but better than for children with other patterns of E&B disorder, such as *Aggression*.

## *Other Considerations*

***Terms.*** Anxiety, fear, phobia, and similar terms have various technical and everyday definitions. Some experts consider the terms interchangeable because they see so much overlap and inconsistent usage among them, and so little benefit for theory or treatment in discriminating them.

Others do perceive some value in discriminating among the negative thoughts, emotions, behaviors, and physiological responses involved (American Psychiatric Association, 2000; Freeman et al., 2002; Wicks-Nelson & Israel, 2006), generally as follows. "Anxiety" (not the *Anxiety* pattern of E&B disorder) covers moderately intense responses to vague or general situations; "fear" refers to more intense forms of these responses and in reaction to narrower circumstances. "Phobia" consists of the same negative responses that (a) far exceed in intensity what would be expected under the circumstances, (b) continue for much longer than could be anticipated, (c) seem unrestrained by reasoning or other attempts at voluntary control, (d) produce vigorous actions to avoid the fear-provoking situation, and (e) are highly maladaptive.

***Anxiety and School Attendance.*** "School phobia" refers to a student's refusal or extreme reluctance to attend school, accompanied by fears about school or specific aspects of it, unease about other aspects of life, and, often, pains or illnesses (Kearney, 2001). Over recent decades, experts have given different and sometimes conflicting meanings to school phobia, varying in usefulness and acceptance. For this reason Kearney (2001) recommended the general term *school refusal* to subsume all situations in which the child refuses or tries to refuse to attend school for part or all of the school day. School refusal would include, for example, begging not to go to school, tantrumming but going, frequent tardiness or class-skipping, absenteeism for a few consecutive days, and absenteeism for many weeks.

In this perspective, many instances of school refusal have little or nothing to do with the *Anxiety* pattern, but others do involve *Anxiety*. For example, school refusal can be accompanied by various behaviors, thoughts, and other responses of the *Anxiety* pattern, including pains, nausea, fast heartbeat and breathing, and other physiological responses (sometimes termed physical complaints or somaticization), or by a phobia involving school or some specific aspect of school.

***Posttraumatic Stress Disorder.*** Children as well as adults can experience a serious, debilitating E&B disorder called posttraumatic stress disorder (PTSD) following a single life-threatening or otherwise highly stressful event or a series of such events (Fletcher, 2003; Pfefferbaum, 2002; Yule, 2002). The traumatic event(s) can include natural or man-made disasters, sexual or physical abuse, life-threatening or chronic serious disease, and observation of a loved one victimized by violence. A person's chance of developing PTSD depends in part on the severity of a traumatic event and how directly involved he or she was.

Young people with PTSD repeatedly reexperience a traumatic event via disturbing, vivid visual and auditory memories that intrude unexpectedly while awake or asleep (Cohen, 2005). They avoid situations associated with the traumatic event, remain almost continuously vigilant and irritable ("hyperarousal"), have sleep problems, and experience new fears. They may feel sad, alienated from people and activities they formerly enjoyed, and incapable of love, enthusiasm, and other positive thoughts. A student with PTSD often shows poor concentration and deteriorating school performance.

## Depression

### *Description*

The *Depression* pattern among students involves the following thoughts, emotions, behaviors, and physical features (Hammen & Rudolph, 2003): inability to sustain attention; decline in educational participation and performance; pervasively sad mood; general irritability; strong feelings of worthlessness or guilt; hopelessness; loss of interest in most or all activities; drastic change in weight, appetite, sleeping pattern, or energy level; prolonged or unpredictable crying; social withdrawal; and thoughts about death and self-destruction, sometimes accompanied by related behaviors (Garber & Horowitz, 2002; Gresham & Kern, 2004; Harrington, 2002; Lewinsohn & Essau, 2002; Weller, Weller, Rowan, & Svadjian, 2002). Display 4-5 presents a case of *Depression*.

Time can be an important consideration in *Depression*. In many cases, periods of distressing and maladaptive emotions, behaviors, and cognitions alternate with periods without these problems. These periods with and without *Depression* last varying amounts of time—from hours to weeks or even longer. Time criteria help determine

**Display 4-5** One manifestation of the *Depression* pattern

---

Three nights ago, Melissa was taken to the hospital emergency room after cutting her wrists with a carpet knife. While at the hospital she was withdrawn and downcast, was crying quietly at times, and nervously avoided eye contact with the psychiatric assessment and treatment personnel.

Melissa did report that she first began feeling miserable and hopeless about 3 months ago. She found herself unable to concentrate at school, and her grades dropped from Bs or Cs to mostly failing. Melissa stopped calling her friends and lost all interest in soccer, despite years of success and being a starting player on her high school team. Two weeks ago she stopped attending school because she had neither the energy nor the interest to continue. Investigation found that the school had been attempting to contact the home for several days.

This 15-year-old eats very little and has lost a few pounds recently. For about a month she has been waking up around 4 a.m., unable to get back to sleep. She thinks frequently of suicide, believing that her family would be better off without her. Her mother and stepfather are both alcoholics. They argue and sometimes fight with each other, but neither has been violent with Melissa. She used to have general plans for college, work, marriage, and a family, but lately Melissa sees nothing good in the future. She has told friends that she will never complete high school, go to college, or obtain a good job.

Melissa has been administered medication that could reduce important aspects of *Depression*. She and her parents have met several times with psychiatric personnel, have prepared to begin counseling, and agree that they want her to come home right away. They have received information about *Depression, Suicidality*, and how to create a situation at home in which a suicide attempt is less likely. Melissa will be sent home tomorrow.

whether a young person with severe *Depression* qualifies for a DSM-IV Mood Disorder.

### *Relation to Classification and Definition*

DSM-IV diagnoses related to *Depression* include several depressive and bipolar Mood Disorders. However, to qualify for these the *Depression* must meet time-related and other criteria (see Chapter 5). *Depression* is a part of several other DSM-IV mental disorders.

Two ASEBA cross-informant syndromes, Anxious/Depressed and Withdrawn/Depressed, partially encompass *Depression*. In the federal definition of ED, characteristic (D), "mood of unhappiness or depression," addresses the *Depression* Pattern of E&B Disorder. That students with ED significantly exceed students without disabilities on characteristic (D) is evident from several studies (e.g., Cullinan et al., 2003, 2004; Cullinan & Sabornie, 2004; Newcomer et al., 1995).

### *Measurement*

Depression is represented by items on various parent- and teacher-completed rating scales (Breen, 2003; Verhulst, 2001). For instance, a teacher could rate the extent to which the following statement applies: "This student does not experience joy or have fun." Other rating scales focus on particular aspects of *Depression* such as hopelessness, poor self-esteem, and loneliness.

Self-completed rating items prompt students to consider and report on their negative thoughts ("Sad ideas pop into my mind when I am trying to work"), feelings ("Every little thing seems to irritate me"), and physiological perceptions ("I am tired all the time"). Depressive behaviors can also be self-reported. Additionally, interview protocols (Angold & Costello, 2002; McConaughy, 2003) facilitate the professional's thorough exploration of a young person's perspectives on variables related to *Depression*.

Depending on how a particular student exhibits *Depression*, target-behavior recording might focus on observables such as happy or sad facial expressions, pessimistic or optimistic statements, and distraction or engagement in class. If interaction or relationship difficulties are an important part of the pattern for the student, the teacher could record social interactions between her and classmates.

### *Prevalence*

Depression characterizes about 2 percent of children through early adolescence. Beginning around age 14, prevalence increases sharply, approaching adult prevalence: 15 to 20 percent of older adolescents have, or have had, *Depression* (Hammen & Rudolph, 2003; Lewinsohn & Essau, 2002; Weller et al., 2002; Zahn-Wexler, Race, & Duggal, 2005).

These prevalence data reflect both less severe and more severe manifestations of *Depression*, including DSM Mood Disorders and Psychotic Disorders. Still, they probably understate the full impact of *Depression*. As noted, in many cases this pattern of E&B disorder varies in intensity over time. Yet even when a period of

*Depression* is over, some young people experience diminished quality of life in ways that seem to have begun with the onset of *Depression*. For example, a student's educational performance will probably be adversely affected by continuing difficulties involving relationships (such as family turmoil or loss of friends) or learning (substantial missed schoolwork, inability to concentrate). Those who know him may recognize that he has generally poor adjustment, but not that it is a consequence of a recent time of *Depression*.

Prevalence of *Depression* does not differ by sex before adolescence. Among adolescents, girls outnumber boys by about 2:1.

## Course

An important predictor of outcome relates to the first appearance of *Depression* (Hammen & Rudolph, 2003). Poor outcome is linked to younger age, greater severity, gradual rather than sudden onset, and the presence of other forms of E&B disorder along with *Depression* (i.e., comorbidity). In a poor outcome, typically there are repeated experiences of *Depression*, unfavorable school functioning, and, in the long run, adverse job, family, and other life functioning. *Depression* comorbid with *Aggression* is prognostic of suicide (Shaffer & Gutstein, 2002).

## Other Considerations

Although the intensity, pervasiveness, and duration of all patterns of E&B disorder vary across individuals, this consideration is especially important in *Depression*. Depressive thoughts, emotions, and behaviors are prominent in several very serious mental disorders, especially DSM-IV Mood Disorders and Psychotic Disorders (see Display 3-13 and Chapter 5). But we do not know whether or not the depressive aspects of these extreme mental disorders are essentially similar to less severe forms of the *Depression* pattern. Do the extreme and the less severe manifestations differ only in terms of the intensity, pervasiveness, or duration with which depressive problems are experienced, or are there other important differences? Experts disagree (Hammen & Rudolph, 2003). Because most of the research on *Depression* of young people has involved DSM Mood Disorders, we are unsure how well existing information applies to *Depression* that does not meet DSM severity, time, and other criteria. It is because this controversy has not been resolved that this chapter addresses *Depression* as a pattern of varying severity, while Chapter 5 discusses it as a component of extreme E&B disorders.

Recognition of and intervention for early indicators of *Depression* might enable educators to prevent a worsening of the pattern or at least reduce some of its harmful effects on the child's development and education. One obstacle to recognition and prevention is that many attributes of *Depression* are not unusual if exhibited to a moderate extent or occasionally. Kazdin and Marciano (1998) recommended special attention to depressive thoughts, feelings, and behaviors (a) for which there seems to be no precipitating event, (b) that have persisted for many days even though others have tried to get the young person to "snap out of it," or (c) that noticeably impair the student's academic learning or participation in school life.

However, *Depression* is still difficult to recognize in many cases. Problems may show ups and downs in the short run that camoflage the fact that they have been gradually worsening for weeks or months. Additionally, some students with *Depression*, particularly of a less severe form or early in a process that is gradually worsening, can avoid obvious impairment. They may get by in school and other aspects of life with considerable effort, while bearing immense personal distress. Without screening programs, many such students probably will not be recognized as experiencing *Depression*.

The foregoing situation suggests a debatable issue. Suppose Pat is clearly experiencing *Depression* but also seems to be functioning adequately in academic subjects and extracurricular activities, with no apparent social problems. Think about Pat as you consider the part of the federal definition (Display 1-4) that seems to reserve ED for the student whose problem "adversely affects" her educational performance. Does Pat qualify for the ED disability?

## Impulsiveness

### *Description*

As a pattern of E&B disorder, *Impulsiveness* refers to failure or inability to delay or interrupt an inappropriate behavior. This pattern becomes evident in a young person's excessive, inappropriate responses to situations that require sustained attention, forethought, and controlled responding to structured tasks or social expectations (Barkley, 2003; Rapport, 2001; Schachar & Tannock, 2002; Weiss & Weiss, 2002). For example, an elementary student with *Impulsiveness* may show hyperactivity (intense, chronic, and pervasive overactivity) in class and on the school bus. This could include nearly continuous motions of hands, feet, head, trunk, or multiple body parts while remaining in one place and/or movement from place to place when prohibited or inappropriate. The student with *Impulsiveness* is likely to attend poorly to explanations, demonstrations, and assignments; procrastinate about and fail to complete assigned tasks; and ignore or disobey teacher directions and school rules.

Many of this young person's decisions and actions seem unplanned because they ignore or disregard foreseeable outcomes, even unpleasant or dangerous ones. In peer interactions this may translate into abrupt intrusions into other children's individual or group activities; failure to share, take turns, or cooperate with peers; exhibiting bossy, selfish interactions; and inability to avoid arguments. Children with *Impulsiveness*, understandably, are disliked and rejected by most peers.

Adolescents with this pattern of E&B disorder exhibit less hyperactivity than preadolescents, although many still feel fidgety and uncomfortable if they have to remain focused, such as while studying. They continue to show hasty, unreflective decisions, choices, and behaviors (Schachar & Tannock, 2002), which tend to produce more detrimental consequences than when they were younger. For instance, they often disregard long-term consequences in favor of immediate satisfaction; perform necessary tasks in disorganized, inadequate ways; say provocative or disrespectful things apparently without any consideration of likely results; and become

**Display 4-6** One manifestation of the *Impulsiveness* pattern

> Nine-year-old John, who has a history of hyperactivity, disruptiveness, and learning problems, has just been placed in a special class for students with ED. For as long as his parents can remember, John has been very active and difficult to manage. As a young child, he often climbed to get forbidden objects; switched activities frequently, usually leaving a mess behind; turned special events into disasters, especially when he tried to help; seldom remained seated through a meal; disregarded instructions; and otherwise was a discipline problem. Because John was not skilled at games, tried to be bossy, and often got into arguments and minor fights, few children would play with him. He had no friends.
>
> John's situation in school has not been much different. His teachers all have noted how poorly he performed in remaining at his desk, listening and looking appropriately, persisting with a task until completion, and waiting his turn in classroom or playground groups. Academically, he was behind his peers in the first grade and has gradually fallen farther behind. When responding in class to book problems or the teacher's questions, John usually answers immediately and thoughtlessly, and classmates often ridicule his mistakes. Sometimes he appears to enjoy the resulting attention and disruption. At other times this seems to make him angry; he may have a tantrum, start an argument or fight with a classmate, and remain noncompliant and impolite to the teacher for the rest of the day. Paradoxically, John sometimes comes to class early to talk with his teacher and is usually respectful and friendly. Occasionally John talks about his social and academic problems and is clearly concerned.
>
> John's mother has sought medical help. The family physician placed 4-year-old John on 10 mg of dextroamphetamine per day. The mother detected some decrease in John's uncontrolled activity, but it disturbed her that he had trouble getting to sleep and often ate very little at meals, so this drug was discontinued after about 7 months. At age 8, John was seen by a psychiatrist, who placed him on 50 mg of methylphenidate daily and provided his parents with weekly counseling and therapy for several months. The parents noticed some improvement in John's behavior at home, and he remains on this drug therapy. Because of continuing educational maladjustment, however, a decision was reached to provide John with intensive school intervention within the special education class for ED.

emotionally moody or agitated. Adolescents with *Impulsiveness* gravitate toward other unpopular adolescents, and make unreflective, ultimately damaging choices about peer groups, illegal acts, and other serious life situations (Anastopoulos & Shelton, 2001; Barkley, 2003; Hinshaw & Blackman, 2005). Display 4-6 illustrates the *Impulsiveness* pattern of E&B disorder.

Children and adolescents with *Impulsiveness* tend to exhibit defiance, opposition, and other behaviors similar to *Aggression*. Their relations with parents and teachers are often marked by conflict. Many show academic achievement that is far below expectations based on their abilities, have speech and language disorders, and fail to advance in grade.

Also, they are prone to risky behaviors. They are much more likely than normal peers to suffer serious injuries from nonvehicle accidents and to ingest poisonous items. As teenagers, their driving records tend to be poor, with speeding tickets, suspended licenses, and accidents, and they are especially likely to use alcohol and drugs (Barkley, 2003; Pelham & Molina, 2003).

### *Relation to Classification and Definition*

Display 4-2 indicates that *Impulsiveness* is similar to two subcategories of DSM-IV Attention Deficit/Hyperactivity Disorder (ADHD): Predominantly Hyperactive-Impulsive and Combined. It is not similar to a third subcategory, Predominantly Inattentive. *Impulsiveness* is related to the ASEBA syndrome Attention Problems (based on that syndrome's items, not its name).

*Impulsiveness* is not one of the specified characteristics of ED in the federal definition. Many students with this pattern may qualify as ED because of their aggressive behavior, peer and teacher relationship problems, or other disorders of behavior and emotion. Also, students with *Impulsiveness* who receive a diagnosis of ADHD following psychological assessment generally qualify for the Other Health Impairments (OHI) education disability. Teachers of students with ED are often assigned students with OHI.

### *Measurement*

Some narrow-focus rating scales (see Anastopoulos & Shelton, 2001; Verhulst & Van der Ende, 2002) are specialized for measuring *Impulsiveness*, along with other aspects of ADHD. Most rating scales designed to measure multiple problems include several *Impulsiveness* items (e.g. "misbehaves without thinking" or "interrupts; does not take turns"), and may have a subscale for impulsive and hyperactive behavior. Structured interviewing (Anastopoulos & Shelton, 2001; Angold & Costello, 2002) to measure this pattern is used frequently by clinicians and less often by educators.

Target-behavior recording can measure behaviors that represent *Impulsiveness* (Rapport, 2001), including disruption via movement and noise (see Display 3-4). Alternatively, the converse of *Impulsiveness* may be measured, such as following the teacher's instructions or performing reflectively (e.g., stating aloud the steps of a problem-solving strategy, then carrying them out to solve the problem).

### *Prevalence*

Prevalence of *Impulsiveness* has to be indirectly estimated because most of the relevant studies have examined ADHD, which contains inattentive as well as impulsive and hyperactive components. (a) Prevalence of ADHD has varied across studies, from 1 to 15 percent of children and adolescents or even higher (Anastopoulos & Shelton, 2001; Barkley, 2003; Frick & Silverthorn, 2001; Hechtman, 2005; Lahey et al., 1999; Schachar & Tannock, 2002). The most representative estimates of prevalence of ADHD are in the 3- to 6-percent range. (b) Only about one third of young people with ADHD exhibit attention problems alone. The other two thirds exhibit impulsive and/or hyperactive behavior, some with attention problems, some without (Anastopoulos & Shelton, 2001; Barkley, 2003). (c) Based on these considerations, the prevalence of the *Impulsiveness* pattern can be estimated at 2 to 4 percent of children and adolescents.

*Impulsiveness* is more prevalent among younger children than adolescents. The male-to-female ratio is at least 3:1.

## Course

Impulsiveness usually first appears before age 7 years. Children who show this pattern before and during the primary grades tend to remain poorly adjusted into adolescence and, often, young adulthood (Barkley, 2003).

Their hyperactive and impulsive behaviors typically decline in severity by adolescence, but other problems develop. By grade 5 about half of students with *Impulsiveness* show extensive problems of disorganized thinking and planning, noncompliance with rules and expectations of teachers and peers, and continued academic failure. Many are increasingly aggressive and rejected by peers.

In high school, young people with *Impulsiveness* tend to be rash in thought and action, often to the point of recklessness. Frequently there is worsening defiance and aggression, school failure, difficulties with peers, poor self-esteem, substance abuse, and juvenile delinquency (Barkley, 2003; Lahey et al., 1999; Pelham & Molina, 2003; Weiss & Weiss, 2002).

## Other Considerations

Combining severe inattention, hyperactivity, and impulsivity into a single category of mental disorder (ADHD) is supported by some research and opposed by other research. To illustrate, research based on teacher ratings of students at school seems to support the idea that attention problems ought to be a separate disorder from impulsive and hyperactive problems. However, parent ratings of the same children in home and community does not support this separation (Achenbach & Rescorla, 2001). Perhaps this means that the *Impulsiveness* pattern is more likely to be a problem at school than elsewhere. Barkley (2003) holds that attention problems should—and before long, will—be classified separately from hyperactivity and impulsivity.

Many students with *Impulsiveness* are inconsistent in their problems (Barkley, 2003). Occasionally they will have a "good day" in which they remain on task, follow rules well, complete work accurately, interact well with classmates, and behave with foresight and good judgment. Such inconsistency naturally suggests that their poor performance on the other days reflects laziness or stubbornness. Probably it would be more fruitful instead to discover what causes the good days.

Extreme E&B disorder, especially bipolar disorder (see Chapter 5), can involve a great deal of *Impulsiveness*, as well as *Aggression*. Bipolar disorder is very rare before adolescence but should be given consideration in attempts to understand and intervene with risky, aggressive behavior among secondary school students.

It is interesting to consider some situational aspects of *Impulsiveness*. Suppose a child exhibits extensive climbing, running, interrupting, squirming, talking, and general excitability, while displaying very little patience, cooperation, reflective thought, and rule following. In the second-grade classroom this may be intolerably hyperactive and impulsive. Yet in some play and other low-structure situations, the student might be considered only exuberant. Or consider circumstances in which a yes-or-no decision must be made immediately, even though the correct decision is unknown. An immediate impulsive response has a 50% chance of succeeding, but a reflective, deliberated response will always be wrong.

The general point is that the meaning of any pattern of E&B disorder depends to some extent on the situations in which it occurs. Regarding *Impulsiveness*, this point has implications for various issues that concern educators, such as measuring this pattern of E&B disorder at school, deciding whether a student with this pattern is qualified for the ED disability, and providing excellent intervention for students with *Impulsiveness* (see Barkley, 2005).

## Relationship Problem
### *Description*
Humans fundamentally are social beings. We perform a wide range of behaviors with or because of other people, and we derive pleasure and tangible benefits from friendships. Children need to interact with other people to develop competence in socially related emotions, communication, cognition, and behavior.

Of course, people have varying degrees of social effectiveness, and the skills required for social competence change over time. In general, however, socially competent children start enjoyable social interchanges, respond positively to others, cooperate, assert themselves appropriately, communicate clearly, and solve interpersonal problems (McFadyen-Ketchum & Dodge, 1998). These behaviors are important for

Relationship problems characterize many students with E&BD.

creating a pleasant, effective group situation, and they help children become accepted by peers and make friends (Rubin, Burgess, Kennedy, & Stewart, 2003).

Socially incompetent behaviors interfere with adjustment (Dickstein, 2005; Kavale, Mathur, & Mostert, 2004). Young people who threaten, annoy, insult, yell at, disrupt activities of, betray, steal from, bully, or assault peers are often rejected—that is, avoided by most individuals and excluded by peer groups (Bierman, 2003; McFadyen-Ketchum & Dodge, 1998). Among the young people who frequently exhibit such behaviors are those with *Aggression* or *Impulsiveness* patterns of E&B disorder. Of course, aggression does not necessarily lead to peer rejection and may even contribute to popularity (Farmer, Goforth, Leung, Clemmer, & Thompson, 2004; Rodkin et al., 2000).

Also likely to be neglected, if not rejected, are children and adolescents whose behaviors signal that they are overly dependent on adults, preoccupied with their own thoughts, wish to avoid interaction with an individual or a group, generally unhappy, afraid or unwilling to communicate, in need of frequent reassurance, and/or unpleasantly strange. Among the children and adolescents who tend to exhibit such behaviors are those with *Anxiety* and *Depression* (Morris, Shah, & Morris, 2002; Rubin, Coplan, Chen, et al., 2005).

In addition to neglect and rejection, socially incompetent behaviors interfere with making friends and keeping them. A lack of friends can promote social withdrawal and deep loneliness, and/or coercion, conflict, and hostility toward peers and adults. In either case, a self-perpetuating cycle often results in which unpopular children and adolescents are further avoided and ignored, thereby restricting their opportunities for appropriate social skill development and for friendship (or even companionship), except perhaps with other rejected peers (Rubin et al., 2003).

Thus, *Relationship Problem* is a somewhat different kind of pattern of E&B disorder than *Impulsiveness, Aggression, Anxiety,* and *Depression,* because it causes and/or is caused by the other patterns. For example, *Relationship Problem* may contribute to *Depression* when the student becomes greatly discouraged over her rejection and lack of a friend. In turn, *Depression* may contribute to *Relationship Problem* when peers tease the student or avoid his sad facial expressions, verbal deficits, and lack of interest in participating in play or other activities. Similarly, *Relationship Problem* may contribute to *Aggression* when a student reacts with physical and verbal antisocial behavior to peers who elect not to associate with her. Such antisocial behavior and its resulting social discord will often cause or aggravate the *Relationship Problem* pattern. Thus a "conflict cycle" (see Chapter 7) may be created. Display 4-7 illustrates *Relationship Problem.*

### *Relation to Classification and Definition*
Many DSM-IV mental disorders involve a general dysfunction in interpersonal relationships, and some feature a more specific relationship dysfunction (e.g., Oppositional Defiant Disorder, Social Phobia). Profound social distortions are a key part of Pervasive

**Display 4-7** One manifestation of the *Relationship Problem* pattern

> On the school bus taking middle schoolers home, the chuckling was changing to laughter. Although Solomon could not hear what they were saying, he was becoming vaguely aware that it might have something to do with him. He asked the kids near him what was going on. The first two just smirked and claimed ignorance; the third said, "Look what's on your jacket." He unzipped and removed it to see the large black letters made by a laundry marker: TOOL
>
> Solomon screamed, turned toward his tormentors, and screamed again, "You dirty shits! You ruined my new jacket! This is my birthday present! I hate you bastards. You're gonna pay for this jacket!"
>
> Solomon cried and screamed more, slammed his open palms against seat backs, and returned to his seat. Solomon has no friends at school, not among the sixth, seventh-, and eighth-graders with whom he attends some classes nor those in his half-day intensive resource room. He has had very few friends in his entire life.
>
> Solomon has received various special education provisions since he was first referred for interpersonal and academic problems at age 8. Teacher reports and formal assessment have consistently shown that he lacks basic skills in getting along with others. He has never been able to start friendly conversations with peers or keep them going. No one remembers Solomon's ever saying "please" or "thank you," or complimenting a peer; instead, he tries to butt into conversations, activities, or games. He rarely shares or takes turns, and when involved in a group activity or sport, he often cheats, makes foolish or clumsy mistakes, or tries to cause his team to lose. When criticized or teased, Solomon calls names, has a tantrum, or (with weaker peers) becomes physically aggressive. He taunts other children when they make an error or get hurt.
>
> Solomon has always been one of the poorest achievers in his regular classes. His achievement varies across subjects, ranging between about second-grade and sixth-grade levels. Intelligence testing consistently places his IQ at about 80. His mother, who says that he is a good son at home, attributes most of Solomon's problems to incapable or personally vindictive teachers and mean peers. She participates little in the special education effort, but has not interfered with any school decisions about her son's education.
>
> Solomon frequently states that assigned work is unimportant or unworthy of his attention, but to several trusted teachers he has admitted great concern and pessimism over his loneliness and failure to learn. Because Solomon's problems are disturbing to everyone involved, additional educational decisions will have to be made soon.

Developmental Disorders, discussed in Chapter 5. Despite these linkages, *Relationship Problem* does not closely correspond to any specific childhood mental disorder (Rubin et al., 2003), with the possible exception of Reactive Attachment Disorder (Boris & Zeanah, 2005; O'Connor, 2002), one of DSM-IV's Other Disorders of Infancy, Childhood, or Adolescence.

In the ASEBA classification, social withdrawal and rejection are addressed by two syndromes, Withdrawn/Depressed and Social Problems. The federal definition of ED deals with this pattern of E&B disorder in characteristic (B), "[poor] relationships with peers and teachers" (see Display 4-2). Students with ED show this characteristic significantly more than nondisabled students (Cullinan et al., 2003, 2004; Cullinan & Sabornie, 2004).

### *Measurement*

Sociometrics (see Chapter 3) that use peer nominations can help us identify students who are rejected (viewed negatively by many classmates, positively by few) or neglected (receiving few if any nominations, negative or positive). Sociometrics measure other aspects of social acceptance as well. Teacher-completed rating scales inform about the student's interpersonal functioning with peers—social skills with other students, participation in instruction, play, and extracurricular activities, popularity among peers, and friendships—as well as social skills involving teachers and other school adults. Interviews can reveal the student's own perspective on his social behaviors and friendships.

Target-behavior recording could focus on the frequency or duration of positive interactions the student has with classmates. Cooperative work and play, friendly conversations, appropriate physical contact, sharing and taking turns, asking to join in a group, and praising or complimenting a peer are examples. Behavior incompatible with good social relationships can also be recorded: not joining a work or play group, refusing to share, bothering others, hovering near a group without participating, and so on.

Sociometrics, behavior rating scales, target-behavior recording, and other methods of measurement may capture divergent or even contradictory aspects of *Relationship Problem*. Teachers and peers sometimes have surprisingly different views about a student's popularity or respect among peers (McFadyen-Ketchum & Dodge, 1998). The need to use multiple methods and sources of information is especially important in measuring *Relationship Problem* (Bierman, 2003).

### *Prevalence*

Social incompetence, withdrawal, and rejection are widespread among children and adolescents. *Relationship Problem* is the chief reason for referral to psychological clinics for at least 15 percent of children and adolescents (U.S. Department of Health and Human Services [USDHHS], 1999). It is a secondary referral reason for many more. A child referred primarily for problems of *Impulsiveness* or *Anxiety*, for example, may also have poor social skills and few, if any, friends.

### *Course*

Socially rejected children and adolescents are at increased risk for social, personal, and learning problems that escalate in severity and probably continue into adulthood (Lewin et al., 1999; Rubin et al., 2003). Among the poor outcomes are other patterns of E&B disorder, school dropout, delinquent and criminal behavior, drug and alcohol misuse, and diagnosed mental disorders (Rubin et al., 2005; Woodward & Fergusson, 1999; Wyrick & Howell, 2004).

### *Other Considerations*

The prevalence and course of *Relationship Problem* are less clear than those of the other patterns of E&B disorder. *Relationship Problem*, as noted, is usually closely linked with one or more other patterns of E&B disorder. One consequence is that it is harder to determine its prevalence apart from the other patterns, and its unique contribution to poor outcomes. A related consequence is that the scientific research needed to answer questions about prevalence and course is infrequent, in large part because of difficulty in finding young people who have *Relationship Problem* but no other patterns.

## LINKAGES BETWEEN AND AMONG PATTERNS OF E&B DISORDER

*Morbid* means diseased. The nosological perspective on classification (e.g., DSM-IV) is derived from medical systems for classifying diseases, in which a person who has two or more diseases is termed *comorbid*. By analogy, a person with two or more E&B disorders is *comorbid* for those disorders.

Advocates of dimensional classification (e.g., ASEBA) consider comorbidity to be a misleading term because E&B disorder is not (usually) a disease. It is, instead, an extreme variation of ordinary emotions, behaviors, and thoughts—so extreme that it is a big problem. Thus they use the term *cooccurrence* to describe having two or more E&B disorders.

Each term has advantages and disadvantages. Both are used widely in the professional literature (Angold et al., 1999; Mattison, 2004; Wicks-Nelson & Israel, 2006). For many purposes, they can be interchanged.

A child may experience multiple patterns of E&B disorder at the same time **(concurrent comorbidity)**, one pattern followed sooner or later by another pattern (successive comorbidity), or both concurrent and successive. Properly conducted research on comorbidity of children's E&B disorder is a difficult challenge, but it has potential to clarify some of the most important issues about E&B disorder of children (Angold et al., 1999; Cullinan, 2004; Wicks-Nelson & Israel, 2006). Comorbidity research to date has suggested what concurrent comorbidities tend to be found among children with E&B disorder and what successive comorbidities are most predictable over the course of development.

*Aggression, Anxiety, Depression,* and *Impulsiveness* are often concurrently comorbid with one another (Angold et al., 1999; Frick & Silverthorn, 2001). There is less research on comorbidity involving *Relationship Problem*, so comorbidity conclusions about this pattern are uncertain. Different pairs of the patterns of E&B disorder are not equally likely to be comorbid. Display 4-8 presents the approximate extent (low, medium, high) of concurrent comorbidity for different pairs. Of course, comorbidity can involve more than two forms of E&B disorder (patterns, mental disorders, or dimensions).

Also of interest is concurrent comorbidity involving the five qualifying characteristics in the federal definition of ED. Display 1-7 illustrated the extent of comorbidity among the characteristics and how this varies according to the student's level in school (Cullinan & Epstein, 2001).

The situation for successive comorbidity is more complicated. For instance, some of the poor outcomes of a pattern of E&B disorder are major problems of adjustment that are not patterns of E&B disorder (e.g., *Law-Breaking Behavior, Suicidality*). A second

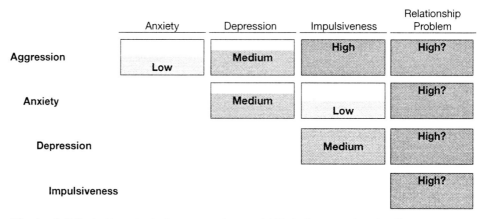

**Display 4-8** Probable extent of concurrent comorbidity between pairs of patterns of E&B disorder

complication: outcome for a child with two concurrently comorbid patterns of E&B disorder may be different from outcome for a child with either pattern alone.

Despite these and other complexities, we do know a few basics about successive comorbidity. Many cases of *Aggression*, especially if evident before school age, tend to become more severe and take on antisocial and illegal forms. Children with the *Anxiety* pattern have a tendency to develop *Depression*. *Depression*, in many cases, tends to become more severe and more clearly meets criteria for a Mood Disorder (see Chapter 5). *Impulsiveness*, as time goes by, tends to lead to academic learning problems and *Aggression*. *Relationship Problem* that involves extensive association with antisocial peers predicts delinquency and gang involvement.

## CONNECTED PROBLEMS

A person can experience social and personal life maladjustment in several ways, and not all are patterns of E&B disorder. Some of these other kinds of maladjustment, even though they are not patterns of E&B disorder, are significantly connected to one or more of the patterns. Four such connected problems are discussed here: *Law-Breaking Behavior, Learning Difficulty, Substance Misuse*, and *Suicidality*.

Each connected problem represents an ominous setback for the young people involved and their families. *Law-Breaking Behavior, Learning Difficulty*, and *Substance Misuse* are large-scale societal disasters as well. These three connected problems are considerably more likely to be present among young people with E&B disorder than without. The most serious aspects of *Suicidality* are not large-scale societal problems, but they are especially closely connected to E&B disorder.

## Law-Breaking Behavior

### *Description*

*Law-Breaking Behavior* refers to a severe, pervasive style of behaving and thinking that disregards or defies standards of the community. The standards may be informal, but more often are formal. Therefore the infringements usually are law violations or "status delinquency"—acts that are illegal for children but not adults, such as using alcohol, performing sexual acts, roaming late at night, or missing school excessively.

*Law-Breaking Behavior* tends to be accompanied by attitudes that reject or scorn laws, moral standards, traditions, and other values endorsed by authorities (e.g., teachers, parents, and community institutions). Such rebellious attitudes can be forcefully expressed in provocative grooming and clothing, interests that overtly conflict with established values, defiant or aggressive talk, selection of standards-violating role models, and participation in risky behaviors with well-known dangerous consequences (Newcomb & Richardson, 2000).

At school, *Law-Breaking Behavior* generally involves victimization of a fellow student or staff member. Often, it is performed in the company of, under encouragement from, or in conformity to expectations of a peer group. Besides peer pressure, *Law-Breaking Behavior* may be motivated by the resources it obtains, power or dominance over others, a desire to show independence, or the thrill associated with exposure to challenges and dangers.

### *Prevalence*

Although some instances of *Law-Breaking Behavior* are readily observable (hall or classroom gang conflict) or create a product (vandalism), most are hidden or go unreported. Prevalence information comes from confidentially self-reported transgressions; reports by peers, teachers, or other adults; behavior observations; and institutional behavior-product records (e.g., school suspensions, police arrest data). Combining data from multiple sources tends to improve confidence in results. The scope of *Law-Breaking Behavior* is suggested by data on victimization in school, and gangs.

**Victimization in School.** There have been unmistakable decreases in victimization in school in recent years (DeVoe et al, 2003; Federal Interagency Forum on Child and Family Statistics [FIFCFS], 2003; National Center for Education Statistics [NCES], 2004a), but nearly everyone would agree that the levels remain unacceptably high. For example, each year about 36 percent of public schools report to police one or more violent crimes; 15 percent report serious violent crimes (mainly assault, threat of assault with a weapon, sexual assault, and robbery); and 28 percent report theft. A great majority of these are middle and high schools, and they tend to be located in large urban areas.

Teachers are the victims of about 260,000 crimes per year at school (DeVoe et al., 2003). A little over one third of these are violent crimes (around 2.1 per 100 teachers), mainly assault without a weapon. Male teachers are 2.5 times as likely as female teachers to be the victim. Most of the nonviolent crimes against teachers are thefts.

Socialized deviance is a challenge to educators.

Approximately 8 percent of adolescent students report recently having been threatened or injured with a weapon at school; 13 percent having been in a fight; 8 percent, bullied by a peer. About 6 percent have recently carried a gun, knife, or club at school; 6 percent sometimes fear for their safety; 5 percent avoid particular areas of school. One in five adolescent students reports that there is a street gang presence at her or his school (DeVoe et al., 2003).

***Gangs.*** A **gang** is an organized, continuing group with identifiable leadership, territory, and communication (including hand signals, clothing, body markings, or graffiti), which engages in illegal acts, often serious and violent crime (Howell, 1997). Much about gangs remains obscure. For instance, except for core participants, gang membership is often unclear because of complications such as part-time members, "wanna-bes," and temporary members (many belong for less than a year). Also, it is hard to discriminate a gang crime from a crime by one or two individuals who belong to a gang. Roughly, 750,000 U.S. adolescents are gang members.

Of the more than 20,000 gangs in the U.S., some are all adolescents, some are all adults, and some are mixed (Egley & Major, 2004; Snyder & Sickmund, 1999). Most "youth gangs" (arbitrarily defined to include persons up to age 24) are located in a few large cities. However, over the past quarter-century they have come to be found in 3,000 to 4,000 U.S. cities, towns, villages, suburbs, and rural areas in every state, including nearly every city over 100,000 in population (Egley & Major, 2004; Miller, 2001). Possible causes of this expanding geographic range include (a) increasingly competitive drug-selling by gangs, prompting a need to spread to new territories; (b) gang formation following recent large increases in immigration from Asia and Latin America; (c) the continuing high rate of young people raised in fatherless households; (d) extensive media coverage—often uncritical, sometimes favorable—of negative aspects of gang culture (see Display 4-9).

Of all violent crimes committed by multiple offenders, approximately half are carried out by people under age 18 (Miller, 2001), many in gangs. Gang involvement in schools remains uncomfortably high, and the rate of violent victimization in schools with gangs is more than twice as high as those without gangs (DeVoe et al., 2003). Teachers of students with ED should be alert to general and local information about gangs.

Among young people, males are more frequently involved than females in illegal and delinquent conduct (Connor, 2002). Sex differences are very large for severe and violent offenses, smaller for nonviolent offenses, and nearly nonexistent for status delinquency (Snyder). Female adolescent participation in gangs is increasing.

Annually, approximately 2 percent of unmarried females under age 18 become mothers (FIFCFS, 2004). This is the lowest rate in many years, but it is still unacceptable because, for one thing, teenage motherhood is strongly associated with the offspring's future involvement in various patterns of E&B disorder and other life adjustment problems, including *Law-Breaking Behavior* (Yampolskaya, Brown, & Greenbaum, 2002; see Chapter 6).

### *Connections of Law-Breaking Behavior to E&B Disorder*

Adolescents with E&B disorder tend to engage in *Law-Breaking Behavior*, including crimes as part of a gang (Thornberry, Huizinga, & Loeber, 2004; Wyrick & Howell, 2004). Detained delinquents are especially prone to E&B disorder (Cauffman, 2004; Domalanta, Risser, Roberts, & Risser, 2003; Garland, et al., 2001; Nelson, Leone, & Rutherford, 2004; Teplin, Abram, McClelland, Dulcan, & Mericle, 2002; Wasserman,

**Display 4-9** Does gangsta rap contribute to the growth of juvenile gangs?

> In the 1990's, the substance of gang life was communicated to national audiences through a new medium known as gangsta rap. For the first time, this lifestyle was portrayed by youthful insiders, not adult outsiders. The character and values of gang life described by the rappers differed radically from the images of "West Side Story". Language was rough and insistently obscene; women were prostitutes ("bitches," "ho's," and "sluts") to be used, beaten, and thrown away; and extreme violence and cruelty, the gang lifestyle, and craziness or insanity were glorified. Among the rappers' targets of hatred, scorn, and murder threats were police, especially black police (referred to as "house slaves" and "field hands"); other races and ethnic groups; society as a whole; and members of rival gangs.
>
> The target audience for gangsta rap was adolescents at all social levels, with middle-class suburban youth constituting a substantial proportion of the market for rap recordings. The medium had its most direct appeal, however, for children and youth in ghetto and barrio communities, for whom it identified and clarified a set of values, sentiments, and attitudes about life conditions that were familiar to them. The obscene and bitterly iconoclastic gangsta rappers assumed heroic stature for thousands of potential gang members, replacing the drug dealer as a role model for many. Gangsta rap strengthened the desire of these youth to become part of a gang subculture that was portrayed by the rappers as a glamorous and rewarding lifestyle.

*Source:* Miller, 2001, p. 46.

McReynolds, Lucas, Fisher, & Santos, 2002). For example, Teplin et al. (2002) found that about two thirds of 10- to 18-year-olds detained for delinquency had at least one DSM mental disorder. The highest proportions had a substance use disorder (about 50%) and/or disruptive behavior disorder (40%), but considerable proportions had an anxiety disorder (20%) or affective disorder (20%).

In the federal definition of ED, a student cannot qualify as ED if his sole problem is that he is "socially maladjusted." If he is socially maladjusted but also exhibits at least one of the five listed characteristics of ED (see Display 1-4), the student can qualify. In other words, whether or not he is socially maladjusted is irrelevant (Cullinan, 2004). Socially maladjusted is neither defined nor described in the federal definition, but its meaning could well be similar to aggressively antisocial forms of *Law-Breaking Behavior*. In any case, students with ED show the socially maladjusted condition significantly more than regular education students (Cullinan & Epstein, 2001; Cullinan et al., 2003; Cullinan & Sabornie, 2004).

### *Other Considerations*

Because *Law-Breaking Behavior* consists of such widely divergent forms of antisocial functioning, prognosis statements are especially tentative. Adolescents involved in frequent, intense delinquency and other serious violations of societal standards tend to experience continued social and personal dysfunction into adulthood (Connor, 2003; Nelson et al., 2004). This dysfunction includes unemployment, isolation from community interaction, marriage and family failure, alcohol and drug abuse, incarceration and other legal trouble, and E&B disorders. Outcome tends to be especially poor if the *Law-Breaking Behavior* is preceded at an early age by *Aggression* and/or *Impulsiveness* patterns of E&B disorder.

## Learning Difficulty

### *Description*

As one would expect, a young person's social and personal adjustment tends to be linked with his school learning performance. One aspect of *Learning Difficulty* is failure to learn what schooling has to offer: basic academics (such as reading, arithmetic, writing), subject-area knowledge (science, history, or literature), vocational preparedness, and other offerings. Students with ED are especially likely to manifest serious language problems (Hooper, Roberts, Zeisel, & Poe, 2003; Kaiser, Cai, Hancock, & Foster, 2002; Nelson, Benner, & Cheney, 2005; Rogers-Adkinson & Hooper, 2003; Toppelberg & Shapiro, 2000), probably in both expressing ideas and understanding what others are trying to communicate. In addition, many children seem to have learned ways of thinking that perpetuate their E&B disorder (Kendall, 2000). For instance, they may respond to disputes by aggressing before considering other solutions (see Chapter 9).

Some *Learning Difficulty* is due to "dyspedagogia"—poor teaching practices and disorderly school environments. Another cause may be the child's inadequate cognitive functioning (Silver & Hagin, 2002) in either general intellectual ability or specific information-processing abilities such as attention, auditory discrimination, memory, and metacognition (awareness and control of one's own thoughts).

### *Prevalence*
Although great variations are found in the learning abilities and achievements of students with ED, most exhibit substantial deficiencies (Lane, 2004; Trout, Nordness, Pierce, & Epstein, 2003). The average IQ score of students with ED is approximately 90. A small proportion has very high intellectual ability. About half are 2 years or more below grade level in fundamental reading, writing, and arithmetic performance.

### *Connections of Learning Difficulty to E&B Disorder*
Students with ED are highly likely to fail in courses and grades, have language deficits, drop out of school, and show other evidence of continuing *Learning Difficulty* (U.S. Department of Education, 1998; Hooper et al., 2003; Kendziora, 2004; Mattison, Hooper, & Glassberg, 2002). *Learning Difficulty* is connected to each of the patterns of E&B disorder (US DHHS, 1999), especially *Aggression, Impulsiveness,* and *Relationship Problem* (Furlong, Morrison, & Jimerson, 2004; Hinshaw & Lee, 2003).

E&B disorder is especially common among children with intellectual ability below 70 IQ (Hodapp & Dykens, 2003). Of course, most often a student with IQ below 70 (and who meets other requirements) will be identified with mental retardation. However, quite a few students with ED have IQ substantially below 70. Evidently, in some identification decisions behavior and emotional problems take precedence over low learning ability.

### *Other Considerations*
In the federal definition of ED, the first characteristic listed, "(A) unexplained inability to learn," encompasses much of the *Learning Difficulty* connected problem. As noted in Chapter 1, the definition states that the presence of any one of the five characteristics is sufficient to identify a student as ED. However, it is hard to find a student identified as ED whose sole characteristic is *Learning Difficulty*. Such a student more likely would be identified with learning disability or mental retardation.

When discussing individual students with ED, educators sometimes debate whether their emotional and behavior problems caused their learning problems, or vice versa. *Learning Difficulty* undoubtedly can lead to personal frustration, negative emotions, conflict with teachers, peers, and parents, and other maladaptive behavior. Conversely, negative emotions or extensive conflict with other people tends to interfere with paying attention, solving problems, remembering, and other cognitive processes needed for learning. Conclusions regarding this are as follows:

1. *Learning Difficulty* and the patterns of E&B disorder can incite and intensify each other,
2. both often coexist with various significant biological and psychosocial risks for unfavorable child and adult adjustment, and
3. it is usually impossible to specify which came first.

Because many students with ED show *Learning Difficulty* along with their patterns of E&B disorder, their teachers in regular and special settings will be unable to serve them without good capabilities for remedial instruction (see Chapter 11).

## Substance Misuse

### Description

Many substances that can be ingested to produce desired psychological, social, or physical effects can also cause unfortunate effects for the person ingesting and for others. As a problem connected to E&B disorder, *Substance Misuse* refers to the young person's unauthorized ingestion of legal or illegal substances, resulting in substantially maladaptive psychosocial functioning.

Information on misused substances often addresses three kinds: alcohol, marijuana, and drugs other than marijuana (Centers for Disease Control and Prevention [CDC], 2004; Chassin, Ritter, Trim, & King, 2003; Simkin, 2005). The latter obviously is very broad. It includes amphetamines (especially methamphetamine and its derivative, "ice"); cocaine and its derivative, "crack"; inhalants (intoxicating fumes and gases from glues, solvents, gasoline, nitrous oxide, amyl nitrite); opiates (opium derivatives and synthetic narcotic analgesics, such as heroin, hydrocodone, oxycodone); hallucinogens (mainly LSD); and a growing list of **club drugs** (including ecstasy, GHB, ketamine, PCP, and Rohypnol) that produce intoxication, feelings of unreality, hallucinations, and/or empathy with other people. Various other substances (e.g., tobacco, body-building steroids) that also may fit the definition of *Substance Misuse* are not addressed in this section.

### Prevalence

The extent of *Substance Misuse* among adolescents is suggested by their anonymous, self-reported use of substances, as well as tabulations of diagnoses of DSM Substance Use Disorder, treatment and consequences of substance overdose, and reporting by parents and others. Large-scale studies of alcohol and drug use have been conducted regularly in the U.S. for several decades. Resulting data have varied over the years and by substance, as suggested by Display 4-10. Differences have also been found by age, gender, race-ethnic status, and other variables (CDC, 2004; DeVoe, et al., 2003; Jaffe & Simkin, 2002; Johnston, O'Malley, Bachman, & Schulenberg, 2004; Substance Abuse and Mental Health Services Administration [SAMHSA], 2004; Weinberg, Harper, & Brumback, 2002).

To note a few details, recent research on U.S. students in grades 9 to 12 (DeVoe, et al., CDC, 2003; 2004) found that within the prior month, 45 percent had used alcohol (5 percent on school property) and 22 percent had used marijuana (6 percent on school property). Around 10 percent acknowledged at least occasional use of other illegal drugs (note that Display 4-10 tracks 12th graders only). About 28 percent acknowledged taking five or more drinks of alcohol ("binge drinking") on at least one occasion within the prior month, 5 percent had used marijuana

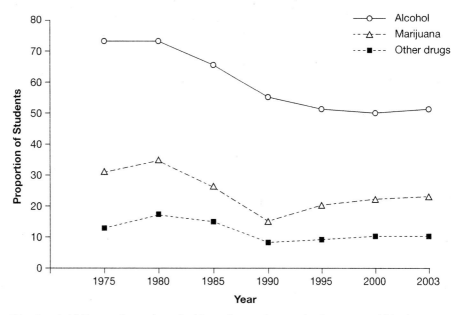

**Display 4-10** Proportions of grade 12 students who used substances within the past month, by substances and years

nearly every day, and 29 percent had been offered, given, or sold an illegal drug at school. Some of these adolescent students reported first using substances before they were 13 years old (alcohol, 28 percent; marijuana, 10 percent). Nationwide, around 12 percent of teachers report student drug and alcohol use as a serious problem at their school (NCES, 2003a). About one sixth of 16- to 18-year olds admitted having driven under the influence of alcohol and/or drugs at least once in the prior 12 months (SAMHSA, 2004).

Young people with *Substance Misuse* ordinarily use multiple substances. A common sequence of multiple substance use is cigarettes, to which is added alcohol, marijuana, and then other drugs (Chassin et al., 2003).

DSM-IV considers some kinds of *Substance Misuse* to be mental disorders (Substance Use Disorders) (Jaffe & Anthony, Chassin 2005; et al., 2003). A subcategory called Dependence involves extended substance use with severe adverse consequences, plus **substance tolerance** (progressive need for larger doses of the substance to get the same effects) and/or withdrawal (unpleasant physical or psychological effects following substance deprivation). A subcategory called Abuse involves less severe but still significant consequences. Each year about 9 percent of 12- to 17-year olds evidence Dependence or Abuse—mostly Abuse—and nearly 1 percent receive treatment at a facility specializing in *Substance Misuse* (SAMHSA, 2004).

Taken together, information on substance use and problems (e.g., Andrews, 2005; Chassin et al., 2003; Johnston et al., 2004; Simkin, 2005) indicate that before age 12 few children evidence *Substance Misuse*; and it peaks soon after age 20, declining thereafter. Between ages 12 and 20 years, about 5 percent of younger adolescents and 15 percent of older adolescents show this serious problem. There is substantially more alcohol misuse than drug misuse.

### Connections of Substance Misuse to E&B Disorder

Obviously, many young people try alcohol and/or drugs but experience little enduring interference with their development, whereas others experience significant setbacks. There is extensive co-occurrence of *Substance Misuse* and the five patterns of E&B disorder among adolescents (Chassin et al., 2003; Jaffe & Simkin, 2002; Solhkhah & Armentano, 2002; US DHHS, 1999). Present knowledge suggests that (a) *Aggression, Anxiety,* and *Depression,* independently or comorbidly, tend to precede and increase the likelihood of *Substance Misuse*. However, (b) *Impulsiveness* and *Relationship Problems* precede and increase the likelihood of *Substance Misuse* mainly when they co-occur with *Aggression*. Aarons, Brown, Hough, Garland, & Wood (2001) found that about one fourth of a group of adolescent students with ED had a DSM Substance Use Disorder.

### Other Considerations

Substance Misuse is linked not only to patterns of E&B disorder but to other Connected Problems (Chassin et al., 2003; Jaffe & Anthony, 2005). For instance, students who use substances are more likely to commit other offenses than those who do not, and much serious *Law-Breaking Behavior* is committed to obtain drugs and while the perpetrator is intoxicated on substances (Crowe, 1998). *Substance Misuse,* tragically, is an important risk factor for suicide.

Over the years there have been changes in social and legal expectations about some substances. Consider changes in the acceptability of tobacco, stimulant and antidepressant prescription drugs for problems of behavior and emotion, and body-building steroids. Acceptability of a substance seems to be related, in part, to how widely it is used—even if used illegally. Could the illegal use of some substances become so common that it is no longer meaningful to view it as *Substance Misuse?*

## Suicidality

### Description

Suicidality refers to the behaviors and thoughts related to an intent to end one's own life. It includes nonspecific ideas about suicide; plans for suicide that are specific about time, place, method, or other aspects; suicidal acts of low **lethality** (likelihood of inflicting death); suicidal acts of high lethality; and completed suicides (Moscicki, 1995; Pfeffer, 2002).

It is possible that *Suicidality* is a continuum on which the least lethal thoughts and behaviors (nonspecific suicidal ideas) are the most common, while progressively more lethal thoughts and behaviors are less and less common (ultimately, completed suicide). A continuum of *Suicidality* implies that research on and interventions for suicidal ideas is relevant to understanding and preventing suicidal acts.

On the other hand, there may not be a continuum of *Suicidality*. Children and adolescents who perform suicidal acts of high lethality, or who complete suicide, may be psychologically different from those who just think about suicide or make attempts of low lethality (Shaffer, 2005; Shaffer & Gutstein, 2002).

### *Prevalence*

Rates of death by suicide among U.S. young people greatly increased between about 1950 and 1990 and have declined somewhat since 1990 (CDC, 2004; Pfeffer, 2002). In recent years, approximately 2,000 persons under 20 years of age have completed suicide annually. Fewer than 300 of these are under 15 years old (Arias, Anderson, Hsiang-Ching, Murphy, & Kochanek, 2003). An average of about five suicides—one quarter of 1 percent of suicides under 20 years of age—take place at school each year (DeVoe et al., 2003). The methods by which young people most frequently complete suicide are guns and hanging.

In one large scale survey, high school students were asked in confidence about various maladaptive experiences over the preceding 12 months (CDC, 2004). About 17 percent reported that they had seriously considered attempting suicide and had made a plan to do so. Nearly 9 percent had made a suicide attempt, one third of which required the attention of a doctor or nurse (overdose, poisoning, injury).

Prevalence of suicidality varies by age, sex, race-ethnic status, and other variables (DeVoe et al., 2003; CDC, 2004; Shaffer & Gutstein, 2002). For instance, suicide attempts among high school students are more likely by 9th than 12th graders, by girls than boys, and by Hispanics than Blacks or Whites. Although females are more likely to perform suicidal acts, including attempts of low or medium lethality (e.g., medication overdose), males are far more likely to complete suicide. The sharp rise in completed suicide among young people from 1950 to 1990 was due largely to increases among older adolescent males (see Display 4-11).

### *Connections of Suicidality to E&B Disorder*

A large majority of children and adolescents who make highly lethal suicide attempts have one or more of the five patterns of E&B disorder, especially *Depression*. There is a diagnosed or diagnosable Mood Disorder or other DSM mental disorder in at least 90 percent of completed suicides (Pfeffer, 2002; Shaffer, 2005). Suicide is also more likely if the young person has comorbid patterns of E&B disorder, especially

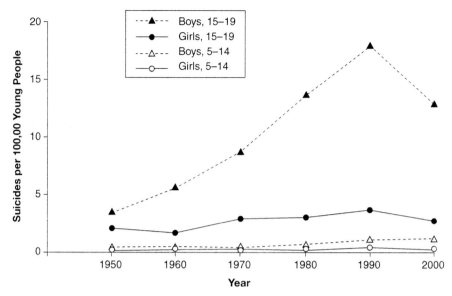

**Display 4-11** Rates of completed suicide among children and adolescents, by age level, sex, and years

*Aggression* and *Depression*, or psychotic symptoms, with or without a Psychotic Disorder. (Mood Disorder and Psychotic Disorder are presented in Chapter 5).

## Other Considerations

***Predictors of Suicidality.*** As noted, a strong predictor of suicides and highly lethal attempts among young people is severe E&B disorder. Among females, this is the strongest risk factor; among males, having made a previous suicide attempt predicts even more powerfully than having a severe E&B disorder.

"Predictors of" or "risk factors for" E&B disorder, or other phenomena, are complex concepts addressed in Chapter 6. To illustrate some complexities, the risk factor that probably most strongly predicts future completed suicide is having the Psychotic Disorder schizophrenia, but schizophrenia is so rare among young people that it accounts for only a small proportion of suicides. On the other hand, a history of *Aggression* characterizes a large proportion of adolescent suicides, but it also characterizes a considerable proportion of adolescents who do not complete suicide. As a result, *Aggression* is a weak risk factor for (has low power to predict) suicide.

Other risk factors for *Suicidality* (Pfeffer, 2002; Shaffer & Gutstein, 2002) can be divided roughly into "background" factors and more immediate, "precipitating" factors. Some background risk factors: (a) family history of suicide, *Law-Breaking*

*Behavior*, or *Substance Misuse;* (b) immediate family was disrupted by marital conflict; (c) father was absent from the family; and (d) young person was a victim of sexual or physical abuse. **Precipitating risk factors** include (a) certain highly stressful life events (such as being in trouble in the community, home, or school; incarceration; rejection, humiliation, or other loss of social connections); (b) awareness of attempted or completed suicide by a peer or a famous person; (c) a readily available gun or medications; and (d) substance use. Regarding substance use, many young suicide completers are intoxicated on some substance when they kill themselves (by a variety of methods, not primarily drug overdose). Background and precipitating factors for *Suicidality* are often so interrelated that the sequence and other details of causation are unclear. However, each risk factor can contribute to *Suicidality* risk, especially in the context of existing E&B disorder.

**Misconceptions.** There are several widespread assumptions about *Suicidality* among young people that are not supported by what incomplete knowledge we have about the subject. It is sometimes proposed that the increase in adolescent suicide over the past few decades has been caused by a proliferation of cheap handguns or by a substantial increase in how stressful life is in the United States. However, about four fifths of suicides by gun involve rifles and shotguns, not pistols (Shaffer & Gutstein, 2002). Further, suicide rates of young people increased in other regions of the world during the same time period.

Another assumption is that harassment, bullying, and persecution pushes many gay, lesbian, and bisexual young people to *Suicidality*. Homosexual adolescents are substantially more likely than heterosexual adolescents to consider, attempt, and complete suicide (Shaffer & Gutstein, 2002). However, they also are more likely to have experienced E&B disorder, *Substance Misuse*, and other strong background risk factors for *Suicidality*. Probably the same risk factors contribute to suicidal thinking and behavior of young people, whether they are heterosexual or homosexual. Of course, rejection and mistreatment by peers are highly stressful precipitating risk factors for suicide.

Suicide attempts of low lethality are sometimes said to be attention-seeking gestures of little if any significance ("parasuicides"). In practice this is a dangerous perspective because the cost of a mistake is so high. It is true that attempts of low lethality are infrequently followed by a completed suicide, but young people, especially males, who have already attempted suicide are many times more likely to complete suicide later than those who have never attempted (Shaffer, 2005).

Suicide among children and adolescents is a rare, tragic occurrence. Because it is so closely connected to E&B disorder, *Suicidality* is of particular concern to school practitioners working with students with ED and other young people with E&B disorder. Chapter 11 describes education practices and programs intended to prevent suicide and address school situations (e.g., student conflict, bullying) that can be risk factors for suicide.

## CHAPTER SUMMARY

Significant forms of E&B disorder of children and adolescents fall into five patterns: *Aggression, Anxiety, Depression, Impulsiveness,* and *Relationship Problem*. Each pattern of E&B disorder has the following:

- Important features that describe it
- Typical ways in which it is measured
- Varying degrees of similarity to DSM-IV categories and ASEBA dimensions
- Research-based information on its prevalence and course
- Other interesting features worth professional consideration

Each of the patterns of E&B disorder involves extremes of behavior, emotion, and cognition.

- *Aggression* emphasizes an intent to inflict injury, harm, pain, and disruption.
- *Anxiety* emphasizes distressing anticipation of harm, escape from threats, and unpleasant physical reactions.
- *Depression* emphasizes sad emotion, hopeless and grim thoughts, and deficits in social behavior.
- *Impulsiveness* emphasizes cognitive problems that result in failure to inhibit inappropriate acts, hyperactivity, and risky behaviors.
- *Relationship Problem* emphasizes insufficient appropriate interaction and/or excessive inappropriate interaction, together with a lack of friendships.

Two kinds of comorbidity are concurrent (more than one E&B disorder at the same time) or successive (more than one in succession).

*Law-Breaking Behavior, Learning Difficulty, Substance Misuse,* and *Suicidality* are kinds of serious social and personal maladjustment that, although not E&B disorders, are significantly linked to the five patterns of E&B disorder of young people.

- Among prominent aspects of *Law-Breaking Behavior* are criminal victimization in school and youth gangs.
- *Learning Difficulty* among young people with E&B disorder encompasses intellectual and language deficits and thinking distortions. Most students with ED are far below grade level in achievement.
- *Substance Misuse* is in a period of slight decline among young people. However, it is more widespread among young people with E&B disorder than those without.
- *Suicidality* includes a range of thoughts and behaviors that vary in probability of causing death. Suicidality is highly associated with E&B disorders, especially Mood Disorder and Psychotic Disorder.

## IDEAS FOR CONSIDERATION AND DISCUSSION

1. For each of the following patterns of E&BD, describe situations in which individuals or organizations might tend to overstate or understate its prevalence.
   - *Aggression*
   - *Anxiety*
2. Should either of the following be considered a pattern of E&BD? For each, present a strong case for and a strong case against.
   - Law-Breaking Behavior
   - Substance Misuse
3. The text states that one task for teachers of students with *Aggression* is to help them achieve a balance between assertiveness and independence on one hand, and cooperation, kindness, and respect on the other. Describe two ways for teachers to accomplish this task.
4. Should a student with *Depression* who has adequate adjustment in academics and extracurriculars be identified with ED? Present a strong case for and a strong case against.
5. Describe the "continuum of suicidality."
6. What specific services should the school offer to a student who shows
   - *Anxiety?*
   - *Depression?*

## RESOURCES FOR FURTHER STUDY

**www.help4adhd.org/faqs.cfm** ADHD frequently asked questions
**www.nimh.nih.gov/publicat/adhd.cfm** ADHD
**www.nmha.org/infoctr/factsheets/82.cfm** Adolescent suicide
**www.keepkidshealthy.com/welcome/conditions/anxiety_disorders.html** Anxiety and young people
**www.adaa.org/GettingHelp/FocusOn/Children&Adolescents.asp** Anxiety Disorders Association of America
**www.befrienders.org/support/warningSigns.php** Befrienders suicide support organization
**www.kidsource.com/kidsource/content5/long.young.child.html#intervention** Children and loneliness
**www.nmha.org/infoctr/factsheets/74.cfm** Conduct Disorder frequently asked questions
**www.aacap.org/publications/factsfam/conduct.htm** Conduct Disorder
**http://www.daap.ca/** Drug Addiction and Advice Project
**www.nmha.org/children/justjuv/index.cfm** E&BD and youth in the juvenile justice system
**www.oas.samhsa.gov/2k4/girlDelinquents/girlDelinquents.htm** Female Youths and Delinquent Behaviors
**http://safestate.org/shop/files/Gangs_comm.resp.pdf** Gangs: A community response
**www.ncptsd.va.gov/facts/specific/fs_children.html** National Center for Posttraumatic Stress Disorder
**www.health.org/features/kidsarea/kidsarea.htm** National Clearinghouse for Alcohol and Drug Information (NCADI)

**www.nida.nih.gov/drugpages.html** National Institute on Drug Abuse (NIDA) Drugs of Abuse
**www.nrscrisisline.org/** National Runaway Switchboard
**www.iir.com/nygc/faq.htm** National Youth Gang Center frequently asked questions
**http://www.ubhonline.com/html/education/cbt/adhdlnChildren/index.html#** Online presentation on ADHD by R. Barkley
**www.aacap.org/publications/factsfam/72.htm** Oppositional Defiant Disorder
**psychcentral.com/library/teen_depression.htm** Psych Central (adolescent depression)
**www.naspcenter.org/factsheets/socialskills_fs.html** Social skills at school
**http://ojjdp.ncjrs.org** U.S. Office of Juvenile Justice and Delinquency Prevention

Chapter **Five**

# *Extreme Emotional and Behavior Disorders*

## Chapter Objectives

**After reading this chapter, you should be able to:**
- Explain three reasons justifying coverage of extreme emotional and behavior disorders apart from the five patterns of E&B disorder.
- List two predictors of especially poor outcome for young people with a Mood Disorder.
- Discriminate positive and negative psychotic symptoms, with one example of each.
- Describe the three phases of schizophrenia.
- State the three major deviant characteristics that define Autistic Disorder.
- Identify two issues in educating students with Mood Disorders or Psychotic Disorders.

## Can You Define These 10 Terms?

early onset
episode
cycle
double depression
electroconvulsive therapy

positive psychotic symptoms
negative psychotic symptoms
active phase
insidious onset
autism spectrum

Chapter 4 described patterns of emotions, behaviors, and cognitions that can be present among most or all children, but when present to a very unusual extent indicate a need to consider whether the child has an emotional and behavior (E&B) disorder. Variations in frequency, duration, intensity, and other aspects of these patterns help separate normal expressions of emotion, cognition, and behavior from abnormal ones. Such variations help professionals discriminate normal functioning from E&B disorder, as well as less severe E&B disorder from more severe. Useful as they are, however, the patterns of E&B disorder alone are not sufficient for us to fully understand some extreme forms of E&B disorder.

For one thing, certain aspects of extreme E&B disorder are difficult to conceptualize in terms of a continuum of severity. Consider a child who believes she hears loud, angry voices criticizing her private thoughts. What would a less severe form of this be—quiet voices offering constructive suggestions? Or think of an adolescent who nearly every day experiences long periods of agitated, impatient excitement, alternating with long periods of deep sadness and immobility. Is the latter situation really no more than an extreme version of moodiness?

Many aspects of extreme E&B disorders undoubtedly can be conceptualized as familiar behaviors that are exhibited to an extreme extent (e.g., very high or low duration, very high or low frequency). But perhaps some aspects represent E&B disorder phenomena that are different in kind as well as in extent. Imagine a young person who sits motionless and stares constantly for 3 to 4 hours. Certainly that is an extremely long duration, but could it also represent a different *kind* of phenomenon than standing and staring for only 1 or 2 minutes? For another example, suppose a child has experienced zero moments of pleasure or fun during the past three months. Such a situation would seem to signify more than just a very low frequency of pleasure.

Moreover, time and the timing of phenomena are important criteria for recognizing extreme E&B disorder. In some cases diagnosis requires that certain behavioral, emotional, or cognitive problems occur in a particular sequence, occur in alternation with another problem, or first appear by a certain age (Boland & Keller, 2002; Wing & Agrawal, 2003). There are many specifications in DSM about problem durations, sequences, age when first observed, and other time-related criteria for various extreme E&B disorders.

Finally, it is a fact that professions other than education—especially psychiatry and clinical psychology—are often extensively involved in assessment, treatment, other services, and research for children with extreme E&B disorder. Educators must understand the concepts and language of these professions to be able to work with them. For these philosophical and practical reasons this chapter presents information about extreme E&B disorder organized mainly according to categories of E&B disorder—specifically, DSM-IV Mood Disorders, Psychotic Disorders, and Pervasive Developmental Disorders—rather than mainly according to the patterns of E&B disorder presented in Chapter 4.

# Background

Extremely deviant expressions of emotion, thinking, and behavior have been reported since ancient times and in various cultures. Centuries-old descriptions exist of adults with profound sadness, exhaustion, guilt, and other negative feelings; language that is strange, is rapid and illogical, or has become extremely slow; beliefs that are bizarre and seemingly unaffected by overwhelming proof to the contrary; unjustifiable fear, anger, or other unpleasant emotions, felt and expressed excessively or changing frequently and unexpectedly; or a lack of any emotional expression (Akiskal, 2005). These and other extraordinary problems that seem to resemble extreme E&B disorder of today have been given various names in the past; for instance, delirium (confused excitement), dementia (deterioration of mental abilities), lunacy (illogical thought and behavior), mania (racing thoughts, inappropriate elation, and risky behavior), and melancholia (extreme despondency and fear) (Wing & Agrawal, 2003). Children with such extreme abnormalities of emotion, cognition, and behavior have been written about for over 200 years (Hollis, 2003; Neve & Turner, 2002).

There have been many attempts to explain these extreme E&B disorders that can be so debilitating to the affected person, so strange to most observers, and so mysterious to researchers and practitioners. One fundamental question has been whether the emotional, behavior, and cognitive problems involved are best described as a single basic disorder with various manifestations or as multiple separate disorders (Kirkpatrick & Tek, 2005; Werry, 1996; Wing & Agrawal, 2003). A related point of dispute involves similarities and differences in adult versus child manifestations of extreme E&B disorder.

## One-Disorder Perspectives

One early viewpoint was that there is one extreme E&B disorder, and that its fundamental nature involves emotions, specifically, very negative or highly changeable moods. This viewpoint recognized that some people with extreme E&B disorder also presented severe thinking problems and behavior problems. However, these were seen as secondary problems that varied greatly, depending on how particular individuals adapted to the core emotional disorder.

Another early perspective agreed that there was only one disorder but held that its fundamental nature was not emotional. Instead it was an intense thought disorder that one clinical pioneer named *schizophrenia* ("madness of conflicting thoughts"). This perspective acknowledged that schizophrenia was often accompanied by serious problems of emotion, attention, social behavior, and willpower. It proposed that the diverse ways people adapted to the core cognitive disorder in schizophrenia caused both these accompanying problems and a false illusion that there are different forms of extreme E&B disorder.

## Two-Disorder Perspective

Around 1900, some experts came to believe that there were indeed two distinct kinds of extreme E&B disorder, one like each of the forms proposed years earlier. That is, one was an emotional disturbance involving negative mood states, usually melancholia but sometimes melancholia alternating with mania. The second extreme E&B disorder was a cognitive disturbance involving deterioration of formerly adequate thinking processes, termed *dementia praecox* ("early loss of mental abilities").

The one-disorder and two-disorders perspectives alternated in dominance during the first few decades of the 20th century. Since about 1970, scientific evidence and changes in theory have tipped the scales in favor of two (or more) disorders.

## Children's Extreme E&B disorder

Similar changes over the years can be seen in viewpoints on extreme E&B disorder of children (Werry, 1996). During the first three decades of the 20th century, extreme E&B disorder of a child was generally considered to be no different from that of an adult, except that the disorder became evident unusually early in life.

In the middle decades of the 20th century clinicians described an increasingly wide variety of extreme problems among children and adolescents. Many appeared to be very different from any extreme E&B disorder of adults. For instance, child specialists Leo Kanner (in 1943) and Hans Asperger (in 1944) reported on children who had social disorders of a severe nature, very strange interests and activities, and communication disabilities ranging in intensity from mild to profound. These problems were evident from very early childhood. Kanner and Asperger referred to these disorders as "autistic," meaning withdrawn into an inner world (Pearce, 2005).

A professional consensus then evolved that extreme E&B disorders of young people should be considered variations of a single, child-specific E&B disorder known as *childhood schizophrenia*. They were not considered to be early-appearing versions of adult mental disorders.

From about 1970, this hypothesis of childhood schizophrenia was contradicted by developing scientific evidence. This research indicated that, as with adults, the very serious problems of young people should be understood in terms of more than one kind of disorder (Asarnow & Asarnow, 2003; Werry, 1996). Some are **early-onset** forms of adult mental disorders such as Mood Disorders and Psychotic Disorders. The phenomena described by Kanner and Asperger, together with other extreme disorders of development, are considered to fall into a different DSM category. This category is pervasive developmental disorder, also referred to as autism spectrum disorders (Lord & Bailey, 2002).

## Extreme E&B Disorder and Education

Changes in clinical perspectives on extreme E&B disorder among young people have influenced education. For example, the federal disability category of emotional disturbance (ED) originally included both autism and schizophrenia. In 1981, at the request of advocates for children with autism, the U.S. Department of Education removed autism from the ED category and placed it into a miscellaneous disability category, Other Health Impairments (OHI). In 1990, amendments to the U.S. special education law created a new category, Autism, and many state education agencies followed a similar course. As a result, students with autism spectrum disorders are usually not assigned to teachers who have prepared and received certification to teach students with ED.

The main thrust of the chapter is a consideration of extreme E&B disorder of children in terms of the DSM-IV categories Mood Disorders and Psychotic Disorders (American Psychiatric Association [APA], 2000). In addition, this chapter briefly addresses autism spectrum disorders because of the historic association of autism with extreme E&B disorder and the ED disability. Another reason is that the problems of some students with autism spectrum disorders who also have high language and intellectual ability resemble the problems of students with extreme E&B disorder (see Simpson & Myles, 2003).

##  KEY INFORMATION

Key information about Mood Disorders and Psychotic Disorders is organized into the following topics: Description, Relation to Classification and Definition, Prevalence, Course, and Interventions. This coverage is similar to that of the patterns of E&B disorder in Chapter 4, with two main differences: (a) considerations of special interest when children rather than adults show a Mood Disorder or Psychotic Disorder and (b) very brief statements of intervention ideas for each disorder.

To elaborate on the first difference, DSM-IV criteria for Mood Disorders and Psychotic Disorders are moderately specific, have undergone some research validation, and, despite some reservations, have received considerable acceptance. However, these categories were developed for diagnostic use with adults, not young people, and they apply to adults better than to children and adolescents. Therefore, material on key information as it applies to Mood Disorders or Psychotic Disorders in general (i.e., among adults) is augmented by special considerations about how the key information applies to children and adolescents.

## MOOD DISORDERS

### Description

In DSM, Mood Disorders are characterized by and defined in terms of **episodes** (periods of severe malfunctioning). Display 5-1 describes four kinds of episode: major depressive, manic, mixed, and hypomanic.

Most people with a Mood Disorder experience more than one episode. That is, the episodes recur. Episodes may last minutes or a few hours or may go on for years. The time between the start of one episode and the start of the next is a **cycle**. If a person has more than about four cycles per year, his disorder is considered to be "rapid cycling."

It is mainly different kinds and sequences of the four kinds of episodes that discriminate the following varieties of Mood Disorders (Akiskal, 2005):

- **Major Depressive Disorder:** One or more major depressive episodes, but no manic episode.
- **Dysthymic Disorder:** A chronic condition involving the *Depression* pattern discussed in Chapter 4, but the problems do not meet criteria for Major Depressive Disorder.

**Display 5-1** Condensed descriptions of episodes in DSM Mood Disorders

**Major depressive episode**
1. For most of the time during a particular two-week period, at least five of the symptoms[1] (a)–(i). At least one of these must be (a) or (b):
   (a) feeling sad or behaving as if sad for most of the two-week period;
   (b) self-reported or observed loss of interest or pleasure in doing anything, and/or depressed mood, lasting at least two weeks;
   (c) substantial decrease or increase in weight or appetite;
   (d) sleeplessness or other sleep disturbance;
   (e) hyperactivity, restless or agitated behavior;
   (f) listlessness, feeling of exhaustion;
   (g) feelings of worthlessness or extreme guilt;
   (h) loss of concentration, or indecisiveness;
   (i) recurring thoughts of or plans for suicide.
2. The symptoms result in substantial disabilities in functioning or personal distress.
3. The symptoms are not caused by mourning.

**Manic episode**
1. For much of the time during a period of at least one week, either:
   (a) an unusual mood of great <u>elation or excitement</u> plus at least three of the symptoms below, or
   (b) an unusual mood of great <u>irritation</u> plus at least four of the symptoms below.
2. To a substantial extent:
   (a) unrealistically excessive egotism or self-appreciation;
   (b) very little sleep needed;
   (c) incessantly, persistently talkative;
   (d) thoughts and stated ideas change rapidly and in uncontrolled succession;
   (e) easily distracted;
   (f) agitated, driven activities;
   (g) high level of participation in personally or financially risky activities.
3. The symptoms result in substantial disabilities in social or personal functioning, or danger to self or others.

**Mixed episode**
1. The person experiences at least one major depressive episode (duration criterion excepted) and at least one manic episode (duration criterion excepted) within the same day.
2. The daily alternation of depressive and manic episodes must occur nearly every day for at least one week.
3. The symptoms result in substantial disabilities in social or personal functioning, or danger to self or others.

**Hypomanic episode**
1. For much of the time during a period of at least four days, either:
   (a) an unusual mood of readily noticeable <u>elation or excitement</u> plus at least three of the symptoms below, or
   (b) an unusual mood of readily noticeable <u>irritation</u> plus at least four of the symptoms below.
2. To a substantial extent:
   (a) unrealistically excessive egotism or self-appreciation;
   (b) very little sleep needed;

>   (c) incessantly, persistently talkative;
>   (d) thoughts and stated ideas change rapidly and in uncontrolled succession;
>   (e) easily distracted;
>   (f) agitated, driven activities;
>   (g) high level of participation in personally or financially risky activities.
> 3. The symptoms result in a readily noticeable change but no substantial disabilities in social or personal functioning.

*Source:* American Psychiatric Association, 2000.

[1]Symptoms caused by taking substances or medical conditions generally do not qualify as Mood Disorders symptoms in any of these episodes.

- ***Bipolar I Disorder:*** One or more manic episodes and/or mixed episodes, often alternating with major depressive episodes (sometimes called "manic depression").
- ***Bipolar II Disorder:*** At least one major depressive episode that is associated with a hypomanic episode.
- ***Cyclothymic Disorder:*** Alternations between hypomanic episodes and periods of *Depression*, but these problems do not meet the criteria for manic episodes or major depressive episodes.

Dysthymic Disorder and other depressive conditions are probably not simply less intense manifestations of Major Depressive Disorder. For instance, Dysthymic Disorder tends to appear earlier in life and be more chronic than Major Depressive Disorder. Although manic features differentiate Bipolar I and Bipolar II from Major Depressive Disorder, the depressive episodes characterizing all these disorders seem to be fundamentally similar (Johnson & Kizer, 2002). People with Mood Disorders often have comorbid mental disorders, and tend to attempt and complete suicide.

### *Special Considerations for Children and Adolescents*

In general, the four kinds of episodes are harder to distinguish among adolescents than adults and among younger children than adolescents (Biederman, 2005; Hammen & Rudolph, 2003; Harrington, 2002). Display 5-2 sketches a young person with a Mood Disorder.

***Depressive Disorders.*** Compared to adults, children and adolescents are more likely to show extensive irritable moods during depressive episodes (Garber & Horowitz, 2002; Hammen & Rudolph, 2003; Lewinsohn & Essau, 2002; Shaffer, 2005; Weller, Weller, Rowan, & Svadjian, 2002). They are more likely to exhibit co-occurring E&B disorder conditions, especially the following:

1. Psychotic symptoms (discussed later in this chapter), especially delusions, hallucinations, and disorganized thinking
2. Body pains and discomforts
3. *Impulsivity* (especially boys)
4. *Anxiety* (especially girls)

**Display 5-2** An adolescent with a mood disorder

On the first Thursday in February the Schoolwide Prevention Team at Kennedy High School met to consider LaTrisha. She had been a good student during ninth grade and, as records indicated, throughout her school career. She had achieved high grades, excellent conduct and citizenship, and election as an officer of her eighth grade. She was a good athlete, was captain of her softball team in middle school, and had made the high school softball and soccer teams.

However, in recent months several teachers had noted that LaTrisha had "gotten an attitude," saying impolite things and otherwise showing irritability and disrespect on several occasions. She frequently had been involved in disciplinary incidents, mainly class attendance violations in which she was found arguing loudly with various other students. School attendance had become erratic, although generally she had a signed excuse from her father. In the fall semester of 10th grade she had failed math, biology, and American literature.

LaTrisha and some of the other students involved had met individually with a school counselor following one of these incidents, and LaTrisha readily agreed to additional meetings. During some meetings she talked a great deal but much of what she said was disorganized. Her replies quickly became sidetracked into tangential topics that did not seem to go anywhere. She did talk coherently about poor grades, seemingly having lost all confidence in her ability to complete 10th grade ("I'm bombing out of school").

The counselor's meetings with the other students indicated that the previously popular LaTrisha began to lose friends early in 10th grade. A consistent complaint was that she started to brag about out-of-school activities and accomplishments that were pretty obviously false. When her statements were challenged, she spoke sharply to her companions and walked away. LaTrisha would make elaborate plans for social events or other adventures, then fail to do her part or show up. These behaviors were behind some of the arguments and minor physical conflicts with the schoolmates. Some of her schoolmates (former friends) recalled comments to them such as, "Nothing is going right for me any more," "All I want is to be left alone," and "I hope I go to sleep tonight and don't wake up in the morning."

The Team meeting resulted in some insight and considerable concern. It became clear what a large change in behavior LaTrisha was showing. Also, although generally LaTrisha was refusing to participate orally in classes, two teachers recalled some of her irrelevant and illogical responses, especially near the end of the semester. The Team decided to urgently ask LaTrisha's father to meet with a school psychologist as soon as possible.

This meeting took place several days later. The father had raised LaTrisha since her mother abandoned them when the girl was 5 years old. The father and daughter were especially close. He had first noticed problems the previous summer when she had shown no interest in the annual family reunion weekend, very much unlike past summers. In the months since, she often said she felt depressed and without energy, and frequently went to bed at 7 or 8 p.m.

LaTrisha told her father about mental blocks that kept her from saying her ideas, even as her thoughts seemed to race as if out of control. She was worried that this made her forget what she was saying right in the middle of a statement. Throughout the first semester of 10th grade there were periods of several days each during which she refused to go to school, instead staying in bed and staring out the window or just sleeping. LaTrisha told him this was due to exhaustion caused by the constant strain of her schoolwork that had become too difficult, fear of getting into conflicts with her peers and teachers, and the uncomfortable "aches in her bones" that came on unexpectedly, especially in the morning.

The school psychologist learned that the father arrived home from work one day after Christmas and found LaTrisha nearly unconscious from consuming every pill in the medicine cabinet (mostly nonprescription pain pills). At the emergency room he and LaTrisha met with a physician, who started a process of clinical treatment for her. Neither father nor the clinicians had informed the school of LaTrisha's treatment.

Additionally, adolescents in depressive episodes are prone to suffer from extremely sad mood and feelings of hopelessness and to engage in *Substance Misuse.*

**Bipolar Disorders.** More commonly than adults, young people with bipolar disorders exhibit intensely irritable behavior, psychotic symptoms, body pains and discomforts, and *Aggression* during manic episodes (Biederman, 2005; Faedda, Baldessarini, Glovinsky, & Austin, 2004; Geller et al., 2003; Hammen & Rudolph, 2003; Lewinsohn, Seeley, & Klein, 2003; Pavuluri, Herbener, & Sweeney, 2004). Amazingly, most preadolescents with bipolar disorder have very short cycles—less than 24 hours.

Manic episodes at any age can involve "driven" (excessive, seemingly unrestrainable) talkativeness, great agitation, and self-centered, risky behaviors such as boasts, threats, indiscriminant sex with multiple partners, and substance abuse (Mitchell & Malhi, 2004; Weller, Weller, & Sanchez, 2002). When young people exhibit such behaviors, it is easy to confuse bipolar disorders with *Aggression* and *Impulsivity.*

Bipolar disorders are not only somewhat similar to ADHD, they are highly comorbid with ADHD. Because these two DSM disorders share important similarities they are commonly misdiagnosed. However, properly discriminating them can improve treatment (Geller et al., 2003).

## Relation to Classification and Definition

DSM-IV Mood Disorders are addressed in part by several syndromes of the ASEBA system, especially Anxious/Depressed and Withdrawn/Depressed. In the federal ED definition, one of the five qualifying characteristics is "pervasive mood of unhappiness or depression."

Obviously the federal ED definition does not express many details of the DSM-IV depressive episodes and disorders, nor does it mention important aspects of bipolar disorders. Still, nearly any student with a Mood Disorder will probably show one or more of the five characteristics in the federal ED definition, at least during an episode of the Mood Disorder. Furthermore, many other students with substantial problems involving depressive and/or manic symptoms, even if their episodes are not long or severe enough to meet DSM-IV criteria, should also qualify under the ED definition.

## Prevalence

Prevalence researchers want to know, among other things, the proportion of people experiencing a Mood Disorder at any one point in time and the proportion that, up to that point, has ever had a Mood Disorder. Obtaining this information is made more difficult by the facts that (a) Mood Disorder episodes occur, then decline in intensity, then (usually) recur, starting another cycle; and (b) episodes and cycles last for varying lengths of time for different individuals.

### *Depressive Disorders*

Depressive disorders are very rare in young children. By the beginning of adolescence, perhaps 1 percent of children have experienced Major Depressive Disorder, with another 1 percent having a different form of depressive disorder (Hammen & Rudolph, 2003; Lewinsohn & Essau, 2002; Weller et al., 2002b).

In early adolescence the rate of new cases begins to increase until late adolescence, at which time it approximates adult rates. About 15 percent of adolescents have experienced Major Depressive Disorder, and an additional 5 percent have experienced a different depressive disorder. At any one time 3 to 5 percent of adolescents are experiencing some form of depressive disorder.

Before adolescence the female:male ratio is 1:1; in late adolescence it is 2:1. Among adolescents, sex differences in co-occurring E&B disorders become prominent (mainly *Anxiety* among females, *Aggression* and *Impulsivity* among males).

### *Bipolar Disorders*

Like depressive disorders, bipolar disorders are also rare before puberty, begin to increase in early adolescence, and occur in older adolescents about as frequently as in adults (Faedda et al., 2004; Geller et al., 2003; Weller et al., 2002a). About 1 percent of older adolescents have ever met criteria for a bipolar disorder, and about 4 percent more have experienced bipolar-like situations involving poor adjustment, suicidality, and other serious problems that do not quite meet DSM criteria (Lewinsohn et al., 2003). Males and females are about equally likely to have a bipolar disorder.

## Course

### *Depressive Disorders*

Most major depressive episodes of children and adolescents last no longer than 2 months, and about 90% last no longer than a year (Hammen & Rudolph, 2003). In a small fraction of cases, recovery does not take place. Another episode takes place within 5 years in about half of cases. Needless to say, depressive episodes have significantly detrimental effects on educational and social functioning (Birmaher, Arbelaez, & Brent, 2002; Lewinsohn et al., 2003). Children and adolescents with a depressive disorder are several times as likely to commit suicide as those without (Shaffer, 2005; U.S. Department of Health and Human Services [US DHHS], 1999).

Age at first depressive episode predicts quality of outcome (Geller et al., 2003; Hammen & Rudolph, 2003; Strober, 1996). When the depressive disorder first appears in adolescence, outcome is likely to be poorer than when it first appears in adulthood. Outcome is poorer still when a depressive disorder first appears in childhood, which predicts a variety of poor life adjustments (not just depressive disorder, but bipolar disorder, other E&B disorders, and/or serious social, marital, and legal problems).

Many young people with a less severe pattern of *Depression* E&B disorder eventually experience a more severe Mood Disorder (Flory, Vance, Birleson, & Luk, 2002). One form of this, the onset of Major Depressive Disorder in a person already suffering Dysthymic Disorder, is called **double depression**; it has especially poor prognosis. Up to 25 percent of children and adolescents who are first identified with a depressive disorder eventually develop a bipolar disorder (Hammen & Rudolph, 2003).

### *Bipolar Disorders*

Based on limited research, course and outcome of a bipolar disorder seem to vary by age at first episode (as with depressive disorders) and by nature of the first episode. When it is a manic or hypomanic episode (no *Depression* involved), chances are better for quick recovery, few or no recurrences, and a fairly good outcome. When the first episode is a mixed episode (see Display 5-1) or other alternation of manic and depressive features, outcome tends to be poor (Strober, 1996).

## Interventions

Three general goals of intervention are (a) to stabilize and improve the current Mood Disorder episode; (b) to help the person's present and future adaptive functioning in family, school, community, and (if applicable) job; and (c) to prevent future Mood Disorder episodes (Kutcher & Marton, 1996; Papatheodorou & Kutcher, 1996). Several medical and psychosocial interventions are available, and most authorities recommend combining them in various ways. In many cases, brief residential placement may be needed.

Some evidence suggests that young children can be identified at high risk for Mood Disorders as young as 3 years old (Faedda et al., 2004). If so, there might be important opportunities for prevention.

### *Medical*

The major medical intervention is psychotropic drug therapy (Konopasek & Forness, 2004; US DHHS, 1999; Weller et al., 2002a, 2002b). For depressive disorders, the main drug therapies are selective serotonin reuptake inhibitors (SSRIs) and tricyclic antidepressants (Hammen & Rudolph, 2003). For manic disorders, they are lithium, carbamazepine, and valproic acid (Ryan, 2003). Teachers have important roles in making drug therapies successful for their students (see Chapter 12).

**Electroconvulsive therapy** (ECT) involves passing a controlled electric current through the skull to induce a seizure. It is about as effective and safe as drug therapy for some Mood Disorders (Prudic, 2005). However, this procedure is controversial because it can have unpleasant side effects (Taieb, Cohen, Mazet, & Flament, 2000), and, frankly, sounds like a form of torture. ECT tends to be used after drug therapy has proven unsatisfactory (Weller et al., 2002b). Light therapy (frequent, regular exposure to bright light) is among the other treatments that may improve some Mood Disorders.

Interventions for mood disorders should educate the child and family about the nature of the mood disorder and its prognosis, as well as providing sources of support.

## *Psychosocial*

It is important for a professional to educate the child and the family about the nature of his mood disorder. This would include its possible course and prognosis, available interventions, and some sources of professional, community, advocate, and other support. The intervention plan should reflect the fact that parents and family play large roles in intervention for young people. Strong and long-lasting intervention efforts probably will be required (Kowatch et al., 2005). Parents and the young person must understand the likely episodic nature of Mood Disorders, the implications for intervention, and the need to obtain and stick to an intervention plan.

In many cases this plan should include special education. A variety of behavioral and cognitive interventions are used in clinical treatments (Gresham & Kern, 2004) and more and more frequently in schools as well (Smith, Lochman, & Daunic, 2005). Cognitive interventions (see Chapter 9) that help people recognize and change dysfunctional thoughts, emotions, and behaviors seem to have particular promise (Harrington, 2002; Weller et al., 2002b). When there are substantial risks to the safety of the individual or others, brief placement in a psychiatric hospital or other residential placement (see Chapter 12) may be appropriate.

At any age an extreme E&B disorder causes deterioration in present functioning, but in a child or adolescent it additionally interrupts the ongoing development of emotions, behaviors, thinking, and other aspects of growing up. Intervention planning should consider how to restore the child's development to a normal course following such an interruption. Among the important aspects of growing up are the young person's role as student and her need to participate in peer systems.

Differences in how adults and children exhibit and experience Mood Disorders can lead to clinical misdiagnosis, sometimes causing intervention mistakes. As noted, manic episodes in children tend to be marked by extreme irritability and disruptiveness, which could lead to misdiagnosis as ADHD. This may be very unfortunate because stimulant psychotropic drugs, prescribed to improve certain aspects of ADHD, can greatly worsen manic symptoms (Hammen & Rudolph, 2003).

Issues of diagnostic confusion have implications for educators. For instance, many students with ED were originally referred for, and continue to show, *Aggression* and *Impulsivity* patterns of E&B disorder. Could some of these students have an unrecognized and untreated mood disorder? How would teachers change education plans and services if they knew that a student with *Aggression* and *Impulsivity* patterns also had a bipolar disorder?

##  PSYCHOTIC DISORDERS

### Description

DSM-IV describes several subcategories of Psychotic Disorders, including schizophrenia. Information about adult-onset schizophrenia, the major psychotic disorder, is relatively firmly established, but the several other subcategories of Psychotic Disorders among adults are not well researched (Pull, Cloos, & Murthy, 2003). As a result, we do not know much about their prevalence, course, outcome, and other features. Pending more definitive information, some authorities refer to Psychotic Disorders other than schizophrenia as "atypical psychoses" or just "other psychoses."

#### *Psychotic Symptoms*

The hallmark of Psychotic Disorders is psychotic symptoms (Cutting, 2003; Fuller, Schultz, & Andreason, 2003), that is, extreme problems of emotion, behavior, and thought. Some authorities subdivide such problems as positive or negative. Positive psychotic symptoms involve the presence of abnormal, maladaptive phenomena, whereas negative psychotic symptoms concern the absence of normal adaptive phenomena. Key psychotic symptoms are described briefly in Display 5-3.

Note that psychotic symptoms are not unique to Psychotic Disorders. Psychotic symptoms sometimes accompany Mood Disorders, and they are found with other E&B disorders as well (e.g., Vickers, 2002).

***Special Considerations for Children and Adolescents.*** Many of the psychotic symptoms are about as prevalent in children and adolescents as in adults. Russell (1994) found that similar percentages of children and adults with schizophrenia had auditory hallucinations (both groups approximately 80 percent), visual hallucinations (40 percent), delusions (60 percent), disorganized spoken language or "thought disorder" (40 percent), and disorganized, deficient, or otherwise inappropriate emotions (80 percent).

**Display 5-3** Positive and negative psychotic symptoms

| Symptom | Description |
|---|---|
| | ***Positive Psychotic Symptoms*** |
| Delusion | Belief about external reality that others do not share, and that the person holds with deep conviction despite overwhelming evidence and argument to the contrary. |
| Hallucination | Perception of a phenomenon when no such phenomenon is present to be perceived, or inaccurate perception of the size, intensity, duration, or other characteristics of a phenomenon that is present. |
| Disorganized Spoken Language | Selected forms of incompetent verbal communication, often indicative of thinking problems. For example: *loosening of associations* (illogical concepts); *neologisms* (words and phrases with unique meanings); *derailment* or *incoherence* (sentences or paragraphs in which different parts appear not to be related to one another). |
| Disorganized or Catatonic Behavior | Various complex, apparently involuntary activities and postures while fully conscious. This symptom may include peculiar mannerisms or grimaces; long-term maintenance of a peculiar posture; automatic imitation of behavior or compliance with commands; and repetitive, meaningless movements. |
| | ***Negative Psychotic Symptoms*** |
| Deficient Spoken Language | Little or no speech; or excess delay in verbal responding; or content of speech is repetitive and contains little information. |
| Deficient Affect | Loss of ability to express joy, fear, anger, and other emotions via language and facial expressions. Eye contact is lacking. |
| Deficient Motivation | Inability to get interested, get started, or persist in daily activities or a particular task. Gives impression of extreme apathy. |

*Sources:* American Psychiatric Association (2000); Cutting (2003); Fuller et al. (2003).

On the other hand, psychotic symptoms of children and adolescents take forms that are different from those typical of adults (see Display 5-4). Generally, psychotic symptoms of adolescents are moderately different, while psychotic symptoms of preadolescents are greatly different (Werry, 1996). Why this is true is not well understood. Some differences (such as sexual content of delusions) may stem from adults' exposure to more and different kinds of life experiences. Other differences may reflect the young person's incomplete cognitive development and thus limited capacities to conceptualize and express abstract ideas.

### *Schizophrenia*
***Criteria.*** DSM-IV criteria for identifying schizophrenia are summarized in Display 5-5. Briefly, schizophrenia is diagnosed, subject to certain exclusions, if the person has experienced a period of at least 6 months of very abnormal functioning that includes at least 1 month in which particular psychotic symptoms have been prominent. This is

**Display 5-4** Positive psychotic symptoms as manifested in children and adolescents

| Symptoms | Example |
|---|---|
| Delusion | "A 9-year-old boy was convinced he was a dog (his parents were German Shepherds) and was growing fur, and on one occasion refused to leave a veterinarian's office unless he received a shot" (Andrews, 1994, p. 635).<br><br>"A 5½-year-old boy . . . believed that a baby was inside his throat telling him to kill himself, and he reached down his throat to try to extract the baby" (Spencer & Campbell, 1994, p. 716). |
| Hallucination | "The good angel and the bad angel are arguing and yelling about me. Most of the time I cannot hear what they are yelling. Sometimes the good angel says that I have been good. She says I am smart. The bad angel says that one night after I fall asleep she is going to take me away forever. Sometimes when they are arguing, I can see them if I stare at the wall." |
| Disorganized Spoken Language | "I wish for Christmas, 15 birthdays, churches, halloween time with I think about Sam or record players or instruments. And hospitals people cops painters. Born 1967 September 19 a cake balloons, card hats blowers presents socks stockings books catalogs magazines. Animals birds circuses parades zoos. Or summer with fall days" [excerpted from a letter by a 15-year old girl with EO/child schizophrenia attempting to update her therapist on what she has been doing lately] (Cantor, 1988, p. 103).<br><br>"I have to take off my socks because we don't have any trees growing in this classroom." |
| Disorganized or Catatonic Behavior | The 17-year-old frequently makes clicking sounds with his mouth and/or flicks his tongue rapidly. He has a peculiar way of shaking hands in which he tries to hold just your index finger, then the index and middle, then index plus middle plus ring, then all four fingers, after which he shakes your hand vigorously. |

accompanied by an obvious deterioration of social, personal, and vocational or educational functioning (Asarnow & Asarnow, 2003; Hollis, 2003; Kirkpatrick & Tek, 2005; Volkmar & Tsatsanis, 2002).

*Phases.* In the DSM-IV system, schizophrenia has three phases: prodrome, active, and residual (APA, 2000; American Academy of Child and Adolescent Psychiatry [AACAP], 2001). Following years or even decades of normality (whatever that may be for each individual), schizophrenia begins with a **prodrome phase** that can last for a few hours up to several months. During prodrome, the person shows decreased adaptive functioning and emotional and behavior problems, sometimes including psychotic symptoms, but not to the extent needed to qualify as the **active phase**. The active phase is a distinct episode of schizophrenia, with particular psychotic symptoms (Display 5-3) prominent for at least 1 month. Following this is the **residual phase**, in which typically the **positive psychotic symptoms** decrease or disappear. However, **negative psychotic symptoms** may continue for months,

**Display 5-5** Condensed description of DSM-IV diagnostic criteria for schizophrenia

1. <u>Psychotic symptoms (active phase)</u>. Either (a) or (b) below must occur for a substantial part of a one-month period. (The criterion length may be less than one month if psychotic symptoms have been successfully treated.)
   (a) at least one of the following:
   - bizarre delusions (example: "my father was born in the empire of Troy, 3,883 years ago")
   - auditory hallucinations in which one voice provides an ongoing or recurrent commentary on the person's behavior, thoughts, or feelings
   - auditory hallucinations in which multiple voices converse with each other
   
   (b) at least two of the following (see Display 5-1):
   - delusions
   - hallucinations
   - disorganized spoken language
   - disorganized or catatonic behavior
   - negative psychotic symptoms
2. <u>Duration</u>. The disturbance must have lasted for at least 6 months, including prodrome, active phase (see criterion 1), and residual phase.
3. <u>Dysfunction</u>: Since the disturbance began, the person shows a marked deterioration in social, self-care, or vocational functioning. (For children, failure to develop may substitute for deterioration.)
4. <u>Special Considerations</u>. Before schizophrenia is diagnosed, the diagnostician must rule out mental disorders of mood that resemble schizophrenia, and the possibility that psychotic symptoms are caused by drugs or medical conditions. If the person has a prior diagnosis of Pervasive Developmental Disorder, specific conditions must be met for an additional diagnosis of schizophrenia.

Adapted from American Psychiatric Association (2000).

along with other emotional, behavior, and cognitive functioning of a maladaptive and distressing nature.

In some cases it is difficult or impossible to identify the point of onset of schizophrenia because the person has a history of significant cognitive, language, emotional, and behavior problems, and these may have been gradually worsening before the active phase became apparent. Therefore the person's *premorbid* (before the disorder's beginning) functioning seems little if at all different from the prodrome phase of schizophrenia. Such a gradual beginning is referred to as **insidious onset**, as opposed to **acute onset** (sudden or clear-cut).

***Special Considerations for Children and Adolescents.*** Schizophrenia occurring before adulthood is referred to as early-onset (EO) schizophrenia. Some authorities (see AACAP, 2001) suggest further differentiating cases as to onset before puberty versus after puberty, because outcome and other important considerations seem to differ between these two groups.

The ways in which EO schizophrenia meets DSM-IV criteria for schizophrenia differ in important aspects from adult-onset schizophrenia (AACAP, 2001; McClellan, 2005; Wicks-Nelson & Israel, 2006).

As noted, psychotic symptoms of children and adolescents often appear different from those of adults. Distinct phases are less likely to be seen in EO schizophrenia (especially among young children), and insidious onset is more common (Werry, 1996).

Third, in addition to deterioration in emotions, behavior, cognition, and other important areas of life functioning, EO schizophrenia is marked by the child's failure to develop in those areas. That is, the disorder often interferes with the child's ability to meet a succession of expectations based on age and ability.

Fourth, EO schizophrenia is associated with severe *Learning Difficulty*. Children with EO schizophrenia tend to have low general intelligence, specific perceptual and cognitive problem such as attention disorders, and thinking-related language dysfunctions such as confused reasoning and incoherent or disjointed statements (Bearden et al., 2000; Caplan, Guthrie, Tang, Komo, & Asarnow, 2000; Volkmar & Tsatsanis, 2002). These cognitive and language dysfunctions are evident not only during the active phase of schizophrenia, but in many cases before and after. They are not restricted to schizophrenia but are found in other psychoses as well. Such problems in cognitive functioning and learning are, of course, a particular concern of special educators.

Additionally, a variety of substantial emotional and behavior problems are exhibited by young people with EO schizophrenia (Asarnow & Asarnow, 2003; McClellan, 2005; Volkmar & Tsatsanis, 2002). More than one third have a second DSM mental disorder (Russell, 1994). Adolescents with schizophrenia tend to become involved in petty crime, sexual misconduct, substance abuse, running away, and homelessness, and they may commit violence or suicide (US DHHS, 1999).

Display 5-6 illustrates several key features of EO schizophrenia. Just as important, it suggests the immense distress endured and courage displayed by children and adolescents with this extreme E&B disorder.

## *Other Psychoses and Other Mental Disorders with Psychotic Symptoms*

Other psychoses covers a wide range of interesting, controversial, and little-understood conditions (Fennig & Fochtmann, 2005; Pull et al., 2003; Wing & Agrawal, 2003). Some people have psychotic symptoms and other problems that meet some but not all of DSM-IV's fairly strict criteria for schizophrenia. For example, a person with Schizoaffective Disorder experiences an enduring, severe psychotic disorder concurrent with one of the mood disorders. The mood disorder is present most of the time but occasionally goes away for a brief period (weeks), leaving only the psychotic symptoms (APA, 2000).

***Special Considerations for Children and Adolescents.*** Many young people with psychotic symptoms do not meet DSM-IV's criteria for schizophrenia or perhaps any other psychotic disorder (Asarnow & Asarnow, 2003; Hollis, 2003). This can happen when they have (a) psychotic symptoms of insufficient duration or

**Display 5-6** Autobiographical account of schizophrenia with childhood onset

I have schizophrenia. I have had problems ever since I started school. I remember trying to hide under the tables in kindergarten so I wouldn't have to do any work. . . . [M]y mom and grandma had to come to school every day to make sure I got my work done. . . . [In] the fourth grade . . . something happened in October. All of a sudden I couldn't read or write or do math any more. Everything was so confusing because I couldn't understand anything that was going on around me. By November I was so sick I couldn't go to school anymore. On November 13 I went to the hospital and I stayed there for 2 months. . . . In the middle of the seventh grade I was proclaimed to be in remission.

It has always been hard for me to have friends. I want friends, but I don't know how to make them. I always think people are being serious when they are just joking around. . . . I get into fights with people all the time. . . . After I got back from the hospital I really couldn't get along with anyone. . . . Finally one girl in my special education class became my friend. . . . I had another friend in junior high who was also nice and kind to me. But my best friend is my dog Cindie. . . . I like to play by myself best. I make up stories and fantasies. . . .

I have trouble getting things done or even getting them started. For example, I bought some beads to make earrings for Christmas gifts. . . . Even though I had time during Thanksgiving break I just couldn't make myself get started. . . . Unless my parents come down hard on me, I never get things done. One of them has to supervise me with all my homework or . . . I just sit there staring off into space. . . . One of the hardest things for me in high school has been trying to get all the extra work done. I managed to convince my junior high teachers that I couldn't do very much work. I would cry or put my head on my desk or act stressed out or take lots and lots of time to do simple assignments. Now I have homework every night in algebra and nobody cares if I have trouble or not. This has been a hard semester, but I am happy because so far I have been able to stay up with my algebra class. My dad works with me every single night. . . .

Sometimes I laugh too much, even when things aren't all that funny. I get too excited and upset about things too. . . . [M]y family thinks I overdramatize almost anything that happens to me. Sometimes I fall down and pretend to faint.

In the seventh grade, I always thought I was sick. I went to the nurse's office two or three times a week and had the nurse call my mom to come and get me. Finally, my mother had a long talk with the nurse and after that . . . I couldn't get out of going to school by having pretend fevers, aches and pains. . . . During the years I was getting sick and then beginning to get better . . . I never smiled or had any expression on my face. I had a blank look in all my school pictures . . . .

[V]oices . . . started in the fourth grade when I was really sick. At first the voices were friendly; then they got mean and scared me to pieces. I got so I couldn't even go into my bedroom because I was so scared that a voice who lived there might get me. . . . [O]ther voices . . . protected me from the bad voices. The good voices were the first to disappear when I started taking medicine. . . .

I always had a terrible headache when the voices came. . . . When I was sickest I could even see the voices . . . (one of them had three heads). . . . I have wallpaper in my bedroom of old-fashioned girls with bonnets, and it used to seem to me that they would come alive and come off the walls to attack me. . . . Whenever I felt a voice attack coming on I would go to my mother. . . . She would say "Distract," and . . . make me lie down and relax. It worked. . . . Once while I was in the hospital the voices told me to jump out of the window . . . (I was on the sixth floor). I told my nurse about this and . . . I had to sleep in two chairs pushed together next to the nurses' station.

Sometimes I go on and on when I talk, and people have a hard time understanding what I am talking about. My family is always saying to me "You're going on and on" . . . [as] a clue to me to stop talking or that nobody is understanding what I am talking about. . . . My first psychiatrist thought I had attention deficit disorder because I had so much trouble paying attention and getting my work done. But one time when I was going on and on, . . . he asked if I was hearing voices. When I said yes he said I needed to be hospitalized for evaluation. . . . My parents were scared out of their wits.

. . . I have trouble writing too. I leave words out of sentences, or I don't finish writing a word. . . . Sometimes my sentences get really long. . . . I cannot write more than one or two paragraphs because I get really confused.

Everyone says I am very immature for my age. I would rather play with younger kids. . . . The best friend I ever had was 5 years younger than I was. We played Pippi Longstocking and house and dressup. Then she moved to Iowa. She visited me last summer, and I still wanted to play our old games. But she had changed. She wanted to do other things that weren't as much fun to me.

My brothers were both in advanced classes . . . in high school. . . . They both get good grades in college now. . . . I am an intelligent person, but because of my illness I won't be doing the things they did. I do want to go to a junior college, and if I can make it there, I want to become either a nurse for children or teach children. . . . I think being really sick makes you grow up in ways other people (like my brothers) don't. There are some things that are more important than getting good grades or being extra smart, like being nice.

I have been in remission for over 2 years. . . . [E]very night I pray that I will stay in remission. So far that has worked along with my therapy, my medicine, and all the help I get from my family and some of my teachers.

Excerpted from *Schizophrenia Bulletin, 1994*, pp. 587–590.

intensity to meet DSM criteria; (b) very substantial depressive or manic characteristics along with their psychotic symptoms, which generally rules out a diagnosis of schizophrenia; (c) co-occurrence of psychotic symptoms with other severe emotional and behavior problems such as *Substance Misuse, Law-Breaking Behavior,* obsessions, or posttraumatic stress disorder, which can camouflage a psychotic disorder. Such cases may be identified as an atypical psychosis or as some other DSM-IV disorder with an acknowledgment of psychotic symptoms. Display 5-7 illustrates a child with other psychosis.

Nurcombe (2005; Nurcombe et al., 1996) described a phenomenon that illustrates psychotic symptoms in conjunction with other severe E&B disorder, resulting in a difficult diagnostic and intervention situation. Called "dissociative hallucinosis," it is characterized by episodes of trancelike nightmares or daydreams (sometimes compulsively self-induced), hallucinations, irrational or disorganized thoughts, disturbing images, extreme anxiety and other emotional arousal, and impulsive behavior that is harmful to others and to self. These disturbed behavior, emotion, and cognitive phenomena generally share a common theme of degrading sexual and physical abuse. Episodes of dissociative hallucinosis last from an hour to several days and recur repeatedly. The young person may come to professional attention for running away, *Suicidality, Substance Misuse,* prostitution, or delinquency.

**Display 5-7** Anthony, a student with an Atypical Psychotic Disorder

> On the strong recommendation of school personnel. Anthony's mother contacted the community-health agency about her 13-year-old son. Since the beginning of this school term 8 weeks ago, this boy has shown serious disorders in thinking, social functioning, emotion, and other areas. He seems confused, for one thing: he often goes to the wrong class or walks the halls instead of attending class, muttering something to himself. This naturally has amused other students and prompted a good deal of ridicule toward Anthony, who either pays no attention or replies angrily, "You leave me alone!"
>
> Anthony occasionally approaches pupils he does not know to ask inappropriate and bizarre questions (e.g., "How much do you trust old Abe Lincoln?"; "When two people kiss, the heat of their lips kills the cancer germs, doesn't it?"). At the same time, he avoids—seems frightened of—classroom and other organized interaction with peers. For example, if someone stares, he can become upset and report the staring incident to the teacher. For weeks, Anthony had come to the office at least once a day, agitated or even panicked, to report incidents of schoolmates' planning to assault or steal from him. On those occasions when the principal discussed these accusations at some length, Anthony supplied details that usually were difficult to follow; for example, "The three boys in that jacket club are going to smother me after school. They want to be in my club which I have for my friends here and at other places which I know about but they have to smother me to tell them." Anthony then described the club's secret oath and activities. Sometimes his speech would speed up and continue almost without any pauses for breathing.
>
> Anthony is the third of five children. His divorced mother is employed as a teaching assistant in the elementary school. No one knows where his father is. The family rents a small house in a deteriorating neighborhood and receives some welfare assistance. The oldest daughter graduated from high school and entered the U.S. Army, and the other three youngsters are progressing satisfactorily in school.
>
> "Progressing satisfactorily" would have probably described Anthony until now. His school career had been unremarkable. His grades were usually average, occasionally low, but never failing. In fact, few of his former teachers remember very much about him. The invariably brief comments in his cumulative school records indicated no notable problems in classroom deportment, peer relationships, or other areas.
>
> His mother says he has always been lovable, manageable, and helpful. She observed that Anthony is "the shy one of the family"—having some acquaintances, no close friends, and preferring to read or do hobby projects alone.
>
> Although further information has to be collected on Anthony's situation, the mental-health agency staff is now considering intervention possibilities. Anthony has remained away from school for 3 days, and a special education teacher and the principal want Anthony to return. But it is not clear to anyone involved how this will be accomplished.

Typically, this young person has endured severe, repeated, inescapable sexual and physical abuse over a long period. Nurcombe et al. (1996) suggested that the prevalence of dissociative hallucinosis among adolescents may be higher than schizophrenia and probably is increasing. Perhaps relatedly, drastic increases in sexual and physical abuse of children have been reported in recent years (Office of Juvenile Justice and Delinquency Prevention [OJJDP], 2000; see Chapter 6).

## Relation to Classification and Definition

DSM-IV Psychotic Disorders is addressed to some extent by the ASEBA syndrome Thought Problems. None of the five characteristics specified in the federal definition of ED explicitly covers a major aspect of Psychotic Disorders. Note that clause (ii) of the federal definition states that ED "includes schizophrenia."

This clause probably was not intended to focus on DSM schizophrenia to the exclusion of students with psychotic symptoms that do not qualify as schizophrenia. The federal definition of ED became official in 1975 with the enactment of PL 94-142 (predecessor of IDEA 2004). As noted earlier, until the 1970s, schizophrenia was a more general term than now. Expert opinion in the U.S. generally held that most if not all extreme E&B disorder of children—even autistic disorder—could be best understood as forms of "child schizophrenia."

At any rate, virtually every student with a DSM-IV Psychotic Disorder exhibits at least one of the five characteristics in the federal ED definition. Many additional students with psychotic symptoms should also qualify as ED according to the federal definition, even if they do not currently meet DSM criteria for Psychotic Disorder. This could include students in prodrome or residual phase of schizophrenia, those experiencing a psychotic disorder of insufficient intensity or duration to meet DSM criteria, or those who have a psychotic disorder that has yet to be recognized and diagnosed.

## Prevalence

Consider all the people born in a certain year. After a few years go by, a small number of them first experience schizophrenia or another Psychotic Disorder each year. About 1 percent will have experienced schizophrenia by the time this cohort reaches age 60.

Schizophrenia can occur in children as young as 4 or 5 years, but EO schizophrenia before puberty is a very rare condition, perhaps 1 child in 10,000 (AACAP, 2001; Asarnow & Asarnow, 2003; Volkmar & Tsatsanis, 2002; Wicks-Nelson & Israel, 2006). Thereafter the number of new cases of schizophrenia increases rapidly throughout the adolescent years. Most cases are first diagnosed between ages 15 and 35.

On average, boys exhibit EO schizophrenia at an earlier age than girls. Until early adulthood there are more new cases of schizophrenia among males than females. After approximately age 25 there are more new female cases annually (Jablensky, 2003; Werry, 1996).

## Course

EO schizophrenia that begins before puberty typically involves insidious onset (Asarnow & Asarnow, 2003; Volkmar & Tsatsanis, 2002). For months or years the child's development may have lagged or may have regressed gradually and, often, unevenly across developmental areas (e.g., physical, motor, cognitive, emotional).

Therefore parents and teachers often have trouble specifying details about early indicators of schizophrenia or stating when the prodrome or active phase started.

In contrast, adolescent-onset EO schizophrenia more often involves acute onset and a definite prodrome. Thus parents and teachers can more readily notice decline in self-care, social, educational, problem-solving, and other activities. In these ways it is similar to adult-onset schizophrenia.

Following the active phase, which is likely to last longer in schizophrenia that begins before puberty than after, the residual phase typically involves months of stabilization or slow recovery. During this time the young person shows relatively mild negative psychotic symptoms such as inappropriately flat emotions and cognitive confusion. Unfortunately, a residual phase is often followed by additional active phases, and there may be further declines in functioning. When the active phases stop recurring, the young person's ability to function will improve somewhat, but rarely to developmentally appropriate levels.

Poor outcome is predicted by several risk factors, especially younger age at onset, insidious onset, an excess of certain negative psychotic symptoms, weak family and social support, and low socioeconomic status (AACAP, 2001; Hollis, 2003; Jablensky, 2003). For schizophrenia overall (without considering age of onset), outcome is "poor" in about 50 percent of cases (Hafner & an der Heiden, 2003; US DHHS, 1999). Poor outcome means continued or repeated hospitalization and intensive treatment for recurring active episodes, and/or lack of independence in major life roles such as family functioning and job.

Outcome of EO schizophrenia is poor in at least two thirds of cases (AACAP, 2001; Hollis, 2003). When it begins before puberty, outcome is poor in nearly all cases.

Adolescents with psychotic disorders may become involved in petty crime, substance abuse, and homelessness.

## Interventions

Generally, intervention efforts should take into account the nature of a person's Psychotic Disorder and its present phase. Efforts may be aimed at reducing the debilitating aspects of the active phase, planning for recovery of adaptive functioning in the short and long term, and preventing future psychotic symptoms.

### *Medical*

Antipsychotic medication (see Chapter 12) improves positive psychotic symptoms in a large majority of adults (Miyamoto, Stroup, Duncan, Aoba, & Lieberman, 2003). They should be tried for children and adolescents with schizophrenia (AACAP, 2001) and other disorders with psychotic symptoms. Antipsychotic drugs have various nuisance or dangerous side effects requiring caution.

### *Psychosocial*

Drug treatment should be carefully integrated with psychosocial interventions (Hollis, 2003; Martindale, Mueser, Kuipers, Sensky, & Green, 2003; Wicks-Nelson & Israel, 2006). These include discussion-oriented therapies (individual, group, family), performance-oriented therapies (such as behavioral, cognitive, social skills training), and social-support–oriented interventions (family-mediated contingency management, community follow-up care, supported employment, support for self-advocacy).

The nature of the psychotic disorder and what its course may be (e.g., probably long, perhaps life-long, with progress, reversals, and other ups and downs) must be explained to these young people and their families. The child or adolescent will likely show one or more of the E&B disorder patterns discussed in Chapter 4 in the home, community, and school, along with positive and/or negative psychotic symptoms. She may need hospitalization for initial treatment and later residential placements of various kinds, especially during additional active phases. Families must understand the importance of adhering to a treatment plan, advocating for other needed services, and securing appropriate education. Much of the psychosocial intervention (e.g., teaching of self-care, social skills, self-advocacy, and other adaptive behaviors) can be delivered in school, along with appropriate academic content and behavior problem management.

# PERVASIVE DEVELOPMENTAL DISORDERS

## Description

Pervasive Developmental Disorders (PDDs) feature extremely deviant social interactions and other disorders with onset in childhood, usually infancy or early childhood (APA, 2000). DSM-IV describes five types of PDD: Autistic Disorder, Rett's Disorder, Childhood Disintegrative Disorder, Asperger's Disorder, and PDD not otherwise specified (PDD-NOS).

Recent research has clarified the nature and validity of Rett's Disorder (see later discussion) and has clarified Autistic Disorder considerably (Volkmar, Klin, & Schultz, 2005; Volkmar, Lord, Bailey, Schultz, & Klin, 2004). However, pending better information about other PDDs, many experts prefer to refer to all PDDs as **autism spectrum** disorders. The other autism spectrum disorders resemble Autistic Disorder, especially in extreme social deficits, but differ in number and severity of Autistic Disorder characteristics, typical age of onset, developmental course, and other ways (Klinger, Dawson, & Renner, 2003; Koenig & Tsatsanis, 2005; Volkmar, Lord, Klin, & Cook, 2002). Display 5-8 highlights a student with an autism spectrum disorder.

**Display 5-8** Angie, a student with an autism spectrum disorder

> Should she return for another year or ought we find some other placement? This was the fundamental decision to be made at the end-of-year conference for Angie, a 6-year-old pupil at a preschool for students with disabilities. Her parents, teachers, psychologist, and a psychiatric social caseworker reviewed Angie's history and progress and considered public school and other service possibilities.
>
> Pregnancy and Angie's birth were normal. Motor development has been normal, and she is healthy and attractive in appearance. But during her first 2 years of life she was very irregular in her eating, sleeping, and elimination. For example, she would often sleep only 2 or 3 hours at night and scream for a long time before sleeping and upon awakening. Holding, rocking, patting, "sweet-talk," and other attempts to calm her were useless and even seemed to agitate her more.
>
> She began to say a few words, mostly echoically, by about age 3, but gave no indication of understanding what others said to her. During these early years she spent much of her time tapping on her crib or other objects and listening intently. She became highly upset at sudden loud noises and when the light was turned on or off. Angie explored toys, floors, furniture, and other things by smelling and touching them with her tongue. She rarely used toys and never did so appropriately. She often walked on tiptoe, held her arms close to the body, and flapped her hands or twirled slowly. During these stereotypies Angie sometimes vocalized odd sequences of wordlike sounds that rhymed (e.g., "ooozoo, voozoo, ooo, zoovoogoo, zoozoo, ooogooo ooo ooo ooo").
>
> When nearly 5 years old, Angie was accepted into the preschool. She was upset by and avoided the other children for a year; she could often be seen holding her hands over her ears—eyes shut—when there was an increase in room activity level. Angie progressed well in using crayons, pencils, and scissors skillfully; copying and drawing; matching words to pictures; stacking, sorting, and manipulating objects; playing simple games with the teacher; and generally learning how to perform in "school readiness" activities.
>
> Soon after her sixth birthday, Angie's ability to produce and understand speech began to improve noticeably. Now, what she says is slow and halting, monotonous, includes only key words and no pronouns, and is quite awkward (e.g., "Angie drink juice. Good juice.")—but she does communicate. She has begun to tolerate other children, occasionally following an instruction or otherwise responding appropriately to what a peer says. She continues to progress in readiness activities, which now involve much more language.
>
> Recent intellectual assessment indicated an overall IQ score of 57, with verbal abilities substantially higher than in the past. This and the modest gains in Angie's social and other functioning elicit an atmosphere of cautious optimism among those at the conference. As well, there is anxiety over the decision that may critically influence this little girl's future.

### Autistic Disorder

In 1943, distinguished child psychiatrist Leo Kanner reported on a small group of children whose disorders seemed to be qualitatively different from other forms of extreme E&B disorder (Kanner, 1943). Kanner's children displayed profoundly deviant social interactions and relationships, language and communication disorders, extensive behavior rituals, an abnormal insistence on preserving "sameness" in their environments, and other characteristics (Klinger et al., 2003). Unlike other children with extreme E&B disorder, this group first showed their abnormalities in infancy. By and large, these three emotional, behavior, and cognitive characteristics, along with the very early onset age, continue to define Autistic Disorder (Klinger et al., 2003; Lord & Bailey, 2002; Volkmar et al., 2004, 2005). In addition, many children with Autistic Disorder experience other major problems, often of an unusual nature, that are not obviously a manifestation of the three core symptoms.

***Interpersonal Relationships.*** Almost all infants engage in "attachment and bonding" behavior cycles with their parents. For example, they make and maintain eye contact, recognize their parents' faces, initiate and reciprocate smiling, converse in prelanguage vocalizations, show enjoyment at being approached and held, and imitate parental language and other behavior. Infants with Autistic Disorder do not do these things, however. They may even avoid eye contact and resist being cuddled.

As children with Autistic Disorder grow older, they develop few cooperative play or other social skills, rarely make friends, and often continue to show indifference to parents and siblings. They may express emotions very ineptly. For most adolescents with Autistic Disorder, social functioning remains a serious problem.

***Language Disorders.*** Youngsters with Autistic Disorder are very much delayed in language development, including babble, speech imitation, and other prelanguage behavior. Many never develop useful speech, and those who do still show various disturbances such as *echolalia* (uncontrolled, immediate repetition of others' words), pronoun reversal, inability to describe events or engage in conversations, and voice disorders.

The language disorders obviously go beyond speech (Volkmar et al., 2004). Language comprehension is poor, and the children have trouble following instructions and answering questions. Additionally, there is evidence for basic cognitive deficits involving the use of symbols. For example, these children rarely play imaginatively or pretend; they show difficulties in abstracting language rules (such as grammar or syntax) even after years of everyday exposure to speech; if they can read, they still comprehend poorly. There are prominent difficulties in understanding the perspectives of other people. Intelligence testing has identified particular difficulties involving symbolic usage of language. Cognitive deficiencies related to language are extensive, severe, and a crucial feature of Autistic Disorder.

***Restricted Behaviors and Interests.*** Children with Autistic Disorder exhibit various repetitive behaviors and restricted interests. For example, they may become intensely attached to a particular object or become highly anxious or upset over a minor change in their environment or routine.

Many of these children concentrate obsessively on knowing facts about a particular topic (such as dates, maps, street names, or animals) or on performing a single activity (such as collecting objects or drawing geographic figures), but show no interest in other topics or activities. Up to 10% of young people with autism may qualify as "savant" (able to perform extraordinary or even incredible memory, calculation, or other cognitive tasks; Volkmar et al., 2005). A large portion of their day may be consumed by repetitious, stereotypical arm flapping, rocking, rubbing, whirling, body posturing, or touching. Many perform ordinary activities, such as eating, dressing, or going to school, only if accompanied by some ritualistic behaviors or object preferences.

***Other Major Problems.*** Among other common problems among people with Autistic Disorder are disturbances in perception, self-injurious behaviors, phobias, and mental retardation (Klinger et al., 2003; Lord & Bailey, 2002; Volkmar et al., 2004). Many of these children overreact or underreact to sights, sounds, and other stimuli. For instance, they may show no reaction at all to loud noises but become distracted by barely audible sounds. A considerable proportion injure themselves, usually in stereotypical ways such as head beating, hand biting, or face scratching. Deviant sleep patterns may create problems for themselves and families. Mental retardation characterizes about half of these young people. This complicates research and diagnosis because some characteristics of Autistic Disorder (e.g., self-stimulation and self-injury) resemble those found among many children with mental retardation.

Many display various patterns of E&B disorder, such as *Anxiety*, to a very severe extent (Sweeney & Hoffman, 2004; Volkmar et al., 2005). For example, the young person may urgently avoid, and scream in the presence of, objects that seem strange as foci of phobia, such as particular household appliances, kinds of clothing material, or toys.

***Early Onset.*** Autistic Disorder appears within the first 2 years of life in most cases and is often apparent from infancy (Volkmar et al., 2004). DSM-IV criteria require appearance by age 3.

***Comments on Autistic Disorder.*** The brief information on characteristics presented above, needless to say, does not cover important variations related to child age, severity of disorder, and other context variables. The specific problems of many young people with Autistic Disorder change as they develop, but the problems usually remain highly noticeable and disabling. There is some evidence that early, intensive psychosocial interventions can improve—perhaps greatly improve—prospects for life adjustment (Rogers, 1998; Rutter, 2005a; Tanguay, 2000; Volkmar et al., 2004, 2005).

### Other Pervasive Developmental Disorders

***Asperger's Disorder.*** DSM-IV criteria for Asperger's Disorder include Autistic Disorder-like dysfunctions in interpersonal relationships and restricted behaviors and interests, but without major deficiencies of language and communication (Klinger et al., 2003; Lord & Bailey, 2002). In DSM, Asperger's Disorder can be diagnosed only if Autistic Disorder is ruled out.

However, several competing definitions of Asperger's Disorder are in general use, because experts disagree about its basic nature (Volkmar et al., 2004). Some doubt that Asperger's is anything other than cases of Autistic Disorder in which language and intelligence are not below the normal range. Young people with Asperger's Disorder do usually have normal intellectual functioning. They also tend to show motor awkwardness and some have psychotic symptoms (Klinger et al., 2003). Recently, considerable popular and professional interest has developed in Asperger's Disorder (Simpson & Myles, 2003).

***PDD-NOS.*** Children with PDD-NOS (also called atypical PDD or atypical autism) show only one or two core symptoms of Autistic Disorder intensively or all three but not intensely enough to qualify as Autistic Disorder. They also may fail to meet other criteria of Autistic Disorder (e.g., onset age). The lack of specific criteria has led to sharp growth in the use of this DSM category, with many cases that are relatively mild and many that are not reliably distinct from Asperger's Disorder.

***Rett's Disorder.*** Girls with Rett's Disorder (boys with Rett's Disorder do not live) show normal development until about 6 to 24 months of age (occasionally later), at which time head growth slows and motor coordination deteriorates. Especially noticeable are loss of purposive hand skills, stereotypic hand movements such as hand wringing, and severe language impairments. Most cases of Rett's Disorder have been linked to the mutation of a specific gene (Volkmar et al., 2004).

***Childhood Disintegrative Disorder.*** Children with Childhood Disintegrative Disorder begin to show severe dysfunction in at least one of the Autistic Disorder core characteristics (social, language, restricted behaviors) after 24 to 48 months of normal development. This means that the child has at least talked in simple sentences and engaged in social play and may have engaged in much more complex social and language functioning before deterioration began. Losses are also seen in walking, other motor skills, self-help behavior, and bladder and bowel control (Klinger et al., 2003).

### Comment on Pervasive Developmental Disorders

***Prevalence Issues.*** The prevalence of PDD appears to be approximately as follows (Fombonne, 2003; Tanguay, 2000; Volkmar et al., 2004, 2005): Autistic Disorder, 10 cases per 10,000 children and adolescents; Asperger's, 2 cases per 10,000; Rett's, 1 case per 10,000; Childhood Disintegrative Disorder, 0.2 cases per 10,000. Volkmar et al. (2004), noting that no good prevalence data exist for PDD-NOS, reasoned that it is probably more common than Autistic Disorder. This suggests 15 or more cases per 10,000. Therefore the total of PPDs would be at least 30 cases per 10,000 young people. Most young people with a PDD are male.

What makes prevalence of PDD especially interesting is that the reported prevalence has roughly tripled in the past quarter-century (Fombonne, 2003; Volkmar et al., 2004). Recent popular and professional media reports have referred to alarming increases in—even epidemics of—PDD (Sweeney & Hoffman, 2004), together with calls for urgent government and professional action to find the causes and deal with the situation.

Among potential reasons for the higher numbers (Koegel, Valdez-Menchaca, Koegel, & Harrower, 2001) are the following:

1. Actual increases in the number of cases of PDD
2. Discovery of many formerly unidentified cases as a result of improved assessment
3. Increased referrals because of greater parental awareness of autism, resulting from media reports and advocacy group activities
4. Increased diagnosis of children whose problems meet the vague criteria of PDD-NOS
5. Prevalence calculations based on cases identified via relaxed criteria for autism spectrum, especially PDD-NOS clinical diagnoses, and education agency counts of students in the Autism category of education disability (see Newschaffer, Falb, & Gurney, 2005)
6. Prevalence studies conducted in regions well-known for good services to people with autism spectrum disorders, to which large numbers of them have relocated.

Although present knowledge does not justify a final conclusion, the balance of evidence indicates that despite the reports, there are no large increases in the proportion of young people with actual Autistic Disorder or other category of PDD (Volkmar et al., 2004).

**Treatment Issues.** It is difficult to imagine that educators of students with ED would be assigned children with Rett's or Childhood Disintegrative Disorder. Infrequently, they may serve a student with Autistic Disorder, Asperger's Disorder, or PDD-NOS who has intellectual and language abilities in the normal range.

Psychosocial interventions with a heavy educational emphasis can substantially improve functioning of young people with PDD (Klinger et al., 2003; Lord & Bailey, 2002). Most of the scientific evidence supports some variation of direct, behavioristic intervention (see Chapter 8). To have much effect it should begin early in life, involve well-trained parents and teachers in the intervention, address core problems (usually language and social disorders) in developmentally appropriate ways, be intensive (many hours per day), directly teach generalization of behavior improvements across situations, and continue for a long time, perhaps into adulthood. Antipsychotic and antidepressant drug treatments can support psychosocial intervention by reducing self-injurious, repetitive stereotyped, and other severe problem behaviors (Konopasek & Forness, 2004; Volkmar et al., 2004).

## OBSERVATIONS ON EXTREME E&B DISORDER

### Classification Uncertainty

As the descriptions and vignettes in this chapter illustrate, youngsters who show extreme E&B disorder deviate greatly from normal functioning. Therefore it is logical to wonder why there has been so much uncertainty and controversy over the years among experts who have observed and studied such children carefully, for decades.

One major reason is the rarity of children and adolescents diagnosed with extreme E&B disorder. It is difficult to identify enough cases to study and even more difficult to identify representative samples. As a result, the groups of children in various studies often have been systematically different, leading the investigators to diverse conclusions.

A second reason has been changes in perspectives on extreme E&B disorder, which has made the results of research from different time periods difficult to compare. Studies of "childhood schizophrenia" from the 1960s and 1970s included children who would now be identified with more specific mental disorders, mainly Mood Disorders, Psychotic Disorders, and Autistic Disorder. Because the earlier studies often did not discriminate these disorders, their results give limited help in understanding differences among them.

A third problem is that early-onset forms of Mood Disorder and Psychotic Disorder are often less distinct from one another than the adult-onset forms are (AACAP, 2001; Asarnow & Asarnow, 2003). To receive a particular clinical diagnosis, the person must manifest fairly specific amounts, repetitions, and sequences of designated behaviors, emotions, and thoughts. However, adolescents and (especially) preadolescents often do not meet such criteria as clearly as adults. This is usually not a question of severity; the children definitely show an extreme E&B disorder, but not exactly in the ways required to qualify for a particular diagnosis. Note that children are more likely than adults to exhibit comorbid mental disorders or other co-occurring E&B disorder. Comorbidity also complicates differentiation of the disorders.

These complications add interest, not to mention frustration, to present and future efforts to understand extreme E&B disorder of children. They excite our admiration of the genius and immense effort of those who have wrestled with and created some order out of the pieces of information about extreme E&B disorder of children. And they caution us against premature closure on this topic: present viewpoints probably will not be the final word.

### Education

DSM-IV criteria for the main subcategories of Mood Disorder and Psychotic Disorder are relatively strict. The use of strict criteria for a disorder almost always produces a smaller number of cases. A person whose extreme E&B disorder does not quite meet strict criteria may be diagnosed as fitting a miscellaneous disorder category or as qualifying for no mental disorder at all. The small number of children and adolescents diagnosed with a DSM-IV Mood Disorder or Psychotic Disorder very likely underestimates a population of children with great needs, especially educational needs, that is generally unrecognized and unserved.

There are probably many children and adolescents with extreme E&B disorder who are not now identified by schools as ED and thus not served as a student with an education disability. Why not?

1. Some of them have problems that meet DSM criteria for a Mood Disorder or a Psychotic Disorder but simply remain undetected by educators or other professionals.
2. Others may have a history of problems that, if carefully examined, would indicate that they qualify for services. They may be at an early stage of what eventually will be clinically diagnosed as Mood Disorder or Psychotic Disorder. They may be in a partial-recovery or residual phase of personal, social, and educational impairment following an episode of major depressive disorder or an active phase of schizophrenia.
3. Still other young people have an extreme E&B disorder that does not quite meet the DSM criteria for Mood Disorders or Psychotic Disorders, but certainly embodies one or more of the characteristics in the federal definition of ED.

In addition to these unidentified students, it is likely that there are students identified with ED who have unrecognized extreme E&B disorders. Many students already identified as ED because of their socially incompetent, aggressive, disorganized, fearful, or other behavior problems probably could qualify for DSM Mood Disorders or Psychotic Disorders (e.g., Faedda et al., 2004). Therefore, even if special educators are adequately addressing these students' recognized behavior problems, the students probably are not being served appropriately because their extreme E&B disorders remain unrecognized and untreated.

Education of students with extreme E&B disorder raises yet-unanswered questions. For instance, would a highly structured, self-contained class or special school provide needed control and support for behavior and academic rehabilitation to a youth being treated for bipolar disorder? What are the significant advantages or disadvantages in serving a student with schizophrenia together with other students with ED?

In light of the fluctuating nature of Mood Disorders (e.g., episodes and cycles) and Psychotic Disorders (e.g., phases), how can educators detect important changes in the student's functioning? And what difference would it make? In what ways can teachers be flexible in changing placements, schedules, instruction content, teaching practices, and other aspects of appropriate education? Co-occurring E&B disorder, interruptions in development, questions of placement and instruction, and sensitivity to changes in a student's functioning are certainly not unique to intervention for students with Mood Disorders or Psychotic Disorders. However, resolving such issues may be especially relevant to serving them appropriately.

## Modifying the Prognosis

As noted, the prognosis for children with Mood Disorders and Psychotic Disorders is poor. Many continue to experience mental disorders and poor adjustment to school, community, job, and life in general. But as Display 5–6 shows, there can be a future of satisfaction and accomplishment for children and adolescents with extreme E&B disorder. Those who teach such students have a mission: to upset the predictions of poor outcome, to create an education environment that will build the child's resilience, and to use knowledge and resourcefulness to change the student's future.

## CHAPTER SUMMARY

After decades of controversy about the nature of extreme E&B disorder of children and adolescents, there is some consensus that three are especially relevant: Mood Disorders, Psychotic Disorders, and Pervasive Developmental Disorders.

- The patterns of E&B disorder described in Chapter 4 do apply to extreme E&B disorders, but cannot explain these disorders entirely.
- Students with Mood Disorders and Psychotic Disorders, if they qualify for special education, should do so under the ED disability category. Students with Pervasive Developmental Disorders generally fall under the Autism category.
- Different kinds of Mood Disorders are distinguished by episodes, or periods of maladaptive functioning that feature depressive and/or manic emotional, cognitive, and behavioral extremes.
- The essential aspects of Mood Disorders apply to both young people and adults, but there are some differences, such as:
  — Defining features of Mood Disorders are less distinct in young people.
  — Sex ratios are different.
- Some young people with Mood Disorders recover most or all of their earlier functioning, but many do not recover fully. One strong predictor of poor outcome is early age when the Mood Disorder first appears.
- Psychotic Disorders are mainly defined by psychotic symptoms, especially:
  — Delusions
  — Hallucinations
  — Language indicating disorganized thought
  — Grossly inappropriate emotions
- The major form of Psychotic Disorder, schizophrenia, is characterized by a three-part sequence of phases. In the active phase, psychotic symptoms are most obvious.
- Other forms of Psychotic Disorders also feature psychotic symptoms and maladaptive characteristics that do not meet the criteria for schizophrenia.

- The essential aspects of Psychotic Disorders apply to both young people and adults, but there are some differences, such as:
  — The three-part sequence of phases is usually less clear among children.
  — Children are more likely to have severe cognitive and language dysfunctions.
- Outcome of Psychotic Disorder is especially poor for preadolescent onset.
- Pervasive Developmental Disorders encompasses a wide range of extreme problems of cognition, behavior, and emotion, including Autistic Disorder and Asperger's Disorder.
- Autistic Disorder features:
  — Extremely deviant interpersonal relationships
  — Language disorders
  — Repetitive behaviors and/or restricted interests
  — First appearance no later than age 3, often much earlier
- Asperger's Disorder and other Pervasive Developmental Disorders include many cases that meet some but not all criteria for Autistic Disorder.
- Treatment of extreme E&B disorders includes drug therapies and psychosocial interventions, including education. The family and child need to understand the E&B disorder they are facing.
- Unresolved issues include the following:
  — Identifying students with extreme E&B disorders accurately
  — Providing them appropriate special education

## IDEAS FOR CONSIDERATION AND DISCUSSION

1. Explain why school professionals might find it difficult to discriminate the *Impulsivity* pattern from some forms of Mood Disorders. What are some things to keep in mind that may help make this discrimination?
2. Create an informal checklist on Mood Disorders for use by general education or special education teachers. This checklist should include characteristics that can suggest that a student has or is developing a Mood Disorder, and so may need closer examination by specialists. How will the teacher obtain information needed to complete each checklist item?
3. Speculate about educational modifications teachers and other school professionals might make upon learning that a student with *Aggression* or *Impulsivity* pattern also has a bipolar disorder.
4. Why has there been uncertainty and controversy about the nature of extreme E&BD of children, even among experts who have intensively studied them?
5. Create an informal checklist on Psychotic Disorders for use by general education or special education teachers. This checklist should include characteristics that can suggest that a student has or is developing a Psychotic Disorder, and so may need closer examination by specialists. How will the teacher obtain information needed to complete each checklist item?

6. Some extreme E&BD are exhibited in ways that vary over time. Give several examples of this phenomenon based on material presented in Chapter 5. State one or more implications of such variations over time for educating students with extreme E&BD.

## Resources for Further Study

**www.aacap.org/publications/factsfam/schizo.htm** AACAP schizophrenia in children
**http://www.ninds.nih.gov/disorders/asperger/asperger.htm** Asperger's Disorder
**www.autism-society.org/site/PageServer?pagename=WhatisAutism** Autism Society of America
**www.nimh.nih.gov/publicat/bipolarupdate.cfm** Bipolar disorder and young people
**www.bpkids.org/** Child & Adolescent Bipolar Foundation
**www.mhsource.com/narsad/pub/win0001childbp.html** Children and bipolar disorder
**www.nimh.nih.gov/healthinformation/schizophreniamenu.cfm** National Institutes of Mental Health, schizophrenia
**www.nimh.nih.gov/healthinformation/autismmenu.cfm** Pervasive Developmental Disorders
**www.nimh.nih.gov/publicat/schizoph.cfm** Schizophrenia (general)
**www.musckids.com/health_library/mentalhealth/schiz.htm** Schizophrenia (child and adolescent)
**www.mentalhealth.com/book/p40-sc02.html#Head_16** Teachers and schizophrenia
**www.bpso.org/practice.htm** Treating children and adolescents with bipolar disorder

# Causes and Models

CHAPTER 6   *Biological and Psychosocial Influences*

CHAPTER 7   *Psychodynamic Model*

CHAPTER 8   *Behavioral Model*

CHAPTER 9   *Cognitive Model*

CHAPTER 10  *Sociological, Ecological, and Values-based/Spiritual Models*

Chapter **Six**

# *Biological and Psychosocial Influences*

## CHAPTER OBJECTIVES

**After reading this chapter, you should be able to:**
- Describe four kinds of measurement of brain disorder.
- Describe one way a genetic error might contribute to E&B disorder.
- State the logic behind comparing monozygotic and dizygotic twins to estimate the contribution of heredity to any form of E&B disorder.
- List five general kinds of family disruption that can contribute to E&B disorder of children.
- Define the Accepting-Rejecting and Permitting-Controlling continua of discipline practices and state how they may be involved in some forms of E&B disorder of children.
- Identify one way that each of the following influences beyond the family can contribute to a child's E&B disorder: peers, community, school, and media.

## CAN YOU DEFINE THESE 10 TERMS?

developmental psychopathology
risk factor
psychosocial
brain disorder

gene
neurotransmitter
physiological assessment
attachment
diathesis-stress
temperament

Child development is the process of growth, maturation, and change during the period from the individual's conception, and to some extent even before, until the beginning of adulthood. Child development authorities recognize that many biological and **psychosocial** (psychological, social, and cultural) variables can powerfully affect the individual child's development (Berk, 2005; DeHart, Sroufe, & Cooper, 2004; Gordon, 2005).

## SOME BASIC CONCEPTS IN CHILD DEVELOPMENT

Biological and psychosocial variables influence child development in complex ways. One complexity is that the relative strength of these variables depends on what aspect of child development is at issue (U.S. Department of Health and Human Services [US DHHS], 1999). For example, especially during early development, *maturation*—changes in physical characteristics and physiological functioning that almost inevitably occur under ordinary environmental conditions—is strongly influenced by biological variables. Additionally, the particular biological and psychosocial variables that are most influential generally change over the course of an individual's development. One familiar example is the increase in the power of peer influence as a child becomes older.

Second, the biological, psychological, social, and cultural influences rarely operate alone; they interact with each other, and they modify each other (Bronfenbrenner & Morris, 1998; Crain, 2005; Moffitt, Caspi, & Rutter, 2005). For instance, learning is generally seen as a psychological process, but learning can produce physical changes in brain structure (DeCicco-Bloom & Sondell, 2005; US DHHS, 1999).

## Developmental Pathways

Some child development theoreticians find it helpful to organize such variables, together with other influences on development, by making analogies to trees, streams, or paths that might branch. The child's functioning over time may be likened to a ball rolling down a hill that is not perfectly smooth. The ball's location and direction at any point in time are determined to a great extent by where it has been (development that has preceded the present instant), plus the forces that may change its pathway (biological and psychosocial variables). The chance that the ball will continue on its present pathway or take a different one depends on the strength of the forces for change and their timing relative to the ball's location. Stronger forces are more likely to produce pathway changes and bigger pathway changes. A given force applied when the ball is traveling slowly (e.g., early in its course) will probably have greater effect than after the ball is traveling faster. Further, the influence of a force will depend on whether or not the ball is located in a channel or groove, how deep the groove is, and whether the grooves have bumps. If this rolling ball analogy seems worthwhile, the reader may wish to consider what biological and/or psychosocial variables might create grooves and bumps.

Such analogies are meant to represent child development in its more usual processes and outcomes, as well as unusual ones, including emotional and behavior (E&B) disorder. They may stimulate thoughts about the nature of normal and abnormal child development, how E&B disorders are defined, how a particular pattern of E&B disorder remains similar over time and how it may change, and what may be done to anticipate and change the course of an E&B disorder, especially from the perspective of an educator of students with ED. For instance, a developmental perspective (DeHart et al., 2004; Friedman & Chase-Lansdale, 2002; Rutter, 2002; Wilmshurst, 2005) emphasizes how important it is to know what constitutes ordinary development at different ages and how a child's present functioning may or may not be a cause for concern, depending on whether that sort of functioning is predictive of later social or personal maladaption.

**Developmental psychopathology** is a multidisciplinary field concerned with the relation of human development to emotional and behavioral maladjustment (Rutter, 2002; Wicks-Nelson & Israel, 2006). The huge, expanding body of research, facts, and theories on child development and on E&B disorder of children permits various interpretations of child developmental psychopathology. This chapter briefly considers key biological and psychosocial variables associated with child development that may cause E&B disorder.

## Risk Factors

What is meant by the phrase, "cause E&B disorder?" Understanding a phenomenon such as E&B disorder of children would be simpler if each biological or psychosocial cause were a "necessary and sufficient condition" that "(a) *must* be present for a particular phenomenon to occur, and (b) *always* leads to the phenomenon" (Achenbach, 1982, p. 103). However, few necessary and sufficient conditions for E&B disorders have been identified. Instead, research has identified quite a few **risk factors**, that is, biological or psychosocial variables that increase the chance that a child will later exhibit an E&B disorder (Cuffe, McKeown, Addy, & Garrison, 2005; US DHHS, 1999). Much of the research on causes of E&B disorder of children involves (a) finding possible risk factors for E&B disorder in general or a specific E&B disorder, (b) determining the extent to which each possible risk factor actually does contribute to the chance of an E&B disorder, (c) finding out *how* the risk factor increases risk, which usually means (d) examining the interactions of multiple risk factors and other biological or psychosocial variables, often as they occur in "pathways" over long periods of time (Rutter, 2002; Wicks-Nelson & Israel, 2006). This chapter considers risk factors noted in Display 6-1.

Risk factors can be subdivided in various ways. For example, distal risk factors operate long before the E&B disorder they promote, and/or in a general, indirect

**Display 6-1** Significant risk factors for E&B disorder

---

**Biological Reasons for Brain Disorder**
   Heredity
   Physical environment

**Psychosocial**
   Family socialization
      Attachment
      Discipline styles
      Disruptions to child-rearing
      Single parenting
      Child maltreatment
   Beyond the family
      Peers
      Community
      School
      Media
      Stress

way (e.g., they create other risk factors that more directly promote the E&B disorder). Proximal risk factors operate nearer to the time the E&B disorder will occur and/or contribute more directly to E&B disorder. A slightly different idea discriminates "background" from "precipitating" risk factors.

Generally, the more risk factors a child experiences, the greater the chance for an E&B disorder (Friedman & Chase-Lansdale, 2002). Some risk factors predict a variety of E&B disorders, whereas others seem to be especially predictive of a particular E&B disorder. Some risk factors are greater for a particular age or gender (e.g., Unruh & Bullis, 2005).

## Protective Factors

Many children have been exposed to strong or multiple risk factors yet remain free of E&B disorder. Such children are said to be *resilient* (able to resist the ill effects of risk factors or rebound from them) (Knapp, 2005; Masten, 2001; Masten & Coatsworth, 1998). These children are thought to have the benefit of *protective factors*, that is, biological or psychosocial variables that decrease the chance a child will later exhibit an E&B disorder. Some protective factors are the converse of risk factors (e.g., supportive community organizations versus lack of community support). To date, scientific understanding of protective factors and resilience in E&B disorder of children is limited (Compas, Connor-Smith, Saltzman, Thomsen, Wadsworth, 2001).

Risk and protective factors are important not only in understanding causes of E&B disorder but in preventing and treating them. Many prevention efforts attempt to undo harmful influences of risk factors, especially those that seem more feasible to change, while strengthening protective factors. Concepts and practices of prevention are discussed in Chapter 11.

Biological and psychosocial influences are discussed separately in this chapter, but in reality they rarely operate separately in E&B disorder. As causes of human functioning, biological and psychosocial influences sometimes counteract each other, sometimes work together, and each may modify the other (Nevid, Rathus, & Greene, 2006; Oltmanns & Emery, 2004; Salkind, 2004). It is true that there are some biological conditions that, alone, produce definite restrictions on a child's functioning regardless of his or her life experiences; as well, there are probably psychosocial risk factors so powerful as to overwhelm even persons with no biological limitations. Generally, however, biological influences seem to establish broad boundaries on behavior, emotional, and cognitive possibilities, boundaries within which the child's actual functioning is influenced mainly by psychosocial influences (Sarason & Sarason, 2005). Some ideas about how biological and psychosocial influences interact are presented later in the chapter.

## BIOLOGICAL INFLUENCES

Because the brain controls most behavior, biological influences on E&B disorder almost invariably involve the brain. The operation of the developing human's brain, the causes and effects of brain disorders, and how the brain and its disorders may help explain E&B disorders of children are topics of fascinating scientific research (e.g., Allen, Bruss, & Damasio, 2004; Anderson & Cohen, 2002; Kalat, 2004; Wagner & Silber, 2004). The term **brain disorder** includes either (a) damage to the brain's physical structure or (b) dysfunction, that is, improper operation of some brain function. The wondrous complexity of the human brain is a major challenge to scientific attempts to understand the conditions under which brain disorders are responsible for E&B disorder of children. Yet research has begun to clarify some of the relationships among brain development, brain disorders, and E&B disorder (Edmondson, 2005; Goodman, 2002; Rosenzweig, Breedlove, & Watson, 2005; Rubenstein & Puelles, 2004; Werry, Zemetkin, & Ernst, 2002). These relationships must be understood in consideration of some key points about the brain and the measurement of brain disorders.

## The Brain

The human brain's physical development begins very soon after conception and continues until about 30 months after birth, and in some ways for years thereafter. The brain is composed of 100 to 150 billion neurons (nerve cells), along with glia cells, blood vessels, cerebrospinal fluid, and other parts (Kalat, 2004; Rosenzweig et al., 2005; Wagner & Silber, 2004).

Neurons communicate with each other across synapses (microscopic gaps between specialized parts of the neuron) mainly by releasing **neurotransmitters** (chemicals that influence the functioning of a nearby neuron). A neuron is connected in this way to many other neurons (often hundreds, sometimes tens of thousands), resulting in trillions of synapses. Communication among neurons takes a split second to occur and is the basis for the brain's control over so many important emotions, behaviors, thoughts, and other aspects of mental functioning.

Glia cells are much more numerous than neurons. They physically support the brain, act as electrical insulators on neurons, nourish the neurons, and deactivate neurotransmitters.

### *Neurotransmitters*

The hundred or more kinds of neurotransmitter can be roughly classified according to their effects on other neurons sharing the synapse. Some influence other neurons to become active, thus transmitting an electrical nerve message; other neurotransmitters inhibit activity; a third kind adjusts the effects of these exciter and inhibitor neurotransmitters. Some E&B disorders are related to abnormalities involving neurotransmitters, especially those of the third kind. For example, schizophrenia is associated with an excess of the neurotransmitter dopamine; depressive states are associated with deficiencies of norepinephrine or serotonin. Details, not well understood now, are being studied vigorously, with special emphasis on implications for drug and other treatments that remedy neurotransmitter abnormalities.

### *Systems*

In the brain's organization, neurons that perform similar functions tend to operate as a system. For example, the limbic system regulates many emotional reactions and aspects of motivation. Limbic system dysfunction can produce uncontrollable excesses or deficits in emotions.

The brain and its systems have varying degrees of resistance to the effects of damage or dysfunction. Built into some systems are safety features, such as more neurons devoted to a particular function than are actually needed or more than one system able to control the same critical function. Despite all this, obviously the brain is vulnerable to dysfunction and damage, with varying effects on a person's development.

## Brain Disorder and Its Relation to E&B Disorder

It is clear that in a general way, brain disorder is related to E&B disorder. We know that the more severe the brain disorder, the greater is the risk of E&B disorder, and that brain disorder can have short-term or long-term effects on emotional and behavioral adjustment. However, despite many decades of scientific research, we have only a partial understanding of the relationship between brain disorders and E&B disorder of children. Knowledge is incomplete about many aspects of brain development and operation, as well as linkages between brain development and brain disorders. A large obstacle to more complete knowledge is the problem of measurement of brain disorders.

### *Incomplete Knowledge of the Brain*

Scientists are only beginning to comprehend some of the amazingly complex aspects of the human brain (Grebb, 2005; Kalat, 2004; Wagner & Silber, 2004; Werry et al., 2002). One kind of complexity is due to the fact that some behavior, emotional, or cognitive functions depend on the correct operation of several brain systems. A disorder in any one of these systems can cause the same malfunction. As a result, disorders located in different places in the brain, or involving different brain systems, can produce similar malfunctions of behaviors, emotions, and cognitions. This makes it difficult to identify what parts of the brain are responsible for what malfunctions.

Another kind of complexity is that sometimes different brain systems separately control the same function. Therefore some brain disorders may have no detectable effects—at least for a while—because a different, properly operating system continues to carry out the function.

Furthermore, it is not well understood how a child's E&B disorder might depend on the total extent of damage to or disorder of the brain, the age when the brain disorder began, and the child's sex (Rhoads, 2004). There seem to be brain disorders that have few if any detectable effects until the individual experiences major stress, at which point an E&B disorder may become obvious (McMahon, Grant, Compas, Thurm, & Ey, 2003; Sandberg & Rutter, 2002). Another unknown is how psychosocial influences such as good support from the child's family, skilled teachers, and other resources can reduce the handicapping effects of brain disorder.

A simple set of facts can illustrate the puzzling relationship of brain disorder to emotional and behavioral problems. Many children with brain disorder exhibit extremely hyperactive behavior; many children with brain disorder exhibit little or no hyperactive behavior; many children with no evidence of brain disorder exhibit extremely hyperactive behavior. Given these three facts, what can we conclude about the relation between brain disorder and extreme hyperactivity?

One recent direction for research assumes that we cannot understand a person's present brain situation—normal or dysfunctional—without knowing in detail how it developed. This assumption has motivated study of the hereditary, prenatal, and early childhood origins of the brain's chemistry, structure, and functions. Greater understanding of brain development should clarify causes of and perhaps potential interventions for brain disorders.

### *Measurement Problems*

A second reason for uncertainty about the relationship of brain disorder to E&B disorder is measurement limitations. Until recently, normal and disordered functioning of the brain have been difficult to measure directly, so indirect indicators of functioning typically have been used. Two indirect indicators of brain disorder include discovering what life experiences the child has had that might have caused brain disorder (developmental history) and measuring abnormal behaviors and cognitions that, logically, could result from brain disorder (neurological examination and neuropsychological testing).

For some decades in research laboratories, and more recently in medical and psychological practice settings, these traditional methods of brain disorder assessment have been supplemented by various physiological procedures (Schultz et al., 2002). Thus brain disorder assessment is moving toward measuring normal and disordered brain functioning directly (see D'Amato, Fletcher-Janzen, & Reynolds, 2005).

A *history* of the young person's development includes social and family history, general medical history, and the history of specific problems thought to be related to brain disorder. Sources of information include the child's and parents' recall, along with medical records, with particular attention to problems during pregnancy and birth, blows to the head, and illnesses. Also, diagnosticians observe the young person's language, attention, memory, and other behaviors and abilities during an interview for indications of problems that need to be addressed further.

A *neurological examination* explores cognitive, motor, and sensory capabilities in order to indicate the existence of dysfunction and its location in the brain. The child may be examined for arousal level, memory, awareness, language, posture and gait, facial expression abnormalities, body strength and coordination, reflexes, and other physical functioning. Because certain areas of the brain influence particular competencies, incompetencies can indicate locations of brain disorder. For instance, some expressive language disorders are often associated with brain dysfunction on one side of the cerebral cortex.

*Neuropsychological testing* uses a variety of tasks intended to measure selected sensory, perceptual, learning, and other abilities thought to be controlled by particular areas or systems of the brain (Jura & Humphrey, 2005). Poor performance on a task or test is assumed to indicate problems in one or more specialized abilities and, therefore, disorders in those particular brain areas or systems. Specially designed neuropsychological tests and modifications of other psychological tests may be used for this kind of assessment.

**Physiological assessment** procedures measure brain structure and functioning more directly (Fitzgerald & Rosenberg, 2005; Rosenzweig et al., 2005; Schultz et al., 2002). The *electroencephalograph* (EEG) detects brain electrical output recorded from locations on the child's scalp that correspond to underlying areas of the brain. Recordings are made under varying circumstances such as high versus low stimulation. Patterns of output can be analyzed by computer or compared to norms to help localize some kinds of abnormal brain functioning. *Computed axial tomography* (CT or CAT) uses X-rays to measure the differing densities of various brain tissues. *Magnetic resonance imaging* (MRI) uses magnetic and radio energy to detect hydrogen atoms. Because hydrogen is present to varying extents in common constituents of the brain, MRI can create an image of brain tissues and chemicals. *Magnetic resonance spectroscopy* (MRS) is similar to MRI except that it detects atoms other than hydrogen (e.g., those in neurotransmitters). CAT, MRI, and MRS are techniques that measure brain structure.

Other neuroimaging techniques measure brain functioning. *Functional MRI* (fMRI) examines changes over time in multiple MRI measurements, to identify brain areas that are active while the child performs various tasks. Practitioners of *positron emission tomography* (PET) and *single photon emission computed tomography* (SPECT) administer small doses of radioactive substances that enter different brain tissues. Energy emissions are measured to display a continually changing image of parts of the brain, which can be color-coded according to levels of metabolic activity. Neuroimaging and other physiological assessment rely on computers to convert measured data into three-dimensional images, cross-sectional "slices" of the brain, depictions of selected brain structures apart from the rest of the brain, and other analyses.

In various fields of science, breakthroughs in understanding natural mysteries often have been due to advances in our ability to measure concepts that are difficult to observe, such as time, distant or small objects, and energies undetectable by human senses. Neuroimaging may be such an advance in measurement. By allowing users to view small details of the brain, normal and abnormal, under various circumstances, brain imaging holds great promise for reducing uncertainty about relationships between brain disorders and E&B disorder (Werry et al., 2002). Additional neuroimaging techniques will develop from new methods to detect brain energies and to analyze and visualize data. Brain imaging will increase in practical relevance as it becomes safer and cheaper and as it suggests intervention tactics for more disability conditions, especially E&B disorder of children.

For now, there continue to be limitations in procedures for measuring brain disorder. In some cases the indications of brain disorder are obvious (e.g., abrupt cognitive deterioration, seizures), and various methods accurately assess brain disorder. But more often the young person's indications of brain disorder are inconsistent, subtle, or otherwise complicated. In many of these cases there are problems of measurement involving uncomfortably low reliability (e.g., measurements that are abnormal at one testing but not at the next) and validity (e.g., results that could be caused by brain disorder but just as well by psychosocial variables such as nervousness). Such limitations mean that in many cases a diagnosis of brain dysfunction continues to be uncertain.

### *Particular E&B Disorders Linked to Brain Disorders*

Despite obstacles such as assessment, the research on brain disorder and E&B disorder is beginning to yield important knowledge. The findings to date can be generally summarized as follows.

1. Brain disorders are not a major contributor in most cases of E&B disorder among children and adolescents.
2. Most children with brain disorders do not show E&B disorder (although many have other disabilities such as mental retardation).
3. However, there is substantial and growing evidence that some E&B disorders of children and adolescents are linked with damage to or dysfunctions of the brain (Rozenzweig et al., 2005; US DHHS, 1999; Weinberger & Marenco, 2003).

At present the evidence for this linkage is strongest for schizophrenia and some Mood Disorders, especially those with onset in childhood. Other evidence indicates that brain disorders are sometimes involved in the developmental pathways leading to each of the five patterns: *Aggression, Anxiety, Depression, Impulsiveness,* and *Relationship Problem.*

Revelations of relationships between brain disorder and E&B disorder are fascinating, so much so that sometimes we have to remind ourselves to keep them in proper perspective. Brain functioning is just one factor—along with psychosocial and other considerations—that operates, in ways now only poorly understood, to determine children's behavior, emotional, and cognitive functioning. In some cases of E&B disorder, brain disorder is a major influence, but in most cases it appears to be no more than a minor one.

## Causes of Brain Disorder

Given that brain disorders can contribute to some E&B disorder, what causes brain disorders? Biological causes can be subdivided into hereditary influences and physical influences, either of which can increase the risk of variations from ordinary brain structure and functioning that may result in maladaptive behaviors, emotions, and thinking.

These brain variations may be readily measured, or they may be undetectable by present measurement technology. Obviously one would be more comfortable applying the term "brain disorder" to readily measured variations than those for which the measurement evidence is unclear.

The behavioral, emotional, and cognitive consequences of brain disorder may be dramatically deviant, or they may fall within or not far outside the normal range of human variation (Rutter, 2002). In the latter case, whether or not there is an E&B disorder would be debatable, and few would make the judgment either way with great confidence. Of course, it is just such uncertain cases and situations that raise some of the toughest issues about defining E&B disorder and identifying individual children.

### *Hereditary Influences*

The idea that human physical and psychological characteristics are transmitted from one generation to the next is an ancient one, and scientific study of the topic has occurred for two centuries. But just in recent years have we begun to glimpse the awesome nature of hereditary transmission and its potential role in brain disorder and E&B disorder (Kalat, 2004; Klug & Cummings, 2005; Lewis, 2005; Lombroso & Leckman, 2002). This heredity research has tended to fall into two categories: direct and indirect research. Direct research involves observing the effects of individual *genes* (submicroscopic physical units of heredity) upon specific human characteristics, including some closely related to brain disorders and E&B disorder. Indirect research examines selected groups of people to estimate the extent that heredity influences such characteristics.

***Direct: Observing Individual Genes.*** Nearly every human cell contains a copy of a person's entire hereditary material, in the form of 23 pairs of chromosomes. Chromosomes consist mainly of molecules of deoxyribonucleic acid (DNA). A gene is a segment of one of these chromosomes. Different human chromosomes contain various numbers of genes, ranging from hundreds to thousands, and totaling approximately 30,000 genes.

Direct genetic research examines the functions of genes operating individually or in combination. Such research has established a human gene "map" by identifying what each gene is made of and the role it plays in controlling various human physical and even psychological characteristics (Display 6-2). This effort is beginning to yield revolutionary developments in the understanding of some hereditary disorders.

Genes operate mainly by communicating with "factory" parts of the cell to dictate the construction of particular kinds of protein. Some of these proteins serve as *enzymes* (modifiers of chemical reactions) that regulate the body's *metabolism* (use and disposal of raw materials such as oxygen, nutrients, and water). But what if a gene has some structural abnormality? The protein it dictates will reflect this genetic error and may not work properly. Given these facts, the following oversimplified scenarios suggest just three of the ways in which a genetic error could possibly contribute to E&B disorder.

1. Imagine a metabolism process that yields a by-product that has the potential to deactivate or kill neurons in the brain. Normally this poisonous by-product is immediately eliminated by the action of an enzyme, but there is an error in gene "A" that dictates the construction of this enzyme. As a result, there is none of this enzyme, so the by-product accumulates and poisons neurons.

**Display 6-2** Human Genome Project

The Human Genome Project was part of a multidisciplinary, international effort to learn the basis of human heredity. A goal of this effort, officially begun in the 1980s and building on earlier work, was to describe the chemical and physical structure, organization, and function of the human genome (entire collection of genetic material). Related research involved developing advanced research techniques to achieve this goal and describing the genomes of other forms of life. In 2000, it was announced that researchers with the Human Genome Project and Celera Genomics, a private biotechnology corporation, had achieved a preliminary description or "map" of the entire human genome. In 2003, an advanced map was completed and the Human Genome Project came to an end.

To understand the human genome, researchers attempt to identify the physical nature and operation of particular genes and other DNA segments, as well as their locations on chromosomes and elsewhere. The genetic processes behind normal human characteristics are studied, of course, but there is particular interest in the genetic basis of abnormal characteristics. Genetic researchers have achieved startling insights about functions and locations of some genetic material, some of which have medical and other uses.

Medically, many gene-based tests for detection of present and future diseases are now available. Researchers expect to develop drugs that have higher effectiveness and lower danger because they will be customized to different people's DNA. Also anticipated is a new form of therapy based on transferring into a patient genes modified to treat a specific disease. In addition to the medical uses, diverse other applications stemming from such research have appeared. They range from identifying perpetrators and exonerating people falsely accused of crimes, modifying plants and animals to be more productive food sources, studying the evolution and migration of human beings and other species, and rapid detection of toxins, including pollution and biological and chemical weapons.

Critics of gene manipulation point to the unprecedented possibilities for control of human structure and functioning, and to humankind's record of often having used scientific and technology developments in ignorant and evil ways. Supporters and critics alike recognize the need to examine ethical, moral, social and legal implications of gene research.

*Sources:* Human Genome Program, U.S. Department of Energy (2003). *Genomics and its impact on science and society: The Human Genome Project and Beyond.* Washington, DC: Author. Retrieved December 21, 2005, at http://www.ornl.gov/hgmis/publicat/primer.

2. Consider a different metabolism process in which raw materials are combined, with the help of an enzyme, to become a particular neurotransmitter that is critical to emotional stability. But an error of gene "B" results in too little of the needed enzyme. Therefore there is a shortage of the critical neurotransmitter, so emotional stability cannot be maintained.
3. Or perhaps another kind of gene error dictates the construction of an abnormal neurotransmitter. This abnormal neurotransmitter causes some neurons or brain systems to operate in disorganized and unusual ways, creating maladaptive effects on behavior, emotions, and cognition.

Situation 1 is similar to a form of mental retardation that involves drastically deviant emotions and behavior. In Lesch-Nyhan syndrome a genetic error causes a defect in an enzyme needed to metabolize key body chemicals (Skuse & Kuntsi, 2002). This enzyme defect allows an excess of uric acid to accumulate in the body, leading to physical abnormalities, mental retardation, and severe behavior disorders such as unusual body posturing, primitive aggression, and pitiful self-mutilation.

Regarding genetic error Situation 3, over the years various experts have theorized that an individual gene error could be the basis for some forms of E&B disorder. One speculation was that a gene error might cause the construction of an abnormal neurotransmitter resembling the hallucinogenic drug LSD. This abnormal neurotransmitter would interfere with brain functioning to produce hallucinations, delusions, or other psychotic symptoms. Logical as this idea is, research to date has not supported it.

In fact, direct gene research to date raises doubts that a single gene will be identified as the cause of any particular E&B disorder (Hallmayer, 2004; McGuffin & Rutter, 2002). Instead, the genetic basis for many of the E&B disorders is probably several genes acting together, in complex ways, to create a biological basis for E&B disorder.

**Indirect: Studying Selected Groups.** Since long before technology enabled the direct study of a single gene, genetic control of human characteristics was indirectly studied. Such research capitalizes on naturally occurring situations that offer insight into the extent of genetic influence on various normal and abnormal characteristics, including common traits of personality as well as E&B disorder (Wicks-Nelson & Israel, 2006). This indirect study is done using pedigree analysis, adoption comparisons, twin comparisons, and other research designs (Moldin, 2005).

1. The *pedigree analysis* design examines the family trees of people who show a particular disorder so as to determine whether there is a pattern based on which relatives share the disorder. Different patterns can suggest various forms of genetic influence. For example, there are many pedigree analyses which show that relatives of people with schizophrenia are more likely to have schizophrenia than nonrelatives, and that closer relatives have a higher risk than more distant ones. Display 6-3 illustrates this relationship.

    The main drawback of pedigree analysis is that it is not well suited to separate the effects of heredity and environment. For example, Display 6-3 could reflect the fact that closer relatives of people with E&B disorder not only share more genetic similarity with them but usually have more social contact with them than do distant relatives or total strangers. Therefore closer relatives have more chances to learn or otherwise be affected by deviant behaviors of people with E&B disorder. Also, the general maladaptive functioning of people with E&B disorder (e.g., ill effects of bad decisions about associates or finances) might create serious adjustment problems for their relatives.

2. An *adoption comparison* involves cases in which the infant of a parent with a particular E&B disorder is adopted by normal parents soon after birth. Such an adoptee is affected by the natural parents' genes but probably cannot have learned any maladaptive cognitions, emotions, or behaviors from them. Therefore, if years later such adoptees are more likely to exhibit the E&B disorder than adoptees born of parents without E&B disorder, the evidence for hereditary causation becomes stronger.

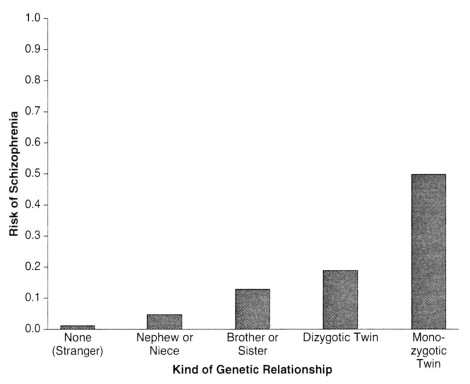

**Display 6-3** Risk of schizophrenia as related to increased genetic similarity
*Source:* Adapted from US DHHS, 1999.

3. *Twin comparison* research attempts to separate heredity and environment as causes of E&B disorder by comparing groups of *monozygotic* (MZ: one-egg, or "identical") twins and *dizygotic* (DZ: two-egg, or "fraternal") twins. The goal is to find out whether either type of twin is more dissimilar on a particular E&B disorder, by applying the following logic (US DHHS, 1999):
   (a) MZ twins are 100 percent alike in their genetic makeup, whereas DZ twins are on average 50 percent alike genetically.
   (b) Nongenetic variables such as family socialization and community influences exert about as much influence on MZ twins as on DZ twins, as long as they are of the same sex.
   (c) Therefore behavior differences between DZ twins may be due to hereditary *and* environmental factors, but behavior differences between MZ twins can be due only to environmental factors, because their heredity is identical.

By measuring many MZ and DZ twin pairs on the E&B disorder or other characteristic being studied, an "average dissimilarity" statistic can be computed separately for MZ twins and DZ twins. If the DZ twins are considerably more dissimilar than the MZ twins, heredity probably affects that particular characteristic.

The size of the difference allows an estimate of *heritability* (how much heredity affects that characteristic). One limitation of twin comparison research is that there may be circumstances under which point (b) above is incorrect (Wicks-Nelson & Israel, 2006).
4. Among other research methods is combining adoption and twin comparison designs by studying MZ and DZ twins who have been either reared together (both twins adopted by the same family) or reared apart (adopted by different families). This is one of the most powerful—and difficult to perform—of the indirect research methods.

These gene research designs may also be applied to study the role of chromosomes in causing E&B disorders. *Chromosomes* are structural arrangements of the genes found in each cell. In human growth and sexual reproduction the 23 pairs of chromosomes separate, duplicate themselves, find and combine with other chromosomes, and perform other complex processes. When these processes do not occur with great precision, one result may be an offspring with abnormal chromosomes that interfere with the normal operation of genes. A small fraction of newborns have a chromosome abnormality of some kind. Some of these are associated with mental retardation, severe behavior and emotional problems, and other physical and/or psychological disorders (Skuse & Kuntsi, 2002).

**Findings on Hereditary Influence.** A large body of persuasive research demonstrates that heredity influences diverse kinds of E&B disorder (McGuffin & Rutter, 2002; Oltmanns & Emery, 2004; Rhee & Waldman, 2002; Rosenzweig et al., 2005). Among them are *Aggression, Anxiety, Depression, Impulsiveness,* and *Relationship Problem* patterns of E&B disorder, and extreme E&B disorders.

But how much influence does heredity have? For some E&B disorders the amount of genetic influence appears to be high, but for most it is moderate to small. No research has found heritability of any E&B disorder to approach 100%, indicating that other biological variables and psychosocial variables are important as well.

In addition to heredity's effect on definite forms of E&B disorder, it appears to have considerable influence on ordinary human behavior and emotion tendencies (Kalat, 2004; McGuffin & Rutter, 2002; Wagner & Silber, 2004). For instance, low or high "sociability" or "emotionality" tendencies may underlie an individual's personality. One of these personality tendencies evidenced to an extreme extent, or some combinations of several of them, could predispose the individual to an E&B disorder (Rutter, 2002). For example, one might speculate that extremely high emotionality could predispose the young person to the *Anxiety* pattern of E&B disorder. Inherited behavior and emotion tendencies are related to the concept of temperament, discussed later in this chapter.

### *Physical Influences*
Various physical events can affect the child's brain and may immediately or eventually harm emotional and behavior development. Physical events may operate before a child is conceived, during the pregnancy, and during childhood and adolescence

(see Goodman, 2002; Mayes, Meteyer, & Granger, 2002; Whitaker, Birmaher, & Williams, 2002).

***Before Conception.*** A maternal history of illness, extreme obesity, substance abuse, or very poor nutrition before a pregnancy puts the developing organism at risk for various problems, including brain disorder. Risk is increased for mothers who are very young or old at the time they become pregnant.

***Prenatal Period.*** Following conception, the fertilized egg begins rapidly doubling and redoubling. Early in the pregnancy, this embryo cell mass differentiates into layers that have specialized functions, including a layer from which the nervous system will form. By about 10 weeks after conception the developing organism—now called a fetus—is unmistakably human in appearance. Major organs and other systems are present and operating by this time, including reflex behaviors important for survival and fetal glandular secretions critical to proper development of the brain. The point is that there are countless complex, precisely timed biological processes occurring throughout pregnancy. These processes usually operate well, but there are many opportunities for flaws.

Numerous risk factors operating during pregnancy are linked to brain disorders in the fetus. These include maternal exposure to general malnutrition or specific dietary deficits; poor maternal health during pregnancy; viral infections and other illnesses; maternal ingestion of toxic substances such as lead, mercury, and other metals; exposure to radiation; maternal ingestion (especially repeated or large-dose ingestion) of a range of substances, including tobacco, alcohol, prescription and nonprescription medications, and various illegal drugs. In general, these prenatal

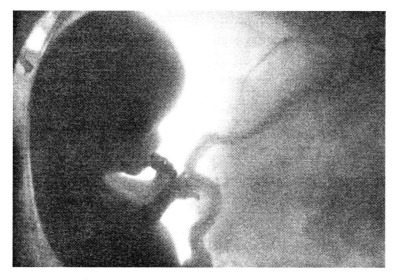

Risk factors at the prenatal period may create brain disorders in the fetus.

risks seem to be more likely to cause brain disorder when they occur early in pregnancy, while body structures are being formed, than later.

***Perinatal Period.*** The perinatal period includes birth and, according to various authorities, several days or weeks before and after. Normally a human pregnancy lasts about 40 weeks and the newborn weighs at least 6 pounds. About 1% to 2% of infants are born "very low birth weight" (less than 3.3 pounds; Federal Interagency Forum on Child and Family Statistics [FIFCFS], 2004), and advanced neonatal treatment permits most to survive. Many have a normal life, but they tend to have a range of physical and mental complications, including, in some cases, brain disorder and E&B disorder (Seidman et al., 2000). Risk for low birth weight is increased by poor maternal health; poor prenatal care; ingestion of alcohol, drugs, and other toxic substances; pregnancy before 20 years of age; and maternal sexually transmitted disease. Other perinatal risks for brain disorder are brain hemorrhage during birth and *asphyxia* (oxygen deprivation; also referred to as *anoxia*), which is more likely in a preterm birth.

It should be emphasized that exposure to prenatal or perinatal risk factors does not necessarily cause brain disorders, and brain disorders do not necessarily lead to E&B disorder. Many low-birth-weight infants do not show brain disorders, and of those who do, mental retardation and other problems are more likely outcomes than E&B disorder.

***Postnatal Risks.*** Continued maturation during childhood is a prerequisite for the youngster's acquisition of behavior, emotion, cognitive, and other capabilities (Berk, 2005; DeHart et al., 2005). These capabilities show progressively increasing specialization of function, along with integration of these specialized functions into complex, coordinated systems. Maturation varies intraindividually (within each child; various body systems mature at different rates) and interindividually (across children; because of differences in heredity, prenatal and perinatal history, and other variables). Maturation and adaptive operation of the brain may be put at risk by unfortunate physical influences such as improper diet, toxic substances, and physical trauma.

Severe and prolonged general undernutrition, especially of very young children, can interfere with brain maturation, increasing the risk of attention and learning disorders and perhaps some forms of E&B disorder. Additionally, deficiencies of specific vitamins, minerals, or other nutrition can be harmful to psychological functioning. A dramatic example: early in the 20th century the diets of many poor people contained too little niacin (a B vitamin), and as a result many developed pellagra, a disease affecting the skin, digestive system, and nervous system. The resulting depression, fearfulness, hallucinations, extreme confusion, loss of sensations (touch, taste, smell), and other symptoms were often misdiagnosed as a psychotic disorder (Colp, 2005).

Not every hypothesis about unfortunate dietary influences on brain disorder is valid. Feingold (1975) hypothesized that salicytic acids, found in many foods and food additives, affect genetically susceptible children by causing an allergic reaction that makes the child hyperactive. Research on Feingold's ideas indicates, however, that dietary salicylates are at most a rare cause of hyperactive children (Conners,

1980). Similarly, there is little scientific support for observations that children's E&B disorder is caused by consuming too much sugar or caffeine (Wolraich, Wilson, & White, 1995).

The ingestion of toxic substances in air, water, or food can result in brain disorders. For instance, prolonged breathing of low doses of lead from auto exhaust and flaking house paint is a suspected cause of brain disorder (US DHHS, 1999). Prolonged alcohol or substance abuse can result in enduring brain dysfunction (American Psychiatric Association, 2000).

Accidental injuries cause brain damage in thousands of children every year (Whitaker et al., 2002), a small proportion of whom show E&B disorder. Physical abuse of children can have similar results. However, child abuse more commonly has psychosocial connections to emotional and behavioral problems of children, as discussed later in this chapter. In IDEA 2004, Traumatic Brain Injury continues to be a category of education disability for students with brain disorder acquired through injury.

## Psychosocial Influences

This section briefly presents a selection of psychological, social, and cultural influences on development that seem most relevant to understanding E&B disorder of children. Although most if not all psychosocial risk factors are compatible with various theories of child development or E&B disorder, there is no attempt here to integrate these influences into any theory. Selected theoretical explanations of E&B disorder are described in Chapters 7 to 10.

It is obvious that the great majority of human behavior occurs in a social context, either in the actual presence of someone or influenced by a significant person or persons not present. Human culture depends in part on children's learning and conforming to expectations about what behaviors, emotions, thoughts, attitudes, and values are appropriate in various situations. How youngsters come to conform to—and vary from—group expectations for behavior and values are major issues in the area of study known as socialization. These issues are, of course, highly relevant to understanding E&B disorder (Karnik, 2004; Kessler, 2005).

### Family Socialization

Families provide for children in various crucial ways, including education, health, and economic support. In the psychosocial realm, families love, nurture, and socialize their children to varying extents and in different ways. Much socialization research has focused on the family because it is generally seen as such a key socializing influence on young people (Combrinck-Graham & Fox, 2002; King, 2002).

For instance, although children can have E&B disorders that do not resemble parental personality or behaviors, parents and children tend to show similarity on many kinds of behaviors, normal and disordered. Research has documented parent–child and sibling–sibling similarity in regard to nearly every pattern of E&B disorder. Some of this similarity can be attributed to heredity, but powerful socializing influences within the family are also prime considerations (Berk, 2005; DeHart et al., 2004; Wicks-Nelson & Israel, 2006).

### *Attachment*

Infancy and earliest childhood have long been seen as especially relevant to a child's psychological development. Over the last half century researchers have explored **attachment:** interactions between infant and mother (or other primary caregiver) and the special kind of affective relationship that ordinarily develops, especially as this influences the infant's interaction with the environment (Bowlby, 1988; DeHart et al., 2004). These interactions and this special relationship seem to control the infant's emerging emotions and behaviors in the first year of life and have far-reaching consequences for emotional and behavioral adjustment as the infant becomes a child, an adolescent, and an adult (Pianta, 1999).

If the infant–mother bond has developed securely, a 12- to 18-month-old child will (a) separate from mother readily to explore or play, (b) seek comfort or reassurance when a distressful situation arises (e.g., appearance of a stranger, disappearance of the caregiver), and (c) resume exploration after a brief period of calming down. However, some youngsters show inadequate attachment as evidenced by little or no exploration, distress with a stranger, or comfort-seeking when the caregiver reappears; and by disorganized, nonfunctional behaviors in response to stressful situations. Caregivers who are insensitive to the infant's needs or rejecting of infant contact, abuse or neglect the infant, or experience depression or other E&B disorder, are more likely to have an infant showing inadequate attachment (DeHart et al., 2004; Wicks-Nelson & Israel, 2006).

Extremely inadequate attachment can itself be classified as E&B disorder of early childhood (APA, 2000). Further, inadequate attachment early in life seems to be a risk factor for later development of E&B disorder (Green & Goldwyn, 2002; Lyons-Ruth, Zeanah, & Benoit, 2003; Olson, Bates, Sandy, & Lanthier, 2000), especially *Aggression* and *Depression* patterns.

### *Discipline Styles*

Developmental psychologists have extensively explored parental discipline practices, especially as they relate to children's behavior and emotional problems. Although families show great variation in discipline practices, much of this variation can be conceptualized in terms of two general kinds of parental behavior that can be termed *Accepting-Rejecting* and *Permitting-Controlling*. The hyphenated terms describe opposite extremes on two continua of discipline practices. Display 6-4 depicts these continua (compare to Becker, 1964; Boyum & Parke, 1999).

A family's typical discipline practices could be placed somewhere along each of the two continua. Parenting practices characterized by expressions of hostility, aloofness, insensitivity, disinterest, criticism, or coolness toward the child would be placed close to the Rejecting extreme of the Accepting-Rejecting continuum. Highly Accepting practices feature affection, understanding, frequent use of reasoning in delivering discipline, and avoidance of physical punishment. On the Permitting-Controlling continuum, highly

## ACCEPTING

**Indulgent Style**
- Give few restrictions or rules
- Give weak consequences for misbehavior
- Encourage dependence on parent(s)
- Tolerate and excuse child's environmental conflict
- Give help for child's personal disturbance
- Give nurturing regardless of child's behavior

**Protective Style**
- Communicate strict standards and rules, as appropriate to child's maturity
- Punish violations consistently; discuss violation and punishment
- Recognize child's strengths, problems, needs
- Commit much interpersonal and tangible nurturing contingent on child's behavior

**PERMITTING** | **CONTROLLING**

**Neglectful Style**
- Give few or illogical restrictions or rules
- Fail to recognize child's conflicts with others
- Fail to recognize child's personal distress
- Commit little interest, nurturing, or emotional involvement to child
- Give inconsistent conseqences for misbehavior

**Domineering Style**
- Impose strict standards and rules
- Recognize but do not tolerate child's conflict with others
- Recognize but do not tolerate child's personal distress
- Disapprove or physically punish violations severely
- Give little interpersonal and tangible nurturing
- Intrude, manage child's life extensively

## REJECTING

**Display 6-4** A simple model of parental discipline styles
*Sources:* Adapted from Becker, 1964; Hetherington & Martin, 1986; and Wicks-Nelson & Israel, 2003.

Permitting discipline practices involve vagueness about expectations, inconsistent enforcement of rules, and considerable toleration of inappropriate behavior. At the Controlling extreme there would be clear expectations, explicit use of rules and control over the child's activities, strict enforcement with few exceptions, and possessiveness.

Display 6-4 also shows that various combinations of these practices result in particular "styles of discipline," depicted in boxes within each quadrant. For example, parents whose practices are both highly Rejecting and highly Permitting could be said to show a neglectful style of discipline. Those who are highly Controlling and highly Accepting show a protective style.

Like many other attempts to classify things, these dimensions and styles are generalizations that should be used with caution. For example, although the domineering style can involve physical punishment, physical punishment does not automatically equal domineering style because a large majority of parents spank or otherwise corporally punish their children (Larzelere, 2000; Straus & Stewart, 1999). Still, the dimensions and styles help summarize a large body of research, including research showing that certain styles of discipline are associated with significant emotional and behavioral problems of children and adolescents (Davis, Sheeber, & Hops, 2002; Loeber,

Farrington, Stouthamer-Loeber & Van Kammen, 1998; Watson & Gross, 2000; Wicks-Nelson & Israel, 2006). The following examples illustrate this.

1. Children who show *Anxiety, Depression,* and *Relationship Problem* tend to come from families with the domineering style of discipline.
2. Disciplinary inconsistency, that is, unpredictable discipline practices, feeble attempts to control that are defeated by the child, or a discrepancy between the styles of mother and father, is often found in the families of children with *Aggression.*
3. *Law-Breaking Behavior* is common among older children whose parents are highly Permitting about behavior away from home (e.g., do not monitor their young person's whereabouts or punish violations). The linkage is especially strong if the parents model antisocial behavior and attitudes and justify their own violations and their children's.

### *Disruptions to Child-Rearing*

Discipline and other aspects of child-rearing and child care can be stable over many years, but they also are subject to modification in response to powerful factors (Hetherington, Bridges, & Insabella, 1998). Among these factors are whether the parents separate as a couple, the degree to which they exhibit conflict, and the psychological adjustment of parents (especially the mother). Such factors are influenced in complex ways by each other and by additional child and family considerations, including the child's age, gender, and temperament (discussed later) and family circumstances such as finances and social support from relatives, friends, and community or social service organizations (Boyum & Parke, 1999).

For instance, suppose a couple whose marriage is strained has a child whose behaviors are difficult to manage. They are coping with this youngster satisfactorily, through the assistance of special education and family counseling. The birth of a second child may (a) further strain the marital relationship and make outside counseling too costly to continue, resulting in a worsening of the behavior problems of the first child; (b) greatly improve the couple's relationship, help the first child feel important as one of the caregivers for the baby, and thus prevent a future case of E&B disorder; or (c) produce no change, because positive and negative effects of the birth offset each other. Despite such complexities, the abundant research in this area has begun to yield some general findings on family conflict and disruption (Emery, 1999; Greene, Anderson, Hetherington, Forgatch, & DeGarmo, 2003; Hetherington et al., 1998).

***Disruptions of the Family.*** Each year for the past three decades, the parents of more than 1 million U.S. children (mostly, young children) have divorced. More than 40 percent of U.S. children and adolescents will experience the divorce of their parents—many, two or more times. Children of divorced and separated parents are at increased risk for E&B disorder (Emery, 1999; Greene et al., 2003; Grych & Fincham, 1999; Watson & Gross, 2000). Other kinds of family disruption such as parental death, parent institutionalization because of mental disorder or crime, and loss of child custody because of neglect or abuse are also associated with children's emotional and behavioral problems.

***Parent Conflict.*** Conflict between parents, especially involving violence, is a strong risk factor for E&B disorder of children—probably stronger than divorce or separation (Kelly, 2000; Osofsky, 2003; Pelcovitz, Kaplan, DeRosa, Mandel, & Salzinger, 2000; Peris & Emery, 2004; Wolfe, Crooks, Lee, McIntyre-Smith, & Jaffe, 2003; Zimet, & Jacob, 2001). Of course, many divorces and separations are marked by bitter conflict. Thus the connection between parent conflict and increased risk for E&B disorder among children probably explains, to a considerable extent, the association between divorce and child E&B disorder.

***Parent E&B Disorder.*** A parent's personal and social maladaptation may impair parenting and increase risk for E&B disorder of the children (Barry, Dunlap, Cotten, Lochman, & Wells, 2005; Farver, Xu, Eppe, Fernandez, & Schwartz, 2005; Friedman & Chase-Lansdale, 2002; Kelley & Fals-Stewart, 2004). It is not hard to imagine that a parent showing home and community aggression, criminal offending, substance abuse, Mood Disorders, or Psychotic Disorders might be an inadequate parent and possibly contribute to the child's E&B disorder.

For example, depressed parents may not enjoy any activities, avoid social interactions, lack energy, become irritable, and openly express their despair. Such characteristics could harm parenting at each phase of child development (Lovejoy, Graczyk, Hammen & Rudolph, 2003; O'Hare, & Neuman, 2000). To illustrate, a joyless, socially avoidant mom may miss critical opportunities for attachment with her infant. Her feeble, inconsistent discipline attempts will be easily defeated by active toddlers and rebellious adolescents alike. Social withdrawal will limit her access to networks of other parents who could give help or at least sympathy. Children of any age would probably be anxious about a mother's statements of hopelessness. The children of depressed mothers are at high risk for *Depression* and other E&B disorders (Hammen & Rudolph, 2003).

***Comment on Disruptions to Child-Rearing.*** Family disruption tends to destabilize children's lives not for the rest of childhood, but for a finite period (often about 2 years), during which time there is increased risk for developing E&B disorder (Emery, 1999). There are sex differences in how children are affected by disruptions to child-rearing (Oltmanns & Emery, 2004; Rhoads, 2004). For example, after a divorce boys and girls may experience different kinds of emotional and behavior problems. Boys are more likely to show problems but less likely to receive professional support.

Finally, although we tend to think first about how parents' behavior affects their children, in fact children and parents powerfully affect each other and thus influence family relationships. Children's behavior can contribute to family disruption and affect its aftermath.

### Single Parenting

Giving birth out of wedlock and divorce are the main causes of single parenthood. Out-of-wedlock birth rate varies greatly by economic circumstances, race-ethnic groups, mother's age, and other factors (Emery, 1999; FIFCFS, 2004). From about 1960 to 1995 the U.S. out-of-wedlock birth rate tripled, to about 4.5 babies born per 100 unmarried females, and has remained at that level. But for females under 18 years, the rate has fallen sharply since 1995. Many single parents eventually marry or remarry, but there are approximately 11 million single-parent families in the U.S., involving 28 percent of all children and adolescents. The vast majority live with their single mothers.

Many of these single parents have difficulty providing for the economic, psychological, and other needs of their children (Chafel & Hadley, 2001; Lerman, 2002; Weitoft, Hjern, Haglund, & Rosen, 2003). The child of a single parent is more than five times as likely to be living in poverty as the child of married parents (FIFCFS, 2004).

### *Child Maltreatment*

Child maltreatment, especially in its less extreme forms, can be difficult to define and measure precisely. To illustrate, many parents apply strong corporal punishment to misbehavior or insist that a young person take care of himself and siblings for considerable time, situations that approach or meet some definitions of maltreatment. Discussions and data from various sources (e.g., Emery & Laumann-Billings, 2002; Office of Juvenile Justice and Delinquency Prevention [OJJDP], 2000; Wekerle & Wolfe, 2003) suggest distinguishing at least four kinds of child maltreatment, as noted in Display 6-5.

***Maltreated Children.*** Prevalence estimates of reported plus unreported maltreatment range from 1% to 10% of U.S. children. Considering just reported cases, in recent years there have been about 3 million U.S. children maltreated per year, involving an

**Display 6-5** Varieties of child maltreatment

| Term | Description | %[1] |
|---|---|---|
| Physical abuse | Physical acts that caused or could have caused physical injury to the child. | 16 |
| Sexual abuse | Involvement of the child in sexual activity to provide sexual gratification or financial benefit to the perpetrator (e.g., prostitution, pornography). | 8 |
| Physical neglect | Abandonment, expulsion from the home, failure or delay in seeking remedial health care, inadequate supervision, disregard for hazards at home, inadequate food, clothing, or shelter. | 35 |
| Nonphysical maltreatment | Extremes of verbal or emotional assaults, inadequate affection, and permitting maladaptive behaviors, including school nonattendance. | 40 |

*Sources:* OJJDP, 2000; Wekerle & Wolfe, 2003.
[1]Approximate proportion of all cases of child maltreatment that were classified as one of the four varieties listed above in 1999.

estimated 150,000 serious injuries, 300,000 sex abuse incidents (Webster & Hall, 2004), and more than 1,000 deaths. These data represent large increases over reports from past decades. About 16% of these reports were made by educators.

Large numbers of homeless, on-the-street adolescents originally left home following maltreatment in a conflicted family (Cauce, Stewart, Whitbeck, Paradise, & Hoyt, 2005). After becoming homeless they are likely to have been abused physically, sexually, or both by predatory adults or peers. Many evidence E&B disorders, especially *Anxiety* (Stewart, Steiman, Cauce, Cochran, Whitebeck, & Hoyt, 2004).

**Maltreaters.** Most maltreaters are the child's birth parent(s). Single parents living in poverty, or their partners, are especially likely to maltreat. Maltreating parents tend to live in temporary family situations, that is, with various partners or other adults with children, in households that last for some time, then dissolve. They are prone to live in violent neighborhoods with few or no social networks such as church and community group activities.

Females are more likely than males to physically abuse boys up to about age 7, and girls up to about age 14. Males are much more likely than females to sexually abuse children at any age. More than 95% of sexual assaults on children under 12 years old are committed by a family member or close acquaintance—nearly 40% by one under age 18. About three quarters of these child victims are girls.

Maltreating parents tend to be unhappy and in conflict with spouse or live-in partner and children. They generally show little ability to handle stress, abuse alcohol and drugs, show a range of antisocial behaviors, and experience depression. They are prone to use harsh criticism and physical punishment (domineering style of discipline) and engage in other unpleasant interactions with their children (see Display 6-4). It is worth emphasizing that many parents with the above characteristics (e.g., unhappy, in conflict, employ harsh discipline) do not engage in child abuse.

**Effects of Maltreatment.** After maltreatment, children often suffer emotion-related problems such as insecure attachment with the caregiver, low self-esteem, sadness, chronic emotional arousal, and anger. In the long run, their social relations tend to be poor, marked by both aggression toward and avoidance of other children (Bernet, 2005; US DHHS, 1999; Wolfe, 1999). Maltreated children, particularly if severely maltreated, are at risk for *Aggression, Anxiety*, and *Depression* patterns of E&B disorder, Law-Breaking Behavior, Learning Disorder, Substance Misuse, Suicidality connected problems, and extreme E&B disorder. They are at risk as well for death by homicide. Sexual abuse puts victims at high risk for *Depression* and *Anxiety*, posttraumatic stress disorder, and other serious problems (Emery & Laumann-Billings, 2002; Glaser, 2002; Trickett, Kurtz, & Noll, 2005; Wekerle & Wolfe, 2003).

**Comments on Child Maltreatment.** Harmful effects of maltreatment on a child's adjustment may depend on some specifics of maltreatment. These probably include kind(s) of maltreatment (many children are maltreated in more than one way), its severity, how long it continued, the child's age when abused, the sex of the child and the abuser, and his or her relationship to the abuser.

Many social and personal problems of maltreated children are similar to those of their maltreaters, suggesting a continuing, intergenerational cycle. However, it is estimated that about two thirds of maltreating parents were not themselves maltreated as children, so clearly other factors must also be important.

Data on the nature of child maltreatment, characteristics of maltreaters, and effects on children have to be viewed with caution for several reasons (US DHHS, 1999; Wekerle & Wolfe, 2003; Wolfe, 1999). Maltreatment is both overreported (most reported cases are false or cannot be substantiated) and underreported (maltreatment is often hidden, denied, and misrepresented). Much of what we know about maltreatment is based on reported cases, but it could be that reported maltreatment is dissimilar in important ways from undetected maltreatment.

## Beyond the Family

### *Peers*

Peer interaction normally begins as early as 6 months of age and evolves throughout childhood and adolescence into complex structured systems that are important socialization influences. Having friends and being a successful member of a peer group can provide social status, build self-esteem, provide the joys of companionship and affection, and offer experience with new roles and ideas that substantially contribute to personal maturity and adjustment. Conversely, unsatisfactory peer relations generally are linked to negative emotional, cognitive, and behavioral functioning (King, 2002; Nishina, Juvonen, & Witkow, 2005; Rubin, Burgess, Kennedy, & Stewart, 2003).

Some kind of problem with peer relations is a common reason for school or clinical referral of children. *Relationship Problem* and other patterns of E&B disorder involve failure to succeed in a peer group or as a friend. Problematic peer relations also are a considerable risk factor; many children with peer problems later experience school failure and dropout and ultimately show various kinds of unfortunate adult adjustment (Bierman, 2005; McFadyen-Ketchum & Dodge, 1998; Rubin et al., 2003).

Moreover, peer influence can contribute to E&B disorder. Some peers and peer groups promote school nonattendance, substance abuse, early sexuality, gang membership, illegal activity, and other attitudes and behaviors associated with patterns of E&B disorder and connected problems, especially Law-Breaking Behavior and Substance Misuse.

### *Community*

Children with emotional and behavior problems are more likely to live and attend school in areas with poverty, welfare, unemployment, dilapidated housing, inferior nutrition and medical care, single parent or unstable families, substance abuse, crime, gang activity, and adult mental illness (Chafel & Hadley, 2001; Evans, Wells, Chan, & Saltzman, 2000; FIFCFS, 2004; Friedman & Chase-Lansdale, 2002; Leventhal & Brooks-Gunn, 2000). People exposed to extremes of these living conditions, especially over many years or if born into them, are sometimes referred to as "socially disadvantaged" or a related term (e.g., socioeconomically disadvantaged, culturally deprived, very low socioeconomic status, member of the permanent underclass).

The linkage between socially disadvantaged communities and E&B disorder is the subject of much societal and professional concern (e.g., Tarnowski, Brown, & Simonian, 1999), as well as many explanatory theories (see Chapter 10). To make a long story short, bad community conditions promote E&B disorder and E&B disorder promotes bad community conditions.

Socially disadvantaged living conditions can contribute to E&B disorder in numerous ways (Karnik, 2004; Wilmshurst, 2005). Often, residents provide multiple, varied examples of violent and otherwise maladaptive behavior. Such conditions also create a pervasive climate of fear, stress, helplessness, and alienation that can complicate patterns of E&B disorder and other problems (McLoyd, 1998).

At the same time, affordable housing prompts mentally ill, unemployed, poor, incompetent, law-violating, and substance-abusing people—and their children—to move to such disadvantaged areas or to remain there while more successful residents leave. In this way, E&B disorder contributes to socially disadvantaged living conditions. Moreover, such communities usually offer few official services (e.g., mental health, medical) or informal community supports that might reduce E&B disorder of the residents (US DHHS, 1999).

Many socially disadvantaged children and adolescents enter school without essential skills expected by teachers (US DHHS, 1999). They tend to lack prerequisite knowledge for early school learning, basic classroom survival (e.g., listening, following instructions, participating with a group of children, and remaining on task), motivation to persist and complete work, and reasonable facility with standard English. These students often endure schools hampered by insufficient finances, supply and equipment problems, and personnel weaknesses such as high turnover, less training, and less experience of teachers. For these and other reasons, poor school achievement of socially disadvantaged students is often evident in first grade and likely to worsen thereafter.

It is a puzzling fact that E&B disorder rates can vary dramatically among living areas with similar degrees of poverty and socioeconomic disadvantage. Those with lower rates of E&B disorder among children tend to have active community institutions (e.g., places of worship, family associations) and leaders. Further, many children in high-risk communities not only avoid developing E&B disorder, they achieve excellent personal and social adaptation. Their resilience allows them to withstand growing up in a conflicted home, a neighborhood filled with undesirable influences, a lack of money and goods, and other conditions predictive of E&B disorder (Knapp, 2005; Rutter, 2002).

### *School*

Schooling is linked with children's adjustment and maladjustment in three general ways. First, many children bring their personal and social problems to school. As noted, many children enter school without important prerequisites to initial success. Additionally, problems stemming from family, community, or other factors are brought to or spill over into the school, presenting emotionally charged, disruptive, or disturbing situations that educators must recognize and handle (Long, Wood, & Fecser, 2001). Theft, assault, robbery, gang violence, and other offenses against students and teachers occur at, going to, or coming from school, creating disruption and fear among students and teachers (DeVoe et al., 2003; National Center for Education Statistics [NCES], 2004). Students who behave maladaptively encourage others to do so as well, by demonstrating and reinforcing misbehavior, especially in classrooms or schools in which there are many who misbehave (Barth, Dunlap, Dane, Lochman, & Wells, 2004).

Second, schooling unfortunately can also contribute to E&B disorder of young people by causing or aggravating emotional and behavioral problems. Critics of U.S. elementary and secondary education point to numerous and diverse shortcomings, including widespread disorder in schools, increases in student cheating, excessive focus on assessment and grading, inadequate college preparation of teachers, obsession with student conformity, weak preparation for noncollege careers, poor classroom instruction practices, and failure to prevent absenteeism. Teachers sometimes inadvertently encourage emotional and behavioral problems (Kauffman, 2001) when they (a) do not allow for the individuality of pupils, (b) hold inappropriately low expectations for achievement and performance that become self-fulfilling prophecies of failure, (c) incompetently manage individual and group behavior, or (d) assign irrelevant and boring tasks. Because remaining in school is a protective factor against later social and personal problems (Ripple & Luthar, 2000), schools that do not strongly oppose truancy and dropout may be, in effect, encouraging those problems to proliferate.

Third, and most importantly, schooling can improve students' emotional and behavior adjustment and reduce E&B disorder. Most educators are committed to children's emotional and behavior adjustment, as well as their learning. Educators can play a significant role in strengthening young people's mental health and preventing the need for special education services by providing an effective learning situation (Jones, Dohrn, & Dunn, 2004; Kerr & Nelson, 2006; Lane & Beebe-Frankenberger, 2004; Martella, Nelson, & Marchand-Martella, 2003; Rosenberg, Wilson, Maheady, & Sindelar, 2004; see Chapter 11) that will promote appropriate cognitive, behavioral, emotional, social, and other educational development. Further, schools can anticipate likely personal and social problems so as to provide appropriate prevention services. Teachers can activate protective factors by calling for specialized educational and other services when E&B disorders are suspected or detected. For students identified as ED, effective special education improves their personal, social, and academic functioning, encourages them to continue to participate in school, and provides support and hope.

### *Media*

Mass electronic media, including movies, radio, video games, music media, Internet websites, and especially television, continue to be powerful influences on children's socialization. Children watch TV 15 to 20 hours per week on average; about one quarter of them watch at least 35 hours per week (NCES, 2004). Electronic media frequently present situations, behaviors, information, and attitudes to which few parents would choose to expose their children, including brutal violence, widespread substance use, extremely antisocial attitudes, and explicit sex (Murray, 2003; Scharrer & Comstock, 2003). But parents are frequently ineffective in restricting such exposure.

Many people are convinced that extensive involvement in electronic mass media (e.g., heavy TV viewing) causes emotional and behavioral problems, either directly in some children or indirectly through erosion of the culture's values (Medved & Medved, 1998). Arousing, casual, explicit, or perverse sexual content on TV, the Internet, films, and video games is common, and is suspected to cause children to experience emotional problems, engage in early sexual behavior, and devalue enduring love relationships; or to prompt sexual abuse of children (Scharrer & Comstock, 2003; Thornburgh & Lin, 2002). However, the scientific evidence is not definitive. There is a growing consensus among scholars and others that electronically mediated violence increases young people's aggression and their acceptance of violence as a way to solve conflicts (Kashani, Jones, Bumby, & Thomas, 1999; Murray, 2003), although the data are not conclusive here either. It is also unclear whether harmful effects vary by child characteristics (e.g., age, sex, having a particular pattern of E&B disorder).

## Stress

Stress is a situation in which external or internal demands strain or overload a person's adaptive resources. Stress can refer to either *stressors*—events that activate, and may overwhelm, the individual's adaptive resources, or *stress effects*—physiological, cognitive, emotional, and behavioral responses, often distressing or disruptive ones, following exposure to stressors (Compas et al., 2001; Sandberg & Rutter, 2002).

### *Stressors*

Stressors include a wide variety of physical events such as hunger or other deprivation of basic needs, illness, injury, and extreme sensory stimulation; social relationship changes (e.g., separation from a loved one, family conflict or disintegration, change of school environment, acquiring a new sibling or parent), and psychological challenges, including threats to physical safety, failure to achieve an important goal, and financial setbacks. In many cases a stressor has physical, social, and psychological aspects. The likelihood that an event will act as a strong stressor depends on whether it is temporary or chronic, the number of other stressors to which the child is exposed, social support he or she receives, personal characteristics of the young person, and other considerations (Knapp, 2005; Rutter, 2002; US DHHS, 1999). Some stressors can be risk factors for E&B disorder of children (Smith, 2004).

### *Stress Effects*

Common undesired short-term stress effects include disruptions of thinking, emotions, behavior, and physiological functioning. These may include confusion, forgetting, terror, anger, hopelessness, guilt, speech dysfluencies, deterioration in behavior skills, and changes in blood circulation, breathing, hormone output, and muscle tension. It appears that long-term disturbances, as well, can be caused by stress, either a single powerful stressor or an accumulation of them (Compas et al., 2001; Dimsdale, Irwin, Keefe, & Stein, 2005; Sandberg & Rutter, 2002).

Separation from a loved one can be a strong stressor.

Scientific research, mostly with adults, has linked exposure to stressors with various emotional, behavior, and cognitive problems involving *Anxiety, Depression, Aggression,* Substance Misuse, and Suicidality. However, a given stressor experienced by different people, or the same child at different ages, may lead to very different stress effects. Of most importance here: some will experience an E&B disorder, others will not. Why this is the case is not known; authorities guess that part of the answer involves protective factors and the interaction of biological and psychosocial variables (Lahey, 2004; Rutter, 2005b).

Please note that some stress effects are not negative. In many circumstances, stressors challenge and bring out the best in people. Additionally, some authorities believe that it is during a highly stressful psychological crisis that people are most likely to critically examine their conventional behaviors, emotions, and thinking and to make adaptive changes in them. This hypothesis is one basis for "crisis-intervention" techniques used by counselors, clinicians, and special educators (Brems, 1999; Long et al., 2001; see Chapter 7).

## Interaction of Biological and Psychosocial Influences

### Diathesis-Stress

One general idea of joint biological-psychological causation of E&B disorder is **diathesis-stress**. Diathesis means a biologically based predisposition to disease or disorder. Therefore the diathesis-stress position on E&B disorder says that some individuals, because of brain disorder or other biological variables, are particularly susceptible to unfortunate effects of stressors. If powerful physical or psychosocial stressors are never encountered, the individual is unlikely to show E&B disorder. On the other hand, exposure to sufficient stressors does produce E&B disorder (Jaffee et al., 2005; McMahon et al., 2003; Murray & Bramon, 2005).

To illustrate, Benes (1995) has examined schizophrenia from a diathesis-stress perspective. In Benes' model, many people inherit a brain disorder involving abnormal functioning mainly in the limbic system, which is closely associated with control of emotions, concentration, motivation, and certain forms of logical thought. As the child develops, this abnormal brain functioning may produce "schizotypal personality," a characteristic pattern of thought, emotion, and behavior that, although noticeably different from ordinary, is not grossly maladaptive. However, if a person with this inherited abnormal brain functioning also experiences the stress of brain damage, schizophrenia may result.

## Temperament

A **temperament** is a biologically based behavior tendency or style that is apparent from birth or very early childhood (Rothbart & Bates, 1998). Temperaments differ from person to person, and some authorities propose them as the basis of individual personality. There are different theories of temperament (e.g., Buss, 1997; Kagan, 2002; Rothbart & Bates 1998). Most agree that temperaments interact with physical and social environments to modify the influence of those environments on the person. Increased risk for E&B disorder arises from only certain temperaments in interaction with some but not all environments (Sanson & Prior, 1999).

### *Thomas and Chess*

One classic theory of temperament is that of Thomas and Chess (Chess & Thomas, 2002; Thomas, Chess, & Birch, 1968), who intensively studied more than 100 children as they developed from birth into adolescence. From data collected through interviewing parents, observing in the home, testing in the clinic, and other methods, these investigators detected nine categories of temperament that, in various combinations, described the children's psychological development. Temperament patterns were fairly stable throughout childhood, and parents tended to adopt management practices that seemed most successful, considering their child's particular temperament makeup. These investigators concluded that children's temperaments, because they influence discipline and other child-rearing practices, are important long-term determinants of child behavior.

Some of the children developed emotional and behavioral difficulties. Thomas and Chess identified several temperament characteristics evident in very early childhood that typified most of these "difficult" young children: irregularity of biological functioning (e.g., sleeping, eating), avoidance of new situations, difficulty in adapting to environmental changes, and frequent, strong, negative moods and behaviors (Chess & Thomas, 2002). Children with difficult temperament tended to have stronger or longer-lasting adjustment problems if their temperament characteristics clashed with parenting practices or after exposure to other stressors (e.g., divorce).

### *Comment on Temperament*

Key issues in the study of temperament have yet to be resolved (Gordon, 2005; Muris & Ollendick, 2005; Rothbart & Bates, 1998; Wicks-Nelson & Israel, 2006), but existing research offers thought-provoking implications. For instance, suppose the effects of different child management practices depend on a child's temperament. If so, some management practices would work better with certain temperaments than with others. In the education realm, it may be possible and desirable to match various teaching and classroom management practices in school to students' temperaments (Carey, 1998; Keogh, 2003).

If temperament theories are correct, a child's temperament, as reflected in his behavior, influences the effectiveness of adult discipline (and other management) practices. If the adult modifies discipline practices based on their effectiveness, the child will have changed the kind of discipline used. Research shows that discipline and other management practices are important psychosocial influences on children's development; but to what extent are adult discipline practices controlled by biologically based child temperaments?

## COMMENT ON BIOLOGICAL AND PSYCHOSOCIAL INFLUENCES

Teachers, psychologists, and others—as school professionals and as curious citizens—are rightly interested in the fascinating research on biological contributors to children's E&B disorder, even though such information has little to do with most educational practices. Perhaps advances in our knowledge about biological factors in E&B disorder will have strong relevance to appropriate education in the future.

Researchers have struggled to isolate the effects of risk and protective factors individually and in combination (Moffit et al., 2005). Many psychosocial risks for children's E&B disorder are overlapping and interrelated. For instance, certain discipline styles are more common in families with parental conflict and among adults who maltreat their children. So what is the fundamental cause of the E&B disorder—the discipline style, the conflict, the maltreatment, or some combination? Protective factors provide another research challenge: for example, harmonious families and good schooling may reduce ill effects of undesirable effects of peers, the community, and electronic media. Which risk factors, when combined, increase the chance of E&B disorder in general or of a particular E&B disorder? Which protective factors counteract which risk factors or lower the likelihood of which E&B disorders?

Until such questions are answered, it will remain difficult to specify biological and/or psychosocial causes of an E&B disorder. But research on risks and related topics will continue to produce fascinating developments, and eventually advance our understanding of E&B disorder of children and adolescents.

## Chapter Summary

The concept of risk factors helps explain causes of E&B disorder of young people. There are biological and psychosocial risk factors.

- Biological risk factors for E&B disorder focus on the brain and disorders of brain functioning.
- Neurons, neurotransmitters, and brain systems are basic concepts related to brain functioning.
- Brain functioning has been measured in several ways, including:
  — History
  — Neurological examination
  — Neuropsychological testing
  — Physiological assessment, especially various kinds of neuroimaging
- Relationships between the brain's dysfunctioning and E&B disorder of children are not well understood at present.
- Hereditary risk factors for brain disorder are explored through:
  — Direct study of individual genes (e.g., Human Genome Project)
  — Indirect study using designs such as twin comparison research
- Physical influences before conception, prenatally, perinatally, and postnatally can increase risk for brain disorder. They include improper nutrition, illnesses, substance abuse, and injuries.
- Psychosocial influences on E&B disorder include risks associated with family socialization and risks beyond the family situation.
- Family socialization risks include:
  — Inadequate attachment of child to caregiver
  — Unfortunate discipline styles
  — Disruptions to child-rearing such as disruption of the family, parent conflict, or a parent with an E&B disorder
  — Single parenting
  — Child maltreatment
- Phenomena beyond the family that may increase risk for E&B disorder include:
  — Peer influences
  — Community socioeconomic disadvantage
  — Unhealthy school influences
  — Destructive media effects
- Many of the biological and psychosocial risk factors may operate as stressors that create maladaptive responses.

- Biological and/or psychosocial risk factors probably operate in interactive ways to yield many instances of E&B disorder.
- In diathesis-stress concepts, a brain disorder leaves the individual vulnerable to biological or psychosocial stressors, but E&B disorder occurs only when and if the individual is subjected to the stressors.
- In theories of temperament, children have biologically conditioned tendencies in their emotions, behaviors, and thinking. These tendencies interact differentially with various environments. If the child's temperament does not fit a parenting or teaching environment, both child and environment may become disordered.

## Ideas for Consideration and Discussion

1. Explore the ball-rolling-downhill analogy of child development by considering various Chapter 6 influences on normal and abnormal development. What biological and psychosocial variables could be likened to short- and long-term destinations? Forces applied to the ball? Changes in the hill's slope? Bumps, grooves, and forks? Other possible features?
2. List and explain some of the obstacles that result in our having only incomplete knowledge of the brain at present.
3. The text states or implies several risk factors for E&B disorder that involve parents. Describe as many of these risk factors as you can. Describe other parent-related risk factors not addressed in Chapter 6.
4. Research indicates that parents can contribute to the risk for their child's E&B disorder. But blaming parents may be unjust, may create resistance and resentment, and rarely leads to benefits for the child. Discuss and try to resolve the apparent contradiction between these two sentences.
5. Describe the complex relationship between a socially disadvantaged community and E&B disorder of children. Use the concepts of risk factors, protective factors, and resilience in your description. Remember that a scientific "relationship" between or among variables is a data-based generality that applies in many, but rarely all, cases.
6. a. Describe three ways that schooling was said to be related to children's emotional and behavior maladjustment. Give your own example of each.
   b. Identify some emotional and behavior problems that are dependent, to a great extent, on the fact that schooling exists.
   c. Identify some emotional and behavior problems that would exist to about the same extent even if there were no schooling.

## Resources for Further Study

www.teenpregnancy.org/whycare/sowhat.asp Adolescent single parents
faculty.washington.edu/chudler/image.html Brain imaging
www.bic.mni.mcgill.ca/ Brain imaging
www.ncptsd.va.gov/facts/specific/fs_child_sexual_abuse.html Child sex abuse

**www.childdevelopmentinfo.com/development/temperament_and_your_child.htm**
  Child temperament
**www.aacap.org/publications/factsfam/divorce.htm** Children and divorce
**www.nimh.nih.gov/publicat/teenbrain.cfm** Developing brain
**www.nlm.nih.gov/research/visible/vhp_conf/toh/abstract.htm** Digital Brain Atlas
**www.ncbi.nlm.nih.gov/books/bv.fcgi?call=bv.View..ShowSection&rid=gnd.chapter.75**
  Genes and brain diseases
**www.genome.gov/10001772** Human Genome Project
**nccanch.acf.hhs.gov/** National Clearinghouse on Child Abuse and Neglect Information
**faculty.washington.edu/chudler/cells.html** Neurons
**web.sfn.org/Template.cfm?Section=PublicResources&Template=PublicResources/ SubCategory.cfm&cat_id=6** Society for Neuroscience brain information

Chapter **Seven**

# *Psychodynamic Model*

## Chapter Objectives

**After reading this chapter, you should be able to:**
- Describe three ways E&B disorder arises, according to psychoanalysis.
- List two ways teachers determine the goal of a student's misbehavior.
- Describe how conditional positive regard creates incongruence.
- Identify ill effects of a failure identity.
- Explain the Conflict Cycle.
- State the six steps in performing Life Space Crisis Intervention.

## Can You Define These 10 Terms?

unconscious
defense mechanism
revenge goal
logical consequences
actualizing tendency

I-message
restitution
managing surface behavior
emotional first aid
clinical exploitation of life events

The psychodynamic model is concerned with the development of intrapsychic functioning—special forms of mental activity—and how this intrapsychic functioning creates normal and abnormal emotions, thoughts, and behaviors (Feist & Feist, 2006; Friedman & Shustack, 2005; Schultz & Schultz, 2005). This model views behavior and emotional problems as the observable indications of hidden intrapsychic disorders. Many variations of the psychodynamic model have been put forward over the years, including several in which its main ideas are adapted for use in school and other intervention situations for children and adolescents with E&B disorder. Psychodynamic interventions are intended to assist the young person to recognize, understand, and overcome the adverse intrapsychic functioning and negative emotions that interfere with his or her personal satisfaction, social and behavior adjustment, and educational success.

# Psychoanalysis

## Theory

The point of origin for the psychodynamic model is Sigmund Freud's psychoanalysis (Karasu, 2005; Lerner & Ehrlich, 2001; Meissner, 2005; Quintar, Lane, & Goeltz, 1998). Freud's early clinical experience with adults suffering from nervous disorders left him dissatisfied with available treatments, so he studied unconventional methods such as hypnotizing patients or encouraging them to talk about their dreams and private thoughts. Freud became convinced that people's behavior, perception of events around us, and conscious awareness of thoughts are just a small portion of human psychology, like the tip of an iceberg. Other portions below the surface—in the **unconscious** mental domain—are most crucial to understanding and correcting problems of emotion and behavior.

Unconscious phenomena are not available to the individual's awareness and cannot be willfully thought about (except under special circumstances). Much of psychoanalysis focuses on the distinction between the organized, logical activities of consciousness and the disorganized, illogical, but powerful unconscious. In understanding the psychoanalytic perspective on how E&B disorders originate and what must be done to change them, two key concepts are the personality's structure and its development through psychological stages.

### *Structure of Personality*

In psychoanalysis, personality has a three-part structure: id, ego, and superego (Friedman & Shustack, 2005; Lerner & Ehrlich, 2001; Quintar et al., 1998). The *id* contains biologically-based sexual and aggressive *drives* that provide the energy to run the entire personality system. When internal or environmental events stimulate a drive, it generates mental energy. The person experiences this higher energy level as uncomfortable psychic tension and is motivated to discharge the tension. In response to this motivation ("need"), the id operates unconsciously to create a *wish* (mental image of how psychic tension can be discharged).

The *ego*, an organization of senses, behavior, thought, and other conscious and unconscious capabilities, must attempt to discharge the psychic tension in such a way that the person will not be physically endangered. Often this means delaying fulfillment of the id's wish or selecting a safe alternative to it. When ego safely and effectively reduces tension, it takes psychic energy from the id. This energy is needed by the ego to further develop its own capabilities (perception, memory, intelligence, behavior skills) and to build defense mechanisms (discussed later) that can restrain overly threatening drives.

Ego does not consider good versus evil, only safe versus unsafe. As personality develops, the child unconsciously adopts parental (and later, societal) attitudes about moral actions and thoughts. This is the beginning of the child's *superego*, the mental referee of right and wrong. Superego emerges gradually and ideally grows powerful enough to make ego refuse an immoral course of action, even if it is safe.

### *Personality Development*

Psychoanalysis emphasizes the gradual development of personality through life stages (Karasu, 2005; Marans & Cohen, 2002; Schultz & Schultz, 2005). Each stage presents different challenges with which the developing personality must struggle. Personality develops appropriately to the extent that the individual overcomes challenges at each stage; otherwise, personality problems start to accumulate. The first stage begins in early life, and stages continue in succession into adulthood. However, Freud believed that the individual's basic personality is nearly complete, for better or worse, by about age 6 years.

When ego is able to discharge id's psychic tension, the person experiences pleasurable relief. During different stages of personality development, this pleasure is associated with different *erogeneous zones* (sensitive areas of the body). Infant pleasure involves sucking, eating, biting, and other mouth activities, which to Freud reflected the *oral* stage of personality development. In the *anal* stage (about 1 to 3 years of age), pleasure stems from elimination of body wastes. Next, pleasure is centered in the child's sex organ. In this *phallic* stage, children experience sex and aggression drive wishes that are so strong and threatening that ego alone cannot handle them, because there is no safe course of action. For instance, the young male unconsiously wishes to copulate with and possess his mother, taking the place of—or even killing—his father (the "Oedipus complex").

Such an id wish that cannot be managed by the ego creates an intense form of psychic tension referred to as *neurotic anxiety*. The neurotic anxiety brought on by the phallic stage of human development constitutes an important developmental challenge that can be resolved only through the gradual emergence of the third personality structure, superego. Superego operates unconsciously to *repress* those id wishes that are the source of neurotic anxiety. To achieve this, superego forces these wishes out of conscious awareness—into the unconscious—and keeps them blocked out.

Once the developmental challenges of the phallic stage are resolved (about age 5 or 6 years) the *latency* stage begins. If development has proceeded normally, the main aspects of personality are already in place: the ego discharges psychic tension safely and appropriately, except for those id wishes that produce neurotic anxiety and so must be repressed through the operation of the superego. One method of repression during latency is *sublimation*, a process by which anxiety-producing wishes are transformed into socially accepted behaviors such as learning, helping, creating, and making friends. Sublimation is one of several methods, collectively termed defense mechanisms, by which the personality protects an individual from consciously experiencing unbearable neurotic anxiety.

This happy, productive balance is upset by the coming of puberty, which boosts sexual and aggressive drive energies so much that they overwhelm sublimation and other established ways of handling id wishes. Thus begins the *genital* stage of development, which blends into adulthood. To master the challenge of this stage, the adolescent must not merely repress sexual and aggressive wishes toward parents, as in the phallic stage. He or she must give up such wishes entirely in order to find persons outside the family to be appropriate objects of sexual and aggressive drives.

By late adolescence, the drive energies that had been localized in various erogenous zones during earlier stages of development combine to yield mature sexual attractions, altruistic motives, adult socialization and citizenship patterns, vocational activities, and preparations for family life. These are ego and superego activities that provide the stability and security necessary for continuation of the human species.

**Display 7-1** Psychoanalytic personality development stages of children

| Name of Stage | Approximate Ages Covered (Years) |
|---|---|
| Oral | Birth to 1 |
| Anal | 1–3 |
| Phallic | 3–6 |
| Latency | 6–12 |
| Genital | 12 and older |

## *Causes of E&B Disorder According to Psychoanalysis*

As described, in the psychoanalytic view there is an ideal course of human personality development that involves a sequence of developmental stages (oral, etc.) that appear according to a fairly strict timetable. Any substantial variation from the ideal sequence and timing results in personality disturbances. Because emotions, thoughts, and behaviors are caused and controlled by unconscious psychic energies and operations, psychoanalysts view maladaptive emotions, cognitions, and behaviors, including E&B disorder, as outward manifestations of some psychic disturbance (Meissner, 2005; Quintar et al., 1998; Schultz & Schultz, 2005). Such a disturbance can result from poorly resolved conflicts, overreliance on defense mechanisms, and gross deviations of personality structure.

***Poorly Resolved Conflicts.*** During each stage of development there is a certain amount of psychic conflict between the mind and the outside world (e.g., id wishes versus practical limitations) or among the personality structures (e.g., id wishes versus superego constraints). If a psychic conflict is not resolved appropriately, it will carry over into later stages of development and even into adulthood. For example, during the anal stage of development, the child's wish to defecate conflicts with the parents' efforts to toilet train their child. If their efforts are too strict, the child may rebel and show "anal expulsive" behavior (intentionally inappropriate defecation). Although in time the child will perform appropriate toileting, the anal expulsiveness remains an unconscious part of the personality, surfacing later in life as disorderliness, cruelty, or destructiveness.

***Defense Mechanisms.*** Neurotic anxiety is produced by psychic conflicts and experienced unconsciously as intense psychic tension. Neurotic anxiety may also be experienced consciously, as extreme doubts about one's ability to control id wishes, along with negative emotions and thoughts about the consequences of such a failure. Psychoanalysis holds that we all cope with some neurotic anxiety realistically by trying to avoid situations that cause it. But when we cannot do this, we may develop **defense mechanisms**, which are unconscious mental strategies to repress neurotic anxiety (force it out of our awareness).

Psychic tension motivates learning, making friends, and other prosocial activities during latency, if the child has overcome the challenges presented by earlier stages of personality development.

However, overreliance on defense mechanisms can be psychologically dangerous. For one thing, defense mechanisms are only temporary solutions to the problem of neurotic anxiety because they do not eliminate the underlying id wishes, which will continue to generate neurotic anxiety in the future. Second, building and maintaining defense mechanisms tie up psychic energy that might otherwise be used for ego development, such as growth in the child's abilities to think and socialize. Third, defense mechanisms often involve behavior patterns that others view as weird or disturbed.

The psychodynamic literature discusses various defense mechanisms; Display 7-2 presents a selection. Besides repressing neurotic anxiety, what all defense mechanisms have in common is that they deny or distort reality and they function unconsciously so that the person is not aware of their operation (Friedman & Shustack, 2005; Meissner, 2005).

For example, in *displacement*, psychic conflict that actually stems from a relationship with person A is converted into external conflict with person B. Suppose a child has strong aggressive wishes toward her parent, but the thought of expressing them generates neurotic anxiety. Displacement of the anxiety may produce aggression, hostility, and negativism in interactions with her teachers. In another defense mechanism, *projection*, neurotic anxiety generated by a psychic conflict is converted into negative emotions about some specific thing or person (real or imagined) in the external world. The result can be a phobia (Display 7-3).

**Gross Deviations of Personality Structure.** What would happen if a part of the personality structure failed to develop properly? Some interpretations of psychosis and other extreme E&B disorders suggest that certain forms of improper parenting

**Display 7-2** Selected psychodynamic defense mechanisms

| Defense Mechanism | Description |
|---|---|
| Repression | Forcing unacceptable thoughts and feelings out of conscious awareness (this is the goal of all defense mechanisms, as well as a defense mechanism in its own right) |
| Displacement | Substituting another person for the actual object of a strong emotion |
| Isolation | Transforming emotion-laden conflicts into abstract, intellectual terms to avoid experiencing the emotions that produce anxiety |
| Reaction formation | Replacing an unacceptable thought or feeling with its opposite |
| Projection | Attributing anxiety that is actually caused by mental conflicts to some convenient pseudocause in the external environment |
| Denial | Denying the existence of unacceptable thoughts and feelings by acting as if the circumstances that produce them have not occurred |
| Regression | Falling back to an immature stage of personality development at which one was successful and comfortable |

**Display 7-3** Projection and phobia

When Ann was three, her father left home to live with his secretary. Ann was upset, but she got over it as her mother came to terms with the situation. . . . When she was four and a half she developed a generalized anxiety, fearing that her mother would disappear or that she herself would die.

She had . . . feelings she had difficulty handling. She felt in competition with her mother for her father's affections, yet she was also angry with her father, who had, after all, deserted both of them. . . . Her . . . anxiety . . . was an expression of her inability to handle her ambivalence towards her parents.

Ann became afraid that a kidnapper would come and get her during the night. . . . She protected herself by moving into her mother's bed. In play therapy sessions Ann repeatedly enacted the same fantasy with a doll family. A girl would go away with her father. A robber would kill the mother. Then the girl, who was also a doctor, would revive the mother and look after her.

She handles the anger she cannot accept by putting it outside herself and into the kidnapper, that is, by projecting it. . . . She projects her angry feelings onto the robber who kills the mother while Ann retains awareness, in the girl representing herself, only of the protective feelings towards her mother. . . . Her generalized anxiety diminished as she structured her neurosis and her life around this one phobia.

*Source:* Steinhauer & Rae-Grant, 1977, pp. 137–138.

drastically interfere with the development of ego (e.g., Mahler & Furer, 1972). This leaves the child unable to recognize his own individuality or discriminate between himself and other persons and objects. The consequences are serious intellectual, language, relationship, movement, and other disturbances found in children with psychosis.

Deficient development of the superego is one psychoanalytic explanation for serious antisocial behavior. A young male who during the phallic stage has an improper father figure, or none at all, may have no opportunity to resolve the Oedipus complex. Therefore he will fail to develop a proper superego. Without superego's restraints, this male's ego is responsive only to id drives and events in the external world. His ego must still satisfy unconscious wishes without endangering him, but it is not limited by any internalized standards for moral behavior. The result might be an adolescent who experiences neither inner anxiety before nor remorse after cheating, injuring, or performing other antisocial acts against people.

### *Other Psychodynamic Theories*

Psychoanalysis is the basis for many other psychodynamic explanations of normal and abnormal human functioning. Freud himself revised psychoanalysis several times (Meissner, 2005), and since the early years of the 20th century numerous other theoreticians and therapists have modified Freud's ideas in diverse and interesting ways (Costa & McRae, 2005; Fonagy, 2004; Merydith, 1999; Mohl, 2005).

For example, (a) while Freud emphasized biological influences on personality, some psychodynamic variations stress the power of social and cultural forces to shape normal and disturbed personality. (b) Although Freud emphasized the importance of the unconscious id in determining personality, other authorities have accentuated the role of the conscious ego, including such powerful capabilities as perceiving, remembering, thinking, acting, reasoning, and creating. (c) Some theory variations have subdivided the age-related phases of development or extended the phases into adulthood. Others have given different interpretations to—or even thrown out—id, ego, and/or superego. (d) Furthermore, many theorists have combined psychoanalytic concepts with those of behavioral, cognitive, sociological, and other models (see Chapters 8, 9, and 10).

However, even though the revisions have involved diverse and often substantial modifications of psychoanalysis, they retain the following essential psychodynamic concepts:

1. Emotional, behavioral, and cognitive functioning reflect motivations (e.g., drives, needs) that are basic to human nature. To some extent these motivations are unconscious.
2. The young child's experiences often create mental conflicts involving those basic motivations. Such conflicts are at least partially unconscious.
3. Unconscious motivations together with unconscious memories of past mental conflicts affect a person's present emotions, cognitions, and behaviors. Both adaptive and maladaptive emotions, cognitions, and behaviors are affected.
4. If understood properly, present emotions, cognitions, and behaviors can reveal the person's unconscious motivations and past conflicts. A child or adult who understands these about himself can attain better adaptation to life.

Of particular interest are psychodynamic variations that have been used in education situations with students who have maladaptive emotions and behaviors. Four of these—the social discipline, person-centered, reality therapy, and psychoeducational approaches—are presented later.

## Psychodynamic Intervention

Teachers of students with ED should be familiar with some aspects of psychodynamic child psychotherapy. However, therapist-administered child psychotherapy (psychodynamic or other) probably is not common among students identified as having ED. Relatively few take part in individual and/or group psychotherapy at school (Knitzer, Steinberg, & Fleisch et al, 1990; US DHHS, 1999), and those who do probably tend to be students in separate schools and residential institutions. Other students with ED—an unknown but probably small proportion—receive psychotherapy at clinics in addition to special education at school.

### *Psychodynamic Assessment*

Psychodynamic assessment for therapy generally requires that a properly trained, sensitive interviewer, usually the therapist herself, establish a special therapeutic relationship with the *client* (child or adult receiving therapy). In this low-structure interview (see Chapter 3), assessment is an integral part of therapy. That is, the therapist alternates within the session between assessment and therapy as she sees fit. The therapeutic relationship enables the client to reveal unconscious information that, interpreted properly by the therapist, will indicate causes of the E&B disorder in terms of past incidents and continuing maladaptive thoughts, emotions, and behaviors (Beresin & Schlozman, 2005).

Such interview assessment may be supplemented by projective personality instruments (see Chapter 3), which are intended to reveal the same kind of information as the therapeutic interview (Adams & Culbertson, 2005). In addition, there are multidisciplinary assessment procedures that explore a wide range of information on the child's past and present functioning in medical, social, personal, school, and other areas. Such multidisciplinary assessments are largely neutral theoretically, but some of the information obtained can be interpreted as indicating intrapsychic causes of E&B disorder that give directions for psychotherapy.

### *Psychodynamic Therapy*

Psychodynamic child psychotherapy may emphasize discussions (as in adult therapy) or other modes of communication, such as play, art, or drama. This depends on the child's intellectual and language competence, the therapist's preferences, limits on the time available for psychotherapy, and other factors (Corsini & Wedding, 2005; Fonagy, 2004; Kaye, 2005; Loughran, 2004; Warren & Messer, 1999). Some use a group format (Thienemann, 2005). Regardless, psychodynamic therapies for children or adolescents generally share the following similar objectives and principles:

1. To analyze unconscious psychic conflicts
2. To bring such conflicts and painful memories to conscious awareness

**Display 7-4** Summary of Psychoanalysis theory

| WHAT | Brief description | Emotions, behaviors, and thoughts reflect unconscious drives, needs, or other deep motivations. Emotional, behavior, and cognitive disturbances indicate conflicts involving these motivations. A person must understand her or his own motivations and conflicts before such disturbances can be corrected. |
|---|---|---|
| | Key terms | <u>Unconscious</u>: Not available to a person's conscious awareness |
| | | <u>Personality structure</u>: Division of psychic functioning into id, ego, and superego parts |
| | | <u>Personality development</u>: Progression through stages involving different unconscious conflicts that challenge the developing personality |
| | | <u>Neurotic anxiety</u>: Unpleasant psychic energy caused by unconscious conflict |
| | | <u>Defense mechanisms</u>: Unconscious psychic strategies to manage neurotic anxiety |
| WHO | Who is intervention appropriate for? | Children whose maladaptive emotions, behaviors, and cognitions indicate abnormal personality structure, development, or defense mechanisms. |
| | Who delivers intervention? | Therapists |
| WHEN | When and how often is intervention delivered? | At scheduled sessions involving client, therapist, and often the family |
| WHERE | In what contexts is intervention delivered? | Clinic office |
| WHY | Rationale/purpose for intervention | To help the child understand maladaptive emotions, behaviors, and cognitions as expressions of psychic conflicts, in order to resolve the conflicts |
| HOW | Selected strategies for intervention | Low-structure discussions and other activities that reveal the nature of the child's conflicts to the therapist and child |

3. To help the young person gain insight into the past and present events that underlie his maladaptive emotions, thoughts, and behaviors
4. To assist the young person toward more appropriate ways of expressing emotions and interacting with other people

To achieve these objectives, psychodynamic therapists typically establish a special relationship in which the child feels free to reveal private information and express strong emotions *(catharsis)*. The child is encouraged to project onto the therapist all the anger, fear, and other negative emotions—previously unexpressed and often unconscious—arising from past mental conflicts, especially those involving parents. When this takes place, the therapeutic process of *transference* is achieved. The therapist may then help the child understand his or her problems and plan more appropriate ways of emotional expression.

***Nonverbal Variations.*** Some child psychotherapists see play as a better therapeutic medium than talking, at least for some children. Play can be arranged by the therapist to give the child insight into her emotional conflicts or to achieve other therapeutic goals (Coppolillo, 2002; Merydith, 1999). The child's insight can then be explored further through discussions. Besides play, other forms of personal expression such as art, music, drama, literature, dance, and other activities may be used as alternative psychotherapeutic media with children and adolescents.

Sometimes educators employ nonverbal media under the direction of therapists. Such expressive therapies have been adapted for use by teachers and other staff in psychodynamically oriented education situations in such situations. It can be difficult to discriminate therapy from education for students with ED.

See Display 7-4 for a summary of the psychoanalysis theory.

## Psychodynamic Approaches for School

### Social Discipline Approach

#### *Theory*

Alfred Adler was a member of the Vienna Psychoanalytic Society, Sigmund Freud's "think tank," who left over theoretical disagreements and founded a psychodynamic variation known as Individual Psychology (Friedman & Schustack, 2005; Kelly, 1999). Some of its main tenets are:

1. People's behavior is always goal-directed, but people are often unconscious of the real goal to which their behavior is directed. Bringing the goal of one's behavior to conscious understanding is a major step toward explaining the behavior and changing it if needed.
2. The basic motivating force for human goals and behaviors is each person's need to progress from a feeling of inferiority (also referred to as inadequacy) to a feeling of mastery (or significance). The feeling of inferiority begins with the infant's helplessness, and it recurs throughout life whenever the person confronts a new challenge.
3. This striving for a feeling of mastery leads to challenges in three areas of life: social relations, vocation (school and work), and intimacy.
4. In dealing with these challenges, especially early in life, the child develops a *lifestyle* that includes goals for behavior, perspectives on one's self, and a view of the nature of other people (e.g., helpful or hurtful, accepting or rejecting, trustworthy or untrustworthy).

Adler and his student and colleague, Rudolph Dreikurs, came to the U.S. to escape the Nazi dictatorship. Dreikurs was especially interested in children's problems, including their misbehavior in school. Adapting Adler's theory, Dreikurs identified four goals of misbehavior: attention seeking, power, revenge, and helplessness (Dreikurs, 1972). When any of these goals dominates the child's lifestyle, he may behave inappropriately, sometimes extremely so (Albert, 1989; Wolfgang, 2005).

An *attention seeking* child or adolescent feels inferior unless he is receiving attention in the form of praise or criticism. Instead of obtaining adult or peer attention via achievements, he acts in ways that he thinks will produce extensive criticism or praise.

The child with a goal of *power* needs to rebel against rules, punishment, and other forms of adult control. The result is defiance, opposition, stubbornness, or laziness. Alternatively, such a student may bully or interfere with peers.

Particularly if power goal behavior has not satisfied the child's striving for mastery, it may be superseded by the **revenge goal**. This involves a child's striking back against adults who are perceived to have wronged him. For example, teachers may win a power battle through punishment and threats, but the student may retaliate by cheating, vandalizing, or other means. The child with a revenge goal may work diligently at finding methods of retaliation that successfully hurt the adult, even if they also hurt the child even more.

Children whose pursuit of attention, power, and revenge has not satisfied their striving for mastery and significance may become passive, discouraged, and unengaged in pursuing any life challenges. Their goal becomes *helplessness*: they take on a lifestyle of inadequacy and disablement, trying to get others to give up on them as well.

### *Intervention*

School intervention with the social discipline method for students with emotional and behavior problems addresses the main points summarized in Display 7-5.

**Display 7-5** Key points in Social Discipline intervention in school

1. Understand the goal of the student's misbehavior. Is it:
   - Attention seeking?
   - Power?
   - Revenge?
   - Helplessness?
2. Uncouple the goal of misbehavior from the student's actual misbehavior.
3. Implement natural and logical consequences for misbehavior.
4. Involve students in the determination of consequences.
5. Give encouragement to the student's strivings for mastery.
6. Hold democratic class meetings to develop students' self-governance and adaptive behaviors.

***Understand the Student's Goal.*** The first step in Dreikurs' social discipline intervention is to determine the goal of his misbehavior (Kelly, 1999; Wolfgang, 2005). Observing the student sometimes clearly reveals what the goal is.

Second, the goal may be evident to a teacher who is sensitive to her own reactions. If the teacher is annoyed at the student's misbehavior, his goal is probably obtaining attention. If her reaction is a feeling of being threatened, the student's goal is probably power. A feeling of being hurt or wronged suggests a revenge goal. If the student's misbehavior makes the teacher feel out-of-touch with the student—unable to communicate with or stimulate him to act adaptively—his goal is probably helplessness (Wolfgang, 2005).

The third way a teacher determines the goal of misbehavior is to talk privately with the student so as to confirm or disconfirm her tentative idea about the goal. The teacher may begin by asking the student why he misbehaved. If he does not identify the reason or misidentifies it, she suggests a possible reason (goal). To illustrate, for a power goal she could say, "Perhaps, like most people, you wanted to make sure that things are done your way?"; for a revenge goal, "Might it be that you feel very hurt about my enforcing the rule about leaving the classroom? And you want to see that I feel just as hurt?" The student may say something that confirms the teacher's hypothesis, or give nonverbal confirmation (e.g., shoulder shrugs, eye contact, or other body language, changes in facial expressions).

***Uncouple the Goal from Misbehavior.*** In the next step the teacher must help the student achieve his goal through behavior that allows him to move from inadequacy toward mastery. Therefore it is crucial to prevent the student from achieving

Disengagement from the pursuit of personal mastery may represent the student's adoption of a lifestyle of helplessness or disablement.

the goal through his misbehavior. With skill and practice the teacher will quickly recognize the goal of many misbehaviors and can respond immediately and without interference to ongoing instruction. In other cases she will have to make a delayed response or decide that his misbehavior is more important than the ongoing instruction.

***Natural or Logical Consequences.*** All people need to recognize that behavior has consequences. There are *natural* consequences for some behaviors: results brought on by a behavior with no teacher intervention necessary (e.g., a person who spits into the wind will get spit upon). For other misbehaviors, Dreikurs called for establishment of **logical consequences** that are determined democratically by students. Usually there must be some teacher input and consideration of factors beyond the teacher's control (e.g., laws, school regulations).

After they are established, the logical consequences must be strictly enforced by the teacher. In this way each student experiences freedom to misbehave, responsibility for the consequences, and a chance to grow in mastery and self-discipline. Isolation of various kinds is an allowable logical consequence, but one to be avoided insofar as possible.

***Encouragement.*** Encouragement means teacher recognition of the student's effort, improvement, independence, self-satisfaction, and other evidence of self-disciplined behavior and feelings of mastery (Dinkmeyer & Dreikurs, 1963; Wolfgang, 2005). In social discipline intervention, competition and praise are not encouragement; in fact, they harm encouragement and should be avoided. Contests and awards (e.g., "student of the week") may discourage all but the winners, undercut cooperation and peer support, and distract the student from self-improvement. Praising the student for competent products, teacher-pleasing behavior, or just "being good" can create dependence on others, imply that the student's value is little more than his output, and confirm feelings of inferiority ("How screwed-up am I? Ordinary kids don't get praised for lining up to go to lunch").

***Democratic Class Meetings.*** Regular and emergency democratic class meetings prepare students for living in a self-governing society. Meetings should be held to establish and modify logical consequences, consider significant misbehavior situations, and allow opportunities for learning desirable social behavior and thinking.

See Display 7-6 for a summary of the social discipline theory.

## Person-Centered Approach

### *Theory*

Psychological and philosophical perspectives called humanistic, existential, and phenomenological address the meaning of human existence, including each person's struggle with questions of life, death, immortality, and personal purpose (Friedman & Shustack, 2005; Gaylin, 1999; Moore, Presbury, Smith, & McKee, 1999;

**Display 7-6** Summary of Social Discipline theory

| WHAT | Brief description of theory | Emotions, behaviors, and thoughts reflect the unconscious need to progress from inferiority toward mastery. This leads each person to characteristic goals and perspectives about life. Some of them cause maladaptive emotions and behaviors. |
|---|---|---|
| | Key terms | <u>Lifestyle</u>: A person's goals in life and perspectives about self and others |
| | | <u>Uncouple</u>: Help the student achieve a goal by adaptive means |
| | | <u>Natural consequences</u>: Consequences directly produced by a behavior |
| | | <u>Logical consequences</u>: Consequences decided by students but enforced by the teacher |
| WHO | Who is intervention appropriate for? | Students whose maladaptive emotions, behaviors, and cognitions indicate a maladaptive lifestyle, especially goals |
| | Who delivers intervention? | Teachers, counselors, school psychologists |
| WHEN | When and how often is intervention delivered? | Ongoing |
| WHERE | In what contexts is intervention delivered? | In classrooms or other group settings |
| WHY | Rationale/purpose for intervention | To help the child learn adaptive behaviors and behavior goals in a social setting |
| HOW | Selected strategies for intervention | 1. Determine the goal of the student's maladaptive behavior<br>2. Uncouple goal from maladaptive behavior<br>3. Apply natural and logical consequences<br>4. Hold democratic class meetings |

Watson & Greenberg, 1998). In these perspectives, actual, objective events are not important in and of themselves. Instead, what is important is how each person subjectively perceives these events. Consequently, (a) every person's unique perceptions, experiences, and conclusions are equally valid; (b) there is no universal meaning or purpose of life; and (c) life's meaning must be discovered anew by each one of us. In fact, a search for meaning is what defines us as human.

Carl Rogers' *person-centered theory* combines some features of psychodynamic theory with a humanistic perspective. Like psychoanalysis, Rogers' theory recognizes a vast, powerful unconscious mental realm in which there is conflict between inherent motivations and realities of life. But in important ways it is the opposite of other psychodynamic perspectives. For example, instead of exploring the client's past, Rogers' therapy emphasizes his present situation, and instead of directively managing therapeutic change through authoritative questions, judgments, and advice, it helps the client to solve his own problems (Gaylin, 1999; Moore, Presbury, Smith, & McKee 1999).

According to person-centered theory, each child is born with an **actualizing tendency** that motivates him to develop all his capacities in positive ways. People are inherently motivated, for instance, to be creative and spontaneous, to freely choose goals and actions, and to pursue ever-higher levels of achievement, pleasure, consciousness, and spiritual growth. Second, the child also has an inborn feedback system that indicates whether or not any particular "experience" (emotion, thought, or behavior) is in accord with the actualizing tendency or in conflict with it. Third, each person has a need for *positive regard*—to be accepted, loved, respected, and supported—that can best be satisfied by significant others such as parents, friends, and other loved ones (Rogers, 1951).

Ideally, the child's experiences that are in accord with the actualizing tendency will generate positive regard *unconditionally*, that is, whether or not significant others are pleased by them. Unconditional positive regard enables the child to risk experiencing all the emotions, thoughts, and behaviors generated by his actualizing tendency, and to accept such experiences as a natural part of his self. Unconditional positive regard allows the child to accept and believe in himself, that is, to have a positive *self-concept*.

Of course, many experiences generated by the actualizing tendency are in conflict with parental wishes, cultural taboos, or religious prohibitions. For these experiences the child typically is not given positive regard; in fact, significant others may reject, doubt, or mistreat him. Rejection and doubt will become incorporated into his self-concept, and such a negative self-concept may result in maladaptive emotions and behavior (Gaylin, 1999; Moore et al., 1999).

At the same time, this child does receive positive regard, but conditionally, that is, when he does something the authorities want him to do. Lacking unconditional positive regard but receiving conditional positive regard, the child's need for positive regard can trap him into distorting or denying some of his actualizing experiences. This unhealthy development causes *incongruence*—psychological tension and alienation from one's true human nature. In extreme cases, incongruence amounts to E&B disorder. For instance, depressive disorders are created when a child or adult does not make free choices and control his own future.

### *Intervention*

Person-centered (also termed client-centered or nondirective) therapy or counseling is intended to help the client understand his own actualizing tendency, revitalize the inborn feedback system for actualizing experiences, and recognize how the need for positive regard has distorted his self-concept and led to incongruence. Because of each person's uniqueness, no one but the client can fully know or make decisions about these things. Therefore the counselor must not direct this process. Instead she must facilitate it by (a) establishing a trusting relationship with the client; (b) encouraging him to explore and discover his feelings, thoughts, and values; (c) communicating empathy in various ways such as *reflecting* (nonjudgmentally summarizing the client's expressed feelings, thoughts, and values); and (d) providing unconditional positive regard (Moore et al., 1999; Watson & Greenberg, 1998).

Rogers was very much concerned with education. He saw typical schooling as directive and authoritarian, providing little unconditional positive regard but much conditional regard (e.g., evaluations of behavior and learning progress, competitions), and failing to emphasize emotional growth (Rogers, 1969). He criticized schooling as a major source of incongruence and thus a major cause of E&B disorder of children.

Rogers therefore proposed reforms in how schools operate. Children should have "freedom to learn" facilitated by teachers who recognize that they cannot determine the education needs of other people, any more than a counselor can dictate her client's life purpose or the steps toward discovering it. The person-centered teacher should establish loosely structured environments that facilitate learning, creativity, and exploration and serve as resources for information and activities. The teacher must share decision making with students, who plan their own learning experiences. She should also incorporate person-centered counseling practices (e.g., trust, encouragement for personal exploration, empathy, unconditional positive regard, reflecting) within the school day. Students with ED, no less than other children and adolescents, need these elements in their education.

***Educational Adaptations.*** There are circumstances in which such ideas can be readily implemented (e.g., alternative school for students with ED), but Rogers' recommendations seem incompatible with most school situations. However, Gordon (1974), Freiberg (1999), and others have adapted them to be more suitable for school use. Some key aspects of a person-centered education are noted in Display 7-7.

Gordon's *teacher effectiveness* approach (1974) presents education and counseling practices based on Rogers' ideas, modified to acknowledge that although teachers should be counselors, they have other roles as well (e.g., managers of

---

**Display 7-7** Key points in Person-Centered intervention in school

1. Establish trust with the student through caring and respect.
2. Prevent behavior and emotional problems by anticipating potential setbacks as well as opportunities for student self-actualization.
3. Establish each student's ownership of classroom operation and of her or his own learning.
4. Provide learning activities that encourage students to explore the world and their own values, think and act creatively, value their own responses, and use the teacher as a resource.
5. Build cooperation, joint responsibility, and connections among students for each other, their schooling, and their community.
6. Respectfully confront acts that threaten individual and group growth by encouraging the offender to consider effects of the behavior on others and himself.

instruction, members of a professional team, employees of an education agency). The teacher should select emotional and behavior problems for counseling, implement problem-solving interactions with students, and help resolve problems that involve teacher and student (Wolfgang, 2005).

Regarding the solving of classroom problems, Gordon emphasized that some problems belong to the teacher, others to the student. The teacher "owns" the problem if the student's behavior causes unwanted effects on the teacher (e.g., causes a safety concern, takes away the teacher's rights or other students' rights). Otherwise, the student owns the problem.

The teacher should try to solve a problem she owns by sending an **I-message** intended to start a person-centered conversation. The I-message is, in effect, a complaint that contains three parts: student behavior, its effect, and teacher's feeling about it. To illustrate, for a student taunting another in class: "A student who taunts another student messes up the learning climate, interferes with my teaching, and may provoke a fight. This makes me feel frustrated and unappreciated, and worries me that someone would get hurt."

Following this I-message, the teacher moves to a person-centered conversation in which she facilitates student exploration of the problem through reflecting and encouraging the student to continue (nodding, "Umm-hmm," "Could you explain just a little more?"). By stating and exploring his own thoughts about the teacher's problem, the student may recognize his role in contributing to it and may learn more about himself (Gordon, 1974; Wolfgang, 2005).

If the problem belongs to the student, the teacher challenges him to try to solve it, again for the purpose of starting a person-centered conversation. The teacher then continues the person-centered conversation as above, helping the student to fully consider the behavior, why he owns this problem, and its ramifications.

Freiberg's *consistency management and cooperative discipline* (CMCD) approach (1999; Freiberg & Driscoll, 2004) recommends classroom and school practices designed to embody Rogers' counseling objectives of establishing trust, encouraging self-discovery, communicating empathy, and providing unconditional support. The key points are caring, cooperation, organization, and community, as well as prevention of problems.

- Teachers practice *caring* by listening reflectively to students, honoring their ideas and displaying their achievements, encouraging their evaluation of class activities and teaching practices, and showing respect for them as people even when correcting their misbehavior. As teachers practice caring, they model it as a way for students to interact with other people.
- *Cooperation* is encouraged by having all students help plan class discipline, assignments, and other learning activities; learn cooperatively; and perform academic and other assignments as teams. By helping create the school environment and becoming involved in it, students experience ownership of and responsibility for classroom functioning.
- Students are expected to assume joint responsibility with the teacher for classroom *organization*. They perform many regular and occasional classroom tasks (e.g., taking roll, getting supplies) and other aspects of classroom management.

- *Community* strength is built by involving families and local persons in the education effort. Parents may participate in selected learning or celebration activities, help teach lessons, and attend meetings with their child to plan, discuss, or do learning activities. Other people come to teach students about institutions, events, and jobs in the community.

Freiberg (1999) also emphasized *prevention*, which is "80 percent of classroom management" (p. 82). Behavior problems often stem from a failure to anticipate obstacles to and opportunities for helping students develop ownership of their own learning and discipline.

See Display 7-8 for a summary of the person-centered approach.

**Display 7-8** Summary of Person-Centered approach

| WHAT | Brief description of theory | Emotions, behaviors, and thoughts reflect the unconscious need to continually develop higher levels of capabilities |
|---|---|---|
| | Key terms | <u>Actualizing tendency</u>: Inherent motivation to develop greater creativity, spirituality, pleasure, freedom, and other capabilities |
| | | <u>Positive regard</u>: Love and acceptance from significant others in one's life |
| | | <u>Incongruence</u>: Maladjustment caused by denial of actualizing tendency in order to satisfy the need for positive regard |
| WHO | Who is intervention appropriate for? | Students whose maladaptive functioning indicates incongruence |
| | Who delivers intervention? | Teachers, counselors, school psychologists |
| WHEN | When and how often is intervention delivered? | At scheduled sessions with counselors and individual students or groups; in classroom activities supplemented by unscheduled counseling between teacher and student |
| WHERE | In what contexts is intervention delivered? | In low structure counseling or classroom settings; can be adapted for any classroom |
| WHY | Rationale/purpose for intervention | To help the child understand her or his maladaptive functioning as incongruence and explore experiences that support the actualizing tendency |
| HOW | Selected strategies for intervention | 1. Establish relationship of trust and caring<br>2. Encourage student to explore values<br>3. Serve as resource to self-directed learning activities<br>4. Prompt misbehaving student to consider effects on self and others |

## Reality Therapy Approach
### *Theory*
Psychiatrist William Glasser, drawing on clinical experience, work with adolescent delinquent girls, and an appreciation of moral therapy concepts (see Chapter 2), discarded or adapted many ideas of psychodynamic theory to create *reality therapy* as a method of helping people act rationally to improve their adaptation (Fuller & Fuller, 1999; Glasser, 1965). Incorporating minor changes, Glasser later renamed his ideas choice theory (Glasser, 2001).

In choice theory, the fundamental human motivation is to achieve identity, that is, a person's vision of herself as separate and distinct from all other persons. To achieve a "success identity," four basic needs must be fulfilled: *love* (giving and receiving love; also belonging, friendship, caring, and social involvement), *power* (important accomplishments, feelings of worth, recognition), *pleasure* (fun, relaxation, satisfaction), and *freedom* (independence, choice).

When these four needs are substantially unmet, the child instead adopts a "failure identity." A child with a failure identity:

1. Believes she is not cared for by, and does not care about, others. Therefore, she has difficult relations with adults and peers.
2. Questions her own performance and value as a person. Therefore, she does not feel worthwhile or recognized, at least not for prosocial or adaptive behavior.
3. Does not accept responsibility for her own life. Instead, she views her problems as caused by others, not by her own choices (Fuller & Fuller, 1999).

Glasser criticized schools (Glasser, 1969) for practices that eliminate the fun of learning, aggravate the failure identity, and block fulfillment of children's four basic needs. Major harmful schooling practices include grading, which brands many students as failures; lecture forms of information presentation, which encourage dependence and passivity; memorization and recitation assignments at the expense of discussion and participation; learning materials that are too hard or too easy for many students; and subjects that have little relevance. Schools create and perpetuate failure identities, especially through practices that encourage dependence and irresponsibility, while discouraging freedom, choice, and responsibility.

However, reality therapy does not emphasize fixing school problems or other environmental deficiencies. Glasser (1965, 1998) generally attributes any person's unhappiness and performance failure to his own irresponsibility. This includes a child or adolescent with E&B disorder, even serious mental disorders. For a student with ED, a major mission of the counselor (or teacher functioning as counselor) is to help him behave responsibly in order to meet the four needs of a success identity.

### *Intervention*
***Individual Reality Therapy.*** Reality therapy operates according to several fairly simple principles. Children with inappropriate behavior and feelings must be helped, in a personal and caring way, to acknowledge their behavior as irresponsible, and then to change it to be logical, responsible, and appropriate. The reality

therapist teaches the student to evaluate her present behaviors, set feasible behavior goals, plan how to achieve them, commit to doing so, and avoid excuses for failure (Fuller & Fuller, 1999; Wolfgang, 2005).

1. *Trust and confidence*. As in many therapies, the counselor's first task is to build a trusting relationship with the student through concerned, supportive involvement with her. He also conveys a climate of responsibility—particularly confidence that the student is able to change and that he has the experience and skills to help her do so.
2. *Present behavior*. The counselor focuses change efforts on present, rather than past, maladaptive behavior. Regarding a student's conflict, distressing behavior, or other target of concern, he may confront the problem by asking the student, "What are you doing?" The object is to require her to think about her behavior and to describe it.
3. *Self-evaluation*. To help the student evaluate her maladaptive behavior, the counselor may say, "How is what you are doing helping you?" or "How does your behavior fulfill your needs?" The counselor insists that the young person think about the outcomes of her behavior until she recognizes that it is ineffective in obtaining what she needs.
4. *Planning*. When the student acknowledges that her present behavior is ineffective and counterproductive, the counselor presses for responsible behavior that will meet one or more success identity needs. To make sure the student recognizes that she is the one responsible for her own behavior, the counselor asks what she is going to do about the situation. He must be ready to help her make specific plans: *what* will be done, *where, when*, involving *whom*, and other specifics. To make success more likely, early plans often focus on just one improvement within a short time frame.

    If appropriate, plans may include **restitution**—remedying the student's misbehavior by righting a harm it caused to another person. Restitution requires the student to recognize the unacceptable behavior and its consequence, plan a course of restitution, and act to make it right (Gossen, 1992). For instance, if the student broke something, she can fix it; if she destroyed something, she can pay for it with earned money; if she taunted or slandered someone, she could say good things about the wronged person. Restitution is favored because it builds responsibility through public acknowledgement of fault, satisfies the offender's need for power because she acquires the power to correct something, and improves her social acceptability to peers.
5. *Commitment*. The counselor must obtain the student's commitment to carry out the plan. A written commitment, perhaps in the form of a brief contract signed by the student and counselor, is preferred, especially if there may be disagreement later over what the student's commitment was.
6. *No excuses*. If the plan does not work, the counselor accepts no excuses or apologies, because these operate to undercut the commitment. Instead, the counselor asks, "When will you do what you agreed to?", insisting that the child follow the plan. If the plan looks flawed, the counselor offers to work with the

student to make a new plan. The counselor does not criticize or punish but does enforce consequences called for by the written commitment or by established discipline procedures (e.g., loss of privilege follows a rule violation).

7. *Do not give up.* From the start the counselor has had confidence that the student is able to change and that he can successfully help her do so. Failure is not acceptable. Unsuccessful attempts are fine, because the student may not really want to change until she sees and is reminded that her maladaptive behavior is ineffective in yielding what she needs. Several recyclings of the reality therapy procedures may be needed.

***Reality Therapy in the Classroom.*** Glasser calls for drastically changing the focus and activities of schools, generally to fulfill children's four needs (Glasser, 1969). For instance, he calls on schools to eliminate grading, lecture, and memorization and to encourage freedom, self-directed learning, and responsibility. Even if such a radically nontraditional form of schooling is unfeasible or undesired, reality therapy can be used in the classroom, especially a separate classroom for students with ED. This would involve practices similar to those described in steps 1 to 7 above, with modifications in recognition of realities of school life (e.g., that the teacher has instruction responsibilities, that other teachers and students share the building). The key points of school intervention according to reality therapy are presented in Display 7-9.

1. *Expectations.* The first thing for the teacher to do is to spend some time considering what he has been doing until now and how it has not succeeded. Then he must resolve to amend past inadequate management practices by applying reality therapy and expecting it to work well.

**Display 7-9** Key points in Reality Therapy intervention in school

1. Expect the student to succeed in the plan to behave responsibly.
2. Correct nuisance misbehaviors by students.
3. Therapeutically confront serious misbehavior. Say:
   "What are you doing?"
   "How is that helping?"
   "What will you do to change?"
   "What are the specifics?"
   "Let's write it down. Will you do it?"
4. Enforce reasonable discipline consequences.
5. Hold scheduled democratic class meetings to help the students practice and pursue personal responsibility.
6. Hold unscheduled meetings at which the class considers and confronts individual irresponsibility and helps the irresponsible classmate resume the pursuit of responsible behavior.

2. *Corrections*. It is neither possible nor desirable to target every discipline infraction for a reality therapy confrontation. Therefore the teacher should use a general discipline technique to correct minor violations of rules and misbehaviors: identify the student and offense, then state an alternative behavior the student ought to perform. For instance, "Brenda, stop talking to José and keep working on your assignment."
3. *Reality therapy confrontations*. Brenda may not comply right away or may even reply disrespectfully to the teacher. When this happens, the teacher should engage her in a therapeutic confrontation designed to build the student's responsibility. The steps are similar to the seven steps already described for individual counseling. The teacher directly but nonpunitively confronts the student by saying, "What are you doing?"; "Explain how that is helping you"; "What will you do to change?"; "Tell me about the what, where, when, and whom"; "Let's write this down"; "Will you do this?"

   Of course, the teacher does not let excuses or apologies substitute for a definite plan of action. If the confrontation goes on for a little while, the teacher may occasionally have the child summarize what has happened in the discussion to make sure she is attending and remembering. The student may have to suffer ordinary classroom consequences (e.g., loss of a privilege) that are part of established classroom discipline consequences or a preexisting contract for this student. Further, if she refuses to take a meaningful part in the confrontation, the student should be separated from full social participation in class activities, so she can ponder her irresponsibility and begin to think of a plan to be responsible. She may be removed to another location in the class, outside the classroom door, or to a remote location. Before reentry she might be required to present a modified plan.
4. *The class meeting*. One of Glasser's main techniques to help students achieve their four basic needs is the class meeting (Fuller & Fuller, 1999; Wolfgang, 2005). The class meeting addresses students' need for love, by having them work on social relationships and friendship; for power, by helping them achieve success and recognition; for pleasure, by making the meetings enjoyable for participants; and for freedom, by insisting that each student become more involved in independently framing goals and actions to pursue them.

   There are different kinds of class meeting. One kind is scheduled regularly. Its purpose is discussion of interesting, important, and controversial issues about school and life (e.g., school rules, preparing for middle school or a career, justice). A second kind is for evaluation of the students' learning and the teacher's instruction practices. The third kind—the social problem-solving meeting—addresses a behavior or personal problem experienced by one or more of the students. It may be scheduled or called on-the-spot if needed.

   To begin, the teacher states the problem that is the reason for the meeting (e.g., "Kendra has been bullying several classmates."). He then calls for the group to help with it, facilitates democratic procedures, and keeps the discussion moving. Each student gives examples of the problem behavior along with their bad results. Next, the problem student explains her behavior and may point out things that could have provoked it. Group members suggest corrective actions, evaluate them, and narrow the possibilities to a few. The problem student or the class as a whole then selects a plan and commits to it.

See Display 7-10 for a summary of reality therapy.

**Display 7-10** Summary of Reality therapy

| | | |
|---|---|---|
| WHAT | Brief description of theory | Emotions, behaviors, and thoughts reflect a motivation to experience a distinct identity, love, power, pleasure, and freedom. If these needs are not satisfied, irresponsible behaviors result. |
| | Key terms | <u>Success identity needs</u>: Love, power, pleasure, and freedom |
| | | <u>Failure identity</u>: Pervasive belief that one is uncared for, has no worth, can experience little joy, and is not free to choose |
| | | <u>Restitution</u>: Correcting or making up for an act that harmed someone |
| WHO | Who is intervention appropriate for? | Students whose maladaptive emotions, behaviors, and cognitions indicate a failure identity |
| | Who delivers intervention? | Teachers, counselors, school psychologists |
| WHEN | When and how often is intervention delivered? | At sessions involving counselors and individuals or groups or in ongoing classroom activities supplemented by group meetings involving all students |
| WHERE | In what contexts is intervention delivered? | In any classroom or other group setting |
| WHY | Rationale/purpose for intervention | To help a student question the value of misbehavior in satisfying love, power, pleasure, and freedom needs; plan adaptive ways to satisfy these needs; and accept responsibility for her or his own emotions, behaviors, and cognitions |
| HOW | Selected strategies for intervention | 1. Prompt student to evaluate misbehavior, especially whether it helps or hinders a success identity<br>2. Help student to accept responsibility for actions and their consequences and plan how to pursue a success identity<br>3. Insist that the student stick to the plan<br>4. Hold class meetings that support students' love, power, pleasure, and freedom needs and encourage the group to help individuals stay with their reality therapy plans |

## Psychoeducational Approach

Perhaps the main way the psychodynamic model has influenced education of students with ED is through the psychoeducational approach (Duggan & Dawson, 2004; Long & Morse, 1996; Long, Wood, & Fecser, 2001; Wood, Brendtro, Fecser, & Nichols, 1999). The psychoeducational approach relies on some key psychoanalytic concepts such as unconscious intrapsychic causes of emotions, thoughts, and behaviors. At the same time, it embraces psychodynamic variations that (a) de-emphasize id while emphasizing ego capacities as especially important for the child's personality development and improvement and (b) de-emphasize past causes while focusing on current and recent events in home and especially school that seem to be immediate causes of the student's E&B disorder.

To elaborate on (a), the psychoeducational approach gives much attention to intrapsychic conflicts associated with a student's cognitive abilities, educational skills and progress, relations with peers, and attitudes toward the teacher. These are mainly ego capabilities. Regarding (b), a main way that psychoeducationists (practitioners of this approach) intervene is by selecting school school situations that are good opportunities for helping the young person to recognize and control his problems. Psychoeducational intervention teaches students with ED how to recognize the problems they have, understand causes and results of their problems, and use this knowledge to control their own emotions, thoughts, and behaviors (Dawson, 2003; Grskovic & Goetze, 2005).

### *Theory*

The psychoeducational explanation of a student's E&B disorder is summarized by Nicholas Long's *Conflict Cycle* (Long, 1974; Long et al., 2001), a succinct depiction of causes of a student's problems. The Conflict Cycle (also called the stress cycle) holds that a student's behavior at any point in time reflects past events, current mental states, and environmental input (see Display 7-11). Every child has a unique personality structure formed early in life. One major influence on personality is how the child strikes a balance between satisfying basic biological and emotional needs and, on the other hand, meeting social requirements (mainly parent expectations). If the biological and social balance is not established, personality distortions will occur. The young person will acquire a negative perception of himself and the world, consciously and unconsciously attributing incompetence, hostility, fear, unhappiness, and other negative characteristics to himself and to others.

The Conflict Cycle depicts how the child brings these negative perceptions to school, where academic, social, and behavior expectations may activate the negative perceptions and create feelings of stress. The student tends to see the school situation as hostile or hopeless and behaves accordingly by showing symptoms of his E&B disorder manifested, for example, as *Aggression, Anxiety, Depression, Impulsiveness*, and *Relationship Problem*.

Not surprisingly, such patterns of E&B disorder typically bring about similar negative emotions and behaviors in people around him (Long & Long, 2002). To illustrate, a student's aggressive talk or behavior often provokes counteraggression and rejection

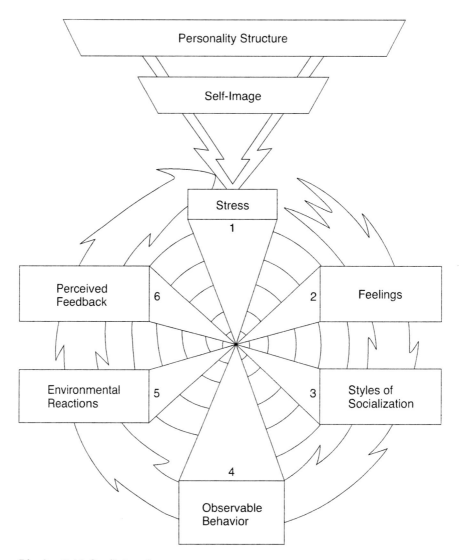

**Display 7-11** Conflict cycle
Source: Adapted from N. J. Long, 1974, p. 181. In J. M. Kauffman & C. D. Lewis (Eds.), *Teaching Children with Behavior Disorders: Personal Perspectives*. Upper Saddle River, NJ: Merrill/Prentice Hall. Reprinted with permission.

by peers, as well as restrictions and penalties by the teacher; a student's nonparticipation and sadness can induce social exclusion by peers and neglect by the teacher. Such negative social reactions serve to confirm to the student that his original negative perceptions were accurate. The situation becomes a self-perpetuating cycle of conflict and stress.

Long's Conflict Cycle streamlines psychodynamic concepts for effective communication to educators and other service providers. It serves not only to explain a psychodynamic interpretation of E&B disorder of students but to guide decisions about psychoeducational intervention.

### Intervention

**Assessment.** Psychodynamic interviewing and multidisciplinary workups can provide information useful to practitioners of the psychoeducational approach. However, because psychoeducationists emphasize recent causes and current solutions, additional information is needed about the student's "life space," that is, recent situations and problems relevant to the child's functioning in school, home, and community.

Morse (1996) described a life space assessment interview procedure between teacher and student with ED. This interview begins before the student enters the intervention situation (special class or other) and continues with additional interview sessions after the student is participating in intervention. The life space assessment interview explores important past events in the student's personal and school life, identifies significant areas of stress and strength, and helps the student formulate an initial plan for educational and personal improvement. The content and sequence of

**Display 7-12** Content and sequence of Life Space Assessment Interview

---

**Step 1: Meet with the student individually before entering the special education class or other situation.**
- Interviewer communicates support for the student.
- Initial questions should be general, such as those related to school record information.
- Knowledge of some details of the student's situation shows interest in the student as an individual and discourages student reporting of misinformation.

**Step 2:** Develop a Personal Life Time Line
- Encourage the student to recall early childhood memories.
- Use existing record to prompt recollections.
- Identify pleasant and unpleasant emotions associated with the memories.
- Gradually move to recent events and emotions.
- Encourage the student to anticipate future events (hopes).

**Step 3:** Develop an Education Time Line
- Encourage recall of school memories from earliest to most recent school events.
- Use school records to prompt recollections.
- Identify pleasant and unpleasant emotions associated with the memories.
- Gradually move to recent school events and emotions, again prompting the student to anticipate future hopes about school and thereafter.

**Step 4:** Create a Stress and Support Diagram
- In light of Personal Life and Education Time Lines, help student describe people and situations that are stressful, and those that are supportive.
- The student specifies his own weaknesses, stressors, and problems, as well as his own strengths, pleasures, and sources of support.

**Step 5:** Build a Student Day Profile
- Consider the sequence of the student's typical day (e.g., waking up, breakfast, getting ready for school, travel to school, each part of the school day, the trip home, after-school activities, chores, play, dinner, going to bed, and dreams).
- Identify hassles, fears, punishments, likes, dislikes, and other emotion-related events.

> **Step 6:** Develop a Mutually Understood Plan
> - In light of the prior steps, help the student to identify needs and goals in the areas of academic growth, other talents and goals (hobbies, sports, art, other skills), and emotional-behavioral growth (past problems to correct, new capabilities desired).
> - Student recommends practices and policies for the teacher to follow to help the student achieve the academic, emotional-behavioral, and other goals.
> - Interviewer helps student develop a set of written plans for some or all goals. If the student is reluctant or resistant, interviewer creates a provisional plan and shows the student how it represents the outcome of Steps 1–5.
> - Student and interviewer keep a copy of the Mutually Understood Plan. Copy also goes into a portfolio, along with records of progress and setbacks as education proceeds.
> - Plan is reviewed and revised in subsequent interviews between student and teacher.

Source: Morse (1996).

Morse's Life Space Assessment Interview is presented in Display 7-12. Note how the emphasis of this interview moves from assessment to education planning and yields broad knowledge about the student's perspective on his own situation.

***Scope of Psychoeducational Intervention.*** Psychoeducational intervention is an umbrella term covering various procedures for incorporating a psychodynamic view of E&B disorder into educational practice (Duggan & Dawson, 2004; Long & Long, 2002; Long & Morse, 1996; Wood et al., 1999). It stresses the building of proper adult–child relationships that can promote corrective emotional development, all in the context of social and academic skill improvement in the school or other intervention setting. As the psychoeducational approach has evolved, it has expanded by adopting useful ideas and practices, including some ordinarily associated with behavioral, cognitive, or other models (see Chapter 8, 9, and 10). Often psychoeducationists interpret in psychodynamic terms the ideas and practices adopted from other models.

***Psychoeducationist Perspective.*** To be a good psychoeducationist, the teacher should develop deep self-awareness of her own emotional strengths and weaknesses, adopt a pervasive attitude of helping and caring about children and adolescents with E&B disorder, and understand discipline as a major tool to help students with ED achieve emotional growth. Further, she must possess other characteristics of a good person (Long & Morse, 1996; Long et al., 2001).

1. ***Self awareness.*** Each teacher reacts to the maladaptive emotions and behaviors of children and adolescents with E&B disorder in personal ways, determined in part by her own personality. To better serve these students the teacher must recognize how she reacts to various emotional situations in different ways and understand why she does so. This requires insight into influential past events that created her own personality.

Another aspect of the teacher's self-awareness is her understanding of the process by which a student's behavior can disturb teachers. By using the Conflict Cycle for this purpose, the teacher can better recognize the following:
   a. The sources of the student's predisposition to disturbance (e.g., home stresses, negative perceptions of self and others)
   b. The role of stressful incidents in activating the student's negative perceptions
   c. How the student's negative perceptions and emotions become translated into maladaptive behaviors at school
   d. The reactions of the teacher and classroom peers to these maladaptive behaviors
   e. How the teacher's reactions can create additional stressful incidents that further disturb the student's emotions, thus perpetuating the Conflict Cycle

2. *Caring as intervention.* Teaching students with ED involves helping them in many ways—instruction, counseling, discipline, encouragement, and therapy, to name a few. The psychoeducational approach emphasizes caring as a major form of helping. Caring requires that teachers develop understanding of and empathy for the individual situations and difficulties of each of their students. Caring is needed to create a therapeutic relationship (Long & Morse, 1996). Caring also motivates kind, compassionate behavior toward the student (Long, 1997), such as respecting the student as a fellow human being, protecting him from his self-destructive emotions, forgiving him for the problems he has caused, persistently teaching him ways to overcome his patterns of E&B disorder, and continuing to give the student support despite his resistance.

3. *Discipline and emotional growth.* Related to caring is the psychoeducational view of discipline. The psychoeducationist conceptualizes discipline as a way to help students leave behind immature reactions to their emotions and develop more adaptive behaviors. Although many students with ED need to be controlled by the teacher at certain times, discipline is not primarily seen as a method of controlling students.

4. *Other teacher characteristics.* Good psychoeducationists should communicate expectations that the students will succeed. For instance, when a student exhibits immaturity, depression, or disruption, the teacher must communicate that she cannot accept such behavior, but that she still values the student and has strong expectations that he will give up such behavior and experience emotional growth. In addition, teachers should model the behaviors and values that they want their students to show. It is also necessary for the teacher to respect the student as a fellow human being and show that respect as often as possible through teaching and other interactions.

**Long-Term Goals of Discipline.** The psychoeducational view of discipline suggests some long-term goals that the teacher should keep in mind in planning and delivering schooling to students with ED. First, disciplinary planning and action must recognize the need to move from external control by the teacher to student self-control of emotions and behaviors. Second, discipline must help the student move from taking no responsibility for his behavior to accepting an appropriate degree of responsibility. Third, the student must move away from disciplinary control based on immediate satisfaction (e.g., via rewards) to motivation for altruistic reasons or to achieve long-term goals.

***Daily Teaching and Management.*** The psychoeducational approach calls for teaching strategies that either provide psychodynamic intervention practices in the classroom or establish the climate necessary for the use of those practices. Among them are preventive planning, group processes, managing "surface behavior," and new behavior "tools."

1. *Preventive planning.* Teachers should anticipate and prevent sources of conflict and frustration in order to prevent problems. For instance, to allay a student's feelings of anxiety due to uncertainty, teachers can give their students *support from routine* with a highly predictable daily schedule and program. Some kinds of items in the classroom (e.g., food, toys, gang clothing or paraphernalia, paints) tend to induce impulsive students to misbehave; *removing seductive objects* avoids power struggles and group disintegration. This prevention effort is an ongoing one (see **managing surface behavior** below), reconsidered regularly and as the situation changes.
2. *Group processes.* The psychoeducational approach emphasizes the need to carefully understand and use social group processes in the education of students with ED. Group processes influence relations among individual students or subgroups; teacher–student interactions; student acceptance, rejection, or isolation; and emotional-behavioral crises. For instance, effective teachers should be aware of multiple events occurring as they present individual or group instruction. They orchestrate smooth activity transitions. They also manage sessions or meetings skillfully to use the positive power of groups of young people to contribute to the emotional growth of individual students.
3. *Managing surface behavior.* Teachers of students with ED must always be ready to deal with "surface" behavior problems generated by the student's negative perceptions. Psychoeducationists recognize that fighting, crying, withdrawing, running away, and defying the teacher, for instance, may represent defense mechanisms or other observable manifestations of "below-the-surface" (unconscious) psychic conflicts. Long and Newman (1976) conceptualized four kinds of surface behavior management strategies to protect the individual student, his classmates, and the education program from harmful effects of surface behavior problems: permitting, tolerating, preventive planning, and interfering.
   - In *permitting*, the teacher clearly identifies behaviors that can and cannot be performed in school. Thus the student is reassured about expectations and does not have to "test the limits" to find out what the rules are.
   - *Tolerating* is useful when the student has yet only imperfectly learned new adaptive skills or prohibitions, or when the behavior problem is a symptom of serious psychic conflicts. In these cases, the teacher makes it clear that she neither approves of nor permits the behavior, but will tolerate it until the student is able to improve.
   - *Preventive planning*, as noted earlier, involves ongoing evaluation and adjustment of schedules, physical structure, seating patterns, and other classroom features that can affect surface behavior.
   - *Interfering* consists of various strategies the teacher uses when behavior problems persist despite permitting, tolerating, and preventing. Fagan (1996), Henley (2003),

and Long and Newman (1976) described a variety of psychoeducational interfering strategies to reduce surface behavior problems on a short-term basis, along with circumstances that might determine when each should be used. Display 7-13 presents some of these, arranged from less intense to more intense.

**Display 7-13** Psychoeducational techniques for interfering with surface behavior

| Management Technique | Description |
| --- | --- |
| Planned ignoring | If the inappropriate behavior is not likely to disrupt or spread to others, and the teacher believes that it will eventually run its course, the behavior can be ignored. |
| Signal interference | Nonverbal communication techniques (e.g., eye contact, hand gestures, facial frowns) can signal to the student a feeling of teacher disapproval and control. |
| Proximity control | Standing near a student or carefully placing one's hand on his shoulder can suppress inappropriate behavior and be a source of protection, strength, and identification for the agitated student. |
| Interest boosting | Showing interest or enthusiasm in a student's work can renew her attention to and interest in the task. |
| Tension decontamination | A humorous comment or joke may alleviate a tense and anxiety-provoking situation. |
| Hurdle lessons | Teacher assistance to a student who is frustrated by a particular assignment can prevent frustration-induced misbehavior and allow him to "hurdle" the assignment. |
| Restructuring the classroom assignment | In situations in which the lesson may be creating irritability, boredom, or conflict, classroom tension can be alleviated by immediately changing the lesson. |
| Direct appeal to values | The teacher attempts to activate whatever values a student has internalized (e.g., mutual respect with or like for the teacher, teacher's position of authority, reality of likely consequences, reaction of peers) in order to re-establish control. |
| Antiseptic bouncing | In an excited or conflictual situation, temporarily removing one of the students involved (e.g., asking her to carry a note to the office) may permit the situation to return to normal. |
| Cooling off | When a student is about to lose or has lost control of his behavior due to a stressful situation, he may leave or the teacher may remove him from the situation to a low-stress location. There he may simply regain control or may receive counseling about the situation. |
| Physical restraint | If the student has lost control of his emotions or if there is a threat of harm to someone, careful physical restraint can interrupt the behavior problem and show the pupil that the teacher cares enough to protect him from his own uncontrolled impulses. |

4. *Teaching new behavior tools.* Some problems of students with E&B disorder stem from their limited repertoire of adaptive emotion and behavior capabilities. This may show up as the repeated use of an unsuccessful way of socializing, solving disputes, dealing with disappointment, or reacting to peer pressure to break rules.

To teach new behavior tools, the teacher may simply suggest a better way of behaving or ask the student to think of several possible behaviors for a given situation. Alternatively, the teacher could schedule regular sessions to encourage behaviors and attitudes that are adaptive in various situations (Wood et al., 1999). For instance, knowing skillful and successful ways of starting conversations, sharing and taking turns, expressing sympathy, and giving genuine compliments should bring a student more joy, success, and self-confidence, along with less rejection, loneliness, anger, and disputes. Teaching social and cognitive skills to students with ED is important to proponents of other models as well.

Two other behavior tools emphasized in the psychoeducational approach are frustration management and self-control (Henley, 2003). Fagen (1996) described the teaching of frustration management, which is broken down into changing (a) the student's attitudes and perceptions toward frustration, (b) his ways of coping with frustration, and (c) his tolerance for frustration. A psychoeducational curriculum for teaching self control is presented later in this chapter.

**Life Space Crisis Intervention.** The most important form of psychoeducational intervention is Life Space Crisis Intervention (LSCI; Long & Morse, 1996; Long et al., 2001). LSCI incorporates various psychoeducational intervention ideas and techniques, including many of those noted previously. Its core technique is the life-space interview (Redl, 1959). The Life Space Interview attempts to create psychodynamic therapy-like encounters that are implemented (a) by the teacher or other practitioner who regularly works with the child (rather than a specialized therapist from outside the school) and (b) at the time of an incident of anger, phobia, hopelessness, or other crisis (rather than in a scheduled therapy session). It is an assumption of LSCI that the emotional turmoil of a crisis often provides the best opportunity for effective intervention.

Redl (1959) outlined two major goals of the Life Space Interview. *Emotional first aid* assists the student in regaining emotional composure after a crisis incident so she can return to regular activities without much delay. The student obtains some therapeutic benefit by experiencing support and comfort from the teacher and perhaps learning more adaptive ways of handling crises. However, emotional first aid is not intended to help the student gain insight about the crisis (e.g., that this incident is part of a maladaptive pattern in her life).

*Clinical exploitation of life events*, on the other hand, is meant to help the student to recognize and gain greater understanding of an emotional conflict or other issue that has eluded her conscious awareness. By skillful interviewing the psychoeducational teacher discovers and leads the student to see how the crisis was not an isolated incident but, instead, just one more instance of a pattern of self-defeating emotions and behaviors (Parese, 2002). The student may gain an insight that the

**Display 7-14** Emotional first aid techniques in Life Space Crisis Intervention

| Emotional First Aid Technique | Description |
| --- | --- |
| Drain-off of frustration acidity | When frustrations accumulate to the point that the student cannot continue in a pleasurable activity, sympathetic communication by the teacher may reduce the hostility-laden emotion. |
| Support during panic, fury, and guilt | When a student is overwhelmed by emotions, the teacher must provide ego support and help the student put the precipitating incident into perspective. |
| Communication maintenance in moments of relationship decay | When a student is so overwhelmed by frustration that he or she is likely to become uncommunicative or even lose touch with reality, the teacher needs to use any and all links possible to keep communication flowing. |
| Regulation of behavioral and social traffic | When a student fails to remember the relevance of a rule or custom, the teacher needs to remind him or her of the social conventions, without moralizing. |
| Umpire services | When a student experiences inner conflict over choices of right and wrong or external conflict with peers, the teacher must assist decision making or even make decisions that promote a "hygienic" (emotionally healthy) situation. |

present incident is a symptom of her own Conflict Cycle, one that may involve not only school but people in the home and community. To pursue either emotional first aid or clinical exploitation, the teacher implements one or more of a variety of therapeutic activities (Displays 7-14 and 7-15).

**LSCI Procedure.** LSCI provides a six-step procedure for decision and action to help the teacher choose which therapeutic activities to carry out following a crisis (Duggan & Dawson, 2004; Long et al., 2001).

In Step 1, *Crisis and De-escalation:* The teacher acknowledges the student's intense emotions stemming from a crisis incident, attempts to reduce these emotions, and keeps communication channels open.

In Step 2, *Clarify:* The teacher encourages the student to reconstruct the entire crisis incident, including what preceded and resulted from it. The teacher must "decode" as appropriate by paying close attention to the student's words and acts—even seemingly tangential ones—that may be clues to understanding the meaning of the crisis.

In Step 3, *Diagnose Central Issue:* The teacher must determine whether the crisis under consideration is (a) a troublesome incident that is not, however, closely related to his psychic conflict or (b) a symptom of the student's fundamental emotional disturbance.

**Display 7-15** Clinical exploitation of life events techniques in Life Space Crisis Intervention

| Clinical Exploitation Technique | Description |
| --- | --- |
| Red flag | When a student disruptively violates rules due to disturbing events elsewhere (in home, community, or another classroom), the teacher must identify the causal events, help the student recognize that these remote events caused his or her misbehavior, and teach the student to deal with such disturbing events. |
| Reality rub-in | When disturbed emotions or behaviors stem from a student's failure to accurately perceive a sequence of events leading to the disturbance, the teacher must correct misperceptions about the actual events that occurred and help the student link events, emotions, and environmental reactions. |
| Symptom estrangement | When a student expresses satisfaction with aggressive, exploitative, or other antisocial behavior, the teacher must contradict his or her rationalizations for these "symptoms," and plant doubts about eventual consequences of such a pattern of living. |
| Massaging numb values | When a student feels guilt and low self-esteem about impulsive misbehavior, the teacher must recall the student's positives, cast a particular failure as a learning event, and teach improved ability to self-control. |
| New-tool salesmanship | When a student truly desires to behave properly but does not know how to do so, the teacher helps him or her to understand what went wrong in particular situations and encourages the use of a wider range of behavior reactions to stress than the student currently possesses (may be paired with social skills training or the teaching of other new behavior tools). |
| Manipulate boundaries of the self | When a student misbehaves for approval of or due to manipulation by another student, the teacher must help him or her understand the nature of real friendship, the sequence of events manipulated by the other student, and, more generally, the various perspectives of several actors in a given situation. |
| Double struggle | When a student's disturbance creates anger, rigidity, fear, depression, or other maladaptive reaction in a staff member, a fellow professional can use the Conflict Cycle to help the staff member realize his or her role in perpetuating the student's disturbance. |
| Antiseptic bouncing | In an excited or conflictual situation, temporarily removing one of the students involved (e.g., asking her to carry a note to the office) may permit the situation to return to normal. |
| Cooling off | When a student is about to lose or has lost control of his behavior due to a stressful situation, he may leave or the teacher may remove him from the situation to a low-stress location. There he may simply regain control or may receive counseling about the situation. |
| Physical restraint | If the student has lost control of his emotions or if there is a threat of harm to someone, careful physical restraint can interrupt the behavior problem and show the pupil that the teacher cares enough to protect him from his own uncontrolled impulses. |

If the Step 3 decision is (a), the teacher ensures that the student is able to resume classroom activities, perhaps after providing additional emotional first aid. If the decision is (b), the teacher performs activities intended to achieve clinical exploitatation of life events. In addition, delivery of emotional first aid is continued as needed.

In Step 4, *Alternatives and Commitment:* The teacher helps the student consider alternative ways to handle the crisis incident and others like it. She secures the student's commitment to try one or more of these alternatives.

In Step 5, *Practice Alternatives:* The teacher helps the student rehearse the words and actions needed to activate those alternatives he has selected, as well as anticipate the outcomes of these behaviors.

In Step 6, *Re-enter and Follow-up:* The teacher helps the student get ready to return to a classroom or other school activity. Because the interview may last only a few minutes, often this is the activity during which the crisis occurred. The teacher may also have to prepare classmates for this return, and enlist other staff members to support the student's alternative way of handling future incidents.

See Display 7-16 for a summary of the psychoeducational approach.

## Psychodynamic Programs and Curricula

### *Program*

Social discipline, person-centered therapy, reality therapy, and psychoeducational practices can be implemented to address problems of students with ED within any education placement. However, as noted, educational interventions derived from the psychodynamic model generally seem to require large changes in the teaching philosophies and practices that are typically found in regular school situations. Thus many such interventions are more compatible with resource rooms, separate classes, separate schools, and residential placements.

***Crisis/Helping Teacher.*** For instance, William Morse's concept of Crisis/Helping Teacher (Morse, 1976) is a resource room program based on the psychoeducational approach. This program can assist regular and special classroom teachers' efforts to manage students with ED and help maintain placement of these students in regular classrooms. Morse envisioned the Crisis/Helping Teacher as a special educator who fills four roles: drop-in relief, therapy, consultation, and advocacy.

First, the Crisis/Helping Teacher is available on an immediate basis for students who are so upset or disruptive that they must temporarily leave their classroom. This drop-in role provides the student, his teacher, and the class with a few minutes or hours of relief from a distressing and perhaps behaviorally contagious situation in which everyone benefits from the student's temporary absence. The emotional first aid function of LSCI is a preferred method of carrying out this first role.

**Display 7-16** Summary of Psychoeducational approach

| WHAT | Brief description of theory | In a student with a negative view of the world, home or school stressors activate negative emotions, which create behaviors that conflict with or disturb teachers and peers. If they reciprocate the adverse behaviors, the student's negative view is confirmed, perpetuating a conflict cycle. |
|---|---|---|
| | Key terms | <u>Managing surface behavior</u>: Reducing nuisance misbehaviors that are not E&B disorder. |
| | | <u>Life Space Crisis Intervention</u>: Techniques in which a student experiencing a seriously upsetting or disruptive classroom incident receives emotional first aid and/or clinical exploitation of life events |
| | | <u>Emotional first aid</u>: Techniques that support an upset or disruptive student and help him calm down in order to resume ongoing activities |
| | | <u>Clinical exploitation of life events</u>: Techniques that promote a student's insight into unconscious reasons for his upset or disruption and recognition that the current incident is part of a self-defeating, maladaptive cycle of conflict |
| WHO | Who is intervention appropriate for? | Students whose emotions, behaviors, and cognitions indicate that they are enmeshed in a cycle of conflict |
| | Who delivers intervention? | Teachers, school psychologists, counselors |
| WHEN | When and how often is intervention delivered? | In ongoing classroom activities and during unscheduled sessions following a behavior crisis incident |
| WHERE | In what contexts is intervention delivered? | In a separate classroom or a regular classroom with access to a Crisis/Helping resource teacher |
| WHY | Rationale/purpose for intervention | To manage behavior problems while delivering instruction to a group, help a student regain composure following an incident, and help a student gain insight into unconscious emotional conflicts |
| HOW | Selected strategies for intervention | 1. Use the classroom group as a social teaching tool<br>2. Manage surface behavior by permitting, tolerating, preventive planning, and teaching appropriate behavior alternatives<br>3. Use emotional first aid and clinical exploitation practices to manage and help the student gain from behavior crises |

The second role is that of therapist. Morse and others believe that during an emotional crisis the child's personality is especially flexible and open to change. Thus crises are excellent times for helping the student recognize and change his maladaptive perceptions and behaviors through techniques such as the clinical exploitation form of LSCI.

Third, the Crisis/Helping Teacher serves as a consultant to other teachers. She coordinates among teachers and other professionals who serve the student with E&B disorder, and she is available to teach them techniques of school and classroom management (e.g., surface behavior management) and other aspects of appropriate education for the student.

The fourth role is that of mental health advocate who examines curricula, teaching and administrative practices, and other features of the school. If policies or practices are counterproductive, the Crisis/Helping Teacher works for improvements that could prevent or reduce E&B disorder.

### *Curricula*

Various curricula have been designed to help teachers translate psychodynamic principles into school activities for promoting students' behavior and emotional adjustment.

***Self-Control Curriculum.*** Fagen, Long, and Stevens (1975; Fagen & Long, 1979) developed the Self-Control Curriculum (S-CC) based on the assumptions that many cases of ED reflect a student's undeveloped ability to control her own mental impulses; that school success depends largely on the student's having positive rather than negative perceptions and emotions about herself, the material, and the teacher; and that cognitions and emotions powerfully influence each other. The S-CC is designed to teach a student self-control of impulses that may activate maladaptive behaviors and to teach positive perceptions of and feelings toward the self and the world (Edwards & O'Toole, 1998).

The S-CC authors conceptualize self-control as resulting from the proper functioning of eight personal "enabling skills," four primarily involving cognitive functioning, the other four primarily affective (emotional) (see Display 7-17). Supporting the S-CC is the *Self-Control Behavior Inventory* (Dembinski, 1979), a behavior rating scale that assesses the eight enabling skills for screening and placing students and checking their progress.

For each enabling skill, there is a rationale, curriculum units, student activities (e.g., games, discussions, role playing), and guidelines for the teacher to develop additional exercises. For example, the enabling skill "Appreciating Feelings" is supported by curriculum units that teach four aspects of appreciating feelings: identifying feelings, developing positive feelings, managing feelings, and reinterpreting feeling events. The curriculum provides advice and information about how the teacher should plan and teach S-CC activities, including how to start easy, proceed in small steps, provide repetition, show appreciation for student effort, make activities enjoyable, prepare students to use their new skills in other situations, and remain flexible.

***Other Curricula.*** A large variety of text series, activity kits, daily programs, board games, teacher and parent guidance material, and related individual and/or group curricula exist that support one or more of the psychodynamic education approaches.

**Display 7-17** Main components of the Self-Control Curriculum

| | |
|---|---|
| **Cognitive Enabling Skills** | |
| Selection | Selectively concentrating on relevant information |
| Storage | Remembering seen and heard information |
| Sequencing and Ordering | Planning and carrying out a sequence of actions |
| Anticipating Consequences | Relating own actions to likely outcomes |
| **Affective Enabling Skills** | |
| Appreciating Feelings | Recognizing, understanding, and managing emotions |
| Managing Frustration | Recognizing sources of frustration and managing reactions to them |
| Inhibition and Delay | Resisting impulses to act prematurely |
| Relaxation | Learning to relax physically and mentally and to know when to begin relaxation |

Many of these curricula present potentially emotionally arousing situations for discussion, prescribe activities intended to increase awareness of self, explore values believed to be important for self-understanding or adaptation to society, and/or teach social interactions of various kinds. A sample: *Developing Understanding of Self and Others* (DUSO; Dinkmeyer & Dinkmeyer, 1982) uses social discipline principles to deliver lessons in personal development for young students. The *Consistency Management and Cooperative Discipline* program (Freiberg, 1999), based on person-centered counseling principles, has been implemented schoolwide and district-wide as a violence and disruption prevention program. *Teaching Self-Control: A Curriculum for Responsible Behavior* (Henley, 2003) presents daily activities by which teachers can implement a classroom reflecting psychoeducational techniques for ordinary classroom management and intervention for a crisis. *Developmental Therapy* (Wood, Davis, Swindle, & Quirk, 1996) provides psychoeducational and other activities to promote appropriate development and functioning in four main realms: communication, socialization, thinking and academics, and other behavior. Activities and goals differ with advancing stages of development, but all provide occasions for therapeutic interactions among the individual child, group, and teachers.

Although such curricula differ in style, activities, and format, all address concerns that are compatible with the psychodynamic model. They teach, for example, emotions and their development, cognitions about self and others, how emotions and cognitions drive behavior, the interplay of cognitive and emotional mental activities, adaptive social interactions with peers and adults, and how awareness of one's own emotions can control behavior—especially problem behavior.

## Chapter Summary

Freud's psychoanalysis and many variations constitute the psychodynamic model. Variations of this model that have strong relevance to education of students with ED include social discipline, person-centered, reality therapy, and the psychoeducational approaches.

- Psychoanalysis proposes a personality structure consisting of id as the energy source of personality, ego as manager of this energy, and superego as influence for moral behavior.
  — Id, ego, and superego develop during childhood stages and operate unconsciously to control emotions, behaviors, and thoughts—abnormal as well as normal.
  — E&B disorder results from conflicts involving the mental structures, excessive use of defense mechanisms, or improper development of id, ego, or superego.
- Nearly all variations of psychoanalysis hold that emotions, behaviors, and thoughts reflect unconscious motivations, and the young person who deeply understands these motivations will better control them.
- In Social Discipline, people need to progress from feelings of inadequacy about challenges to feelings of mastery over them.
  — Children's misbehavior reflects perversions of this need into the goals of seeking attention, power, revenge, or helplessness.
  — The teacher determines which goal misbehavior serves, helps the student progress from inadequacy to mastery, and provides natural or logical consequences for misbehavior.
- In the Person-Centered approach, an inborn actualizing tendency motivates human attempts to pursue ever-continuing personal growth.
  — This motivation is perverted by social pressures, creating incongruence between the actualizing tendency and reality, leading to maladaptive emotions and behaviors.
  — Intervention helps the student discover and support her actualizing tendency, and reject experiences that cause incongruence. The teacher builds trust and student involvement to help the student make changes.
- In Reality Therapy, people have four needs: love, power, pleasure, and freedom.
  — A young person whose needs are not fulfilled will not accept responsibility for his own life and may exhibit E&B disorder.
  — Reality Therapy helps the student recognize personal responsibility for behavior, plan improvements, and put the plan into action. When the student behaves irresponsibly, the teacher uses confrontation to help him recognize this and commit to improve.
- In the Psychoeducational approach, the Conflict Cycle explains a student's E&B disorder and suggests interventions.
  — Teachers should understand themselves, care about their students, plan so as to prevent problems, design group activities to help individuals, manage

surface behavior problems, teach adaptive behavior, and use curricula that aid student self-understanding.
— To use Life Space Crisis Intervention for a crisis, the teacher decides whether to defuse it through emotional first aid or use clinical exploitation of life events to help the student deeply understand his own E&B disorder.

## IDEAS FOR CONSIDERATION AND DISCUSSION

1. Explain three ways by which E&B disorders are caused, according to psychoanalysis.
2. Consider the defense mechanisms listed in Display 7-2. For each, present an emotional and behavior problem that seems to illustrate the defense mechanisms. (For these illustrations you can overlook the fact that, to produce E&B disorder, defense mechanisms generally operate at the unconscious level.)
3. Describe at least three points that psychoanalysis, the social discipline approach, the person-centered approach, reality therapy, and the psychoeducational approach have in common.
4. Consider how the person-centered approach could be used to educate students with ED in regular class and separate class education environments. Illustrate how this approach would be put into effect in each environment. In what ways might it need to be modified for use in each?
5. Consider how the reality therapy approach could be used to educate students with ED in regular class and separate class education environments. Illustrate how this approach would be put into effect in each environment. In what ways might it need to be modified for use in each?
6. Describe each of the six phases of the Conflict Cycle as a possible explanation of the origin and continuation of emotional and behavior problems at school. At each step, state one or more actions the teacher, counselor, or school psychologist can take to prevent or reduce such problems.

## RESOURCES FOR FURTHER STUDY

**ourworld.compuserve.com/homepages/hstein/** Alfred Adler Institute
**www.maginationpress.com/bbytopic.html** Bibliotherapy
**www.infed.org/thinkers/et-rogers.htm** Carl Rogers, core conditions and education
**www.BehaviorAdvisor.com/** Dr. Mac's psychoeducational interventions for teachers
**www.lsci.org/** Life Space Crisis Intervention
**maxweber.hunter.cuny.edu/pub/eres/EDSPC715_MCINTYRE/why_web_page_insert.html** Mistaken goals illustrated
**www.angelfire.com/ab/brightminds/** Reality therapy and choice theory
**wik.ed.uiuc.edu/index.php/Dreikurs,_Rudolf** Rudolph Dreikurs
**www.childanalysis.org/** The Association for Child Psychoanalysis
**www.gordontraining.com/tgorigins.asp** Thomas Gordon and TET
**www.itaa-net.org/** Transactional analysis
**www.wglasser.com/** William Glasser Institute

Chapter **Eight**

# *Behavioral Model*

## CHAPTER OBJECTIVES

**After reading this chapter, you should be able to:**
- State how positive and negative reinforcement are alike, and how they are opposite.
- State how a teacher can inadvertently teach inappropriate behavior through positive reinforcement.
- State how a teacher can inadvertently teach inappropriate behavior through negative reinforcement.
- Describe how applied behavior analysis supports the behavioral model.
- Discriminate interdependent and dependent group contingencies.
- Identify three forms of behavioral self-management.

## CAN YOU DEFINE THESE 10 TERMS?

operant
consequence
antecedent
schedule
ABAB research design

differential reinforcement
timeout from reinforcement
matching
levels system
behavioral contract

### Summary of Behavioral Model

| WHAT | Name of Theory | Operant Conditioning |
|---|---|---|
| | Brief description of theory | Behavior is controlled by stimuli that precede or follow it. E&B disorders of children consist of behaviors that occur too much or too little, and are thus judged as inappropriate. Educators can modify behavior to be more appropriate by decreasing behaviors that occur too much and increasing those that occur too little. |
| | Key terms | <u>Operant</u>: A behavior affected by its consequence<br><u>Consequence</u>: A stimulus that follows and affects the operant<br><u>Antecedent</u>: A stimulus that precedes and affects the operant<br><u>Positive reinforcement</u>: Strengthening of an operant by a consequence that involves the addition of a stimulus<br>*(continued)* |

## Summary of Behavioral Model (Continued)

| WHAT | Name of Theory | Operant Conditioning |
|---|---|---|
| | | Negative reinforcement: Strengthening of an operant by a consequence that involves the subtraction of a stimulus |
| | | Punishment: Process in which an operant is weakened by a consequence |
| | | Positive reinforcement (as cause of E&B disorder): Social attention allocated to a student's maladaptive behaviors |
| | | Negative reinforcement (as cause of E&B disorder): A student's aggression or fearfulness may coerce others to withdraw requests for adaptive behavior or otherwise give in to the student |
| | | Applied behavior analysis: Use and experimental evaluation of procedures for improving important human behaviors |
| WHO | Who is intervention appropriate for? | A student who performs behaviors that are inappropriate because their frequency, intensity, or duration is far too low or high |
| | Who delivers intervention? | Teachers, school psychologists, other school personnel, parents, and fellow students |
| WHEN | When and how often is intervention delivered? | In most applications, continuously in the education setting |
| WHERE | In what contexts is intervention delivered? | Some behavioral interventions suit any education setting; others are better suited to resource rooms, separate classrooms, separate schools, or residential settings |
| WHY | Rationale/purpose for intervention | To increase the student's desirable, adaptive behaviors and decrease undesirable, maladaptive behaviors |
| HOW | Selected strategies for intervention | 1. Positive reinforcement through social attention, preferred activities, or tokens<br>2. Extinction through withholding teacher and peer social attention<br>3. Aversive punishment through penalty marks or positive practice<br>4. Forfeiture punishment through response cost or timeout from reinforcement<br>5. Positive approaches to behavior reduction such as DRL and DRI<br>6. Group contingencies<br>7. Antecedent control strategies<br>8. Behavioral self-management<br>9. Behavior modification packages or programs |

The behavioral model includes several theories and points of view about the nature and control of behavior (Jacob & Pelham, 2005; Schultz & Schultz, 2005; Vitulano & Tebes, 2002). Despite interesting disagreements among these variations, there are two key points that clearly mark the behavioral model: (a) its assumption that behavior—including maladaptive behavior of students—is determined by certain scientifically demonstrated principles of learning and (b) its commitment to scientific methods of studying behavior and behavior change. Although the behavioral model owes much to the contributions of various pioneers, B.F. Skinner's work on *operant conditioning* went far beyond others in its amount, detail, and impact on how educators and psychologists view human behavior and treat emotional and behavior (E&B) disorder (Kazdin, 1978; Miltenberger, 2004; Tryon, 2001).

## BEHAVIORAL THEORY

Operant conditioning recognizes that people's behavior is influenced by some biological and psychosocial factors. However, this theory focuses on understanding behavior in terms of its relationships to environmental stimuli of various kinds that precede or follow the behavior (Miller, 2006; Miltenberger, 2004; Skinner, 1969). In operant conditioning, a researcher or practitioner "understands" a behavior when she can control it by manipulating environmental stimuli.

Skinner found that there are two varieties of behavior: respondents and operants. Respondents are behaviors that temporarily adapt the person to stimuli that are intense, or otherwise help improve his chances for survival. **Operants** are behaviors that operate on and are affected by stimuli that follow them.

### Respondents

A *respondent* is a behavior that is almost invariably *elicited* by (produced in reaction to) a stimulus that precedes it. This stimulus may originate in the external environment or from within the person. Respondents include behaviors of the autonomic nervous system as well as the glands and muscles it controls. For instance, bright light can elicit reflexive contraction of the eye's pupils; food in the mouth can elicit salivation; intense stimuli (e.g., loud sounds, physical blows) can elicit changes in breathing, blood circulation, hormone levels, and muscular activity. A respondent ordinarily is not affected by a stimulus that follows it.

Respondent conditioning and respondent extinction are learning processes concerned mainly with changes in the stimuli that elicit a respondent. In respondent conditioning, a stimulus that originally could not elicit some particular respondent acquires the power to do so. In respondent extinction, a stimulus loses its acquired power to elicit a respondent.

For instance, respondent extinction is a basis for systematic desensitization, an intervention long used by clinical behavior therapists to reduce *Anxiety* of adults

(Head & Gross, 2003; Jacob & Pelham, 2005). This procedure involves gradual exposure to the stimuli that elicit anxious behaviors, thoughts, and physiological reactions. As a result, over time those stimuli no longer elicit the maladaptive responses. Although this intervention can be highly effective, few students with E&B disorder receive systematic desensitization or any other intervention based on respondent conditioning, in school.

## Operants

An *operant* is a behavior that can be affected by its **consequence** (a stimulus that follows and influences the operant). An operant is *emitted* by the person, and depending on what consequence follows, that operant behavior may become more likely to be emitted again or it may become less likely.

Operant behavior is a very broad category. It includes behaviors that are necessary for individual survival (e.g., traveling to a source of water), those that are important for the individual or his group to flourish (acting cooperatively to perform large or complex tasks), other behaviors that may imperil the individual and those around her (needlessly consuming scarce resources), as well as many behaviors of which the benefits or detriments, if any, are not easy to determine (watching a little television). Operants are the more relevant variety of behavior for understanding E&B disorder of children and adolescents.

*Operant conditioning* involves principles that describe the relationship between operants and the stimuli that influence them. These stimuli include not only several forms of consequences, but **antecedents** (stimuli that precede and influence operants) as well. The relationship of operant behaviors to their antecedent and consequent stimuli is called the three-term contingency or A-B-C model (Display 8-1). Operant conditioning is based on a great amount of research in laboratories and real-life settings (Agras, & Wilson, 2005; Fink & Lotspeich, 2004; Jacob & Pelham, 2005; Lewis, Lewis-Palmer, Newcomer, & Stichter, 2004; Skinner, 1953, 1969; Tryon, 2001).

### *Consequences*

A consequence may *strengthen* the operant it follows (i.e., increase the probability that the operant will recur in the future), or may *weaken*, it (decrease its probability of recurrence). For a consequence to strengthen or weaken the behavior it follows, it must be *contingent* upon the occurrence of that behavior. A contingent consequence is one that takes place only after a particular behavior is performed. A noncontingent consequence—one that happens whether or not that behavior is performed—ordinarily does not affect behavior.

**Reinforcement.** Reinforcement is the process by which a behavior is strengthened because it currently results in a contingent consequence. Contingent consequences that do strengthen behavior are called *reinforcers*. Certainly many reinforcers are perceived as pleasant by the behaver; but not all reinforcers are pleasant, and

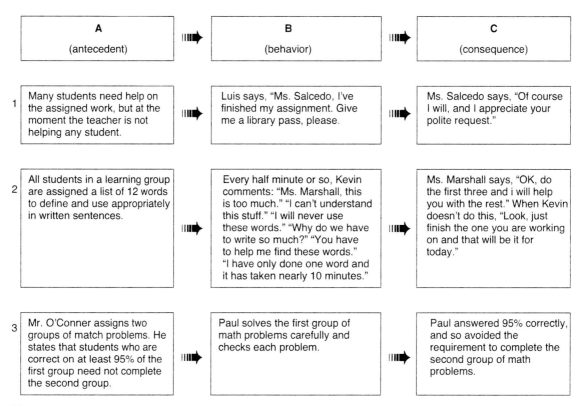

**Display 8-1** A-B-C contingency, with examples

pleasant stimuli do not necessarily reinforce behavior. Instead, reinforcement is defined objectively by two facts: a contingency between the behavior and its consequences, and a strengthening of the behavior.

There are two variations of reinforcement: positive reinforcement and negative reinforcement. In *positive reinforcement*, the consequence for the strengthened operant behavior involves the addition of something (a positive reinforcer) after the behavior occurs. Suppose that a student says "please" when he asks the teacher to use the classroom library, and that if the teacher gives permission and praises the student for saying "please," the student is more likely to say "please" when making a library request in the future (see Example 1 of Display 8-1). The teacher's compliance with the request and his praise for saying "please" act as a positive reinforcer for the operant verbal behavior "please."

In the *negative reinforcement* process, the consequence for a strengthened behavior involves the subtraction of something (a negative reinforcer) after the behavior occurs. Suppose that when a student is instructed to complete a number of vocabulary practice items independently, he complains that it is too much to do. The teacher decides to reduce the number of items required of that student. In the future the student is more likely to complain when requested to do vocabulary practice. The practice assignment is a negative reinforcer because its subtraction (removal and replacement by an easier requirement) strengthens the preceding operant behavior (complaining when presented with a practice assignment).

*Extinction* is the process in which a behavior that once received reinforcing consequences is no longer reinforced. Extinction weakens the operant, returning its strength to about the level that existed before it was on the reinforcement contingency.

**Punishment.** Operant conditioning also includes procedures for weakening behavior. Punishment is a process in which a behavior is followed by a consequence, and thereafter that behavior is less likely to occur. As with reinforcement, punishment is defined by the effect of a contingent consequence on the strength (future probability) of a behavior. It is not defined by how unpleasant the consequence seems to be. To put it another way, admonitions, penalties, and pain do not necessarily work as punishment, and punishment of an operant can occur without any pain or coercion.

Also as with reinforcement, there are two varieties of punishment. Behavior can be weakened by a consequence that adds something to the environment (usually a negative reinforcer) after the behavior occurs or by a consequence that subtracts something (usually a positive reinforcer) from the environment.

Operant conditioning research with humans has examined punishment less frequently than reinforcement. Unquestionably, human behavior can be weakened through punishment, and some school interventions for E&B disorder are improved by the careful application of punishment (e.g., Conyers et al., 2004; Walker, Ramsey, & Gresham, 2004). However, there are many unanswered questions about how punishment works (Kazdin, 2001; Miller, 2006). Also, punishment may produce unintended and undesirable results, especially when used improperly or unscrupulously. Of course, this is also true of reinforcement, as well as any powerful intervention technique.

Once a punishment contingency is discontinued, the operant behavior often shows *recovery*. The behavior's strength increases to about what it was before the punishment contingency.

Display 8-2 summarizes the operant conditioning processes and their relation to consequences. It shows that the processes in the boxes are determined by (a) the effect the consequence has on the status of the postbehavior environment, and (b) the future likelihood of occurrence of the behavior.

**Schedules.** An operant may be reinforced according to many different rules: every instance it occurs, every 17th instance it occurs, the first instance it occurs after 6 minutes have elapsed, and numerous other possibilities. A rule that specifies the details of such relationships between a behavior and its consequences is called a **schedule**. Schedules powerfully determine how consequences affect operants: well-controlled laboratory research has demonstrated that an investigator can predict and control behavior on the basis of the reinforcement schedule put into effect. However, in practical settings such as classrooms, most reinforcement schedules are difficult to put into effect with precision.

**Display 8-2** Operant conditioning processes as related to behavior strength and consequences

| Operant Conditioning Process | Behavior Strength (Future Likelihood) | Consequences (Stimulus Change Following Behavior) |
|---|---|---|
| • Positive Reinforcement | Increased[1] | Stimulus added |
| • Negative Reinforcement | Increased[1] | Stimulus subtracted |
| • Recovery[2] | Increased | No change |
| • Aversive Punishment[3] | Decreased[4] | Stimulus added |
| • Forfeiture Punishment[3] | Decreased[4] | Stimulus subtracted |
| • Extinction[5] | Decreased | No change |

[1] Or maintained at high strength if the behavior's strength is already high.
[2] Assuming that the behavior formerly was on a punishment contingency.
[3] Aversive punishment is also termed positive punishment (stimulus added contingent on behavior); forfeiture punishment is also called negative punishment (stimulus subtracted).
[4] Or maintained at low strength if the behavior's strength is already low.
[5] Assuming that the behavior formerly was on a reinforcement contingency.

From the behaver's point of view, there are two general types of schedule: predictable and unpredictable. For instance, sooner or later a student will be able to predict what the schedule is if she is reinforced:

1. Every instance that she emits a particular behavior (*continuous* schedule)
2. Every $n^{th}$ instance she does so (*fixed-ratio* schedule)
3. The first instance she emits the behavior after a specific interval of time (*fixed-interval* schedule)
4. If reinforcement is never provided for the behavior (*extinction* schedule).

On the other hand, the student will not be able to predict which instance of a reinforceable behavior will actually be reinforced if:

5. The behavior must occur a variable number of instances before the next instance is reinforced (*variable-ratio* schedule)
6. Variable periods of time must elapse before the next instance can be reinforced (*variable-interval* schedule)

For many learning situations, behaviorists recommend that teachers use the continuous predictable schedule during the early stages of learning and gradually change to an unpredictable schedule. The continuous schedule is most likely to facilitate behavior improvement in the early stages. An unpredictable schedule tends to cause the behavior to be emitted persistently even when reinforcement becomes very infrequent, as it often does in real life. For this reason, unpredictable schedules promote behavior maintenance (durable responding). This is crucial because all too often interventions improve students' adaptive behaviors but these improvements do not last. Alberto and Troutman (2006) and Martella, Nelson, and Marchand-Martella (2003) summarized practices to support behavior maintenance.

***Behavior Classes.*** The discussion of reinforcement referred to "the strengthening of operants" as if the identical operant would occur again in the future. Actually, the physical aspects of an operant are rarely identical from occurrence to occurrence. For example, each instance of a student's complaining will differ at least slightly in wording, intensity, tone, and so on. Still, if different instances of complaining are followed by a reduced assignment, they all serve the same "function." In this example the function is negative reinforcement. Reinforcement for one instance of complaining strengthens other ways of complaining as well. The various ways of complaining constitute a *functional behavior class* (also called functional response class).

When reinforcement for a particular behavior also strengthens other behaviors, the phenomenon is known as *behavior generalization*. The other behaviors may be slight variations of the reinforced behavior ("I hate this vocabulary practice crap," and "I ain't gonna do vocabulary work today"), but they might be physically dissimilar (e.g., student turns over his desk or reports an excruciating, assignment-prohibitive headache). If reinforcement for complaining increases the likelihood of other behaviors that avoid vocabulary work, behavior generalization has taken place. Complaining, physically disrupting, and reporting pain are instances of the same functional behavior class.

That behaviors and behavior classes function to produce reinforcement is the basis for functional behavioral assessment (FBA; see Chapter 3). An FBA performed on a student's problem behavior (Shippen, Simpson, & Crites, 2003) is intended to discover, among other things, what tangible, social, preferred activity, or other consequences the problem behavior obtains (its positive reinforcement function) or what consequences the problem behavior escapes (its negative reinforcement function). Many problem behaviors have both positive and negative reinforcement functions.

## *Antecedents*

The discussion so far has emphasized consequences, but an operant behavior can also be influenced by its antecedents. For instance, an antecedent that is consistently present before a particular behavior is reinforced may become that behavior's *discriminative stimulus for reinforcement*. It is, in effect, a signal that the behavior is likely to be reinforced, and its presence makes that behavior more likely to occur.

For example, suppose that when her classmate Randall's face appears happy, Kendra's request to play with his GameBoy is usually granted. Randall's happy face is a discriminative stimulus for reinforcement of her request for the toy. Thus this request is more likely to be made in the presence of the happy face.

## *Other Concepts in Operant Conditioning*

Antecedents are closely involved in other important concepts of behavioral theory. For example, antecedents operate to link sequences of behaviors (*behavior chains*); acquire reinforcing power as discriminative stimuli for other reinforcers (*conditioned reinforcers*); prompt operant behaviors reinforced in one setting to be performed in other settings (*stimulus generalization*); and facilitate a person's performance of appropriately different operants in different situations (*discrimination*). Display 8-3 briefly describes these and some other operant conditioning concepts.

**Display 8-3** Additional concepts in operant conditioning

**Behavior Chains**
Because discriminative stimuli indicate that reinforcement is likely, they become reinforcers for behaviors that produce them. Continuing with the GameBoy example, suppose that when Kendra makes a joke it produces a smile on Randall's face, then the request for GameBoy is made, and Randall agrees. This sequence constitutes a *chain* of behaviors: operant 1 (making a joke) produces a consequence (Randall's happy face) that reinforces operant 1 while it serves as a discriminative stimulus for operant 2 (requesting GameBoy). Operant 2 produces a reinforcing consequence (request is granted).

In this example, Kendra emitted only two operants. But many complex human behaviors are chains of multiple operants. Regardless of how many operants are involved in a chain, each behavior "link" is reinforced by the environmental changes it produces—changes that function as discriminative stimuli signaling that the next behavior in the chain has become reinforceable. For the last behavior in the chain, the reinforcer is some established reinforcing item or activity (here, getting the GameBoy).

**Conditioned and Primary Reinforcers**
In a behavior chain, discriminative stimuli are *conditioned* reinforcers (also call learned or secondary reinforcers). That is, they are formerly neutral stimuli (without any reinforcing value) that have become reinforcing because they signal that some further behavior is reinforceable. In addition to conditioned reinforcers there are also *primary* reinforcers—food, water, tastes, and other stimuli with a reinforcing capability that exists without having been learned.

**Conditioned Punishers**
Just as they can become conditioned reinforcers, neutral events can become *conditioned punishers*. An antecedent that reliably precedes behavior that is punished is a discriminative stimulus for punishment. Likewise, an antecedent that reliably precedes behavior that is not reinforced is a discriminative stimulus for nonreinforcement. In either case, because the antecedent signals that there will be no reinforcing consequence for a particular behavior, it decreases the probability that the person will emit those behaviors.

For instance, if Randall's unhappy, frowning face typically precedes an angry denial of the request to use his GameBoy, Kendra is unlikely to make that request as long as there is an unhappy face. Discriminative stimuli for punishment are common in our lives: safety warning signs, angry screams, religious and moral prohibitions, and some classroom rules are a few examples. Like conditioned reinforcers, conditioned punishers are important behavior regulators.

**Stimulus Generalization**
Behaviors prompted to occur by a particular discriminative stimulus may also be prompted by other stimuli that are similar in some way to the original one. *Stimulus generalization* refers to the development of a collection of discriminative stimuli, any of which increase the probability that a particular behavior will occur. Thus, behaviors reinforced in one situation (i.e., in the presence of the original discriminative stimulus) may also be performed in other situations (in the presence of other, similar discriminative stimuli), even if reinforcement is not provided in these other situations. For example, because requests are successful when Randall's face is happy, Kendra is likely to make requests of other persons when they look happy, even though not every person will reinforce the requests.

*(continued)*

**Display 8-3 (Continued)**

**Discrimination**
Obviously, no behavior is appropriate in every situation. An operant will seldom or never be reinforced in the presence of discriminative stimuli for punishment or nonreinforcement. When a behavior is reliably performed in the presence of its discriminative stimuli for reinforcement, but not in the presence of its discriminative stimuli for punishment or nonreinforcement, the person has made a *discrimination*.

**Generalized Reinforcers**
Some stimuli are discriminative stimuli for one specific kind of reinforcer. Others signal the availability of various reinforcers, and are called *generalized reinforcers*. One important generalized reinforcer for children is adult approval, which usually signals the availability of a wide variety of specific reinforcers. Of course, approval by others is a generalized reinforcer for most people.

Money is a generalized reinforcer; it has no intrinsic value (except to misers) but is a discriminative stimulus for access to many specific reinforcers. One important feature of a generalized reinforcer is that it is reinforcing in many more situations than is a specific reinforcer. Although a hungry person might be reinforced by either access to food or money, someone who is not hungry can still probably be reinforced by money.

**Verbal Behavior and Covert Behavior**
In operant conditioning theory, speech and language involve verbal operants that are regulated just as other operants are, that is, by antecedents, reinforcers, and other environmental stimuli. Moreover, thinking, sensing, and experiencing emotions are considered to be covert or "private" operant behaviors—again, influenced by antecedents and consequences similarly to how overt or public behaviors are.

**Complex Behavior**
Antecedents, behaviors, consequences, and other concepts have been described separately above. Of course, in real life these and other concepts of operant conditioning operate simultaneously. To cite a few possibilities:
1. The same stimulus can be a consequence for one behavior while an antecedent for another.
2. The same antecedent may function as a discriminative stimulus for reinforcement of behavior X, but at the same time as a discriminative stimulus for nonreinforcement of behavior Y.
3. A behavior or behavior chain may produce both reinforcing consequences and punishing consequences.
4. The immediate consequence of a behavior may be reinforcing but the eventual consequence punishing (and vice versa).

The possibilities are numerous, as they must be to encompass the marvelously complex nature of human behavior.

*Sources:* Jacob & Pelham, 2005; Miltenberger, 2004; Skinner, 1969.

## Operant Conditioning and E&B Disorder

In the behavioral model, an adolescent or child with E&B disorder is one whose behaviors have been judged by authorities to be very inappropriate. Of course, rarely would a designation of E&B disorder be made based on just one behavior, but if several are considerably inappropriate, the designation could be made.

Some behaviors are inappropriate because they occur too little (behavior deficiencies). For instance, suppose that nearly all students in one elementary school interact with peers at recess in the range of 62 to 91 minutes per week, but Kenneth interacts an average of 4 minutes per week. Assisted by the peer comparison, his teacher decides this duration is inappropriately low. Some behaviors are inappropriate because they occur too much (behavior excesses). Suppose that Crandell interrupts an average of 7.8 times per day when the teacher or a classmate is speaking. The teacher decides that is considerably more than the upper limit for effective group learning.

Many young people with E&B disorder exhibit behavior excesses. Behaviorists have attempted to understand them in terms of a variety of operant conditioning concepts. Two explanations are based on positive reinforcement and negative reinforcement.

***Positive Reinforcement via Misallocated Attention.*** Many kinds of disturbing behaviors of children—physical aggression, expressions of anxiety, verbal disruption, bizarre statements and activities, social withdrawal, and so on—naturally attract the attention of other children and adults. Observations show that teachers typically pay a lot of attention to inappropriate behavior while largely ignoring behavior that is industrious, quiet, or otherwise prosocial (Walker et al., 2004). This teacher attention can take a variety of forms, including reprimands, appeals to the child's sense of fairness to others, therapeutic dialogs, sarcasm, reminders about classroom rules, sympathy, threats, and so on. But as diverse as these teacher reactions to unwanted behavior may appear to be, they are similar in one important way: they all provide attention from an adult as a contingent consequence for inappropriate behavior.

Often, the immediate result of these different kinds of teacher attention is that the student stops the misbehavior. However, if this misbehavior is recorded over several days, it is seen to occur more often. What has happened is that the teacher's response "works" (stops the misbehavior) every time it has been used. The removal of the misbehavior negatively reinforces the teacher attention that prompted its removal. The teacher may be unaware that the misbehavior and her attention to it are both growing more frequent. The teacher has unintentionally but powerfully expanded the extent of a student's disruptive, careless, or defiant behaviors with positive reinforcement via contingent attention (Furlong, Morrison, & Jimerson, 2004; Kerr & Nelson, 2006; Walker et al., 2004).

Positive reinforcement via teacher attention can support behaviors reflecting E&B disorder other than *Aggression* and *Impulsiveness.* Student verbal behaviors expressing self-doubt, terror, hopelessness, delusions, physical discomfort, and worthlessness, for example, often draw much attention from educators. Nonverbal behaviors such as crying, nonparticipation, apathetic behavior, and facial expressions of distress do so as well. In some cases teachers and counselors, even as they are providing necessary encouragement, comfort, hope, and consolation to students in personal distress, may be positively reinforcing maladaptive behaviors indicative of *Anxiety, Depression Relationship Problem, Mood Disorders,* and *Psychotic Disorders.*

It is not only adults who provide social attention contingent on problem behavior. Fellow students and other peers may supply words and body language expressing approval, elevated status in a peer group, and other social behaviors contingent on a student's maladaptive behavior. In addition to social reinforcement, other kinds of positive reinforcement—contingent preferred activities, tangible items, or conditioned reinforcers, for example—can increase or maintain inappropriate behavior of young people.

Positive reinforcement for inappropriate behavior generally occurs alongside nonreinforcement of appropriate behavior. Most if not all students with emotional disturbance (ED) have deficiencies of important appropriate behaviors as well as excesses of inappropriate behaviors. Thus, insufficient positive reinforcement for one or more appropriate behaviors is another way positive reinforcement is implicated in ED (Walker et al., 2004).

**_Negative Reinforcement via Coercion-Compliance._** Patterson and his co-workers (Patterson, 1982; Patterson & Yoerger, 2002; Snyder, 2002) have studied the origins and operation of a collection of aggressive, disruptive behaviors such as whining, screaming, arguing, insulting, threatening, pushing, and hitting. These seemingly different behaviors were found to have an important similarity: each can force other people to comply with the behaver's demands. Patterson labeled this functional response class *coercion* and showed how people teach each other to be coercive via negative reinforcement. Research that has followed children into adulthood has supported this coercion process as a major source of *Aggression* and Law-Breaking Behavior (Hinshaw & Lee, 2003; Loeber, Farrington, Stouthamer-Loeber, & Van Kammen, 1998; Walker & Severson, 2002).

To illustrate, suppose two students both wish to use some object at the same time. One may claim to have "had it first," and the other may say that it is her turn to use it. If neither gives in right away, one may threaten the other, who may scream and push the first, and so on as further hostile behaviors occur. Each child responds to the other's behavior by escalating the level of coercion so as to make it more likely that the other will comply with her coercive behavior. But such escalation cannot continue forever; eventually someone will have to give in.

When this happens, the successful coercive behavior is negatively reinforced by having eliminated the other child's coercive behavior. This coercive behavior is also positively reinforced by acquisition of the disputed resource and perhaps in other ways. Further, the unsuccessful coercer is negatively reinforced for giving in and complying, which also terminates coercive behavior. Finally, both participants learn that mild forms of coercion do not work as well as intense forms.

The coercion analysis also applies to interactions between child and adult, and for E&B disorders other than *Aggression* (Davis, Sheeber, & Hops, 2002; Wicks-Nelson & Israel, 2006). Suppose (a) the teacher gives the class instructions for an academic or social interaction assignment. (b) A student states that he is not able to do the assignment. (c) The teacher encourages and cajoles. (d) Eventually the student begins crying, saying that he hates himself for not being able to do the assignment. (e) At this point the teacher withdraws the original demand, and (f) the student begins to calm down. In this scenario, the student's coercive behavior, which might be termed "poor self-concept," has been negatively reinforced by the teacher's removal of a requirement. This strengthens the student's coercion. The teacher's behavior, giving in, also is strengthened: he has been negatively reinforced by the student's ceasing (temporarily) his poor self-concept behavior. Thus teacher and student have taught one another to behave maladaptively.

## Behavioral Interventions

Inappropriately excessive or deficient behaviors of a young person with E&B disorder are controlled, like other operants, mainly by stimuli in the environment that act as consequences and antecedents. Behaviorists change these controlling stimuli in order to modify the inappropriate behaviors (Alberto & Troutman, 2006; Kavale, Forness & Walker, 1999). In fact, a behavioral procedure called *functional analysis* can identify controlling stimuli in the environment and thus indicate environment changes that can be made to modify the behaviors (Fox & Gable, 2004; Kazdin, 2001; Skinner, 1953). Functional analysis, along with less formal methods of identifying motivators for misbehavior, are considered a part of FBA (see Barnhill, 2005; Fox & Gable, 2004).

The behavioral model has influenced intervention for children and adolescents with E&B disorder through two related but separate routes: scientific applied behavior analysis and practioner-oriented behavior modification. *Applied behavior analysis* is the use and experimental evaluation of procedures for improving important human behaviors in "natural" (nonlaboratory) settings (Baer, Wolf, & Risley, 1968). *Behavior modification* is the use of behavioral principles, mainly operant conditioning, to make substantial improvements in the behavior of people, including children with E&B disorder, in natural settings such as schools, homes, communities, and institutions. Applied behavior analysis findings have provided much of the scientific basis for behavior modification and have led to new or improved behavior modification techniques.

### Applied Behavior Analysis

Two major features of applied behavior analysis (Kazdin, 2001; Lewis et al., 2004) are a strong emphasis on measurement of behavior and other variables and a requirement that interventions be experimentally evaluated, especially through the use of "single-case" research designs.

#### *Measurement*
***Definition.*** Like other scientific activities, applied behavior analysis is mainly concerned with *measurable* phenomena, especially observable behaviors. (Antecedents to and consequences of observable behaviors are other measurable phenomena of concern). A first priority is that the behavior(s) of interest be given an operational definition, that is, an objective, clear, and complete statement of the behavior to observe (Kazdin, 2003; Martin & Pear, 2003; see Chapter 3). This helps produce reliable measurement. When a behavior selected for modification is given an

**Display 8-4** Patterns of E&B disorder with some target behavior definitions relevant to them

| Pattern of E&B Disorder | Representative Target Behavior Definition |
|---|---|
| Aggression | • Instances of verbal abuse (taunting, teasing, verbal bullying) of classroom peers (improvement = decrease)<br>• Percentage of teacher instructions with which student complies within 20 seconds (improvement = increase) |
| Anxiety | • Percentage of 2-minute intervals in which the student bites fingernails, picks at skin, or exhibits other specific nervous habits (improvement = decrease)<br>• Number of teacher questions during which student maintains eye contact with the teacher (improvement = increase) |
| Depression | • Number of times per day in which student states pessimism or hopelessness about school or other matters (improvement = decrease)<br>• Percentage of 5-minute intervals in which the student smiles at least once (improvement = increase) |
| Impulsiveness | • Total number of minutes student keeps his face oriented toward math assignment, eyes open (improvement = increase)<br>• Number of 2-minute intervals in math class during which student remains seated and performs no unpermitted talking (improvement = increase) |
| Relationship Problem | • Total number of seconds student remains within 4 feet of any other student while class is at recess (improvement = increase)<br>• Number of 15-minute intervals during which the student exhibits one or more instances of rude, threatening, sarcastic, or aggressive verbal or nonverbal behavior toward a fellow student (improvement = decrease) |

operational definition, it is called a *target behavior*. Display 8-4 presents examples of selected target behaviors related to E&B disorder of children and adolescents, together with potential recording strategies.

**Recording.** The next step is to select a suitable measurement method for the target behavior. Target behavior recording along with behavior-products recording methods (see Chapter 3) are strongly favored in applied behavior analysis (Alberto & Troutman, 2006; Miltenberger, 2004). Selection of a recording method may be affected by setting considerations such as classroom schedule and availability of extra staff (Gunter & Denny, 2004). Regardless of which recording method is selected, the behavior should be measured frequently and regularly (e.g., every day), before and after the intervention is put into effect.

Results of measurement before intervention, called *baseline* data, represent the ordinary but inappropriate level (too high or too low) of the target behavior.

Baseline data can be compared to measurement results recorded after the intervention has begun, in order to indicate whether behavior has improved and how much.

***Reliability.*** To address measurement reliability, applied behavior analysis includes procedures to check interobserver agreement. On several occasions during baseline and intervention phases, target behaviors are recorded simultaneously by independent observers (Kennedy, 2005). If their records differ more than a little, the target behavior may be poorly defined and need to be improved.

***Social Validity.*** Social validity means measuring the appropriateness of the target behavior, intervention method, and/or amount of behavior change achieved by intervention (Kazdin, 2003; see Chapter 3). The subjective evaluation method is one way to measure social validity. It requires obtaining judgments, preferably wise and informed, about the appropriateness of target behaviors selected, intervention methods used, and behavior changes achieved. Teachers, parents, other adults, peers, and the student herself may be asked to provide subjective evaluations.

Peer comparison is a second way to assess social validity. This involves measuring the target behavior not only of the selected student but also of one or more peers whose behavior is appropriate. Target student and peer data are then compared. For example, an applied behavior analysis of Julian's compliance might evaluate social validity of improvement in this target behavior by using both types of social validity. Peer group data on how much Julian's peers complied with teacher instructions would help determine whether Julian's level of compliance after intervention became normal. Subjective evaluation interviews with Julian's teachers would determine whether they had noticed his improvement in compliance.

### *Experimental Evaluation*

If a target behavior has been defined properly and recorded regularly, both in a baseline period and after intervention is begun, the applied behavior analyst can determine the extent of behavior change simply by comparing target behavior in baseline to that in intervention. If data show behavior improvement, it is tempting to say that the improvement must have been due to the intervention used. But isn't it possible that the observed improvement was due to home, medical, community, spiritual, or other unexpected influences unrelated to the intervention? The probability that observed behavior changes were caused by the intervention can be evaluated through the use of an applied behavior analysis experimental design (Kennedy, 2005).

The most common applied behavior analysis design is the **ABAB research design** (also referred to as "reversal" design), in which target behavior is repeatedly measured while phases A (baseline) and B (intervention) are alternated every few days. Other designs include the multiple baseline, alternating treatments, and changing criterion (Kazdin, 2003; Kennedy, 2005; Lewis, Hudson, Richter, & Johnson, 2004; Martin & Pear, 2003). Each of these designs involves different research activities, but they share the same basic logic: if a behavior change might be caused by our intervention but potentially by other variables as well, we can be confident in our intervention only if the other variables are ruled out.

Educators know that there are many methods of intervention that may be suitable for use with students having E&B disorder. As described in coursework, journal articles, textbooks, websites, advertisements, workshops, and elsewhere, most of these methods sound reasonable. Yet it is not hard to find two methods for dealing with the same problem that call for totally different or even opposite actions by the teacher. Can all these intervention methods be worthwhile?

In the applied behavior analysis perspective, educators of students with ED should prefer intervention methods for which there is supporting scientific evidence (Lewis et al., 2004; Witt, VanDerHeyden, & Gilbertson, 2004). Applied behavior analyses have produced a good deal of scientific evidence for many of the behavior modification methods (e.g., Fink & Lotspeich, 2004). Such research, including research conducted by teachers in their own classrooms, has built a body of knowledge about changing students' behavior and has helped give a scientific basis to the professions serving students with ED.

## Behavior Modification

Behavior modification includes various interventions based on operant conditioning and other aspects of the behavioral model. Behavior modification involves carefully defining and measuring target behavior, then controlling the environmental stimuli that precede behavior (antecedents) and/or follow behavior (consequences) in order to improve that target behavior (Alberto & Troutman, 2006; Martin & Pear, 2003; Miltenberger, 2004). Note that the term "behavior modification" has been used inaccurately to refer to drug therapy, brainwashing prisoners of war, self-help mind control techniques, and various other concepts, leading to confusion.

### *Behaviorist Perspective on Modifying Behavior*

Because E&B disorder is, in essence, behavior that is emitted to an inappropriate extent (frequency, duration, intensity, etc.), it will be corrected if the practitioner arranges for the young person to emit the behavior to an appropriate extent. This behaviorist perspective leads to clear guidelines for modifying E&B disordered behavior:

1. If a target behavior's frequency, duration, or intensity is too low, do something to increase it.
2. If frequency, duration, or intensity is too high, do something to decrease it.

To implement this perspective properly requires careful judgment in conceptualizing a student's problem and defining one or more target behaviors. This is because the choice of a behavior modification procedure often depends on how the target behavior is defined for recording and intervention. For example, should a student's pattern of *Aggression* in the classroom be conceptualized as too low a frequency of resisting provocations or too high a frequency of hitting? If the former, the teacher would define and record "resisting provocations" and select an intervention to increase this behavior. If the latter, the teacher would define and record hitting, then intervene to decrease it. Of course, some of the most effective interventions increase behaviors that are deficient while also decreasing behaviors that are excessive (Tryon, 2001).

### *Increasing Target Behaviors*
Important aspects of the patterns of E&B disorder can be conceptualized as involving a deficit in the frequency, duration, and/or intensity of some behavior. For instance, *Impulsiveness* sometimes reflects a deficit in the student's remaining on task and following rules. *Anxiety* can involve too few approaches toward a feared situation. *Relationship Problem* might stem from a deficit in verbal interactions such as greetings, compliments, and requests to play. If taught or encouraged to perform these adaptive behaviors (e.g., follow rules, approach scary situations, start conversations with peers) more frequently, a student probably would show less *Impulsiveness, Anxiety,* or *Relationship Problem.* The student might even be judged as no longer needing to be identified as having ED. Using various methods, teachers of students with ED often must increase certain target behaviors.

***Positive Reinforcement.*** A basic behavior modification procedure for increasing behavior is positive reinforcement. To implement positive reinforcement, the teacher arranges things so a reinforcer will be delivered contingent on target behavior by the student. In practice, positive reinforcement of a behavior to be increased is often combined with extinction (mainly, ignoring) of other (unwanted or neutral) behaviors. This combined procedure is termed **differential reinforcement**.

Teachers who wish to use differential reinforcement can select various kinds of reinforcers. These include social attention (e.g., eye contact, praise, recognition, physical proximity, touch), preferred activities (e.g., classroom privileges, extra recreation time, school duties), and tokens (check marks, stickers, points, play money, and other conditioned reinforcers redeemable for a range of items and activities), as well other reinforcers such as consumables (candy, gum, sodas, etc.) and performance feedback.

1. *Social attention.* Differential reinforcement with adult social attention is a commonly used behavioral intervention (Lewis et al., 2004). In this technique, the teacher gives attention to the student contingent on his performing the desired target behavior, but avoids paying attention when he performs other (especially unwanted) behaviors (Bell, Boggs, & Eyberg, 2003).

    Hall, Lund, and Jackson (1968) studied how differential attention could be used in simple but effective ways. One particularly disruptive boy, Robbie, studied very little during a 30-minute period each day when all students were to be working on an assignment at their desks. Instead, Robbie typically talked and laughed with other students, played with objects, and generally interfered with his own and others' education. Rather than record these disruptive behaviors, however, it was decided to record Robbie's "on task study behavior," which was inappropriately low. Study behavior was first recorded for 7 days under a baseline condition in which the teacher managed Robbie as he typically did—urging

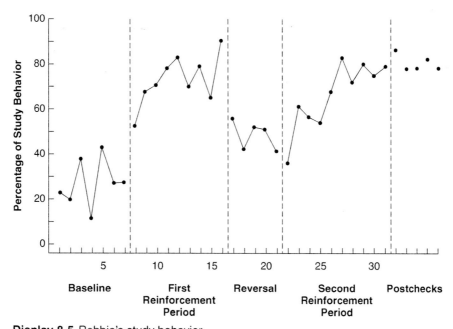

**Display 8-5** Robbie's study behavior
Source: Adapted from R. V. Hall, D. Lund, & D. Jackson, 1968. "Effects of Teacher Attention on Study Behavior," *Journal of Applied Behavior Analysis, 1,* p. 3. Copyright 1968 by the Society for the Experimental Analysis of Behavior, Inc. Adapted by permission.

him to work on assignments, put away other objects, and so on, when he was being disruptive.

On days 8 through 16, a differential reinforcement intervention was put into effect. Whenever Robbie showed study behavior continuously for 1 minute, the teacher gave social attention (approached and praised him). Also, the teacher ignored disruptive and other nonstudy behaviors. Display 8-5 shows that Robbie's study behavior rose dramatically during days 8 to 16.

The implication that differential attention to study behavior caused it to increase was experimentally evaluated with the ABAB design. Beginning with day 17, the intervention was discontinued for a few days while the teacher again behaved as he did during the first baseline. The result was an obvious decline in study behavior. On days 21 to 31, differential reinforcement by social attention was reapplied, and Robbie's study behavior improved again. The final "postchecks" phase shows Robbie's study behavior on five measured occasions after day 31. Robbie's behavior improvement endured for at least 3 months.

Many teachers of students with ED are skeptical—justifiably—that their social attention has much controlling power over these students. Perhaps this means that teacher social reinforcement must be applied more consistently and persistently than for typical students. The fact is that social attention has been shown to improve various behavior problems of young people (Kerr & Nelson, 2006;

Martella et al., 2003; Walker et al., 2004). Not only teachers but psychologists, counselors, nurses, teacher assistants, principals, classmates, and others at school can use social reinforcement to improve a student's behavior (Alberto & Troutman, 2006; Lee & Axelrod, 2005).

2. *Preferred activities.* Of any two separate activities in which a person is free to engage, the activity performed more frequently can serve to reinforce the less frequent one, according to the *Premack Principle.* Thus a student will probably perform a less preferred activity in order to gain the opportunity to engage in a more preferred one (Kerr & Nelson, 2006; Lee & Axelrod, 2004). To use preferred activities in positive reinforcement, the teacher must first identify preferred activities by (a) asking the student to name activities and people she prefers and likes, (b) asking other people to name the student's preferred activities and people, or (c) observing the student's activity and people preferences when free to engage in them. The teacher then arranges the learning situation so that the student has access to preferred activities and people contingent on her performance of a less preferred activity (i.e., one the teacher wants her to perform and practice).

Teachers can use the Premack Principle by scheduling periods of more difficult, longer, and/or less interesting student activities to alternate with periods of novel, more fun, or otherwise preferred activities. Students who complete the former to an appropriate degree can engage in the latter. Appropriate social behavior (e.g., cooperation with a peer) can be made a part of classroom learning assignments so that a student who needs to practice cooperation must do so to complete an assignment that is a prerequisite for a preferred activity that follows (Bos & Vaughn, 2006).

The teacher can reinforce students' rule-following
and academic work progress with checkmark tokens.

3. ***Tokens.*** A token is a generalized conditioned reinforcer (see Display 8-3), that is, an item with little inherent value that becomes a reinforcer because it signals the availability of a variety of other reinforcers. Money is the prototype token. More common in education are check marks, poker chips, embossing stamps, stickers, play money, paper clips, and smiling faces drawn by the teacher. In token reinforcement interventions, the teacher dispenses a token after a desired target behavior occurs. The student accumulates tokens to redeem later for desired items or activities (Kerr & Nelson, 2006).

Tokens may help the teacher involve other school personnel or parents in the student's intervention. She can communicate the student's earned and lost tokens via daily or frequent report cards to people who will reinforce or withhold reinforcers accordingly (Kelley, 2003).

Token reinforcers have been used to improve various problems of emotion and behavior by increasing corresponding adaptive behaviors (Kazdin, 2001; Kerr & Nelson, 2006; Miltenberger, 2004). For example, token reinforcers can address the social withdrawal that can be a part of *Anxiety, Depression,* or *Relationship Problem.* Suppose Yvette virtually never initiates or responds to a social interaction from her third-grade classmates. The teacher could play a token game, beginning by teaching all the students some good ways to start and respond to social interactions. Next, the teacher could implement two rules for earning tokens: (a) Yvette earns a token each time a classroom peer initiates a social interaction toward her, and (b) the rest of the class earns a token each time Yvette initiates a social interaction toward any peer. Once both Yvette and the class peers earn a certain number of tokens, they can exchange their tokens for rewards.

## *Decreasing Target Behaviors*

Behaviors are excessive if they occur too often, too intensively, too long in time, in too many settings, or a combination of these. For instance, students with *Anxiety* may too frequently ask for teacher assistance and reassurance when independent functioning is more appropriate. Students with *Aggression* may too intensively threaten peers and argue with teachers. Students with *Depression* may too often state the belief that they are worthless and error prone. Based on this perspective, behavioral interventions for excessive behavior problems attempt to decrease the frequency, intensity, duration, or some other aspect of target behaviors. These methods include extinction, punishment, "positive approaches," and antecedent control.

***Extinction.*** Behavior that was once effective in achieving reinforcement, but is effective no more, tends to decrease in frequency over time. That is, the behavior undergoes extinction. To implement extinction in the classroom, the teacher must select the target behavior to be extinguished, identify reinforcers that have been maintaining the target behavior, and control these reinforcers. Teacher and/or peer social attention to the behavior of a student with ED often are major reinforcers that must be controlled. This means that the teacher must not only stop paying attention to the target behavior, she must encourage peers of the inappropriately behaving student to do so as well (Lee & Axelrod, 2005). Obviously these requirements can be a challenge in many classrooms where students with ED are taught. One possible solution is to apply a separate intervention for the peers, for example, rewarding them for ignoring the student with ED when he displays the target behavior or rewarding them as the target behavior improves.

Extinction of an undesired behavior is rarely used by itself. It is most often combined with reinforcement of a desired behavior. As stated earlier, this is one application of the differential reinforcement procedure. Differential reinforcement techniques are presented in the discussion of *positive approaches*.

**Punishment.** Barrish, Saunders, and Wolf (1969) described a punishment procedure for reducing classroom disruption (unpermitted seat leaving and talking out) during individual work assignment periods in math and reading instruction. For intervention, the teacher specified a few simple rules, including one requiring each student to ask permission to leave his seat or talk, and introduced the class to the "Good Behavior Game." The classroom was divided into two teams, and when a member of either team broke a rule, his team received a penalty mark on the chalkboard. At the end of class, the team with fewer marks won privileges (victory tags and stars, lining up first for lunch, extra free time). Both teams could win if neither received more than five penalty marks.

The penalty marks in the Good Behavior Game were intended to punish unpermitted seat leaving and talking out. This intervention decreased disruptive behaviors to very low, tolerable levels within a few days. Based on a review of research on the Good Behavior Game and its variations, Embry (2002) called for educators to implement it much more widely to prevent and remediate classroom behavior problems.

Punishment may be subdivided according to the nature of the consequence that follows target behavior (Alberto & Troutman, 2006; Kazdin, 2001; Miltenberger, 2004). As Display 8-2 shows, these are aversive punishment (also referred to as positive punishment) and forfeiture punishment (also termed negative punishment).

1. *Aversive punishment* involves a decrease in the target behavior caused by the contingent addition of a stimulus to the environment. The Good Behavior Game illustrates this: a penalty mark was added to a group's "environment" (chalkboard column) following a rule violation by that group. Reprimands may also function as aversive punishment.

    Other aversive punishment applications involve contingent activity. For example, in *positive practice* intervention (Martella et al., 2003), the student is required to repeatedly practice appropriate behaviors that are alternatives to the inappropriate target behavior. Azrin and Besalel (1999) described how positive practice could be used in a separate classroom for students with ED who often disruptively violate rules. To intervene, the teacher requires each rule-violator to

engage in positive practice at the beginning of recess or other preferred activity time, by doing the following:
(a) Reciting the rule he broke
(b) Raising his hand until called on by the teacher
(c) Asking for permission to talk or leave his seat

This sequence is repeated several times, after which the student can join his peers in the preferred activity. In another contingent activity punishment, each time the student exhibits an inappropriate target behavior, she is required to carry out a planned program of vigorous exertion, chores, or other nonpreferred activity (Kazdin, 2001; Martella et al., 2003).

2. The other form of punishment involves a decrease in the target behavior caused by the contingent removal of a stimulus from the environment. This *forfeiture punishment* has two variations: response cost and timeout from reinforcement.
    (a) In *response cost*, a specified amount of reinforcer is forfeited contingent on the occurrence of the target behavior (e.g., Conyers et al., 2004). Imagine a separate class for students with ED, all of whom show *Aggression*. Suppose a target behavior to be reduced is defined as particular aggressive statements or acts directed toward a peer. Each student is given a supply of points to begin each day and loses a point for engaging in a target behavior. At day's end, students exchange their unlost points for items or privileges. Similarly, in many token economy interventions for students with ED (described below), fines for rule infractions exemplify response cost.
    (b) In **timeout from reinforcement** (or "timeout"), access to any reinforcer is forfeited for a specified period of time, contingent on occurrence of the target behavior. In classroom applications, the student may be removed from the reinforcing environment for a while or the reinforcing environment may be withdrawn from the student (Friman & Finney, 2003; Martella et al., 2003). Timeout differs from traditional seclusion or exclusion from school in two ways: the loss of opportunity for reinforcement is contingent on the occurrence of a specific target behavior, and the period of time involved is typically brief. Display 8-6 presents guidelines for using timeout from reinforcement in school.

**Comment on Punishment.** Applying punishment to modify behavior is controversial (Alberto & Troutman, 2006; Lewis et al., 2004; Wacker, Harding, Berg, Cooper-Brown, & Barretto, 2003). Many child service professionals and many behaviorists are philosophically opposed to techniques that are unpleasant to, or may offend, a young person. Punishment procedures can be misused and abused: it is easy to imagine aversive and forfeiture punishment practices that involve more disagreeable consequences than getting a chalkboard penalty mark or briefly losing a chance to earn tokens. Critics of punishment, or of a particular program that uses aversive or forfeiture punishment, can easily portray such procedures as abusive even when properly and benevolently applied. Various punishment procedures (e.g., timeout) are restricted in some localities.

**Display 8-6** Guidelines for school use of timeout from reinforcement

| | |
|---|---|
| 1. Timeout location | • Consider nearness, physical and other features of possible locations.<br>• Make selected location free from dangerous and distracting circumstances.<br>• Consider using an in-classroom location for minor offenses and an out-of-classroom location for major offenses. |
| 2. Decide timeout procedure details | • What violations deserve timeout?<br>• What is the standard timeout length or lengths?<br>• What time will be added for timeout procedure violations?<br>• What privileges will be removed for certain timeout procedure violations? |
| 3. Explain timeout to students, others | • State violations that will receive timeout (e.g., selected rule violations, verbal or physical aggression).<br>• State (optionally, practice) appropriate student behavior when teacher assigns timeout.<br>• State how timeout procedure violations yield extra penalties (extra minutes in timeout, loss of privileges). |
| 4. Implement timeout for stated violations | • State the violation clearly and tell student to go to timeout.<br>• When student enters timeout location, set timer for standard timeout length.<br>• When timeout length has been served, tell student to rejoin the group.<br>• If student fails to enter timeout right away (suggestion: 15 seconds), state the violation (refusal) and extend timeout 1 minute. Other 1-minute extension violations: verbal or physical disruption before or while in timeout.<br>• If student receives 5 extensions on a particular timeout, he loses a privilege.<br>• Avoid physical force in enforcing timeout. |
| 5. Implement timeout properly | • Remain calm in voice and gesture when stating violations, adding extensions, removing a privilege, and all aspects of timeout.<br>• Follow through on timeout, extensions, privilege removal. Do not reinforce arguments, pleas, accusations, threats, or other attempted coercion by replying to it or changing timeout procedure. Verbal or physical disruption calls for a timeout extension.<br>• Do not delay any aspect of timeout, including privilege removal.<br>• Perform normal classroom procedures during timeout. Do not talk to or check up on the student during timeout. Prevent others from doing so.<br>• After timeout is served, move on. Do not discuss the violation or require an apology. |

*Sources:* Miltenberger, 2004; Walker et al., 2004.

Further, educators using punishment for inappropriate behavior should think about the coercion concept presented earlier. Many situations in which punishment might be used tend to induce impulsive behavior in adults as well as children and may trap them into escalating coercive behaviors. This can result in arguments, damaged relationships, and unplanned words and deeds, including physical conflict.

On the other hand, current punishment of maladaptive behavior by a teacher may prevent more intense future punishment from other sources. Punishment may be essential for successful intervention with E&B disorder in some cases (e.g., Fabiano & Pelham, 2003; Walker et al., 2004). Educational use of punishment procedures requires care: the teacher must care for the students, and he must act with care (anticipate, plan, follow the plan).

***Positive Approaches.*** Although it may seem paradoxical, inappropriate behaviors can be decreased with the use of reinforcement, via procedures that have been called positive approaches to decreasing behavior. Positive approaches rely on differential reinforcement of behaviors that are adaptive alternatives to inappropriate behaviors (Bos & Vaughn, 2005; Martin & Pear, 2003). That is, while the inappropriate behaviors are decreased through extinction, appropriate alternative behaviors are reinforced (Meadows & Stevens, 2004). Two of the positive approaches are differential reinforcement of low rates of behavior (DRL) and differential reinforcement of incompatible behavior (DRI).

1. ***DRL.*** A behavior's frequency can be decreased with the DRL procedure, in which a behavior is reinforced only if it occurs at less than a specified frequency (Tarbox & Hayes, 2003). The target behavior is occurring at too high a rate, and this high rate receives extinction. The alternative, desired response is the same behavior occurring at a lower rate; this lower rate is reinforced. In effect, DRL encourages moderation.

   One way to implement DRL is to provide a reinforcer only if the target behavior has occurred no more than some criterion number of times during a particular time frame (e.g., no more than four times in 30 minutes). DRL can be used in this way to reduce a high frequency of obscene statements in a classroom for students with ED, warnings from a lunchroom monitor that Table 17's noise volume is too great, or expressions of self-doubt and worthlessness. To apply DRL in these examples, the teacher might inform the students that they will earn reinforcers only if the recorded data indicate no more than 20 obscene statements per day, 2 warnings per lunch period, or 5 self-doubting statements per hour.

   Educators who use DRL often include an announced, gradual lowering of the criterion for reinforcement, in steps over several days. The final limit can be set at a tolerably low level, even zero if that is reasonable.

   Similar intervention procedures can be applied to target behaviors that are excessive not in frequency, but in duration or some other aspect. A student with ED could earn praise, preferred activity time, or tokens contingent on reducing the duration of her lengthy trips to the pencil sharpener or bathroom. A group could earn a special privilege contingent on decreasing the latency between the beginning-of-class bell and the moment that all students are on task.

2. ***DRI.*** In the DRI procedure, differential reinforcement is provided for a particular behavior alternative to the undesirable target behavior. After the teacher designates the target behavior to be reduced, she also identifies desirable behaviors that are physically incompatible—or at least very unlikely to occur simultaneously—with the target behavior. For example, suppose the target behavior was being out of seat; working at one's desk is incompatible and might be selected for reinforcement. Likewise, sharing and taking turns are incompatible alternatives to fighting over the use of materials. Saying confident, self-appreciative things in an authentic manner is incompatible with claiming to be worthless, stupid, and hopeless. Relaxed breathing and face muscles, along with calm talk, is nearly incompatible with *Aggression* and *Anxiety.*

Other forms of differential reinforcement include differential reinforcement of other (any behavior that is not the target behavior, called DRO) (e.g., Conyers et al., 2004; Wallace & Robles, 2003) and reinforcement of functional equivalents (Kazdin, 2001; see Meadows & Stevens, 2004). A functional equivalent is an acceptable behavior that achieves the same function as an inappropriate behavior. The idea behind functional equivalents is related to FBA, which attempts to discover an inappropriate behavior's function.

### *Group Contingencies*

Many applications of behavior modification focus on the behavior of a single student, but behavior modification procedures have also been developed that involve groups of students or even entire classrooms (Hansen & Lignugaris/Kraft, 2005; Lee & Axelrod, 2005; Martella et al., 2003; Salend, 2005). Generally, group contingencies achieve at least two important ends: (a) the power of the peer group is harnessed to encourage cooperation and support rather than inappropriate behavior, and (b) teacher time and effort can be more efficiently utilized. Two variations are interdependent and dependent group contingencies.

***Interdependent.*** In the interdependent group contingency, the performance of the group as a whole determines the consequences for every member of that group. This contingency can be arranged so that the group must meet a criterion selected by the teacher (e.g., 24 or more helpful peer interactions per period; all group members attentive and on task at least 70% of the school day; no more than 2 arguments per recess). Alternatively, the criterion for reinforcement may be that to win today, the group must meet or beat its performance of yesterday.

In a popular variation of the interdependent group contingency, the class is divided into teams whose members cooperate with each other while competing against the other team(s). An example is the Good Behavior Game described earlier, in which teams of students compete for desirable consequences by avoiding point losses for broken rules. All members of the winning team receive rewards, whereas members of the losing team may not.

A dependent group contingency can encourage peers to support the behavior improvements of a student with E&B disorder.

**Dependent.** In a dependent group contingency (also called "consequence sharing"), the consequence for the entire group is determined by the performance of one designated student. The student usually earns items, free time, or other positive reinforcers that she must share with all group members. A main rationale is that classmates who stand to benefit from a student's behavior improvement tend to encourage it or at least refrain from prompting inappropriate behavior. In a variation of dependent group contingency it is not one but two students who earn reinforcers that all share.

For example, a dependent group contingency might help teach an elementary school student experiencing *Relationship Problem* to interact prosocially during a 20-minute recess. First, the teacher describes and shows him prosocial recess behaviors and helps him practice. Next, a large picture is cut into 10 parts. The student earns a picture part for each 2-minute interval during which he performs at least one prosocial interaction. Each part the student earns qualifies his class for a minute of a fun group activity later in the day. There could be a 5-minute bonus for earning all 10 parts.

The CLASS behavior management program (Walker et al., 2004) is described later in this chapter. In it, a disruptive student can earn privileges to share with his entire class by complying with specified rules.

### *Antecedent Control of Behavior*

Some behavior problems are responses to antecedents that signal that inappropriate behavior probably will be reinforced. For instance, when students are disorganized and disruptive in starting and completing their assignments, interacting with the teacher, and moving about hallways, teachers may need to build proper antecedent control over such behaviors. To do so the teacher could establish a regular schedule and specific routines, arrange classroom space to improve learning and management, give very clear requests and corrections, specify reasonable rules for classroom and school, and present assignments that are appropriate to each student's learning needs (e.g., Bos & Vaughn, 2005; Darch & Kameenui, 2004; Kerr & Nelson, 2006; Poling & Gaynor, 2003; Witt, VanDerHeyden, & Gilbertson, 2004). The teacher must support these antecedents for appropriate behavior by reinforcing student behavior that complies with them (e.g., following schedules, requests, and rules) while preventing reinforcement for noncompliance.

One intervention based on antecedent control is *precorrection* (Lewis, Colvin, & Sugai, 2000; Martella et al., 2003). In precorrection, the teacher anticipates and manages antecedents of appropriate behaviors so the student will avoid inappropriate behaviors and perform the appropriate ones, as follows. The teacher:

1. Identifies the problem behavior and specifies the appropriate behavior
2. Identifies antecedents that probably are supporting the problem behavior (e.g., locations, activities preceding it, people present when it occurs, teacher instructions that seem to set it off)
3. Hypothesizes what antecedents should be changed to promote the appropriate behavior
4. Requires the student to state and/or practice the appropriate behavior ahead of time
5. Provides strong reinforcement contingent on the student's performing the appropriate behavior.
6. Gives extra help via signals, reminders, or other prompts to perform correctly if the problem behavior recurs.

Antecedent control plays a large role in an important approach to prevention and intervention of behavior and emotional problems called schoolwide positive behavior support (e.g., Liaupsin, Jolivette, & Scott, 2004), discussed in Chapter 11.

### *Self-Management*
The discussion of behavior modification so far has assumed that the behavior modifier is someone other than the behaver. This behavior modifier (teacher, school psychologist, classroom peer, teacher assistant, principal, or other) records target behaviors and manages antecedents and consequences, in order to modify the student's behavior. But of course it is possible for a person to serve as modifier of his own behavior. People commonly select behavior goals, observe their own behavior, evaluate it, and reward or penalize themselves according to how closely their performance approaches their goals. Behavioral intervention techniques similar to these everyday behavior change efforts are collectively termed behavioral *self-management* (optionally, self-control or self-regulation; see Bradley-Klug & Shapiro, 2003; Lewis et al., 2004; Martin & Pear, 2003; Polsgrove & Smith, 2004; Reid, Trout, & Schartz, 2005; Smith & Daunic, 2004).

Behavioral self-management means behavior modification methods administered substantially (not necessarily entirely) by the behaver. It is difficult to draw a clear line between certain behavioral self-management interventions and other ones best considered cognitive management (addressed in Chapter 9). This chapter includes the methods of antecedent self-control, self-monitoring, self-reinforcement, and self-punishment. Of course, in real classrooms behavioral self-management, other behavior modification techniques, and nonbehavioral intervention practices may be combined (e.g., Cancio, West, & Young, 2004; Crum, 2003).

***Antecedent Self-Control.*** As noted, antecedent stimuli make particular behaviors more likely or less likely. Young people can seek or create situations containing antecedents that make their own adaptive behavior more likely, and they can avoid or change antecedents that often prompt maladaptive behavior. For instance, a study room with noise, confusion, and disruptive behavior sets up stimulus conditions that make study behavior less likely. To increase his own study behavior, a student might control these maladaptive stimuli by moving to a corner of the room, a study carrel, or another room.

Setting goals and selecting priorities are antecedent self-control techniques (Lovitt, 2000; Martella et al., 2003; Polsgrove & Smith, 2004). A student can be taught to identify personal and academic improvements he wants (e.g., have more friends) and to describe actions needed to pursue those improvements (e.g., do something together with some new acquaintances). The student could specify the actions in the form of behavioral objectives, using clear, observable terms including time, amount, and other criteria (e.g., in the next 10 days, do something with 3 new acquaintances). Finally, the student monitors his pursuit of the behavioral objective. Teacher assistance will be needed with some steps, early in the process, but the intervention is still self-management.

***Self-Monitoring.*** Systematically observing, recording, and/or graphing one's behavior can affect that behavior, including the educational behavior of students with ED (Levendoski & Cartledge, 2000). Target behavior recording methods (e.g., event, time-sampling, duration; see Chapter 3) ordinarily used to measure someone else's behavior can be used to measure one's own as well. Students are more likely to use self-monitoring when they are taught simple and clear target behavior definitions, methods of self-recording, and directions for how to self-monitor, perhaps supplemented by teacher-prepared recording forms and graphs on which to display progress (Daly & Ranalli, 2003; Martella et al., 2003; Miltenberger, 2004; Vanderbilt, 2005). Rating scales are another simple measurement method suitable for self-monitoring.

An early applied behavior analysis examined a highly inattentive junior high student who was taught to self-monitor her own on-task work behavior during class (Broden, Hall, & Mitts, 1971). Every few minutes she marked herself "+" on a paper if, in her own judgment, she was engaged in appropriate study behavior, or a "−" if she was not. This procedure substantially increased her appropriate classroom behavior. A similar self-monitoring procedure was reported by Todd, Horner, and Sugai (1999). Self-monitoring may have special value in efforts to modify physiological, cognitive, and other phenomena that are observable only by the student (e.g., nausea, self-derogatory thoughts, fearful images, angry urges).

One potential drawback to self-monitoring is that the student may not observe and record his own behavior properly. Although a target behavior might improve despite careless or falsified self-monitoring, it is usually important that self-monitoring be accurate. One way to improve accuracy is matching, which is not a self-management procedure but one that can strengthen self-management.

In *matching*, the teacher records the same behavior as the student who is self-monitoring (Peterson, Young, West, & Peterson, 1999). At selected times (e.g., the end of each hour, or when a timer unpredictably rings) the teacher compares the student's record to her own. She reinforces the student if his record nearly or exactly matches hers. Gradually, and as accuracy of matching improves and remains high, the teacher schedules fewer comparisons, until the student self-monitors with rare or no matching.

***Self-Reinforcement.*** In self-reinforcement, someone (preferably the student herself) specifies the target behavior and its defining criteria (e.g., percentage accuracy, time limits). The student administers a reinforcer contingent on her own behavior that meets the criteria. Obviously, self-monitoring in some form is a prerequisite to self-reinforcement.

Self-reinforcement can bring about behavior modifications of various kinds, but special interest is given to this technique's potential to promote behavior maintenance and setting generalization (Alberto & Troutman, 2006; Kerr & Nelson, 2006; Miltenberger, 2004). *Behavior maintenance*, as noted, refers to retention of behavior improvements well after the original intervention has been reduced or discontinued entirely. *Setting generalization* refers to behavior improvements that occur outside the setting in which the original intervention took place. To use self-reinforcement for behavior maintenance and setting generalization, Schloss and Smith (1998) recommended a four-part teaching sequence.

1. *Establish the behavior improvements desired*. The teacher records target behavior and implements an intervention to increase the student's adaptive behaviors and/or decrease his maladaptive behaviors to an appropriate extent.
2. *Implement self-monitoring*. The teacher continues to record the target behaviors while teaching the student to self-record these same target behaviors, using essentially the same recording method as she is.
3. *Implement the self-reinforcement* procedure. The teacher teaches the student to self-reinforce. She should allow the student considerable latitude in selecting the reinforcers and the criteria for reinforcement. The student should administer reinforcers contingent on his own behavior meeting the criteria.
4. *Carry out matching* to heighten the accuracy of student self-monitoring and self-reinforcement. Matching is gradually discontinued ("faded") at a rate based on the target behavior.

## Package Interventions

Even a "simple" behavior modification intervention may involve more than one procedure (e.g., differential reinforcement equals positive reinforcement for one behavior plus extinction for another). Many school behavior modification interventions (e.g., token economy, behavioral contracting) are packages of several behavioral techniques (e.g., Kehle, Bray, Theodore, Jenson & Clark, 2000), or a combination of behavioral and nonbehavioral techniques.

### Token Economy

A token economy is a simulated economic system based on token reinforcers (Kazdin, 2001). This highly versatile procedure can manage and motivate a wide range of behavior problems in schools and other intervention settings (Kerr & Nelson, 2006; Rosenberg et al., 2004). Individuals or groups may earn tokens for some target behaviors and lose them for others. Tokens are redeemed for various attractive items and privileges. Teachers using a token economy can simulate features of a national economy such as saving, credit, interest, investment, and inflation, as well as sales promotions such as clearance sales, mystery prizes, auctions, rebates, double-value days, lotteries, and so on. A token economy can be a powerful motivation system for difficult-to-motivate students and can help students learn about some features of adult finances. It does require investments of time and effort to start and maintain. Ghezzi, Wilson, Tarbox, and MacAleese (2003) and Jones, Dohrn, and Dunn (2004) describe procedures, advantages, limitations, and other issues of a token economy.

Many school token economies incorporate a **levels system**, which organizes student responsibilities and corresponding privileges into a hierarchy of contingency arrangements or levels (Cruz & Cullinan, 2001; Jones et al., 2004; Kerr & Nelson, 2006). Students complete responsibilities at a less demanding level before they are promoted to the next higher level of responsibilities and privileges.

Display 8-7 illustrates a behavior management program in a separate classroom for students with E&B disorder. It uses points as token reinforcers within a levels system; therefore it is called a points-and-levels system. When a student is enrolled in this classroom she would begin on *Level 1, Orientation*, and stay at least 8 days, longer if she failed to meet *Criteria to Advance a Level*. She meets those criteria by earning points for completing *Behavior Responsibilities* and *Study Responsibilities*. Points can also be spent to lease privileges, such as brief use of a personal headphone radio. She must also avoid performing *Freeze Level Offenses* (e.g., aggression). Freeze Level is a restricted situation resulting from specified offenses. Depending on the nature and context of the offense, Freeze varies in duration, extent of lost privileges, level to which the student returns after freeze, and other factors that insofar as possible are specified clearly, in advance, to the student.

Once Criteria to Advance are met, the student enters Level 2, which works similarly to Level 1, except Criteria, Responsibilities, and Privileges are greater. The student may progress through a third and fourth level as well, by which time she will be spending most or all of the school day in general education settings. Although in a classroom based on a points-and-levels system all students at a given level are subject to similar criteria, responsibilities, and privileges, the teacher may need to add individualized features to meet unique needs of particular students.

In many level systems (e.g., Display 8-7) the highest level not only offers extra privileges, it calls for the student to participate in regular education for some, much, or even all of the school day. Conversely, lower levels typically involve little or no participation in regular education, under the logical assumption that until a student demonstrates acceptable behaviors, emotions, and academic functioning she will not do well in general education. In some localities this use of the highest level in a level system may violate rulings of due process hearings or courts, or education agency policies, that restrict linking a student's participation in regular education to his progress in special education settings.

### *Behavioral Contracting*

A **behavioral contract** (or contingency contract) is a written specification of relationships between a person's target behaviors and the consequences for performing those behaviors. A behavioral contract should clearly state:

1. *Responsibilities:* The target behaviors to be performed by the student, including specific times, places, and other particulars of the target behaviors
2. *Monitoring:* Exactly how the student's performance of these responsibilities is to be observed and recorded
3. *Privileges:* Reinforcers available to the student on performance of the responsibilities, together with how and when privileges are to be given for completed responsibilities

In some cases, contracts may be made more effective by the addition of bonus and penalty clauses.

4. *Bonus clauses:* Provide special privileges for outstanding or highly consistent performance of responsibilities
5. *Penalty clauses:* Indicate what will be lost for unusually poor performance of responsibilities

Contracting practices vary a great deal. It may be best to conceptualize responsibilities and privileges as small, discrete units of target behavior and reinforcers. Bonus and penalty consequences should be kept separate from privileges. Privileges earned by completion of responsibilities should not be subject to loss due to a penalty clause or offenses not addressed by the contract.

If possible, the various aspects of the behavioral contract should be agreeable to both teacher and student. Some negotiation may be required, and agreement is indicated when student and adult (teacher, parent) sign the contract. Concepts of behavioral contracting are available in Houmanfar, Maglieri, and Roman (2003), Kerr and Nelson (2006), and Miltenberger (2004).

Display 8-7 Summary of main considerations, by level, in a middle school points-and-levels system

| Consideration | Level | | | |
|---|---|---|---|---|
| | 1. "Orientation" | 2. "Next Step" | 3. "Moving On" | 4. "Back On Track" |
| Minimum stay | 8 days | 20 days | 20 days | Until decertified |
| Point checking | Every 15 minutes | Every 30 minutes | Every 60 minutes, or ratings of teachers or supervisors after integrated activities | Ratings of teachers or supervisors after day's activities |
| Criteria to stay at level | No Freeze Level offenses | Earn 70 points per day No Freeze Level offenses | Earn 85 points per day No Freeze Level offenses | Weekly ratings by general education staff: <u>Unacceptable</u>, maximum = 2; <u>Good</u> or <u>Very Good</u>, minimum = 25 |
| Criteria to advance a level | Earn 800 points 5 consecutive days of 80 points No Freeze Level offenses | Earn 2,000 points 10 consecutive days of 90 points No Freeze Level offenses | Earn 2,000 points 10 consecutive days of 95 points No Freeze Level offenses | Determined by progress toward decertification No Freeze Level offenses |
| Behavior responsibilities | Attend school on time State/do group rules daily State/do personal goals daily Common decency to peers Common decency to staff In the circle at group events | All Orientation Level, plus: Do specified social skill 3 times daily | All Next Step Level, plus: Do specified social skill once daily in general education academic classes; Have general education teacher(s) rate conduct and participation on Daily Class Progress Note | Those of students in general classes or vocational sites, as indicated by staff members' ratings at end of class or each 60 minutes |

| | | | | |
|---|---|---|---|---|
| Study responsibilities | Return 1 homework at 80% correct; Start assignment in 60 seconds; On task 75% of work time; Complete assignment 80% correct; Record school and home assignments | All Orientation Level, plus: Do specified learning strategy 3 times daily; Read library book, 2 pages daily; Assigned activities related to classes in which student will be reintegrated (about 30 minutes/day) | All Next Step Level, plus: Read library book 5 pages daily; Assigned activities related to classes in which student will be reintegrated (about 60 minutes/day); Reintegration, 1 or 2 general education academic classes | Those of students in general classes or vocational sites, as indicated by staff members' ratings at end of class or each 60 minutes, and daily grade reports as appropriate |
| Level privileges | | All Orientation levels, plus: Unescorted bathroom breaks; Outside breaks with regular classes | All Next Step level, plus: Unescorted walk to classes; Field trips with classes; Club extracurriculars | Those of students in general classes or vocational sites |
| Privileges for lease with points | | Audiotape license; Cafeteria pass; Earphone radio license | Gym/playground time with staff; In-class free time; In-class snack license | In-school pass; Off-campus meal with staff; VCR license |
| Freeze Level offenses | | Physical aggression to staff members; Physical aggression to students | Leaving your assigned area (class, playground, cafeteria, work site) without staff permission | Destroying someone else's property; Stealing |

**Display 8-8** Behavioral contracting for homework completion

> Barbie was a 13-year-old enrolled for part of her school day in a resource room for middle school students with emotional disturbance and learning disabilities. Her school problems included academic underachievement in most subjects, noncompliance and negativism toward teacher authority, unpermitted absenteeism from school or particular class periods, and frequent failures to complete assignments.
>
> As an initial target behavior for the behavioral contracting procedures, Barbie's resource room teacher, Mr. Carter, selected completion of the reading comprehension homework that he assigned daily. Each of these assignments consisted of a brief reading exercise that did not exceed Barbie's reading abilities, followed by 10 to 15 comprehension questions to which she was to write responses. She had to turn in the assignment before the beginning of school the following day to the resource teacher, who graded it by the time Barbie came for her daily period of resource room assistance.
>
> Typically, Barbie did not turn in these assignments, and when she occasionally did there were seldom more than a few correct. The resource teacher recorded the percentage of correct items on this daily homework assignment for 7 days (baseline) before applying a behavior contract.
>
> Mr. Carter prepared to contract with Barbie by determining responsibilities, privileges, bonus and penalty clauses, and other details. For responsibilities he established percentage levels of correctness (e.g., 50 percent, 60 percent) on the homework. Finding privileges for which Barbie would work was a problem, but the teacher decided to try to use the girl's attraction to popular music by offering up to 10 minutes of listening to music through earphones as the privilege. The amount of listening time available each day was linked to the level of correctness on the homework assignment, up to a maximum of 10 minutes of music listening time for a 100 percent correct paper. Consistently good performance could earn a special bonus, such as a gift certificate at a nearby fast-food restaurant. Backsliding was penalized by a loss of recess time. The contract (see Display 9-10) was discussed with Barbie on Friday. She agreed to give it a try, and it went into effect on the following Monday.
>
> The resource teacher continued to record daily percentage correct on the reading-comprehension assignment and was pleased with the improvements in Barbie's performance. She was over the 50-percent level and therefore received music listening time on most days. On the third day of contracting she lost her recess. On days 10 and 15, she earned a gift certificate. After about 3 weeks on this contract, it was renegotiated to include mathematics computation homework assignments. Later in the year additional types of homework assigned by some of Barbie's other teachers were included in the contracting procedure.

### *Social Skills Training*

Social skills are behaviors that enable a person to start and maintain positive social interactions, to be accepted by others, and to achieve appropriate adjustment to school and other significant social environments (Elksnin & Elksnin, 2006; Gresham, 2002; Kavale, Mathur, & Mostert, 2004; Walker et al., 2004). Students who are unable or unwilling to perform social skills adequately, and/or are not accepted by peers, are at risk for continuing personal and social maladjustment. Teaching social skills is designed to improve students' interactions, social acceptance, and adjustment in school and life.

One behavioral approach to teaching social skills is to increase prosocial behaviors and decrease behaviors that interfere with social competence. The teacher identifies the student's existing prosocial behaviors (e.g., introducing oneself, asking to

**Display 8-9** Contract for Barbie

# DEAL

for _Barbie Dominguez_

## Main Exchange

| Responsibility Completed | Privilege Earned |
|---|---|
| For each daily reading-comprehension homework assignment completed at these percentages correct: | Barbie is entitled to listen to the MP3 player or radio for a period of: |
| at least 50% correct | 1 minute |
| at least 60% correct | 2 minutes |
| at least 70% correct | 3 minutes |
| at least 80% correct | 4 minutes |
| at least 90% correct | 5 minutes |

## Bonus Clause

| Good Accomplishment | Bonus Delivered and Accepted |
|---|---|
| (a) For a 100% correct assignment | (a) 10 minutes of MP3 or radio |
| (b) For 5 days in a row of at least 90% correct assignments | (b) a $2.00 gift certificate good at Burgers R Us |

## Penalty Clause

| Poor Performance | Penalty Delivered and Accepted |
|---|---|
| (a) For any assignment graded 0 percent correct | (a) spend recess that day in the assistant principal's office |

## Fine Print (below or attached)

Definitions and details of responsibilities, privileges, and other contract provisions are on the back of this contract. Specifics of monitoring are also on the back.

Today's date: _November 12_ This deal lasts from (start date): _November 15_ to (end date): _December 7_

Deal will be renegotiated (when, where): _December 7_          This deal suits me. I agree to take part in it.

_Barbie Dominguez_, Student          _R. L. Dominguez_, Parent

_Kendrick Carter_, Teacher

participate, complimenting, cooperating, sharing, taking turns, and conversing appropriately), however infrequently they may occur. He also identifies behaviors that interfere with social interactions and peer acceptance, such as arguing, interrupting, acting maladaptively strange, or withdrawing from the group. Then the teacher applies DRI by reinforcing the prosocial skills while reducing interfering behaviors via extinction and, perhaps, punishment (Meadows & Stevens, 2004).

What if there were an important prosocial behavior the student simply did not perform (thus there is nothing to reinforce)? The teacher might teach this behavior by describing its simple parts in proper sequence and asking the student to do these. She could show him by demonstrating the behavior and having him imitate it immediately. She could require the student to practice this prosocial skill in her presence and elsewhere (Meadows & Stevens, 2004). These and other teaching techniques are involved in *social skills training*.

Social skills training is the systematic, directive teaching of specific skills needed for appropriate social interaction. There are many behavioristic social skills training procedures and/or curricula available (e.g., Alberg, Petry, & Eller, 1994; Battalio & Stephens, 2005; Kavale et al., 2004). They are generally similar as to intervention goals and skills covered, varying somewhat more as to teaching procedures used.

***Goals.*** Nearly all social skills training is designed to promote the learning of new skills. Other goals of social skills training should be to improve poor skills (e.g., partially accurate, infrequently performed), reduce obstacles to socialization (e.g., withdrawal from peers, bullying, aversive body odor), support "natural" performance (e.g., skills performed fluently and authentically), and encourage behavior maintenance and setting generalization in classrooms, buses, and other situations outside of training.

***Skill Coverage.*** Most social skills training packages address, to varying degrees, behaviors that please teachers, please peers, and control interferences. (a) Students' school adjustment is linked to their performance of teacher-pleasing behaviors, especially prerequisites to academic success such as coming to class on time, bringing materials, paying attention, asking and responding to questions, following directions, and requesting help (Gresham, 2002; Lane, Wehby & Cooley, 2006). (b) Perhaps even more crucial are peer-pleasing behaviors—starting verbal and behavior interactions, complimenting, keeping interactions going, cooperating, sharing, and following formal or informal peer group rules. (c) In addition, many social skills training packages cover skills to counteract temptations, provocations, harrassments, strong emotions, negative thoughts, and other situations that are likely to interfere with good performance of social skills or with acceptance by peers (Elksnin & Elksnin, 2005; Hazel, Schumaker, Sherman, & Sheldon, 1996). Some skills serve more than one of these purposes.

Of course, it is usually illogical to teach a particular skill to a child or adolescent who already knows it, and not all students with ED are lacking in social skills (Wagner, Kutash, Duchnowski, Epstein, & Sumi, 2005). Thus many social skill packages recommend or provide assessment procedures to help match students to the particular skills they need to be taught (Elksnin & Elksnin, 2006). Assessment is especially helpful when students will be taught individually or in small groups homogeneous for the social skill.

***Teaching Procedures.*** Systematic, directive teaching of specific social skills generally relies on demonstration, imitation, consequences, and practice. If the social skill to be taught is fairly simple (e.g., asking the teacher's permission, taking turns with peers when talking, maintaining eye contact with peers or teacher), few or no additional procedures may be needed. After getting the student's attention, the teacher (a) demonstrates the social skill; (b) calls for the child to imitate it immediately; (c) provides feedback, praise, or other consequences, or has the group do so; and (d) arranges for the student to practice the social skill in the training situation and elsewhere.

However, many important social skills are complex, and/or for other reasons require additional actions to help the student with ED learn and perform the skill.

1. *Preparation* before teaching may include analysis of a complex skill into teachable components, assessment of students to select skills and establish teaching groups, and training in specialized teaching procedures for a particular curriculum.
2. *Demonstration* may be enhanced by giving students a justification of its value with examples and by presenting multiple demonstrations, in each of which the model is reinforced (i.e., is socially successful). In some cases erroneous demonstrations, clearly identified as such, can build the concept of what the appropriate social skill is, and is not.
3. *Imitation* by the student may be facilitated by "leading," in which the teacher co-performs during the student's initial imitations. This gives an additional demonstration and may prompt a reluctant participant to try. The teacher should require multiple imitations, with verbal corrections and reminders of the skill components.
4. *Consequences* should be mainly accuracy feedback from the teacher or other students in the group and student self-evaluation of his own imitation.
5. *Practice* is an extension of imitation. A student should practice the social skill several times during the session, perhaps in a simulated situation in which other group members act various parts. After identifying real situations in which the skill could be relevant for her, the student may be assigned to practice it elsewhere in the school or community.

Social skills training is presented here as a behavioral intervention, and it is possible to interpret most of steps 1 to 5 in terms of behavioral theory. However, some social skills teaching practices appear to be better understood in cognitive terms. For instance, under the *Imitation* step, a student can learn to give herself thought reminders for each component of the overall social skill, or help herself perform a complex behavior by recalling a moving image of the model demonstrating it. Quite a few social skills training packages have elements of both behavior modification and cognitive interventions, as illustrated in Chapter 9.

Social skills training is widely recommended and used. Its effectiveness seems to vary across different situations, E&B disorders, and teaching methods (e.g., Bullis,

Walker, & Sprague, 2001; Kavale et al., 2004). Gresham (2002; Gresham, Crews, & Kern, 2004) described ways to increase the value of social skills training through improvements in measuring social skills, selecting interventions that match skills problems, eliminating maladaptive interfering behaviors, and arranging for generalization.

## Behavior Modification Programs

### Regular Education

#### CLASS

Contingencies for Learning Academic and Social Skills (CLASS) is designed to help elementary school teachers control defiant, disruptive, and aggressive behaviors of a student at risk for identification with ED. This program integrates dependent group contingency, social, activity, and token reinforcement, timeout, and other intervention techniques (Hops & Walker, 1988; Walker et al., 2004). In the group contingency, the target student earns tokens (points) for displaying appropriate classroom behavior and following the teacher's rules. If he earns enough points during the day, his entire class shares in a reward (e.g., extra recess, playing a game). Second, the teacher also dispenses social reinforcement (praise) to the student each time a point is earned. A third component is timeout for instances of severe disruption. Fourth, arrangements are made with the student's parents to provide a home reward (e.g., extra TV time, treats, privileges), along with praise, when the student brings home a satisfactory daily report card, which is provided only if he has earned sufficient points at school.

CLASS is compatible with a range of curricula, teaching styles, and other features of classrooms. It is designed to be completed in under 2 months. For the first few days it is put into effect by a consultant trained in the CLASS procedures. During this time the classroom teacher learns how to carry out CLASS by observing the consultant, supplemented by reading and discussion. The teacher very soon begins to take over the implementation of CLASS with feedback from the consultant, and within several days is maintaining CLASS with little or no consultant help. As this program moves to completion, the teacher's use of points is phased out while teacher praise is continued to maintain the student's appropriate behavior. Similarly, in the later stages of the program, parents continue contingent praise for good school reports but no longer give other home rewards. Careful research on the use of CLASS by many teachers in a variety of locations strongly supports the power of this program to normalize the behavior of aggressive and disruptive elementary-age students.

#### First Step to Success

CLASS has been adapted for use as a main component of *First Step to Success* (Beard, & Sugai, 2004; Golly, Stiller, & Walker, 1998; Walker, Kavanagh, Stiller, Golly, Severson, & Feil, 1997; Walker et al., 2004), a prevention program for students

**Display 8-10** Hill M. Walker profile

> Hill Walker is a behavioral psychologist and special educator, with a doctorate in special education, from University of Oregon. He has maintained a career-long focus on applied research designed to develop solutions to social, emotional, and behavior problems of young people and to create assessment and intervention tools that make educators more effective.
>
> Among Walker's accomplishments are the development of assessment procedures and curricula for improving the placement and integration of students with behavior and learning disorders, along with practical, valid procedures for early screening of and intervention with emotional and behavioral problems of children and youth at risk for continuing antisocial behavior. With colleagues at CORBEH, Walker utilized a three-stage process to develop and refine interventions. First, individual treatment techniques were studied and modified in experimental education situations. Techniques thus validated were combined into a standard package for use in ordinary schools by teachers of students with behavior and learning disorders, still under close supervision from the researchers. Finally, refined by research, the treatment package was field-tested in many school districts away from the developers' control, to determine its usability and acceptability. Through this process treatment packages were developed to solve the problems of acting out behavior (CLASS), poor academic survival skills (PASS), social withdrawal (PEERS), and out-of-classroom aggression and bullying (RECESS).
>
> Since 1990, Walker has devoted substantial effort to school safety, student violence reduction, and prevention of E&B disorder. He helped create a guide for schools to recognize early signs of troubled students (*Early Warning, Timely Response*), violence intervention programs identified as national models of best practice, and an influential agenda to identify and help very young students at high risk for developing E&B disorder (*First Step to Success*).
>
> He founded the Institute on Violence and Destructive Behavior at University of Oregon, where he serves on the faculty in Education. Walker has published many influential research and discussion journal articles, book chapters, and books that address children with E&B disorder, especially aggressive and other antisocial behavior. He also serves on the editorial boards of several professional journals. Among Walker's professional honors are the Outstanding Researcher Award of the Council for Exceptional Children, for career achievements of a researcher in special education.

in grades K to 3 who are at risk for chronic antisocial functioning, including *Aggression, Impulsiveness*, and Law-Breaking Behavior. *First Step to Success* includes three interrelated components—proactive screening, school intervention, and home intervention—implemented by teachers, parents, and peers in an approximately 3-month program.

***Proactive Screening.*** The screening component uses well-established screening procedures applied to classrooms, schools, or other large groups. The purpose is to identify young students whose present problems predict high likelihood of antisocial behavior several years in the future. Preferred screening procedures are Systematic Screening for Behavior Disorders (SSBD; described in Chapter 3) and Early Screening Project (ESP; Walker, Severson, & Feil, 1995), a modification of SSBD for preschool settings. Both SSBD and ESP involve three stages of assessment in which more resource-intensive procedures are reserved for later in the process, at which point fewer students remain under consideration. Other screening procedures can be used as well.

***School Intervention.*** The school intervention component is CLASS, modified as appropriate for age and other special circumstances. Skilled consultants provide demonstrations, other instruction, and support to the targeted student's classroom teacher. Gradually the classroom teacher assumes control of the school intervention, while support remains available.

***Home Intervention.*** In the home intervention component ("Homebase"), program consultants train the parents of an at-risk student how to teach their child crucial prosocial skills, manage antisocial behavior at home, support the school intervention component of First Step to Success, and take an active role in school life. The parent training includes six weekly in-home lessons on teaching the child to cooperate with peers and adults, comply with adult directives, and solve problems. Program consultants contact the parents for other purposes and arrange parent group events to encourage mutual support and overcome obstacles to success.

## Separate Classes

### *Engineered Classroom*

Probably the most influential program for educating students with E&B disorder was Frank Hewett's Engineered Classroom (Hewett, 1968; see Chapter 2). In this elementary school separate class program, time and physical aspects were highly structured. Praise, token reinforcers exchangeable for rewards, timeout from reinforcement, and other behavior modification methods were used to encourage appropriate learning and social behavior. As a guide for learning and social goals for student progress over time, Hewett created a "developmental sequence" of steps toward ever higher personal and educational capabilities. Since the late 1960s, the Engineered Classroom has been the prototype for many separate classes for students with E&B disorder, often without the developmental sequence (i.e., using ordinary curriculum goals instead).

### *Franklin-Jefferson Program*

The Franklin-Jefferson (F-J) Program (Schloss, Holt, Mulvaney, & Green, 1988) is a multifaceted program for elementary, middle, or high school age students with E&B disorder. Its main components involve multiple behavior modification practices, supplemented by cognitive interventions. Together these components amount to a comprehensive plan for self-contained classrooms in regular and alternative schools. The components are the School Note, activities and breaks, relaxation, social skills, aggression management, a levels system, staff training, and family involvement.

***School Note.*** The F-J Program day is organized clearly for teachers and students through the use of each student's School Note. This identifies periods of education activities and breaks, specifies what each student's activity is each period, ties daily activities to IEP and other goals, lists behaviors for which points are awarded and docked (fined) for the student, and provides appropriate spaces for teachers and other staff members to mark award and dockage points, by behavior.

***Activities and Breaks.*** The F-J Program day is subdivided into activity periods and breaks. In each activity period the student carries out an assignment or activity that pursues goals identified in his IEP or other goals negotiated with the teacher. Each period's activity is specified in his individualized School Note. For starting, continuing, and good achievement on these activities, and for prosocial behavior, the teacher awards points; for disruptive, aggressive, and other inappropriate behavior, the teacher docks points. Physical aggression results in a high fine and possible placement in a restriction room.

After several activity periods there is a scheduled break of about 15 minutes. Breaks offer students the opportunity to engage in specific preferred activities or free time. A student earns a break if, since the last break, his points awarded exceed his points docked. Excess award points give him opportunities for special activities. A student who does not earn a break must continue to work on assigned tasks during break period. After the break, students' point totals, awarded and docked, are reset to zero in order to create a "clean slate."

***Relaxation.*** Students are taught via regular sessions to relax muscles, breathe deeply, talk normally and with control, keep a relaxed facial expression, sit or stand without excess motion or excitement, and other behaviors that increase emotional control and project low levels of excitement to others (see Ferguson, 2003; Jacob & Pelham, 2005). Relaxation is largely incompatible with behaviors, thoughts, and physiological responses characteristic of strong emotional states such as anger or fear.

***Social Skills.*** Social skills appropriate to the students' needs and problems are taught. Throughout the school day, staff members recognize and reinforce these skills.

***Aggression Management.*** Students may aggress or disrupt for many reasons, including to escape disliked requirements, achieve goals they value above those of the teacher, and frighten or annoy peers and staff members. The F-J Program has a special set of consequences designed to ensure that aggressive behavior has a high cost to the aggressor and to require positive practice in relaxation, social skills, and

**Display 8-11** The 10 Rs of the Franklin-Jefferson aggression management intervention

| Step | Action Taken |
|---|---|
| 1. Response Cost | • From the student's School Note, the staff member docks a high point fine. |
| 2. Relax | • Student engages in previously taught relaxation skills. For a minimum of 3 minutes, student must talk in a normal tone of voice, keep calm instead of being agitated, breathe deeply through the nose, and maintain normal face expression. |
| 3. Rectify | • Student corrects the physical or emotional disruption caused. |
| 4. Recognize | • Student names events that led to her aggression, as well as appropriate behaviors that could be alternatives to aggression. |
| 5. Rehearse | • Student performs alternative prosocial or other appropriate behavior(s) identified in Step 4. |
| 6. Reinforce | • Staff member praises the student's performance in Step 5. |
| 7. Reflect | • Student compares aloud the consequences of the aggressive way she actually behaved (e.g., points and privileges lost, the hassle of having to rectify her misdeed) versus the behavior alternative to aggression that she just practiced. |
| 8. Reenter | • Student returns to class and "picks up" at the least preferred activity on her schedule that was missed due to the aggressive episode. If necessary, her breaks are lost to do so. |
| 9. Record | • (Antecedents and consequences of aggressive reactions are recorded) |
| 10. Repeat | • This same sequence is repeated every time the student performs a physically aggressive act. |

*Source:* Schloss, Holt, Mulvaney, & Green (1988).

other adaptive behaviors (see Display 8-11). For aggression to staff members the student is placed in a restriction room for at least one day.

***Levels System.*** The F-J Program token reinforcement arrangement incorporates a levels system. The program as described so far constitutes Level 1, at which all students begin. Students who earn at least 80% of points for 3 consecutive weeks move to Level 2. At this level the student neither earns nor loses points, but has automatic access to breaks and privileges. At Level 3 students attend regular classes. This level is for those who for 2 consecutive weeks in Level 2 have completed at least 80% of their assignments and have exhibited zero instances of aggression or violation of other major rules.

***Staff.*** Teachers and other staff members are trained in F-J procedures so that all adults involved will consistently implement the various techniques. This is intended to improve setting generalization. For example, students are less likely to "shop" for staff members who are lax in awarding points or implementing the aggression management strategy.

***Family Involvement.*** Parents help determine in-school goals for their student. Also, they receive the School Note and are asked to give nightly verbal feedback to the youth based on his points earned on the School Note.

## CHAPTER SUMMARY

The behavioral model consists mainly of Skinner's operant conditioning and the intervention techniques derived from it.

- In operant conditioning, behaviors are emitted. If followed by a consequence, the behavior's strength may be increased through reinforcement or decreased through extinction or punishment.
- Besides consequences, other key aspects of operant behaviors include:
  — Schedules
  — Behavior classes
  — Antecedents
- Behaviorists view E&B disorders as behaviors judged to be inappropriate.
- Children learn inappropriate behaviors mainly via:
  — Positive social reinforcement (adult or peer attention) for misbehaviors and
  — Negative social reinforcement (giving in to coercion).
- School practitioners use behavioral interventions to increase students' appropriate behavior and decrease their inappropriate behavior.
- Many behavioral interventions have been validated through applied behavior analysis.
- Appropriate student behaviors are increased through contingent social attention, preferred activities, and tokens.
- Inappropriate student behaviors are decreased by:
  — Extinction
  — Punishment via positive practice, response cost, and timeout
  — Positive approaches such as DRL or DRI
- Variations on the basic techniques include:
  — Interdependent or dependent group contingencies
  — Changing antecedents that control inappropriate behavior
  — Student self-management
  — The token economy with levels of increasing expectations and privileges
  — Behavioral contracting
  — Social skills training
- The CLASS program is designed to prevent a student's disruptive behavior from escalating into a referral for special education.

- *First Step to Success* is a prevention program for young students at risk for antisocial behavior. It includes CLASS plus screening and parental involvement components.
- The Franklin-Jefferson Program combines several behavioral and other intervention components, integrated by use of a School Note.

## IDEAS FOR CONSIDERATION AND DISCUSSION

1. Consider Displays 8-1 and 8-2. Think of school situations that illustrate the following phenomena:
   a. Teacher unintentionally supports the student's nonparticipation with peers, through her use of positive reinforcement.
   b. Teacher uses positive reinforcement to encourage the student's cooperation with peers on a group project.
   c. Teacher uses negative reinforcement to encourage the student's compliance with classroom rules about talking and remaining seated during independent work on an assignment.
2. Briefly state the concept of discrimination. Based on your examination of Display 8-3, suggest how discrimination could help explain why Roland, a middle school student, is frequently defiant, disrespectful, and disobedient with Mr. Sanchez in Period 3 but typically compliant, upbeat, and on task with Ms. Washington-Obidi in Period 4.
3. Name and explain two ways in which E&B disorders are caused, according to operant conditioning. Create one example of a behavior problem that illustrates each way.
4. Select one of the five patterns of E&B disorders (see Chapter 4). Develop two target behavior definitions for this pattern, one involving a behavior that needs to be increased to achieve improvement, the other involving a behavior that needs to be decreased to achieve improvement. Your target behavior definitions should address behaviors that are unlike those already in Display 8-4.
5. a. How might group contingencies be used in the regular class and the separate school education environments? Describe an example of group contingencies applied in each education environment.
   b. How might token economy be used in the resource room and the separate class education environments? Describe an example of token economy applied in each education environment.
6. Select one of the patterns of E&B disorder (see Chapter 4). Develop a list of four social skills that might be especially helpful to students showing this pattern. Analyze each of the four skills into two component subskills that can be taught separately.

## RESOURCES FOR FURTHER STUDY

www.abainternational.org Association for Behavior Analysis
www.bfskinner.org/ B.F. Skinner Foundation
www.usu.edu/teachall/text/behavior/LRBIpdfs/Behavioral.pdf Behavior contracting

**www.journals.apa.org/prevention/volume4/pre0040001app13.html** First Step to Success
**www.specialconnections.ku.edu/cgibin/cgiwrap/specconn/main.php?cat=behavior&section=main&subsection=classroom/positive#ques4** Group contingencies
**seab.envmed.rochester.edu/jaba/** Journal of Applied Behavior Analysis
**www.state.ky.us/agencies/behave/bi/TO.html** Recommendations for implementing timeout
**www.usu.edu/teachall/text/behavior/LRBlpdfs/Token.pdf** Token economy

Chapter **Nine**

# *Cognitive Model*

## CHAPTER OBJECTIVES

**After reading this chapter, you should be able to:**
- Describe the four subprocesses of modeling.
- State similarities and differences between reciprocal determinism and operant conditioning.
- List four ways by which children may develop E&B disorder, according to the social cognitive theory.
- Discriminate cognitive deficits and cognitive distortions.
- Describe five stages of teaching cognitive problem solving.
- State how the A-B-C concept of Rational-Emotive Therapy applies to E&B disorder.

## CAN YOU DEFINE THESE 10 TERMS?

modeling
vicarious effects
perceived self-efficacy
response access
cognitive distortion

transfer homework
problem-solving set
triggers
negative cognitive triad
disputing

### Summary of Cognitive Theory and Intervention

| WHAT | Name of Theory | Cognitive Theory |
|---|---|---|
| | Brief description of theory | Cognitions, behaviors, and environmental stimuli interact with and control each other. Thinking about past events, planning for the future, self-regulating, and learning new behaviors by observing models are some ways that cognitions affect behaviors. Cognitions contribute to E&B disorder when, for instance, children ruminate about unhappy setbacks, anticipate a hopeless future, misinterpret the meaning of peers' actions and words, cannot think of nonaggressive responses to conflicts, misjudge the outcomes of behaviors they could perform, or acquire maladaptive behaviors or emotions from models. |
| | Key terms | <u>Observational learning</u>: Acquisition of capabilities to behave or experience emotions by observing a model<br><u>Reciprocal determinism</u>: Theory about how cognitions, behaviors, and environmental stimuli interact to influence each other |

(*continued*)

## Summary of Cognitive Theory and Intervention (Continued)

| WHAT | Name of Theory | Cognitive Theory |
|---|---|---|
| | | <u>Dysfunctional self-efficacy</u>: Mistaken judgment about what will result from performing some behavior |
| | | <u>Cognitive deficit</u>: Absence of some important cognitive process, leading to E&B disorder |
| | | <u>Cognitive distortion</u>: Faulty operation of some important cognitive process, leading to E&B disorder |
| | | <u>Self-instruction</u>: Intervention in which the student says or thinks statements that guide her or his own actions |
| | | <u>Cognitive problem-solving</u>: Intervention in which the student determines what the problem is, then selects responses that will solve it |
| | | <u>Irrational belief</u>: Unrealistic belief linked to maladaptive emotions and behaviors |
| WHO | Who is intervention appropriate for? | Students who exhibit cognitive deficits or cognitive distortions related to their E&B disorder |
| | Who delivers intervention? | The student herself or himself, after instructional intervention by educators or other professionals |
| WHEN | When and how often is intervention delivered? | At training sessions involving groups of students and one or more educators; and/or in ongoing classroom and school activities that may be extensions of the training sessions |
| WHERE | In what contexts is intervention delivered? | Some cognitive interventions can be used in any classroom; others involve activities better suited to resource and separate classrooms, or counseling sessions |
| WHY | Rationale/purpose for intervention | To correct cognitive deficits and distortions that play a role in a student's E&B disorder |
| HOW | Selected strategies for intervention | 1. Model appropriate behaviors and thoughts (aloud)<br>2. Teach self-instruction<br>3. Teach cognitive problem-solving<br>4. Teach students to recognize and correct social misperceptions and other distortions of information processing<br>5. Dispute and teach students to dispute irrational beliefs and other distortions of attitudes and beliefs |

The cognitive model (also called "cognitive-behavioral") is a group of ideas about how cognition plays a role in emotions and behaviors, how E&B disorders originate, and what to do about them. Diverse developments that took place mainly after the mid-20th century set the stage for today's cognitive explanations of and interventions for E&B disorders of children and adolescents (Albano, 2005; Braswell & Kendall, 2001; Dobson & Dozois, 2001; D'Zurilla & Nezu, 2001; Erickson & Achilles, 2004; Mayer, Lochman, & Van Acker, 2005).

For one thing, there was a sharp increase in the scientific study of children's attention, memory, imagery, language as a mediator of behavior, and other aspects of thinking (e.g., Berk, 2006; DeHart, Sroufe, & Cooper, 2004; Meichenbaum & Goodman, 1971). Important threads of this research explored cognition associated with emotional and behavior problems of children (Reinecke, Dattilio, & Freeman, 2003). Another contributor was the widespread, successful use of psychotherapies for adults that relied heavily on the client's thoughts and mental images (e.g., Beck & Newman, 2005; Dryden & Ellis, 2001).

During this same period, researchers were extending operant conditioning into the realms of thoughts (conceptualized as "covert operants") and self-behavior modification (e.g., Homme, 1965; Kanfer & Karoly, 1972). Many of these projects were direct extrapolations of behavior modification, but others were not easily explained by operant conditioning. They appeared to require cognitive explanations.

Finally, the research and theory of Albert Bandura (1969, 1986, 1997) clarified and expanded the case for a strong cognitive role in E&B disorder. Bandura studied cognitive aspects of imitation and demonstrated that cognitive variables can control a wide range of behavior and behavior change. This work led to the creation of social cognitive theory, Bandura's influential explanation of how cognition interacts with various kinds human performance and external forces.

##  MODELING AND SOCIAL COGNITIVE THEORY

Beginning in the 1960s, Bandura explored human imitation and related psychological phenomena. His scholarship yielded a thorough explanation of imitation from a cognitive perspective (Bandura, 1969, 1971), referred to as modeling theory. The implications of modeling led to a more general theory of human functioning (Bandura, 1973, 1986, 1997) called social cognitive theory. Modeling and social cognitive theory are complex, and they address many areas of human functioning, but let us consider in brief a few aspects that have implications for the cognitive model.

### Modeling

**Modeling** refers to changes in one person's thoughts, behaviors, and emotions that result from her observing another person (the model). Bandura found that psychodynamic, behavioral, and other theories could not adequately explain many of the everyday facts about imitation and modeling. For instance, most people see and hear numerous different models every day—whenever they are with other people or viewing television programs, for example. But what determines which models and behaviors they will or will not imitate? How are people able to imitate behavior not only immediately but after hours or even years have passed since they observed it?

### Acquisition Versus Performance

Bandura's research showed that observers of a model acquire and retain mental representations of a model's behaviors. He distinguished two effects of observing a model:

1. The cognitive *acquisition* of mental representations that provide to the observer new behavior capabilities
   *versus*
2. The imitative *performance* of already-existing behavior capabilities

**Acquisition: Observational Learning.** Bandura analyzed modeling into a sequence of four subprocesses. The first three—attention, retention, and response reproduction—are mainly concerned with the acquisition of new behavior capabilities by observing a model. Bandura called this acquisition effect of modeling *observational learning*.

Observational learning plays a crucial role in child development. Many language, social, and other critical human behavior patterns are so complex that they would be very difficult to learn without observing a model's demonstration. Other important behaviors are simple enough to learn through trial-and-error, but are so dangerous that just one mistake would end all learning attempts. Fortunately, most children acquire a vast range of important behavior capabilities during developing years, by seeing, hearing, and otherwise observing behaviors modeled by parents, peers, teachers, and others.

Besides behaviors, children acquire emotions through observational learning. This is because emotions involve observable cognitive, behavior, and physiological aspects. These can be acquired by the child through observing another person's words, actions, facial expressions, gestures, voice pitch, breathing rate, and other indicators of emotional response.

**Performance: Vicarious Effects.** Bandura's fourth subprocess of modeling—motivation—is not principally involved in the acquisition of mental representations of a model's behavior. Instead, motivation subprocess has to do with whether, and under what circumstances, an observer's behavior changes as a result of observing a model. For example, how does observation of a model affect the observer's motivation to imitate that model? Changes in the observer's behavior that result from observation of a model are called **vicarious effects**.

One kind of vicarious effect involves an observer's behavior becoming more likely or less likely due to his observing the consequences of a model's behavior. If the model's behavior obtained favorable consequences, the observer will probably be more likely to imitate that behavior. Bandura would say that the observer's behavior is "vicariously reinforced." If the model's behavior received unfavorable consequences, the observer probably will not behave similarly (his imitative behavior will have been vicariously punished). In either case, modeling has not taught the observer a new behavior capability. Instead, through a vicarious effect it has informed him about what consequences will probably follow a behavior. That is why it may affect motivation to perform that behavior.

A different vicarious effect involves characteristics of the model. Suppose that one or more model characteristics (e.g., age, sex, race-ethnic status, style of dressing or speaking, apparent physical prowess, expressed interests) resemble those of the observer. On this basis the observer might decide to imitate the model, reasoning that because of their similarity, a behavior for which the model was rewarded will probably be rewarded for her as well. On the other hand, if the model has dissimilar characteristics the observer may assume that she and the model are subject to different rules and rewards. Again, modeling provides information that can affect the observer's motivation to actually perform an existing behavior capability.

## From Modeling to Social Cognitive Theory

Bandura and colleagues expanded modeling theory, incorporating research on the role of cognition in self-regulation while retaining the crucial distinction between acquisition and performance. This evolution resulted in social cognitive theory, which features Bandura's overall view of human functioning reflected in the concept of *reciprocal determinism.*

In social cognitive theory, there are three kinds of phenomena that exert influence over each other: the individual's behavior (**B**), environmental (**E**), and personal (**P**) (especially cognitive) phenomena (see Display 9-1). The social cognitive

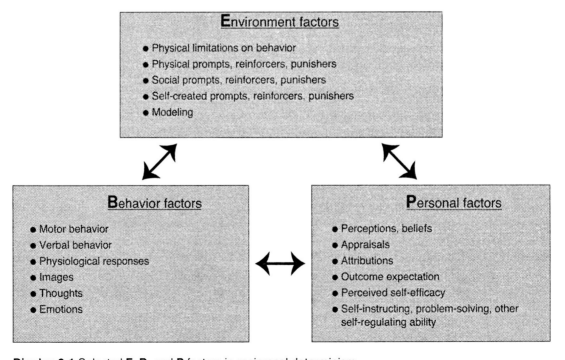

**Display 9-1** Selected **E, B,** and **P** factors in reciprocal determinism

view of reciprocal determinism (back and forth control) between **B** and **E** is compatible in some ways with operant conditioning. For instance, some behaviors function to change (add or subtract) environmental events, while environmental events act as antecedents and consequences to change behaviors.

However, reciprocal determinism differs from operant conditioning in significant ways. For one thing, **B** includes not only motor and verbal operants, but mental phenomena such as thoughts and images. Also, **E** often does not affect **B** automatically or directly but via **P** phenomena. For instance, many environmental events provide information that the young person cognitively processes, usually in light of existing beliefs, attributions, and other information. These cognitive processing results guide his decisions about behavior to enact.

To some extent the cognitive processing of **E** information accounts for the fact that different people, exposed to the same information, may attend to and remember different things, and therefore respond to the information differently. Other **P** activities enable people to learn new behaviors and control them through cognitive processes such as symbolizing, planning, self-regulating, and learning from models (Cervone, 2000; Williams & Cervone, 1998).

For illustration, controlling one's own behavior through planning might involve (a) symbolizing various possible future situations; (b) anticipating different responses one might make to each situation; and (c) attempting to foresee outcomes expected of the different responses. These response outcome expectancies can greatly affect motivation: a child tends to be strongly motivated to perform a behavior that she expects will result in privileges, compliments from peers, and other desired outcomes.

A further aspect of planning is judging how adequately one can perform a particular behavior. Bandura called this **P** variable *perceived self-efficacy*. It has significant implications for motivation and performance. For instance, no matter how desirable the outcomes of a particular behavior may be, a child will probably not try to perform that behavior if she judges that she lacks skills needed to do it. Perceived self-efficacy is relevant to an understanding of some emotional and behavior problems.

## Social Cognitive Theory and E&B Disorder

Social cognitive theory indicates several explanations for how children acquire and perform maladaptive behaviors, emotions, and cognitions (Bandura, 1969, 1986; Hallenbeck & Kauffman, 1995). Among them are two based on observational learning, two based on vicarious effects, and one based on perceived self-efficacy.

***Observational Learning of Maladaptive Behavior.*** Children who observe people exhibiting hostile, phobic, sad, impulsive, withdrawn, law-denigrating, drug-taking, suicidal, bizarre, or other kinds of disordered behavior are likely to learn how to perform such behavior. Observational learning of maladaptive behavior is particularly likely when a young person (a) is exposed to a variety of inappropriate behaviors (b) that are repeatedly exhibited by numerous models, (c) who are observed to benefit from the inappropriate behaviors. In this way, family members, community adults, peers, schoolmates, Internet displays, video games, films, and television can be rich sources of information on how to behave maladaptively.

***Observational Learning Failure.*** Conversely, a lack of observational learning of appropriate behaviors can also contribute to E&B disorder. Developing children need to acquire various skills that enable them to master challenges that life will bring. But homes and communities may have few or no persons who model such critical skills. Or, the child may experience a failure in a subprocess of observational learning (attention, retention, response reproduction). In either case, children may be delayed in learning important skills such as how to comply with rules, start or continue social interactions, solve conflicts without violence, anticipate and plan for setbacks and opportunities, and solve social problems. Without skills expected of age peers, this child could experience social and personal problems.

***Vicarious Behavior Disinhibition.*** Models can powerfully encourage misbehavior even when they do not teach new misbehavior capabilities. For example, after observing that others readily violate standards while suffering few ill effects, a young person's reluctance to violate those standards may be weakened. He may begin to freely engage in inappropriate behaviors that previously he avoided.

***Vicarious Emotional Arousal.*** By observing someone's responses to a particular situation a child can experience joy, disgust, sadness, anger, dread, or other strong emotional arousal. Later in a similar situation, the child may experience the same emotion as before, even if the model is not there. If this emotional reaction interferes with social relationships or other developmental opportunities, it is a maladaptive emotion. For example, children can learn to be very angry about a certain person by observing the angry behaviors, ideas, and emotions directed toward that person by loved ones, schoolmates, or teachers.

***Dysfunctional Self-Efficacy.*** Emotional and behavioral problems can be caused by dysfunctionally low or high perceptions of **self-efficacy.** A student with the *Anxiety* pattern often has low perceived self-efficacy about making friends (Boegels & Zigterman, 2000). That young person believes he will appear awkward and be ineffective in making friends. Therefore, even if he really knows how, he is not likely to perform the responses necessary for meeting people and making a friend.

On the other hand, an adolescent with *Aggression* might have very high perceived self-efficacy about her capability to inflict hurt on peers. She will probably be much more likely than other children to rely on bullying and violent methods of settling disagreements.

## Other Cognitive Explanations of E&B Disorder

Two other cognitive explanations of children's emotional and behavior problems, Social Information Processing and Cognitive Deficits/Distortions, are helpful. Both are compatible with significant ideas in social cognitive theory (e.g., distinction between acquisition and performance, concepts of outcome expectancy and perceived self-efficacy).

### *Social Information Processing*

Dodge and colleagues (Crick & Dodge, 1994; McFadyen-Ketchum & Dodge, 1998) developed a model of social information processing (SIP) to explain behavior problems often found in the *Aggression* pattern of E&B disorder. Examples of social information include people's acts, words, tone of voice, appearance, face expressions, behavior products, and other obvious or subtle information generated by the behavior of people. The SIP model has six key steps that operate in a sequence, as described below.

1. *Encoding* involves seeking, attending to, and retaining social information. Aggressive children are less likely than nonaggressive ones to seek social information and to pay attention to relevant social information. Instead, they tend to pay attention to less relevant social information such as that which is sensational or most recent.
2. *Interpretation* requires comparing the social information to one's own experience in order to judge its meaning. Aggressive children and adolescents are often poor in understanding the thoughts and emotions of other people in a given situation. Nor are they good at judging how others are likely to treat them. They are prone to incorrectly perceive hostile intentions in the neutral or even friendly words and deeds of adults and peers.
3. **Response Access** requires a mental search for possible responses to the situation or the creation of suitable responses if no familiar response is found. Many aggressive young people have little knowledge of the behaviors and thoughts needed for good social relationships, such as conversation skills and problem-solving ideas that can peacefully resolve disagreements. They tend to remember or construct fewer possible responses to a challenging situation, but more aggressive ones.
4. *Response Decision* involves selecting a response. To select adequately the child must foresee the likely outcomes of each response remembered or created in Step 3, and he must consider what goals he wants the response to accomplish. Aggressive children and adolescents tend to select revenge and deterrence as goals, fabricate or exaggerate despicable characteristics about other people in order to justify attacks on them, and judge a victim's suffering to be an acceptable—even desirable— response outcome. They also perceive themselves as capable of aggressing successfully, but only incompletely foresee the outcomes of aggression.
5. *Enactment* involves performance of the selected response. Aggressive children tend to lack competence in prosocial verbal and motor skills. They may expect little good to come of prosocial behaviors, but much success of aggression.
6. *Outcome Evaluation* entails observing response outcomes to evaluate the effectiveness of one's enactment. This enables the child to decide whether he needs to modify the process when similar circumstances arise again. Aggressive youths are prone to overlook the poor results of an aggressive response. For instance,

they minimize negative response outcomes for victims of aggression, and pay attention to only a few aspects of the entire outcome situation.

## *Cognitive Deficits/Distortions*

Kendall (Braswell & Kendall, 2001; Kendall, 1991; Kendall, Choudhury, Chung, & Robin, 2002) recommends discriminating two kinds of problem that may result in E&B disorder of children: cognitive deficit and cognitive distortion. In a **cognitive deficit**, E&B disorder results from a partial or complete absence of some necessary cognitive process. To illustrate, Sharone may not know what she could say or do that would defuse a conflict while not showing weakness. Lacking negotiation or sharing skills, she would probably say and do something aggressive.

In a **cognitive distortion**, E&B disorder is caused by the faulty operation of a cognitive process. Example: suppose Williard misinterprets an innocent statement as a strong personal attack. He then becomes anxious, confrontational, or depressed. Although one or a few such incidents reflecting cognitive deficits or distortions may not be noteworthy, the young person who typically thinks and behaves like this could be identified with *Aggression, Anxiety*, or another pattern of E&B disorder.

Kendall (1991) proposed that E&B disorder involving *Aggression* and *Impulsiveness* entail mainly cognitive deficits, and *Anxiety* and *Depression* stem mainly from cognitive distortions. He recognized that many cases of E&B disorder reflect cognitive deficits and cognitive distortions.

## *SIP-by-Deficits/Distortions*

Although Dodge designed his SIP model with *Aggression* in mind, it has implications for other patterns of E&B disorder. For example, adolescents with *Depression* may show Encoding problems, by paying greater attention to unhappy events than happy ones; Interpretation problems, by exaggerating the importance of impolite remarks by peers or their own minor personal failures; Response Decision problems, by underestimating their own self-efficacy to perform adaptive behaviors; and Outcome Evaluation problems, by minimizing potential benefits of their own well-performed behaviors, instead maintaining that nothing can be done to avoid their hopeless future (Hammen & Rudolph, 2003).

Combining the SIP and Deficit/Distortion concepts may help organize cognitive explanations of E&B disorder. This combination also implies directions for intervention. Display 9-2 presents possible cognitive deficits at each of the SIP steps, with corresponding intervention goals. Display 9-3 presents similar information for cognitive distortions. (For brevity, Response Access and Response Decision SIP Steps [3 and 4] are combined.)

To illustrate, the consistently obnoxious and mistake-prone behavior of a student with *Impulsiveness* may stem from cognitive deficits involving the Response Access and Decision step (see Display 9-2). Perhaps this student does not foresee outcomes or consequences of her decisions and behaviors or does not consider the unfortunate social and learning implications of them. This suggests an intervention to teach her to (a) think of various consequences of different responses to important school

**Display 9-2** Selected cognitive deficits by social information processing steps, with some corresponding intervention goals

| Step | Cognitive Deficits | Intervention Goals |
|---|---|---|
| Encoding | • Does not seek enough external cues (social, physical)<br>• Does not seek enough internal cues (e.g., own moods, thoughts, and physiological responses) | • Observe social information (e.g., words, facial expressions, body language)<br>• Observe own moods, thoughts, physiological responses |
| Interpretation | • Does not recognize other people's intentions, emotions, and perspectives<br>• Does not recognize own responses to a situation | • Infer others' intentions, emotions, and perspectives from social information<br>• Identify own behaviors, thoughts, and emotions<br>• Identify social information being sent by own behaviors, thoughts, and emotions |
| Response Access and Decision | • Does not identify sufficient adaptive responses to challenging situations<br>• Does not identify consequences of various responses<br>• Does not consider consequences of various responses | • Recall several familiar responses to challenges<br>• Create several new responses to challenges<br>• Identify desirable and undesirable consequences of alternative responses<br>• Consider desirable and undesirable consequences of alternative responses |
| Enactment | • Cannot perform adaptive physical or verbal responses | • Identify verbal and motor skills needed to perform adaptive responses<br>• Perform adaptive responses in training situations<br>• Perform adaptive responses in challenging situations |
| Outcome Evaluation | • Does not recognize many outcomes of own behavior<br>• Does not recognize relation between own responses and response consequences | • Identify effects of own responses on oneself and on other people<br>• Evaluate the appropriateness of own responses |

situations, and (b) consider the plusses and minuses of the various consequences. The objective of this intervention would be to prompt the young person to be more planful before behaving.

Or, suppose a student with *Depression* typically exhibits cognitive distortions involving Outcome Evaluation (see Display 9-3), such as stating that he always says

**Display 9-3** Selected cognitive distortions by social information processing steps, with some corresponding intervention goals

| Step | Cognitive Distortions | Intervention Goals |
|---|---|---|
| Encoding | • Concentrates on some social information cues (e.g., obvious, sensational, or familiar) while ignoring others (e.g., subtle or novel) | • Observe and identify many cues (especially subtle and novel) |
| Interpretation | • Perceives neutral behaviors and other cues as negative<br>• Exaggerates the importance of negative social and other events | • Accurately infer others' intentions, emotions, and perspectives from cues<br>• Accurately assess the importance of social cues and other events |
| Response Access and Decision | • Identifies maladaptive responses to situations<br>• Establishes inappropriate goals for response<br>• Overvalues potential outcomes of maladaptive responses<br>• Undervalues potential outcomes of appropriate responses<br>• Is not concerned about unfortunate effects of responses upon others | • Identify adaptive responses to situations<br>• Set appropriate goals for response<br>• Accurately value potential outcomes of maladaptive and appropriate responses<br>• Appreciates unfortunate effects of responses upon others |
| Enactment | • Thinks and says maladaptive things | • Perform adaptive responses in training situations and in natural situations<br>• Provide motivational help (e.g., behavioral self-management strategy) |
| Outcome Evaluation | • Denies responsibility for effects of own responses<br>• Overvalues actual outcomes of maladaptive responses<br>• Undervalues actual outcomes of appropriate responses<br>• Inappropriately attributes negative consequences of own actions to external influences (e.g., personal discrimination, bad luck)<br>• Inappropriately attributes negative events beyond personal control to internal influences (e.g., "I'm nothing but a loser.") | • Accurately evaluate the positive and negative outcomes of own responses<br>• Dispute own false attributions |

and does the wrong things. This is why God is punishing him with sadness and loneliness, and things will get worse as time goes by, finally reaching the point where he will not be able to stand living. One intervention may be to teach him how to recognize and appreciate the good as well as the bad outcomes of his behavior and to dispute his own pessimistic forecasts.

## COGNITIVE INTERVENTION

### Modeling

Most cognitive interventions rely heavily on modeling (Naugle & Maher, 2003). They typically utilize observational learning, vicarious effects, and other aspects of modeling to heighten its power as a teaching tool. For example, special efforts may be made to increase the learner's attention to particular details of the model's behavior and to help her retain newly learned adaptive behaviors with the help of mnemonic strategies. Some cognitive interventions use vicarious punishment and reinforcement by showing children videos that demonstrate good consequences of appropriate cognitive performance but bad consequences of inappropriate thinking. Similarly, in role-play skits, trainers and students can model desirable and undesirable behaviors and their outcomes.

However, as powerful as modeling can be for improving cognitive, behavior, and emotional problems, it is rarely used alone. Instead, modeling is an important part of general teaching practices and specialized cognitive interventions. For instance, it is used along with or to enhance explanations of new skills, skills practice and role playing, corrective feedback, behavior maintenance, and setting generalization activities in which the skill is practiced beyond the teaching session. Further, modeling is combined with specialized cognitive interventions such as those involving self-instruction, social problem solving, and modifying distorted information processing and attributions.

### Interventions for Cognitive Deficits

Suppose that a youth, when faced with a social conflict or problem, is unable to think of a nonaggressive way to resolve the conflict. He does know aggressive ways to resolve the conflict, and he acts on this knowledge by behaving aggressively. Perhaps another young person is unable to slow down her decision-making process or consider various important aspects of social and learning situations that confront her. As a result she interrupts conversations and refuses to take turns, which leaves her peers in agreement that they do not want her as a friend and her teachers in agreement that she is hyperactive.

As Display 9-3 indicates, the cognitive deficit perspective sees *Aggression, Impulsiveness,* and other patterns of E&B disorder as deficits in the young person's ability to recognize the nature of a challenging problem situation, think of alternative ways to meet the challenge, evaluate each alternative especially in terms of its consequences, and select one alternative to try first. Cognitive interventions for deficits attempt to help the young person acquire a way to resolve such challenges through their own adaptive actions (Albano, 2005; Krain & Kendall, 1999). Two kinds of interventions for cognitive deficits are *self-instruction* and *social problem solving* strategies (Beck & Newman, 2005; Merrell, 2001).

## *Self-Instruction*

Self-instructions are statements a person makes to herself that guide her execution of decisions and actions needed for successful performance of a task. First, this task is analyzed into the steps needed to complete it, in sequence. Each step becomes the basis for an instruction, like a simple assembly manual or recipe. The instructions form a sequence of self-instructions, each one a reminder to perform some decision or action that is the next step in the task. When the student has performed every decision and action dictated by the sequence of self-instructions, he has completed the task.

To successfully self-instruct, a student must first recognize circumstances that call for the task to be done. Thus the student may be taught to recognize circumstances calling for self-instruction. When circumstances do dictate, the student must activate the sequence of self-instructions. To help the student remember them, a memory aid (e.g., word, acronym, image) may be taught. Third, the student must say and/or think each self-instruction in proper sequence as he activates its corresponding decision or action. Finally, the student evaluates the outcome of self-instruction, to know whether additional actions are needed. This general four-step sequence—recognize circumstances, activate self-instructions, perform acts while self-instructing, and evaluate outcome—may be modified to accommodate various tasks and individual needs of particular students, including academic, social, and other tasks.

To help the student learn self-instruction, the teacher first describes the sequence of self-instructions, including the task it helps accomplish, some circumstances calling for the use of this sequence, and how to evaluate its success. Next she models the sequence of self-instructions, including "cognitive modeling" (stating crucial thoughts aloud or pantomiming them). Third, after the student performs, the teacher gives feedback about the adequacy of the student's self-instruction.

Such teaching attempts to encourage error-free student performance by gradually removing teacher assistance, via a teaching sequence such as that of Display 9-4 (see also Kendall, 1991; Krain & Kendall, 1999). One objective of this sequence is orderly change from teacher-directed performance to shared direction, then to student self-directed performance. A second objective is for the student to adopt self-instruction as a general way to succeed independently at other tasks that have not been taught. For simple tasks the sequence can be made shorter and less gradual by omitting some of the phases (e.g., II, IV, VI).

## *Example: Skillstreaming*

Modeling and self-instruction are fundamental aspects of many interventions and curricula for social skills training (Segrin, 2003). For instance, structured learning is a cognitive-behavioral procedure developed by Arnold Goldstein for teaching

**Display 9-4** Phases in teaching self-instruction

|  | |
|---|---|
| Phase I | • The teacher performs the observable steps (decisions and actions) needed to complete the task successfully. Simultaneously, the teacher states aloud the self-instructions corresponding to the observable steps.<br>• The student observes (watches and listens).<br>• The teacher may require the student to use a reminder card with the steps written on it, create a reminder card by writing each step on a blank card, or teach some other memory strategy. |
| Phase II | • The teacher states aloud self-instructions corresponding to the observable steps of the task.<br>• The student performs the observable steps needed to do the task (may consult reminder card).<br>• The teacher gives feedback as needed (e.g., prompts, corrections) to help the student imitate the teacher's performance of observable steps. |
| Phase III | • The student performs the observable steps needed to do the task. Simultaneously, the student also states aloud the corresponding self-instructions. The student begins to discontinue use of reminder card.<br>• The teacher gives feedback as needed (e.g., prompts, corrections) to help the student imitate observable steps and self-instructions. |
| Phase IV | • The teacher performs the steps needed to do the task successfully. Simultaneously, the teacher whispers corresponding self-instructions.<br>• The student observes. |
| Phase V | • The student performs the steps while simultaneously whispering the self-instructions.<br>• The teacher gives feedback as needed to help the student imitate observable steps and whispered self-instructions. |
| Phase VI | • The student performs the steps while simultaneously making soundless lip movements corresponding to the appropriate self-instructions. |
| Phase VII | • The teacher performs the steps. Simultaneously, she mimes thinking about the self-instructions by pausing before performing each step while stroking her chin, looking away as if in thought, or the like.<br>• The student observes. The student may be required to state aloud the appropriate self-instruction each time the teacher pauses. |
| Phase VIII | • The student performs the steps while simultaneously pausing and thinking the appropriate self-instructions.<br>• The student may self-evaluate process and outcome; peers may evaluate same. |

prosocial skills. Structured learning has been adapted for various intervention situations (Gibbs, Potter, & Goldstein, 1995; Gibbs, Potter, Goldstein, & Brendtro, 1998; Goldstein, 1999; Goldstein & Glick, 1987; Goldstein, Glick, & Gibbs, 1998; Goldstein, Reagles, & Amann, 1990; Goldstein & McGinnis, 1997; McGinnis & Goldstein, 1997).

**Display 9-5** Arnold Goldstein profile

Arnold P. Goldstein (1933–2002) specialized in understanding and reducing school and community violence, delinquency, and harmful gang activity. He created significant, innovative interventions for conflict and other problems in schools, corrections facilities, and other treatment settings for young people. After receiving his doctoral degree in clinical psychology at Pennsylvania State University, Goldstein served on the faculty in the Psychology Department and School of Education at Syracuse University, where he founded the Center for Research on Aggression.

Early in his career, Goldstein found that typical psychotherapies had little value for poor clients, who needed less to ponder their own mental conflicts than to learn social behavior skills that would help them function adaptively in the community. This prompted him to develop an alternative termed "structured learning therapy," which emphasizes social skills training through modeling and other cognitive interventions. Goldstein then adapted structured learning therapy for use with groups of children and adolescents in schools and detention facilities: *Skillstreaming*.

To address various problems of young people, Goldstein and colleagues developed multipart interventions that feature Skillstreaming supported by other forms of intervention. For example, Aggression Replacement Training, designed to decrease violence and rule-breaking and to increase prosocial behavior, consists of Skillstreaming plus cognitive anger control and moral education.

Goldstein wrote more than 60 books and 100 journal articles. He was invited to present his ideas and practices to many professional, parent, and other organizations. The American Psychological Association honored Goldstein's contributions with the Senior Scientist Award and with the School Psychology Division's Career Achievement Award.

*Sources:* Gibbs, Potter, & Goldstein, 1995; Goldberg, 1997; U.S. Center for Aggression Replacement Training. Available at: http://www.uscart.org/maingoldstein.htm. Accessed Sept. 3, 2005.

An adaptation with special relevance for young people with *Aggression, Impulsiveness,* Law-Breaking Behavior, and Substance Misuse is called *Skillstreaming* (Goldstein, Sprafkin, Gershaw & Klein, 1980; Goldstein & McGinnis, 1997; McGinnis & Goldstein, 1997). To implement Skillstreaming appropriately, the teacher must attend to three program features: preparation, conducting the group, and managing behavior problems.

***Preparation.*** *Preparation* addresses selecting and preparing trainers, choosing the prosocial skills, selecting students, organizing the group, and preparing students for group participation. Often, trainers are selected from among staff members at the school or other site. Trainers are sought who have good abilities in understanding adolescents, talking, teaching, modeling and role-playing in front of a group, listening, being enthusiastic, giving honest feedback, and showing sensitivity. Also, trainers are given additional preparation in these general qualities, as well as in teaching skills specific to delivering Skillstreaming.

Skillstreaming encompasses approximately 50 social skills organized into areas such as Dealing with Feelings, Alternatives to Aggression, and Planning. If assessment shows that students do not exhibit deficits in all the social skills, or if there are time constraints, a subset of skills can be selected for training.

**Display 9-6** Skill card for a hypothetical social skill similar to Dealing with Group Pressure in Skillstreaming

> **Skill: Handling Peers Urging You to Break Rules**
> Step 1: Think about what the group wants you to do and why.
> Step 2: Decide what you want to do.
> Step 3: Decide how to tell the others what you want to do.
> Step 4: Tell the others what you have decided to do.

*Source:* Adapted from information in Goldstein et al. (1998) and Goldstein & McGinnis (1997).

A Skillstreaming group should consist of about six students and two trainers. Ideally, sessions last about one hour each and occur a few days apart, one or two times per week. The final preparation step is for trainers to meet with each student to describe the purposes of the group, the training procedures, and rules for group operation (e.g., attendance, confidentiality, participation).

***Conducting the Group.*** After preparations are completed, the initial session is devoted to orientation. Except for this one, each Skillstreaming session is conducted according to a set format covering seven activities: homework checking, skill presentation, trainer role-play, student roleplay, evaluation, homework assignment, and recycling.

1. *Homework checking*. At the beginning of each session the trainers review and check each student's *transfer homework* (described below).
2. *Skill presentation*. Next, the trainers present activities related to the selected social skill. In the first session devoted to a new social skill they introduce and briefly explain it. Then each student gets a *skill* card that lists, in order, the components of that social skill. The students are to follow along and recognize each component as it is modeled. The skill card summarizes key self-instructions that the student should give himself in order to perform the social skill effectively. An illustrative skill card for a prosocial skill similar to "Dealing with Group Pressure" is presented in Display 9-6.
3. *Trainer role-play*. The trainers model the social skill as it applies to two different situations that should be relevant to the trainees. This modeling situation ("role-play" in Skillstreaming terminology) is used to demonstrate (a) the major behaviors of the main actor, (b) subtle behavior nuances of all the role players, and (a) what the main character is thinking and deciding in order to implement the social skill. Such information might be lengthy and difficult to transmit through written or spoken material only, but is quickly and accurately presented through the role play. Display 9-7 presents a possible role-play of an important social skill. It involves two trainers and three Skillstreaming group students who have agreed to play the remaining parts.
4. *Student role-play*. Trainers prompt the students to discuss situations in their lives in which they could have used the skill that has just been modeled. Based on these situations, the trainers select a student to repeat the role play, except this

time as it applies to his own situation as he stated it. The selected student is joined in the role-play by one or more peers who agree to play minor characters in that situation. The remaining students use their skill cards to check the main actor's performance of the skill components.
5. *Evaluation.* After the role-play is performed the trainers call for evaluation of the selected student's performance by all other students and finally by the selected student himself. Students are encouraged to evaluate how accurately the main actor's behavior has followed the instructions found on the skill cards.
6. *Homework assignment.* The trainers discuss how the student might practice the social skill before the next session. It is a key premise of Structured Learning that social skills learned in the controlled, "safe" group sessions must be practiced under actual conditions in which they will be needed. Situations and people that may provide practice opportunities are noted, and these become the basis for the student's transfer homework assignments. The student makes a record of out-of-session skill practice and brings it to the next Skillstreaming session for review and discussion.
7. *Recycling.* After assigning transfer homework to this student, the trainer selects another student to role-play the social skill as applied to his situation. This procedure is repeated until all students have had a turn at role-playing the social skill as applied to a personally relevant, challenging social situation. It may take more than one session to allow every student to be the main actor for a particular social skill.

**Managing Group Problems.** The students for whom Skillstreaming is selected as an intervention will probably show a range of problems during training. Students may be apathetic or reluctant to participate in the group. They may get off task or refuse to role-play, give feedback, or otherwise take part. Some will be restless, digress from the role-playing, or disrupt other group activities. Some may seem unable to understand the role-plays. The Structured Learning materials present possible corrective actions for trainers faced with such problems.

### Social Problem Solving
Social problem solving as therapy for adults was pioneered by D'Zurilla and Goldfried (1971), who conceptualized emotional and behavior problems as social challenges for which the person cannot or does not perform an effective solution (D'Zurilla & Nezu, 1999, 2001; Nezu, Nezu, & Lombardo, 2003). Likewise, Spivack and Shure (e.g., Shure, 1992, 1999; Spivack & Shure, 1974) found that children with poor peer relationships typically do not use cognitive skills that could solve their interpersonal problems (Bierman, 2005). They tend to lack, for instance, "means-end thinking" (thinking of the steps necessary to move toward a desired goal) and "alternate solution thinking" (conceiving of various possible solutions to interpersonal conflicts). Therefore these professionals designed interventions to teach social problem solving processes.

**Display 9-7** Role-play vignette for a social skill similar to a Skillstreaming social skill, Dealing with Group Pressure

| | |
|---|---|
| Main Actor: | Andrew, a 15-year-old student. |
| Co-Actors: | Benjamin, Carlene, DeShaun, and Elvin, classmates and associates of Andrew |
| Scene: | Andrew is in the hall just after school, talking to Carlene, a girl with whom he plans to walk downtown. Benjamin and DeShaun, classmates and associates, come up to Andrew appearing excited and begin to tell this story about Elvin. |
| Benjamin: | Andrew, you ain't gonna believe what Elvin said about you today. |
| DeShaun: | Not once but all day long! |
| Benjamin: | He said he has had it with your crap, and he is telling everyone he's gonna whip you. |
| Deshaun: | Yeah, he's in the gym now, saying the same thing to Robby and Vernell. |
| Benjamin: | Man, don't let him keep talking like that. You have got to stop that stuff at the beginning or a lot of guys will start to say the same thing. |
| DeShaun: | Come on, Andrew, shut him up now. |
| Carlene: | You ain't gonna let him get by with this, are you, Andrew? |

**Skill Card Step 1: Think about what the group wants you to do and why.**

| | |
|---|---|
| Andrew (thinking to himself): | They are excited but it could be an act. What are Benjamin and DeShaun trying to get me to do? Could Elvin really be saying that? I haven't done anything much to him. What did Elvin really say, if anything? Are Benjamin and DeShaun trying to get me into another fight? |
| Andrew: | What's happening with Elvin? Why is he threatening me and telling the other kids all of this? |
| DeShaun: | This has been coming on all week, Andrew. He has been talking about putting you down in front of everybody, and whipping you in public if you don't like it. |
| Carlene: | My brother wouldn't let no one talk that way about him. No man would. What are you gonna do, Andrew? |

**Skill Card Step 2: Decide what you want to do.**

| | |
|---|---|
| Andrew (thinking to himself): | It makes me mad to hear what Elvin said about me—if Benjamin and DeShaun are telling the truth. They are trying to get me to argue and maybe fight Elvin, and Carlene seems to, also. |
| | I could just ignore them and tell Carlene we need to go now, but they would make fun of me and call me a chicken. |
| | I could wait outside the gym and just confront Elvin, but Benjamin and DeShaun would boost us into a fight for sure. |
| | If I could talk to Elvin by himself, I could probably find out the truth about what he has been saying or even if he has been saying anything. I need to talk to Elvin alone, and I'd better do it right away. |

| | |
|---|---|
| DeShaun: | What are you waiting for, Andrew? Are you losing your nerve? |
| Benjamin: | Hey, I'll go to the gym and tell him to get his butt out here right now! |
| Andrew: | No! This is my problem and I'm gonna solve it my way. |

**Skill Card Step 3: Decide how to tell the others what you want to do.**

| | |
|---|---|
| Andrew (thinking to himself): | They are all pushing me real hard. I think they are making this up. Should I say so? |
| | If I accuse them of boosting me, they will deny it and call me afraid. This is not a good idea. |
| | Maybe I should find Elvin by myself and talk to him. That would be the best idea. I will tell these three that I will go talk to Elvin by myself. |
| Carlene: | It's now or never. Don't let this guy get away with this crap, Andrew. |

**Skill Card Step 4: Tell the others what you have decided to do.**

| | |
|---|---|
| Andrew: | I need to talk to Elvin by myself. You wait at the east porch while I find Elvin and talk to him man-to-man. |
| Benjamin: | Forget that, Andrew! We want to be there when this goes down. |
| Carlene: | Yeah, we're behind you against that chump. |
| DeShaun: | He may have some guys there with him. He was talking to Frank when I saw him. We'll keep this thing fair. |
| Andrew: | No, this is my problem. You said he is talking about me. I will talk to him straight up and find out what the problem is. |
| Andrew (in the lunchroom): | Hey, Elvin! What's happening, man! Hey, you got a minute to talk with me? |
| Elvin: | No problem, man. S'up? |
| Andrew: | Listen, Elvin, don't take any offense here, but I've been told that you are talking trash about me. I don't believe it but I just had to come to you to find out for myself. You would tell me straight out if you had any problem with me, wouldn't you? |
| Elvin: | Sure, man, I don't know what you are talking about. Who is lying to you? I haven't been talking about you. |
| Andrew: | That's what I thought, but I had to ask. I'm going to walk downtown now. You interested in going with me? |

Social problem solving has been adapted for a range of problems, ages, cognitive ability levels, and other considerations. Yet across adaptations, five stages generally summarize how it is implemented (D'Zurilla & Nezu, 1999; Merrell, 2001; Shure, 1999): problem solving set, problem definition, alternatives generation, decision making, and implementation and verification.

1. *Problem solving set.* To begin, the teacher presents a hopeful "set" (outlook or orientation) about emotional and behavior problems. Students are taught to look at their personal and social problem as just another challenge of life that people

can and do solve, to view themselves as capable of solving such challenges, and to approach personal and social problems in a reflective way rather than giving up or acting hastily. The teacher shows them how to identify various components of problems, especially the behavior of other people, physical (nonsocial) events, and their own thoughts and feelings.

Participants learn about unsuccessful forms of social problem solving that nearly everyone uses to some extent, and that can be especially common and problematic among young people with E&B disorder. Merrell (2001) summarized four of the most important of these "maladaptive styles of dealing with conflict": avoidance, dominance, pliancy, and trivialization (elaborated in Display 9-8). These problem solving strategies rarely work in the long run. Worse, they often aggravate the social problem. Thus they can contribute to E&B disorders and connected problems, especially *Aggression, Depression*, Learning Difficulty, and Substance Misuse (Merrell, 2001).

Typically, social problem solving participants learn to recognize such maladaptive strategies and how to avoid using them. Other strategies that are more likely to solve the problem are taught, illustrated, and practiced. Once participants understand and (hopefully) begin to adopt the problem solving set, including maladaptive and adaptive problem solving styles, intervention proceeds.

**Display 9-8** Four maladaptive styles of dealing with conflict

| Style | Description | Solution |
|---|---|---|
| Avoidance | Person may be very uncomfortable with conflict, or act in a "passive-aggressive" manner. Changes the subject, stays away from the problem situation, and vents frustration in other ways. | Learn to deal with conflict directly. |
| Dominance | Person has a need to feel in control and to "be right." Will not let others respond in a conflict situation. May resort to intimidation or threats to silence the other person. | Learn to slow down, to listen to the point of view of others, and not have to "be right." |
| Pliancy | Person may feel responsible or take responsibility for the problem, even when it is not his fault. May be overly shy and self-critical. | Learn to be more assertive and direct. |
| Trivialization | Person laughs or shrugs off problems. Does not take problems seriously. Minimizes things and says, "It's not a big deal." | Learn to respect the other person and take the problem seriously. |

*Source:* Merrell, 2001, p. 134.

2. *Problem definition.* Next, the youth is taught to examine external and internal aspects of the problem situation and to focus on those aspects that are most relevant to a solution. In consideration of these relevant aspects only, the youth is assisted to identify changes in external or internal aspects that would help resolve the problem.
3. *Alternatives generation.* At this point the student is taught to brainstorm alternative ways to achieve the changes identified in stage 2. Evaluation of each alternative solution is temporarily delayed so as to avoid premature closure that may prevent finding a better alternative.
4. *Decision making.* The leader teaches the group to consider likely consequences and outcomes of each alternative (if individual intervention, the teacher and student do so). Moreover, using realistic or student-generated real situations, they take into account the likelihood that a participant will actually implement each alternative. At this point the teaching process frequently shifts back and forth between stages 3 and 4 until an alternative is selected as the first problem solving strategy to try.
5. *Implementation and verification.* In this last stage the young person tries the selected solution. He keeps a log of information about challenging situations, problem solving attempts, thoughts and emotions during problem situations and solutions, and outcomes of the strategy. These records are considered in an evaluation of the strategy.

If his first strategy was successful, the student rewards himself in various ways. If unsuccessful, he is encouraged to recognize that the alternative he selected and his attempt to apply it were worthy efforts, and that he and the trainer need to return to an earlier stage in the process and try again.

Although described separately, social problem solving stages overlap. Participants review parts of stages and recycle as needed and otherwise are not bound by sharp boundaries between stages.

### Example: Adolescent Anger Control Program

The Adolescent Anger Control Program (AACP; Feindler, 1991; Feindler & Ecton, 1986) has been used with groups of impulsive, aggressive adolescents. Its goals are anger prevention, anger regulation, and anger alternatives. Each goal is a component of the social problem solving training.

The *prevention* component involves encouraging adolescents not to get angry when anger and acting out will not resolve the conflict or problem. The *regulation* component is designed to teach adolescents to reduce intensity and duration of anger when they do get angry. They learn that extreme anger interferes with the skillful performance of alternatives to anger, and rumination on negative ideas creates a cycle of anger. The AACP presents specific ways to control intensity and interrupt the cycle. Third, the *alternatives* component teaches skills for responding to provocations with talk and action that are not angry or aggressive. Social problem solving is a significant part of all three components.

1. *Problem solving set.* In the initial AACP stage of *problem orientation*, adolescents learn what anger is and that a person can control it. Anger is a problem when it leads to uncontrolled behavior and maladaptive results. Anger contains cognitive, physiological, and behavior aspects. The adolescents learn details of these aspects and how all three aspects influence each other. They are taught that they can control these components to some extent.
2. *Problem definition.* The AACP teaches young people to identify external **triggers**—the behavior of certain people as well as other external situations—that provoke their anger. The details of a trigger vary from person to person. Common examples include taunts from classmates and repeated instructions or demands from a teacher. They are also shown how to recognize internal *cues* such as thoughts, feelings, and physiological responses that signal the experience of anger. Triggers and cues are usually part of the youth's problem in controlling anger.

   Another part of the problem for some students is failure to discriminate inappropriate and appropriate responses. Therefore, AACP participants are taught a distinction between maladaptive and adaptive responses to anger.
3. *Alternatives generation.* Students are encouraged to think of and discuss adaptive responses when angered. Further, trainers teach skills that can facilitate these adaptive responses. For example, the adolescents learn to be vigilant for triggers, as well as the irrational thoughts and negative emotions that accompany triggers. They learn to be prepared with private reminder statements that help them remain in control of their responses, such as, "That guy is trying to pull me into an argument again," or "This teacher is going to hassle me, but I can handle it."

   The adolescents learn a variety of self-controlling, adaptive responses to provocation. Examples include self-relaxation skills (e.g., deep breaths), response-delay strategies (e.g., counting to 10), negotiation with an antagonist, and acts of pacification. Additionally, they learn self-instructions that guide sequencing and timing as they use their self-controlling skills.
4. *Decision making:* To help them make better decisions, adolescents are taught to consider various courses of action that they might take. They consider immediate and delayed outcomes, both good and bad. For instance, they describe in writing several anger-provoking situations from their recent experience. Then, AACP trainers use these situations to help each adolescent foresee and discuss potential results of impulsive, uncontrolled aggression.

   Likewise, the students are helped to anticipate probable consequences of using the alternative ways of coping with provocation they learned in Step 3. They weigh drawbacks and benefits of different alternatives, rank these alternatives, and select an anger control strategy based on their own analysis.
5. *Implementation and verification.* At this step each student rehearses his selected strategy, then uses it to solve one of the problems recorded from his experience. The students evaluate their anger control strategies according to three considerations: (a) how well did it solve the problem? (b) what were other good outcomes? and (c) what were other bad outcomes?

If the first selected alternative works, all can rejoice. If it does not solve the anger problem, or does solve the problem but generates other outcomes that are unacceptable, the youth selects his second-ranked alternative and repeats this problem solving stage.

Other examples of social problem solving (e.g., Hune & Nelson, 2002; Merrell, 2001) vary as to method details and adaptations for the young person's cognitive level. However, they retain the essence of the social problem solving technique.

## Interventions for Cognitive Distortions

Suppose a student's peers make a joke about drunken men they have recently seen. This student's father has long abused alcohol and is an unreliable parent and provider. The student falsely assumes that his peers were taunting him. Thus he reacts angrily and causes an argument immediately, as well as a fight later in the school day. It is reasonable to conceptualize this episode as arising from the student's cognitive distortion about his peers' joke.

The cognitive model holds that in many cases, E&B disorder can be traced to a person's distorted thoughts and perspectives about other people, himself, or impersonal environmental events. Such inaccurate, maladaptive perspectives are cognitive distortions that arise from errors in social information processing and from mistaken beliefs (Bierman, 2005; Guerra, Boxer, & Kim, 2005; Krain & Kendall, 1999). They can lead to distressing, strange, and destructive acts that most other people understandably judge to exemplify one of the patterns of E&B disorder. Several cognitive interventions for E&B disorder are designed to teach people to recognize such maladaptive perspectives and to substitute adaptive ones.

### *Modifying Distorted Information Processing*

Children and adolescents with various patterns of E&B disorder frequently perceive social information inaccurately or selectively and therefore maladaptively. Young people with *Aggression* and/or *Impulsiveness* patterns are especially likely to misperceive peers' nonaggressive, neutral behavior as provocative and hostile (Feindler, 1991; Smith, Lochman, & Daunic, 2005). Of course, this sort of attribution may be essentially accurate and even highly adaptive in some of the child's environments, such as the home or neighborhood in which he may have learned it from adult or peer models. In any case, that kind of distortion of social information predisposes the student to conflict with peers and adults in the school environment.

Distorted processing of social information can prevent the young person from realizing that different people can interpret a given social situation in different ways—let alone what some of these alternative interpretations might be. This is unfortunate because the ability to understand the interpretations and perspectives of others involved in a disagreement or conflict often can help prevent aggression. Therefore, some cognitive interventions for aggressive disorders feature activities to teach children how to consider different perspectives for a range of situations.

### *Example: Anger Coping*

The *Anger Coping* program (Larson & Lochman, 2002; Lochman & Wells, 1996; Pardini & Lochman, 2003; Smith et al., 2005) was designed for use with small groups of older elementary school students evidencing the *Aggression* pattern to a high degree. A main goal of Anger Coping is to address social misperceptions that could lead to strong emotional arousal and aggressive behavior.

Anger Coping has evolved over two decades of research (e.g., Lochman, White, & Wayland, 1991; Lochman & Wells, 2004). In two recent versions there are about 18 lessons (Anger Coping) and more than 30 (Coping Power). Each lesson lasts about one hour and is designed to be delivered about weekly. Each contains explicit objectives, activities, and directions for proceeding to teach the lessons, getting the group to work together, and managing behavior incidents.

The five main concepts taught in these lessons are goal-setting, self-talk, anger concepts, alternatives to anger, and social perspective taking. In addition, the students are taught a simple strategy for activating (recalling and using) these concepts to control anger. The concepts are introduced gradually, reviewed frequently, and integrated with one another as the lessons proceed. They are practiced in and outside of sessions to increase behavior maintenance and generalization to real-life settings.

1. *Goal-setting* is the basis for weekly Anger Coping homework that is reviewed at the beginning of each lesson. Early in the program the children are taught how

Teachers can model self-talk or thinking to teach cognitive strategies that may help students resist triggers of anger.

to set, pursue, and evaluate goals related to the lessons. For example, a goal may be, "To stop my angry talk and actions when I am taunted."
2. *Self-talk* is taught, using modeling by puppets and role-playing, as a way to resist taunts and other precipitants of anger. Self-talk (similar to self-instruction) enables the young person to "stay cool" and control anger.
3. *Anger concepts* include behaviors (e.g., face expressions, postures), emotions, thoughts, and physiological responses (e.g., feeling "hot," muscle tenseness) associated with anger. These personal responses are defined, discussed, and explored via audiovisual media.
4. *Alternatives to anger* in a conflict are explored. The teacher or other group leader also helps the students to think of probable consequences of each of these alternative courses of action.
5. *Social perspective taking* is a key feature of the Anger Coping Program. The teacher uses various lessons and techniques to explore different perspectives that a student might take in a variety of situations. These lessons also address potential results of these different perspectives.

   For instance, group members take turns giving different interpretations of pictures, stories involving hypothetical situations, narratives based on the young person's actual home and school problems, and role-plays of hypothetical and actual episodes. The intent of teaching social perspective taking is to reduce the misperceptions, misinterpretations, and other distortions of social information processing that can lead to aggressive, disruptive talk and action.
6. *Activating*. In addition to the concepts, students are taught a strategy for activating Anger Coping practices. Each learns to ask himself four questions: (a) What is the problem? (b) What do I feel? (c) What alternatives do I have? and (d) What are the consequences? Actual wording of each step in this strategy can be adapted to reflect the particulars of the students' problems and situations, as revealed by the discussions within the group.

Coping Power is an enhanced version of Anger Coping. It has more sessions, individual as well as group sessions, additional training goals and activities, scheduled consultation with teachers, and an extensive parent training component (Pardini & Lochman, 2003).

## *Modifying Distorted Attributions and Beliefs*

Various hypotheses assign an important role to distorted attributions and beliefs in the *Anxiety* and *Depression* patterns of E&B disorder (Compton et al., 2004). Abramson, Seligman, & Teasdale (1978), for example, observed that people with *Depression* tend to attribute bad things that happen to them to their own generalized, enduring shortcomings ("I don't blame people for rejecting me because I have nothing to offer, and never will."). However, they attribute good things to temporary, limited events beyond their personal control ("I got this good grade because of a one-time lucky break.").

According to Beck (1976; Beck & Newman, 2005), early in life each person begins to establish cognitions about himself, his environment, and his future.

If these cognitions are based on false information that leads to erroneous conclusions, he may develop maladaptive beliefs about himself as an inadequate person, about his world as a place of endless obstacles to satisfaction, and about his future as an unchanging continuation of the hopeless present (DeRubeis, Tang, & Beck, 2001; Laird & Metalsky, 2003). This despairing view of self, world, and future, termed the **negative cognitive triad,** is found commonly among people with *Depression.*

Similarly, Ellis (1962) concluded that *irrational beliefs* create many forms of E&B disorder. A belief is irrational if it is inflexible and illogical, is concerned with what life should be rather that what it actually is, and interferes with achievement of one's goals in life (DiGiuseppe, 1999).

### *Example: Rational-Emotive Therapy/Education*

***Rational-Emotive Therapy.*** Albert Ellis created Rational-Emotive (R-E) Therapy, the general objective of which is to replace the client's irrational beliefs with rational ones. Rational beliefs are the opposite of irrational ones: they are flexible and logical in the face of changing circumstances, consistent with the realities of the situation rather than how one wishes it were, and helpful to the person in achieving her goals (Dryden & Ellis, 2001; Ellis, 1962, 2003).

R-E Therapy assumes that emotion and cognition are not separate systems but instead are closely linked. To a great extent, thinking causes emotions. An important corollary is that negative situations do not directly create our emotional and behavioral problems; it is our irrational beliefs about those situations that create our problems. This is understood within R-E Therapy's "A-B-C" framework: Activating events, Beliefs, and Consequences (Display 9-9). People tend to attribute their unpleasant emotions and maladaptive behaviors (Cs) to unfortunate events that preceded (As), but R-E Therapy emphasizes that it is people's irrational beliefs (Bs) that actually cause the distressing, maladaptive Cs.

What are these irrational beliefs? In general they are rigid, dogmatic perspectives about what should or must take place, often linked with unrealistically high standards or demands about oneself, others, or life in general. Specific irrational beliefs, of course, can vary depending on particular people and situations, but Ellis and others have described a few categories into which many irrational beliefs fit, including the colorfully named ones in Display 9-10.

**Display 9-9** A-B-C framework for understanding problems in Rational-Emotive Therapy

| | | |
|---|---|---|
| A | Activating events | Observable circumstances in the external world, as well as some of the person's interpretations of such circumstances |
| B | Beliefs | A variety of evaluations of and perspectives on particular situations that occur, as well as larger beliefs or philosophies of life that a person may hold |
| C | Consequences | The emotions and behaviors that follow from one's beliefs |

*Sources:* Dryden & Ellis, 2001; Ellis, 2003.

**Display 9-10** Illustrative irrational and rational beliefs in RET

| Term | Irrational Belief | Alternative Rational Belief |
|---|---|---|
| Awfulization | This Activating Event is nothing less than a catastrophe. | It is very inconvenient, highly distasteful, even detrimental to me, but not a catastrophe. |
| I-can't-stand-it-itis | This Activating Event is beyond my ability to bear. | It is going to be painful and difficult, and will require me to make big changes, but I can get through this. |
| Magical thinking | This Activating Event is unjust, incompatible with how the world should work, extremely unfair, and ought never to have happened. | I wish it had not happened but it did, and now I have to correct it, tolerate it, or deal with it in some other way. |
| Damnation | The wicked person who caused this Activating Event must be blamed and punished for the vicious misdeed. | I am in control of my thoughts and other reactions to the way he treats me. |
| All-or-noneness | I will always be unhappy. I will never be accepted by the people I love. Because I was unsuccessful on this important task, my other accomplishments—including my life—are worthless. | Like nearly everyone else, I will experience happiness as well as sadness, love as well as rejection, and success as well as failure. |

*Sources:* Dryden & Ellis, 2001; Ellis, 2003.

The main R-E Therapy intervention is *cognitive restructuring*, which means converting the client's Bs from irrational to rational. The therapist facilitates cognitive restructuring by **disputing** the client's irrational Bs. Disputing techniques include explaining how irrational Bs lack logic, evidence, and usefulness, challenging the client to justify his irrational Bs, and emphasizing that others (perhaps including the therapist herself) formerly had similar irrational Bs but overcame them. If successful, cognitive restructuring changes the person's system of thinking that has produced the E&B disorder. This kind of change is necessary for generalized, durable improvement.

R-E Therapy begins with the therapist and client exploring various possible personal and social dissatisfactions in order to agree upon a target problem. The therapist then assesses, in turn, the C aspects of the target problem, the A aspects, and finally the client's Bs. When the therapist understands the A-B-Cs of the problem, she teaches the client a connection between B and C, then disputes irrational Bs. At the appropriate time she assigns appropriate home, job, community, and other activities to help the client learn to dispute his own irrational Bs.

***Rational-Emotive Education.*** Zionts (1996) and others (see Gonzalez et al., 2004) have shown how to adapt R-E Therapy to be a group intervention appropriate to the education of students with emotional disturbance (ED). Rational-Emotive Education (R-E Education) calls for the teacher (preferably) or other counseling adult to function as R-E therapist and group behavior manager. Zionts recommended a regular schedule of R-E Education sessions, perhaps three or four per week totaling about four hours.

The teacher's preliminary steps are crucial: she insists on mutual respect among all group members, emphasizes the need for children to commit to change and treat the sessions seriously, and stays focused and directive during sessions so that the students will, too. Another important preliminary is teaching key R-E Therapy concepts to the children and adolescents. These include As, Bs, and Cs, how to dispute irrational ideas, and to recognize the adaptive behaviors and cognitions brought about by new, rational thinking).

After preliminaries are attended to, the teacher prompts group members to bring up and explore Cs and As. This enables her to select one target problem as the initial group project. The A-B-C aspects of this problem are thoroughly examined, especially with regard to the links between Bs and Cs. The group is taught and encouraged to dispute the target peer's irrational Bs respectfully (Zionts & Fox, 1998).

Zionts recommends a variety of activities to help students learn to dispute. For instance, suppose a student makes an irrational assertion and another student or the teacher disputes it. Naturally, the first student often rejects the disputation, and the process could become little more than an argument. At this point the teacher could call for a "Rational Role Reversal," in which the first student takes the role of disputer, while the original disputer switches to being a strong supporter of the irrational assertion or belief.

At each session's end, the students are given homework designed to help the one with the target problem learn to dispute his own irrational Bs and to help all students in the group develop general disputing skills. Homework is checked at the next session. When it is decided that work has progressed appropriately on the first target problem, this R-E Education process is recycled for subsequent target problems.

## Cognitive Interventions for Particular E&B Disorders

Most intervention practitioners realize that they rarely will be able to focus an intervention on a single problem of emotion and behavior. For one thing, a large proportion of young people with E&B disorder experience comorbidity among the patterns, or between patterns and connected problems (see Chapter 4). Moreover, many interventions are applied to groups of children or adolescents, which usually ensures a diversity of problems represented.

Even so, some cognitive interventions are used primarily for a particular pattern of E&B disorder or connected problem. Examples that have been used in education situations, or seem highly applicable to school use, are presented below.

### Aggression
The Skillstreaming, Adolescent Anger Control, and Anger Coping/Coping Power programs described earlier target *Aggression* and/or Law-Breaking Behavior. Other cognitive interventions for similar problems are discussed by DiGiuseppe and Li (1999); Hune and Nelson (2002); Kavale, Forness, and Walker (1999); Kellner, Bry, and Colletti (2002); Robinson, Smith, and Miller (2002); and Smith et al. (2005).

### Anxiety
Cognitive interventions for child and adolescent fears, phobias, obsessions, and other *Anxiety* problems are discussed by Albano (2003), Baer and Garland (2005), Compton et al. (2004), Fisher, Masia-Warner, and Klein (2004), Franklin, Rynn, Foa, & March (2003), Kendall and Suveg (2005), King Heyne, and Ollendick (2005), and Merrell, (2001). For instance, Fisher et al. (2004) described Skills for Academic and Social Success (SASS), a program for adolescent students with strong social fears. Participants attend group sessions lasting about 40 minutes in which leaders manage social skills training and exposure to feared social situations. Other SASS features: each participant receives a few individual sessions, her or his teachers are informed how to help with the program, and parents are taught about managing their teen's social anxieties.

### Depression
Curry and Reinecke (2003), Maag and Swearer (2005), Merrell (2001), Lewinsohn, Clarke, Rohde, Hops, & Seeley (1996), Mufson, Dorta, Olfson, Weissman, and Hoagwood (2004), Possel, Horn, Groen, and Hautzinger (2004), Rehm and Adams (2003), and Schwartz, Kaslow, Racusin, and Carton (1998) have described cognitive interventions for child and adolescent *Depression*. To illustrate, the Adolescent Coping with Depression Course (Lewinsohn et al., 1996) features social problem solving along with several other cognitive and noncognitive components. Small groups of adolescents attend weekly learning sessions for about four months, totaling approximately 32 hours. Intervention is delivered at school, a mental health facility, or other community location. Parents can play a relatively small role, but the focus is on young people learning to solve problems linked to their *Depression*. The young people learn to set realistic goals, recognize and change negative thoughts, observe and evaluate their thoughts and behavior, perform self-instruction, and use social problem-solving strategies.

### Impulsiveness
Self-instruction (e.g., Anastopoulos & Gerrard, 2003; Krain & Kendall, 1999; Merrell, 2001) has been described and recommended for decades to help students control their pervasively impulsive style of responding. Bloomquist (2005), Green and Albion (2005), and Gresham, Sugai, Horner, Quinn, and McInerney (1998) noted other cognitive interventions and curricula for students with problems similar to *Impulsiveness*. Anastopoulos and Gerrard (2003) and Gresham (2005) have pointed out that scientific support of cognitive interventions, especially self-instruction, for ADHD is limited.

Cognitive problem-solving and other techniques are used in cognitive interventions for depression.

### *Relationship Problem*

Severe problems involving social interaction and friendship are addressed in some programs and techniques noted in this chapter. Some of them use social skills training, which is usually focused on more friendly social interactions. Other intervention programs employ techniques such as self-instruction or social problem solving that directly address other problems (Bierman, 2005). Helping the young person think through a situation in order to select and perform adaptive behaviors ought to improve friendships and social interactions, too.

### *Other Problems*

As noted, Law-Breaking Behavior is addressed by many of the cognitive interventions for *Aggression*. There are several cognitive interventions for Learning Difficulty, especially learning and study strategies (e.g., Bradley-Klug & Shapiro, 2003; Friend & Bursuck, 2006; Polloway, Patton, & Serna, 2005; also see Chapter 11).

Cognitive interventions addressing Substance Misuse include *Life Skills Training* (Botvin & Dusenbury, 1987; Griffin, Botvin, Nichols, & Doyle, 2003; Trudeau, Spoth, Lillehoj, Redmond, & Wickrama, 2003). This scientifically supported program employs modeling, self-instruction, mental rehearsal of adaptive words and actions, and other techniques. Other programs for Substance Misuse are described by Goldstein, Reagles, and Amann (1990) and Patterson and O'Connell (2003).

Few cognitive or other interventions address Suicidality directly. Some components of cognitive treatments for *Anxiety, Depression*, and Substance Misuse may be relevant. Relatedly, there are cognitive interventions for poor self-esteem (e.g., Pope, McHale, & Craighead, 1988; Scott and Cervone, 2003; Shirk, Burwell, & Harter 2003). Pope et al. (1988) described a self-esteem building program for individual or group use with students age 9 years and older. It teaches social problem solving, modification of maladaptive attributions, taking the cognitive and emotional perspectives of others, disputing negative thoughts about oneself, and self-instruction. Objectives are to help the young person develop adaptive relations with family and peers, success in school, and positive body image.

Most of the interventions described in this chapter have obviously involved more than one cognitive technique. The chapter concludes with an intervention program that relies on several cognitive techniques, along with other practices. Three different aspects of a complex, significant emotional and behavior maladjustment are thereby targeted.

## Separate School Program: Aggression Replacement Training

Aggression Replacement Training (ART) is a multifaceted program designed to improve young peoples' problems in prosocial behavior skills, control of anger, and moral reasoning (Goldstein & Glick, 1987; Goldstein, Glick, & Gibbs, 1998). In the authors' view these three problems are significant causes of aggression and violent delinquency in school and society, and all three possess significant cognitive aspects. Each of these problems is addressed in ART through a different cognitive intervention: *Structured Learning, Anger Control Training*, and *Moral Education.*

ART is suited for use in schools, but Goldstein and Glick (1987) described how it was applied to adolescent male delinquents in residential correctional facilities. It was provided to groups of six 14- to 17-year-old delinquent boys within a 10-week program featuring ten Structured Learning social skills, ten Anger Control lessons, and ten moral dilemma lessons for the Moral Education part.

### *Structured Learning*

Ten critical social skills were selected and adapted from the several dozen available in *Skillstreaming the Adolescent.* These were: Expressing a Complaint, Responding to Others' Feelings, Getting Ready for a Stressful Conversation, Responding to Anger from Others, Keeping Out of Fights, Helping Other People, Dealing with an Accusation, Responding to Group Pressure, Expressing Affection, and Responding to Failure. The authors point out that with other groups and more time with which to work, ART program users might select more skills or different ones, and might involve the youths in selecting social skills.

### *Anger Control*

The Anger Control aspect of ART is an adaptation of the Adolescent Anger Control Program described earlier in this chapter. It included teaching the cognitive and other components of anger and some external and internal triggers for anger. To reduce anger and the aggression to which it may lead, students were taught relaxation, reminders, considering some maladaptive consequences of aggression, and use of social skills and social problem solving as alternatives to aggression. Lessons for Structured Learning and Anger Control were coordinated in content and sequence, especially during the last few weeks, when social skills taught in Structured Learning sessions were used as alternatives to anger within the same week's Anger Control sessions.

## *Moral Education*

The third component of ART is Moral Education, based on moral reasoning theories and curricula of Kohlberg and others (e.g., Power, Higgins, & Kohlberg, 1989). In brief, this line of thought holds that the individual's concepts of morality develop through a sequence of moral stages, each more mature and advanced than the preceding. This moral advancement takes time because it is substantially linked to biological determinants of the youth's cognitive development, but it can be accelerated through proper experiences. Moral education gives such experiences by having him engage in group discussions of "moral dilemmas"—situations that raise at least two different moral values which are in conflict because they call for incompatible courses of action.

As an example of a moral dilemma, suppose a teen has recently discovered that a 20-year-old young woman he knows is selling a highly addictive drug in his neighborhood. He has tried to tell her to stop doing this because it is illegal, can get the seller into trouble, and can harm people who buy it. However, she continues to sell. What should the boy do? Ignore it? Turn her in to the cops? Warn other community people? Something else? After some discussion, the leader might change the scenario a bit: What difference would it make if the young woman were his older brother's fiancée? His own sister? If it were a less-addictive, widely used drug? What if the sole purpose of selling the drug was to finance medical treatment for the young woman's very sick grandmother? Participants in a moral dilemma discussion take turns stating what should be done in these cases and justifying their decisions.

Common sense and some scientific research indicate that children and adolescents who engage in antisocial, aggressive behavior tend to operate at less advanced stages of moral reasoning. Moral Education was installed as a component of ART in the hope that it would prompt the antisocial adolescent to think about moral issues from various perspectives, and to examine his own as well as others' moral judgments. This in turn might raise his level of moral development, thereby improving his use of social skills and anger control abilities.

In the ART Moral Education, groups consisted of two trainers and about 12 youths meeting for one hour, two or three times per week. Each youth's beginning level of moral reasoning was assessed so that each group could be assigned members who were reasoning at different moral stages. In the group meetings, trainers presented moral dilemmas that were highly relevant to the young people involved. Next, each youth was prompted to say *what* action the person in the dilemma should take, and *why* that was the proper action. In consideration of the "what and why" information, trainers set up and managed debates between adolescents who were reasoning at different moral reasoning stages. In each debate, the youth(s) at a less-advanced stage were exposed to the fact that other rationales were not only possible but perhaps better than their own. Youths showing the most advanced moral reasoning on a particular dilemma were debated by the trainers.

## Comment on Cognitive Interventions

Cognitive interventions of various kinds are important aspects of numerous psychotherapy and counseling treatments for a range of E&B disorders of children and adolescents. Unfortunately, existing education programs for students with ED still do not commonly use cognitive interventions (Mayer et al., 2005). Such interventions deserve a larger role in such efforts (see Polsgrove & Smith, 2004). As indicated in this chapter, there are many promising developments in this direction.

## CHAPTER SUMMARY

The cognitive model assumes that cognitive events are important influences on the origins and improvement of E&B disorder.

- Social cognitive theory explains human functioning, including some E&B disorder of children, in terms of the modeling and the reciprocal determinism of B, E, and P factors—roughly, behaviors, environmental stimuli, and cognitions.
- People can influence their own behavior in various ways, especially by:
  — Learning new behavior capabilities from models
  — Evaluating their own past behavior
  — Imagining and choosing from among different future goals
  — Evaluating their own progress toward chosen goals
- Many cognitive causes of E&B disorder involve modeling.
  — A young person who observes violent, unsociable, fear-stricken, rule-violating, sad, or self-destructive behaviors may learn how to perform them, especially if they are modeled repeatedly and by various persons.
  — Inappropriate behavior may be disinhibited if a child observes someone behave inappropriately but still obtain rewards.
  — Emotions such as anger, fear, and sadness can be experienced and learned through observation.
- Other cognitive influences on E&B disorder involve attention, memory, and decision-making. Many aggressive young people tend to:
  — Pay little attention to social information
  — Perceive threatening intent where there is none
  — Remember mostly aggressive responses to disagreements
  — Excuse their own violence by attributing contemptible characteristics to victims
  — Evaluate aggression unrealistically by ignoring the bad outcomes for others and themselves
- To simplify and summarize a variety of such cognitive influences on E&B disorder, Kendall suggested discriminating two overall kinds: cognitive deficits and cognitive distortions.

- To address cognitive deficits, interventionists teach adaptive cognitive processes and behaviors. They use:
  — Modeling
  — Self-instruction
  — Cognitive problem-solving, perhaps through programs such as Skillstreaming and Adolescent Anger Control
- To address cognitive distortions, one can teach a student to:
  — Correct errors in social information processing
  — Use strategies to understand the perspectives of other children involved in a disagreement, perhaps through a program such as Anger Coping
  — Give up irrational beliefs about her or his life
  — Participate in rational-emotive therapy or education to learn to recognize and change irrational beliefs and the maladaptive behaviors they cause
- Many cognitive interventions are specialized to address a particular pattern or other specific form of E&B disorder.

## IDEAS FOR CONSIDERATION AND DISCUSSION

1. Explain how observational learning, failure of observational learning, vicarious behavior disinhibition, vicarious emotional arousal, and dysfunctional self-efficacy can be involved in students' E&B disorder, according to Bandura's Social Cognitive Theory.
2. Present a cognitive explanation of *Impulsiveness* that addresses most or all of the steps found in the cognitive-<u>deficits</u>-by-social-information-processing table (Display 9-2). What intervention actions are suggested by each step of your explanation?
3. Present a cognitive explanation of *Anxiety* that addresses most or all of the steps found in the cognitive-<u>distortions</u>-by-social-information-processing table (Display 9-3). What intervention actions are suggested by each step of your explanation?
4. a. Create skill cards for the following social skills for children and adolescents with E&B disorder:
   Responding to Criticism from a Teacher
   Asking a Peer to Join You in a Play Activity
   Apologizing to Your Teacher for Misbehavior.
   b. Imagine a different social skill needed by some children and adolescents with E&B disorder. Create a skill card for your social skill.
5. Consider how <u>Skillstreaming</u> could be used with students with ED in a resource room and a separate class education environment. Give an example of how it could be used within each environment. Anticipate possible obstacles or other problems in using <u>Skillstreaming</u> in these environments with students with ED.
6. a. What is an "irrational belief"?
   b. What is the relationship of irrational beliefs to E&B disorders?

c. Consider Display 9-10, and think of a different irrational belief that is not in the display. Name and describe this new irrational belief, including its possible ill effects on a young person's emotions and behavior. Finally, describe an alternative, rational belief for your irrational belief.

## Resources for Further Study

**www.emory.edu/EDUCATION/mfp/bandurabio.html** Albert Bandura biographical sketch

**www.psychologyinfo.com/depression/cognitive.htm#cognitivefactors** Cognitive influences on depression

**www.psychologymatters.org/shure.html** Cognitive problem solving

**www.beckinstitute.org** Cognitive therapy (Beck)

**www.temple.edu/psychology/FacultyWebs/Kendall/kendall.html** Philip Kendall biographical sketch

**www.rebt.org/WhatisREBT.htm** Rational-emotive therapy (Ellis)

**www.emory.edu/EDUCATION/mfp/effpage.html** Self-efficacy

Chapter **Ten**

# *Sociological, Ecological, and Values-Based/ Spiritual Models*

## CHAPTER OBJECTIVES

**After reading this chapter, you should be able to:**
- State the two major social group variables in sociological perspectives on E&B disorder.
- Discriminate social drift and social causation explanations of the link between SES and E&B disorder.
- Say how labeling contributes to E&B disorder.
- Describe physical, social, cognitive, and time aspects of an ecosystem.
- List teacher roles in broad ecological intervention.
- Identify the four circle of courage needs, and results of failure to satisfy each need.

## CAN YOU DEFINE THESE 10 TERMS?

conflict theory
functionalism theory
labeling
child advocacy
ecosystem

goodness-of-fit
character education
spirituality
12-step program
need for generosity

This chapter describes some key aspects of sociological, ecological, and values perspectives on E&B disorder of children. Each perspective conceptualizes the nature of and interventions for E&B disorder at a different level than the psychodynamic, behavioral, and cognitive models. The sociological perspective examines social aspects of groups of people, whether societies or smaller groups, that result in the identification of certain of its members as having E&B disorder. The ecological perspective is mainly concerned with smaller environments such as classrooms and schools. It emphasizes how social, physical, and other influences of these environments contribute to E&B disorder or can be changed to reduce it. The values perspective considers the role of values and spiritual considerations in intervention.

## SOCIOLOGICAL PERSPECTIVE

### Theory

Sociology is the study of large and small human groups, with particular attention to interactions between groups and the results of such interactions (Albrow, 1999; Shepard, 2005; Wallace & Wolf, 2006). Sociologists study entire societies, groupings based on social class and race-ethnic cultures, settings for work and school, neighborhoods, families, and other groups. Among the wide range of issues addressed in sociology is *deviance* (behavior that differs from group expectations) of individuals and subgroups. Deviance includes E&B disorder. Sociological explanations of deviance explore how E&B disorder is defined and identified, different ways it is exhibited, and differences in prevalence rates across groups (Aneshensel & Phelan, 1999; Cockerham, 2006; Gallagher, 2002; Karnik, 2004).

### *Sociological Considerations*
***Socioeconomic Status.*** The terms social class and socioeconomic status (SES) refer to levels of social resources under an individual's or a family's control. Financial, occupational, and educational circumstances are the main social resources of interest. They can be measured and combined via formulas in order to identify the SES level (e.g., upper, upper middle, lower middle, working, lower) that best describes any individual or family.

There is abundant research showing that social class is related to all sorts of variables pertaining to people's physical and psychological well-being, attitudes, and behaviors (Gallagher, 2002; Shepard, 2005). Research conducted in various societies around the world shows that the prevalence, patterns, and treatment of E&B disorder are associated with SES (Aneshensel & Phelan, 1999; Desjarlais, Eisenberg, Good, & Kleinman, 1995). People of low SES have greater-than-average rates of many forms of E&B disorder, especially extreme E&B disorders and antisocial disorders (Aneshensel & Phelan, 1999; Cockerham, 2006; Gallagher, 2002; Kessler, 2005; U.S. Department of Health and Human Services [USD HHS], 1999).

Of course, these relationships are generalities. High SES does not innoculate a person against E&B disorder, and many people of low SES lead productive, satisfying, well-adjusted lives.

Ability to benefit from available interventions for E&B disorder is also associated with SES. People of lower SES are less likely to have access to mental health services, continue with interventions they receive, and benefit from these interventions (Gallagher, 2002; Osher et al., 2004; Wicks-Nelson & Israel, 2006). Students with disabilities are disproportionately of low SES, especially students with ED (USD Education, 2002; Wagner, Kutash, Duchnowski, Epstein, & Sumi, 2005).

***Race-Ethnic Culture.*** Culture can be defined as the sum of a group's history, language, beliefs, customs, and technology (Gallagher, 2002; Wallace & Wolf, 2006). The term is usually applied to an entire society, but is also used, along with "subculture" and "community," to describe groups within a larger culture or society (Valsiner, 2000).

In publications and other official actions, the U.S. government often designates four minority race-ethnic groups: African American, Asian/Pacific Islander, Hispanic, and Native American (USD HHS, 1999), as well as the majority White race-ethnic group. This way of designating has loopholes and requires disclaimers: for instance, there are various alternative terms (e.g., Black, Latino/a, European-American), and each race-ethnic group subsumes very diverse subgroups, including substantial numbers of multiracial members. But other ways of classifying people by race-ethnic status also are problematic.

It is often said that various race-ethnic groups in the U.S. constitute different cultures (e.g., Torres-Valasquez, 2000). Some would disagree, claiming that race-ethnic subculture differences are small compared to their similarities within U.S. culture. In any event it is clear that group norms, beliefs, and values have much relevance to understanding cultural considerations for E&B disorder in the community and the school (Lau et al., 2004; Obiakor et al., 2002; Osher et al., 2004).

1. *Normality is relative.* Standards for normal behavior exist in most if not all cultures in the world, but exactly what is normal often varies across places and times (Gallagher, 2002; Wicks-Nelson & Israel, 2006). Cultures vary in what sorts of functioning they support and deter and how they interpret violations of standards. For example:
   (a) Some cultures encourage expression of emotions in general or certain emotions, whereas other cultures discourage displaying emotions.
   (b) A person who hears the voice of or who sees a dead person suddenly feels extreme confidence and joy and experiences a dreamlike state while awake, may be considered a transcendant prophet in one culture, but a person with extreme E&B disorder in another.
   (c) Cultures that emphasize individual responsibility tend to perceive abnormal functioning as a disruption of individual self-development, while cultures that view the person primarily as a member of a family or clan perceive such problems as mainly a shame on the group.

2. *Disorders vary across cultures.* Some forms of E&B disorder, such as schizophrenia and manic forms of Mood Disorders, are present in many if not all nations and cultures of the world (Nevid, Rathus, & Greene, 2006). Even in these cases, however, cultural variables influence how disorders are expressed (e.g., Greenberger, Chen, Tally, & Dong, 2000; Pineda et al., 2000).

3. *Disorders may vary across subcultures.* To some extent, similar phenomena are observed across subcultures within a society (Nevid et al., 2006; Satel & Redding, 2005). For instance, American race-ethnic groups show varying rates of different problems related to E&B disorder, such as Mood Disorders, *Anxiety*, alcoholism, serious school behavior problems, and Suicidality (Cockerham, 2006; Kilpatrick et al., 2000; Pigott & Cowen, 2000; USD HHS, 1999). As Display 1-9 shows, Black students show a disproportionately high prevalence of the ED education disability, whereas other minority race-ethnic students show a low prevalence. The prevalence of White students is about proportionate. In addition, there are race-ethnic differences in how much and what kinds of assistance people with E&B disorder and their families seek (USD HHS, 1999; Wicks-Nelson & Israel, 2006).

**Comment on SES and Race-Ethnic Culture in E&B Disorder.** SES and race-ethnic status overlap considerably in many places, of course, including the U.S. Research attempting to separate their influence on E&B disorder has generally found that SES is a stronger determinant than race-ethnic group membership (Cockerham, 2006; USD HHS, 1999). In fact, SES seems to be the single strongest demographic correlate of mental illness (Cockerham, 2006; Gallagher, 2002). Besides SES and race-ethnic culture, sociologists are interested in possible relationships between E&B disorder and variables such as gender (e.g., Foster, 2005), conditions of residence (e.g., urban versus rural), and religious cultures.

### *Sociological Explanations*
Why are SES and race-ethnic status linked with E&B disorder? There are various sociological interpretations, and theorists draw on ideas from psychology and other disciplines as well (Aneshensel & Phelan, 1999; Kessler, 2005; Valsiner, 2000). Two main explanations are referred to as social drift and social causation. Social causation theories are supplemented by a consideration of the influences of stress and labeling.

**Social Drift.** Social drift (also termed social selection) holds that people of low SES are disproportionately likely to experience E&B disorder because in many cases both E&B disorder and low SES come about for similar reasons (Sarason & Sarason, 2005). Primarily, people with very maladaptive emotional, behavioral, or cognitive functioning tend to be identified with E&B disorders *and* they tend to have great difficulty obtaining and maintaining material aspects of well-being. Their problems dispose them to loss of wealth, employment, friends and other helpful aspects of a social network, good housing and neighborhoods, health and health care, education, and other assets. This leads to a decline in their SES, or if SES originally was low it remains that way. This decline may be hastened if these people also engage in high-risk behaviors such as misusing substances, bearing children without a husband or life partner, or committing law violations. Most tragically, children experience the detrimental effects of their parents' problems.

**Social Causation.** In social causation interpretations, harmful societal conditions create obstacles for people to achieve their economic, social, educational, health, political, and other important life goals. Principal among these harmful conditions are economic problems (e.g., poverty, unemployment) and injustice, race-ethnic discrimination, and apathy or malevolence of social institutions (e.g., mental health and education bureaucracies), along with the unhealthy psychological stresses they create. E&B disorder and low SES are two of the sad but predictable outcomes of these societally created obstacles (Costello, Compton, Keeler, & Angold, 2003; Hudson, 2005). Alternative interpretations of how these outcomes happen are provided by conflict theory and functionalism theory.

1. In ***conflict theory***, a fundamental characteristic of a society or culture is that groups within the society are continuously in a state of struggle (Cockerham, 2006; Gallagher, 2002). Some of these groups are very powerful, others nearly powerless. To maintain their power, the former exploit and oppress the latter by restricting their access to work and economic opportunities, education, political strength, and other social resources. When the powerless oppose these efforts,

powerful groups arrange for their behavior to be identified as criminal, mentally ill, or otherwise officially deviant. They further oppress the powerless by proclaiming theories of E&B disorder that hide the true cause of their problems (oppression), controlling them through isolation and harmful therapies while limiting their access to meaningful help.

Conflict theory is based in part on Karl Marx's philosophy of economic class struggle, so it has focused mainly on economic reasons for group conflict (Gallagher, 2002). However, it has also been applied to between-groups conflict based on race-ethnic cultures or subcultures, genders, age-groups, and other subgroups in societies (e.g., Chesney-Lind & Shelden, 1998; Cockerham, 2006; Karenga, 1980; Myers, 1999; Osher et al., 2004).

2. **Functionalism theory** holds a different view of a society: that it is an inherently stable organization of social parts (e.g., families, economies, religions, various social groups). These parts are interdependent, so major changes in one often cause others to change as well. After the change, society evolves to a new equilibrium. Each part has a "function" (contribution to the stability of society).

   Sometimes, what stabilizes the society as a whole may not be good for a part of the society or for an individual. Regarding individual deviance, for instance, a person may be unable or unwilling to pursue socially approved goals (e.g., school or work failure, withdrawal from reality). Or he may pursue socially approved goals by disapproved means, such as violence, fraud, prostitution, or theft. By identifying this person as deviant, the society attempts to maintain an important aspect of its stability: expectations or norms for desirable and undesirable behavior.

   Functionalism theory is also applied to small social systems. In family systems theory, certain undesirable child-rearing practices maintain family stability by creating E&B disorder in an offspring (Gallagher, 2002). The function of the child with E&B disorder is to keep the family from disintegrating. For example, a mother who is unable to parent a normally active child effectively because she is depressed may encourage the child's fears, low self-esteem, passivity, pessimism, or social isolation in order to maintain her parental control. A father may exaggerate an adolescent's deviance and reject her as a negative example in attempting to persuade younger siblings to avoid the same problems.

3. The role played by *social stress* (see Chapter 6) in causing E&B disorder is emphasized in some social causation explanations (Gallagher, 2002; Kessler, 2005). These stressors, created or magnified by disadvantageous societal conditions, may work directly or indirectly.
   (a) Directly, stress associated with poverty and discrimination based on gender, race-ethnic status, religion, and immigrant status has been linked to E&B disorder (Nevid et al., 2006; Sarason & Sarason, 2005).
   (b) Indirectly, stress can have destructive effects on small social organizations such as neighborhoods, schools, and families. Physically and socially deteriorated neighborhoods, chaotic, unsafe schools, loss of social support from loved ones, and dysfunctioning of the family (e.g., disturbed attachment, problematic discipline styles) are prominent risk factors for E&B disorders.

4. **Labeling** is the process of publicly designating a person as deviant. This concept explains how some forms of deviance can originate and be perpetuated (Gallagher, 2002; Wallace & Wolf, 2006). Like stress, labeling is compatible with both conflict and functionalism theories.

In explaining how E&B disorder *originates* through labeling, Szasz (1960, 1970) provocatively asserted that mental illness is no more than a myth that legitimizes the labeling and manipulation of children and adults who think and act deviantly. He reasoned that all people have "problems in living" of various kinds and degrees. But society's official labelers—psychiatrists, psychologists, educators, judges—will designate as deviant any person whose problems in living involve behaviors that threaten powerful organizations and individuals. People with little power are especially likely to be labeled (Laing, 1967). In addition, a labeled person who accepts the label begins to suffer stress, which can lead to E&B disorder (Cockerham, 2006).

Moreover, labeling *perpetuates* deviance by establishing social expectations for further deviance (Gallagher, 2002). Once a person is labeled, many of her behaviors may be seen as yet more evidence of deviance, even though the very same behaviors might not be considered deviant when exhibited by others. Social expectations also may pressure the labeled person to adopt behaviors compatible with the label (Cockerham, 2006; DesJarlais & Paul, 1978). For instance, once a student is labeled as tough, mean, defiant, or a troublemaker, he may increasingly act in accord with this label (e.g., by associating exclusively with other troublemakers). At the same time his appropriately assertive behavior may be ignored, especially by official labelers whose power would be threatened by such evidence of an inaccurate diagnosis (Scheff, 1975).

**Comment on Social Drift and Social Causation.** In their basic assumptions, social drift and social causation are contradictory, but many sociologists recognize that both effects could be operating simultaneously to produce the disproportionately high prevalence of E&B disorder among persons of low SES (Cockerham, 2006). Social causation seems to be of greater interest to sociologists, perhaps because it implies more need for and possibilities of changing social phenomena (e.g., oppressive conditions that lead to poverty, race-ethnic group discrimination, sexism) that may cause E&B disorder. Social drift suggests the need to address E&B disorder directly and implies that successful interventions for a person's E&B disorder may also reduce, halt, or reverse declining SES.

## Intervention

Sociological perspectives have shaped the views of educators, other helping professionals, and society in general about how membership in a social subgroup (especially low SES and African American race-ethnic subgroups) can contribute to an individual's deviance, including E&B disorder. These perspectives also imply directions for assessment and intervention to improve economic and race-ethnic problems and reduce E&B disorder. However, sociological implications tend to be general, not focused on classroom actions.

|  | Name of Theory | Sociological Perspective |
|---|---|---|
| WHAT | Brief description of theory | The behavior of individuals is controlled by variables involving groups in society and interactions between those groups. E&B disorder is caused by powerful groups' oppression of low socioeconomic status and minority race-ethnic groups, by stress effects resulting from oppression and other harmful societal conditions, and/or by labeling. |
|  | Key terms | Socioeconomic status: Degree of financial and other social resources<br>Social causation: Hypothesis that harmful social conditions lead to various forms of deviance, including E&B disorder<br>Labeling: Publicly designating someone as deviant, often producing oppression of that person |
| WHO | Who is intervention appropriate for? | Students with E&B disorder due to oppression, societally induced stress, or labeling |
|  | Who delivers intervention? | Teachers, school psychologists, other school personnel; on a larger scale, citizens, governments, and charitable organizations |
| WHEN | When and how often is intervention delivered? | When assessment, curriculum, and instruction decisions are made; thereafter, continuously |
| WHERE | In what contexts is intervention delivered? | School, school system, community, nation |
| WHY | Rationale/purpose for intervention | To reduce oppression based on socioeconomic and race-ethnic status, societally created stress, and labeling |
| HOW | Selected strategies for intervention | 1. Consider socioeconomic and race-ethnic differences in assessment and diagnosis of ED<br>2. Consider socioeconomic and race-ethnic differences in educational and community prevention and intervention<br>3. Advocate government and other societal changes to reduce oppressive conditions<br>4. Reduce labeling effects by serving students identified as ED solely in general education classes, or by serving students with E&B disorder without identifying them as ED |

## *Assessment*

Sociologists warn that failure to understand or consider social class and race-ethnic cultural considerations may lead to bias in assessment, classification, and diagnosis of E&B disorder (Osher et al., 2004; Pumariega, 2003; USD HHS, 1999). Assumptions behind the development and use of assessment procedures may apply more accurately to some U.S. subcultures than others. Recognizing such issues may reduce the use of assessment procedures that yield culturally biased outcomes, either improperly identifying a student as having ED or improperly failing to identify the student.

Avoiding this problem was one of the objectives of the definition proposed by the National Mental Health and Special Education Coalition (e.g., Forness & Kavale, 2000) as an alternative to the federal definition of ED. The Coalition's proposal calls for judging a student's problems against norms specific to her or his culture or ethnicity (Cullinan, 2004; see Display 1-4).

## *Intervention*

Problems and solutions related to undesirable social and cultural effects on people go far beyond E&B disorder of children and the professionals who serve them. Countless prophets, philosophers, revolutionaries, politicians, journalists, and everyday people—as well as various child service professionals—have thought of highly diverse solutions to these problems. Teachers, school psychologists, and other education professionals can play important parts in some interventions that are compatible with the sociological perspective (McIntyre, 1996; Wilson, 2004).

The sociological perspective is reflected in a variety of steps to prevent or reduce E&B disorder among children from societal groups at high risk (Sarason & Sarason, 2005). Some of these ideas and actions are associated with school-based services for children's emotional and behavior problems (Jacobs, Randall, Vernberg, Roberts, & Nyre, 2005; Porter, Pearson, Keenan, & Duval-Harvey, 2003) and the school's place in a "system of care" (Eber & Keenan, 2004; Stroul, 2003).

Child and family support services such as special education, counseling, therapy, medical treatment, public health, and economic assistance should be provided in local community settings (Powell & Dunlap, 2005; Smith-Boydston, 2005; USD HHS, 1999). In some cases this should be the local school. Individuals and agencies must deliver these services in a "culturally competent" manner that respects race-ethnic, SES, and other cultural features of the children and communities (McIntyre, 1996; Osher et al., 2004; Pumariega, 2003). To empower individuals, families, and communities to assist themselves, such services often use family and community members to help identify needs, plan services, and advocate for the clients. Systems of care, cultural competence, and related concepts are described in Chapters 11 and 12.

In their attempts to improve services to children plagued by societal problems, many education professionals adopt a child advocate role. **Child advocacy** can be defined as a collection of beliefs that produce action intended to promote causes that benefit children. This role involves diverse actions taken individually or through professional organizations to address public and private aspects of the societal problems.

In the public realm, child advocates may work for changes in procedures and regulations of schools and other child service agencies or in laws, regulations, and government practices. They push for increased government funding where needed.

In the private sector, child advocates attempt to increase citizen awareness and charitable organization support of the issues on which they are working. They also try to expand opportunities for economic improvement and other forms of self-improvement of families. Whether directed to public or private targets, what these and other child advocacy efforts generally have in common is the effort to modify social conditions linked to discrimination or disadvantage based on poverty, minority race-ethnic status, or other cultural situations that diminish the benefits of education for students with ED or at risk for ED.

The concept of labeling has alerted special educators to sometimes unrecognized but potentially strong social expectations in school and society that may have destructive effects on students identified with ED. Some have proposed that labeling effects can be reduced by educating all students with ED in general education classes ("full inclusion") or by serving students with emotional and behavior problems without identifying them with ED or any other education disability.

The next section describes the ecological perspective, which is based in part on two sociological ideas, functionalism theory and labeling. The ecological perspective addresses learning and adjustment considerations for students with ED in smaller social systems such as the classroom, and its interventions closely resemble sociological ones.

# ECOLOGICAL PERSPECTIVE

## Theory

Ecology is the study of relationships within an **ecosystem**. An ecosystem consists of an organism and its environment(s), including the behavior of other organisms. Ecological psychology draws on insights from biology, sociology (especially functionalism theory and labeling), and other disciplines (Bronfenbrenner, 2004) to conceptualize how environmental variables create and destroy **goodness-of-fit** (stable relationships among a young person's development, behavior, and environments). As applied to E&B disorder of children and adolescents, the ecological perspective is concerned with how an ecosystem loses goodness-of-fit, how this may lead to E&B disorder, and what can be done to restore goodness-of-fit (Cantrell, Cantrell, Valore, Jones, & Fecser, 1999; Rhodes, 1967).

### Ecosystems

Children's ecosystems include the child's behavior plus physical, social, cognitive, time, and other aspects that provide opportunities for and limits on those behaviors (Guerra, Boxer, & Kim, 2005; Howard, Barton, Walsh, & Lerner, 1999). Classrooms, playgrounds, meetings, athletic contests, parties, places of worship, and other ecosystems have characteristic structures, objects, schedules, actors, and activities. That is, a particular ecosystem may bring forth similar behaviors from very different participating individuals, even if these individuals are located far apart and separated in time by decades (e.g., spectator behavior at baseball games, worshipper behavior at religious services). The aspects of ecosystems include the following:

1. *Physical* aspects of an ecosystem are clearly important. For example, students grouped at a table are more likely to converse and discuss than those seated in rows.
2. *Social* aspects include how the ecosystem affects cooperative, conflictual, and other interactions among children and adults. It also is concerned with different purposes for which children participate in it.
3. There are *cognitive* aspects to ecosystems. Regardless of the absolute nature of physical and social variables, the way one thinks about them can be important. For instance, how a student perceives her school may control learning and behavior more significantly than the actual quality of buildings, curricula, and social opportunities.
4. *Time* affects ecosystems. Some remain stable over time while their participants are changing, as happens each new year in a middle school. Further, the physical, social, cognitive, and other variables that strongly determined an ecosystem at one age may be superseded by other variables at a later age (Howard et al., 1999). Other ecosystems change over time in various ways, and still others just disappear.
5. Various other aspects of ecosystems are seen as important by different authorities.

It is evident that an ecosystem is modified by naturally occuring changes in physical, social, cognitive, time, and other variables. These ecosystem modifications can create, improve, or disrupt goodness-of-fit. Of course, educators and other intervention agents also modify ecosystems intentionally to create or improve goodness-of-fit.

Students behavior is strongly influenced by physical, social, cognitive, and other aspects of school ecosystems.

### Multiple Ecosystems

Children do not function in only one ecosystem, but in many. Not surprisingly, varied ecosystems tend to bring forth different behaviors, emotions, and thinking. Behavior that is adaptive in one ecosystem may not be adaptive in another. To illustrate, polite assertive behavior maintains goodness-of-fit in most classrooms but may destroy it in some children's community peer groups. Some of a child's ecosystems may be unrelated, but often they are linked to some extent; that is, a change in one can affect the others. For example, an incident involving threats and arguing in one class a student attends may destabilize the ecosystem of another class. Also, substantial disturbance at home can affect the child's school ecosystem, and vice versa.

Some ecosystems operate within other ecosystems. For instance, families, churches, a park and shelter, a school, two gangs, a small business area, and a neighborhood crime watch network may each be a small ecosystem included within a larger ecosystem, the neighborhood. Of special interest as ecosystems are agencies and services that address children with E&B disorder, especially education, mental health, child and family welfare, and juvenile justice systems. These systems are themselves composed of smaller ecosystems (e.g., the education system subsumes schools, a teacher's organization, special education services, etc.). The teacher may need to become familiar with these ecosystems and subecosystems in order to maximize his value to students identified as ED.

### Ecological Explanation of E&B Disorder

To the extent that a person does not show goodness-of-fit in a given ecosystem, she will be perceived as different, perhaps even alarmingly abnormal. As applied to education, the ecological perspective views E&B disorder as a deficiency in goodness-of-fit between the student and one or more education ecosystems (Cantrell et al., 1999). Rhodes' (1970) classic ecological definition of ED described how this happens:

1. Some characteristic of a child (usually, behavior) agitates an educational ecosystem.
2. The ecosystem responds in ways that lead the child to react, thereby creating further agitation.
3. Reciprocally disturbing interactions are set into motion within the ecosystem.

Therefore, deficient goodness-of-fit is a property of the classroom, school, or other education ecosystem as a whole, not the individual student's behavior or any other single aspect of the ecosystem. Or as Munger (1998, p. 18) expressed it: "There are no high-risk children, only high-risk circumstances." Despite this, educators often mistakenly focus responsibility on an individual student. As a result she may be labeled as having the ED disability.

## Assessment and Intervention

Ecological assessment is designed to clarify how the young person's ecosystems ordinarily function and how they become discordant. It explores variables within the classroom(s) where goodness-of-fit is lacking, as well as in other important ecosystems of which the child is part. To capture valid indicators of behavior and environment, assessment data should be collected within natural ecosystems, not artificial ones. For instance, to remove a student from class and administer a paper-and-pencil test of personality probably would not yield information about a natural ecosystem.

That there are many potentially important variables within and across students' ecosystems can make it difficult to conceptualize how these variables operate, singly and in combination. This makes it hard to decide what variables should be assessed. One approach is to begin with a general assessment of an ecosystem, then move to assessing more specific variables. The particular variables may be suggested by the general assessment, or they may be called for by the assessor's preferred model of E&B disorder (e.g., psychoeducational, behavioral).

Ecological intervention for students with E&B disorder attempts to restore goodness-of-fit and to prevent its loss in the future. Because E&B disorder arises from or is perpetuated by exposure to high-risk circumstances (Munger, 1998), the educator should lower the student's exposure to high-risk circumstances while arranging more exposure to helpful circumstances. Of course, a very wide range of educational intervention activities are said to provide helpful circumstances (e.g., Bos & Vaughn, 2006; Davis et al., 2004; Jones, Dohrn, & Dunn, 2004; Polloway, Patton, & Serna, 2005).

### *Initial Assessment: General*

The initial assessment should measure a range of target student behaviors and physical, social, cognitive, time, and other important aspects of an ecosystem. In any particular case this might involve (a) the target student's behavior, emotions, thoughts, medical situation, and temperament (Carey, 1998); (b) her peers, the teacher, and interactions among them; and (c) physical features, structure, and scheduling in the classroom and other school ecosystems.

In many ecosystems there are potential resources that are currently underutilized but might be helpful in establishing goodness-of-fit. Ecological assessors can exploit this idea by identifying and assessing support resources in the ecosystem (Munger, 1998) by place (e.g., quiet areas for study), activity (e.g., ones preferred by the student), and people (e.g., principal). This may point to resources that can modify ecosystems to be more supportive of the young person. Display 10-1 presents a simple way to survey social support possibilities in school.

Given the ecological model's concern with interactions among multiple ecosystems, home, neighborhood, and other ecosystems of the student may need to be considered for assessment. Finally, assessment results within each ecosystem and across several ecosystems are examined for patterns and trends that may suggest changes teachers or others can make to improve goodness-of-fit.

In Chapter 3, Display 3-7 presented areas of potential interest in assessing education environments. Many of these classroom physical, schoolwide physical, personnel, student and teacher social, scheduling, grouping, instruction, and behavior management variables can be of interest in assessing stable and disturbed goodness-of-fit. Published lists and inventories of education environment variables may also guide a general ecological assessment (e.g., Munger, 1998; Ysseldyke & Christenson, 2002).

**Display 10-1** Identifying people who may give social support for an ecological intervention

|  | Name of person: _____ |
|---|---|
| Nature of existing social interaction with student _____ | _____ |
| Nature of social support this person could give _____ | _____ |
| Present and potential frequency of social support _____ | _____ |
| How willing to help is the person? _____ | _____ |
| How able and reliable in delivering help is the person? _____ | _____ |
| Obstacles to social support from this person _____ | _____ |
| Summarize positive and negative aspects about this person; make decision _____ | _____ |
| If this person is to provide social support, how will it work? _____ | _____ |

*Source:* Adapted from Munger, 1998.

### *Intervention: General*

Many important aspects of ecological intervention are not specific to a particular model of E&B disorder. Instead, ecological practitioners use a range of practices drawn from various models, disciplines, or other sources, as long as those practices advance the ecological intervention goals of establishing and maintaining goodness-of-fit. But in addition to general practices, some ecological practitioners add methods drawn mainly from a particular model (e.g., psychoeducational or behavioral), as illustrated below.

Ecological intervention emphasizes correcting deficiencies in goodness-of-fit by changing physical, social, cognitive, time, and other variables in the classroom ecosystem (Cantrell et al., 1999; Rhodes, 1967). Attempts to change the student directly are acceptable but should not be the main effort. If places, activities, and people have been identified as potential resources, they may be incorporated into an intervention plan that changes the target student's school ecology.

Practitioners also take responsibility to work for changes in other important ecosystems in which the child operates (e.g., Eber & Keenan, 2004; Pumariega, 2005; Stroul, 2003). This often requires knowledge of and cooperation with mental health, child and family welfare, juvenile justice, and other systems of human service. A child advocacy role may be adopted.

### *Follow-up Assessment: Specific*

As the ecological assessor moves from general to more specific assessment, she must decide which particular variables need to be measured in order to make intervention decisions. At this point the decision maker's preferred model of E&B disorder will probably come into play, because different models emphasize different variables as most important for intervention.

For example, psychoeducationists may assess pleasant and unpleasant memories the student has about school, stressful situations and people in his daily schedule, and maladaptive emotions and self-perceptions (Long, Wood, & Fecser, 2001; Morse, 1996). Behaviorists may record the student's adaptive and maladaptive behaviors, as well as the classroom antecedents, consequences, and functions of them (Alberto & Troutman, 2006; Lewis, Lewis-Palmer, Newcomer, & Stichter, 2004). Proponents of other models would focus on different reasons that goodness-of-fit is disturbed. Regardless of model, as long as the assessment is designed to clarify what ecological variables might be changed to restore a stable ecosystem, it is probably compatible with the ecological perspective.

Classroom social interactions are of special importance in specific ecological assessment (Barth, Dunlap, Dane, Lochman, & Wells, (2004). Different ways that the teacher and student, or student and peers, talk and act toward each other can be analyzed to reveal important sequences or other patterns of classroom interaction, and to indicate what ecological variables might be changed to modify social interaction in ways that improve goodness-of-fit.

Sometimes sociometric assessment (see Chapter 3) is used to identify relatively popular and unpopular students, those who are not noticed much, and other aspects of social status within the group. Sociometric information may suggest social ecology changes needed to improve group functioning. Students' feelings and attitudes related to social interaction can be measured through self-reported rating scales or objective personality tests.

### *Assessing Multiple Ecosystems*

Important as understanding the ecosystems of classroom and school are, ecological assessment is also concerned with other ecosystems. Assessment procedures similar to those for school use are available or can be adapted for assessing the student's home and other important ecosystems (Munger, 1998). Once assessed, ecosystems can be contrasted and otherwise analyzed to provide information that is not available when assessment is focused solely on the student being considered for identification as having ED.

To illustrate, suppose at least one ecosystem shows goodness-of-fit. It can be studied intensively for hints as to how other, disturbed ecosystems can be changed to encourage goodness-of-fit there. In any case, the results of multiple-ecosystem assessment may be helpful in planning the pupil's overall intervention program, completing the IEP, and integrating the teacher's activities into an overall treatment effort covering multiple settings.

### *Intervention: Psychoeducational-Ecological*

Rhodes (1967) called for a set of three successively broader psychoeducational-ecological interventions. Student-focused interventions are short term and narrowly tailored to a particular student. School-focused interventions are meant to modify classroom and school ecology to improve goodness-of-fit for students in general. Broad interventions deal with ecosystems beyond the classroom and even the school.

***Student Focused.*** The student with ED is likely to undergo severe stress when goodness-of-fit does not exist between his behavior and the classroom ecosystem (Rhodes, 1967). The teacher must recognize this and, in the short term, serve as the student's emotional support and buffer against stress. Psychoeducational teaching strategies such as surface behavior management and emotional first aid could satisfy this (Long et al., 2001; Wood, Brendtro, Fecser, & Nichols, 1999).

***School Focused.*** Other interventions address classroom and school goodness-of-fit. The teacher should extend curriculum coverage beyond academic content. A wide range of materials, instruction strategies, and activities is necessary to teach the student with ED how to live and cope in a complex world. Some areas that would be particularly helpful in a modified classroom ecosystem include creative art and drama, crafts, physical education and guided play, other structured and unstructured group interaction, and training in appropriate social behavior. Also, the teacher should increase motivation by relying on more independent research, field trips, group projects, and other appealing instructional practices, along with assignments individualized for a particular student, while relying less on lecture and class-wide assignments.

Not surprisingly, psychoeducational-ecological educators believe that curriculum should encourage students to express feelings and psychic conflicts. These might provide opportunities for the clinical exploitation kind of Life Space Crisis Intervention (e.g., Long et al., 2001); see Chapter 7.

***Beyond the Classroom.*** Rhodes' broad ecological interventions involve the teacher's working in various roles beyond the classroom and school. These roles are not specific to psychoeducational intervention, and so are discussed after behavioral-ecological interventions.

Parenthetically, many of Rhodes' ecological recommendations for schooling (e.g., extending curriculum coverage, instructional activities, locations for learning) would appear to conflict with mandates for higher academic achievement among all students, including those with ED. Any teaching activity not obviously contributing to academic achievement might be viewed as an expendable luxury in light of federal and state education laws, mandates for high-stakes testing, and penalties for schools in which specified student subgroups lag in achievement (Katsiyannis & Yell, 2004; Sitlington & Neubert, 2004).

### Intervention: Behavioral-Ecological

The ecological perspective is also compatible with the behavioral model, especially interventions focusing on antecedents that influence behavior (e.g., Stormshak & Dishion, 2002; Sugai et al., 2000). Disorderly student behavior and inefficient learning are reduced by well-structured physical, social, and time aspects of the classroom and school (e.g., specified classroom areas, equipment, rules, class scheduling, and transitions among activities). If these are lacking, behaviorists might institute them as one kind of ecosystem change.

The teacher often must serve as an emotional buffer against stress for a student with E&B disorder.

The ecological emphasis on multiple ecosystems meshes well with behavioristic concepts of generalization across settings. The "ecobehavioral" approach assesses different settings to identify variables that can help and hinder generalization, then creates interventions based on this information (Cantrell et al., 1999; Harvey, Lewis-Palmer, Horner, & Sugai, 2003). Various school settings (e.g., other classrooms, hallways, school playground, community, home) may contain similar physical, social, and other antecedents that prompt similar inappropriate behaviors. Modifying such antecedents may make it more likely that the student with E&B disorder will perform appropriate behaviors in each setting.

### *Ecological Intervention Beyond the Classroom*

Teachers, school psychologists, and others concerned with education of students with ED must influence ecosystems beyond the classroom (Harvey et al., 2003; Munger, 1998). One way to accomplish this is to modify the attitudes and behaviors of fellow educators, the student's parents, and other important individuals and groups in the student's various ecosystems. Another is to improve these young people's access to services.

As *consultant to school* ecosystems, the ecological special educator provides information, encourages other people's involvement in intervention, and helps decision-making. He works with fellow teachers and administrators to improve how the school perceives and deals with disturbed ecosystems, inform them about the needs of specific students with ED, and help them increase their skills in educating such students (Bos & Vaughn, 2006; Jones et al., 2004; Polloway et al., 2005; Salend, 2005).

| | Name of Theory | Ecological Perspective |
|---|---|---|
| WHAT | Brief description of theory | Ecosystems include people's behavior and other components that interact to either sustain the ecosystem's goodness-of-fit or destabilize it. Powerful persons in the ecosystem incorrectly blame a loss of goodness-of-fit on the behavior of some powerless person. In a classroom or other education ecosystem, professionals blame lost goodness-of-fit on the behavior of a student, who may then be labeled as ED. |
| | Key terms | <u>Ecosystem:</u> Interactive system involving the child and his behaviors, other people and their behaviors, and other aspects of the environment<br><u>Goodness-of-fit:</u> Condition of stable relationships among the aspects of an ecosystem |
| WHO | Who is intervention appropriate for? | Education ecosystem in which goodness-of-fit has been lost, and one or more students have been identified as ED or the cause of lost goodness-of-fit |
| | Who delivers intervention? | Teachers, school psychologists, other school personnel |
| WHEN | When and how often is intervention delivered? | When assessment occurs; when ecosystem change decisions are made; when advocacy actions are taken |
| WHERE | In what contexts is intervention delivered? | Classrooms and other significant ecosystems of the student |
| WHY | Rationale/purpose for intervention | To restore goodness-of-fit by changing the student and other aspects of the education ecosystem |
| HOW | Selected strategies for intervention | 1. Assess many school and other ecosystem variables to identify various possible modifications that may restore the original or a different goodness-of-fit without removing a student from existing ecosystems<br>2. Modify curriculum, instruction practices, classroom structure and schedules, support for inclusion in general education classes, and other aspects to improve stability of school ecosystems.<br>3. Adopt roles as consultant to school and home, facilitator of access to needed services, and student advocate. |

As *consultant to home* ecosystems, the teacher understands that parents may have information about the child's ecosystems that can make or break an intervention and seeks such information. The teacher should offer and facilitate intervention between home and school. Recognizing that parents are often best positioned to provide continuity across services, agencies, and time, the ecological special educator helps parents interact productively with education and the other service delivery systems (Pogloff, 2005; Seligman, 2000). The teacher may know of parent groups that can provide nonspecific support and share specific helpful information.

As facilitator of *access to services*, the practitioner must understand the nature of child service systems, adopt a child-advocacy stance, and take positive actions based on this knowledge and attitude (Eber & Keenan, 2004). The service systems with which students with ED are most likely to interact are mental health, child and family welfare, and juvenile justice, along with education. These organizations are ecosystems; their physical, social, and other characteristics help determine how services are defined, provided, and perceived. A teacher should understand the nature of such systems—not just in general, but as operated locally—to have the best chance of obtaining their services for her students and changing them if needed.

As *child advocate*, the educator recognizes that even the best-intentioned service system can respond improperly to the needs of its clients. Advocacy for students with ED may require pursuit of their Individuals with Disabilities Education Improvement Act (IDEA) and other rights to an appropriate program of education and related services (see Chapter 1); monitoring the social validity of service goals, methods, results; and making certain that service is provided in ways that respect the student's human worth (Scheuermann & Guetzloe, 2002; Scheuermann & Johns, 2002; Smith & Katsiyannis, 2004; Zionts & Callicott, 2002).

The teacher-as-child advocate sometimes faces difficult issues. He must pursue effective advocacy while avoiding alienating colleagues through self-righteous or disrespectful methods. He must remain willing to confront powerful persons and organizations while avoiding a reduction in overall effectiveness (e.g., "winning the battle but losing the war") and in professional opportunities (e.g., loss of job or raises). It can be helpful to obtain support from advocates external to the service systems, such as parent and professional organizations (e.g., Council for Children With Behavioral Disorders; National Association for the Mentally Ill).

## VALUES AND SPIRITUAL PERSPECTIVES

Opinion surveys often find the American public concerned about child and adolescent behaviors and attitudes indicative of undesirable values, character, and morals. Some of these behaviors and attitudes are related to patterns of E&B disorder and connected problems such as Law-Breaking Behavior, Substance Misuse, and Suicidality. That many young people decline to label school and community vandalism, sexual behavior and pregnancy, stealing, dishonesty, bullying vulnerable peers, and other transgressions as unacceptable or morally wrong also contributes to the concern. Perhaps adults are motivated to create for the next generation a society characterized by more good and less evil than the current one. At any rate, public concern has been one of the motivators for renewed emphasis on incorporating values into U.S. education.

Discussions of values and similar terms (e.g., morality, character, ethics, virtues) begin in controversy because there is considerable disagreement as to what these concepts mean (Lickona, 2004; Nucci, 1989; Walberg & Wynne, 1989). Some experts define *values* as emotional and/or cognitive dispositions to act, or to refrain from acting, in certain ways; and *character* as a persistent tendency to say and do things in accord with one's values. In this view, values are a main basis for character, but character additionally requires actual behavior and perhaps volition (internal motivation, will power).

Another controversial issue involves what values should be selected. Values differ, of course, across cultures, time periods, philosophies, religions, and other influences, and these differences are reflected in disagreements about what (and even whether) values should be taught in schools. Some perspectives, such as the person-centered approach (Moore, Presbury, Smith, & McKee, 1999; Rogers, 1969) and values clarification (e.g., Kirschenbaum, 1995), hold that counselors and educators should not teach particular values. Instead they should help children explore a variety of values and learn to internalize those that they discover to be worthwhile. However, most perspectives specify desired values and character attributes, along with teaching activities designed to help students achieve them.

## Teaching Morality, Character, and Values

### *Moral Reasoning*

Building on the observed relation of children's moral reasoning to their level of cognitive development, Kohlberg held that moral reasoning ideally progresses through a hierarchy of six stages that vary in social and moral values (Power, Higgins, & Kohlberg, 1989). An individual operating in the lowest stage values avoidance of unpleasant consequences for his or her actions. This person may suppress antisocial actions for that reason, but gives little if any consideration to how such actions may hurt other people. The individual who progresses to the highest stage is motivated by ultimate principles about life, human welfare, and justice. These are values above laws and social norms—in fact, values on which good laws and norms should be based.

Progress toward higher stages of moral reasoning comes about through maturation of cognitive abilities together with social interaction, especially cooperative problem-solving. People vary as to how fast and far they progress through these moral stages—some may remain at the lowest stage through adulthood. Educators using Kohlberg's approach attempt to facilitate the development of advanced moral reasoning by encouraging children to consider logical flaws in their current form of moral reasoning, often through "moral dilemma" scenarios. Kohlberg's approach has been used in conjunction with other interventions (e.g., Goldstein, Glick, & Gibbs, 1998).

### Character Education

More direct ways of teaching values are illustrated by the work of Lickona (1996, 2004; Lickona, Schaps, & Lewis, 2003), whose position is that

1. citizens generally know what values and character traits we want our children to manifest,
2. children can, want, and need to learn good character as well as academic knowledge, and
3. good character will best develop when educators planfully teach it.

Good values and character traits are generally those that we would want others to exhibit in similar situations (i.e., act toward others as you would have them act toward you). Primary among these are courage, compassion, fairness, honesty, hope, integrity, justice, loyalty, love, respect, responsibility, and self-control.

The *character education* approach holds that educators must go beyond exposing young people to moral reasoning situations that eventually may help them infer noble values. Instead they should plan a comprehensive program in which most aspects of the school day are considered and used to develop values and character. Such a program should encompass the subjects and topics taught, teacher behavior, classroom management, schoolwide discipline, extracurricular activities, relations with families and communities, and other aspects.

Lickona and others have presented specific practices for achieving such a comprehensive program. Display 10-2 illustrates a selection. An after-school program of character education for young students with behavior and learning problems was described by Muscott and O'Brien (1999).

### Religion, Spirituality, and Values

Religion can be defined as "a set of beliefs concerning the cause, nature, and purpose of the universe, especially when considered as the creation of a superhuman agency or agencies, . . . often containing a moral code for the conduct of human affairs" (Random House Webster's College Dictionary, 1991, p. 1138). Religion has existed in all times and societies in history and, perhaps, prehistory (Parrinder, 1983), and at present there are thousands of religions in the world. Polls generally find that more than 90% of U.S. adults say religion is important in their lives and state a belief in God or a supernatural, spiritual force (e.g., Taylor, 2003).

**Spirituality** is the concept that humans have an essential component that is associated with the mind or soul but is distinct from the physical body (Miller & Thoresen, 1999). This spirit can achieve a purpose or destiny through beliefs, meditation, service, accomplishments, self-deprivation, or other means. Spirituality is a central feature of most religions, as well as numerous nonreligious philosophies.

**Spirituality and Intervention.** Intervention for E&B disorder has several linkages with religion and spirituality. Religion and spirituality are important historical contributors to therapies for physical and mental health problems (Foskett, 1996; Kurtz, 1999). Many contemporary interventions, as well, rely on religious and spiritual

**Display 10-2** Concepts and practices compatible with Lickona's approach to character education

| | |
|---|---|
| School staff are moral models and mentors | Teacher and other staff members treat students with respect, exemplify proper values, and support student behavior showing good character while correcting that showing bad character. |
| Academic learning is a "conscience of craft" | Encourage values favoring learning and school accomplishment, including participation, setting and meeting high standards, persistence, pride of accomplishment, and discovery. |
| Values are taught through academic curricula | Use subject area content opportunities to present value issues, moral dilemmas, and discussions of ways to put good values into action. |
| Democracy is created in the classroom and school environment | Involve individual students, whole classrooms, student organizations, and the student body in making decisions (e.g., rules, learning activities), exploring values, and taking steps to build good character. |
| Service to school and community gives practice in good character | Initiate or expand if necessary student participation in service projects to school and community that are and have been explicitly linked to values and character development. |

*Sources:* Adapted from Lickona, 1996, 2004.

values about how a person should behave, think, and feel toward other people (Everson, 1997; Richards, Rector, & Tjeltveit, 1999; Wells, 1999). Like religion, many therapies are concerned with subjective mental phenomena; personal versus biological determinants of emotions, thoughts, and behaviors; and enduring issues involving the essential nature of humankind, such as free will, individual responsibility, and how a person can control her or his future (Cole & Pargament, 1999; Cox, 1996; Ewen, 2003; Feist & Feist, 2006; Nayani & Bhugra, 1996).

Of course, many theories and therapies do not rely on religion or spirituality—and may even reject them—as a basis for understanding or improving E&B disorder (Fulford, 1996). Still, advocates of a greater role for religious and spiritual considerations in intervention for students with E&B disorder (e.g., Benson, 1996; Brendtro & Long, 1996; Coles et al, 1995; Dowd, 1997) point to evidence suggesting that belief in God and participation in religion is associated with positive mental health (Bhugra, 1996; Miller & Thoresen, 1999), is a protective factor among children at high risk for E&B disorder (Miller, Davies, & Greenwald, 2000; Smith & Denton, 2005; Werner & Smith, 1992), and increases the success rate of some kinds of treatment (e.g., Brendtro, 1997; Larson, 1996).

*Example: 12-Step programs.* Spirituality is a key element of 12-Step programs, especially those of or closely based on Alcoholics Anonymous. 12-Step programs are the most common method of treatment for drug and/or alcohol abuse among adults, with participants in the millions (Lawson, 1992; Tonigan, Toscova, & Connors, 1999). It is also widely used with adolescents. Moreover, 12-Step programs are widely available for people with various other out-of-control behaviors (e.g., gambling, eating), and whose loved ones cannot stop using alcohol or drugs.

Fundamental to 12-Step programs is acknowledgement of a "higher power," that is, the creator of the universe and a source of help outside oneself or any person (the higher power is not specified in detail). One must develop a personal relationship with the higher power through prayer, meditation, making amends to one's past victims, and service to people.

In 12-Step programs, groups of abusers meet to help each other pursue a set of "steps" or principles (see Display 10-3). There are numerous slight variations in wording of the 12 steps, but all variations address the same concepts. The meeting format also varies, but usually group fellowship and mutual support activities are prominent. Often the meeting is guided by a former abuser with substance abuse training, or by group members on a rotating basis. Group members

1. volunteer to reveal how substance misuse has harmed them and their loved ones,
2. learn to decrease their guilt over such harm,
3. obtain information about how to avoid abusing substances,
4. confront other members who try to deceive about substance use or deny their own responsibility for it, and
5. encourage each other to keep pursuing the twelve steps and stay substance-free, one day at a time.

Members can contact each other and designated "sponsors" at any time for support (e.g., when tempted to use substances or to enter situations where others will be using). 12-Step programs may be combined with other substance abuse treatment

**Display 10-3** Steps in a 12-step program

1. We admitted we were powerless over alcohol and drugs, that our lives had become unmanageable.
2. We came to believe that a power greater than ourselves could restore us to sanity.
3. We made a decision to turn our will and our lives over to the care of God, as we understand God.
4. We made a searching and fearless moral inventory of ourselves.
5. We admitted to God, to ourselves, and to another human being the exact nature of our wrongs.
6. We became ready to have God remove all our shortcomings of character.
7. We humbly asked God to remove our shortcomings.
8. We made a list of all persons we had harmed and became willing to make amends to them all.
9. We made direct amends to such people wherever possible, except when to do so would injure them or others.
10. We continued to take personal inventory, and when we were wrong promptly admitted it.
11. We sought through prayer and meditation to improve our conscious contact with God as we understand God, praying only for knowledge of God's will for us and the power to carry that out.
12. Having had a spiritual awakening as the result of these steps, we tried to carry this message to alcoholics and addicts and to practice these principles in all our affairs.

*Sources:* Lawson, 1992; Tonigan, Toscova, & Connors, 1999.

elements, and tend to be offered to young people in residential, day treatment, and other more restrictive education and mental health settings.

***Concerns About Religion.*** Whether or not religion can benefit intervention, there are other potential interactions between religion and education of students with ED that special educators need to contemplate (compare to Bhugra, 1996). Students and/or their parents may seek or have already sought the counsel of religious personnel or spiritual helpers. They may view behavior, emotional, or cognitive problems in mainly spiritual terms (e.g., separation from God, struggle with supernatural forces of evil, punishment for parental misdeeds). Students and families may resist school interventions they perceive as opposed to their religious convictions, or to religious and spiritual interventions in which they participate. Resistance could be especially problematic if the teacher's values conflict strongly with those of students and parents. School professionals should be aware of these and other possible issues involving the religion beliefs and practices of their students with ED to better be able to avoid and defuse unnecessary conflicts.

***Cautions About Religion.*** Assuming that teachers want to incorporate religious and spiritual considerations into interventions for students with E&B disorder, there are potential problems with doing so in public school settings. For instance, many believe that a "wall of separation" does and ought to exist between religion and government activities, including tax-supported education. Apart from this, in a society built on religious freedom and encompassing numerous religious variations, how can religion and spirituality be incorporated into education in a way that does not favor some religions and disfavor others? Can we teach values based on spirituality but not based on religion?

The wall of separation issue is controversial on many levels. Specifically regarding religion and public education, the U.S. Department of Education has guidelines that provide some basis for education decisions (unless further government action changes the legalities). Display 10-4 presents key aspects of these guidelines.

The issue of even-handedly addressing various religions probably cannot be resolved entirely. Some approaches have attempted to deemphasize concern with the exact nature of the human spirit and its relation to supernatural forces, instead focusing on spiritual values (see Long, 1997). One example of this is the *circle of courage*, which incorporates some psychoeducational, sociological (conflict theory), and ecological features, along with spiritual ones.

### *Spiritual Values Program: Circle of Courage*

Brendtro and others (Brendtro, Brokenleg, & Van Bockern, 1990, 1991; Brendtro, Ness, & Mitchell, 2001; Brendtro & Shahbazian, 2003, Brokenleg, 1996, Cross, 2002) proposed that many cases of E&B disorder arise because the European culture prevalent in North America encourages inappropriate child-rearing values and practices. These practices do not adequately meet four basic needs of all humans: *belonging, mastery, independence,* and *generosity*. When family, community,

**Display 10-4** U.S. Department of Education position on religious expression in public schools

| | |
|---|---|
| Student religious activity during school | Students have the right to engage in prayer and religious discussion during the school day (e.g., read scriptures, say prayers, attempt to persuade others about religious topics). |
| Religious literature | Students may distribute religious literature to schoolmates on the same terms (e.g., restrictions) as nonreligious literature. |
| Assignments | Students may express their beliefs about religion in written and oral assignments, free of discrimination based on religious content. |
| Teaching about religion | Schools may teach about religion, history of religion, comparative religion, sacred scriptures as literature, the influence of religion on history, art, literature, and other topics. They may teach about religious holidays and celebrate secular aspects of holidays. Schools may not provide religious instruction, nor promote observance of holidays as religious events. |
| Teaching values | Schools may teach civic values, virtue, and morality, even if some of these values are held also by religions. |
| Religious excusals | Federal law and court decisions do not require that schools excuse students from lessons to which they or their parents object on religious or moral grounds. |
| Official neutrality | Teachers and other school officials may not encourage religious activity, participate with students, discourage religious activity, nor encourage antireligious activity. |
| Worship at school events | School officials may not mandate or organize religious activities at graduation or related ceremonies. |
| School facilities | Student religious activities have the same access to school facilities as do student clubs and other secular activities (e.g., before and after school, noninstructional time during school, announcements). |
| | School facilities must be available to nonreligious and religious private groups on the same terms. Students may participate in, before or after school, religious events at school, subject to the same rules of order as apply to other student activities. |

*Source:* Abstracted, with considerable verbatim quotation, from the following public domain source (revised May, 1998): http://www.ed.gov/Speeches/08-1995/religion.html.

and other cultural institutions do not meet these needs, or meet them in a distorted, unhealthy way, children show it through attitudes and behaviors such as those in Display 10-5. Such attitudes and behaviors generally provoke alarm, contempt, pity, and discouragement among other people and often are designated E&B disorder.

To be effective, schools and other services for students with E&B disorder must use practices that advance a *theme* (philosophical direction). To create their theme, Brendtro et al. (1990, 1991; Brendtro & Van Bockern, 1998) drew on Native

**Display 10-5** Basic needs and related behaviors in the circle of courage

| Belonging | | |
|---|---|---|
| **Normal** | **Distorted** | **Absent** |
| Attached | Gang loyalty | Unattached |
| Loving | Craves affection | Guarded |
| Friendly | Craves acceptance | Rejected |
| Intimate | Promiscuous | Lonely |
| Gregarious | Clinging | Aloof |
| Cooperative | Cult vulnerable | Isolated |
| Trusting | Overly dependent | Distrustful |

Some youth who feel rejected are struggling to find artificial, distorted belonging through behavior such as attention seeking or running with gangs. Others have abandoned the pursuit and are reluctant to form human attachments. In either case, their unmet needs can be addressed by corrective relationships of trust and intimacy.

| Mastery | | |
|---|---|---|
| **Normal** | **Distorted** | **Absent** |
| Achiever | Overachiever | Nonachiever |
| Successful | Arrogant | Failure oriented |
| Creative | Risk seeker | Avoids risks |
| Problem solver | Cheater | Fears challenges |
| Motivated | Workaholic | Unmotivated |
| Persistent | Perseverative | Gives up easily |
| Competent | Delinquent skill | Inadequate |

Frustrated in their attempts to achieve, children may seek to prove their competence in distorted ways, such as skill in delinquent activity. Others have learned to retreat from difficult challenges by giving up in futility. The remedy for these problems is involvement in an environment with abundant opportunities for meaningful achievement.

| Independence | | |
|---|---|---|
| **Normal** | **Distorted** | **Absent** |
| Autonomous | Dictatorial | Submissive |
| Confident | Reckless/macho | Lacks confidence |
| Assertive | Bullies others | Inferiority |
| Responsible | Sexual prowess | Irresponsible |
| Inner control | Manipulative | Helplessness |
| Self-discipline | Rebellious | Undisciplined |
| Leadership | Defies authority | Easily led |

Fighting against feelings of powerlessness, some youth assert themselves in rebellious and aggressive ways. Those who believe they are too weak or impotent to manage their own lives become pawns of others. These young people need opportunities to develop the skills and the confidence to assert positive leadership and self-discipline.

*(continued)*

> **Display 10-5 (Continued)**
>
> | | Generosity | |
> |---|---|---|
> | **Normal** | **Distorted** | **Absent** |
> | Altruistic | Noblesse oblige | Selfish |
> | Caring | Overinvolved | Affectionless |
> | Sharing | Plays martyr | Narcissistic |
> | Loyal | Codependency | Disloyal |
> | Empathic | Overinvolvement | Hardened |
> | Prosocial | Servitude | Antisocial |
> | Supportive | Bondage | Exploitative |
>
> Without opportunities to give to others, young people do not develop as caring persons. Some may be involved in pseudo-altruistic helping or they may be locked in servitude to someone who uses them. Others plunge into lifestyles of hedonism and narcissism. The antidote for this malaise is to experience the joys that accrue from helping others.

*Source:* Adapted from L. K. Brendtro, M. Brokenleg, & S. Van Bockern, 1991, "The Circle of Courage," *Beyond Behavior,* 2(1), 5–12. Copyright 1991 by the Council for Exceptional Children. Reprinted by permission.

American Indian child-raising philosophy, "the most effective system of positive discipline ever developed" (Brendtro et al., 1991, p. 6). They also incorporated selected European and American child development and intervention ideas (mainly psychoeducational and ecological perspectives), and called their theme the *circle of courage.*

**Theory.** Circle of courage encompasses the four basic needs toward which intervention planning and delivery must be directed. Properly addressing these needs allows practitioners to "reclaim" children and adolescents whose circle of courage is broken.

1. *Belonging.* In traditional American Indian societies, all adults taught and cared for all children, thus children developed a sense of belonging to other people and to the tribe. These children became affectionate, cooperative, friendly, respectful, sympathetic, and trusting. Their emotions and behavior showed that their need for belonging was satisfied in a positive way.

   In contrast, the families and communities of many students with E&B disorder have not nurtured or provided a supportive environment for their child. Some feel rejected and seek to meet their need through gangs or sexual misbehavior; others give up on the chance for close personal relationships. Schools must do what they can to satisfy *belonging,* because changing children is nearly

|  | Name of Theory | Values and Spiritual Perspective |
|---|---|---|
| WHAT | Brief description of theory | Values, character, and spiritual development are important determinants of young peoples' emotions, behaviors, and cognitions. Some E&B disorder stems from absent or improper values and spirituality |
|  | Key Terms | <u>Character:</u> Personal tendency to behave according to one's values<br><u>Spiritual:</u> Aspect of oneself associated with mind or soul, but separate from one's physical being<br><u>Circle of courage:</u> Program for personal improvement of children and adolescents derived from Native American concepts of basic spiritual needs |
| WHO | Who is intervention appropriate for? | Students who exhibit deficient values, character, or spiritual development, as evidenced by their E&B disorder and in other ways |
|  | Who delivers intervention? | Teachers, other school personnel, and fellow students |
| WHEN | When and how often is intervention delivered? | Varies with particular actions or programs used |
| WHERE | In what contexts is intervention delivered? | Classroom, school |
| WHY | Rationale/purpose for intervention | To improve the student's character or satisfy the student's spiritual needs |
| HOW | Selected strategies for intervention | 1. Recognize values, character, and spiritual needs of children with E&B disorder, and provide activities that develop those needs<br>2. Implement a program of moral or character education<br>3. Implement a spiritually oriented program such as circle of courage |

    impossible unless this need is met and a positive attachment develops between adults and youth.

2. *Mastery.* American Indians satisfied the need for mastery in their children by offering plenty of opportunities for developing physical, cognitive, social, creative, and spiritual competence. Children learned that someone with more competence is not a rival but a resource from whom to learn. High achievement is to be pursued for personal reasons, not to be better than others. Unfortunately, schools often impede children's need for *mastery* by breaking learning into fragmented subject areas, emphasizing external control and motivation over personal striving, and encouraging competition and jealousy.

3. ***Independence.*** Indian teaching used inner discipline to encourage children to make decisions, solve problems, and show personal responsibility. Masterful adults modeled, nurtured, taught values, and gave feedback, while the children were presented with many opportunities to make free choices. Children exposed to this kind of education feel respected and powerful.

   Families and schools often deprive children and adolescents of significant opportunities for free choice, respect, and power. To attempt to satisfy this *independence* need, many young people will disobey to demonstrate freedom from authority, harm others to coerce respect, and use subterfuge and dishonesty to attain power.

4. ***Generosity.*** In Indian culture, young people proved their own virtue by helping other people. By contributing to someone else's life, they demonstrated power and purpose, and met their fundamental need for generosity.

   In our society, many children and adolescents perform no necessary roles, spend ever-increasing time and effort seeking pleasure, and become addicted to possessions. Without having learned to be unselfish they cannot know a purpose in life, and we should expect that this distortion will continue throughout adulthood unless educators and others intervene.

***Intervention.*** The circle of courage provides a theme that directs the planning and practices of intervention personnel toward meeting the young person's basic *belonging, mastery, independence,* and *generosity* needs. Traditional interventions based on Western civilization's obedience-oriented model cannot reclaim young people because they incorporate some of the same mistaken objectives that produced the young people's problems in the first place (Brendtro & Long, 1996; Brendtro & Van Bockern, 1998). The circle of courage reclaims young people by empowering them and meeting their basic needs.

To implement this theme, educators must adopt, and, if need be, adapt, practices from whatever sources advance the circle of courage theme (Pike, Millspaugh, & DeSalvatore, 2005). This could include ideas from psychodynamic, ecological, and selected aspects of other models. Curricula and other aspects of schooling can be based on the circle of courage theme (Bock, 1997).

1. ***Meeting the need for belonging.*** A wide variety of approaches to intervention rely on building trust, attachment, caring, and mutual concern for adults and peers. Teachers must outlast the frustrating behavior of students who test teachers by goading them to become hostile. Teachers also must communicate acceptance of the student (while rejecting the misbehavior), remain a dependable source of support, and model behaviors and attitudes of trust, caring, and concern. Supportive practices include statements of understanding and empathy, peer student teams for cooperation, and unity-building exercises such as retreats, socials, and working partnerships with families (Brendtro & Van Bockern, 1998; Brendtro & Shahbazian, 2003).

2. ***Meeting the need for mastery.*** Brendtro et al. (1990, 1991) recommend building creativity and self-expression through art, literature, dance, and other activities

that can help the student experience and know his own emotions. Teachers of students with ED should use problem incidents as learning opportunities, as in Life Space Crisis Intervention (see Chapter 7). Further, the *mastery* need is supported by teaching social skills (e.g., accepting criticism), logical and adaptive cognitions that replace irrational thoughts and maladaptive self-talk, and skills for peer groups to cooperatively solve problems. Intervention programs should also capitalize on adolescents' high-spirited tendency to take risks through activities such as outdoor adventure challenges (see Chapter 12).

3. *Meeting the need for independence.* To meet this need, teachers must be ready to provide temporary external controls so students will have the opportunity to build self control. This need is also supported by teaching self-management, recognition of emotions and what triggers them, and self-instruction strategies for controlling behaviors, emotions, and thoughts. Students with ED should be given as many opportunities as feasible to decide classroom rules and other group expectations.

4. *Meeting the need for generosity.* The teacher of students with ED can meet their **need for generosity** and give them purpose in various ways. Using Life Space Crisis Intervention, she can massage numb values of students to help them activate their dormant altruism, empathy, and caring. Cognitive moral education activities that build higher levels of moral reasoning may also support altruistic thinking. The teacher should provide opportunities and projects involving volunteering that will make caring fashionable and selfishness unacceptable through, for example, adopting senior citizens, coaching community children, and collecting goods and money to help needy families.

## Chapter Summary

Sociological, ecological, and values or spiritual approaches offer diverse interpretations of E&B disorders of young people.

- The sociological perspective considers the role of social group variables such as socioeconomic and race-ethnic status in creating and perpetuating human deviance, including E&B disorder.
- In social drift explanations, maladaptive functioning leads to both identification as E&B disorder and low SES.
- In social causation explanations, low SES leads to E&B disorder, or at least the labeling of a young person as such. Two variations of social causation are functionalism and conflict theory.
- If a person's deviance threatens society's powerful groups, they may label her or him as having E&B disorder, as a means of control. Thereafter, other people's expectations may pressure the person to behave deviantly, in accord with the label.

- Sociological interventions attempt to correct oppressive social conditions and minimize labeling and its bad effects.
- The ecological perspective is concerned with goodness-of-fit within ecosystems such as classrooms and schools.
- When goodness-of-fit is lost, authorities tend to focus on how a particular student contributed to the problem, instead of looking at the entire ecosystem. That student is the one likely to be labeled as ED.
- Ecological interventions assess classrooms and other ecosystems to identify social, physical, and other variables that might be changed to improve goodness-of-fit.
- Because the ecological perspective is compatible with psychodynamic, behavioral, and other intervention practices, it is difficult to specify ecological practices. Within limits, different educators see the need for various changes in ecologies, and they use a range of methods. Interventions often involve home and community, as well as classroom and school.
- Values and spiritual perspectives hold that many personal and social problems, including E&B disorder of children and adolescents, are due to deficiencies in values and spiritual development.
- Teaching and otherwise helping young people to develop values, character, and spiritual strength can reduce their conflict with others, their personal distress, and other manifestations of E&B disorder.
- Values and spiritual approaches to intervention can be combined with other interventions, as in the circle of courage.

## Ideas for Consideration and Discussion

1. a. Describe the social drift explanation of E&B disorders among children of low SES.
   b. Describe the social causation explanation of E&B disorders among children of low SES.
   c. State ways in which the two explanations agree, and ways in which they disagree.
2. Explain how the labeling process can create E&B disorder in the first place. How can labeling perpetuate E&B disorder?
3. Imagine and describe how ecological intervention could be put into action for students with ED in the regular class education environment. Anticipate possible obstacles in using your ecological intervention in this education environment. Consider how persistent educators could overcome these obstacles.
4. Imagine and describe how character education intervention could be put into action for students with ED in the separate class education environment. Anticipate possible obstacles problems in using a character education intervention in this education environment. Consider how persistent educators could overcome these obstacles.

5. Imagine and describe how a 12-step intervention could be put into action for students with ED in a separate school education environment. Anticipate possible obstacles in using a 12-step intervention in this education environment. Consider how persistent educators could overcome these obstacles.
6. Regarding the Circle of Courage:
   a. Discuss the meanings of the <u>Normal</u>, <u>Distorted</u>, and <u>Absent</u> columns of Display 10-5. Why is each set (row) of terms under its respective column heading (e.g., for the Belonging box, Attached, Gang Loyalty, Unattached)?
   b. Assume that some expressions of the four needs have been left out of Display 10-5. Think of one Normal behavior or attitude that expresses the Belonging need, but has been omitted. Write this behavior or attitude in the <u>Normal</u> column below, under the *Belonging Need* heading. Now think of a behavior or attitude that expresses this in a distorted way. Write this under the <u>Distorted</u> column. In the <u>Absent</u> column, put a behavior or attitude that expresses its absence.

   Complete the table below by repeating the above process for the *Mastery Need*, *Independence Need*, and *Generosity Need*.

**Belonging Need**

| Normal | Distorted | Absent |
|---|---|---|
|  |  |  |

**Mastery Need**

| Normal | Distorted | Absent |
|---|---|---|
|  |  |  |

**Independence Need**

| Normal | Distorted | Absent |
|---|---|---|
|  |  |  |

**Generosity Need**

| Normal | Distorted | Absent |
|---|---|---|
|  |  |  |

## Resources for Further Study

www.al-anon.alateen.org/ Alateen of Al-Anon
www.abpsi.org/ Association of Black Psychologists
www.childrensdefense.org/ Children's Defense Fund
www.augie.edu/dept/nast/Projects/doc6.htm Circle of Courage

**www.confidentkids.com/about_confident_kids.htm** Confident Kids Spiritual Support Groups

**www.surgeongeneral.gov/library/mentalhealth/cre/** Mental Health: Culture, Race, and Ethnicity

**www.charityadvantage.com/aacld/HomePage.asp** National Association for Education of African American Children w/LD

**cpmcnet.columbia.edu/dept/nccp/** National Center for Children in Poverty

**www.mediacampaign.org/faith/Faithbrochure.pdf** Substance abuse prevention for faith-based organizations

# Prevention and Intervention

CHAPTER 11   *Intervention in the Education System*
CHAPTER 12   *Intervention in Other Systems*

Chapter **Eleven**

# *Intervention in the Education System*

## CHAPTER OBJECTIVES

**After reading this chapter, you should be able to:**
- List two ways to classify prevention activities.
- Identify six fundamental aspects of preventive classroom management.
- Describe three forms of conflict resolution education.
- Explain why post-suicide crisis intervention is selective prevention.
- Say two arguments for full inclusion and two for full continuum.
- Describe five areas of competency often needed by students with ED.

## CAN YOU DEFINE THESE 10 TERMS?

least restrictive environment
universal prevention
Primary Mental Health Project
prereferral intervention
collaboration

Combined Classroom Model
full inclusion
survival-and-success behaviors
learning strategies
career education

There are various ways in which we can respond to the emotional, behavior, and cognitive problems of children and adolescents. We might act as individuals to help them in a personal way. We can join other concerned people to pursue goals through private organizations. We could work through government agencies that are responsible for helping young people with such problems. Many of the government agencies involved in these efforts can be considered systems of services, such as education, mental health, child and family welfare, and juvenile justice.

This chapter briefly, selectively addresses the education system. Chapter 12 does so for other systems of child service with which educators of students with ED are likely to interact.

### *Least Restrictive Environment*
Within each service system there are a variety of interventions and settings in which services are delivered. Interventions and settings are often classified in terms of "restrictiveness," generally meaning the degree to which they intrude on or interfere with a person's ordinary life. A basic principle in many service systems is that intervention should be provided in the least restrictive environment (LRE) that is appropriate (U.S. Department of Health and Human Services [USD HHS], 1999).

**Display 11-1** What is the least restrictive environment (LRE)?

> Deciding what the LRE is can be more complex than it might appear. Often, restrictiveness of an intervention environment is judged in terms of its location. A service provided in an ordinary environment or placement (e.g., regular class in a neighborhood school) is generally viewed as less restrictive than the same service provided in an extraordinary environment (e.g., special school). However, some services (e.g., token economy with a freeze level) are difficult to deliver except in extraordinary environments, so it is not always possible to untangle services and placements.
>
> Moreover, it is conceivable that the short-term value of a service may be different from its long-term value. For example, an intervention setting may seem to be less restrictive at present because it permits a child to interact with more peers who have no disabilities. However, if this setting offers inadequate opportunities for the interventions required for that young person's improved academic, social, personal, vocational, or other functioning, it might come to be recognized as having been more restrictive in the long run.

The LRE principle is described in IDEA 2004 and other laws and regulations governing special education, in terms of physical integration with nondisabled students (Display 11-1). IDEA 2004 assumes that the regular class is the appropriate setting for special education intervention unless it is determined that another setting is appropriate. As noted in Display 1-7, the U.S. Department of Education classifies special education settings ("education environments") with this in mind. In order of less restrictive to more restrictive, they are: regular class, resource room, separate class, separate school, residential facility, and homebound/hospital. These settings, including variations on them, make up the "continuum" of special education environments (Hallahan & Kauffman, 2006). This chapter describes education services for students with ED mainly in terms of this continuum.

### *Prevention*

Most people would agree that preventing E&B disorders is more desirable than even the most effective intervention after a child has developed an E&B disorder. Like intervention, prevention is a major concern of education and other child service agencies, as well as many other individuals and organizations (Greenberg, Domitrovich, & Bumbarger, 1999; Quinn & Poirer, 2004). There is quite a variety of school-based efforts to prevent E&B disorder and connected problems. As with interventions, prevention efforts differ as to how much they intrude into ordinary schooling.

Prevention is a concern of most education professionals, and practically all teachers of students with ED. For example, educators try to prevent the need to identify a student as having ED by taking part in prereferral intervention; to prevent a student's recognized problems from getting worse; and to prevent problems from interfering with the student's participation in regular classes, vocational placements, beneficial social occasions, and other opportunities for positive school and life adjustment. This chapter describes three forms of school-based prevention of E&B disorder. This is followed by a discussion of interventions for students with ED in various education environments (Display 11-2).

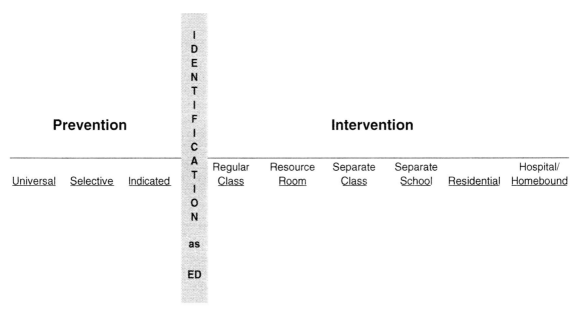

**Display 11-2** Three categories of prevention activity and six education environments for intervention

## FORMS OF PREVENTION

Professionals involved in prevention are sometimes uncertain about exactly what they are supposed to be preventing. For example, some school prevention activities are explicitly intended to prevent E&B disorder, while others are meant to prevent personal and social adjustment problems that could lead to E&B disorder or to other seriously adverse outcomes (e.g., delinquency, suicide). Some prevention efforts are geared toward groups of children, and others focus on an individual. Also, it can be confusing that many of the same methods, materials, activities, settings, and professions may be used to deliver prevention or intervention.

The Institute of Medicine (IOM), a national expert organization that advises the U.S. government on health issues, has made recommendations to help organize how we understand prevention of E&B disorder (Mrazek & Mrazek, 2005). The IOM pointed out that important ideas about prevention come from the field of public health, especially ideas about prevention of infectious diseases. Without modifications, these ideas may have limited relevance for E&B disorder.

### *Primary, Secondary, Tertiary*

Probably the best known way of classifying disease prevention activities is based on the point in a disease's course at which such activities are implemented. *Primary* prevention is implemented before any sign of the disease; it is intended to prevent new cases. *Secondary* prevention is designed to reduce the number of future total cases. *Tertiary* prevention is meant to reduce complications and disability caused by the disease in existing cases. Although the primary/secondary/tertiary perspective is often used to describe educational and psychological prevention efforts, it is not clear how well this public health perspective applies to E&B disorders of young people. To what extent is an E&B disorder similar to an infectious disease? How well do we know the E&B disorder's causes, early course, and outcome?

Because of such uncertainties the IOM recommended a different system of classifying prevention activities, one that considers risk for E&B disorder, as well as benefits and drawbacks of the activities. The IOM considered these points:

1. An individual may be at risk because he shows one or more biological and psychosocial risk factors for E&B disorder (see Chapter 6). Multiple at-risk individuals contitute an at-risk "group."
2. A prevention activity can have benefits, drawbacks, and both (Lorion, 2000; Mrazek & Mrazek, 2005). Different prevention activities have different kinds and amounts of benefits and drawbacks.
3. In deciding which individuals or groups receive which, if any, prevention activities, professionals should weigh potential benefits and drawbacks of the activities.

Some possible drawbacks of prevention activities (and interventions, as well) are listed in Display 11-3.

### *Universal-Selective-Indicated*

The IOM system recommended a system with three forms of prevention (Mrazek & Mrazek, 2005). A *universal* prevention activity is applied to the general public or another broadly defined set (e.g., all students in a school district, a school, the seventh grade). The activity may be desirable for all individuals in the set or, more likely, for just some of them, but it cannot be predicted which individuals will benefit. Therefore, a universal prevention activity is not targeted to any individual or at-risk group—all students in the set take part in it. There is no need to target, anyway, because a universal prevention activity has no drawbacks.

A *selective* prevention activity is targeted to a defined at-risk group whose members do not exhibit E&B disorder now, but share biological and/or psychosocial

**Display 11-3** Potential drawbacks and costs of prevention activities

- Unacceptability of the activity to the student who is participating in it
- Unacceptability of the activity to professional colleagues, students and parents, and the general public
- Financial cost to implement the activity
- Student time required to implement the activity
- Staff time required to implement the activity
- Staff training required to implement the activity properly
- Chance that the activity will unexpectedly cause a worsening of the problem that is to be prevented
- Chance that the activity will unexpectedly cause other problems
- Extent of negative perceptions and labeling by peers and professionals related to the young person's participation in the activity

characteristics that are substantial risk factors for developing E&B disorder. A biological risk might be family history of extreme E&B disorder; a psychosocial risk might be residing in a dysfunctional neighborhood (see Chapter 6).

It is not expected that all young people in the at-risk group will actually develop E&B disorder. Generally, most will not but no one can predict which ones will or will not. The main anticipated benefit of a selective prevention activity is that it will reduce the chance that individuals in the at-risk group will develop E&B disorder. The prevention activity has potential drawbacks but its benefit is judged to be greater than its drawbacks. On the other hand, for young people not in the at-risk group there are few or no anticipated benefits, yet the potential drawbacks remain. Such a prevention activity should not be applied to all students, as a universal prevention is, but selectively to young people who show the relevant risk factor(s).

Third, an *indicated* prevention activity is targeted specifically to individual children or adolescents who show emotional, behavior, cognitive, or other problems known to be precursors, preliminary stages, or early forms of the serious problem. The indicated prevention activity, whether administered individually or in group format, is designed to interrupt the targeted individual's trend toward E&B disorder or other serious problem, and/or reduce its severity and complications.

This activity has substantial potential drawbacks, but they are judged to be an acceptable cost in light of anticipated benefits to the targeted individual. However, these drawbacks make an indicated prevention activity inappropriate for the general school population or even at-risk groups.

The IOM's universal-selective-indicated system was designed to classify prevention of mental disorders, but it seems just as relevant for educational efforts to prevent ED of students. What follows is a sample of techniques and programs designed to prevent maladaptive emotions, behaviors, and cognitions, E&B disorders of young people, and/or ED of students. They are presented according to the universal-selective-indicated prevention categories.

A few disclaimers are in order about this way of classifying prevention. First, many of the prevention techniques and programs are used in educational interventions as well. Also, many of the techniques and programs can or do fall into more than one category of prevention. To illustrate, the Primary Mental Health Project is described below as a selective prevention program because it is implemented in schools with many young students at high psychosocial risk (e.g., low SES, single parent families, dysfunctional neighborhoods). But it also qualifies as indicated prevention because participating students are chosen from the at-risk group based on high levels of behavior and learning problems.

Sugai et al. (2000; see also USD Education, 2000) described and recommended an adaptation of the universal-selective-indicated concept to link school management efforts that address problems of different levels of severity. The appropriate behavior of most students (represented by the largest area of the triangle in Display 11-4) is encouraged and managed by universal school prevention procedures, especially schoolwide positive behavior support (Liaupsin, Jolivette, & Scott, 2004; Stormont, Lewis, & Beckner, 2005). Additional teaching and treatment procedures requiring more resources are also in place or available to manage the small

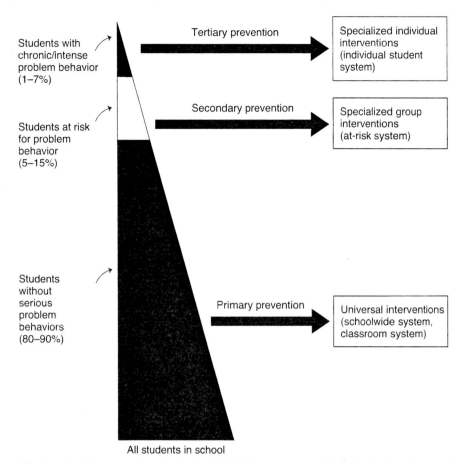

**Display 11-4** Integrated levels of school discipline to serve multiple levels of student problems
*Source:* USD Education, 2000, p. III-16.

proportions of students that will need additional specialized group interventions and specialized individual interventions (e.g., Lane & Beebe-Frankenberger, 2004; Lane, Wehby, Menzies, Doukas, Munton, & Gregg, 2003). "Schoolwide positive behavior support"—mainly, universal prevention via proactive classroom and school management practices—has become a widely used method to anticipate and prevent students' behavior problems.

## Universal Prevention

Universal educational prevention is applied to all students in a domain (e.g., classroom, school, grade level, district-wide, state) in an attempt to reduce future ED among students or prevent the development of patterns of E&B disorder and connected problems among children in the community. Diverse problems have been addressed by universal prevention, many involving verbal and physical conflict, violence, and related problems. This is because an alarming number of students harass, threaten, pick fights with, assault, bully, and otherwise aggress against fellow students (Fannery & Huff, 1999; Furlong, Morrison, & Jimerson, 2004; Smith, Schneider, Smith, & Ananiadou, 2004; Walker et al., 2004). Relatedly, there are many interpersonal conflicts in schools involving, for instance, contested resources, race-ethnic antagonism, and gang-related disputes. Not only are violence and conflict problematic in and of themselves, they can lead to further emotional and behavior problems, such as students' fear of and withdrawal from social situations or their anger accompanied by counter-violence. Among the many school applications of universal prevention are techniques and programs to improve classroom and school management, teach prosocial competencies, resolve conflict, and prevent Substance Misuse.

### *Preventive Classroom and School Management*

Various ordinary aspects of education in the classroom and school can be managed to increase learning, reduce disruption, and thus prevent emotional and behavior problems. Preventive classroom and school management mainly operates proactively, to encourage appropriate behavior among all students, rather than reactively, to respond to incidents (Darch & Kameenui, 2004; Sugai, Sprague, Horner, & Walker, 2000).

**Classroom Management.** The details of good classroom management can differ, of course, depending on grade level, subject area, characteristics of the students and staff, teacher's philosophy of education, and other considerations. Many authorities emphasize the need for a high degree of structure, with particular attention to classroom expectations, rules, routines, scheduling, opportunities for students to respond, and evaluation (for details see, e.g., Bos & Vaughn, 2006; Cangelosi, 2003; Colvin, 2002; Emmer, Evertson, & Worsham, 2006; Evertson, Emmer, & Worsham, 2006; Friend & Bursuck, 2006; Polloway, Patton, & Serna, 2005; Strout, 2005; Swanson, 2005; Van Acker, 2002; Wolfgang, 2005).

To begin with, a teacher's *expectations* about her student's potential may affect his performance for better or for worse. Teachers who maintain and communicate high expectations for learning, conduct, and other aspects of student performance will probably have more students who show good effort and achievement and fewer with emotional, learning, and behavior problems.

*Rules, routines,* and *schedules* can provide comforting stability to the school day and reduce wasted time. Most teachers want all of their students to perform ordinary activities about the same way each day, using efficient and disruption-free *routines* (Maroney, 2004; Olive, 2004). Just a few examples: enter and leave the classroom, interact with peers, distribute materials, respond during lectures, group discussions, individual work, other kinds of instruction, make transitions, and begin work. Along similar lines, teachers can create, perhaps with student input, a few *rules* to cover key aspects of daily activities and interactions. Typically, rules and routines need to be taught, reminded, and posted.

A related good practice is *scheduling* various learning activities, which may alternate within the class period (e.g., intermixing periods of independent work, lecture, peer tutoring, and group work). The rules, routines, and any particular roles expected of students in different scheduled learning activities should be distinct so the student knows what to do, for instance, when in a small group for cooperative learning or discussion, when assigned independent work, and so on.

Many students learn behaviors and concepts best if they frequently perform and receive feedback about them. Preventive classroom management includes techniques to increase students' *opportunities to respond* actively to instructional material (Darch & Kameenui, 2004; Sutherland, Alder, & Gunter, 2003). Among such techniques are asking the group a question and waiting for each student to prepare an answer before calling on a particular student, group unison responding as drill and practice, peer tutoring, and ungraded pop quizzes.

Teachers should give students clear feedback about both learning and conduct (Alexandrin, 2003; Konold, Miller, & Konold, 2004). They should make certain that *grading* and *evaluation* are readily understandable and clearly linked to assigned work (Friend & Bursuck, 2006) and, if desired, specific behavior.

**School Management.** Educators' decisions and actions about physical, time, social, and other variables affecting the entire school can strongly influence disruptive and other unwanted student behavior (Leedy, Bates, & Safran, 2004; Lewis, Hudson, Richter, & Johnson, 2004; Peterson, Miller, & Skiba, 2004). A schoolwide *discipline policy*, preferably created with input from parents, students, and school staff, can reduce disorderliness (Liaupsin et al., 2004; Sugai, Horner, & Gresham, 2002). A good policy should clearly describe the school's:

1. Philosophy and mission of discipline
2. Expectations for and roles of students, parents, and the various school staff members in different discipline situations
3. Rules and procedures for discipline in halls, bus areas, and other common areas of the school
4. Procedures covering student behavior, such as student recognition, rewards, parent contacts, penalties, and referral for remedial or special education

School staff must faithfully implement the policy. Student behavior that complies must be encouraged, and a schoolwide or other penalty for significant discipline violations can strengthen such a policy. The management of student problems should be monitored to give early warning of needed changes (Martella, Nelson, & Marchand-Martella, 2003; Van Acker, 2002).

*Safety* considerations may be another aspect of school management (e.g., Cangelosi, 2003). Among the considerations is a thorough analysis of (a) school physical plant, policy, and other variables affecting safety, with corrective action as needed; (b) community risks to and resources for school safety, again followed by action; (c) staff and student training in safety procedures; (d) a well-understood process for resolution of conflicts involving students; (e) appropriate procedures, personnel, and technology to enable immediate communication about and reaction to a safety threat.

One universal prevention practice for emotional and behavior problems is a schoolwide discipline policy.

## *Teaching Prosocial Competencies*

Some prevention experts assume that children and adolescents aggress because they do not know other behaviors by which they can succeed. Therefore, programs to teach aggressive students these other behaviors are recommended. Because there are various ideas as to what the "other behaviors" should be, programs differ as to what is taught (Brewer, Reid, & Rhine, 2003; Meadows & Stevens, 2004). Many emphasize cognitive skills such as those described in Chapter 9.

For example, *Second Step* (Frey, Hirschstein, & Guzzo, 2000; Grossman et al., 1997) is a universal school prevention program designed to develop children's social and emotional skills so they can succeed in school and life and avoid violence. Second Step draws on cognitive interventions, including social problem solving and anger control strategies, for children's aggressive and antisocial behavior.

Using age-appropriate versions of Second Step, teachers and other school personnel in preschool through middle school levels deliver the program on a schoolwide basis. Lessons are scheduled about twice per week. Lessons and supportive materials are designed to teach three main cognitive competencies: empathy, social problem-solving, and anger management.

1. In *empathy* lessons, students learn how to identify emotions, recognize the emotions of others, and communicate their own emotions.
2. In *social problem-solving*, they learn to identify problems, choose and evaluate solutions, and deal with their own impulsive behaviors and those of others.
3. *Anger management* lessons teach students what triggers their anger, how to control anger, and how to avoid conflict with peers.

Teachers develop students' behavior skills needed to put these competencies into action by using discussions, modeling, role-playing accompanied by teacher and peer evaluation, and extensive practice of competencies and skills, with coaching by the teacher. Teachers also exploit real classroom problem situations as opportunities for students to generalize their learning.

The scope of Second Step is such that the principal and other school authorities must be strongly committed to it on a schoolwide basis and over time. All teachers, other professionals, and paraprofessionals in the school deliver the program, and/or encourage students' use of its competencies and behavior skills. Second Step is intended for continuous use over several school years.

Another universal prevention program for sustained, schoolwide use, and intended to prevent violence, is Promoting Alternative THinking Strategies (PATHS). PATHS (Conduct Problems Prevention Research Group, 1999; Greenberg, Kusché, & Riggs, 2004; Kam, Greenberg, & Kusché, 2004) is a curriculum for behavior self-control, awareness of emotions, and social problem solving. Age-appropriate lessons are taught to students in grades K to 6, several times per week. PATHS is the school-based component of Fast Track, a comprehensive program to prevent antisocial behavior in childhood, adolescence, and beyond (Conduct Problems Prevention Research Group, 2004). Out-of-school components of Fast Track include social skills training, reading remediation, parent training for behavior management, school involvement, and personal support counseling.

### *Resolving Conflict*

Severe, chronic conflict characteristic of *Aggression* and *Relationship Problem* is addressed in many psychodynamic, behavioral, cognitive, and other interventions for students with ED (e.g., Bullock & Foegen, 2002). However, schools implement universal programs to prevent ordinary peer–peer and peer–adult conflicts in various ways (e.g., Smith, Schneider, Smith, & Ananiadou, 2004). For example, PeaceBuilders is a universal prevention program that attempts to create a nonviolent climate in the whole school. This program builds a school culture that teaches and encourages prosocial words and deeds, while discouraging antisocial ones (Flannery et al., 2003). These and other skills are also applied to conflicts that do arise.

Another widespread approach is conflict resolution. Many school conflict resolution programs assume that to prevent conflict and the harmful behavior and emotional outcomes of it, students must understand what conflict is and know particular methods to resolve it (Crawford & Bodine, 1996). These programs often teach two kinds of conflict resolution skills: foundation abilities and problem-solving process. Students then use these skills to resolve conflicts among peers.

1. *Foundation abilities* are prerequisite skills that enable students to use and profit from the problem-solving process. Foundation abilities include learning to do the following:
   (a) Value empathy, fairness, justice, tolerance, and respect for others.
   (b) Recognize and communicate frustration and anger.
   (c) Manage these strong emotions.
   (d) Examine situations from the points of view of other people, while delaying any judgments.

(e) Listen carefully to and be able to clearly state others' points of view.
(f) Brainstorm alternative solutions to conflict, along with changes in the current situation needed to put solutions into effect.
(g) Create fair, explicit criteria to evaluate each solution that is tried.

2. The *problem-solving process* may take the form of negotiation, mediation (negotiation assisted by a neutral person), or group consensus building. Each of these forms relies on skill at performing foundation abilities, and each is generally based on four key principles of conflict resolution: (a) separate the issues from the personalities, (b) focus on real interests, (c) brainstorm options, and (d) use objective standards (Display 11-5). The problem-solving process begins with a presentation of issues, problems, and points of view. Next it proceeds to the identification of each side's real interests. Then, optional solutions are created and these options are evaluated. Ultimately this generates an agreed-on solution.

Foundation abilities and problem-solving process come into play in three forms of conflict resolution education (Bodine & Crawford, 1999; Crawford & Bodine, 1996). (a) In the *process curriculum* form, foundation abilities and the problem-solving process are taught during specific instructional periods much like other school subjects. (b) The *peaceable classroom* form teaches conflict resolution skills not as a separate subject but infused into various subjects and aspects of the school day. This is supplemented by other instruction practices designed to reduce competition and conflict, such as cooperative learning and opportunities for students to practice conflict resolution skills. (c) In *mediation programs*, selected teachers

**Display 11-5** Principles of conflict resolution

| Principle | Description |
|---|---|
| Separate issues from personalities | Conflicts usually involve substantive issues as well as interpersonal and relationship problems. If issues are clearly discriminated from personality clashes, participants in the problem-solving process can work together on the issue while setting aside personal antagonisms. |
| Focus on real interests | In conflict resolution problem solving it is important to discover and discriminate each party's positions (what someone has decided he wants) and real interests (the motivation for or need behind his position). Lasting, useful conflict resolution moves beyond positions to identify and satisfy interests. |
| Brainstorm options | Imagine several possible courses of action that might satisfy both or all parties to the dispute; do not evaluate the possibilities at this point. |
| Use objective standards | Create objective, fair standards to judge the efficacy of the various possibilities, and apply these standards to help select a mutually agreeable course of action. |

*Source:* Crawford & Bodine, 1996.

and/or students are taught to be mediators who can use conflict resolution concepts to help settle interpersonal conflicts arising in the school. Mediators learn how to establish neutrality and trust, which are important to problem solving. They listen without bias to all perspectives, discover each disputant's real interests, help devise possible solutions, and help the disputants evaluate possibilities to come up with a solution to which all can agree.

### *Drug Prevention Education*

*Life Skills Training* (LST) is a school-based universal prevention program for substance abuse and violence avoidance (Botvin & Dusenbury, 1987; Botvin, Griffin, Diaz, & Ifill-Williams, 2001; Trudeau, Spoth, Lillehoj, Redmond, & Wickrama, 2003). It is designed to teach students to do the following:

1. Avoid substance use and other risky behaviors
2. Resist pressure from peers and media
3. Gain self-confidence
4. Assert themselves appropriately
5. Behave adaptively in a range of social situations
6. Perform social problem solving

Students use the social problem-solving skill, once they learn it, to activate other skills (e.g., self-confidence, assertion) as appropriate.

LST is typically delivered via a set of lessons that address Resistance, Self-Management, and Social Skill components. Resistance teaches misconceptions about substances and ways to withstand alluring or forceful incitements to use them. Self-Management teaches introspective examination of self-image in relation to social pressures, self-management via goal-setting and self-monitoring, social problem-solving tactics, and techniques to recognize and reduce stress. The Social Skill component teaches good ways to start and maintain adaptive social interactions, express oneself clearly (including refusals), and behave assertively without performing or projecting aggression.

There are elementary and middle school versions of LST, each designed to be presented over a three-year period (typically, grades 3 to 5 or 6 to 8). They differ somewhat in structure, but both prepare students for the next level of challenges to adaptive development, especially maintaining resistance to Substance Misuse and avoiding violent situations. Evaluations have demonstrated benefits of LST on substance resistance not only of students in general but students at high risk for Substance Misuse as well (Griffin, Botvin, Nichols, & Doyle, 2003).

## Selective Prevention

Individuals who have similar biological or psychosocial risk factors for an E&B disorder are considered to be part of a group that is at risk for that E&B disorder. An at-risk child or adolescent may never have exhibited any behaviors or emotions indicative of that disorder. Selective prevention activities are directed to young people in such at-risk groups.

## *Early Intervention*
Many and varied prevention activities have been implemented to achieve early recognition of and supportive programming for young children at risk for significant adjustment problems, especially aggressive, antisocial behavior (e.g., Conroy & Brown, 2004; Gunn, Smolkowski, Biglan, Black, & Blair, 2005; Joseph & Strain, 2003; Justice, 2004; Kendziora, 2004; Raver, 2004; see Sandall, Hemmeter, Smith, & McLean, 2004; Serna, Nielsen, Mattern, & Forness, 2003; Stormont, Lewis, & Beckner, 2005; Strain & Timm, 2001; Trout, Epstein, Mickelson, Nelson, & Lewis, 2003; Webster-Stratton & Reid, 2003). They generally provide emotional, behavior, and learning support for the children, often with a prominent parent training component. School is a significant part of the prevention activities in many of these programs.

Sometimes called "early intervention," these prevention activities usually attempt to improve school readiness, basic academics, appropriate school conduct, and other personal, social, and learning shortcomings of the young children in a designated at-risk group (Conroy, Hendrickson, & Hester, 2004). Usually the assumption is that early school success will prevent later academic, social, and personal problems in the school and community. A range of specific practices have been used in such efforts.

The *Primary Mental Health Project* (PMHP) is an early intervention project for primary grade students at high risk for developing significant learning, emotional, and behavior disorders (Cowen et al., 1996). The developers of PMHP realized that such high-risk students are far too numerous to be served adequately by traditional mental health services. As an alternative, the PMHP provides low-cost help to many at-risk children. Over several decades the PMHP became a systematic prevention network, located in many school districts.

Each high-risk student is assigned to a *child-aide*, a paraprofessional (often a homemaker in the local community) selected for her desire to help children and her relationship skills. A child-aide works with about 12 high-risk pupils for about two hours each per week, providing help that is appropriate to each child's problems. The child-aide develops a trusting relationship with the boy or girl, discusses the problems, tutors basic academic skills, and sets behavior limits for disruptive students. A PMHP specialist coordinates activities of teachers, child-aides, and other program participants and extends PMHP into the student's home via communication, parent training, and assistance in crisis situations.

## *Suicide Prevention*
The continued high extent of suicide and Suicidality among young people has prompted urgent attention to its prevention (Pfeffer, 2002; Shaffer, 2005), including school-based prevention (Centers for Disease Control and Prevention, 1992; IOM, 2002). Suicide prevention programs have proliferated in variety, in part because effectiveness is difficult to evaluate.

A school-based suicide prevention program can be universal. In *suicide education*, for example, all students are taught facts about suicide, simple warning signs, and methods of getting help when needed by peers or oneself. However, many school-based prevention programs are selective, directed toward subgroups of students at risk for taking their own lives (e.g., Possel, Horn, Groen, & Hautzinger, 2004). Among these risk factors (see Chapter 4) are Mood Disorders, Psychotic Disorders, and other E&B disorders involving *Depression;* participation in Substance Misuse or Law-Breaking Behavior; and being the relative or close friend of a person who has recently committed suicide.

*Peer support* selective prevention programs aim to increase social competencies of and friendship opportunities for young people at risk for suicide. In *school gatekeeping* programs, teachers and other education personnel are taught to identify and monitor students at risk for suicide in order to offer various forms of help when needed, such as counseling the student or bringing in suicide counseling experts.

*Post-suicide crisis intervention* is designed to assist students in coping with strong emotional reactions over a peer's suicide or other tragedy and to prevent subsequent suicides (e.g., "cluster suicides"). Crisis intervention is generally offered to all students in a postsuicide situation, but at the same time it is more intensively targeted to the higher risk subgroups. The crisis intervention approach may involve a coordinating committee that meets to consider the situation when a student commits suicide, perhaps to take some or all of the actions described in Display 11-6.

Many school-based suicide prevention efforts combine parts of more than one kind of program. Moreover, school suicide prevention programs often coordinate with community efforts (IOM, 2002; Shaffer & Craft, 1999) such as crisis hotlines and, of course, clinical treatment referral.

## Indicated Prevention

Individuals may participate in indicated prevention activities if their present emotional or behavioral functioning probably is an early form of E&B disorder (Mrazek & Mrazek, 2005). Education programs of indicated prevention vary in nature and intensity, some being as complex and intense as many interventions for students already identified as ED. For instance, CLASS was described in Chapter 8 as a dependent group contingency applied to elementary students whose acting-out behavior put them at risk for identification as ED (and the school component of First Step to Success; Walker et al., 2004). But similar dependent group contingencies are used in separate education environments for students with ED.

### *Check & Connect*

*Check & Connect* is an indicated prevention program for adolescents who have behavior problems, along with inadequate home support and other risk factors for dropout (Christenson & Havsy, 2004; Sinclair, Christenson, & Thurlow, 2005). It is designed to promote engagement with school, in order to prevent dropping out. *Check & Connect* assumes that a protective factor against such risks is the persisting

**Display 11-6** Steps in performing postsuicide crisis intervention

| Recommended Action | Description |
|---|---|
| Decide and disseminate | After a suicide, determine the school's response, including how to announce the death, to counsel classmates, and to give special support to high-risk peers of the victim. Identify teachers, counselors, and other persons who will directly communicate with friends and peers of the suicide victim. Communicate the school response to these key contact persons. |
| Avoid sensationalism | Public statements and private remarks to students should not glorify the deceased or sensationalize the suicidal act. |
| Identify high-risk persons | Students who were sweethearts, close friends, or relatives of the deceased, along with those having a tendency to depression, history of suicidality, or other high-risk characteristic, should be considered for additional counseling and other preventive action. |
| Communicate with media | An official contact person, and only that person, should provide accurate information, updated as frequently as necessary, to newspapers and electronic media. |
| Influence environment | Reduce available means of further suicides, especially guns, alcohol, and drugs. |
| Improve suicide prevention | Problems in the postsuicide prevention program exposed by this particular case should be examined to determine needed changes in the program |

*Sources:* Adapted from Centers for Disease Control and Prevention 1992; Shaffer, 2005.

presence of an adult who cares about the adolescent completing high school. *Check & Connect* provides such an adult, referred to as a "Monitor."

***Monitors.*** The Monitor is selected for and trained to exhibit the following characteristics: attitude that all young people can succeed in school, willingness to work closely with families and to refrain from blaming the student or his family for problems, skills in negotiation and advocacy, ability to work independently and document project activities, and commitment to remain a Monitor for several years. Each Monitor manages about 45 students. A coordinator (e.g., special educator or school psychologist) consults with multiple Monitors and supervises their professional development, duties, and meetings.

***Checking.*** Approximately weekly, the Monitor checks students' school engagement based on information that is easy to obtain and hard for the student to dispute. This is mainly school records on problems of attendance (class and school), behavior (office referrals, detention, suspension, other disciplinary record), and academics (grades, credits, course failures). School record data may be supplemented by information from school staff members. A student is considered "disengaged" (at risk for imminent dropout) when his problems of attendance, behavior, or academics exceed specified criteria (e.g., 15 or more percent of classes skipped in one month; or sum of office referrals, detentions, and in-school suspensions exceeds three in a month).

***Connecting: Basic Intervention.*** All *Check & Connect* students receive basic intervention, which is primarily a monthly meeting with each student. Besides general conversation and information exchange, the Monitor (a) reiterates the importance of staying in and completing school and the relationship between school completion and the "check" indicators of engagement; (b) presents the student's monthly status on these indicators, expressing praise and dissatisfaction as appropriate; and (c) reviews a simple cognitive problem-solving strategy.

This five-step strategy is reiterated in each monthly meeting to help the student resolve conflicts and cope with other problems. The Monitor, using real or hypothetical problems, goes over the following easy-to-remember strategy (similar to social problem-solving strategies):

1. Stop and think.
2. What choices?
3. Choose one.
4. Do it.
5. How did it work?

***Connecting: Intensive intervention.*** Most *Check & Connect* students are disengaged a good deal of the time. The Monitor responds by ascertaining what is needed to restore engagement with school. To do so the Monitor uses existing school and agency services, family and community relationships and connections, and other means. Resulting intensive interventions are, therefore, individualized, but they tend to involve strategies to cope with disruptive conflicts, as well as support for academics, including alternative ways to complete school.

***Connecting: Relationships.*** Relationships with the student and his family constitute an important component. Most importantly, the Monitor is persistent. She performs check, connect, and other regular and special role duties over several years, through repeated periods of student disengagement. The student can count on contact with a person who knows his situation well, yet still projects the belief that he can succeed. Additionally, the Monitor advocates and otherwise works for the student, especially during disengagement, when others may be willing to tolerate his dropping out of school.

The Monitor also cultivates a relationship with each student's family. She conveys the *Check & Connect* perspective that family members are not blamed for general or specific problems of the student; instead they are resources and partners for intervention. The Monitor keeps the family informed about the student's situation, obtains family perspectives on obstacles to his engagement in school, encourages family support for the student remaining in school and his specific accomplishments, helps the family make changes that may support his completing school, consults about possible intensive interventions, and helps families share ideas about discipline.

### *General School Procedure for Behavior Problems*

Schools should have a general plan of action for preventing escalation of a particular student's emotional and behavior problems. Jones (1991; Jones, Dohrn, & Dunn, 2004) described such a plan that allocates responsibilities to teachers and other school personnel. This plan's seven steps describe in general terms what should be done, in sequence (see Display 11-7). Within each step, any of a variety of specific activities could accomplish the responsibilities (see also Bahr et al., 2006).

**Display 11-7** Seven-step behavior problem management plan

| Step | Description |
|---|---|
| **Step 1:** Enhanced classroom management and/or teacher–student problem solving | Teacher attempts to solve problem by examining own classroom management practices, considering the settings in which problems occur, and engaging in problem-solving discussions with the student. |
| **Step 2:** Teacher contacts parents | Teacher enlists help of parents by increasing communication with home, helping parents teach and manage their kid, and involving the parents in classroom and school activities. |
| **Step 3:** Teacher refers student for counseling | If appropriate, teacher links student to individual or group counseling opportunity. |
| **Step 4:** Teacher requests help in managing the student from school assistance team | Teachers and other staff members at the school consult with the teacher to generate a variety of possible interventions for the problem at hand. |
| **Step 5:** Teacher refers student to office | If problem continues, discipline delivered by the school administration may be justified. Detention or other consequences should be those specified in an existing, well-advertised school discipline policy. |
| **Step 6:** School develops personalized education plan for student | If multiple office referrals occur, the student should receive a carefully crafted plan for intervention that identifies problems, interventions, educators or other professionals responsible for each intervention, and other needed details. |
| **Step 7:** Teacher refers student for special education consideration | If the personalized education plan step does not resolve the problem satisfactorily, the teacher should refer the student for possible identification as having ED and special education services. |

*Sources:* Friend & Bursuck (2006), Jones (1991), Jones et al. (2004).

Step 1 is enacted when a student begins showing a significant behavior problem. Depending on how the teacher manages the classroom, he may consider modifying physical and social ecological aspects of the classroom, his own verbal interactions with the student, classroom antecedents of and consequences for the inappropriate behavior, or other aspects of the situation. Step 1 continues until it is clearly not working, at which point Step 2 is enacted along with or in place of Step 1. Likewise, each step is tried until there is a clear need to move up to the subsequent step.

Beginning with Step 3, teachers are offered assistance in moving through the stepwise plan. This is similar to the concept of *prereferral intervention*, discussed below.

### *Prereferral Intervention*

A regular classroom teacher may consider referring a student for special education services when the student's emotional, learning, behavior, and other problems are seen to surpass the teacher's ability to manage them (see Display 3-8). Other ways through which students may be selected for special education consideration include parent request, a screening process for identification of problems, or a referral activated automatically upon a certain number of absences, poor grades, or disciplinary incidents involving the student.

Receiving special education may have strong benefits for the student, but there are potential drawbacks as well. For example, students in special education may be stigmatized by peers and teachers, feel humiliated, receive a significantly different education than other students, and cost the public considerably more to educate than nondisabled students. Thus, after a recognition that the student is having problems and the teacher's informal efforts to solve them have not succeeded, but before the student is actually referred for special education services, it is good policy to implement *prereferral intervention*. The main purpose of a prereferral intervention is to help the student while preventing his identification as having ED (or other disability). This reduces the chance that he or she will needlessly receive special education assessment, placement, intervention, and other services.

If the problem has reached a point at which referral for special education is being considered, the regular teacher(s) involved probably need assistance in considering and implementing prereferral intervention (Friend & Bursuck, 2006; Hammill & Bartel, 2004; Smith, Polloway, Patton, & Dowdy, 2006). Two modes of prereferral intervention assistance are consultation and collaboration (Truscott, Cohen, Sams, Sanborn, & Frank, 2005). In consultation, the regular teacher presents and clarifies the problem in order to receive advice from an expert or group of experts. In collaboration, the regular educator joins fellow professionals to work together as equals to solve the problem. Often a special educator is the consultant or manages the collaborating group.

***Consultation.*** As consultant to a regular educator, the special educator, school psychologist, or other professional functions as a specialist advising a general practitioner. She must be able to offer practical and acceptable interventions for behavior, emotional, learning, and other education problems of students with ED

A prereferral consultant helps the regular class teacher consider, select, and evaluate interventions for emotional and for behavior problems.

(Bos & Vaughn, 2006; Bostic & Bagnell, 2005; Jones et al., 2004; Kerr & Nelson, 2006; Mercer & Mercer, 2005; Sabornie & DeBettencourt, 2004). In addition to offering intervention advice, the consultant may play a part in some interventions (e.g., coordinate their use across different regular classes the student attends), observe in the regular classroom to monitor the student's functioning, or train the regular educator in use of an intervention.

There are various modes of consultation in prereferral intervention (Brown, Pryzwansky, & Schulte, 2006; Friend & Bursuck, 2006). For instance, in one direct approach with elements of functional assessment of behavior, the consultant helps the regular teacher:

1. Define the student's problem(s) in terms of specific student behaviors of concern
2. Identify classroom or school situations that may be prompting, rewarding, or otherwise supporting these behaviors
3. Consider interventions, especially those involving changes in these school situations, that the teacher can undertake to improve problem behaviors
4. Commit to carrying out one or more of the interventions considered
5. Evaluate the selected intervention by measuring behaviors defined in Step 1 before, during, and after the intervention is put into effect

***Collaboration.*** Collaboration approaches to prereferral call for mutual involvement of teachers and other participants in a group process of defining the prereferral problem, creating possible solutions, selecting a solution, acting to carry it out, evaluating this solution, and trying other solutions if necessary. The membership of this group (called a child study team, prereferral team, teacher assistance team, professional support team, or other term) varies from case to case. Not infrequently a special educator or school psychologist manages the group's composition, communication, and meetings, and monitors implementation of group decisions. However, contributions of all participants are given respectful consideration in order to build a commitment to group decisions and the continued use of this approach. It is advisable to adjust the "breadth" (number of persons and settings involved in planning and implementation) and "depth" (intensity of intervention method), depending on problem severity and other considerations.

Although it is helpful to conceptualize consultation and collaboration as different forms of assistance, in practice they overlap and are combined in various ways. Consultation and collaboration are used not only in prereferral interventions but to support special education of students already identified with ED, especially those educated in regular classrooms.

## Comment on Prevention

### *Refinements Needed*

The universal-selective-indicated concept is a good organizer for a wide range of school-based activities to prevent E&B disorder. However, there are aspects that need improvement.

Imperfect discriminations between the three categories of prevention were noted earlier. In addition, we know too little about the predictive power of many risk factors for E&B disorder. For this reason we cannot always be confident about correctly identifying the at-risk individuals for programs of prevention, especially selective prevention. As a result, prevention programs will include too many students who do not benefit, and may exclude too many others who could have benefitted.

Another problem aspect is that we do not yet know enough about the extent of benefits and drawbacks of many prevention activities. Yet benefit and drawback calculations are supposed to be a key basis for discriminating universal, selective, and indicated prevention.

These reservations point to important directions for research that may improve prevention of E&B disorder of children and adolescents. Among other key issues, we need to learn more about (a) the linkage between various risk factors and different patterns of E&B disorder that may result; (b) emotional, behavioral, cognitive, and other benefits of different prevention activities for students, broken down by relevant student characteristics (e.g., age, sex, SES); (c) emotional, behavioral, cognitive, and other drawbacks of diverse prevention activities.

**Preventing Prevention.** Despite the fact that we have evidence of the effectiveness of some school-based efforts to prevent emotional and behavior problems (Conroy et al., 2004; Witt, VanDerHeyden, & Gilbertson, 2004), schools generally seem to employ few prevention activities. Many students who eventually are identified with ED belong to at-risk groups or have shown behavior and emotional problems resembling ED for some time. Their eventual identification as ED could have been predicted and perhaps prevented (Kauffman, Brigham, & Mock, 2004).

Reluctance to implement school prevention programs has been called "preventing prevention" (Kauffman, 1999). Its causes may include inappropriate concern over harmful effects of labeling, unwillingness to support programs that may identify a disproportionate number of race-ethnic minority students, and high immediate costs of implementing prevention of E&B disorder in schools (Quinn & Poirier, 2004). Perhaps teachers of students with ED are the professionals that can and should advocate strongly for greater use of effective prevention programs in schools.

## INTERVENTION

If prereferral interventions do not solve the problems, the student will usually be considered for special education. This involves a decision-making process that calls for obtaining additional information on behavior, emotional, learning, and other problems and needs of the student, then determining appropriate education and related services (see Display 3-8). There is a great variety of ways through which schools deliver services to students with ED or at risk for ED. One reason for this is the need to individualize education for these students' many needs. Another is the diversity in preparation and skills of their teachers.

As noted, despite this variety, forms of service delivery can be classified into a small number of education environments (placements) based on their extent of restrictiveness. How often each is used varies by the age of the student with ED (Display 11-8). Before discussing each placement, let us consider a significant issue related to placements.

### *Full Continuum and Full Inclusion*

One controversial issue in special education is perhaps especially important for educators of students with ED: the "full continuum versus full inclusion" debate (Kavale & Forness, 2000). IDEA 2004 and related regulations indicate that placement with nondisabled peers is the preferred LRE for any student with an education disability, unless the evidence in a particular case shows otherwise (Hallahan & Kauffman, 2006; Yell, 2006). Appropriate services and placements are to be determined individually for each student, and a continuum of different education environments must be available to serve the student's needs.

***Full Inclusion.*** The situation is viewed differently by advocates for *full inclusion* (e.g., Lipsky & Gartner, 1997), defined as the delivery of special education services solely within the regular education environment. In full inclusion, all students with disabilities, including all students with ED, receive their individualized, appropriate education in regular classrooms alongside age peers who do not have disabilities. There, needed personnel and other resources are provided to ensure appropriate education.

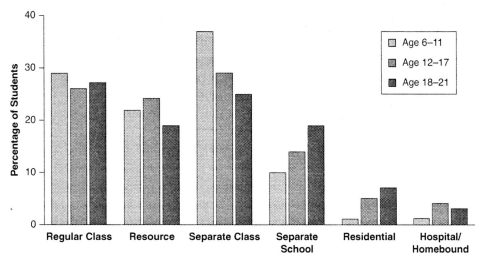

**Display 11-8** Percentage of students with ED served in each of six education environments, by three age levels
*Source:* USD Education, 2005.

The main argument for full inclusion is that placing the student with education disabilities in any setting other than the regular classroom violates his rights by segregating him to some extent from nondisabled peers. This is not only immoral, it is unconstitutional in the same sense that governmentally required racial segregation in public education was. Full inclusion supporters also state that there is little scientific evidence for the value of special education outside the regular education classroom.

Further, recent U.S. legal and societal developments show that people with disabilities will increasingly interact in employment and other important aspects of adult life with people without disabilities. Educating students with disabilities and nondisabled students together will prepare them to better accept such new realities about disability.

***Full Continuum.*** Advocates for a continuum of placements (see Crockett & Kauffman, 1999) counter that to place all students with disabilities in regular classes without considering their individual needs is unethical and illegal (violates IDEA 2004). To appropriately prepare a student with ED for success in school and life sometimes requires specialized interventions that are unfeasible in the regular class. In the view of full continuum supporters, there is modest scientific evidence supporting more restrictive placements for some students with ED, but virtually none for full inclusion.

The position taken here is that a full continuum of appropriate education and related services, including a variety of education placement options, is required for the well-being of students with ED. Although full continuum is sensible and conventional and corresponds to IDEA 2004 dictates, advocates of this position recognize that many students with ED should be educated largely if not entirely with nondisabled peers, and that more restrictive settings have potentially serious drawbacks (e.g., Arnold & Hughes, 1999) along with benefits. Certainly there is great need for more research that clarifies positive and negative aspects of different education services and settings for students with ED (Simpson, 2004; Tankersley, Landrum, & Cook, 2004).

## Regular Class

Students with disabilities are served in the regular classroom environment if they receive special education and related services outside the regular classroom for no more than 20 percent of the school day. The IDEA 2004 assumption that this placement is the preferred education environment (Yell, 2006) is one basis for efforts to enable students with ED who are placed in more restrictive settings to return to a regular classroom as soon as appropriate.

### Consultation or Collaboration

Special education in the regular classroom typically is provided through consultation and/or collaboration arrangements. The special educator's activities are similar to those of the consultant or collaborator in prereferral intervention, as discussed earlier in this chapter. However, the issue is not how to prevent the student's identification as ED but how to teach the student with ED in the regular classroom (Friend & Bursuck, 2006; Landrum, Katsiyannis, & Archwamety, 2004; Myles, 2005; Polloway et al., 2005; Salend, 2005; Villa, Thousand, & Nevin, 2004).

### Modified Regular Class

Educating students with ED outside the regular class is, in part, a response to the fact that regular classes have not adapted education in ways that would encourage those students to succeed. But there have been explorations of how to modify regular classes so that they accommodate students with disabilities as well as students with no disabilities.

For instance, the Combined Classroom Model (CCM) is a modified classroom in which students with ED are integrated with other elementary school students (Flicek, Olsen, Chivers, Kaufman, & Anderson, 1996). A regular elementary teacher and a special educator coteach, with help from teacher assistants and a multidisciplinary support team. Classroom management features a points-and-levels system, other behavior modification procedures, social skills training, and group activities to teach students to tolerate and respect each other. Mental health counseling is available primarily to the students with ED. In an evaluation of CCM, the students with ED made modest improvements in achievement, conduct, and social skills, while the nondisabled students experienced no adverse effects and their parents were satisfied with the CCM program.

## Resource Room

Students are in a resource room program if they receive education outside the regular classroom for 21 to 60 percent of the school day. The main purpose of a resource program is to strengthen academic, behavior, and other functioning of students who have a regular class placement for the balance of their school day. Parenthetically, it can serve the same purpose for students with ED assigned to separate classes, at the same time offering them opportunities for social interaction with other students in the resource room. Thus the resource room can serve as a step toward their integration into regular classes.

Three forms of resource program are common. *Categorical* programs serve students with a particular disability only, while *cross-categorical* programs serve students with various education disabilities (e.g., ED, mild mental retardation, and learning disabilities). *Noncategorical* programs serve students needing educational help, often of a fairly specific nature (e.g., math, study skills), whether or not the student is identified for special education. In effect, noncategorical resource programs can achieve inclusion outside the regular classroom.

The resource teacher provides instruction directly to students with disabilities (Bos & Vaughn, 2006; Haager & Klingner, 2005). This may include remediation in academics, study strategies, social skills, brief counseling, and other areas of educational need. In addition to instructing students, the resource teacher often has responsibilities as consultant and assessor (Hammill & Bartel, 2004; Friend & Bursuck, 2006).

Responsibilities of a consultant were described earlier. In the assessor role, resource teachers assess students, coordinate measurement results to help plan appropriate education, and manage the IEP process. The resource teacher must be familiar with instruments and procedures to measure emotions, behaviors, and cognitions related to a student's adjustment in school (see Chapter 3), as well as academic achievement, school records, and other aspects of educational functioning. Further, resource teachers often take the lead in creating and maintaining IEPs, including managing IEP team meetings, securing educational and related services, finalizing measurement issues (e.g., outcomes, accommodations), and addressing potentially thorny IDEA 2004 issues such as disciplinary exclusion from school.

A specialized form of resource program, the Crisis/Helping Teacher, was designed for students with significant behavior and emotional problems (see Morse, 1998, and Chapter 7). Crisis/Helping Teacher services are available to students who become so disturbed or disturbing that they must leave their assigned regular or separate classroom for a brief time. This offers the Crisis/Helping Teacher an opportunity to provide Life Space Crisis Intervention or other counseling to the student, and gives him, his teacher, and fellow students temporary relief from a potentially explosive situation.

## Separate Classroom

The most common placement for students with ED is a separate ("self-contained") classroom. Nearly all separate classrooms have a few general aspects in common. There is a low student-to-teacher ratio (often, 5 to 12 students and one teacher;

sometimes one or more teaching assistants) and considerable latitude for the teacher to modify space, time, curriculum, and other dimensions of instruction.

Beyond general similarities, separate classrooms show great variation in physical structure, location, time scheduling, rules, motivation systems, curriculum and instructional offerings, and other key features (Bradley, Henderson, & Monfore, 2004; Davis et al., 2004; Kern, Bambara, & Fogt, 2002; Kerr & Nelson, 2006; Lewis, Hudson, Richter, & Johnson, 2004; Miller, Gunter, Venn, Hummel, & Wiley, 2003). Among the reasons for such variation are teachers' preferences for different models to guide their intervention, diverse amounts and kinds of preparation for their role, state-by-state dissimilarities in requirements for educating students with ED, administrative decisions about how resources will be deployed, and the particular emotional and behavior characteristics of the students being taught.

Some authorities are concerned that the latitude and variability found among separate classrooms for students with ED may be decreasing since implementation of the federal No Child Left Behind (NCLB) education law. NCLB requires that the average academic achievement of students with disabilities must improve to nearly the level of students without disabilities. Informal reports indicate that many students with ED now spend more of the school day in academic remediation activities. Also, NCLB mandates considerable achievement testing. One concern is that time for academic teaching and testing could be obtained by reducing nonacademic activities such as Reality Therapy classroom meetings, behavior contracting sessions, social problem-solving exercises, or Circle of Courage discussions. Katsiyannis and Yell (2004), Mooney, Denny, & Gunter (2004), and Sitlington and Neubert (2004) discuss implications of NCLB for students with ED.

### *Structured Environment*
Most students with ED placed in self-contained classrooms exhibit *Aggression* and *Impulsiveness* patterns, along with Learning Difficulty. Many students additionally show the other patterns of E&B disorder as well as one or more connected problems. Self-contained classroom teachers are often advised to establish a structured, teacher-directed setting to maintain an orderly learning environment. Among its objectives are the following:

1. Facilitate the delivery of academic, social-emotional, and other needed instruction, especially that which is unfeasible in less restrictive settings
2. Reduce disruption to other students and teachers who share the school
3. Simulate some of the features and expectations of regular education classrooms that the student may soon rejoin

Some general aspects of such a self-contained classroom for students with ED (Display 11-9) are similar to those recommended earlier (see the examination of classroom management, in the discussion of universal prevention). In the following section some key points are reiterated or elaborated (for details, see Colvin, 2002; Darch & Kameenui, 2004; Jones et al., 2004; Kerr & Nelson, 2006; Martella et al., 2003; Walker et al., 2004). Of course, there are other ways of managing self-contained classrooms that feature less apparent structure and teacher-directedness (see Chapter 7).

**Display 11-9** Selected features of a structured separate class for students with ED

- Physical aspects
- Scheduling
- Behavior management
- Survival-and-success
- Fundamental academics
- Subject content
- Study skills
- Transition
- Social competence

The teacher should consider the influence of *physical aspects* of the classroom, including placement and spacing of desks and tables, designation of activity and reward areas, and transitions within and outside the classroom. He generally has flexibility in *scheduling* needed education opportunities as well as other activities she judges to be appropriate (e.g., extra physical activity or free time periods, therapeutic discussions, and meetings). Activities generally should be scheduled as multiple short periods rather than long periods, because interspersing varied activities can improve the performance of students who have problems of attention and motivation.

A *behavior management system* often includes unambiguous rules, frequent clear feedback to students about their rule compliance and other performance, and specified consequences for appropriate and inappropriate performance. A token economy with or without levels is well suited to address these criteria and can be supplemented with behavioral contracting, self-control techniques, and other behavior management practices (Bear, 2005; Bos & Vaughn, 2006; Colvin, 2002; Kerr & Nelson, 2005; Polloway et al., 2005; Salend, 2005).

### *Other Key Features*

It is a high priority to teach students with ED to perform *survival-and-success* behaviors (see Display 11-10). Such behaviors are typically expected of most students by regular educators and will help them perform adaptively at present, upon return to a regular class environment and in other education situations. There are generic survival-and-success behaviors—those typically exhibited by successful students in most classrooms—as well as specific ones that may be needed to succeed in a particular regular classroom in which the student with ED will participate. Self-control strategies noted in Chapters 7, 8, and 9 may help the student generalize survival-and-success behaviors from separate classroom to regular classroom.

An important justification of self-contained classrooms for students with ED is their flexibility to assess and teach a range of adaptive competencies related to each student's individual educational needs. Each student's needed competencies should be identified through individual assessment, but among those commonly addressed in the separate classroom are fundamental academics, school subject content, study skills, vocational and transition skills, and social competence (e.g., Hoover & Patton, 1999; Johns, Crowley, & Guetzloe, 2002; Kerr & Nelson, 2006; Sabornie & DeBettencourt, 2004; Schmid & Evans, 1998).

**Display 11-10** General survival-and-success behaviors typical of regular class environments

---

*Attending* school and classes regularly and punctually

*Being ready* with materials at hand and prepared for class participation

*Interacting* with peers in positive ways

*Watching* teacher-presented tasks, teacher presentations, teacher-approved tasks, and children answering teacher questions

*Following directions* given by the teacher

*Answering questions* from the teacher about academic or other matters

*Volunteering information* related to academic or management matters, according to teacher's rules and expectations

*Working* on assignments or approved tasks by responding (e.g., writing, drawing, reading, speaking) appropriately

*Interacting* with teachers in respectful ways

*Transitioning* into and out of school, and among different school settings

*Learning* independently by using appropriate study skills to complete assignments

---

*Sources:* Kerr & Nelson (2006); Walker et al. (2004).

The teacher must build and maintain good *relationships* with students. Ideas vary greatly about the nature of that relationship (e.g., Brendtro, Ness, & Mitchell, 2001; Davis, Nelson, & Gauger, 2000; Johns et al., 2002; Long, 1997; Martella et al., 2003; Sterba & Dowd, 1998; Van Acker, 2002). Maybe it should be like one the teacher would have with a student without ED. Davis et al. (2000) recommend being friendly and warm, showing concern for the student and his life, helping the student feel good about himself, and emphasizing that he is in a community of students in the school. Such relationship-building teacher behaviors may strengthen the effectiveness of instructions and consequences, enable learning and stability to resume more quickly after a crisis, open counseling possibilities, decrease absences and dropout, model a way to interact with people, and yield other benefits to teacher and student.

### *Fundamental Academics*

Key areas of fundamental academic skills remediation include reading word attack, reading comprehension, oral language, written language, and mathematics. Remediation practices are described by Al Otaiba & Rivera (2006); Bos, Coleman, and Vaughn (2002), Carnine, Silbert, Kame'enui, and Tarver (2004), Friend & Bursuck (2006), Gersten, Jordan, and Flojo (2005), Polloway et al. (2005), Lane (2004), Meese (2001), Mercer and Mercer (2005), Noell and Gansle (2002), Regan, Mastropieri, & Scruggs (2005), Shippen, Houchins, Steventon, and Sartor (2005), Tindal and Crawford (2002), among many.

***Reading Word Attack.*** Many students with reading problems cannot decode printed letters well. They need instruction in phonic word attack skills to learn to say the sounds of individual letters and groups of letters, then blend those elements to correctly say the printed word. Word attack skills are supplemented by instruction in recognizing irregular words and other fundamental reading skills.

***Reading Comprehension.*** Additional teaching practices can improve the student's understanding of reading material. For example, *before* reading a passage the teacher can lead activities that activate or supplement the student's existing knowledge of the topic or go over key vocabulary items. Also, the student can be taught various strategies to use *during* reading, such as self-questioning (e.g., "Who is this passage about?"; "What is her main problem?"; "How does she try to solve the problem?"; "How does the situation end?") or writing the main ideas of each paragraph. Comprehension exercises *after* reading a passage might include responding to questions about it, retelling the passage, or outlining it.

***Oral Language.*** Problems involving understanding or producing oral language are important in their own right and as impediments to reading and writing. Depending on the student's assessed needs, a teacher may work to improve her receptive and expressive vocabulary, syntax (e.g., verb tense, subject–verb agreement), and other aspects of oral language.

***Written Language.*** Written language is a complex instructional area covering many skills. Self-contained class teachers need to help many students with the mechanics of writing (e.g., capitalization, spelling, punctuation), syntax, sentence and paragraph organization, and elaboration of written ideas (e.g., increased length and complexity).

***Mathematics.*** To remediate mathematics problems of students with ED, teachers may need to instruct in beginning math skills such as counting, operations (e.g., addition, division), math facts and concepts, place values, measurement, and solving simple word problems. Older students often need to learn fractions, proportions, and decimals, simple geometry and algebra, and more advanced applications such as word problems involving job or independent living situations.

### *Subject Content*

To prepare students with ED for participation in regular classes, their special teachers often have to teach and even be licensed in content area subjects. In many cases, they teach several subjects to numerous students operating at different grade levels. This responsibility is frequently made more challenging by students' deficiencies in fundamental academics and effective study skills, along with little apparent motivation to learn. On the positive side, teachers in separate classes (as well as separate schools and residential education environments) may have considerable flexibility to modify lessons and innovate in other ways. Choate (2000), Edwards and Chard (2000), Hoover and Patton (1999), Lenz, Deshler, and Kissam (2004), Mercer and Mercer (2005), and Schmid and Evans (1998) describe instruction in content areas.

### *Study Skills*
Teachers desire and expect students to learn more independently as they become older. Students with ED must learn to use *study skills* such as managing time, making notes, outlining, memorizing, using references, writing reports, completing homework, and taking tests (Bradley-Klug & Shapiro, 2003; Friend & Bursuck, 2006; Kerr & Nelson, 2006; Lenz et al., 2004; Rogan, 2000; Sabornie, 2002). For example, to help the student manage learning time, he can be taught to use a notebook to track assignment details and due dates, divide assignments into subtasks, prioritize and schedule the subtasks, and check them off as he completes them.

Related to study skills are *learning strategies*, which are planned, step-by-step methods of completing assigned tasks. Learning strategies are linked to prerequisite skills and information needed for the learning strategy to work. This is supplemented by instruction in how to select the right learning strategy for a particular task or problem.

Different kinds of learning strategies teach the student to acquire, remember, or demonstrate knowledge and behavior. For example, *Paraphrasing* helps a student acquire information from text (i.e., comprehend reading). Students are taught to read a single paragraph, think of the main idea and key details, and restate them before reading the next paragraph. *FIRST-Letter* is a strategy to help the student remember lists. Students learn how to use the first letter of each list item to create a memorable phrase or sentence that will help them recall the entire list. *DEFENDS* teaches how to demonstrate knowledge by writing a report, essay test, or similar position statement. Students use DEFENDS to identify, arrange, and edit main and supporting ideas for their statement.

### *Transition Skills*
Many students with ED—perhaps most—adjust poorly to life after leaving high school, emphasizing the great need for transition education for these students. By law, transition services must be stated in the IEPs of older students with ED. Their teachers should provide three overlapping aspects of transition education: career, vocational, and life skills education (see Brolin & Loyd, 2004; Cheney & Bullis, 2004; Polloway et al., 2005).

*Career education* addresses productive attitudes toward work, adaptive work behaviors, exposure to a variety of kinds of work, and strategies for selecting possible career directions. *Vocational education* involves teaching the knowledge and skills that are specific to particular kinds of jobs or careers, arranging supported job placements, and assisting the student's transition to a job, vocational or technical school, or vocational services agency. *Life skills education* is concerned with the student's functioning as an independent adult in such areas as housing, transportation, finances, health, postsecondary education, leisure activities, friends and associates, marriage and family success, and general citizenship.

Providing appropriate transition services can be complex. It calls for cooperative service from educators and professional in other fields. Not infrequently, the separate class teacher or other special educator must actively initiate and maintain this cooperation. If adequate services are not available, she may need to find ways to provide some of the services herself.

### *Social Competence*

Many students with ED fail to perform behaviors that would enable them to interact successfully with peers and adults. A major thrust of appropriate education for these students is social skills instruction (Battalio & Stephens, 2005; Gresham, 2002; Kavale, Mathur, & Mostert, 2004). Social skills teaching should be infused and incorporated into multiple aspects of instruction and other school activities for students with ED. At the same time social skills should be taught on a regular schedule, several times per week.

## More Restrictive Education Settings

About one in five students with ED are served in separate public schools, public and private residential facilities, and homebound or hospital settings (see Display 11-8). Education programs for students with ED in separate public schools (often called "alternative" schools) and residential facilities vary greatly in philosophy and emphasis (Gagnon & Leone, 2005; Tobin & Sprague, 2000). Often they involve more kinds of services, of a more intensive nature, than found in separate classes. Many educators in separate environments report that they enjoy working where colleagues understand what they do, share an interest in students with ED, and cooperate in delivering special education and other services. Not all regular schools offer such a supportive climate.

The entire school environment may be arranged to support intensive intervention. Such a therapeutic milieu might feature, for example, an emphasis on academic remediation, the same points-and-levels system in each classroom, a schoolwide discipline plan, individual and group counseling, anger management and social skills instruction groups, and vocational services.

Jacobs, Randall, Vernberg, Roberts, and Nyre (2005) described a program in which students with severe E&B disorders spent half the day in a separate school and the other half in a regular class at a neighborhood school. The separate environment provided intensive intervention, including a token economy, social skills training, and individual psychotherapy. Staff at the separate school provided intervention for behavior maintenance and setting generality, as well as support and training for the student's family. This was facilitated by a 1 to 2 ratio of staff to students.

In residential placements, the school program may be integrated with that of the entire institution via common counseling techniques, consequences for student behavior, and other means. Psychologists, social service and court caseworkers, medical personnel, and other professionals may work with teachers to provide the intensive services. Chapter 12 presents selected noneducational interventions that the teacher should understand and be able use.

Based on an examination of relevant literature, Tobin and Sprague (2000) synthesized a collection of recommended alternative education practices for teaching students with ED in separate schools and residential placements. They probably apply to similar alternative school students not identified as ED (e.g., dropouts, institutionalized delinquents). Among the Tobin and Sprague recommendations are a highly structured classroom environment, teacher-directed instruction of academics and learning strategies, behavioral and cognitive interventions, social skills instruction, and parent involvement.

## Chapter Summary

Education activities for students with ED include universal, selective, and indicated prevention, as well as various forms of school intervention.

- Universal education prevention efforts are offered to all students, and are expected to prevent E&B disorder for some students. Examples:
  — Classroom and school management
  — Drug use education
  — School violence and conflict programs
- Selective prevention is provided to students with risk factors for E&B disorder, and is expected to prevent E&B disorder of some at risk students. Examples:
  — Early intervention
  — Some kinds of suicide prevention
- Indicated prevention is targeted to individual students with early forms of E&B disorder. Examples:
  — Seven-step problem escalation prevention
  — Prereferral intervention
- School intervention for students with ED takes place in regular, resource, separate, and more restrictive education settings.
- Full inclusion advocates call for use of regular education only, whereas full continuum advocates want to use different education environments.
- Tools for serving students with ED in regular and resource classes are:
  — Consultation
  — Collaboration
  — Modified regular classes
  — Crisis-ready resource rooms
- Education in separate classrooms often emphasizes a structured environment.
- The teacher manages classroom physical aspects and scheduling, implements a program of behavior management, and teaches survival-and-success behaviors.
- This structure facilitates teaching the range of competencies many of these students need, including fundamental academics, subject content, study skills, vocational and transition skills, and social competence.

- More restrictive education settings may also provide a structured education environment in which some teaching procedures may be integrated with other services and programs.

## IDEAS FOR CONSIDERATION AND DISCUSSION

1. Describe the Institute of Medicine recommended way of classifying prevention efforts. Illustrate each of the three categories of prevention with an education example from this chapter or elsewhere. Justify your examples by stating why each example illustrates its category of prevention.
2. a. Create in outline form a school-wide discipline policy for an elementary school, keeping in mind the main points in the section of this chapter entitled, *Preventive classroom and school management*. State the purpose(s) of each aspect of your policy.
   b. Do the same for a middle school (policy in outline form, state purpose of each outline entry). Comment on differences between middle school and elementary school policies.
   c. Do the same for a high school (policy in outline form, state purpose of each outline entry). Comment on differences between policies for high school and those for middle school and elementary school.
3. Develop policies and related forms that would give needed details to implement Step 4 and Step 6 of the *Seven-step behavior problem management plan* (Display 11-7).
4. Imagine that you are the teacher who has been employed to develop and implement a new categorical resource program for about 25 students with ED at a middle school.
   a. Describe the problems you want the program to solve and the purposes you want it to serve.
   b. What resources will you need to address these problems and purposes?
   c. Create five daily schedules that summarize your activities as teacher and manager of this resource program during the second week of October.
5. On a 3 × 5 card, create in outline form a three- to five-minute talk on the issue of full inclusion and full continuum for students with ED. Assume that you will give the talk in one of your school's staff meetings. Practice your talk on your classmates, who will evaluate its strengths and weaknesses.
6. Extend Display 11-10 by identifying three additional survival-and-success behaviors.

## RESOURCES FOR FURTHER STUDY

**www.acde.org/common/Contents.htm** American Council for Drug Education information
**www.smhp.psych.ucla.edu/** Center for Mental Health in Schools
**www.safeyouth.org/scripts/teens/conflict.asp** Conflict resolution

**cecp.air.org/guide/guide.pdf** Early warning, timely response
**www.ideapartnership.org/** IDEA Partnership
**curry.edschool.virginia.edu/sped/projects/ose/information/interventions.html**
  Intervention techniques reviewed
**idea.uoregon.edu/%7Encite/index.html** National Center to Improve the Tools of Educators
**www.uni.edu/coe/inclusion/philosophy/philosophy.html** Philosophy for inclusion
**www.reclaiming.com/** Reclaiming youth (circle of courage)
**www.pbis.org/main.htm** Schoolwide positive behavior interventions and supports
**www.nwrel.org/scpd/sirs/5/cu9.html** Schoolwide and classwide discipline
**www.nasdse.org/directors.cfm** State directors of special education, by state
**www.air.org/cecp/resources/stateconsul.htm** State education consultants in emotional and behavior disorders
**www.metanoia.org/suicide/** Suicide—read this first
**www.teachernet.com/htm/classroomresources.htm** Teacher Net materials, curricula, ideas, and issues
**www.cdc.gov/nccdphp/dash/violence/index.htm** U.S. agency activities addressing school violence
**www.cdc.gov/ncipc/dvp/bestpractices_table.htm** Violence prevention curriculum
**www.yellowribbon.org/** Yellow Ribbon Suicide Prevention Program

Chapter **Twelve**

# *Intervention in Other Systems*

## Chapter Objectives

**After reading this chapter, you should be able to:**
- List three systems, in addition to education, that serve students with ED.
- Name five classes of psychotropic drugs.
- State two roles of the teacher in psychotropic drug therapy.
- Identify six features of the Teaching-Family Model.
- Describe teen courts.
- Explain three core values of a system of care.

## Can You Define These 10 Terms?

day treatment
milieu therapy
Project Re-Ed
outdoor challenges
psychotropic drug

therapeutic group home
status offense
system of care
cultural competence
Multisystemic Therapy

This chapter describes systems, in addition to the education system, that serve children and adolescents with E&B disorder. Their educators are especially likely to interact with the mental health, child and family welfare, and juvenile justice systems. Other service systems with which the teacher may interact include vocational, medical/health, recreation, and legal services.

As noted in Chapter 11, the concept of least restrictive environment applies to various systems of intervention in addition to the education system. The continuum of settings and services in the mental health system (Olfson, 2005; U.S. Department of Health and Human Services [USD HHS], 1999), from least to most restrictive, encompasses outpatient treatment, day treatment, residential treatment, and psychiatric hospitalization. There are other mental health service settings as well, and psychotropic drug therapy is an important intervention used in conjunction with other services in all settings. In the child and family welfare system, children may be removed from their homes and placed into respite or shelter care settings briefly, or into foster homes, therapeutic foster care, or group homes for longer periods. In the juvenile justice system, services are sometimes associated with a range of dispositions including probation, special courts, restitution, and detention institutions of numerous kinds.

This chapter describes services and settings according to the different systems, but in reality many services and settings are offered by more than one system. For instance, residential placements emphasizing intervention are found in the mental health, child welfare, and juvenile justice systems.

Coverage of the systems and the services within systems presents general information. Localities may offer some but not all these services and/or additional services not described below. Local terms for a particular service can vary. In some localities a particular service may be available only "in theory"—few knowledgable professionals use it because of long wait times, inadequate performance, and so on. Educators of students with ED should know the local terms and services.

Interesting variations of service to children with E&B disorder continue to emerge (Steele & Roberts, 2005). An especially significant recent development that involves mental health, child welfare, juvenile justice, education, and considerably more, is the concept of a "system of care" for children with E&B disorder. It is presented, with some other emerging interventions, after consideration of the traditional systems of service.

# PREVENTION

Prevention of children's E&B disorder is an important goal of mental health, child and family welfare, and juvenile justice, as well as education and other systems of service (Mrazek & Mrazek, 2005). A large number of efforts to prevent each of the patterns of E&B disorder and connected problems (see Chapter 4) have been reported (e.g., Donovan & Spence, 2000; Greenberg, Domitrovich, & Bumbarger, 1999). Work directed toward preventing *Aggression*, Law-Breaking Behavior, and related problems such as bullying, gang participation, and violence has been extensive (Graczyk & Tolan, 2005; Kashani, Jones, Bumby, & Thomas, 1999; Reid & Eddy, 2002; Walker, Ramsey, & Gresham, 2004) and illustrates some current thinking on prevention in general.

A variety of risk factors for antisocial behavior have been identified, including those in prenatal, infancy, early childhood, middle childhood, and adolescence developmental periods (Guerra, Attar, & Weissberg, 1997; Loeber, Farrington, Stouthamer-Loeber, & Van Kammen, 1998; Reese, Vera, Simon, & Ikeda, 2000; Thomas, 2005). Significant risk factors by developmental periods are indicated in Display 12-1.

Total risk for serious antisocial behavior seems to accumulate as exposure to one risk predisposes the individual to additional, powerful, more proximal risks. Often the result is a "life trajectory" that leads gradually but predictably to antisocial behavior (Munger, 1997; Patterson & Yoerger, 2002). In the life trajectory conceptualization, prevention is an effort to reduce either the ultimate undesired outcome (antisocial behavior) or exposure to one of the developmentally later risk factors.

Universal, selective, and indicated techniques and programs to prevent antisocial behavior have been implemented at various developmental periods. These prevention efforts usually seek to reduce or counteract one or more risk factors, such as those noted in Display 12-1.

The *Fast Track* intervention/prevention program (Conduct Problems Prevention Research Group, 2004) illustrates the strategy. Fast Track is a comprehensive

**Display 12-1** Selected risk factors for antisocial behavior in successive developmental periods

| Developmental Period | Risk Factors |
|---|---|
| Prenatal | • *Mother*: Young and unmarried, poor nutrition, poor health care; tobacco, alcohol, and drug use |
| Infancy | • *Baby*: Illness, difficult temperament<br>• *Parent(s)*: Poor attachment, abuse, neglect |
| Early childhood | • *Child*: High activity level<br>• *Parent*: Coercive discipline, inconsistent discipline, rejection |
| Middle childhood | • *Child*: Lack of school readiness, impulsive behavior and learning style, aggressive behavior toward peers, rejection by peers, defiant behavior toward adults<br>• *Parent*: Low involvement, insufficient supervision<br>• *Teachers*: Rejection of troublesome student |
| Adolescence | • *Adolescent*: School failure, nonattendance, aggressive and bullying toward peers and adults, extensive time spent away from home, participation in antisocial peer group, early sex, substance use, delinquency<br>• *Parents*: Low involvement, ineffective discipline<br>• *Education system*: School removal |
| Late adolescence and adulthood | Chronic antisocial behavior |

*Sources:* Connor, 2002; Loeber et al., 1998.

program to intervene with aggressive, defiant, and disruptive behavior in very young children, to prevent serious antisocial behavior in adolescence and later. The logic of the Fast Track intervention is to target some important risk factors for antisocial behavior.

For this reason the home and community components of *Fast Track* include social skills training, tutoring in reading and building friendships, as well as parent training and home visits to promote good child discipline, good relationships with school, and skills for personal growth. Older participants' intervention is more individualized (e.g., mentoring, tutoring). The main school component of *Fast Track* is a universal curriculum based program called PATHS, noted in Chapter 11. Fast Track has demonstrated modest success, and illustrates a way to coordinate educational and other service systems to address E&B disorders of young people.

# Mental Health System

Psychosocial intervention, including verbal psychotherapy or counseling, constitutes a major treatment offering in the mental health system. This is provided mainly in outpatient, day treatment, and residential mental health settings, but also occurs in other formal and informal settings such as schools, private homes, foster homes, detention institutions, medical or health clinics, churches and temples, shelters for homeless families, and via telephone hotlines (Olfson, 2005). The form, intensity, and settings of psychosocial treatments are influenced by the nature and severity of the E&B disorder, the young person's age and reasoning ability, theoretical preferences and training of the therapist, family involvement, availability of appropriate services, and personal or agency financial considerations. Psychotherapy is often supplemented by psychotropic drug therapy and other supplementary services (e.g., parent training, liaison with schools).

## Outpatient Treatment

Almost any activity the reader can imagine has been used somewhere, sometime, by some therapist as a way to provide psychosocial intervention. In most cases, however, it is based on one or a combination of the models of E&B disorder (see Chapters 7 to 10).

Each year, 5 to 10 percent of U.S. children and adolescents take part in psychotherapy and other psychosocial intervention (Burns, Hoagwood, & Maultsby, 1998; Landolf, 2005; Substance Abuse and Mental Health Services Administration [SAMHSA], 2004), a large proportion as outpatients. Outpatient psychotherapy is provided in private practices or in public and private clinics, which may be attached to medical offices, hospitals, drug treatment centers, community mental health centers, or other institutions. Psychotherapy may take the form of individual, peer group, and family therapy, and it is provided by psychiatrists, psychologists, psychiatric social workers and nurses, counselors, and other licensed practitioners. It may consist of a few sessions or numerous sessions lasting many months (see Erickson & Palmer, 2004; Hibbs, 2005; Josephson, 2005; Smith-Boydston, 2005; Thienemann, 2005).

Some young people receive psychotherapy for an E&B disorder, while others participate for different reasons (e.g., child–parent conflict). In some cases psychotherapy can qualify under IDEA 2004 as a related service (Etscheidt, 2002), but probably just a small proportion of students with ED receive psychotherapy in addition to special education.

## Day Treatment

**Day treatment** (also termed partial hospitalization) is mental health treatment provided in a special setting for several hours each day, with the young person residing at home. Day treatment is designed to be more intensive than outpatient therapy, but less restrictive than residential treatment or hospitalization. It allows for a broad range of therapies (individual, group, family) and other services (e.g., academic, vocational, substance abuse) delivered by various mental health and other professionals. Among its purposes are to prevent residential placement and to ease transition to home and school following residential placement (Kiser, Heston, & Pruitt, 2005).

Many day treatment programs employ **milieu therapy** (or *therapeutic milieu*), the use of key aspects of daily life in the intervention environment to teach adaptive skills, facilitate emotional growth or self-understanding, and provide other kinds of support for the young person's recovery. Different forms of milieu therapy utilize different aspects of daily life, often reflecting a favored psychological model. For instance, psychodynamic milieu therapy might encourage intense relationships with several staff members to simulate and help resolve the child's conflicts with her parents, whereas behavioral milieu therapy might rely on an elaborate token economy to reward her improved social and academic behavior.

In many day treatment programs the milieu includes extensive education in which teachers provide remedial academics, coursework in subject areas, and tutoring to help the student maintain or catch up to levels of educational functioning that

Teachers, psychologists, and other professionals collaborate to provide day treatment.

will facilitate reentry into regular or special education at the conclusion of day treatment. Teachers collaborate with therapists in delivering various group and individual psychosocial interventions such as Life Space Crisis Intervention, reinforcement and other consequences for adaptive and maladaptive behavior, social skills training, social problem solving, transition to adult independence (Cook, Solomon, Farrell, Koziel, & Jonikas, 1997), and other aspects of the treatment program. Additionally, families are invited to take part, mainly through counseling and training in child management.

Day treatment often resembles separate or alternative school services in the education system that include an extensive therapy component. As with separate school programs, it is possible to locate day treatment programs within regular schools (Milin, Coupland, Walker, & Fisher-Bloom, 2000).

The focus of many day treatment programs for adolescents is Substance Misuse. In addition to the components noted above, these often feature 12-step or other recovery programs, random drug and alcohol screening, and curricula for teaching adaptive skills such as assertive refusal and resistance to pressure. Of course, treatment for Substance Misuse is not restricted to day treatment, but occurs in various mental health and other settings (Pringle & Flanzer, 2005).

## Residential Settings

Children may be placed in general hospitals, small community or larger remote residential treatment centers, or psychiatric hospitals when community-based treatment is unavailable or judged to be inappropriate (DeAntonio, 2005; USD HHS, 1999). Short-term placement in the psychiatric unit of a hospital is often a response to some disturbing crisis such as a suicide attempt, depressive episode, severe antisocial offense, or family conflict. Treatment typically features psychotherapy and psychotropic drug therapy, with psychiatric diagnosis and planning for longer-term treatment elsewhere. Educators may provide services to maintain continuity of learning in collaboration with the child's school. There are about 18,000 identified students with ED in residential environments (USD Education, 2005).

Residential treatment centers and psychiatric hospitalization placements may be public or private and vary greatly in number of clients, range of services offered, and length of stay (a few weeks to many months or even several years). Often a stay begins with extensive psychological, social, medical, educational, and/or other assessment of the youth. As in day treatment, a range of interventions are delivered by specialized personnel, typically according to the institution's defined philosophy or model (Becker & DeAntonio, 2004; Chamberlain, 1999; Vargas & Brambila, 2005). As the time approaches for the young person's stay to end, psychiatric hospitals and residential treatment centers increase their interactions with families, schools, community agencies, and other components of a reintegration plan.

Psychiatric hospitals must be licensed medical institutions. Thus medical perspectives, personnel, and activities are much more prominent at psychiatric hospitals than residential treatment centers. Also, psychiatric hospitals tend to serve some children and adolescents that residential treatment centers decline to admit, such as those who evidence psychotic symptoms, Suicidality, extensive *Aggression*, or otherwise seem to need medical or very restrictive treatment (Menninger, 2005). Psychiatric and residential treatment institutions may cooperate by planning a period of control and stabilization in the former setting, followed by longer term treatment in the latter.

Residential treatment of Substance Misuse may take place in units of psychiatric hospitals or separate institutions specialized to treat this problem. Their treatment programs typically resemble those described previously in the discussion of day treatment, sometimes with the addition of physician-supervised detoxification, psychotropic drugs, other medical options, or a "therapeutic community" (therapeutic milieu specialized to support substance recovery; Pringle & Flanzer, 2005).

Residential institutions must provide lodging, food, medical care, and recreation, as well as treatment and education. All these aspects may be self-contained within the institution, or some may be provided by arrangement with other agencies (e.g., local schools).

### *Project Re-ED*

Nicholas Hobbs, a pioneering advocate for children's mental health, began in the 1960s to apply an ecological psychology perspective to the development of residential treatment for children with E&B disorder (Hobbs, 1966, 1974). He saw the need to remove the young person from his disturbed home and other ecosystems, then change them to better support the child upon return home. Hobbs believed that personal attributes of treatment personnel are as important as their intervention skills. Hobbs helped establish **Project Re-ED** "schools," actually residential treatment centers, with strong emphases on education and improved environments.

Children attended Re-ED schools from Sunday evening to Friday afternoon. Each day was carefully structured to facilitate learning, social, and academic responsibilities. Interdisciplinary staff teams featured the teacher-counselor. This was a unique Re-Ed professional who lived with a group of children, serving as their teacher, supervisor, counselor, friend, surrogate parent, and main treatment planner. Each teacher-counselor was selected as being "a decent adult . . . able to give and receive affection, to live relaxed, and to be firm; a person of hope, quiet confidence, and joy; one who has committed . . . to the proposition that children who are emotionally disturbed can be helped by the process of re-education" (Hobbs, 1966, p. 1107). Other staff members included the social worker and the liaison teacher, who facilitated each student's reentry into the community school.

Project Re-ED viewed parents as important partners. They attended group meetings and received training in parenting skills.

Project Re-ED concepts and practices have been widely adopted, often with modifications for application in other situations (Cantrell & Cantrell, 2002). Some of Hobbs' ideas inspired innovations in service to children with E&B disorders, such as the ecological concepts in "systems of care" and multisystemic therapy, described later.

### *Outdoor Challenges*
**Outdoor challenges** (also referred to as wilderness or adventure experiences) can be conceptualized as a form of residential treatment center relying heavily on an unusual kind of milieu therapy, usually without a physical structure. In outdoor challenges, small groups of adolescents travel to isolated, remote locations to be exposed to a series of increasingly demanding, unfamiliar adventure tasks that require courage and prosocial behaviors to master (Bacon & Kimball, 1989; Brown, 2005). The original program, Outward Bound, came to the U.S. in the 1960s. Although not intended to help troubled youths, it and similar programs are used for this purpose.

Outdoor challenge programs take many forms. Many last several weeks to several months, depending on purposes and participants. The unfamiliar adventure tasks (e.g., rock climbing, whitewater rafting, wilderness survival) are meant to seem difficult and dangerous while remaining low in actual risk. As successive adventures unfold, the student increasingly must learn camping and wilderness survival skills, cooperate with others to achieve goals, engage in individual and group problem-solving, and show the ability to lead as well as follow instructions.

The adult leader of a wilderness challenge functions as instructor, model, and therapist. He is an instructor of the physical skills needed to meet the outdoor challenges, a model of confidence, encouragement, problem-solving, leadership, and other desirable adult traits, and therapist who helps each youth recognize and understand the significance of his new accomplishments and behavior patterns. Therapy relies heavily on the natural consequences inherent in adventure tasks and the wilderness to reveal the futility of maladaptive social behaviors, clarify personal responsibility, and generally cause the teen to examine his thoughts, emotions, and behaviors. Throughout the program the leader encourages students to consider the implications of their actions and accomplishments, especially their development of new personal strengths, cooperation with others in solving significant problems, mastery of natural challenges, and growth of self confidence.

## Psychotropic Drug Therapy

A **psychotropic drug** is one administered to change a person's behavior, thinking, and/or emotions (Konopasek & Forness, 2004). Traditionally, a psychotropic is classified according to the main kind of changes observed in the early days of its use (usually with adults). Thus there are stimulant, antidepressant, antipsychotic, antimanic, and antianxiety classes. Additionally, there are drugs that do not fit well into even these general classes (Birmaher & Axelson, 2005; Scahill & Martin, 2002). Also, classes are sometimes subdivided: for example, "typical" antipsychotics (also termed traditional or first-generation) versus "atypical" (novel or second-generation) antipsychotics.

There are other ways to classify psychotropic drugs, but authorities do not agree on a preferred way. In part this is because new drugs and new uses for existing drugs frequently become available (Sussman, 2005). In fact, the major effect for which for some drugs are administered was neither predicted by its developers nor noted by its early prescribers.

A class name (e.g., stimulant) should not be taken too literally. For one thing, most drugs have several different effects, and these effects vary—a little or a lot, depending on the drug—across individuals. Different drugs in the same class would not be interchanged from day to day.

Obviously, some drug effects are beneficial—they are the reason for prescribing the drug. Others are detrimental "side effects," that is, undesired psychological or health consequences ranging from annoying to harmful or even life threatening. Based on reports from large numbers of patients administered a particular drug, the approximate chances of a beneficial or detrimental effect can be estimated. However, results for a particular person are often unpredictable.

Aside from individual variations, the effects of a drug on children and adolescents can be very different than its effects on adults (Birmaher & Axelson, 2005). While immature or undergoing growth spurts, human metabolism may incorporate or eliminate chemicals at a slower or faster rate than usual. This can change drug dosing (e.g., require higher or lower doses per pound and more or fewer doses per day). A drug effect may be negligible to mature body structures but damaging to those under development. Even a minor side effect may have different consequences for children and adults (e.g., weight gain may be so aversive to adolescents that they will not take the medication). Adult versus child drug effects is a big issue because most research on this topic involves adults only.

Selection of any medication should be based on not only beneficial and detrimental effects of the drug in general (i.e., based on research or at least reliable clinical reports), but individual circumstances. Significant examples include a young person's health conditions, medications she is already taking, and support for drug treatment available from her family.

Key psychotropic drugs used to treat young people are briefly summarized in Display 12-2 (see Birmaher & Axelson, 2005; Konopasek & Forness, 2004). About 50 percent of students with ED are prescribed one or more psychotropic drugs (Bradley, Henderson, & Monfore, 2004).

### Classes

Stimulants are mainly prescribed to treat *Diagnostic and Statistical Manual of Mental Disorders IV (DSM)* attention deficit/hyperactivity disorder (AD/HD) and the E&B disorder pattern *Impulsiveness*. They do so effectively in about 75 percent of cases. Detrimental side effects are uncommon even when stimulants are taken for many months. Typically, methylphenidate is tried first. If the young person's response is not satisfactory, a physician may prescribe other stimulants, then other psychotropics (e.g., tricyclic antidepressants, bupropion, atamoxetine).

*Antidepressants* are prescribed for young people experiencing *Depression*, depressive aspects of *DSM* Mood Disorders, and some problems involving *Anxiety*. Less commonly, antidepressants are used to treat AD/HD or *Impulsiveness* when other medications have failed, as well as other conditions. For *Depression*, SSRIs are often the first choice, followed by bupropion, venlafaxine, and monoamine oxidase inhibitors (MAOIs).

**Display 12-2** Main psychotropic drugs used to treat emotional and behavior disorders of young people

| Drug Class | Generic and Brand Name[1] | Potential Improvements | Potential Detriments[2] |
|---|---|---|---|
| Stimulant | dextroamphetamine (**Dexedrine**)<br>dextroamphetamine plus other amphetamine derivatives (**Adderall**)<br>methylphenidate (**Ritalin**) | • Impulsive behavior and cognition<br>• Hyperactivity<br>• Attention | Sleeplessness, reduced appetite, weight loss, increased blood pressure |
| Antidepressant (SSRI)[3] | fluoxetine (**Prozac**)<br>paroxetine (**Paxil**)<br>sertraline (**Zoloft**) | • Depression | Irritability, sleeplessness, nausea, headaches |
| Antidepressant (tricyclic) | amitriptyline (**Elavil**)<br>desipramine (**Norpramine**)<br>imipramine (**Tofranil**) | • Depression<br>• Anxiety<br>• Attention | Dry mouth, blurred vision, weight loss |
| Antidepressant (MAOI)[4] | phenelzine (**Nardil**) | • Depression<br>• Anxiety | Weight gain, sleeplessness, diet restrictions, blood pressure complications |
| Antidepressant (other) | venlafaxine (**Effexor**) | • Depression<br>• Anxiety | Nausea |
| | bupropion (**Wellbutrin**) | • Depression<br>• Hyperactivity<br>• Attention | Irritability, sleeplessness, nausea, headaches, seizures |
| Antipsychotic (typical) | chlorpromazine (**Thorazine**)<br>fluphenazine (**Prolixin**)<br>haloperidol (**Haldol**)<br>thioridazine (**Mellaril**)<br>thiothixene (**Navane**) | • Social, cognitive, and language functioning in psychotic disorders<br>• Mania<br>• Extreme aggression<br>• Social, cognitive, and other functioning in pervasive developmental disorders | Dry mouth, constipation, blurred vision, weight gain, restless feelings and behavior, tremors, rigidity, other involuntary muscle complications, heart problems |
| Antipsychotic (atypical) | aripiprazole (**Abilify**)<br>clozapine (**Clozaril**)<br>olanzapine (**Zyprexa**)<br>risperidone (**Risperdal**)<br>quetiapine (**Seroquel**)<br>ziprasidone (**Geodon**) | • Social, cognitive, and language functioning in psychotic disorders<br>• Mania<br>• Extreme aggression<br>• Social, cognitive, and other functioning in pervasive developmental disorders | Seizures, sedation, weight gain, blood problems |

| Drug Class | Generic and Brand Name[1] | Potential Improvements | Potential Detriments[2] |
|---|---|---|---|
| Antimanic | carbamazepine (**Tegretol**) lithium carbonate (**Eskalith**) valproate (**Depakote**) | • Mania<br>• Depression<br>• Aggression | Kidney problems, liver problems, tremors, memory problems, confusion, dizziness, sleeplessness, nausea |
| Antianxiety (benzo-diazepines) | alprazolam (**Xanax**) clonazepam (**Klonipin**) diazepam (**Valium**) lorazepam (**Ativan**) | • Anxiety | Drowsiness, agitation, confusion, nausea, heart irregularities, drug tolerance and abuse |
| Antianxiety (other) | buspirone (**BuSpar**) | • Anxiety | Dizziness, nausea |
| Miscellaneous | clonidine (**Catapres**) | • Aggression<br>• Hyperactivity<br>• Attention | Drowsiness, dry mouth, depression, nausea, heart irregularities; asthma worsened by propranolol |
| | propranolol (**Inderal**) | | Heart and blood pressure changes |
| | gabapentin (**Neurontin**) atamoxetine (**Strattera**) | • Anxiety<br>• Impulsive behavior and cognition<br>• Hyperactivity<br>• Attention | Nausea, sleepiness Mild heart and blood pressure changes |

[1] Many generic compounds are sold under more than one brand name. Brand given is for example only.

[2] Includes common and some uncommon problems, but not all problems reported. Usually problems can be reduced or eliminated by lowering dosage.

[3] Selective serotonin reuptake inhibitor

[4] Monoamine oxidase inhibitor

Sources: Birmaher & Axelson, 2005; Brown, 2005; Konopasek & Forness, 2004; Kubiszn, Carlson, & DeHay, 2005; Sussman, 2005.

*Antipsychotic* agents are administered to reduce delusions, illogical thought and language, hallucinations, and other positive psychotic symptoms in schizophrenia and other Psychotic Disorders. Certain antipsychotics can improve the value of antidepressants in the treatment of Mood Disorders and are sometimes used to reduce mania or agitation (intense, disorganized verbal and motor behavior), whether or not a person has a psychotic disorder.

*Antimanics* (mood stabilizers) include lithium, carbamazepine, valproate, certain antipsychotics, and several other drugs. Their main use is in controlling manic symptoms of *DSM* bipolar disorders. Also, they may be prescribed to reduce agitation or high levels of *Aggression*.

*Antianxiety* agents (anxiolytics) are widely prescribed for diverse psychological problems of adults, and they are often abused (e.g., Valium). For children and adolescents, their use is generally restricted to improvement of *Anxiety*.

*Miscellaneous psychotropics* do not seem to fit into a class or fit multiple classes. For instance, clonidine and propranolol are used for adult hypertension, but they are sometimes prescribed to reduce children's agitation, *Aggression*, and *Impulsiveness* when other treatments have not succeeded. Atamoxetine is prescribed as a substitute for stimulants that is less subject to improper use.

Various drugs are available that may ease withdrawal or other aspects of substance abuse treatment among adults. Their use with young people is not well researched (McLeer & Wills, 2000). Another kind of drug, *anticonvulsants*, is mainly used to control seizures. They are not considered psychotropics but occasionally are used as such if other medications have failed. Display 12-3 lists selected medications by the problems for which they are likely to be prescribed.

## *Concerns*

A main concern about psychotropics is safety. Research and the experience of clinicians indicate that stimulants and selective serotonin reuptake inhibitors (SSRIs), the most frequently prescribed psychotropics for children and adolescents, are relatively unlikely to produce serious side effects. The same may not be true about other psychotropics, on which there is relatively little research with young people.

Display 12-2 indicates some of the more commonly observed undesired effects. Rarely, there can be very serious effects such as skin, blood, liver, circulatory, respiratory, and neurological disorders and death. Serious side effects generally occur at high doses, in interaction with other drugs, or if the child has certain preexisting health conditions. They can be minimized through proper drug administration and monitoring, and most are reversible. On the other hand, effects such as those noted previously and in Display 12-2 refer mainly to short-term effects. There is little research on desired and undesired long-term effects of most psychotropics on children.

A related concern involves the prescribing of multiple psychotropics (Jensen et al., 1999). No particular psychotropic is invariably effective with a given pattern of E&B disorder, and except for stimulants and perhaps SSRI antidepressants, the success rate is probably less than 50%. As a result, physicians often try more than one psychotropic in sequence or at the same time to try to find a successful drug regimen. Another reason to prescribe multiple psychotropics is to address multiple E&B disorders (e.g., comorbidity). This can be effective and safe, but little is known about the effects, desired and undesired, of two or more psychotropic drugs in combination (or psychotropics combined with other kinds of medication).

Another concern can arise when psychotropics are not prescribed or administered as they should be. Recommended prescribing practices for psychotropics may

**Display 12-3** Psychotropic drugs with good or fair scientific support for effectiveness with E&B disorders of children and adolescents[1,2]

| Disorder | Good or Fair Support |
| --- | --- |
| Aggression | Antipsychotic class |
| | Antimanic class |
| Anxiety | Antidepressant (SSRI) |
| | Antianxiety class |
| Depression | Antidepressant (SSRI) |
| | Antidepressant (other) |
| | Antidepressant (MAOI) |
| Impulsiveness | Stimulant class |
| | Antidepressant (tricyclic) |
| | atamoxetine |
| | bupropion |
| Relationship Problem | |
| Mood Disorders (depressive aspects) | Antidepressant (SSRI) |
| Mood Disorders (manic aspects) | Antimanic class |
| Psychotic Disorders | Antipsychotic class |

[1] Judgement of "good or fair" is based on the author's assessment of reviews of psychotropic drug research with children and adolescents, including Birmaher and Axelson (2005) and Konopasek and Forness (2004).
[2] See Chapters 4 and 5 for descriptions of disorders.

call for thorough assessment, psychosocial intervention along with medication, and follow-up care, but such recommendations are not always followed (Hoagwood, Kelleher, Feil, & Comer, 2000). Also, patients do not always follow the prescribed regimen. The child or parents may forget doses or decide to discontinue without consulting the physician. The student may intentionally skip medications due to embarrassment or belief that it interferes with his performance (e.g., academic, sports). Children sometimes give or sell their medications to peers.

## *Teacher's Role*

Although the recommendation and implementation of drug therapy is the responsibility of physicians and parents, teachers have crucial roles as well. One is observation. Teachers can provide important feedback to the physician and parents by describing the child's behavior, thinking, emotions, and other aspects of functioning. The teacher may use informal reporting or various measurement procedures such as rating scales and target behavior recording.

The teacher's feedback when a psychotropic is being considered can help determine the need for medication. In the early stages of administration, or after changes in a medication, teacher observations can clarify good and bad effects and thus guide the physician's decisions. During and after the course of drug therapy the teacher's observations can help the physician judge the desirability of modifying dosage, changing psychotropics, or combining the drug with additional forms of intervention.

While monitoring the intended effects of a medication, teachers also need to know and recognize its unwanted side effects. Otherwise, drug side effects may be mistaken for new emotional or behavior problems, which could prompt a teacher to take actions that are not necessary (e.g., implement additional interventions, refer the student for different services or placement). Teachers should report troubling or persistent side effects to the parent or physician and be ready to adjust instruction (e.g., schedules, assignments) to accommodate temporary problems the student experiences due to side effects.

Another key teacher contribution is continuing to provide the most effective educational program possible. Psychotropic drug therapy cannot substitute for education. Teachers should try to ensure that parents and physicians understand the student's educational program and that they involve educators appropriately in drug therapy.

Finally, school systems ought to have a policy addressing the educator's role in drug therapy. It should reflect input from parents, teachers, physicians, legal experts, and others as appropriate. Such a policy might cover (a) required, allowed, and prohibited actions of school personnel; (b) procedures for encouraging increased communication between school and the prescribing physician; and (c) a school record-keeping system on drug therapy-by-student.

## CHILD AND FAMILY WELFARE SYSTEM

The child and family welfare system intervenes when parental care is insufficient (due to, e.g., physical or mental illness, substance abuse, incarceration, or other family crisis), neglectful, or abusive. Professionals may offer training and support to parents of such families. However, a child may be removed from his home if, following legal processes, it is determined that remaining at home will have significantly adverse effects on his health or development (Benoit, Nickman, & Rosenfeld, 2005; USD HHS, 1999).

In cases of parental illness or crisis, brief shelter or respite care is available until the home situation is stabilized or a longer term placement is arranged. The welfare system also provides for long-term removal in some cases of parental abuse or neglect. Among the placement options are foster homes, therapeutic foster care, therapeutic group homes, and larger child-care institutions (including residential mental health settings) (Benoit et al., 2005; Chamberlain & Friman, 1997; Rosenfeld, Altman, & Kaufman, 1997).

A considerable proportion of children entering the child and family welfare system have emotional and behavior problems and/or were maltreated, frequently by a drug abusing parent (Armsden, Pecora, Payne, & Szatkiewicz, 2000; Lyons & Rogers, 2005; Marx, Benoit, & Kamradt, 2003; McMillen et al., 2005). Also, the processes of removal from the home and foster placement can, understandably, generate further disturbances. Many foster children have been involved with the juvenile justice system and other service systems (Smith, 2004). However, most foster placements do not offer appropriate treatment and services for young people with E&B disorder. There has been some progress in addressing this problem (e.g., Webb & Harden, 2003).

### Foster Placements

Generally, a *foster home* is a natural family with one or a few children and two parents who are expected to provide a stable family situation for the foster child. Although by necessity many children and adolescents with E&B disorder are placed in foster homes, foster parents generally receive little training in providing treatment for E&B disorder. In some cases it is hoped that the stable family situation and parent-like care will deflect a trajectory toward emotional and behavior problems. Younger children are more likely to be placed in a foster home.

*Therapeutic foster care* (Chamberlain, 1999; Chamberlain & Friman, 1997) usually involves a home that serves just one young person who has considerable emotional and behavior problems. The parents are trained as mental health treatment providers, receive ongoing support and supervision from a child welfare agency, and may participate in a supportive network of fellow therapeutic foster parents. These parents use the family living situation as milieu therapy while implementing an individualized plan to improve the child's emotional and behavior functioning in home, community, and school. Together with the agency supervisor, they manage other needed services and requirements (e.g., contact with probation officers) and work with the child's family or guardian to facilitate reunion or with a family that will adopt.

A **therapeutic group home** involves several adolescents or children cared for by trained mental health providers, often a married couple, who establish a family-like environment in a local community. Therapeutic parents give intensive treatment in the home for emotional and behavior problems, and they maintain linkages with other needed services. The young person attends school locally. If she is expected to return to her family, family living becomes a major focus of psychosocial intervention. If feasible, parents are taught discipline and other parenting skills and given other support for keeping the family together.

### Teaching-Family Model

The Teaching-Family (T-F) Model of intervention (Blase, Fixsen, Freeborn, & Jaeger, 1989; Braukmann & Wolf, 1987; Kirigin & Wolf, 1998; Larzelere, Daly, Davis, Chmelka, & Handwerk, 2004) was developed by behaviorist psychologists as a community-based therapeutic group home program ("Achievement Place") for delinquent or otherwise antisocial young adolescents (Phillips, Fixsen, Phillips, & Wolf, 1979). A typical T-F program involves 6 to 10 adolescents residing with Teaching Parents, a specially trained husband-wife team. Teaching Parents provide a simulated home atmosphere; instruct a variety of academic, social, self-management, vocational, and other adaptive skills; and teach the young people to recognize the consequences of their behaviors.

The T-F Model has evolved (Larzelere et al., 2004) as it has been adapted to other groups (e.g., adolescents with E&B disorder, abused or homeless children) and settings (e.g., larger foster institutions or residential mental health settings) and in response to data from scientific evaluations (some treatment features have been added, modified, or discarded). Details vary from application to application, but the T-F Model embodies six major components.

***Functional Skills.*** First, a range of skills needed for successful adjustment in school, home, community, and other environments is identified. Upon entry, each young person's standing on these skills is assessed to find those that need special attention.

***Teaching.*** Teaching is the principal form of therapy in the T-F Model. Functional skill needs are taught through highly structured educational techniques. Teaching Parents must recognize adaptive and maladaptive behavior accurately and consistently in order to calmly enact the appropriate teaching response. The youth's adaptive behavior is encouraged, while maladaptive behavior is the opportunity for a specialized technique termed a *teaching interaction* (Display 12-4) in which the Teaching Parents encourage the youth to substitute prosocial behaviors for the maladaptive one.

***Points-and-Levels System.*** Participation and improvement are motivated through a token economy with levels (see Chapter 8). There is a most structured level for entering youths, in which the privileges of a comfortable life (e.g., opportunity to watch TV) must be earned on a daily or weekly basis by completing home and

**Display 12-4** Steps in the Teaching Family Model teaching interaction

1. Give initial praise
2. Describe maladaptive behavior
3. Provide negative consequence
4. Describe alternative adaptive behavior
5. Require practice of adaptive behavior
6. Provide feedback for practice
7. Provide positive consequence
8. Praise youth for participation in teaching interaction

school learning assignments and avoiding infractions that lose tokens (points). As a youth shows the capability to perform well in more structured levels of the token economy, he or she is advanced to less structured levels and eventually to no token system at all.

***Self-Government.*** Time is set aside for the adolescents to voice concerns that affect their relations with others and their progress toward leaving the T-F home. In self-government sessions, youths assist in the development of family rules, arbitrate rule violations, solve peer conflicts, and otherwise jointly take responsibility for the operation of the T-F home.

***Counseling.*** Teaching Parents provide counseling to help youths recognize, explore, and solve problems related to their parents, social conflicts, legal difficulties, and other personal issues. Relatedly, they manage each youth's participation in additional therapeutic services needed from community agencies.

***Community Generalization and Integration.*** A sixth component focuses on the generalization of behavior improvement to school, the youth's real home, and other settings. Because these children's adjustment problems often involve conflict with community people such as teachers, peers, police officers, employers, merchants, and neighbors, as well as parents and siblings, special efforts are made to address their community social conflicts.

Teaching Parents maintain close contacts with the local school in which a youth is enrolled (in fact, school-related behavior accounts for the majority of opportunities for a youth to earn points). Teaching Parents work with school staff in defining and assessing academic or conduct problems, and in maintaining a school-to-home feedback system. Additionally, the youth's natural family is given substantial training and follow-up consultation to help them maintain behavior improvements brought about in the T-F home.

## JUVENILE JUSTICE SYSTEM

Juvenile justice that is separate from the adult justice system, more lenient, and protective, rehabilitative, or therapeutic in nature has evolved for well over a century (Bartollas & Miller, 2005; Jackson & Knepper, 2003). Juvenile justice has many variations across jurisdictions, but in general (and in greatly simplified terms) there are several steps in common (Snyder & Sickmund, 1999).

### Juvenile Justice Process

Persons under a certain age (18 in most areas, for most offenses) can come to the attention of the juvenile court through police apprehension for an offense (80 to 90 percent of cases). Most of these offenses are *delinquencies*—law violations regardless of a person's age. Others, probably around 3 in 10, are **status offenses** (Snyder & Sickmund, 1999) involving behavior that is illegal only if performed by juveniles (e.g., beyond control of parents, curfew violations, truancy). There may also be a court referral from a private citizen (e.g., parent, neighbor, teacher) or a public agency (e.g., education). The vast majority of status offenses do not advance to juvenile court.

Many offenses are handled by law enforcement personnel who may warn and release the offender, offer informal supervision, or use another diversion option (described below). In other cases, law enforcement personnel refer the case to juvenile court.

A designated individual or group decides whether the referral justifies a request to the court for an adjudication hearing. Among options at this point are dismissing the referral for lack of evidence, handling it informally using a diversion option, requesting that the case be transferred to adult court jurisdiction, or requesting a juvenile court hearing.

The juvenile court may grant the request for an adjudication hearing but, before the hearing, offer diversion. This decision often depends on the youth's prior legal record and an admission of guilt.

If there is a hearing and the court determines that the child committed the offense, it may either elect probation with or without other diversion activities or adjudicate the youth as delinquent, making her or him (80 percent are males) a ward of the court.

## Diversion

Diversion is any disposition that prevents a juvenile experiencing the ordinary consequences of a particular offense. Diversion may be simple (officer warns, then releases) or complex (e.g., counseling plus social skills training plus 7 p.m. curfew plus requirement to pass all school subjects). Some diversion activities are listed in Display 12-5.

*Probation* is a form of diversion in which sentencing is postponed or sentencing occurs but activation of the sentence is postponed, contingent on a person's completion of specified requirements. Probation ordinarily involves a period of regular supervision. Often, probation is combined with other diversion activities.

### *Teen Court*

One interesting example of diversion is teen court (also referred to as youth or peer court). A teen court is a legally established agency of the court system that is empowered to provide sanctions and services to offenders. It uses adolescent volunteers in court roles ordinarily filled by professionals (Butts, Buck, & Coggeshall, 2002; Godwin, Steinhart, & Fulton, 1996). In different variations, they function as jurors, prosecuting and defending attorneys, or even judges. Some teen courts actually determine innocence or guilt; most decide consequences for youths who have acknowledged their guilt (Godwin et al., 1996). Consequences often include exposure to impact statements by the offender's victim or by other young people who

**Display 12-5** Examples of diversion activities that may be required of a juvenile offender

- Apologizing to victims
- Attending a trial
- Listening to impact statements by the victim of the offender
- Listening to panels of youth who have been harmed by behavior similar to that of the offender (e.g., substance abuse, dangerous driving)
- Making financial or other restitution to victims
- Meeting requirements such as school attendance and home curfews
- Participating in activities designed to increase awareness that illegal behavior can have serious consequences
- Participating in skill training sessions
- Paying a fine
- Performing community service
- Receiving a warning from police, judge, other court officers, with release and no conditions
- Receiving evaluation and/or treatment by a mental health service agency
- Taking part in a teen court case
- Touring police and detention facilities
- Writing essays on the harm created by one's offense

Source: Snyder & Sickmund, 1999.

have been harmed by behavior (e.g., shoplifting, vandalism, extortion, online slander, Substance Misuse, dangerous driving) similar to the offender's, teen court jury duty, and other diversion options.

Teen courts offer a way to hold juvenile offenders accountable for relatively minor offenses—mainly those involving vehicles, alcohol and drugs, shoplifting, vandalism, and fighting—that otherwise might receive no attention from juvenile courts engulfed by more serious offenses. Teen courts communicate to victims and the general public that the justice system is taking action, and they train and encourage youth volunteers—including some former offenders—to develop decision-making skills, leadership, and citizenship.

## Residential Placement

About 25 to 30 percent of young people adjudicated as delinquent are detained in a residential placement for a defined or indeterminate period, sometimes specified as a minimum length plus additional time that depends on behavior while in detention. Detention occurs at placements of widely varying sizes, degrees of security, regimentation, and harshness. These placements include residential treatment centers, therapeutic foster homes, and therapeutic group homes, as well as corrections institutions. When a delinquent is released from a residential placement he often remains for some time under "aftercare" (parole) supervision by juvenile justice personnel (Snyder & Sickmund, 1999).

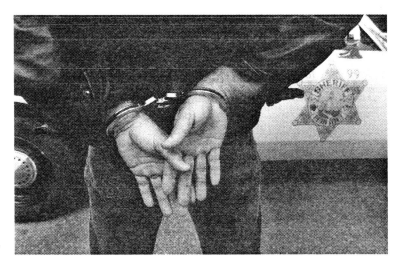

Perhaps two-thirds of adolescents with E&B disorder have been involved with the juvenile justice system.

## Delinquency and E&B Disorder

As indicated in Chapter 4, juvenile delinquency and E&B disorder are linked (Grisso, 2005). Many young people are juvenile offenders because they have exhibited behaviors that are not only illegal but can be indicative of E&B disorder, especially the *Aggression* pattern. An uncertain but large proportion of detained juvenile delinquents (variously estimated at 20 to 80 percent) have E&B disorders (Cocozza & Skowyra, 2000; Heffron, Pumariega, Fallon, & Carter, 2003; Leone & Cutting, 2004), largely involving conduct and defiant disorders and substance abuse. From a different perspective, disproportionately many adolescents with E&B disorder are suspected of having committed a crime; have had one or more court appearances, adjudications, or convictions; or have other direct experience with the juvenile justice system (Greenbaum et al., 1998; Wagner, 1995).

# NEW DIRECTIONS IN INTERVENTION SYSTEMS

## Need for Reform

Throughout the 20th century there were frequent alarms about the great numbers of poorly served children and adolescents with E&B disorder (Lourie, 2003; Zigler, Finn-Stevenson, & Tanner, 2002; see Display 2-4). For example, the Joint Commission on the Mental Health of Children (1969) called for a system that would deliver a range of effective, coordinated services to address the complex needs of children with E&B disorder. *Unclaimed Children* (Knitzer, 1982) documented chaotic, inappropriate services (e.g., residential placement far from home was the only choice for many families) and found that many government agencies were more concerned with self-preservation than children's welfare.

There were six main problems uncovered by the reformers (Henggeler and Santos, 1997; Oswald & Singh, 1996).

1. Many children and adolescents needed mental health services, but a large fraction—perhaps most—who needed services did not receive them.
2. Services within and across systems were poorly coordinated; especially for children who needed multiple services, this severely limited adequate intervention.
3. Use of more restrictive residential placements was encouraged by a lack of a continuum of treatment options in most localities, as well as by law, tradition, and other influences.
4. Collaboration between a family and service agencies, and among agencies, was discouraged by duplicate offerings in multiple agencies, as well as competition for funding and "turf."
5. In most efforts to provide services to children with E&B disorder the family was ignored or disregarded and sometimes excluded (e.g., required to give up custody for treatment, blamed for the E&B disorder).
6. Services were most deficient for race-ethnically diverse families whose proportion of the U.S. population was increasing.

To one extent or another all of these problems persist in the 21st century.

However, such criticisms and related events have brought reform (Stroul, 2003). In 1984, the Child and Adolescent Service System Program (CASSP) was created as a part of the federal National Institute of Mental Health. It was designed to help states and communities develop children's mental health services by:

1. Requiring mental health agencies to work collaboratively with other public agencies serving children
2. Encouraging community-based services
3. Including family members in the advocacy for and planning of child services
4. Addressing special needs of race-ethnically diverse children and families
5. Improving leadership and administration of children's mental health

Private charitable organizations have funded community and state efforts to develop, implement, and evaluate programs that address the CASSP recommendations. Federal agencies and regulations have further prompted states to establish community-based services for children with E&B disorder and have funded services all around the U.S. that exemplify principles and concepts developed under CASSP (Lourie, 2003).

## System of Care

Most of this wide variety of reforms in policy and practice for serving young people with E&B disorder are encompassed by the concept of **system of care**. CASSP supported the development of an influential monograph, *A System of Care for Children* *and Youth With Severe Emotional Disturbance* (Stroul & Friedman, 1986), that defined a system of care, presented its philosophy, identified main elements of such a system, and described how it might operate in local communities. The system of care and related concepts have given direction to parents, professionals, and policy makers who wish to implement system of care principles (e.g., Friedman, 2003; Pumariega, 2005; Stroul, 2003).

## *Definition and Philosophy*

A *system of care* is "a comprehensive spectrum of mental health and other necessary services which are organized into a coordinated network to meet the multiple and changing needs of severely emotionally disturbed children and adolescents" (Stroul & Friedman, 1986, p. iv). Differences in location, other circumstances, and guiding theoretical assumptions create variations among different systems of care (Stroul, 2003). However, all should reflect the system of care philosophy, which is captured by three core values (see Display 12-6) along with 10 guiding principles associated with them.

In brief, the guiding principles state that there must be a sufficient variety of services to address individual problems and strengths, provided in the least restrictive environment, and governed by family decisions. Services and other help should be coordinated across agencies and over time by case managers (Winters & Terrell,

**Display 12-6** Eight dimensions of service function in a system of care

| Service Function Dimension | Representative Services |
|---|---|
| 1. Mental health | Prevention, early intervention, home-based services, outpatient services, day treatment, residential treatment, independent living services |
| 2. Social | Protective services, financial help, respite for family, therapeutic foster care, adoption |
| 3. Educational | Assessment and planning, resource teaching, self-contained classes, special schools, residential schools |
| 4. Health | Preventive education, screening, acute care, long-term care |
| 5. Substance abuse | Prevention, outpatient or day treatment, detoxification, community residential, hospitalization |
| 6. Vocational | Career education, assessment, vocational training, work experiences, employment services, supported employment |
| 7. Recreational | Relationships with significant others, after-school programs, summer camps, special recreational projects |
| 8. Operational | Case management, transportation, family support groups, juvenile justice services, advocacy, legal services |

*Sources:* Stroul, 2003; Stroul & Friedman, 1986.

2003). Systems of care must provide for early detection and intervention, protect against race-ethnic and cultural discrimination, and advocate for family and child rights (see Cook-Morales, 2002; Eber & Keenan, 2004; Stroul & Friedman, 1986).

### Core Value 1: Child-Centered and Family-Focused

***Problems Addressed.*** Over the years professionals and agencies have tended to base service efforts on the assumption that parents cause their child's problems. As a result, service providers rarely allowed parents to contribute to planning for services, helped them find and choose from a range of services, or supported their efforts to raise the child (e.g., by teaching specialized discipline techniques or providing respite care). Providers offered servicers on a "take-it-or-leave-it" basis, requiring individual family needs to fit available services. Rarely did service agencies advocate for these children's or families' rights and interests.

***Solutions.*** The system of care concept puts children and families first, at the family level and at the system level.

1. At the *family level*, there is no focus on family members as causes of the E&B disorder. Instead, families are targets for change, partners in the process of selecting and obtaining services, providers of services for their child, advocates for their own needs and their child's, and evaluators of services. To enable them to play these roles in the system of care, families are taught and helped to take a major role in assessing their own needs and strengths; identifying barriers to service and service possibilities; and planning, implementing, and evaluating services.

   Problems, strengths, and obstacles are assessed. The problems and, importantly, strengths of young people and their families are assessed so that service decisions can be made on an individual, case-by-case basis. Traditional services (e.g., mental health system) as well as community or other nontraditional support possibilities are considered as intervention resources. Obstacles that may affect services are also inventoried.

   Professionals, families, and others who may be involved jointly decide needed services, desired outcomes, and other steps in the plan. Families' identified needs are emphasized, and the system of care plan is individualized. The broad scope of possible services is suggested by Display 12-7 (see also Epstein et al., 2005; Stroul, 2003). Some are provided by the traditional service systems, others by nontraditional organizations or persons, official or informal, public or private. Special education services may be prominent in the system of care plan (Eber & Keenan, 2004).

   Once a plan is developed, its implementation is often characterized by the concepts of "whatever it takes," strength-based services, unconditional care, and wraparound. *Whatever it takes* means that services reach across traditional systems and beyond them. Services traditionally associated with mental health, child and family welfare, juvenile justice, education, and other systems are often supplemented by help recruited from among friends, neighbors, extended family members, church, volunteer organizations, and other sources in the natural environment.

**Display 12-7** Core values for the system of care

The system of care must be:
1. Child Centered and Family Focused — With the needs of the child and family determining the number and kinds of services provided
2. Community Based — With the location of services, management, and decision-making responsibility remaining at the community level
3. Culturally Competent — With agencies, programs, and services that are responsive to the cultural, racial, and ethnic differences of the populations they serve

*Sources:* Stroul, 2003; Stroul & Friedman, 1986.

Some barriers to a successful outcome can be eliminated through creative use of resources. For example, "flexible funds" (Elliott, Koroloff, Koren, & Friesen, 1998) can facilitate access to mental health services or to solve family problems that impede intervention goals. Possible uses of flexible funds are suggested in Display 12-8.

The *strength-based* concept focuses on strengths or assets of the child, family, and other aspects of the situation. Strength-based assessment of the child might measure emotional and behavioral skills and characteristics important to the child's personal, social, and academic development, satisfactory relationships, ability to deal with stress, and feelings of accomplishment. For example, the *Behavioral and Emotional Rating Scale–Revised* (Epstein, 2004) assesses the young person's social strengths, family involvement, inner strengths, school functioning, and affective strengths. Other strength-based assessment may identify supportive possibilities in family, neighborhood, school, and community (e.g., extended family, positive peer group possibilities, church recreation opportunities). Strength-based assessment often facilitates informal, community-based solutions to problems.

*Unconditional care* dictates that service will continue regardless of setbacks. In a system of care, problems such as aversive or self-defeating behavior by the child or family do not justify suspending services.

*Wraparound* (Epstein et al., 2005; Smith-Boydston, 2005; Walker & Schutte, 2004) places the child and family within an array of coordinated mental health and other services. A case manager integrates these services by working closely with the family in assessment, planning, and delivery of individualized services and modification of the plan as needed.

2. At the *system level*, families have considerable input into the development, evaluation, and implementation of a system of care. They help develop and adjust the system by, for instance, participating in focus groups and interviews that identify their good and bad experiences with and preferences for various services.

**Display 12-8** Illustrative uses and purposes of flexible funds

| Use | Purposes | Example of Expenditure |
|---|---|---|
| Respite | Relieve stress of living with a child with E&B disorder; strengthen parents' marriage; strengthen relationships between parents and the sibling(s) of the child with E&B disorder | Payment for child care while parents enjoy an evening or a weekend away from child-raising; family passes to an amusement park |
| Transportation | Enable attendance by the child or family at intervention services where there is no public transit | Bus or cab fare, gasoline and repairs to family automobile |
| Family sustenance | Keep the family in treatment | Rent payment to prevent forced moving during temporary threat of housing loss |
| Child care | Allow the child and family to participate in intervention services | In-home or out-of-home child care for the child's siblings |
| Recreation and leisure | Support the development of a young person's or family's social competence; enable the young person's participation in positive adjustment activities in the school and community | Music or martial arts lessons, summer camp fees, sports or recreation equipment, prom dress |

Source: Elliott et al., 1998.

Participating families help evaluate the system by identifying worthwhile service outcomes, considering evaluation instruments, and helping collect data.

Further, many systems of care hire family members to help implement the system in various capacities. For instance, parents who formerly were clients might be hired to advocate for new families and to help the parents understand and obtain services, access informal community networks, solve family management and financial problems, and develop self-reliance (Elliott et al., 1998).

### Core Value 2: Community Based

**Problems Addressed.** There are roughly three quarters of a million U.S. children in out-of-home placements at some time during each year (see Benoit et al., 2005; Snyder & Sickmund, 1999). Most are in child and family welfare (e.g., foster care) and juvenile justice placements. An unknown but probably large proportion have E&B disorder (Benoit et al., 2005; Leone & Cutting, 2004). Traditionally, many children with E&B disorder and their families have had to travel significant distances to receive mental health services. Sometimes this involves placement in a distant residential treatment center or psychiatric hospital. Some residential placements require parents to give custody of their child to a government agency.

Residential placements are costly (Vargas & Brambila, 2005). In recent years roughly three quarters of financial resources for children's mental health services were used to serve the minority of young people in residential treatment or hospital placements (Burns et al., 1998). Moreover, there is not much evidence for the overall effectiveness of residential placements for young people with E&B disorder (USD HHS, 1999). Cost and effectiveness problems aside, many system-of-care advocates maintain strong philosophical opposition to distant residential placements, because they are highly restrictive treatment environments (Pumariega, 2005).

**Solutions.** The system of care strives for services provided in the youth's local community. Key decisions regarding types, coordination, management, and funding of services are to be made at the community level.

To increase community ownership of community problems and solutions, a system of care places local persons on its boards, committees, and other planning and policy bodies. As noted, parents and other community people are employed as service staff. Natural, informal helping networks are built and strengthened by getting input and support for families from community sources such as churches, other organizations, and neighborhood leaders.

### *Core Value 3: Culturally Competent*

**Problems Addressed.** There are insufficient services for E&B disorder available to race-ethnic minority children and families. The relationship between minority race-ethnic status and E&B disorder of U.S. children is complex, but it is clear that many race-ethnic minority children grow up in family, neighborhood, educational, and economic situations associated with high risk for patterns of E&B disorder, the connected problems described in Chapter 4, and other forms of maladjustment (Osher et al., 2004).

Additionally, race-ethnic minority persons tend to experience obstacles to treatment and service availability (Pumariega, 2003, 2005; USD HHS, 1999), such as unfamiliarity with the services available and mistrust of agencies staffed mostly by European American professionals. Services to treat E&B disorder often do not meet the mental health, educational, and related needs of children and adolescents of diverse race-ethnic status or address such needs in ways that violate Core Values 1 and 2 (Isaacs-Shockley, Cross, Bazron, Dennis, & Benjamin, 1996).

**Solutions. Cultural competence** for a system of care has been defined as a set of "behaviors, attitudes, and policies that come together in a system, agency, or amongst professionals . . . [enabling them] to work effectively in cross-cultural situations" (Cross, Bazron, Dennis, & Isaacs, 1989, p. iv). To achieve cultural competence an individual may first need to attain awareness of traditions, beliefs, and value systems of her or his own culture and other cultures, in order to appreciate cultural differences without making any judgments of superiority or inferiority (Singh, 1998). Recommended actions and policies for achieving a culturally competent system of care are presented in Display 12-9 (see also Benjamin & Isaacs-Shockley, 1996; USD HHS, 1999).

**Display 12-9** Steps in a system of care's achieving cultural competence

| Step | System of Care Action or Recognition |
| --- | --- |
| 1. Value diversity | Recognize that the children and families it serves are from different race-ethnic cultures and that they will make service and treatment choices based on their culture. |
| 2. Conduct cultural self-assessments | Assess the system's values and attitudes toward culture and how values and attitudes affect beliefs and behaviors of staff. |
| 3. Understand dynamics of diversity | Recognize that when professionals from one race-ethnic culture provide services to consumers of a different race-ethnic culture, communications and behaviors are likely to be misinterpreted. |
| 4. Institutionalize cultural knowledge | Through staff training and development activities, systematically incorporate information about cultures and how culture influences the behavior of staff and consumers. |
| 5. Adapt to diversity | Adapt system of care policies, services, assessments, and interactions with families based on knowledge about cultural diversity. |

*Sources:* Hernandez & Isaacs, 1998; Stroul & Friedman, 1986.

Although this core value was meant to address subcultural differences involving race-ethnic minority status, implicitly cultural competence is relevant to religious or spiritual beliefs, socioeconomic status, and other cultural differences (Singh, 1998). This core value directs service providers' attention to the subcultural context in which a child is raised and a family makes its choices (Coatsworth, Szapocznik, Kurtines, & Santisteban, 1997; Wright & Phillips-Smith, 1998). This makes it fundamental to carrying out Core Values 1 and 2. Cultural competence issues may influence referrals for services, assessment of problems and strengths, hiring and training of staff, kind and degree of family involvement in delivering services, the nature and location of services (McCabe et al, 1999), and other essential aspects of a system of care.

### *Developing a System of Care*

A variety of system of care programs have been and continue to be developed, supported by federal, state, and local governments and private organizations. Some have been statewide programs, others local. Many have creative features, often installed as adjustments to obstacles, political realities, and other particulars (see, e.g., Epstein, Kutash, & Duchnowski, 2005; Holden et al, 2003; Stroul, 2003). A strength of the system of care approach is the general nature of its Core Values and guiding principles, because they accommodate a wide range of specific circumstances.

Epstein et al. (1993) identified six points of special concern in the development and operation of a good system of care. These points help developers put system of care Core Values and guiding principles into action.

1. *Interagency collaboration* requires participating child service agencies to specify responsibilities, finances, planning, and collaboration in service delivery. Agencies and family members meet regularly about services to adjust treatment strategies as needed.
2. *Define the target population.* Systems of care focus on locally defined groups. Localities and special interests differ as to what needs they see as most important.
3. *Principles of care.* Professionals, families, and policy makers should agree on "principles of care" that address goals, accessibility, family involvement, coordination across services, evaluation, and other points of importance.
4. *Needs and resources assessment.* It is essential to understand the needs of children and families, the positives and negatives of existing services, and the community assets that might be a resource in the system of care.
5. *Individualized care* requires tailoring a program to the child's needs rather than fitting the child into existing services. Individualized care is delivered through case management, guided by the unconditional care concept (Winters & Terrell, 2003).
6. *Commitment to evaluation.* To hold services accountable, responsive, and effective, evaluation should address child and family functioning, family involvement in planning and treatment, interagency collaboration (Doucette-Gates, 2000), use of various services, family satisfaction with the system, and cost.

### *Education in the System of Care*

Education continues to be an important part of some systems of care (Eber & Keenan, 2004; Porter, Pearson, Keenan, & Duval-Harvey, 2003). Some call for system of care services or comprehensive mental health services to be based in and coordinated from the school (Jacobs, Randall, Vernberg, Roberts, & Nyre, 2005; Nastasi, Moore, & Varjas, 2003; Porter et al., Weist, 1997), pointing out advantages such as coverage (schools are located nearly everywhere and attended by nearly all children), reduced stigma (schools already deliver a variety of services, including services for students with ED), and other benefits. However, integrating special and regular education with the other aspects of a system of care can encounter significant obstacles, such as funding complications, training issues, and disputes over the control of school policies and practices.

System of care projects in which schools have played a large role can provide demonstrations and lessons for reform efforts (see Eber & Keenan, 2004; Epstein et al., 2005). Woodruff et al (1999) summarized the following important features of successful school-based systems of care:

1. Schoolwide prevention is a main emphasis.
2. Educators contact, advocate for, and empower families to participate in system of care efforts.

3. The student is served at school, home, and in the community by diverse professions, including those in mental health, child and family welfare, and juvenile justice.
4. Using the concept of wraparound, a school-based case manager coordinates agency and informal services to support the student.

## Other Reforms in Service to Children with E&B Disorder

### Home-Based Services
Home-based services (also referred to as family preservation, family reunification, or intensive family services) refers to intensive intervention in the home of a young person at risk for or presently in a residential placement (Adnopoz, 2002). Home-based services are designed to prevent placement out of the home or return out-placed (often abused) children to their families (Fraser, Nelson, & Rivard, 1997). Like many system of care interventions, home-based services offer family involvement at all stages; coordination of all services by a case manager; 24-hour-a-day crisis and backup services; assistance with family economic needs; individualized counseling for parenting, marital, and other needs; and strengthening of the family's ability to independently obtain services and community supports on their own (USD HHS, 1999).

***Multisystemic Therapy.*** **Multisystemic Therapy** (MST) is a home-based service that is aligned with the ecological model of E&B disorder. The creators of MST view deviant child behavior as stemming from dysfunctional interactions among the child and the ecosystems in which the child operates (see Huey, Henggeler, Brondino, & Pickrel, 2000). MST begins by assessing each of these ecosystems to identify components that contribute to deviant functioning and other components that do or could support adaptive functioning. From such information, intervention is designed to modify ecosystems in ways that reduce dysfunctional interactions and support adaptive behavior (Henggeler, Schoenwald, Borduin, Rowland, & Cunningham, 1998; Randall & Henggeler, 1999; Rowland et al., 2005; Schoenwald, Borduin, & Henggeler, 1998; Schoenwald & Henggeler, 1999).

MST is designed to enable families to modify and control ecosystems so as to help their children behave adaptively immediately, avoid a correctional or other residential placement, and achieve adequate adjustment in the long run. The specific intervention techniques used vary depending on the diverse situations of children and families served, but all such techniques reflect MST's guiding principles (see Display 12-10). MST has been used mainly with adolescent antisocial behavior (e.g., chronic, violent delinquency, substance use, sex offenses). It has also been modified to fit other problems (e.g., adolescents at risk of psychiatric emergencies, experiencing *Anxiety, Depression*, and Suicidality).

### Support Organizations
There are strong national and local support and advocacy organizations for young people with E&B disorder and their families. The Federation of Families for Children's Mental Health is a national organization run by parents, focused on the

**Display 12-10** Guiding principles in delivering Multisystemic Therapy

| | | |
|---|---|---|
| 1. | Ecological assessment | Multisystemic Therapy (MST) assessment clarifies how ecosystems interact with each other and with the young person's behavior to promote behavior problems and adaptive behavior. |
| 2. | Strength focus | MST intervention is based on strengths of the child and his ecosystems. |
| 3. | Responsibility | MST intervention encourages responsible behaviors and discourages irresponsible behaviors on the part of the child and the family. |
| 4. | Specific behaviors | MST intervention addresses specific child and family actions that will improve specific problems with present and future adaptation. |
| 5. | Ecosystem changes | MST intervention attempts to change identified ecosystem interactions that encourage continuation of the child's behavior problems. |
| 6. | Developmental adaptation | MST intervention is adapted to the child's age and developmental level. |
| 7. | Frequent efforts | MST intervention requires frequent, regular, specific, verifiable acts of effort on the part of the child and the family. |
| 8. | Data-based decisions | MST intervention is evaluated through data collected in multiple ways from multiple sources to judge progress, identify obstacles, and make needed intervention changes. |
| 9. | Generalization | MST intervention teaches and enables families to affect multiple ecosystems and service systems so that they can continue to raise their child in ways that will maintain generalized behavior improvement across situations and over time. |

*Source:* Randall & Henggeler, 1999.

needs of children and youth with E&B disorder and their families. The Federation provides leadership in maintaining a network of family-directed organizations around the nation. It supports families, ensures access to community-based services, and advocates prevention, education, and other appropriate services for children and youth with E&B disorder and their families.

*NAMI* (formerly National Alliance for the Mentally Ill) is a nonprofit, grassroots organization of people with severe mental illness and their families and friends. With more than 1,200 branches mainly in the U.S., NAMI works at national, state, and local levels to support children and adults with E&B disorder, especially severe forms of E&B disorder, through advocacy, education, research, networking, taking public positions on relevant issues, and other ways. NAMI has special services for children and adolescents and their families.

The National Mental Health Association is a nonprofit organization with a nationwide network of affiliate groups that addresses mental health and mental disorders through advocacy, education, research, and service. Advocacy for children's E&B disorder issues is one of its thrusts.

# CHAPTER SUMMARY

Educators of students with ED interact with other service systems, especially mental health, child and family welfare, and juvenile justice.

- Services in these systems:
  — Are organized according to the least restrictive environment
  — Often combine with each other and with education services
  — Work for prevention as well as intervention
  — Overlap considerably
- Mental health services feature verbal interaction psychotherapies, other forms of psychosocial intervention, and psychotropic drug therapy, delivered in outpatient, day treatment, and residential settings.
- Six classes of psychotropic drug are:
  — Stimulant
  — Antidepressant
  — Antipsychotic
  — Antimanic
  — Antianxiety
  — Miscellaneous
- Educators have significant roles to play in psychotropic drug therapy.
- Child and family welfare services support children whose parental care is insufficient.
- Welfare services work with the parents and/or remove the child from the home. If removed, the child is probably placed in a foster home, therapeutic foster care, therapeutic group home, or institution. In the latter three placements, children with E&B disorder may receive mental health treatment.
- Many children and adolescents with E&B disorder commit legal offenses and enter the juvenile justice system.
- They may receive probation, teen court, or other diversion option before or after reaching juvenile court, or may be adjudicated and placed in detention. Some diversion and detention options include mental health treatment.
- Decades of criticism of services for young people with E&B disorder led to major innovations, especially networks of services termed systems of care.
- A system of care is committed to services that are:
  — Child-centered and family-focused
  — Community based
  — Culturally competent
- Systems of care emphasize:
  — Collaboration across agencies
  — Responsiveness to families served and other local community concerns
  — Individualized services
  — Evaluation

## Ideas for Consideration and Discussion

1. Examine the listing of risk factors for antisocial behavior by developmental periods (Display 12-1). Propose a different prevention activity for each developmental period that might interrupt the undesired life trajectory. Justify your proposed activities.
2. a. Describe appropriate roles for teachers, school psychologists, and other education professionals in psychotropic drug therapy for young people.
   b. State possible issues and obstacles that may arise in regard to these educator roles.
   c. Create in outline form a school district policy that addresses these roles.
3. On a 3 × 5 card, create in outline form a three- to five-minute talk on psychotropic medications for students with ED. Assume that you will give the talk in one of your school's staff meetings. Practice your talk on your classmates, who will evaluate its strengths and weaknesses.
4. Name and describe three kinds of foster placement.
5. Describe the several steps commonly found in the juvenile justice process.
6. Name and describe the three core values in a system of care. For each core value,
   a. state problems it is intended to address.
   b. imagine problems that may arise in implementing it.

## Resources for Further Study

www.aecf.org/ Annie E. Casey Foundation
www.kidsmentalhealth.org/ Center for the Advancement of Children's Mental Health
www.aacap.org/publications/factsfam/86.htm Child psychotherapies
www.cwla.org/whowhat/default.htm Child Welfare League of America
www.apa.org/divisions/div37/ Child, Youth, and Family Services Division of American Psychological Association
gucchd.georgetown.edu/programs/ta_center/topics/early_childhood.html Early childhood mental health support
www.FFCMH.ORG/ Federation of Families for Children's Mental Health
www.mentalhealth.samhsa.gov/databases/ Locate U.S. mental health services
www.aacap.org/Announcements/psychiatricmeds.htm Medications and children
www.mstservices.com/ Multisystemic Therapy
www.nami.org/Template.cfm?Section=Child_and_Adolescent_Action_Center National Alliance for the Mentally Ill (NAMI)
www.nasponline.org/index.html National Association of School Psychologists
gucchd.georgetown.edu/nccc/ National Center for Cultural Competence
www.nmha.org/children/index.cfm National Mental Health Association (child concerns)
www.kidspeace.org/contact.htm National support for troubled children and adolescents
gucchd.georgetown.edu/programs/ta_center/index.html National Technical Assistance Center for Children's Mental Health
www.nimh.nih.gov/publicat/childmed.cfm NIMH: Your child and medication
cecp.air.org/prev-ei/best.asp Prevention in community and school

**www.rtc.pdx.edu/** Research and Training Center for Children's Mental Health
**www.apa.org/about/division/div16.html** School Psychology Division of American Psychological Association
**www.air.org/cecp/resources/statemh.htm** State contacts for mental health programs for children
**www.teaching-family.org/tfamodel.html** Teaching-Family Model
**www.teencentral.net/preview/default.asp** Teen-friendly site for sharing problems and solutions
**www.girlsandboystown.org/hotline/index.asp** Toll free hotline for kids with problems
**www.mentalhealth.samhsa.gov/** U.S. Center for Mental Health Services
**ojjdp.ncjrs.org/** U.S. Office of Juvenile Justice and Delinquency Prevention

# References

Aarons, G. A., Brown, S. A., Hough, R. L., Garland, A. F., & Wood, P. A. (2001). Prevalence of adolescent substance use disorders across five sectors of care. *Journal of the American Academy of Child and Adolescent Psychiatry, 40*, 416–426.

Abramson, L. Y., Seligman, M. E. P., & Teasdale, J. (1978). Learned helplessness in humans: Critique and reformulation. *Journal of Abnormal Psychology, 87*, 49–74.

Achenbach, T. M. (1982). *Developmental psychopathology* (2nd ed.). New York: Wiley.

Achenbach, T. M. (1995). Developmental issues in assessment, taxonomy, and diagnosis of child and adolescent psychopathology. In D. Cicchetti & D. J. Cohen (Eds.), *Developmental psychopathology: Vol. 1. Theory and methods* (pp. 57–80). New York: Wiley.

Achenbach, T. M. (2000). Assessment of psychopathology. In A. J. Sameroff, M. Lewis, & S. M. Miller (Eds.), *Handbook of developmental psychopathology* (2nd ed.) (pp. 41–56). New York: Kluwer Academic/Plenum.

Achenbach, T. M., & Edelbrock, C. S. (1978). The classification of child psychopathology: A review and analysis of empirical efforts. *Psychological Bulletin, 85*, 1275–1301.

Achenbach, T. M., & McConaughy, S. H. (2003a). *School based practitioners' guide for the ASEBA*, Burlington, VT: University of Vermont, Research Center for Children, Youth, & Families.

Achenbach, T. M., & McConaughy, S. H. (2003b). The Achenbach System of Empirically Based Assessment. In C. R. Reynolds & R. W. Kamphaus (Eds.), *Handbook of psychological and educational assessment of children: Personality, behavior, and context* (2nd ed., pp. 406–432). New York: Guilford.

Achenbach, T. M., & Rescorla, L. A. (2001). *Manual for ASEBA school-age forms and profiles*. Burlington, VT: University of Vermont, Research Center for Children, Youth, and Families.

Adams, H. E., Luscher, K. A., & Bernat, J. A. (2001). The classification of abnormal behavior: An overview. In P. B. Sutker & H. E. Adams (Eds.), *Comprehensive handbook of psychopathology* (3rd ed., pp. 3–28). New York: Kluwer Academic/Plenum.

Adams, R. L., & Culbertson, J. L. (2005). Personality assessment: Adults and children. In B. J. Sadock & V. A. Sadock (Eds.), *Kaplan & Sadock's comprehensive textbook of psychiatry* (Vol. I, pp. 874–895). Philadelphia: Lippincott Williams & Wilkins.

Adnopoz, J. (2002). Home-based treatment for children with serious emotional disturbance. In D. T. Marsh & M. A. Fristad (Eds.), *Handbook of serious emotional disturbances in children and adolescents* (pp. 334–350). New York: Wiley.

Agras, W. S., & Wilson, G. T. (2005). Learning theory. In B. J. Sadock & V. A. Sadock (Eds.), *Kaplan & Sadock's comprehensive textbook of psychiatry,* (Vol. I, pp. 541–552). Philadelphia: Lippincott Williams & Wilkins.

Aichhorn, A. (1965). *Wayward Youth*. New York: Viking Press.

Akiskal, H. S. (2005). Mood disorders: Clinical features. In B. J. Sadock & V. A. Sadock (Eds.), *Kaplan & Sadock's comprehensive textbook of psychiatry,* (Vol. I, pp. 1611–1651). Philadelphia: Lippincott Williams & Wilkins.

Albano, A. M. (2003). Treatment of social anxiety disorder. In M. A. Reinecke, F. M. Dattilio, & A. Freeman (Eds.), *Cognitive therapy with children and adolescents* (2nd ed., pp. 128–161). New York: Guilford.

Albano, A. M. (2005). Cognitive-behavioral psychotherapy for children and adolescents. In B. J. Sadock & V. A. Sadock (Eds.), *Kaplan & Sadock's comprehensive textbook of psychiatry* (Vol. II, pp. 3332–3341). Philadelphia: Lippincott Williams & Wilkins.

Albano, A. M., Chorpita, B. F., & Barlow, D. H. (2003). Childhood anxiety disorders. In E. J. Mash & R. A. Barkley (Eds.), *Child psychopathology* (2nd ed., pp. 279–329). New York: Guilford.

Albano, A. M., & Krain, A. (2005). Anxiety and anxiety disorders in girls. In D. J. Bell, S. L. Foster, & E. J. Mash (Eds.), *Handbook of behavioral and emotional problems in girls* (pp. 79–116). New York: Kluwer Academic/Plenum.

Alberg, J., Petry, C., & Eller, S. (1994). *A social skills planning guide*. Longmont, CO: Sopris West.

Albert, L. (1989). *A teacher's guide to Cooperative Discipline: How to manage your classroom and promote self-esteem.* Circle Pines, MN: American Guidance Service.

Alberto, P. A., & Troutman, A. C. (2006). *Applied behavior analysis for teachers* (7th ed.). Upper Saddle River, NJ: Merrill/Prentice Hall.

Albrow, M. (1999). *Sociology: The basics*. London: Routledge.

Alexandrin, J. R. (2003). Using continuous, constructive, classroom evaluations. *Teaching Exceptional Children, 36*, 52–57.

Allen, D. E., Hart, B. M., Buell, J. S., Harris, T. R., & Wolf, M. M. (1964). Effects of social reinforcement on isolate behavior of a nursery school child. *Child Development, 35*, 511–518.

Allen, J. S., Bruss, J., & Damasio, H. (2004). The structure of the human brain. *American Scientist, 92*, 246–253.

Allen, J. C., & Hollifield, J. (2003). Using the Rorschach with children and adolescents: The Exner Comprehensive System. In C. R. Reynolds & R. W. Kamphaus (Eds.), *Handbook of psychological and educational assessment of children: Personality, behavior, and context* (2nd ed., pp. 182–198). New York: Guilford.

Al Otaiba, S., & Rivera, M. O. (2006). Individualizing guided oral reading fluency instruction for students with emotional and behavioral disorders. *Intervention in School and Clinic, 41*, 144–149.

American Academy of Child and Adolescent Psychiatry (AACAP). (2001). Practice parameter for the assessment and treatment of children and adolescents with schizophrenia. *Journal of the American Academy of Child and Adolescent Psychiatry, 40* (Suppl.), 4S–23S.

American Psychiatric Association. (1952). *Diagnostic and statistical manual of mental disorders*. Washington, DC: Author.

American Psychiatric Association. (2000). *Diagnostic and statistical manual of mental disorders, fourth edition text revision (DSM-IV-TR)*. Arlington, VA: American Psychiatric Publishing.

Anastopoulos, A. D., & Gerrard, L. M. (2003). Facilitating understanding and management of attention-deficit/hyperactivity disorder. In M. A. Reinecke, F. M. Dattilio, & A. Freeman (Eds.), *Cognitive therapy with children and adolescents* (2nd ed., pp. 19–42). New York: Guilford.

Anastopoulos, A. D., & Shelton, T. L. (2001). *Assessing attention-deficit/hyperactivity disorder*. New York: Kluwer Academic/Plenum.

Anderson, G. M., & Cohen, D. J. (2002). Neurochemistry of childhood psychiatric disorders. In M. Lewis (Ed.), *Child and adolescent psychiatry: A comprehensive textbook* (3rd ed., pp. 46–60). Philadelphia: Lippincott Williams & Wilkins.

Andrews, J. A. (2005). Substance abuse in girls. In D. J. Bell, S. L. Foster, & E. J. Mash (Eds.), *Handbook of behavioral and emotional problems in girls* (pp. 181–210). New York: Kluwer Academic/Plenum.

Aneshensel, C. S., & Phelan, J. C. (1999). *Handbook of the sociology of mental health*. New York: Kluwer Academic/Plenum, 1999.

Angold, A. (2002). Diagnostic interviews with parents and children. In M. Rutter & E. Taylor (Eds.), *Child and adolescent psychiatry* (4th ed., pp. 32–51). Malden, MA: Blackwell Science.

Angold, A., & Costello, E. J. (2002). Structured interviewing. In M. Lewis (Ed.), *Child and adolescent psychiatry: A comprehensive textbook* (3rd ed., pp. 544–555). Philadelphia: Lippincott Williams & Wilkins.

Angold, A., Costello, E. J., & Erkanli, A. (1999). Comorbidity. *Journal of Child Psychology and Psychiatry and Allied Disciplines, 40,* 57–87.

Arias, E., Anderson, R. N., Hsiang-Ching, K., Murphy, S. L., & Kochanek, K. D. (2003). *Deaths: Final data for 2001* (National vital statistics reports, 52[3]). Hyattsville, MD: National Center for Health Statistics.

Armsden, G., Pecora, P. J., Payne, V. H., & Szatkiewicz, J. P. (2000). An examination of psychotropic drug treatment for children with serious emotional disturbance. *Journal of Emotional and Behavioral Disorders, 8,* 49–64.

Arnold, M. E., & Hughes, J. N. (1999). First do no harm: Adverse effects of grouping deviant youth for skills training. *Journal of School Psychology, 37,* 99–115.

Asarnow, J. R., & Asarnow, R. F. (2003). Childhood-onset schizophrenia. In E. J. Mash & R. A. Barkley (Eds.), *Child psychopathology* (2nd ed., pp. 455–485). New York: Guilford.

Azrin, N. H., & Besalel, V. A. (1999). *How to use positive practice, self-correction, and overcorrection* (2nd ed.). Austin, TX: PRO-ED.

Bacon, S. B., & Kimball, R. (1989). The wilderness challenge model. In R. D. Lyman, S. Prentice-Dunn, & S. Gabel (Eds.), *Residential and inpatient treatment of children and adolescents* (pp. 115–144). New York: Plenum.

Baer, D. M., Wolf, M. M., & Risley, T. R. (1968). Some current dimensions of applied behavior analysis. *Journal of Applied Behavior Analysis, 1,* 91–97.

Baer, S., & Garland, E. J. (2005). Pilot study of community-based cognitive behavioral group therapy for adolescents with social phobia. *Journal of the American Academy of Child and Adolescent Psychiatry, 44,* 258–264.

Bahr, M. W., Walker, K., Hampton, E. M., Buddle, B. S., Freeman, T., Ruschman, N., et al. (2006). Creative problem solving for general education intervention teams: A two-year evaluation study. *Remedial and Special Education, 27,* 27–41.

Bandura, A. (1969). *Principles of behavior modification*. New York: Holt, Rinehart, & Winston.

Bandura, A. (1971). Analysis of modeling processes. In A. Bandura (Ed.), *Psychological modeling: Conflicting theories* (pp. 1–62). Chicago: Aldine-Atherton.

Bandura, A. (1973). *Aggression: A social learning analysis*. Englewood Cliffs, NJ: Prentice-Hall.

Bandura, A. (1986). *Social foundations of thought and action*. Englewood Cliffs, NJ: Prentice-Hall.

Bandura, A. (1997). *Self-efficacy: The exercise of control*. New York: W. H. Freeman.

Barkley, R. A. (2003). Attention-deficit/hyperactivity disorder. In E. J. Mash & R. A. Barkley (Eds.), *Child psychopathology* (2nd ed., pp. 75–143). New York: Guilford.

Barkley, R. A. (Ed.)(2005). *Attention-deficit hyperactivity disorder: A handbook for diagnosis and treatment* (3rd ed.). New York: Guilford.

Barnhill, G. P. (2005). Functional behavioral assessment in schools. *Intervention in School and Clinic, 40,* 131–143.

Barrish, H. H., Saunders, M., & Wolf, M. M. (1969). Good behavior game: Effects of individual contingencies for group consequences on disruptive behavior in a classroom. *Journal of Applied Behavior Analysis, 2,* 119–124.

Barry, T. D., Dunlap, S. T., Cotten, S. J., Lochman, J. E., & Wells, K. C. (2005). The influence of maternal stress and distress on disruptive behavior problems in boys. *Journal of the American Academy of Child and Adolescent Psychiatry, 44,* 265–273.

Barth, J. M., Dunlap, S. T., Dane, H., Lochman, J. E., & Wells, K. C. (2004). Classroom environment influences on aggression, peer relations, and academic focus. *Journal of School Psychology, 42,* 115–133.

Bartollas, C., & Miller, S. J. (2005). *Juvenile justice in America* (4th ed.). Upper Saddle River, NJ: Prentice Hall.

Battalio, R., & Stephens, J. T. (2005). Social skills training: Teacher practices and perceptions. *Beyond Behavior, 14*, 15–20.

Bear, G. G. (2005). *Developing self-discipline and preventing and correcting misbehavior*. Boston: Allyn and Bacon.

Beard, K. Y., & Sugai, G. (2004). First step to success: An early intervention for elementary children at risk for antisocial behavior. *Behavioral Disorders, 29*, 396–398.

Bearden, C. E., Rosso, I. M., Hollister, J. M., Sanchez, L. E., Hadley, T., & Cannon, T. D. (2000). A prospective cohort study of childhood behavioral deviance and language abnormalities as predictors of adult schizophrenia. *Schizophrenia Bulletin, 26*, 395–410.

Beck, A. T., (1976). *Cognitive therapy and the emotional disorders*. New York: International Universities Press.

Beck, A. T., & Newman, C. F. (2005). Cognitive therapy. In B. J. Sadock & V. A. Sadock (Eds.), *Kaplan & Sadock's comprehensive textbook of psychiatry* (Vol. II, pp. 2595–2609). Philadelphia: Lippincott Williams & Wilkins.

Becker, D. F., & DeAntonio, M. (2004). Hospital treatment of adolescents. In H. Steiner (Eds.), *Handbook of mental health interventions in children and adolescents: An integrated developmental approach* (pp. 872–884). San Francisco: Jossey-Bass.

Becker, W. C. (1964). Consequences of different kinds of parental discipline. In M. L. Hoffman & L. W. Hoffman (Eds.), *Review of child development research* (Vol. 1). New York: Russell Sage Foundation.

Becker, W. C., Madsen, C. H., Arnold, C. R., & Thomas, D. R. (1967). The contingent use of teacher attention and praise in reducing classroom behavior problems. *Journal of Special Education, 1*, 287–307.

Bell, S. K., Boggs, S. R., & Eyberg, S. M. (2003). Positive attention. In W. O'Donohue, J. E. Fisher, & S. C. Hayes (Eds.), *Cognitive behavior therapy: Applying empirically supported techniques in your practice* (pp. 294–300). Hoboken, NJ: Wiley.

Benes, F. M. (1995). A neurodevelopmental approach to the understanding of schizophrenia and other mental disorders. In D. Cicchetti & D. J. Cohen (Eds.), *Developmental psychopathology*: Vol. 1: Theory and methods (pp. 227–253). New York: Wiley.

Benoit, M. B., Nickman, S. L., & Rosenfeld, A. (2005). Adoption and foster care. In B. J. Sadock & V. A. Sadock (Eds.), *Kaplan & Sadock's comprehensive textbook of psychiatry* (Vol. II, pp. 3406–3411). Philadelphia: Lippincott Williams & Wilkins.

Benson, H. (1996). *Timeless healing: The power and biology of belief*. New York: Scribner.

Beresin, E. V., & Schlozman, S. C. (2005). Psychiatric treatment of adolescents. In B. J. Sadock & V. A. Sadock (Eds.), *Kaplan & Sadock's comprehensive textbook of psychiatry* (Vol. II, pp. 3395–3400). Philadelphia: Lippincott Williams & Wilkins.

Berk, L. E. (2005). *Infants, children, and adolescents* (5th ed.). Needham Heights, MA: Allyn & Bacon.

Berk, L. E. (2006). *Child development* (7th ed.). Needham Heights, MA: Allyn & Bacon.

Berkowitz, P. H. (1974). Pearl H. Berkowitz. In J. M. Kauffman & C. D. Lewis (Eds.), *Teaching children with behavior disorders: Personal perspectives*. Upper Saddle River, NJ: Merrill/Prentice Hall.

Berkowitz, P. H., & Rothman, E. P. (1960). *The disturbed child: Recognition and psychoeducational therapy in the classroom*. New York: New York University Press.

Bernet, W. (2005). Child maltreatment. In B. J. Sadock & V. A. Sadock (Eds.), *Kaplan & Sadock's comprehensive textbook of psychiatry* (Vol. II, pp. 3412–3424). Philadelphia: Lippincott Williams & Wilkins.

Bhugra, D. (1996). Religion and mental health. In D. Bhugra (Ed.), *Psychiatry and religion: Context, consensus and controversies* (pp. 1–4). London: Routledge.

Biederman, J. (2005). Early-onset bipolar disorders. In B. J. Sadock & V. A. Sadock (Eds.), *Kaplan & Sadock's comprehensive textbook of psychiatry* (Vol. II, pp. 623–634). Philadelphia: Lippincott Williams & Wilkins.

Bierman, K. L. (2005). *Peer rejection: Developmental processes and intervention strategies*. New York: Guilford.

Birmaher, B., Arbelaez, C., & Brent, D. (2002). Course and outcome of child and adolescent major depressive disorder. *Child and Adolescent Psychiatric Clinics of North America, 11*, 619–638.

Birmaher, B., & Axelson, D. (2005). Pediatric psychopharmacology. In B. J. Sadock & V. A. Sadock (Eds.), *Kaplan & Sadock's comprehensive text-book of psychiatry* (Vol. II, pp. 3363–3375). Philadelphia: Lippincott Williams & Wilkins.

Birnbrauer, J. S., Bijou, S. W., Wolf, M. M., & Kidder, J. D. (1965). Programmed instruction in the classroom. In L. P. Ulman & L. Krasner (Eds.), *Case studies in behavior modification* (pp. 358–363). New York: Holt, Rinehart & Winston.

Blase, K. A., Fixsen, D. L., Freeborn, K., & Jaeger, D. (1989). The behavioral model. In R. D. Lyman, S. Prentice-Dunn, & S. Gabel (Eds.), *Residential and inpatient treatment of children and adolescents* (pp. 43–59). New York: Plenum.

Bloomquist, M. L. (2005). *Skills training for children with behavior problems*. New York: Guilford.

Bock, M. A. (1997). Jesse: A profile of courage. *Intervention in School and Clinic, 33*, 43–55.

Bockoven, J. S. (1963). *Moral treatment in American psychiatry*. New York: Springer.

Bodine, R. J., & Crawford, D. K. (1999). *Developing emotional intelligence*. Champaign, IL: Research Press.

Boegels, S. M., & Zigterman, D. (2000). Dysfunctional cognitions in children with social phobia, separation anxiety disorder, and generalized anxiety disorder. *Journal of Abnormal Child Psychology, 28*, 205–211.

Boland, R. J., & Keller, M. B. (2002). Course and outcome of depression. In I. H. Gotlib & C. L. Hammen (Eds.), *Handbook of depression* (pp. 43–60). New York: Guilford.

Boris, N. W., & Zeanah, C. H. (2005). Reactive attachment disorder of infancy and early childhood. In B. J. Sadock & V. A. Sadock (Eds.), *Kaplan & Sadock's comprehensive textbook of psychiatry* (Vol. II, pp. 3248–3253). Philadelphia: Lippincott Williams & Wilkins.

Bornstein, M. R., Bellack, A. S., & Hersen, M. (1977). Social-skills training for unassertive children: A multiple-baseline analysis. *Journal of Applied Behavior Analysis, 10*, 183–196.

Borstin, D. J. (1974). *The Americans: The democratic experience.* New York: Vintage Books/Random House.

Borstin, D. J. (1983). *The discoverers.* New York: Random House.

Bos, C. S., & Coleman, M., & Vaughn, S. (2002). Reading and students with E/BD: What do we know and recommend? In K. L. Lane, F. M. Gresham, & T. E. O'Shaughnessy (Eds.), *Interventions for children with or at risk for emotional and behavioral disorders* (pp. 87–103). Boston: Allyn & Bacon.

Bos, C. S., & Vaughn, S. (2006). *Strategies for teaching students with learning and behavior problems* (6th ed.). Boston: Allyn and Bacon.

Bostic, J. Q., & Bagnell, A. (2005). School consultation. In B. J. Sadock & V. A. Sadock (Eds.), *Kaplan & Sadock's comprehensive textbook of psychiatry* (Vol. II, pp. 3503–3512). Philadelphia: Lippincott Williams & Wilkins.

Botvin, G. J., & Dusenbury, L. (1987). Life skills training: A psychoeducational approach to substance-abuse prevention. In C. A. Maher & J. E. Zins (Eds.), *Psychoeducational interventions in the schools* (pp. 46–65). New York: Pergamon.

Botvin, G. J., Griffin, K. W., Diaz, T., & Ifill-Williams, M. (2001). Drug abuse prevention among minority adolescents: Posttest and one-year follow-up of a school-based preventive intervention. *Prevention Science, 2*, 1–13.

Bower, E. M. (1969). *The early identification of emotionally handicapped children in school* (2nd ed.). Springfield, IL: Charles C. Thomas.

Bowlby, J. (1988). *A secure base: Parent-child attachment and healthy human development.* New York: Basic Books.

Boyum, L. A., & Parke, R. D. (1999). Family. In W. K. Silverman & T. H. Ollendick (Eds.), *Developmental issues in the clinical treatment of children* (pp. 141–155). Needham Heights, MA: Allyn & Bacon.

Bradley, C. (1937). The behavior of children receiving Benzedrine. *American Journal of Psychiatry, 94*, 577–585.

Bradley, R., Henderson, K., & Monfore, D. A. (2004). A national perspective on children with emotional disorders. *Behavioral Disorders, 29*, 211–223.

Bradley-Klug, K. L. & Shapiro, E. L. (2003). Treatment of academic skills problems. In M. A. Reinecke, F. M. Dattilio, & A. Freeman (Eds.), *Cognitive therapy with children and adolescents* (2nd ed., pp. 281–303). New York: Guilford.

Braswell, L., & Kendall, P. C. (2001). Cognitive-behavioral therapy with youth. In K. S. Dobson (Ed.), *Handbook of cognitive-behavioral theories* (2nd ed., pp. 246–294). New York: Guilford.

Braukmann, C. J., & Wolf, M. M. (1987). Behaviorally based group homes for juvenile offenders. In E. K. Morris & C. J. Braukmann (Eds.), *Behavioral approaches to crime and delinquency: A handbook of application, research, and concepts* (pp. 135–159). New York: Plenum.

Breen, M. J. (2003). Parent-, teacher-, and youth-completed child-behavior questionnaires. In M. J. Breen & C. R. Fiedler (Eds.), *Behavioral approach to assessment of youth with emotional/behavioral disorders* (2nd ed., pp. 189–223). Austin, TX: PRO-ED.

Brems, C. (1999). *Psychotherapy process and techniques.* Boston, MA: Allyn & Bacon.

Brendtro, L. K. (1997). Mending broken spirits of youth. *Reclaiming Children and Youth, 5*, 197–202.

Brendtro, L. K. (2001). About Fritz Redl and David Wineman. *Reclaiming Children and Youth, 10*, 70.

Brendtro, L. K., Brokenleg, M., & Van Bockern, S. (1990). *Reclaiming youth at risk: Our hope for the future.* Bloomington, IN: National Education Service.

Brendtro, L. K., Brokenleg, M., & Van Bockern, S. (1991). The circle of courage. *Beyond Behavior, 2*, 5–12.

Brendtro, L. K., & Long, N. J. (1996). A crisis of conscience. *Reclaiming Children and Youth, 5*, 129–135.

Brendtro, L. K., & Long, N. J. (1998). Wayward youth: Aichhorn's practical psychology of reconciliation. *Reclaiming Children and Youth, 7*, 66–70.

Brendtro, L. K., Ness, A., & Mitchell, M. (2001). *No disposable kids.* Longmont, CO: Sopris West.

Brendtro, L. K., & Shahbazian, M. (2003). *Troubled children and youth: Turning problems into opportunities.* Champaign, IL: Research Press.

Brendtro, L. K., & Van Bockern, S. (1998). Courage for the discouraged: A psychoeducational approach to troubled and troubling children. In R. J. Whelan (Ed.), *Emotional and behavioral disorders: A 25 year focus* (pp. 229–252). Denver: Love.

Brewer, R. D., Reid, M. S., & Rhine, B. G. (2003). Peer coaching students: Teaching to learn. *Intervention in School and Clinic, 39*, 113–126.

Broden, M., Hall, R. V., & Mitts, B. (1971). The effects of self-recording on the classroom behavior of two eighth grade students. *Journal of Applied Behavior Analysis, 4*, 191–199.

Brokenleg, M. (1996). Unshackled by visions and values. *Reclaiming Children and Youth, 5*, 136–139.

Brolin, D. E., & Loyd, R. J. (2004). *Career development and transition services: A functional life skills approach.* Upper Saddle River, NJ: Merrill.

Bronfenbrenner, U. (2004). *Making human beings human: Bioecological perspectives on human development.* Thousand Oaks, CA: Sage.

Bronfenbrenner, U., & Morris, P. A. (1998). The ecology of developmental processes. In R. M. Lerner (Ed.), *Handbook of child psychology: Vol. 1: Theoretical models of human development* (5th ed., pp. 233–273). New York: Wiley.

Brown, D., Pryzwansky, W. B., & Schulte, A. B. (2006). *Psychological consultation: Introduction to theory and practice* (6th ed.). Needham Heights, MA: Allyn & Bacon.

Brown, K. J. (2005). Therapeutic camping programs. In R. G. Steele & M. C. Roberts (Eds.), *Handbook of mental health services for children, adolescents, and families* (pp. 305–315). New York: Kluwer Academic/Plenum.

Brown, R. T. (2005). Recent advances in pharmacotherapies for the externalizing disorders. *School Psychology Quarterly, 20*, 118–134.

Bukatko, D., & Daehler, M. W. (2004). *Child development: A thematic approach* (5th ed.). Boston: Houghton Mifflin.

Bullis, M., Walker, H., & Sprague, J. (2001). A promised unfulfilled: Social skills training with at-risk and antisocial children and youth. *Exceptionality, 9*, 69–92.

Bullock, C., & Foegen, A. (2002). Constructive conflict resolution for students with behavioral disorders. *Behavioral Disorders, 27*, 289–299.

Bullock, L. M., & Menendez, A. L. (1999). *Historical chronology of the council for children with behavioral disorders: 1964–1999.* Reston, VA: Council for Exceptional Children.

Burns, B. J., Hoagwood, K., & Maultsby, L. T. (1998). Improving outcomes for children and adolescents with serious emotional and behavioral disorders: Current and future directions. In M. H. Epstein, K. Kutash, & A. Duchnowski (Eds.), *Outcomes for children and youth with emotional and behavioral disorders and their families* (pp. 685–707). Austin, TX: PRO-ED.

Buss, A. H. (1997). Evolutionary perspectives on personality traits. In R. Hogan, J. Johnson, & S. Briggs (Eds.), *Handbook of personality psychology* (pp. 345–366). San Diego, CA: Academic Press.

Butcher, J., Mineka, S., & Hooley, J. M. (2004). *Abnormal psychology* (12th ed.). Boston: Allyn and Bacon.

Butcher, J. N., Williams, C. L., Graham, J. R., Archer, R. P., Tellegen, A., Ben-Porath, Y. S., et al. (1992). *Minnesota Multiphasic Personality Inventory–Adolescent.* Minneapolis: National Computer Systems.

Butts, J., Buck, J., & Coggeshall, M. (2002). *The impact of teen court on young offenders.* Research Report. Washington, DC: U.S. Department of Justice.

Cancio, E. J., West, R. P., & Young, K. R. (2004). Improving mathematics homework completion and accuracy of students with EBD through self-management and parent participation. *Journal of Emotional and Behavioral Disorders, 12*, 9–22.

Cangelosi, J. S. (2003). *Classroom management strategies: Gaining and maintaining students' cooperation* (5th ed.). New York: Wiley Jossey-Bass.

Cantor, S. (1988). *Childhood schizophrenia.* New York: Guilford.

Cantrell, M. J., Cantrell, R. P., Valore, T. G., Jones, J. M., & Fecser, F. A. (1999). *A revisitation of the ecological perspectives on emotional/behavioral disorders: Underlying assumptions and implications for education and treatment.* Reston, VA: Council for Exceptional Children.

Cantrell, M. L., & Cantrell, R. P. (2002). Re-Ed: Forty years young, alive and lively! *Reclaiming Children and Youth, 11*, 66–67.

Caplan, R., Guthrie, D., Tang, B., Komo, S., & Asarnow, R. F. (2000). Thought disorder in childhood schizophrenia: Replication and update of concept. *Journal of the American Academy of Child and Adolescent Psychiatry, 39*, 771–778.

Carey, W. B. (1998). Temperament and behavior problems in the classroom. *School Psychology Review, 27*, 522–533.

Carnine, D. W., Silbert, J., Kame'enui, E. J., & Tarver, S. (2004). *Direct instruction reading* (4th ed). Columbus: Merrill Prentice Hall.

Cauce, A. M., Stewart, A., Whitbeck, L. B., Paradise, M., & Hoyt, D. R. (2005). Girls on their own: Homelessness in female adolescents. In D. J. Bell, S. L. Foster, & E. J. Mash (Eds.), *Handbook of behavioral and emotional problems in girls* (pp. 439–462). New York: Kluwer Academic/Plenum.

Cauffman, E. (2004). A statewide screening of mental health symptoms among juvenile offenders in detention. *Journal of the American Academy of Child and Adolescent Psychiatry, 43*, 430–439.

Centers for Disease Control and prevention. (1992). *Youth suicide prevention programs: A resource guide.* Atlanta: Author.

Centers for Disease Control and Prevention. (2004). *Youth risk behavior surveillance: United States, 2003 (Morbidity and Mortality Weekly Report, 53* (SS-2), 1–96). Washington: U.S. Government Printing Office.

Cervone, D. (2000). Thinking about self efficacy. *Behavior Modification, 24*, 30–56.

Chafel, J. A., & Hadley, K. G. (2001). Poverty and the well-being of children and families. In C. E. Walker & M. C. Roberts (Eds.), *Handbook of clinical child psychology* (3rd ed., pp. 48–71). New York: Wiley.

Chamberlain, P. (1999). Residential care for children and adolescents with Oppositional Defiant Disorder and Conduct Disorder. In H. C. Quay & A. E. Hogan (Eds.),

Handbook of disruptive behavior disorders (pp. 495–506). New York, NY: Kluwer Academic/Plenum.

Chamberlain, P., & Friman, P.C. (1997). Residential programs for antisocial children and adolescents. In D.M. Stoff, J. Breiling, & J.D. Maser (Eds.), *Handbook of antisocial behavior* (pp. 416–424). New York: Wiley.

Chandler, L. A. (2003). The projective hypothesis and the development of projective techniques for children. In C. R. Reynolds & R. W. Kamphaus (Eds.), *Handbook of psychological and educational assessment of children: Personality, behavior, and context* (2nd ed., pp. 51–65). New York: Guilford.

Charney, D. S. (2005). Anxiety disorders: Introduction and overview. In B. J. Sadock & V. A. Sadock (Eds.), *Kaplan & Sadock's comprehensive textbook of psychiatry* (Vol. I, pp. 1718-1719). Philadelphia: Lippincott Williams & Wilkins.

Chassin, L., Ritter, J., Trim, R. S., & King, K. M. (2003). Adolescent substance use disorders. In E. J. Mash & R. A. Barkley (Eds.), *Child psychopathology* (2nd ed., pp. 199–230). New York: Guilford.

Cheney, D., & Bullis, M. (2004). The school-to-community transition of adolescents with emotional and behavioral disorders. In R. B. Rutherford Jr., M. M. Quinn, & S. Mathur (Eds.), *Handbook of research in behavioral disorders* (pp. 369–384). New York: Guilford.

Chesney-Lind, M., & Shelden, R. G. (1998). *Girls, delinquency, and juvenile justice* (2nd ed.). Belmont, CA: Wadsworth.

Chess, S., & Thomas, A. (2002). Temperament and its clinical applications. In M. Lewis (Ed.), *Child and adolescent psychiatry: A comprehensive textbook* (3rd ed., pp. 220–227). Philadelphia: Lippincott Williams & Wilkins.

Choate, J. S. (2000). *Successful inclusive teaching: Proven ways to detect and correct special needs* (3rd ed.). Needham Heights, MA: Allyn & Bacon.

Christenson, S. L., & Havsy, L. H. (2004). Family-school-peer relationships: Significance for social-emotional and academic learning. In J. E. Zins, R. P. Weissberg, M. C. Wang, & H. J. Walberg (Eds.), *Building academic success on social and emotional learning: What does the research say?* (pp. 59–75). New York: Teachers College Press.

Coatsworth, J. D., Szapocznik, J., Kurtines, W., & Santisteban, D. A. (1997). Culturally competent psychosocial interventions with antisocial problem behavior in Hispanic youths. In D. M. Stoff, J. Breiling, & J. D. Maser (Eds.), *Handbook of antisocial behavior* (pp. 395–404). New York: Wiley.

Cockerham, W. C. (2006). *Sociology of mental disorder* (7th ed.). Upper Saddle River, NJ: Prentice Hall.

Cocozza, J. J., & Skowyra, K. (2000). Youth with mental health disorders: issues and emerging responses. *Juvenile Justice, 7*, 3–13.

Cohen, J. A. (2005). Posttraumatic stress disorder in children and adolescents. In B. J. Sadock & V. A. Sadock (Eds.), *Kaplan & Sadock's comprehensive textbook of psychiatry* (Vol. II, pp. 3286–3291). Philadelphia: Lippincott Williams & Wilkins.

Cole, B. S., & Pargament, K. I. (1999). Spiritual surrender: A paradoxical path to control. In W. R. Miller (Eds.), *Integrating spirituality into treatment: Resources for practitioners* (pp. 179–198). Washington: American Psychological Association.

Coles, R., Elkind, D., Shelton, C., Mendez, V., Warfield-Coppock, N., Ng, D., et al. (1995). *The ongoing journey: Awakening spiritual life in at-risk youth*. Boys Town, NE: Boys Town Press.

Colp, R. (2005). History of psychiatry. In B. J. Sadock & V. A. Sadock (Eds.), *Kaplan & Sadock's comprehensive textbook of psychiatry* (Vol. II, pp. 4013–4046). Philadelphia: Lippincott Williams & Wilkins.

Colvin, G. (2002). Designing classroom organization and structure. In K. L. Lane, F. M. Gresham, & T. E. O'Shaughnessy (Eds.), *Interventions for children with or at risk for emotional and behavioral disorders* (pp. 159–174). Boston: Allyn & Bacon.

Combrick-Graham, L., & Fox, G. (2002). Development of school-age children. In M. Lewis (Ed.), *Child and adolescent psychiatry: A comprehensive textbook* (3rd ed., pp. 324–332). Philadelphia: Lippincott Williams & Wilkins.

Compas, B. E., Connor-Smith, J. K., Saltzman, H., Thomsen, A. H., Wadsworth, M. E. (2001). Coping with stress during childhood and adolescence: Problems, progress, and potential in theory and research. *Psychological Bulletin, 127*, 87–127.

Compton, S. N., March, J. S., Brent, D., Albano, A.-M., Weersing, V. R., & Curry, J. (2004). Cognitive-behavioral psychotherapy for anxiety and depressive disorders in children and adolescents: An evidence-based medicine review. *Journal of the American Academy of Child and Adolescent Psychiatry, 43*, 930–959.

Conduct Problems Prevention Research Group. (1999). Initial impact of the fast track prevention trial for conduct problems. II: Classroom effects. *Journal of Consulting and Clinical Psychology, 67*, 648–657.

Conduct Problems Prevention Research Group. (2004). The effects of the Fast Track program on serious problem outcomes at the end of elementary school. *Journal of Clinical Child and Adolescent Psychology, 33*, 650–661.

Conners, C. K. (1980). *Food additives and hyperactive children*. New York: Plenum.

Conners, C. K., & Wells, K. (1997). *Conners-Wells Adolescent Self-Report Scale*. North Tonowanda, NY: Multi-Health Systems.

Connor, D. F. (2002). *Aggression and antisocial behavior in children and adolescents: Research and treatment*. New York: Guilford.

Conroy, M. A., & Brown, W. H. (2004). Early identification, prevention, and early intervention with young children at risk for emotional or behavioral disorders: Issues, trends, and a call for action. *Behavioral Disorders, 29,* 224–236.

Conroy, M. A., Hendrickson, J. M., & Hester, P. P. (2004). Early identification and prevention of emotional and behavioral disorders. In R. B. Rutherford Jr., M. M. Quinn, & S. Mathur (Eds.), *Handbook of research in behavioral disorders* (pp. 199–215). New York: Guilford.

Conyers, C., Miltenberger, R., Maki, A., Barenz, R., Jurgens, M., Sailer, A., et al. (2004). A comparison of response cost and differential reinforcement of other behavior to reduce disruptive behavior in a preschool classroom. *Journal of Applied Behavior Analysis, 37,* 411–415.

Cook, J. A., Solomon, M. L., Farrell, D., Koziel, M., & Jonikas, J. (1997). Vocational initiatives for transition-age youths with severe mental illness. In S. W. Henggeler & A. B. Santos (Eds.), *Innovative approaches for difficult-to-treat populations* (pp. 139–163). Washington, DC: American Psychiatric Press.

Cook-Morales, V. J. (2002). The home-school-agency triangle. In D. T. Marsh & M. A. Fristad (Eds.), *Handbook of serious emotional disturbances in children and adolescents* (pp. 392–411). New York: Wiley.

Coppolillo, H. P. (2002). Use of play in psychodynamic psychotherapy. In M. Lewis (Ed.), *Child and adolescent psychiatry: A comprehensive textbook* (3rd ed., pp. 992–998). Philadelphia: Lippincott Williams & Wilkins.

Corsini, R. J., & Wedding, D. (2005). *Current psychotherapies* (7th ed.). Belmont, CA: Wadsworth.

Costa, P. T., & McCrae, R. R. (2005). Approaches derived from philosophy and psychology. In B. J. Sadock & V. A. Sadock (Eds.) *Kaplan & Sadock's comprehensive textbook of psychiatry* (Vol. I, pp. 778–793). Philadelphia: Lippincott Williams & Wilkins.

Costello, E., Compton, S., Keeler, G., & Angold, A. (2003). Relationships between poverty and psychopathology: A natural experiment. *Journal of the American Medical Association, 290,* 2023–2029.

Coutinho, M. J., & Oswald, D. P. (2005). State variation in gender disproportionality in special education: Findings and recommendations. *Remedial and Special Education, 26,* 7–15.

Cowen, E. L., Hightower, A. D., Pedro-Carroll, J. P., Work, W. C., Wyman, P. A., & Haffey, W. G. (1996). *School-based prevention for children at risk: The primary mental health project.* Washington, DC: American Psychological Association.

Cox, J. L. (1996). Psychiatry and religion: A general psychiatrist's perspective. In D. Bhugra (Ed.), *Psychiatry and religion: Context, consensus and controversies* (pp. 157–166). London: Routledge.

Crain, W. (2005). *Theories of development* (5th ed.). Upper Saddle River, NJ: Prentice Hall.

Crawford, D., & Bodine, R. (1996). *Conflict resolution education* (NCJ 160935). Washington, DC: U.S. Department of Justice.

Cremin, L. A. (1961). *The transformation of the school.* New York: Knopf.

Crick, N. R., & Dodge, K. A. (1994). A review and reformulation of social information-processing mechanisms in children's social adjustment. *Psychological Bulletin, 115,* 74–101.

Crockett, J. B., & Kauffman, J. M. (1999). *The least restrictive environment: Its origins and interpretations in special education.* Mahwah, NJ: Erlbaum.

Cross, T. (2002). Spirituality and mental health: A Native American perspective. *Beyond Behavior, 12,* 10–11.

Cross, T., Bazron, B., Dennis, K., & Isaacs, M. (1989). *Towards a culturally competent system of care: A monograph on effective services for minority services for minority children who are severely emotionally disturbed.* Washington, DC: Georgetown University Child Development Center, National Technical Assistance Center.

Crowe, A. H. (1998). *Drug identification and testing in the juvenile justice system: Summary.* Washington, DC: Office of Juvenile Justice and Delinquency Prevention, U.S. Department of Justice.

Crum, C. F. (2003). Using a cognitive-behavioral modification strategy to increase on-task behavior of a student with a behavior disorder. *Intervention in School and Clinic, 39,* 305–309.

Cruz, L., & Cullinan, D. (2001). Awarding points, using levels to help children improve behavior. *Teaching Exceptional Children, 33,* 16–23.

Cuffe, S. P., McKeown, R. E., Addy, C. L., & Garrison, C. Z. (2005). Family and psychosocial risk factors in a longitudinal epidemiological study of adolescents. *Journal of the American Academy of Child and Adolescent Psychiatry, 44,* 121–129.

Cullinan, D. (2004). Research issues in classification and definition of emotional and behavioral disorders. In R. B. Rutherford, Jr., M. M. Quinn, & S. R. Mathur (Eds.), *Handbook of research in behavioral disorders* (pp. 32–53). New York: Guilford.

Cullinan, D., & Epstein, M. H. (1995). Behavior disorders. In N.G. Haring & L. McCormick (Eds.), *Exceptional children and youth* (6th ed.). Columbus, OH: Merrill.

Cullinan, D., & Epstein, M. H. (2001). Comorbidity among students with emotional disturbance. *Behavioral Disorders, 26,* 200–213.

Cullinan, D., Evans, C., Epstein, M. H., & Ryser, G. (2003). Characteristics of emotional disturbance of elementary school students. *Behavioral Disorders, 28,* 94–110.

Cullinan, D., Harniss, M. K., Epstein, M. H., & Ryser, G. (2002). The Scale for Assessing Emotional Disturbance: Concurrent validity. *Journal of Child and Family Studies, 10,* 449–466.

Cullinan, D., Osborne, S., & Epstein, M. H. (2004). Characteristics of emotional disturbance of female students. *Remedial and Special Education, 25,* 276–290.

Cullinan, D., & Sabornie, E. J. (2004). Characteristics of emotional disturbance in middle and high school students. *Journal of Emotional and Behavioral Disorders, 12*, 157–167.

Curry, J. F., & Reinecke, M. A. (2003). Modular therapy for adolescents with major depression. In M. A. Reinecke, F. M. Dattilio, & A. Freeman (Eds.), *Cognitive therapy with children and adolescents* (2nd ed., pp. 95–127). New York: Guilford.

Cutting, J. (2003). Descriptive psychopathology In S. R. Hirsch & D. R. Weinberger (Eds.), *Schizophrenia* (2nd ed., pp. 15–24). Malden, MA: Blackwell.

D'Amato, R. C., Fletcher-Janzen, E., & Reynolds, C. R. (Eds.). (2005). *Handbook of school neuropsychology*. New York: Wiley.

D'Zurilla, T. J., & Goldfried, M. R. (1971). Problem solving and behavior modification. *Journal of Abnormal Psychology, 78*, 107–126.

D'Zurilla, T. J., & Nezu, A. M. (2001). Problem-solving therapies. In K. S. Dobson (Ed.), *Handbook of cognitive-behavioral theories* (2nd ed., pp. 211–245). New York: Guilford.

Daly, P. M., & Ranalli, P. (2003). Using countoons to teach self-monitoring skills. *Teaching Exceptional Children, 35*, 30–35.

Darch, C. B., & Kameenui, E. J. (2004). *Instructional classroom management: A proactive approach to behavior management*. Upper Saddle River, NJ: Merrill Prentice Hall.

Davis, B., Sheeber, L., & Hops, H. (2002). Coercive family processes and adolescent depression. In J. B. Reid, G. R. Patterson, & J. Snyder (Eds.), *Antisocial behavior in children and adolescents* (pp. 173–194). Washington: American Psychological Association.

Davis, C. A., Lane, K. L., Sutherland, K., Gunter, P. L., Denny, R. K., Pickens, P., & Wehby, J. (2004). *Differentiating curriculum and instruction on behalf of students with emotional and behavioral disorders within general education settings*. Arlington, VA: Council for Exceptional Children.

Davis, J., Nelson, C. S., & Gauger, E. S. (2000). *Safe and effective secondary schools*. Boys Town, NE: Boys Town Press.

Dawson, C. A. (2003). A study on the effectiveness of life space crisis intervention for students identified with emotional disturbances. *Reclaiming Children and Youth, 11*, 223–230.

DeAntonio, M. (2005). Residential and inpatient treatment. In B. J. Sadock & V. A. Sadock (Eds.), *Kaplan & Sadock's comprehensive textbook of psychiatry* (Vol. II, pp. 3384–3389). Philadelphia: Lippincott Williams & Wilkins.

DeCicco-Bloom, E., & Sondell, M. (2005). Neural development and neurogenesis. In B. J. Sadock & V. A. Sadock (Eds.), *Kaplan & Sadock's comprehensive textbook of psychiatry* (Vol. I, pp. 33–49). Philadelphia: Lippincott Williams & Wilkins.

DeHart, G. B., Sroufe, L. A., & Cooper, R. G. (2004). *Child development* (5th ed.). New York: McGraw-Hill.

Dembinski, R. J. (1979). The reliability of the Self-Control Behavior Inventory. *Behavioral Disorders, 4*, 136–142.

DeRubeis, R. J., Tang, T. Z., & Beck, A. T. (2001). Cognitive therapy. In K. S. Dobson (Ed.), *Handbook of cognitive-behavioral theories* (2nd ed., pp. 349–392). New York: Guilford.

DesJarlais, D. C., & Paul, J. L. (1978) Labeling theory: Sociological views and approaches. In W. C. Rhodes & J. L. Paul (Eds.), *Emotionally disturbed and deviant children: New views and approaches*. Englewood Cliffs, NJ: Prentice-Hall.

Desjarlais, R., Eisenberg, L., Good, B., & Kleinman, A. (1995). *World mental health*. New York: Oxford University Press.

DeVoe, J. F., Peter, K., Kaufman, P., Miller, A. K., Noonan, M., Snyder, T. D., et al. (2004). *Indicators of school crime and safety: 2004* (NCES 2005-002/NCJ 205290). Washington, DC: U.S. Departments of Education and Justice.

DeVoe, J. F., Peter, K., Kaufman, P., Ruddy, S. A., Miller, A. K., Planty, M., et al. (2003). *Indicators of school crime and safety: 2003* (NCES 2004-004/NCJ 201257). Washington, DC: U.S. Departments of Education and Justice.

Dickstein, L. J. (2005). Relational problems. In B. J. Sadock & V. A. Sadock (Eds.), Kaplan & Sadock's comprehensive textbook of psychiatry (Vol. II, pp. 2241–2246). Philadelphia: Lippincott Williams & Wilkins.

DiGiuseppe, R. (1999). Rational emotive behavior therapy. In H. T. Prout & D.T. Brown (Eds.), *Counseling and psychotherapy with children and adolescents: Theory and practice for school and clinical settings* (3rd ed., pp. 203–301). New York: Wiley.

DiGiuseppe, R., & Li, C. E. (1999). Treating aggressive children with rational-emotive behavior therapy. In S. W. Russ & T. H. Ollendick (Eds.), *Handbook of psychotherapies with children and families* (pp. 281–300). New York: Kluwer Academic/Plenum.

Dimsdale, J. E., Irwin, M., Keefe, F. J., & Stein, M. B. (2005). Stress and psychiatry. In B. J. Sadock & V. A. Sadock (Eds.), Kaplan & Sadock's comprehensive textbook of psychiatry (Vol. II, pp. 2180–2195). Philadelphia: Lippincott Williams & Wilkins.

Dinkmeyer, D., & Dreikurs, R. (1963). *Encouraging children to learn: The encouragement process*. Englewood Cliffs, NJ: Prentice Hall.

Dinkmeyer, D., & Dinkmeyer, D. (1982). *DUSO: Developing understanding of self and others*. Circle Pines, MN: American Guidance Service.

Dobson, K. S., & Dozois, D. J. A. (2001). Historical and philosophical bases of the cognitive-behavioral therapies. In K. S. Dobson (Ed.), *Handbook of cognitive-behavioral theories* (2nd ed., pp. 3–39). New York: Guilford.

Dols, M. W. (1992). *Majnun: The madman in medieval Islamic society*. Oxford, England: Clarendon Press.

Domalanta, D. D., Risser, W. L., Roberts, R. E., & Risser, J. M. H. (2003). Prevalence of depression and other psychiatric disorders among incarcerated youths. *Journal of the American Academy of Child and Adolescent Psychiatry, 42*, 477–484.

Donohue, E., Hersen, M., & Ammerman, R. T. (2000). Historical overview. In M. Hersen & R. T. Ammerman (Eds.), *Advanced abnormal child psychology* (2nd ed., pp. 3–13). Hillsdale, NJ: Lawrence Erlbaum.

Donovan, C. L., & Spence, S. H. (2000). Prevention of childhood anxiety disorders. *Clinical Psychology Review, 20*, 509–531.

Doucette, A. (2002). Child and adolescent diagnosis: The need for a model-based approach. In L. E. Beutler & M. L. Malik (Eds.), *Rethinking the DSM: A psychological perspective* (pp. 201–220). Washington, DC: American Psychological Association.

Doucette-Gates, A. (2000). Capturing data: Negotiating cross agency systems. *Education and Treatment of Children, 23*, 5–19.

Dowd, T. (1997). Spirituality in at-risk youth. *Reclaiming Children and Youth, 5*, 210–212.

Dreikurs, R. (1972). *Discipline without tears*. New York: Harper & Row.

Dryden, W., & Ellis, A. (2001). Rational emotional behavior therapy. In K. S. Dobson (Ed.), *Handbook of cognitive-behavioral theories* (2nd ed., pp. 295–348). New York: Guilford.

Duggan, D., & Dawson, C. A. (2004). Positive behavior support infused by life space crisis intervention in New York city's special education district. *Reclaiming Children and Youth, 13*, 37–43.

D'Zurilla, T. J., & Nezu, A. M. (1999). *Problem-solving therapy: A social competence approach to clinical intervention* (2nd ed.). New York: Springer.

Eber, L., & Keenan, S. (2004). Collaboration with other agencies: Wraparound and systems of care for children and youths with emotional and behavioral disorders. In R. B. Rutherford Jr., M. M. Quinn, & S. Mathur (Eds.), *Handbook of research in behavioral disorders* (pp. 502–516). New York: Guilford.

Eckert, T. L., DuPaul, G. J., & Carson, P. M. (2003). Youth-completed and narrow-band child-behavior questionnaires. In M. J. Breen & C. R. Fiedler (Eds.), *Behavioral approach to assessment of youth with emotional/behavioral disorders* (2nd ed., pp. 225–296). Austin, TX: PRO-ED.

Edmondson, J. C. (2005). Psychiatric aspects of child neurology. In B. J. Sadock & V. A. Sadock (Eds.), *Kaplan & Sadock's comprehensive textbook of psychiatry* (Vol. I, pp. 498–511). Philadelphia: Lippincott Williams & Wilkins.

Edwards, L., & Chard, D. J. (2000). Curriculum reform in a residential treatment program: Establishing high academic expectations for students with emotional and behavioral disorders. *Behavioral Disorders, 25*, 259–263.

Edwards, L. L., & O'Toole, B. (1998). Application of the self-control curriculum with behavior disordered students. In R. J. Whelan (Ed.), *Emotional and behavioral disorders: A 25 year focus* (pp. 349–361). Denver: Love.

Egger, H. L., Costello, E. J., Erkanli, A., & Angold, A. (1999). Somatic complaints and psychopathology in children and adolescents: Stomach aches, musculoskeletal pains, and headaches. *Journal of the American Academy of Child and Adolescent Psychiatry, 38*, 852–860.

Egley, Jr., A., & Major, A. K. (2004). *Highlights of the 2002 National Youth Gang Survey* (Office of Juvenile Justice and Delinquency Prevention, FS-200401). Washington, DC: U.S. Department of Justice.

Eisler, I. (2002). Family interviewing: Issues of theory and practice. In M. Rutter & E. Taylor (Eds.), *Child and adolescent psychiatry* (4th ed., pp. 128–140). Malden, MA: Blackwell Science.

Elksnin, L. K., & Elksnin, N. (2006). *Teaching social-emotional skills at school and home*. Denver: Love.

Elliott, D. J., Koroloff, N. M., Koren, P. E., & Friesen, B. J. (1998). Improving access to children's mental health services: The family associate approach. In M. H. Epstein, K. Kutash, & A. Duchnowski (Eds.), *Outcomes for children and youth with emotional and behavioral disorders and their families* (pp. 581–609). Austin, TX: PRO-ED.

Elliott, S. N., & Busse, R. T. (2004). Assessment and evaluation of students' behavior and intervention outcomes: The utility of rating scale methods. In R. B. Rutherford Jr., M. M. Quinn, & S. Mathur (Eds.), *Handbook of research in behavioral disorders* (pp. 123–142). New York: Guilford.

Ellis, A. (1962). *Reason and emotion in psychotherapy*. New York: Lyle Stuart.

Ellis, A. (2003). Cognitive restructuring of the disputing of irrational beliefs. In W. O'Donohue, J. E. Fisher, & S. C. Hayes (Eds.) *Cognitive behavior therapy: Applying empirically supported techniques in your practice* (pp. 79–83). Hoboken, NJ: Wiley.

Embry, D. (2002). The Good Behavior Game: A best practice candidate as a universal behavioral vaccine. *Clinical Child and Family Psychological Review, 4*, 273–297.

Emery, R. E. (1999). *Marriage, divorce, and children's adjustment* (2nd ed.). Thousand Oaks, CA: Sage.

Emery, R. E., & Laumann-Billings, L. (2002). Child abuse. In M. Rutter & E. Taylor (Eds.), *Child and adolescent psychiatry* (4th ed., pp. 325–339). Malden, MA: Blackwell Science.

Emmer, E. T., Evertson, C. M., & Worsham, M. E. (2006). *Classroom management for middle and high school teachers* (7th ed.). Needham Heights, MA: Allyn & Bacon.

Epstein, M. H. (2004). *Behavioral and Emotional Rating Scale (BERS-2): A strength-based approach to assessment* (2nd ed.). Austin, TX: PRO-ED.

Epstein, M. H., & Cullinan, D. (1998). *Scale for Assessing Emotional Disturbance*. Austin, TX: PRO-ED.

Epstein, M. H., Cullinan, D., Ryser, G., & Pearson, N. (2002). Development of a scale to assess emotional disturbance. *Behavioral Disorders, 28*, 5–22.

Epstein, M. H., Kutash, K., & Duchnowski, A. J. (Eds.). (2005). *Outcomes for children and youth with emotional disorders and their families* (2nd ed.). Austin, TX: PRO-ED.

Epstein, M. H., Nelson, C. M., Polsgrove, L., Coutinho, M., Cumblad, C., & Quinn, K. (1993). A comprehensive community-based approach to serving students with emotional and behavior disorders. *Journal of Emotional and Behavioral Disorders, 1*, 127–133.

Epstein, M. H., Nordness, P. D., Gallagher, K., Nelson, J. R., Lewis, L. & Schrepf, S. (2005). School as the entry point: Assessing adherence to the basic tenets of the wrap-around approach. *Behavioral Disorders, 30*, 85–93.

Erickson, S. J., & Achilles, G. (2004). Cognitive behavioral therapy with children and adolescents. In H. Steiner (Ed.), *Handbook of mental health interventions in children and adolescents: An integrated developmental approach* (pp. 525–556). San Francisco: Jossey-Bass.

Erickson, S. J., & Palmer, L. L. (2004). Group therapy and interventions with children and adolescents. In H. Steiner (Ed.), *Handbook of mental health interventions in children and adolescents: An integrated developmental approach* (pp. 824–848). San Francisco: Jossey-Bass.

Etscheidt, S. (2002). Psychotherapy services for students with emotional or behavioral disorders: A legal analysis of issues. *Behavioral Disorders, 27*, 386–399.

Evans, G. W., Wells, N. M., Chan, H. Y. E., & Saltzman, H. (2000). Housing quality and mental health. *Journal of Clinical Child Psychology, 29*, 526–530.

Everson, T. J. (1997). *Pathways: Fostering spiritual growth among at-risk youth*. Boys Town, NE: Boys Town Press.

Evertson, C. M., Emmer, E. T., & Worsham, M. E. (2006). *Classroom management for elementary teachers* (7th ed.). Needham Heights, MA: Allyn & Bacon.

Ewen, R. B. (2003). *An introduction to theories of personality* (6th ed.). Mahway, NJ: Erlbaum.

Fabiano, G. A., & Pelham, W. E., Jr. (2003). Improving the effectiveness of behavioral classroom interventions for attention-deficit/hyperactivity disorder: A case study. *Journal of Emotional and Behavioral Disorders, 11*, 122–124.

Faedda, G. L., Baldessarini, R. J., Glovinsky, I. P., & Austin, N. B. (2004). Pediatric bipolar disorder: Phenomenology and course of illness. *Bipolar Disorders, 6*, 305–313.

Fagan, S. A. (1996). Fifteen teacher intervention skills for managing classroom behavior problems. In N. J. Long & W. C. Morse (Eds.), *Conflict in the classroom* (5th ed., pp. 273–287). Austin, TX: PRO-ED.

Fagen, S. A., & Long, N. J. (1979). A psychoeducational curriculum approach to teaching self-control. *Behavioral Disorders, 4*, 68–82.

Fagen, S. A., Long, N. J., & Stevens, D. J. (1975). *Teaching children self-control*. Columbus, OH: Merrill.

Fannery, D. J., & Huff, C. R. (Eds.). (1999). *Youth violence: Prevention, intervention, and social policy*. Washington, DC: American Psychiatric Press.

Farmer, T. W., Goforth, J. B., Leung, M. C., Clemmer, J. T., & Thompson, J. H. (2004). School discipline problems in rural African American early adolescents: Characteristics of students with major, minor, and no offenses. *Behavioral Disorders, 29*, 317–336.

Farmer, T. W., Quinn, M. M., Hussey, W., & Holahan, T. (2001). The development of disruptive behavioral disorders and correlated constraints: Implications for intervention. *Behavioral Disorders, 26*, 117–130.

Farver, J. A. M., Xu, Y., Eppe, S., Fernandez, A., & Schwartz, D. (2005). Community violence, family conflict, and preschoolers' socioemotional functioning. *Developmental Psychology, 41*, 160–170.

Federal Interagency Forum on Child and Family Statistics. (2003). *America's children: Key national indicators of well-being, 2003*. Washington, DC: U.S. Government Printing Office.

Federal Interagency Forum on Child and Family Statistics. (2004). *America's children in brief: Key national indicators of well-being, 2004*. Washington, DC: Author. [online] Available: http://childstats.gov.

Feindler, E. L. (1991). Cognitive strategies in anger control interventions for children and adolescents. In P.C. Kendall (Ed.), *Child and adolescent therapy: Cognitive-behavioral procedures* (pp. 66–97). New York: Guilford.

Feindler, E. L., & Ecton, R. B. (1986). *Adolescent anger control: Cognitive-behavioral techniques*. New York: Pergamon.

Feingold, B. F. (1975). *Why your child is hyperactive*. New York: Random House.

Feist, J., & Feist, G. J. (2006). *Theories of personality* (6th ed.). Boston: McGraw-Hill.

Fennig, S., & Fochtmann, L. J. (2005). Psychosis not otherwise specified. In B. J. Sadock & V. A. Sadock (Eds.), *Kaplan & Sadock's comprehensive textbook of psychiatry* (Vol. I, pp. 1542–1543). Philadelphia: Lippincott Williams & Wilkins.

Ferguson, K. E. (2003). Relaxation. In W. O'Donohue, J. E. Fisher, & S. C. Hayes (Eds.) *Cognitive behavior therapy: Applying empirically supported techniques in your practice* (pp. 330–340). Hoboken, NJ: Wiley.

Ferster, C. B., & DeMyer, M. K. (1962). A method for the experimental analyses of the behavior of autistic children. *American Journal of Orthopsychiatry, 32*, 89–98.

Fiedler, C. R. (2003). Legal and ethical issues in the educational assessment and programming for youth with emotional/

behavioral disorders. In M. J. Breen & C. R. Fiedler (Eds.), *Behavioral approach to assessment of youth with emotional/behavioral disorders* (2nd ed., pp. 21–69). Austin, TX: PRO-ED.

Finch, A. J., Deardoff, P. A., & Montgomery, L. E. (1974). Individually tailored behavior rating scales: A possible alternative. *Journal of Abnormal Child Psychology, 2,* 209–216.

Fink, B. C., & Lotspeich, L. (2004). Behavior analysis and child and adolescent treatments. In H. Steiner (Eds.), *Handbook of mental health interventions in children and adolescents: An integrated developmental approach* (pp. 498–524). San Francisco: Jossey-Bass.

Fischer, T. A. (2003). Conducting functional behavioral assessments and designing behavior intervention plans for youth with emotional/behavioral disorders. In M. J. Breen & C. R. Fiedler (Eds.), *Behavioral approach to assessment of youth with emotional/behavioral disorders* (2nd ed., pp. 73–121). Austin, TX: PRO-ED.

Fisher, P. H., Masia-Warner, C., & Klein, R. G. (2004). Skills for Academic and Social Success: A school-based intervention for social anxiety disorder in adolescents. *Clinical Child and Family Psychology Review, 7,* 241–249.

Fitzgerald, K. D., & Rosenberg, D. R. (2005). Neuroimaging in child and adolescent psychiatry. In B. J. Sadock & V. A. Sadock (Eds.), *Kaplan & Sadock's comprehensive textbook of psychiatry* (Vol. II, pp. 3519–3535). Philadelphia: Lippincott Williams & Wilkins.

Flannery, D. J., Liau, A. K., Powell, K. E., Vesterdal, W., Vazsonyi, A. T., Guo, S., et al. (2003). Initial behavior outcomes for the PeaceBuilders universal school-based violence prevention program. *Developmental Psychology, 39,* 292–308.

Fletcher, K. E. (2003). Childhood posttraumatic stress disorder. In E. J. Mash & R. A. Barkley (Eds.), *Child psychopathology* (2nd ed., pp. 330–371). New York: Guilford.

Flicek, M., Olsen, C., Chivers, R., Kaufman, C. J., & Anderson, J. A. (1996). The combined classroom model for serving elementary students with and without behavioral disorders. *Behavioral Disorders, 21,* 241–248.

Flory, V., Vance, A. L. A., Birleson, P., & Luk, E. S. L. (2002). Early onset dysthymic disorder in children and adolescents: Clinical implications and future directions. *Child and Adolescent Mental Health, 7,* 79–84.

Fombonne, E. (2002). Case identification in an epidemiological context. In M. Rutter & E. Taylor (Eds.), *Child and adolescent psychiatry* (4th ed., pp. 52–69). Malden, MA: Blackwell Science.

Fombonne, E. (2003). Epidemiological surveys of autism and other pervasive developmental disorders: An update. *Journal of Autism and Developmental Disorders, 33,* 365–382.

Fonagy, P. (2004). Psychodynamic therapy with children. In H. Steiner (Ed.), *Handbook of mental health interventions in children and adolescents: An integrated developmental approach* (pp. 621–657). San Francisco: Jossey-Bass.

Fonseca, A. C., & Perrin, S. (2001). Clinical phenomenology, classification and assessment of anxiety disorders in children and adolescents. In W. K. Silverman & P. D. A. Treffers (Eds.), *Anxiety disorders in children and adolescents: Research, assessment, and intervention* (pp. 126–158). New York: Cambridge University Press.

Forness, S. (1995). In memoriam: Frank M. Hewett. *Behavioral Disorders, 20,* 86.

Forness, S. R. (2004). Introduction to Part III. In R. B. Rutherford Jr., M. M. Quinn, & S. Mathur (Eds.), *Handbook of research in behavioral disorders* (pp. 235–242). New York: Guilford.

Forness, S. R., & Kavale, K. (2000). Emotional or behavioral disorders: Background and current status of the E/BD terminology and definition. *Behavioral Disorders, 25,* 264–269.

Forness, S. R., & Knitzer, J. (1992). A new proposed definition and terminology to replace "Serious Emotional Disturbance" in Individuals with Disabilities Education Act. *School Psychology Review, 21,* 12–20.

Foskett, J. (1996). Christianity and psychiatry. In D. Bhugra (Ed.), *Psychiatry and religion: Context, consensus and controversies* (pp. 51–64). London: Routledge.

Foster, S. L. (2005). Aggression and antisocial behavior in girls. In D. J. Bell, S. L. Foster, & E. J. Mash (Eds.), *Handbook of behavioral and emotional problems in girls* (pp. 149–180). New York: Kluwer Academic/Plenum.

Fox, J. J., & Gable, R. A. (2004). Functional behavioral assessment. In R. B. Rutherford Jr., M. M. Quinn, & S. Mathur (Eds.), *Handbook of research in behavioral disorders* (pp. 143–162). New York: Guilford.

Franklin, M. E., Rynn, M., Foa, E. B., & March, J. S. (2003). Treatment of obsessive-compulsive disorder. In M. A. Reinecke, F. M. Dattilio, & A. Freeman (Eds.), *Cognitive therapy with children and adolescents* (2nd ed., pp. 162–188). New York: Guilford.

Fraser, M. W., Nelson, K. E., & Rivard, J. C. (1997). Effectiveness of family preservation services. *Social Work Research, 21,* 138–153.

Freeman, J. B., Garcia, A. M., & Leonard, H. L. (2002). Anxiety disorders. In M. Lewis (Ed.), *Child and adolescent psychiatry: A comprehensive textbook* (3rd ed., pp. 821–834). Philadelphia: Lippincott Williams & Wilkins.

Freiberg, H. J. (1999). Consistency management and cooperative discipline: From tourists to citizens in the classrooms. In H. J. Freiberg (Ed.), *Beyond behaviorism: Changing the classroom management paradigm* (pp. 75–97). Needham Heights: Allyn and Bacon.

Freiberg, H. J., & Driscoll, A. (2004). *Universal teaching strategies* (4th ed.). Boston: Allyn and Bacon.

Frey, K. S., Hirschstein, M. K., & Guzzo, B. A. (2000). Second Step: Preventing aggression by promoting social competence. *Journal of Emotional and Behavioral Disorders, 8,* 102–112.

Frey, L. M., & Wilhite, K. (2005). Our five basic needs: Application for understanding the function of behavior. *Intervention in School and Clinic, 40,* 156–160.

Frick, P. J., & Loney, B. R. (1999). Outcomes of children and adolescents with oppositional defiant disorder and conduct disorder. In H. C. Quay & A. E. Hogan (Eds.), *Handbook of disruptive behavior disorders* (pp. 507–524). New York: Kluwer Academic/Plenum.

Frick, P. J., & Silverthorn, P. (2001). Psychopathology in children. In P. B. Sutker & H. E. Adams (Eds.), *Comprehensive handbook of psychopathology* (3rd ed., pp. 881–920). New York: Kluwer Academic/Plenum.

Friedman, H. S., & Schustack, M. W. (2005). *Personality: Classic theories and modern research* (3rd ed). Boston: Allyn & Bacon.

Friedman, R. J., & Chase-Lansdale, P. L. (2002). Chronic adversities. In M. Rutter & E. Taylor (Eds.), *Child and adolescent psychiatry* (4th ed., pp. 261–276). Malden, MA: Blackwell.

Friedman, R. M. (2003). A conceptual framework for developing and implementing effective policy in children's mental health. *Journal of Emotional and Behavioral Disorders, 11,* 11–18.

Friend, M. (2005). *Special education: Contemporary perspectives for school professionals.* Boston: Allyn and Bacon.

Friend, M., & Bursuck, W. D. (2006). *Including students with special needs: A practical guide for classroom teachers* (4th ed.). Needham Heights, MA: Allyn and Bacon.

Friman, P. C., & Finney, J. W. (2003). Time-out (and time-in). In W. O'Donohue, J. E. Fisher, & S. C. Hayes (Eds.), *Cognitive behavior therapy: Applying empirically supported techniques in your practice* (pp. 429–435). Hoboken, NJ: Wiley.

Fulford, K. W. M. (1996). Religion and psychiatry: Extending the limits of tolerance. In D. Bhugra (Ed.), *Psychiatry and religion: Context, consensus and controversies* (pp. 15–22). London: Routledge.

Fuller, G. B., & Fuller, D. L. (1999). Reality therapy approaches. In H. T. Prout & D. T. Brown (Eds.), *Counseling and psychotherapy with children and adolescents: Theory and practice for school and clinical settings* (3rd ed., pp. 302–350). New York: Wiley.

Fuller, R. L. M., Schultz, S. K., & Andreasen, N. C. (2003). The symptoms of schizophrenia. In S. R. Hirsch & D. R. Weinberger (Eds.), *Schizophrenia* (2nd ed., pp. 25–33). Malden, MA: Blackwell.

Furlong, M. J., Morrison, G. M., & Jimerson, S. R. (2004). Externalizing behaviors of aggression and violence and the school context. In R. B. Rutherford Jr., M. M. Quinn, & S. Mathur (Eds.), *Handbook of research in behavioral disorders* (pp. 243–261). New York: Guilford.

Gable, R., Hendrickson, J. M., & Sealander, K. (1997). Ecobehavioral assessment to identify classroom correlates of students' learning and behavior problems. *Beyond Behavior, 8,* 25–27.

Gagnon, J. C., & Leone, P. E. (2005). Elementary day and residential schools for children with emotional and behavioral disorders: Characteristics and entrance and exit policies. *Remedial and Special Education, 26,* 141–150.

Gallagher, B. J. (2002). *The sociology of mental illness* (4th ed.). Englewood Cliffs, NJ: Prentice Hall.

Garber, J., & Horowitz, J. L. (2002). Depression in children. In C. L. Hammen & I. H. Gotlib (Eds.), *Handbook of depression* (pp. 510–540). New York: Guilford.

Garland, A. F., Hough, R. L., McCabe, K. M., Yeh, M., Wood, P. A., & Aarons, G. A. (2001). Prevalence of psychiatric disorders in youths across five sectors of care. *Journal of the American Academy of Child and Adolescent Psychiatry, 40,* 409–418.

Gaylin, N. L. (1999). Client-centered child and family therapy. In S. W. Russ & T. H. Ollendick (Eds.), *Handbook of psychotherapies with children and families* (pp. 107–120). New York: Kluwer Academic/Plenum.

Geller, B., Craney, J. L., Bolhofner, K., DelBello, M. P., Axelson, D., Luby, J., et al. (2003). Phenomenology and longitudinal course of children with a prepubertal and early adolescent bipolar disorder phenotype. In B. Geller & M. P. DelBello (Eds.), *Bipolar disorder in childhood and early adolescence* (pp. 25–50). New York: Guilford.

Gershon, S. (2002). Historical perspective on child and adolescent psychopharmacology. In D. R. Rosenberg, P. A. Davanzo, & S. Gershon (Eds.), *Pharmacotherapy for child and adolescent psychiatric disorders* (2nd ed., pp. 1–6). New York: Marcel Dekker.

Gersten, R., Jordan, N. C., & Flojo, J. R. (2005). Early identification and interventions for students with mathematics difficulties. *Journal of Learning Disabilities, 38,* 293–304.

Ghezzi, P. M., Wilson, G. R., Tarbox, R. S. F., & MacAleese, K. R. (2003). Token economy. In W. O'Donohue, J. E. Fisher, & S. C. Hayes (Eds.), *Cognitive behavior therapy: Applying empirically supported techniques in your practice* (pp. 436–441). Hoboken, NJ: Wiley.

Gibbs, J. C., Potter, G. B., & Goldstein, A. P. (1995). *The EQUIP program.* Champaign, IL: Research Press.

Gibbs, J. C., Potter, G. B., Goldstein, A. P., & Brendtro, L. K. (1998). How EQUIP programs help youth change. *Reclaiming Children and Youth, 7,* 117–122.

Gilbert, G. M. (1957). A survey of "referral problems" in metropolitan child guidance centers. *Journal of Clinical Psychology, 13,* 37–42.

Glaser, D. (2002). Child sexual abuse. In M. Rutter & E. Taylor (Eds.), *Child and adolescent psychiatry* (4th ed., pp. 340–358). Malden, MA: Blackwell Science.

Glasser, W. (1965). *Reality therapy.* New York: Harper & Row.

Glasser, W. (1969). *Schools without failure.* New York: Harper & Row.

Glasser, W. (2001). *Choice theory in the classroom* (Rev. ed.). New York: HarperCollins.

Godwin, T. M., Steinhart, D. J., & Fulton, B. A. (1996). *Peer justice and youth empowerment: An implementation guide for teen court programs* (415–471/60188). Washington, DC: U.S. Government Printing Office.

Goldstein, A. P. (1999). *The prepare curriculum: Teaching prosocial competencies* (2nd ed.). Champaign, IL: Research Press.

Goldstein, A. P., & Glick, B. (1987). *Aggression replacement training: A comprehensive intervention for aggressive youth.* Champaign, IL: Research Press.

Goldstein, A. P., Glick, B., & Gibbs, J. C. (1998). *Aggression replacement training: A comprehensive intervention for aggressive youth* (2nd ed.). Champaign, IL: Research Press.

Goldstein, A. P., & McGinnis, E. (1997). *Skillstreaming the adolescent: New strategies and perspectives for teaching prosocial skills* (2nd ed.). Champaign, IL: Research Press.

Goldstein, A. P., Reagles, K. W., & Amann, L. L. (1990). *Refusal skills: Preventing drug use in adolescents.* Champaign, IL: Research Press.

Goldstein, A. P., Sprafkin, R. P., Gershaw, N. S., & Klein, P. (1980). *Skillstreaming the adolescent.* Champaign, IL: Research Press.

Golly, A. M., Stiller, B., & Walker, H. M. (1998). First Step to Success: Replication and social validation of an early intervention program. *Journal of Emotional and Behavioral Disorders, 6,* 243–250.

Gonzalez, J. E., Nelson, J. R., Gutkin, T. B., Saunders, A., Galloway, A., & Shwery, C. S. (2004). Rational emotive therapy with children and adolescents: A meta-analysis. *Journal of Emotional and Behavioral Disorders, 12,* 222–235.

Goodman, R. (2002). Brain disorders. In M. Rutter & E. Taylor (Eds.), *Child and adolescent psychiatry* (4th ed., pp. 241–260). Malden, MA: Blackwell Science.

Gordon, M. F. (2005). Normal child development. In B. J. Sadock & V. A. Sadock (Eds.), *Kaplan & Sadock's comprehensive textbook of psychiatry* (Vol. II, pp. 3018–3034). Philadelphia: Lippincott Williams & Wilkins.

Gordon, T. (1974). *T.E.T.: Teacher Effectiveness Training.* New York: McKay.

Gossen, D. (1992). *Restitution: Restructuring school discipline.* Chapel Hill, NC: New View Publications.

Graczyk, P. A., & Tolan, P. H. (2005). Implementing effective youth violence prevention programs in community settings. In R. G. Steele & M. C. Roberts (Eds.), *Handbook of mental health services for children, adolescents, and families* (pp. 215–230). New York: Kluwer Academic/Plenum.

Grebb, J. A. (2005). Neural sciences: Introduction and overview. In B. J. Sadock & V. A. Sadock (Eds.), *Kaplan & Sadock's comprehensive textbook of psychiatry* (Vol. I, pp. 1–3). Philadelphia: Lippincott Williams & Wilkins.

Green, C. D., & Groff, P. R. (2003). *Early psychological thought: Ancient accounts of mind and soul.* Westport, CT: Praeger.

Green, J., & Goldwyn, R. (2002). Annotation: Attachment disorganisation and psychopathology: New findings in attachment research and their potential implications for development psychopathology in childhood. *Journal of Child Psychology and Psychiatry, 43,* 835–846.

Greenbaum, P. E., Dedrick, R. R., Friedman, R. M., Kutash, K., Brown, E. C., Lardieri, S. P., & Pugh, A. M. (1998). National Adolescent and Child Treatment Study (NACTS): Outcomes for children with serious emotional and behavioral disturbance. In M. H. Epstein, K. Kutash, & A. Duchnowski (Eds.), *Outcomes for children and youth with emotional and behavioral disorders and their families* (pp. 21–54). Austin, TX: PRO-ED.

Greenberg, M. T., Domitrovich, C., & Bumbarger, B. (1999). *Preventing mental disorders in school-age children: A Review of the effectiveness of prevention programs.* Washington, DC: Center for Mental Health Services, U.S. Department of Health and Human Services. [Online] Available: http://www.psu.edu/dept/prevention/CMHS.html.

Greenberg, M. T., Kusché, C. A., & Riggs, N. (2004). The PATHS curriculum: Theory and research on neurocognitive development and school success. In J. E. Zins, R. P. Weissberg, M. C. Wang, & H. J. Walberg (Eds.), *Building academic success on social and emotional learning: What does the research say?* (pp. 170–188). New York: Teachers College Press.

Greenberger, E., Chen, C., Tally, S. R., & Dong, Q. (2000). Family, peer, and individual correlates of depressive symptomatology among U.S. and Chinese adolescents. *Journal of Consulting and Clinical Psychology, 68,* 209–219.

Green, R. W., & Ablon, J. S. (2005). *Treating explosive kids: The collaborative problem-solving approach.* New York: Guilford.

Greene, S. M., Anderson, E. R., Hetherington, E., Forgatch, M. S., & DeGarmo, D. S. (2003). Risk and resilience after divorce. In F. Walsh (Ed.), *Normal family processes: Growing diversity and complexity* (3rd ed., pp. 96–120). New York: Guilford.

Gresham, F. M. (2002). Social skills assessment and instruction for students with emotional and behavioral disorders. In K. L. Lane, F. M. Gresham, & T. E. O'Shaughnessy (Eds.), *Interventions for children with or at risk for emotional and behavioral disorders* (pp. 242–258). Boston: Allyn & Bacon.

Gresham, F. M. (2005). Methodological issues in evaluating cognitive-behavioral treatments for students with behavioral disorders. *Behavioral Disorders, 30,* 213–225.

Gresham, F. M., Crews, S. D., & Kern, L. (2004). Social skills training for children and youth with emotional and behavioral disorders: Validity considerations and future directions. *Behavioral Disorders, 30*, 32–46.

Gresham, F.M., & Elliott, S.N. (1990). *Social Skills Rating System*. Circle Pines, MN: American Guidance Service.

Gresham, F. M., & Kern, L. (2004). Internalizing behavior problems in children and adolescents. In R. B. Rutherford Jr., M. M. Quinn, & S. Mathur (Eds.), *Handbook of research in behavioral disorders* (pp. 262–281). New York: Guilford.

Gresham, F. M., Sugai, G., Horner, R. H., Quinn, M. M., & McInerney, M. (1998). *Classroom and schoolwide practices that support students' social competence: A synthesis of research*. Washington, DC: U.S. Department of Education.

Griffin, K. W., Botvin, G. J., Nichols, T. R., & Doyle, M. M. (2003). Effectiveness of a universal drug abuse prevention approach for youth at high risk for substance use initiation. *Preventive Medicine, 36*, 1–7.

Grisso, T. (2005). Why we need mental health screening and assessment in juvenile justice programs. In T. Grisso, G. Vincent, & D. Seagrave (Eds.), *Mental health screening and assessment in juvenile justice* (pp. 3–21). New York: Guilford.

Grob, G. N. (1994). *The mad among us*. New York: Free Press.

Grossman, D. C., Neckerman, H. J., Koepsell, T. D., Liu, P., Asher, K. N., Beland, K., et al. (1997). Effectiveness of a violence prevention curriculum among children in elementary school: A randomized controlled trial. *Journal of the American Medical Association, 277*, 1605–1612.

Grskovic, J. A., & Goetze, H. (2005). An evaluation of the effects of Life Space Crisis Intervention on the challenging behavior of individual students. *Reclaiming Children and Youth, 13*, 231–235.

Grych, J. H., & Fincham, F. D. (1999). Children of single parents and divorce. In W. K. Silverman & T. H. Ollendick (Eds.), *Developmental issues in the clinical treatment of children* (pp. 321–357). Needham Heights, MA: Allyn & Bacon.

Guerra, N. G., Attar, B., & Weissberg, R. P. (1997). Prevention of aggression and violence among inner-city youths. In D. M. Stoff, J. Breiling, & J. D. Maser (Eds.), *Handbook of antisocial behavior* (pp. 375–383). New York: Wiley.

Guerra, N. G., Boxer, P., & Kim, T. E. (2005). A cognitive-ecological approach to serving students with emotional and behavioral disorders: Application to aggressive behavior. *Behavioral Disorders, 30*, 277–288.

Guetzloe, E. (2004). Introduction (to Part V). In R. B. Rutherford Jr., M. M. Quinn, & S. Mathur (Eds.), *Handbook of research in behavioral disorders* (pp. 519–521). New York: Guilford.

Gunn, B., Smolkowski, K., Biglan, A., Black, C., & Blair, J. (2005). Fostering the development of reading skill through supplemental instruction: Results for Hispanic and non-Hispanic students. *Journal of Special Education, 39*, 66–85.

Gunter, P. L., & Denny, R. K. (2004). Data collection in research and applications involving students with emotional and behavioral disorders. In R. B. Rutherford Jr., M. M. Quinn, & S. Mathur (Eds.), *Handbook of research in behavioral disorders* (pp. 582–595). New York: Guilford.

Haager, D., & Klingner, J. K. (2005). *Differentiating instruction in inclusive classrooms: The special educator's guide*. Boston: Pearson Education.

Hafner, H., & ander Heiden, W. (2003). Course and outcome of schizophrenia. In S. R. Hirsch & D. R. Weinberger (Eds.), *Schizophrenia* (2nd ed., pp. 101–141). Malden, MA: Blackwell.

Hall, R. V., Lund, D., & Jackson, D. (1968). Effects of teacher attention on study behavior. *Journal of Applied Behavior Analysis, 1*, 1–12.

Hallahan, D. P., & Kauffman, J. M. (2006). *Exceptional learners: Introduction to special education* (10th ed.). Boston: Allyn and Bacon.

Hallenbeck, B. A., & Kauffman, J. M. (1995). How does observational learning affect the behavior of students with emotional or behavioral disorders? A review of research. *Journal of Special Education. 29*, 45–71.

Hallmayer, J. (2004). Genetics and psychopathology: How far have we come and where are we going? In H. Steiner (Ed.), *Handbook of mental health interventions in children and adolescents: An integrated developmental approach* (pp. 193–221). San Francisco: Jossey-Bass.

Hammen, C., & Rudolph, K. D. (2003). Childhood mood disorders. In E. J. Mash & R. A. Barkley (Eds.), *Child psychopathology* (2nd ed., pp. 233–278). New York: Guilford.

Hammill, D. D., & Bartel, N. R. (2004). *Teaching students with learning and behavior problems* (7th ed.). Austin, TX: PRO-ED.

Hansen, S. D., & Lignugaris/Kraft, B. (2005). Effects of a dependent group contingency on the verbal interactions of middle school students with emotional disturbance. *Behavioral Disorders, 30*, 170–184.

Haring, N. G., & Phillips, E. L. (1962). *Educating emotionally disturbed children*. New York: McGraw-Hill.

Harrington, R. (2002). Affective disorders. In M. Rutter & E. Taylor (Eds.), *Child and adolescent psychiatry* (4th ed., pp. 463–485). Malden, MA: Blackwell Science.

Harvey, M. T., Lewis-Palmer, T., Horner, R. H., & Sugai, G. (2003). Transsituational interventions: Generalization of behavior support across school and home environments. *Behavioral Disorders, 28*, 299–312.

Hawkins, R. P. (1990). The life and contributions of Burrhus Frederick Skinner. *Education and Treatment of Children, 13*, 258–263.

Hazel, J. S., Schumaker, J. B., Sherman, J. A., & Sheldon, J. (1996). *ASSET: A social skills program for adolescents* (2nd ed). Champaign, IL: Research Press.

Head, L. S., & Gross, A. M. (2003). Systematic desensitization. In W. O'Donohue, J. E. Fisher, & S. C. Hayes (Eds.), *Cognitive behavior therapy: Applying empirically supported techniques in your practice* (pp. 417–422). Hoboken, NJ: Wiley.

Hechtman, L. (2005). Attention-deficit/hyperactivity disorder. In B. J. Sadock & V. A. Sadock (Eds.), *Kaplan & Sadock's comprehensive textbook of psychiatry* (Vol. II, pp. 3183–3204). Philadelphia: Lippincott Williams & Wilkins.

Heffron, W. M., Pumariega, A. J., Fallon, T., & Carter, D. R. (2003). Youth in the juvenile justice system. In A. J. Pumariega & N. C. Winters (Eds.), *The handbook of child and adolescent systems of care: The new community psychiatry* (pp. 224–249). San Francisco: Jossey-Bass.

Henggeler, S. W., & Santos, A. B. (1997). Introduction, overview, and commonalities of innovative approaches. In S. W. Henggeler & A. B. Santos (Eds.), *Innovative approaches for difficult-to-treat populations* (pp. xxiii–xxxiii). Washington, DC: American Psychiatric Press.

Henggeler, S. W., Schoenwald, S. K., Borduin, C. M., Rowland, M. D., & Cunningham, P. B. (1998). *Multisystemic treatment of antisocial behavior in children and adolescents*. New York: Guilford.

Henley, M. (2003). *Teaching self-control: A curriculum for responsible behavior* (2nd ed.). Bloomington, IN: National Educational Service.

Hernandez, M., & Isaacs, M. (1998). *Promoting cultural competence in children's mental health services*. Baltimore, MD: Brookes.

Hetherington, E. M., Bridges, M., & Insabella, G. (1998). What matters? What does not? Five perspectives on the association between marital transitions and children's adjustment. *American Psychologist, 53*, 167–184.

Hetherington, E. M., & Martin, B. (1986). Family factors and psychopathology in children (pp. 332–390). In H.C. Quay & J.S. Werry (Eds.), *Psychopatholgical disorders of childhood* (3rd ed.) New York: Wiley.

Heward, W. L. (2006). *Exceptional children: An introduction to special education*. Upper Saddle River, NJ: Merrill Prentice Hall.

Hewett, F. M. (1968). *the emotionally disturbed child in the classroom*. Boston: Allyn & Bacon.

Hewett, F. M. (1974). Frank M. Hewett. In J. M. Kauffman & C. D. Lewis (Eds.), *Teaching children with behavior disorders: Personal perspectives*. Upper Saddle River, NJ: Merrill/Prentice Hall.

Hewett, F. M., & Taylor, F. D. (1980). *The emotionally disturbed child in the classroom* (2nd ed.). Boston: Allyn & Bacon.

Heyman, I., & Santosh, P. (2002). Pharmacological and other physical treatments. In M. Rutter & E. Taylor (Eds.), *Child and adolescent psychiatry* (4th ed., pp. 998–1018). Malden, MA: Blackwell Science.

Hibbs, E. D. (2005). Short-term psychotherapies for the treatment of child and adolescent disorders. In B. J. Sadock & V. A. Sadock (Eds.). *Kaplan & Sadock's comprehensive textbook of psychiatry* (Vol. II, pp. 3322–3331). Philadelphia: Lippincott Williams & Wilkins.

Hinshaw, S. P., & Blackman, D. R. (2005). Attention-deficit/hyperactivity disorder in girls. In D. J. Bell, S. L. Foster, & E. J. Mash (Eds.), *Handbook of behavioral and emotional problems in girls* (pp. 117–148). New York: Kluwer Academic/Plenum.

Hinshaw, S. P., & Lee, S. S. (2003). Conduct and oppositional defiant disorders. In E. J. Mash & R. A. Barkley (Eds.), *Child psychopathology* (2nd ed., pp. 144–198). New York: Guilford.

Hoagwood, K., Kelleher, K. J., Feil, M., & Comer, D. M. (2000). Treatment services for children with ADHD: A national perspective. *Journal of the American Academy of Child and Adolescent Psychiatry, 39*, 198–206.

Hobbs, N. (1966). Helping disturbed children: Ecological and psychological strategies. *American Psychologist, 21*, 1105–1115.

Hobbs, N. (1974). Nicholas Hobbs. In J. M. Kauffman & C. D. Lewis (Eds.), *Teaching children with behavior disorders: Personal perspectives*. Columbus, OH: Merrill.

Hodapp, R. M., & Dykens, E. M. (2003). Mental retardation (intellectual disabilities). In E. J. Mash & R. A. Barkley (Eds.), *Child psychopathology* (2nd ed., pp. 486–519). New York: Guilford.

Holden, E. W., Santiago, R. L., Manteuffel, B. A., Stephens, R. L., Brannan, A. M., Soler, R., et al. (2003). Systems of care demonstration projects: Innovation, evaluation, and sustainability. In A. J. Pumariega & N. C. Winters (Eds.), *The handbook of child and adolescent systems of care: The new community psychiatry* (pp. 432–458). San Francisco: Jossey-Bass.

Hollis, C. (2003). Child and adolescent onset schizophrenia. In S. R. Hirsch & D. R. Weinberger (Eds.), *Schizophrenia* (2nd ed., pp. 34–53). Malden, MA: Blackwell.

Homme, L. E. (1965). Perspectives in psychology: XXIV—Control of coverants, the operants of the mind. *Psychological Record, 15*, 501–511.

Hooper, S. R., Roberts, J. E., Zeisel, S. A., & Poe, M. (2003). Core language predictors of behavioral functioning in early elementary school children: Concurrent and longitudinal findings. *Behavioral Disorders, 29*, 10–24.

Hoover, J. J., & Patton, J. R. (1999). *Curriculum adaptations for students with learning and behavior problems: Principles and practices*. Reston, VA: Council for Exceptional Children.

Hops, H., & Walker, H. M. (1988). *CLASS: Contingencies for learning academic and social skills*. Seattle, WA: Educational Achievement Systems.

Houmanfar, R., Maglieri, K. A., & Roman, H. R. (2003). Behavioral contracting. In W. O'Donohue, J. E. Fisher, & S. C. Hayes (Eds.), *Cognitive behavior therapy: Applying empirically supported techniques in your practice* (pp. 40–45). Hoboken, NJ: Wiley.

Howard, K. A., Barton, C. C., Walsh, M. E., & Lerner, R. M. (1999). Social and contextual issues in interventions with children and families. In S. W. Russ & T. H. Ollendick (Eds.), *Handbook of psychotherapies with children and families* (pp. 45–66). New York: Kluwer Academic/Plenum.

Howell, J. C. (1997). *Juvenile justice & youth violence.* Thousand Oaks, CA: Sage.

Huberty, T. J. (2003). Integrating interviews, observations, questionnaires, and test data: Relationships among assessment, placement, and intervention. In M. J. Breen & C. R. Fiedler (Eds.), *Behavioral approach to assessment of youth with emotional/behavioral disorders* (2nd ed., pp. 587–633). Austin, TX: PRO-ED.

Hudson, C. G. (2005). Socioeconomic status and mental illness: Tests of the social causation and selection hypotheses. *American Journal of Orthopsychiatry, 75,* 3–18.

Huey, S. J., Henggeler, S. W., Brondino, M. J., & Pickrel, S. G. (2000). Mechanisms of change in multisystemic therapy: Reducing delinquent behavior through therapist adherence and improved family and peer functioning. *Journal of Consulting and Clinical Psychology, 68,* 451–467.

Huizinga, D., Loeber, R., Thornberry, T., & Cothern, L. (2000). *Co-occurrence of delinquency and other problem behaviors* (Office of Juvenile Justice and Delinquency Prevention, NCJ 182211). Washington: U.S. Department of Justice.

Hune, J. B., & Nelson, C. M. (2002). Effects of teaching a problem-solving strategy on preschool children with problem behavior. *Behavioral Disorders, 27,* 185–207.

Hyatt, K. J., & Howell, K. W. (2004). Curriculum-based measurement of students with emotional and behavioral disorders: Assessment for data-based decision making. In R. B. Rutherford Jr., M. M. Quinn, & S. Mathur (Eds.), *Handbook of research in behavioral disorders* (pp. 181–198). New York: Guilford.

Institute of Medicine. (2002). *Reducing suicide: A national imperative.* Washington, DC: National Academies Press.

Isaacs-Shockley, M., Cross, T., Bazron, B. J., Dennis, K., & Benjamin, M. P. (1996). Framework for a culturally competent system of care. In B. A. Stroul (Ed.), *Children's mental health: Creating systems of care in a changing society* (pp. 23–40). Baltimore: Brookes.

Jablensky, A. (2003). The epidemiological horizon. In S. R. Hirsch & D. R. Weinberger (Eds.), *Schizophrenia* (2nd ed., pp. 203–231). Oxford, England: Blackwell.

Jackson, M. S., & Knepper, P. (2003). *Delinquency and justice.* Boston: Allyn and Bacon.

Jacobs, A. K., Randall, C., Vernberg, E. M., Roberts, M. C., & Nyre, J. E. (2005). Providing services within a school-based intensive mental health program. In R. G. Steele & M. C. Roberts (Eds.), *Handbook of mental health services for children, adolescents, and families* (pp. 47–61). New York: Kluwer Academic/Plenum.

Jacob, R. G., & Pelham, W. E. (2005). Behavior therapy. In B. J. Sadock & V. A. Sadock (Eds.), *Kaplan & Sadock's comprehensive textbook of psychiatry* (Vol. II, pp. 2498–2547). Philadelphia: Lippincott Williams & Wilkins.

Jaffe, J. H., & Anthony, J. C. (2005). Substance-related disorders: Introduction and overview. In B. J. Sadock & V. A. Sadock (Eds.), *Kaplan & Sadock's comprehensive textbook of psychiatry* (Vol. I, pp. 1137–1167). Philadelphia: Lippincott Williams & Wilkins.

Jaffe, S. L., & Simkin, D. R. (2002). Alcohol and drug abuse in children and adolescents. In M. Lewis (Ed.), *Child and adolescent psychiatry: A comprehensive textbook* (3rd ed., pp. 895–911). Philadelphia: Lippincott Williams & Wilkins.

Jaffee, S. R., Caspi, A., Moffitt, T. E., Dodge, K. A., Rutter, M., Taylor, A., et al. (2005). Nature x nurture: Genetic vulnerabilities interact with physical maltreatment to promote conduct problems. *Development and Psychopathology, 17,* 67–84.

Jensen, P. S., Bhatara, V. S., Vitiello, B., Hoagwood, K., Feil, M., & Burke, L. B. (1999). Psychoactive medication prescribing practices for U.S. children: Gaps between research and clinical practice. *Journal of the American Academy of Child and Adolescent Psychiatry, 38,* 557–565.

Johns, B., Crowley, E. P., & Guetzloe, E. (2002). *Effective curriculum for students with emotional and behavioral disorders.* Denver: Love.

Johnson, S. L., & Kizer, A. (2002). Bipolar and unipolar depression: A comparison of clinical phenomenology and psychosocial predictors. In C. L. Hammen & I. H. Gotlib (Eds.), *Handbook of depression* (pp. 141–165). New York: Guilford.

Johnston, L. D., O'Malley, P. M., Bachman, J. G., & Schulenberg, J. E. (2004). *Monitoring the Future national results on adolescent drug use: Overview of key findings, 2003* (NIH Publication No. 04-5506). Bethesda, MD: National Institute on Drug Abuse.

Joint Commission on the Mental Health of Children. (1969). *Crisis in child mental health: Challenge for the 1970s.* New York: Harper & Row.

Jones, V. (1991). Responding to students' behavior problems. *Beyond Behavior, 2,* 17–21.

Jones, V., Dohrn, E., & Dunn, C. (2004). *Creating effective programs for students with emotional and behavior disorders.* Boston: Allyn and Bacon.

Jones, V. F., & Jones, L. S. (1998). *Comprehensive classroom management: Creating communities of support and solving problems* (5th ed). Needham Heights, MA: Allyn & Bacon.

Joseph, G., & Strain, P. (2003). Comprehensive evidence-based social-emotional curricula for young children: An analysis of efficacious adoption potential. *Topics in Early Childhood Special Education, 23*, 65–76.

Josephson, A. M. (2005). Family therapy. In B. J. Sadock & V. A. Sadock (Eds.), *Kaplan & Sadock's comprehensive textbook of psychiatry*, (Vol. II, pp. 3352–3362). Philadelphia: Lippincott Williams & Wilkins.

Jura, M. B., & Humphrey, L. A. (2005). Neuropsychological and cognitive assessment of children. In B. J. Sadock & V. A. Sadock (Eds.), *Kaplan & Sadock's comprehensive textbook of psychiatry*, (Vol. I, pp. 895–915). Philadelphia: Lippincott Williams & Wilkins.

Justice, L. M. (2004). Creating language-rich preschool classroom environments. *Teaching Exceptional Children, 37*, 36–45.

Kagan, J. (2002). The contribution of temperament to developmental profiles. In M. Lewis (Ed.), *Child and adolescent psychiatry: A comprehensive textbook* (3rd ed., pp. 211–220). Philadelphia: Lippincott Williams & Wilkins.

Kaiser, A. P., Cai, X., Hancock, T. B., & Foster, E. M. (2002). Teacher-reported behavior problems and language delays in boys and girls enrolled in head start. *Behavioral Disorders, 28*, 23–39.

Kakar, S. (1982). *Shamans, mystics and doctors*. Chicago: University of Chicago Press.

Kalat, J. W. (2004). *Biological psychology* (8th ed.). Belmont, CA: Wadsworth.

Kam, C. M., Greenberg, M. T., & Kusché, C. A. (2004). Sustained effects of the PATHS curriculum on the social and psychological adjustment of children in special education. *Journal of Emotional & Behavioral Disorders, 12*, 66–79.

Kanfer, F. H., & Karoly, P. (1972). Self-control: A behaviorist excursion into the lion's den. *Behavior Therapy, 3*, 398–416.

Kanner, L. (1943). Autistic disturbances of affective contact. *Nervous Child, 2*, 217–250.

Karasu, T. B. (2005). Psychoanalysis and psychoanalytic psychotherapy. In B. J. Sadock & V. A. Sadock (Eds.), *Kaplan & Sadock's comprehensive textbook of psychiatry* (Vol. II, pp. 2472–2497). Philadelphia: Lippincott Williams & Wilkins.

Karenga, M. (1980). *Kawaida theory: An introductory outline*. Inglewood, CA: Kawaida Publications.

Karnik, N. S. (2004). The social environment. In H. Steiner (Ed.), *Handbook of mental health interventions in children and adolescents* (pp. 51–72). San Francisco: Jossey-Bass.

Kashani, J. H., Jones, M. R., Bumby, K. M., & Thomas, L. A. (1999). Youth violence: Psychosocial risk factors, treatment, prevention, and recommendation. *Journal of Emotional and Behavioral Disorders, 7*, 200–210.

Katsiyannis, A., & Yell, M. L. (2004). Critical issues and trends in the education of students with emotional or behavioral disorders. *Behavioral Disorders, 29*, 209–210.

Kauffman, J. M. (1976). Nineteenth century views of children's behavior disorders: Historical contributions and continuing issues. *Journal of Special Education, 10*, 335–349.

Kauffman, J. M. (1999). How we prevent the prevention of emotional and behavioral disorders. *Exceptional Children, 65*, 448–468.

Kauffman, J. M. (2001). *Characteristics of emotional and behavioral disorders of children and youth* (7th ed.). Upper Saddle River, NJ: Merrill/Prentice Hall.

Kauffman, J. M., Brigham, F. J., & Mock, D. R. (2004). Historical to contemporary perspectives on the field of emotional and behavioral disorders. In R. B. Rutherford Jr., M. M. Quinn, & S. Mathur (Eds.), *Handbook of research in behavioral disorders* (pp. 15–31). New York: Guilford.

Kauffman, J. M., & Landrum, T. J. (2006). *Children and youth with emotional and behavioral disorders: A history of their education*. Austin, TX: PRO-ED.

Kavale, K. A., & Forness, S. R. (2000). History, rhetoric, and reality: Analysis of the inclusion debate. *Remedial and Special Education, 21*, 279–296.

Kavale, K. A., Forness, S. R., & Walker, H. M. (1999). Interventions for oppositional defiant disorder and conduct disorder in the schools. In H. C. Quay & A. E. Hogan (Eds.), *Handbook of disruptive behavior disorders* (pp. 441–454). New York, NY: Kluwer Academic/Plenum.

Kavale, K. A., Mathur, S. R., & Mostert, M. P. (2004). Social skills training and teaching social behavior to students with emotional and behavioral disorders. In R. B. Rutherford Jr., M. M. Quinn, & S. Mathur (Eds.), *Handbook of research in behavioral disorders* (pp. 446–461). New York: Guilford.

Kaye, D. L. (2005). Individual psychodynamic psychotherapy. In B. J. Sadock & V. A. Sadock (Eds.), *Kaplan & Sadock's comprehensive textbook of psychiatry* (Vol. II, pp. 3315–3321). Philadelphia: Lippincott Williams & Wilkins.

Kazdin, A. E. (1978). *History of behavior modification: Experimental foundations of contemporary research*. Baltimore: University Park Press.

Kazdin, A. E. (2001). *Behavior modification in applied settings* (6th ed.). Belmont, CA: Wadsworth/Thompson Learning.

Kazdin, A. E. (2003). *Research design in clinical psychology* (4th ed.). Needham Heights, MA: Allyn & Bacon.

Kazdin, A. E. (Ed.). (2000). *Encyclopedia of psychology* (Vol. 3). Washington, DC: American Psychological Association.

Kazdin, A. E., & Marciano, P. L. (1998). Childhood and adolescent depression. In E. J. Mash & R. A. Barkley (Eds.), *Treatment of childhood disorders* (pp. 211–248). New York, NY: Guilford.

Kearney, C. A. (2001). *School refusal behavior in youth*. Washington, DC: American Psychological Association.

Kehle, T. J., Bray, M. A., Theodore, L. A., Jenson, W. R., & Clark, E. (2000). A multi-component intervention designed to reduce disruptive classroom behavior. *Psychology in the Schools, 37*, 475–481.

Kelley, M. L. (2003). Daily report cards: Home-school contingency management procedures. In W. O'Donohue, J. E. Fisher, & S. C. Hayes (Eds.), *Cognitive behavior therapy: Applying empirically supported techniques in your practice* (pp. 114–120). Hoboken, NJ: Wiley.

Kelley, M. L., & Fals-Stewart, W. (2004). Psychiatric disorders of children living with drug-abusing, alcohol-abusing, and non-substance-abusing fathers. *Journal of the American Academy of Child and Adolescent Psychiatry, 43*, 621–628.

Kellner, M. H., Bry, B. H., & Colletti, L. A. (2002). Teaching anger management skills to students with severe emotional or behavioral disorders. *Behavioral Disorders, 27*, 400–407.

Kelly, F. D. (1999). Adlerian approaches to counseling with children and adolescents. In H. T. Prout & D. T. Brown (Eds.), *Counseling and psychotherapy with children and adolescents: Theory and practice for school and clinical settings* (3rd ed., pp. 108–154). New York: Wiley.

Kelly, J. B. (2000). Children's adjustment in conflicted marriage and divorce: A decade review of research. *Journal of the American Academy of Child and Adolescent Psychiatry, 39*, 963–973.

Kendall, P. C. (2000). Guiding theory for therapy with children and adolescents. In P. C. Kendall (Ed.), *Child and adolescent therapy: Cognitive-behavioral procedures* (2nd ed., pp. 3–27). New York: Guilford.

Kendall, P. C. (Ed.). (1991). *Child and adolescent therapy: Cognitive-behavioral procedures*. New York: Guilford.

Kendall, P. C., Choudhury, M., Chung, H. L., & Robin, J. A. (2002). Cognitive-behavioral approaches. In M. Lewis (Ed.), *Child and adolescent psychiatry: A comprehensive textbook* (3rd ed., pp. 154–164). Philadelphia: Lippincott Williams & Wilkins.

Kendall, P. C., & Suveg, C. (2005). Treating anxiety disorders in youth. In P.C. Kendall (Ed.), *Child and adolescent therapy* (3rd ed.) (pp. 243–294). New York: Guilford.

Kendziora, K. T. (2004). Early intervention for emotional and behavioral disorders. In R. B. Rutherford Jr., M. M. Quinn, & S. Mathur (Eds.), *Handbook of research in behavioral disorders* (pp. 327–351). New York: Guilford.

Kennedy, C. H. (2005). *Single-case designs for educational research*. Boston: Allyn and Bacon.

Keogh, B. (2003). *Temperament in the classroom: Understanding individual differences*. Baltimore: Brookes.

Kern, L., Bambara, L., & Fogt, J. (2002). Class-wide curricular modification to improve the behavior of students with emotional or behavioral disorders. *Behavioral Disorders, 27*, 317–326.

Kerr, M. M., & Nelson, C. M. (2006). *Strategies for addressing behavior problems in the classrooms* (6th ed.). Columbus: Merrill Prentice Hall.

Kessler, R. C. (2005). Sociology and psychiatry. In B. J. Sadock & V. A. Sadock (Eds.), *Kaplan & Sadock's comprehensive textbook of psychiatry* (Vol. I, pp. 623–634). Philadelphia: Lippincott Williams & Wilkins.

King, N. J., Heyne, D., & Ollendick, T. H. (2005). Cognitive-behavioral treatments for anxiety and phobic disorders in children and adolescents: A review. *Behavioral Disorders, 30*, 241–257.

King, R. A. (2002). Adolescence. In M. Lewis (Ed.), *Child and adolescent psychiatry: A comprehensive textbook* (3rd ed., pp. 332–342). Philadelphia: Lippincott Williams & Wilkins.

Kirigin, K. A., & Wolf, M. M. (1998). Application of the Teaching-Family Model to children and adolescents with conduct disorder. In V. B. Van Hasselt & M. Hersen (Eds.), *Handbook of psychological treatment protocols for children and adolescents* (pp. 359–380). Mahwah, NJ: Erlbaum.

Kirkpatrick, B., & Tek, C. (2005). Schizophrenia: Clinical features and psychopathology concepts. In B. J. Sadock & V. A. Sadock (Eds.), *Kaplan & Sadock's comprehensive textbook of psychiatry* (Vol. I, pp. 1416–1435). Philadelphia: Lippincott Williams & Wilkins.

Kirschenbaum, H. (1995). *100 ways to enhance values and morality in schools and youth settings*. Needham Heights, MA: Allyn & Bacon.

Kiser, L. J., Heston, J. D., & Pruitt, D. B. (2005). Partial hospital and ambulatory behavioral health services. In B. J. Sadock & V. A. Sadock (Eds.), *Kaplan & Sadock's comprehensive textbook of psychiatry* (Vol. II, pp. 3376–3383). Philadelphia: Lippincott Williams & Wilkins.

Klein, R. G., & Pine, D. S. (2002). Anxiety disorders. In M. Rutter & E. Taylor (Eds.), *Child and adolescent psychiatry* (4th ed., pp. 486–509). Malden, MA: Blackwell Science.

Klinger, L. G., Dawson, G. D., & Renner, P. (2003). Autistic disorder. In E. J. Mash & R. A. Barkley (Eds.), *Child psychopathology* (2nd ed., pp. 409–454). New York: Guilford.

Klug, W. S., & Cummings, M. R. (2005). *Essentials of genetics* (5th ed.). Upper Saddle River, NJ: Prentice Hall.

Knapp, P. (2005). Resilience and vulnerability: Adaptation in the context of childhood adversities. *Journal of the American Academy of Child and Adolescent Psychiatry, 44*, 399–400.

Knitzer, J. (1982). *Unclaimed children: The failure of public responsibility to children and adolescents in need of mental health services*. Washington, DC: Children's Defense Fund.

Knitzer, J., Steinberg, Z., & Fleisch, B. (1990). *At the schoolhouse door*. New York: Bank Street College of Education.

Kode, K. (2002). *Elizabeth Farrell and the history of special education.* Arlington, VA: Council for Exceptional Children.

Koegel, L. K., Valdez-Menchaca, M., Koegel, R. L., & Harrower, J. K. (2001). Autism. In M. Hersen & V. B. Van Hasselt (Eds.), *Advanced abnormal psychology* (2nd ed., pp. 165–189). New York: Kluwer Academic/Plenum.

Koenig, K., & Tsatsanis, K. D. (2005). Pervasive developmental disorders in girls. In D. J. Bell, S. L. Foster, & E. J. Mash (Eds.), *Handbook of behavioral and emotional problems in girls* (pp. 211–238). New York: Kluwer Academic/Plenum.

Konold, K. E., Miller, S. P., & Konold, K. B. (2004). Using teacher feedback to enhance student learning. *Teaching Exceptional Children, 36,* 64–66.

Konopasek, D. E., & Forness, S. R. (2004). Psychopharmacology in the treatment of emotional and behavioral disorders. In R. B. Rutherford Jr., M. M. Quinn, & S. Mathur (Eds.), *Handbook of research in behavioral disorders* (pp. 352–368). New York: Guilford.

Kowatch, R. A., Fristad, M., Birmaher, B., Wagner, K. D., Findling, R. L., & Hellander, M. (2005). Treatment guidelines for children and adolescents with bipolar disorder. *Journal of the American Academy of Child and Adolescent Psychiatry, 44,* 213–235.

Krain, A. L., & Kendall, P. C. (1999). Cognitive-behavioral therapy. In S. W. Russ & T. H. Ollendick (Eds.), *Handbook of psychotherapies with children and families* (pp. 121–135). New York: Kluwer Academic/Plenum.

Kubiszyn, T., Carlson, J. S., & Dettay, T. (2005). Pediatric psychopharmacology for prepubertal internalizing disorders. *School Psychology Quarterly, 20,* 135–154.

Kupfer, D. F., First, M. B., & Regier, D. A. (Eds.) (2002). *A research agenda for DSM-V.* Washington, DC: American Psychiatric Association.

Kurtz, E. (1999). The historical context. In W. R. Miller (Eds.), *Integrating spirituality into treatment: Resources for practitioners* (pp. 19–46). Washington, DC: American Psychological Association.

Kutcher, S. P., & Marton, P. (1996). Treatment of adolescent depression. In K. I. Shulman, M. Tohen, & S. P. Kutcher (Eds.), *Mood disorders across the life span* (pp. 101–126). New York: Wiley.

La Greca, A. M., & Prinstein, M. J. (1999). Peer group. In W. K. Silverman & T. H. Ollendick (Eds.), *Developmental issues in the clinical treatment of children* (pp. 171–198). Needham Heights, MA: Allyn & Bacon.

Lachar, D. L., & Gruber, C. P. (2003). Multisource and multidimensional objective assessment of adjustment: The Personality Inventory for Children, Second Edition; Personality Inventory for Youth; and Student Behavior Survey. In C. R. Reynolds & R. W. Kamphaus (Eds.), *Handbook of psychological and educational assessment of children: Personality, behavior, and context* (2nd ed., pp. 337–368). New York: Guilford.

Lahey, B. B. (2004). Commentary: Role of temperament in developmental models of psychopathology. *Journal of Clinical Child and Adolescent Psychology, 33,* 88–93.

Lahey, B. B., Miller, T. L., Gordon, R. A., & Riley, A. W. (1999). Developmental epidemiology of the disruptive behavior disorders. In H. C. Quay & A. E. Hogan (Eds.), *Handbook of disruptive behavior disorders* (pp. 23–48). New York: Kluwer Academic/Plenum.

Laing, R. D. (1967). *The politics of experience.* New York: Pantheon.

Laird, R. S., & Metalsky, G. I. (2003). Attribution change. In W. O'Donohue, J. E. Fisher, & S. C. Hayes (Eds.) *Cognitive behavior therapy: Applying empirically supported techniques in your practice* (pp. 23–27). Hoboken, NJ: Wiley.

Lamiell, J. T. (1997). Individuals and the differences between them. In R. Hogan, J. Johnson, & S. Briggs (Eds.), *Handbook of personality psychology* (pp. 117–141). San Diego, CA: Academic Press.

Landolf, B. M. (2005). Outpatient-private practice model. In R. G. Steele & M. C. Roberts (Eds.), *Handbook of mental health services for children, adolescents, and families* (pp. 117–131). New York: Kluwer Academic/Plenum.

Landrum, T., Katsiyannis, A., & Archwamety, T. (2004). An analysis of placement and exit patterns of students with emotional or behavioral disorders. *Behavioral Disorders, 29,* 140–153.

Lane, K. L. (2004). Academic instruction and tutoring interventions for students with emotional and behavioral disorders: 1990 to the present. In R. B. Rutherford Jr., M. M. Quinn, & S. Mathur (Eds.), *Handbook of research in behavioral disorders* (462–501). New York: Guilford.

Lane, K. L., & Beebe-Frankenberger, M. (2004). *School-based interventions: The tools you need to succeed.* Boston: Allyn and Bacon.

Lane, K. L., Wehby, J., Menzies, H. M., Doukas, G. L., Munton, S. M., & Gregg, R. M. (2003). Social skills instruction for students at risk for antisocial behavior: The effects of small-group instruction. *Behavioral Disorders, 28,* 229–248.

Lane, K. L., Wehby, J. H., & Cooley, C. (2006). Teacher expectations of students' classroom behavior across the grade span: Which social skills are necessary for success? *Exceptional Children, 72,* 153–167.

Larson, S. J. (1996). Meeting needs of youthful offenders through the spiritual dimension. *Reclaiming Children and Youth, 5,* 167–172.

Larson, J., & Lochman, J. E. (2002). *Helping school children cope with anger: A cognitive-behavioral intervention.* New York: Guilford.

Larzelere, R. (2000). Child outcomes of nonabusive and customary physical punishment by parents: An updated literature review. *Clinical Child and Family Psychology Review, 3,* 199–221.

Larzelere, R. E., Daly, D. L., Davis, J. L., Chmelka, M. B., & Handwerk, M. L. (2004). Outcome evaluation of Girls and Boys Town's Family Home Program. *Education and Treatment of Children, 27,* 130–149.

Lau, A. S., Garland, A. F., Yeh, M., McCabe, K. M., Wood, P. A., & Hough, R. L. (2004). Race/ethnicity and inter-informant agreement in assessing adolescent psychopathology. *Journal of Emotional and Behavioral Disorders, 12,* 145–156.

Lawson, G. W. (1992). Twelve-step programs and the treatment of adolescent substance abuse. In G. W. Lawson & A. W. Lawson (Eds.), *Adolescent substance abuse: Etiology, treatment, and prevention* (219–229). Gaithersburg, MD: Aspen.

Lee, D. L., & Axelrod, S. (2005). *Behavior modification: Basic principles* (3rd ed.). Austin, TX: PRO-ED.

Leedy, A., Bates, P., & Safran, S. P. (2004). Bridging the research-to-practice gap: Improving hallway behavior using positive behavior supports. *Behavioral Disorders, 29,* 130–139.

Lenz, B. K., Deshler, D. D., & Kissam, B. R. (2004). *Teaching content to all: Evidence-based inclusive practices in middle and secondary schools.* Boston: Allyn and Bacon.

Leone, P. E., & Cutting, P. E. (2004). Appropriate education, Juvenile corrections, and No Child Left Behind. *Behavioral Disorders, 29,* 260–265.

Lerman, R. I. (2002). *Marriage and the economic well-being of families with children: A review of the literature* [Online]. Available: http://www.urban.org/url.cfm?ID=410541.

Lerner, H. D., & Ehrlich, J. (2001). Psychoanalytic model. In M. Hersen & V. B. Van Hasselt (Eds.), *Advanced abnormal psychology* (2nd ed., pp. 65–92). New York: Kluwer Academic/Plenum.

Levendoski, L. S., & Cartledge, G. (2000). Self-monitoring for elementary school children with serious emotional disturbances: Classroom applications for increased academic responding. *Behavioral Disorders, 25,* 211–224.

Leventhal, T., & Brooks-Gunn, J. (2000). The neighborhoods they live in: The effects of neighborhood residence on child and adolescent outcomes. *Psychological Bulletin, 126,* 309–337.

Lewin, L. M., Davis, B., & Hops, H. (1999). Childhood social predictors of adolescent antisocial behavior: Gender differences in predictive accuracy and efficacy. *Journal of Abnormal Child Psychology, 27,* 277–292.

Lewinsohn, P. M., Clarke, G. N., Rohde, P., Hops, H., & Seeley, J. R. (1996). A course in coping: A cognitive-behavioral approach to the treatment of adolescent depression. In E. D. Hibbs & P. Jensen (Eds.), *Psychosocial treatments for child and adolescent disorders: Empirically based strategies for clinical practice* (pp. 109–135). Washington, DC: American Psychological Association.

Lewinsohn, P. M., & Essau, C. A. (2002). Depression in adolescents. In C. L. Hammen & I. H. Gotlib (Eds.), *Handbook of depression* (pp. 541–559). New York: Guilford.

Lewinsohn, P. M., Seeley, J. R., & Klein, D. N. (2003). Bipolar disorder in adolescents: Epidemiology and suicidal behavior. In B. Geller & M. P. DelBello (Eds.), *Bipolar disorder in childhood and early adolescence* (pp. 7–24). New York: Guilford.

Lewis, M., & King, R. A. (2002). Psychiatric assessment of infants, children, and adolescents. In M. Lewis (Ed.), *Child and adolescent psychiatry: A comprehensive textbook* (3rd ed., pp. 525–544). Philadelphia: Lippincott Williams & Wilkins.

Lewis, R. (2005). *Human genetics: Concepts and applications* (6th ed.). New York: McGraw-Hill.

Lewis, T. J., Colvin, G., & Sugai, G. (2000). The effects of precorrection and active supervision on the recess behavior of elementary students. *Education and Treatment of Children, 23,* 109–121.

Lewis, T. J., Hudson, S., Richter, M., & Johnson, N. (2004). Scientifically supported practices in emotional and behavioral disorders: A proposed approach and brief review of current practices. *Behavioral Disorders, 29,* 247–259.

Lewis, T. J., Lewis-Palmer, T., Newcomer, L., & Stichter, J. (2004). Applied behavior analysis and the education and treatment of students with emotional and behavioral disorders. In R. B. Rutherford Jr., M. M. Quinn, & S. Mathur (Eds.), *Handbook of research in behavioral disorders* (pp. 523–545). New York: Guilford.

Liaupsin, C. J., Jolivette, K., & Scott, T. M. (2004). Schoolwide systems of behavior support: Maximizing student success in schools. In R. B. Rutherford Jr., M. M. Quinn, & S. Mathur (Eds.), *Handbook of research in behavioral disorders* (pp. 487–501). New York: Guilford.

Lickona, T. (1996). Teaching respect and responsibility. *Reclaiming Children and Youth, 5,* 143–151.

Lickona, T. (2004). *Character matters: How to help our children develop good judgment, integrity, and other essential virtues.* New York: Simon & Schuster.

Lickona, T., Schaps, E., & Lewis, C. (2003). *CEP's eleven principles of effective character education.* Washington, DC: Character Education Partnership.

Lippman, H. S. (1962). *Treatment of the child in emotional conflict* (2nd ed.). New York: McGraw-Hill.

Lipsky, D. K., & Gartner, A. (Eds.). (1997). *Inclusion and school reform: Transforming American classrooms.* Baltimore: Brookes.

Lochman, J. E., & Wells, K.C. (1996). A social-cognitive intervention with aggressive children: Prevention effects and contextual implementation issues. In R. D. Peters & R. J. McMahon (Eds.), *Preventing childhood disorders, substance abuse, and delinquency* (pp. 111–143). Thousand Oaks, CA: Sage.

Lochman, J. E., & Wells, K. C. (2004). The Coping Power Program for preadolescent aggressive boys and their parents: Outcome effects at the 1-year follow-up. *Journal of Consulting and Clinical Psychology, 72,* 571–578.

Lochman, J. E., White, K. J., & Wayland, K. K. (1991). Cognitive-behavioral assessment and treatment with aggressive children. In P. C. Kendall (Ed.), *Child and adolescent therapy: Cognitive-behavioral procedures* (pp. 25–65). New York: Guilford.

Loeber, R., Farrington, D. P., Stouthamer-Loeber, M., & Van Kammen, W. B. (1998). *Antisocial behavior and mental health problems.* Mahwah, NJ: Lawrence Erlbaum Associates.

Lombroso, P. J., & Leckman, J. F. (2002). Molecular basis of childhood psychiatric disorders. In M. Lewis (Ed.), *Child and adolescent psychiatry: A comprehensive textbook* (3rd ed., pp. 11–22). Philadelphia: Lippincott Williams & Wilkins.

Long, N. J. (1974). Nicholas J. Long. In J. M. Kauffman & C. D. Lewis (Eds.), *Teaching children with behavior disorders: Personal perspectives* (pp. 171–196). Upper Saddle River, NJ: Merrill/Prentice Hall.

Long, N. J. (1997). The therapeutic power of kindness. *Reclaiming Children and Youth, 5,* 242–246.

Long, N. J., & Long, J. E. (2002). *Managing passive-aggressive behavior of children and youth at school and home: The angry smile.* Austin, TX: PRO-ED.

Long, N. J., & Morse, W. C. (1996). *Conflict in the classroom* (5th ed.). Austin, TX: PRO-ED.

Long, N. J., & Newman, R. G. (1976). Managing surface behavior of children in school. In N. J. Long, W. C. Morse, & R. G. Newman (Eds.), *Conflict in the classroom* (3rd ed.). Belmont, CA: Wadsworth.

Long, N. J., Wood, M. M., & Fecser, F. A. (2001). *Life Space Crisis Intervention: Talking with students in conflict* (2nd ed). Austin, TX: PRO-ED.

Lord, C., & Bailey, A. (2002). Autism spectrum disorders. In M. Rutter & E. Taylor (Eds.), *Child and adolescent psychiatry* (4th ed., pp. 636–663). Malden, MA: Blackwell Science.

Lorion, R. P. (2000). Community, prevention, and wellness. In M. Hersen & R. T. Ammerman (Eds.), *Advanced abnormal child psychology* (2nd ed., pp. 251–266). Hillsdale, NJ: Lawrence Erlbaum.

Loughran, M. J. (2004). Psychodynamic therapy with adolescents. In H. Steiner (Ed.), *Handbook of mental health interventions in children and adolescents: An integrated developmental approach* (pp. 586–620). San Francisco: Jossey-Bass.

Lourie, I. (2003). A history of community child mental health. In A. J. Pumariega & N. C. Winters (Eds.), *The handbook of child and adolescent systems of care: The new community psychiatry* (pp. 1–16). San Francisco: Jossey-Bass.

Lourie, I. S., & Hernandez, M. (2003). A historical perspective on national child mental health policy. *Journal of Emotional and Behavioral Disorders, 11,* 5–9.

Lovaas, O. I. (1996). A program for the establishment of speech in psychotic children. In J. K. Wing (Ed.), *Early childhood autism: Clinical, educational, and social aspects.* New York: Pergamon.

Lovejoy, M. C., Graczyk, P. A., O'Hare, E., & Neuman, G. (2000). Maternal depression and parenting behavior: A meta analytic review. *Clinical Psychology Review, 20,* 561–592.

Lovitt, T. C. (2000). *Preventing school failure* (2nd ed). Austin, TX: PRO-ED.

Lyons, J. S., & Rogers, L. (2005). The U.S. child welfare system: A de facto public behavioral health care system. *Journal of the American Academy of Child and Adolescent Psychiatry, 43,* 971–973.

Lyons-Ruth, K., Zeanah, C. H., & Benoit, D. (2003). Disorder and risk for disorder during infancy and toddlerhood. In E. J. Mash & R. A. Barkley (Eds.), *Child psychopathology* (2nd ed., pp. 589–631). New York: Guilford.

Maag, J. W. (2003). Targeting behaviors and methods for recording their occurrences. In M. J. Breen & C. R. Fiedler (Eds.), *Behavioral approach to assessment of youth with emotional/behavioral disorders* (2nd ed.) (pp. 297–333). Austin, TX: PRO-ED.

Maag, J. W., & Swearer, S. M. (2005). Cognitive-behavioral interventions for depression: Review and implications for school personnel [sic]. *Behavioral Disorders, 30,* 259–276.

Mahler, M. S., & Furer, M. (1972). Child psychosis: A theoretical statement and its implications. *Journal of Autism and Childhood Schizophrenia, 2,* 213–218.

Marans, S., & Cohen, D. J. (2002). Child psychoanalytic theories of development. In M. Lewis (Ed.), *Child and adolescent psychiatry: A comprehensive textbook* (3rd ed., pp. 196–211). Philadelphia: Lippincott Williams & Wilkins.

Maroney, S. A. (2004). Increasing the odds for successful transitions. *Beyond Behavior, 13,* 29–31.

Martella, R. C., Nelson, J. R., & Marchand-Martella, N. E. (2003). *Managing disruptive behaviors in the schools.* Boston: Allyn & Bacon.

Martin, G., & Pear, J. (2003). *Behavior modification: What it is and how to do it.* Upper Saddle River, NJ: Prentice Hall.

Martindale, B. V., Mueser, K. T., Kuipers, E., Sensky, T., & Green, L. (2003). Psychosicial treatments of schizophrenia. In S. R. Hirsch & D. R. Weinberger (Eds.), *Schizophrenia* (2nd ed., pp. 657–687). Malden, MA: Blackwell.

Marx, L., Benoit, M., & Kamradt, B. (2003). Foster children in the child welfare system. In A. J. Pumariega & N. C. Winters (Eds.), *The handbook of child and adolescent systems of care: The new community psychiatry* (pp. 332–350). San Francisco: Jossey-Bass.

Mash, E. J., & Dozois, D. J. A. (2003). Child psychopathology: A developmental-systems perspective. In E. J. Mash & R. A. Barkley (Eds.), *Child psychopathology* (2nd ed., pp. 3–71). New York: Guilford.

Mash, E. J., & Wolfe, D. A. (2002). *Abnormal child psychology* (2nd ed.). Belmont, CA: Wadsworth.

Masten, A. S. (2001). Ordinary magic: Relilience processes in development. *American Psychologist, 56,* 227–238.

Masten, A. S., & Coatsworth, J. D. (1998). The development of competence in favorable and unfavorable environments: Lessons from research on successful children. *American Psychologist, 53,* 205–220.

Mattison, R. M. (2004). Psychiatric and psychological assessment of emotional and behavioral disorders during school mental health consultation. In R. B. Rutherford Jr., M. M. Quinn, & S. Mathur (Eds.), *Handbook of research in behavioral disorders* (pp. 163–180). New York: Guilford.

Mattison, R., Hooper, S., & Glassberg, L. (2002). Three-year course of learning disorders in special education students classified as behavioral disorder. *Journal of the American Academy of Child and Adolescent Psychiatry, 41,* 1454–1461.

Mayer, M., Lochman, J., & Van Acker, R. (2005). Introduction to the special issue: Cognitive-behavioral interventions with students with EBD. *Behavioral Disorders, 30,* 197–212.

Mayes, L. C., Meteyer, K., & Granger, R. H. (2002). Teratologic and developmental effects of prenatal drug exposure: Alcohol, heroin, marijuana, and cocaine. In M. Lewis (Ed.), *Child and adolescent psychiatry: A comprehensive textbook* (3rd ed., pp. 447–458). Philadelphia: Lippincott Williams & Wilkins.

McCabe, K. Yeh, M., Hough, R. L., Landsverk, J., Hurlburt, M. S., Culver, S. W., et al. (1999). Racial/ethnic representation across five public sectors of care for youth. *Journal of Emotional and Behavioral Disorders, 7,* 72–82.

McCarney, S. B., & Leigh, J. E. (1990). *The Behavior Evaluation Scale* (2nd ed.). Columbia, MO: Hawthorne Educational Services.

McClellan, J. M. (2005). Early onset schizophrenia. In B. J. Sadock & V. A. Sadock (Eds.), *Kaplan & Sadock's comprehensive textbook of psychiatry,* (Vol. II, pp. 3307–3314). Philadelphia: Lippincott Williams & Wilkins.

McConaughy, S. H. (2003). Interviewing children, parents, and teachers. In M. J. Breen & C. R. Fiedler (Eds.), *Behavioral approach to assessment of youth with emotional/behavioral disorders* (2nd ed., pp. 123–169). Austin, TX: PRO-ED.

McConaughy, S. H., & Achenbach, T. M. (2001). *Manual for the Semistructured Clinical Interview for Children and Adolescents* (2nd ed.). Burlington: University of Vermont, Research Center for Children, Youth, and Families.

McConville, D. W., & Cornell, D. G. (2003). Aggressive attitudes predict aggressive behavior in middle school students. *Journal of Emotional and Behavioral Disorders, 11,* 179–187.

McFadyen-Ketchum, S. A. & Dodge, K. A. (1998). Problems in social relationships. In E. J. Mash & R. A. Barkley (Eds.), *Treatment of childhood disorders.* (pp. 338–365). New York, NY: Guilford.

McGinnis, E., & Goldstein, A. P. (1997). *Skillstreaming the elementary school child: New strategies and perspectives for teaching prosocial skills* (2nd ed.). Champaign, IL: Research Press.

McGuffin, P., & Rutter, M. (2002). Genetics of normal and abnormal development. In M. Rutter & E. Taylor (Eds.), *Child and adolescent psychiatry* (4th ed., pp. 185–204). Malden, MA: Blackwell Science.

McIntyre, T. (1996). Guidelines for providing appropriate services to culturally diverse students with emotional and/or behavioral disorders. *Behavior Disorders, 21,* 137–144.

McLeer, S. V., & Wills, C. (2000). Psychopharmacological treatment. In M. Hersen & R. T. Ammerman (Eds.), *Advanced abnormal child psychology* (2nd ed., pp. 219–250). Hillsdale, NJ: Lawrence Erlbaum.

McLoughlin, J. A., & Lewis, R. B. (2005). *Assessing students with special needs* (6th ed.). Columbus: Merrill Prentice Hall.

McLoyd, V. C. (1998). Socioeconomic disadvantage and child development. *American Psychologist, 53,* 185–204.

McMahon, S., Grant, K., Compas, B., Thurm, A., & Ey, S. (2003). Stress and psychopathology in children and adolescents: is there evidence of specificity? *Journal of Child Psychology and Psychiatry, 44,* 107–133.

McMillen, J. C., Zima, B. T., Scott, L. D., Auslander, W. F., Munson, M. R., Ollie, M. T., et al. (2005). Prevalence of psychiatric disorders among older youths in the foster care system. *Journal of the American Academy of Child and Adolescent Psychiatry, 44,* 88–95.

Meadows, N. B., & Stevens, K. B. (2004). Teaching alternative behaviors to students with emotional and behavioral disorders. In R. B. Rutherford Jr., M. M. Quinn, & S. Mathur (Eds.), *Handbook of research in behavioral disorders* (pp. 385–398). New York: Guilford.

Medved, M., & Medved, D. (1998). *Saving childhood: Protecting our children from the national assault on innocence.* New York: HarperCollins.

Meese, R. L. (2001). *Teaching learners with mild disabilities: Integrating research and practice* (2nd ed.). Belmont, CA: Wadsworth.

Meichenbaum, D., & Goodman, J. (1971). Training impulsive children to talk to themselves: A means of developing self-control. *Journal of Abnormal Psychology, 77,* 115–126.

Meissner, W. W. (2005). Classic psychoanalysis. In B. J. Sadock & V. A. Sadock (Eds.), *Kaplan & Sadock's comprehensive textbook of psychiatry* (Vol. I, pp. 701–745). Philadelphia: Lippincott Williams & Wilkins.

Menninger, K. (1963). *The vital balance.* New York: Viking Press.

Menninger, W. W. (2005). Role of the psychiatric hospital in the treatment of mental illness. In B. J. Sadock & V. A. Sadock (Eds.), *Kaplan & Sadock's comprehensive textbook of psychiatry* (Vol. II, pp. 3875–3883). Philadelphia: Lippincott Williams & Wilkins.

Mercer, C. D., & A. R. Mercer (2005). *Teaching students with learning problems* (6th ed.). Upper Saddle River, NJ: Merrill/Prentice Hall.

Merikangas, K. R. (2005). Anxiety disorders: Epidemiology. In B. J. Sadock & V. A. Sadock (Eds.), *Kaplan & Sadock's comprehensive textbook of psychiatry* (Vol. I, pp. 1720–1727). Philadelphia: Lippincott Williams & Wilkins.

Merrell, K. W. (2001). *Helping students overcome depression and anxiety: A practical guide.* New York: Guilford.

Merrell, K. W. (2003). *Behavioral, social, and emotional assessment of children and adolescents* (2nd ed.). Mahwah, NJ: Erlbaum.

Merydith, S. P. (1999). Psychodynamic approaches. In H. T. Prout & D. T. Brown (Eds.), *Counseling and psychotherapy with children and adolescents: Theory and practice for school and clinical settings* (3rd ed., pp. 74–107). New York: Wiley.

Mezzich, J. E., & Ustun, T. B. (2005). Epidemiology. In B. J. Sadock & V. A. Sadock (Eds.), *Kaplan & Sadock's comprehensive textbook of psychiatry* (Vol. I, pp. 656–671). Philadelphia: Lippincott Williams & Wilkins.

Milin, R., Coupland, K., Walker, S., & Fisher Bloom, E. (2000). Outcome and follow up study of an adolescent psychiatric day treatment school program. *Journal of the American Academy of Child and Adolescent Psychiatry, 39,* 320–328.

Miller, L., Davies, M., & Greenwald, S. (2000). Religiosity and substance use and abuse among adolescents in the National Comorbidity Survey. *Journal of the American Academy of Child and Adolescent Psychiatry, 39,* 1190–1197.

Miller, L. K. (2006). *Principles of everyday behavior analysis* (4th ed). Belmont, CA: Wadsworth.

Miller, K. A., Gunter, P. L., Venn, M. L., Hummel, J., & Wiley, L. P. (2003). Effects of curricular and materials modifications on academic performance and task engagement of three students with emotional or behavioral disorders. *Behavioral Disorders, 28,* 130–149.

Miller, W. B. (2001). *The growth of youth gang problems in the United States: 1970–1998* (NCJ 181868). Washington, DC: U.S. Department of Justice.

Miller, W. R., & Thoresen, C. E. (1999). Spirituality and health. In W. R. Miller (Eds.), *Integrating spirituality into treatment: Resources for practitioners* (pp. 3–18). Washington, DC: American Psychological Association.

Miltenberger, R. G. (2004). *Behavior modification: Principles and procedures* (3rd ed.). Belmont, CA: Wadsworth.

Mitchell, P. B., & Malhi, G. S. (2004). Bipolar depression: Phenomenological overview and clinical characteristics. *Bipolar Disorders, 6,* 530–539.

Miyamoto, S., Stroup, T. S., Duncan, G. E., Aoba, A., & Lieberman, J. A. (2003). Acute pharmacological treatment of schizophrenia. In S. R. Hirsch & D. R. Weinberger (Eds.), *Schizophrenia* (2nd ed., pp. 442–473). Malden, MA: Blackwell.

Moffitt, T. E., Caspi, A., & Rutter, M. (2005). Strategy for investigating interactions between measured genes and measured environments. *Archives of General Psychiatry, 62,* 473–481.

Mohl, P. C. (2005). Other psychodynamic schools. In B. J. Sadock & V. A. Sadock (Eds.), *Kaplan & Sadock's comprehensive textbook of psychiatry* (Vol. I, pp. 755–777). Philadelphia: Lippincott Williams & Wilkins.

Moldin, S. O. (2005). Population genetics and genetic epidemiology. In B. J. Sadock & V. A. Sadock (Eds.), *Kaplan & Sadock's comprehensive textbook of psychiatry* (Vol. I, pp. 236–252). Philadelphia: Lippincott Williams & Wilkins.

Mooney, P., Denny, R. K., & Gunter, P. L. (2004). The impact of NCLB and the reauthorization of IDEA on academic instruction of students with emotional and behavioral disorders. *Behavioral Disorders, 29,* 237–246.

Moore, H. B., Presbury, J. H., Smith, L. W., & McKee, J. E. (1999). Person-centered approaches. In H. I. Prout & D. T. Brown (Eds.), *Counseling and psychotherapy with children and adolescents: Theory and practice for school and clinical settings* (3rd ed., pp. 155–202). New York: Wiley.

Morris, R. J., Shah, K., & Morris, Y. P. (2002). Internalizing behavior disorders. In K. L. Lane, F. M. Gresham, & T. E. O'Shaughnessy (Ed.), *Interventions for children with or at risk for emotional and behavioral disorders* (pp. 223–241). Boston: Allyn & Bacon.

Morse, W. C. (1976). The helping teacher/crisis teacher concept. *Focus on Exceptional Children, 8*(4), 1–11.

Morse, W. C. (1996). Knowing your students: The initial and ongoing dialogue. In N. J. Long & W. C. Morse (Eds.), *Conflict in the classroom* (5th ed., pp. 150–158). Austin, TX: PRO-ED.

Morse, W. C. (1998). The helping teacher/crisis teacher concept. In R. J. Whelan (Ed.), *Emotional and behavioral disorders: A 25 year focus.* Denver: Love.

Morse, W. C. (2001). A half century of children who hate: Insights for today from Fritz Redl. *Reclaiming Children and Youth, 10,* 75–78, 82.

Morse, W. C., Cutler, R. L., & Fink, A. H. (1964). *Public school classes for the emotionally handicapped: A research analysis*. Washington, DC: Council for Exceptional Children.

Moscicki, E. K. (1995). Suicide in childhood and adolescence. In F. C. Verhulst & H. M. Koot (Eds.), *The epidemiology of child and adolescent psychopathology* (pp. 291–308). New York: Oxford University Press.

Moss, N. E., & Racusin, G. R. (2002). Psychological assessment of children and adolescents. In M. Lewis (Ed.), *Child and adolescent psychiatry: A comprehensive textbook* (3rd ed., pp. 555–572). Philadelphia: Lippincott Williams & Wilkins.

Mrazek, D., & Mrazek, P. J. (2005). Prevention of psychiatric disorders in children and adolescents. In B. J. Sadock & V. A. Sadock (Eds.), *Kaplan & Sadock's comprehensive textbook of psychiatry* (Vol. II, pp. 3513–3518). Philadelphia: Lippincott Williams & Wilkins.

Mufson, L. H., Dorta, K. P., Olfson, M., Weissman, M. M., & Hoagwood, K. (2004). Effectiveness research: Transporting interpersonal psychotherapy for depressed adolescents (IPT-A): From the lab to school-based health clinics. *Clinical Child and Family Psychology Review, 7,* 251–261.

Munger, R. L. (1997). Ecological trajectories in child mental health. In S. W. Henggeler & A. B. Santos (Eds.), *Innovative approaches for difficult-to-treat populations* (pp. 3–25). Washington, DC: American Psychiatric Press.

Munger, R. L. (1998). *The ecology of troubled children: Changing children's behavior by changing the places, activities, and people in their lives*. Cambridge, MA: Brookline.

Muris, P., & Ollendick, T. H. (2005). The role of temperament in the etiology of child psychopathology. *Clinical Child and Family Psychology Review, 8,* 271–289.

Murphy, K. R., & Davidshofer, C. O. (2005). *Psychological testing: Principles and applications* (6 ed.). Englewood Cliffs, NJ: Prentice Hall.

Murray, J. P. (2003). The violent fact of television: Research and discussion. In E. L. Palmer & B. M. Young (Eds.), *The faces of televisual media: Teaching, violence, selling to children* (pp. 143–160). Mahwah, NJ: Lawrence Erlbaum Associates.

Murray, R. M., & Bramon, E. (2005). Developmental model of schizophrenia. In B. J. Sadock & V. A. Sadock (Eds.), *Kaplan & Sadock's comprehensive textbook of psychiatry* (Vol. I, pp. 1381–1395). Philadelphia: Lippincott Williams & Wilkins.

Muscott, H. S., & O'Brien, S. T. (1999). Teaching character education to students with behavioral and learning disabilities through mentoring relationships. *Education and Treatment of Children, 22,* 373–390.

Musto, D. F. (2002). History of child psychiatry. In M. Lewis (Ed.), *Child and adolescent psychiatry: A comprehensive textbook* (3rd ed., pp. 1446–1449). Philadelphia: Lippincott Williams & Wilkins.

Myers, L. J. (1999). Therapeutic processes for health and wholeness in the 21st century: Belief systems analysis and the paradigm shift. In R. L. Jones (Ed.), *Advances in African American psychology* (pp. 313–355). Hampton, VA: Cobb & Henry.

Myles, B. S. (2005). *Children and youth with Asperger syndrome: Strategies for success in inclusive settings*. Thousand Oaks, CA: Corwin.

Nastasi, B. K., Moore, R. B., & Varjas, K. M. (2003). *School-based mental health services: Creating comprehensive and culturally specific programs*. Washington, DC: American Psychological Association.

National Center for Education Statistics. (2003a). *Digest of Education Statistics, 2002* (NCES 2003-060). Washington, DC: U.S. Department of Education.

National Center for Education Statistics. (2003b). *The condition of education, 2003* (NCES 2003-067). Washington, DC: U.S. Department of Education.

National Center for Education Statistics. (2004a). *Digest of education statistics, 2003* (NCES 2005-025). Washington: Government Printing Office.

National Center for Education Statistics. (2004b). *The condition of education, 2004* (NCES 2004-077). Washington, DC: U.S. Department of Education.

Naugle, A. E., & Maher, S. (2003). Modeling and behavioral rehearsal. In W. O'Donohue, J. E. Fisher, & S. C. Hayes (Eds.), *Cognitive behavior therapy: Applying empirically supported techniques in your practice* (pp. 238–246). Hoboken, NJ: Wiley.

Nayani, T., & Bhugra, D. (1996). Guilt, religion, and ritual. In D. Bhugra (Ed.), *Psychiatry and religion: Context, consensus and controversies* (pp. 198–213). London: Routledge.

Nelson, C. M., Leone, P. E., & Rutherford, R. B. Jr. (2004). Youth delinquency: Prevention and intervention. In R. B. Rutherford Jr., M. M. Quinn, & S. Mathur (Eds.), *Handbook of research in behavioral disorders* (pp. 282–301). New York: Guilford.

Nelson, J. R., Benner, G. J., & Cheney, D. (2005). An investigation of the language skills of students with emotional disturbance served in public school settings. *Journal of Special Education, 39,* 97–105.

Neve, M., & Turner, T. (2002). History of child and adolescent psychiatry: In M. Rutter & E. Taylor (Eds.), *Child and adolescent psychiatry* (4th ed., pp. 382–395). Malden, MA: Blackwell Science.

Nevid, J. S., Rathus, S. A., & Greene, B. (2006). *Abnormal psychology in a changing world* (6th ed.). Upper Saddle River, NJ: Prentice Hall.

Newcomb, M. D., & Richardson, M. A. (2000). Substance use disorders. In M. Hersen & R. T. Ammerman (Eds.), *Advanced abnormal child psychology* (2nd ed., pp. 467–492). Hillsdale, NJ: Erlbaum.

Newcomer, P. L., Barenbaum, E., & Pearson, N. (1995). Depression and anxiety in children and adolescents with learning disabilities, conduct disorders, and no disabilities. *Journal of Emotional and Behavioral Disorders, 3*, 27–39.

Newschaffer, C. J., Falb, M. D., & Gurney, J. G. (2005). National autism prevalence trends from United States special education data. *Pediatrics, 115*, 277–282.

Nezu, A. M., Nezu, C. M., & Lombardo, E. (2003). Problem-solving therapy. In W. O'Donohue, J. E. Fisher, & S. C. Hayes (Eds.) *Cognitive behavior therapy: Applying empirically supported techniques in your practice* (pp. 301–307). Hoboken, NJ: Wiley.

Nishina, A., Juvonen, J., & Witkow, M. R. (2005). Sticks and stones may break my bones, but names will make me feel sick: The psychosocial, somatic, and scholastic consequences of peer harassment. *Journal of Clinical Child and Adolescent Psychology, 34*, 37–48.

Noell, G. H., & Gansle, K. A. (2002). Mathematics: Screening, assessment, and intervention. In K. L. Lane, F. M. Gresham, & T. E. O'Shaughnessy (Eds.), *Interventions for children with or at risk for emotional and behavioral disorders* (pp. 125–143). Boston: Allyn & Bacon.

Nucci, L. (Ed.). (1989). *Moral development and character education: A dialogue.* Berkley, CA: McCutchan.

Nurcombe, B. (2005). Dissociative disorders in children and adolescents. In B. J. Sadock & V. A. Sadock (Eds.), *Kaplan & Sadock's comprehensive textbook of psychiatry* (Vol. II, pp. 3449–3456). Philadelphia: Lippincott Williams & Wilkins.

Nurcombe, B., Mitchell, W., Begtrup, R., Tramontana, M., LaBarbera, J., & Pruitt, J. (1996). Dissociative hallucinosis and allied conditions. In F. R. Volkmar (Ed.), *Psychoses and pervasive developmental disorders in childhood and adolescence* (pp. 107–128). Washington, DC: American Psychiatric Press.

O'Connor, T. G. (2002). Attachment disorders of infancy and childhood. In M. Rutter & E. Taylor (Eds.), *Child and adolescent psychiatry* (4th ed., pp. 776–792). Malden, MA: Blackwell Science.

Obiakor, F., Algozzine, B., Thurlow, M., Gwalla-Ogisi, N., Enwefa, S., Enwefa, R., et al. (2002). *Addressing the disproportionate representation issue.* Arlington, VA: Council for Exceptional Children.

Office of Juvenile Justice and Delinquency Prevention (OJJDP). (2000). *1999 national report series: Children as victims* (NCJ 180753). Washington, DC: U.S. Department of Justice.

Offord, D. R., & Bennett, K. J. (2002). Epidemiology and prevention. In M. Lewis (Ed.), *Child and adolescent psychiatry: A comprehensive textbook* (3rd ed., pp. 1320–1335). Philadelphia: Lippincott Williams & Wilkins.

Olfson, M. (2005). Mental health services. In B. J. Sadock & V. A. Sadock (Eds.), *Kaplan & Sadock's comprehensive textbook of psychiatry* (Vol. I, pp. 686–691). Philadelphia: Lippincott Williams & Wilkins.

Olive, M. A. (2004). Transitioning children between activities: Effective strategies for decreasing challenging behavior. *Beyond Behavior, 14*, 11–16.

Ollendick, T., King, N., & Muris, P. (2002). Fears and phobias in children: Phenomenology, epidemiology, and aetiology. *Child and Adolescent Mental Health, 7*, 98–106.

Olson, S. L., Bates, J. E., Sandy, J. M., & Lanthier, R. (2000). Early developmental precursors of externalizing behavior in middle childhood and adolescence. *Journal of Abnormal Child Psychology, 28*, 119–133.

Oltmanns, T. F., & Emery, R. E. (2004). *Abnormal psychology* (4th ed). Upper Saddle River, NJ: Prentice Hall.

Osgood, R. L. (2000). *For "children who vary from the normal type": Special education in Boston, 1838–1930.* Washington, DC: Gallaudet University Press.

Osher, D., Cartledge, G., Oswald, D., Sutherland, K. S., Artiles, A. J., & Coutinho, M. (2004). Cultural and linguistic competency and disproportionate representation. In R. B. Rutherford Jr., M. M. Quinn, & S. Mathur (Eds.), *Handbook of research in behavioral disorders* (pp. 54–77). New York: Guilford.

Osofsky, J. D. (2003). Prevalence of children's exposure to domestic violence and child maltreatment: Implications for prevention and intervention. *Clinical Child and Family Psychology Review, 6*, 161–170.

Ost, L.-G., & Treffers, P. D. A. (2001). Onset, course, and outcome for anxiety disorders in children. In W. K. Silverman & P. D. A. Treffers (Eds.), *Anxiety disorders in children and adolescents: Research, assessment, and intervention* (pp. 273–292). New York: Cambridge University Press.

Oswald, D. P., & Singh, N. N. (1996). Emerging trends in child and adolescent mental health services. In T. H. Ollendick & R. J. Prinz (Eds.), *Advances in clinical child psychology* (Vol. 18, pp. 331–365). New York: Plenum.

Papantheodorou, G., & Kutcher, S. P. (1996). Treatment of bipolar disorder in adolescents. In K. I. Shulman, M. Tohen, & S. P. Kutcher (Eds.), *Mood disorders across the life span* (pp. 159–186). New York: Wiley.

Pardini, D. A., & Lochman, J. (2003). Treatments for oppositional defiant disorder. In M. A. Reinecke, F. M. Dattilio, & A. Freeman (Eds.), *Cognitive therapy with children and adolescents* (2nd ed., pp. 43–69). New York: Guilford.

Parese, S. B. (2002). "It ain't like she's my mother": Tyanna's red flag intervention. *Reclaiming Children and Youth, 10*, 246–250.

Parrinder, G. (Ed.). (1983). *World religions from ancient history to the present.* New York: Facts on File.

Patterson, G. R. (1965). An application of conditioning techniques to the control of a hyperactive child. In L. P. Ullman & L. Krasner (Eds.), *Case studies in behavior modification.* New York: Holt, Rinehart & Winston.

Patterson, G. R. (1982). *Coercive family process: A social learning approach* (Vol. 3). Eugene, OR: Castalia.

Patterson, G. R., & Yoerger, K. (2002). A developmental model for early- and late-onset delinquency. In J. B. Reid, G. R. Patterson, & J. Snyder (Eds.), *Antisocial behavior in children and adolescents* (pp. 147–172). Washington: American Psychological Association.

Patterson, H. O., & O'Connell, D. F. (2003). Recovery maintenance and relapse prevention with chemically dependent adolescents. In M. A. Reinecke, F. M. Dattilio, & A. Freeman (Eds.), *Cognitive therapy with children and adolescents* (2nd ed., pp. 70–94). New York: Guilford.

Pavuluri, M. N., Herbener, E. S., & Sweeney, J. A. (2004). Psychotic symptoms in pediatric bipolar disorder. *Journal of Affective Disorders, 80,* 19–28.

Peacock Hill Working Group. (1991). Problems and promises in special education and related services for children and youth with emotional or behavioral disorders. *Behavioral Disorders, 16,* 299–313.

Pearce, J. M. S. (2005). Kanner's infantile autism and Asperger's syndrome. *Journal of Neurology, Neurosurgery, and Psychiatry, 76,* 205.

Pelcovitz, D., Kaplan, S. J., DeRosa, R. R., Mandel, F. S., & Salzinger, S. (2000). Psychiatric disorders in adolescents exposed to violence and physical abuse. *American Journal of Orthopsychiatry, 70,* 360–369.

Pelham, W. E., & Molina, B. S. G. (2003). Childhood predictors of adolescent substance use in a longitudinal study of children with ADHD. *Journal of Abnormal Psychology, 112,* 497–507.

Peris, T. S., & Emery, R. E. (2004). A prospective study of the consequences of marital disruption for adolescents: Predisruption family dynamics and postdisruption adolescent adjustment. *Journal of Clinical Child and Adolescent Psychology, 33,* 694–705.

Peterson, L. D., Young, K. R., West, R. P., & Peterson, M. H. (1999). Effects of student self management on generalization of student performance to regular classrooms. *Education and Treatment of Children, 22,* 357–372.

Peterson, R. L., Miller, C., & Skiba, R. J. (2004). A framework for planning safe and responsive schools. *Beyond Behavior, 13,* 12–20.

Pfeffer, C. R. (2002). Suicidal behavior in children and adolescents: Causes and management. In M. Lewis (Ed.), *Child and adolescent psychiatry: A comprehensive textbook* (3rd ed., pp. 796–805). Philadelphia: Lippincott Williams & Wilkins.

Pfefferbaum, B. (2002). Posttraumatic stress dis-order. In M. Lewis (Ed.), *Child and adolescent psychiatry: A comprehensive textbook* (3rd ed., pp. 912–925). Philadelphia: Lippincott Williams & Wilkins.

Phillips, E. L., Fixsen, D. L., Phillips, E. A., & Wolf, M. M. (1979). The teaching family model: A comprehensive approach to residential treatment of youth. In D. Cullinan & M. H. Epstein (Eds.), *Special education for adolescents.* Columbus, Ohio: Merrill.

Pianta, R. C. (1999). Early childhood. In W. K. Silverman & T. H. Ollendick (Eds.), *Developmental issues in the clinical treatment of children* (pp. 88–107). Needham Heights, MA: Allyn & Bacon.

Piers, E. V. (1984). *Revised manual for the Piers-Harris Children's Self-Concept Scale.* Los Angeles: Western Psychological Services.

Pigott, R. L., & Cowen, E. L. (2000). Teacher race, child race, racial congruence, and teacher ratings of children's school adjustment. *Journal of School Psychology, 38,* 177–196.

Pike, D. R., Millspaugh, C. M., & DeSalvatore, G. (2005). Controlling behavior or reclaiming youth? Creating a behavior management system based on the circle of courage. *Reclaiming Children and Youth, 13,* 213–235.

Pineda, D. A., Ardila, A., Rosselli, M., Arias, B. E., Henao, G.C., Gomez, L.F., et al. (2000). Prevalence of attention deficit/hyperactivity disorder symptoms in 4 to 17 year old children in the general population. *Journal of Abnormal Child Psychology, 28,* 455–462.

Pogloff, S. M. (2005). Facilitate positive relationships between parents and professionals. *Intervention in School and Clinic, 40,* 116–119.

Poling, A., & Gaynor, S. T. (2003). Stimulus control. In W. O'Donohue, J. E. Fisher, & S. C. Hayes (Eds.), *Cognitive behavior therapy: Applying empirically supported techniques in your practice* (pp. 396–401). Hoboken, NJ: Wiley.

Polloway, E. A., Patton, J. R., & Serna, L. (2005). *Strategies for teaching learners with special needs* (8th ed.). Upper Saddle River, NJ: Merrill Prentice Hall.

Polsgrove, L., & Smith, S. W. (2004). Informed practice in teaching self control to children with emotional and behavioral disorders. In R. B. Rutherford Jr., M. M. Quinn, & S. Mathur (Eds.), *Handbook of research in behavioral disorders* (pp. 399–425). New York: Guilford.

Pope, A. W., McHale, S. M., & Craighead, W. E. (1988). *Self-esteem enhancement with children and adolescents.* Elmsford, NY: Pergamon.

Porter, G. K., Pearson, G. T., Keenan, S., & Duval-Harvey, J. (2003). School-based mental health services: A necessity, not a luxury. In A. J. Pumariega & N. C. Winters (Eds.), *The handbook of child and adolescent systems of care: The new community psychiatry* (pp. 250–275). San Francisco: Jossey-Bass.

Possel, P., Horn, A. B., Groen, G., & Hautzinger, M. (2004). School-based prevention of depressive symptoms in adolescents: A 6-month followup. *Journal of the American Academy of Child and Adolescent Psychiatry, 43,* 302–309.

Powell, D., & Dunlap, G. (2005). Mental health services for young children. In R. G. Steele & M. C. Roberts (Eds.), *Handbook of mental health services for children, adolescents, and families* (pp. 15–30). New York: Kluwer Academic/Plenum.

Power, C., Higgins, A., & Kohlberg, L. (1989). *Lawrence Kohlberg's approach to moral education*. New York: Columbia University Press.

Pringle, B., & Flanzer, J. (2005). Treatment services for adolescent substance abuse. In R. G. Steele & M. C. Roberts (Eds.), *Handbook of mental health services for children, adolescents, and families* (pp. 181–200). New York: Kluwer Academic/Plenum.

Prudic, J. (2005). Electroconvulsive therapy. In B. J. Sadock & V. A. Sadock (Eds.), *Kaplan & Sadock's comprehensive textbook of psychiatry* (Vol. II, pp. 2968–2982). Philadelphia: Lippincott Williams & Wilkins.

Pull, C. B., Cloos, J. M., & Murthy, N. V. (2003). Atypical psychotic disorders. In S. R. Hirsch & D. R. Weinberger (Eds.), *Schizophrenia* (2nd ed., pp. 54–67). Malden, MA: Blackwell.

Pumariega, A. J. (2003). Cultural competence in systems of care for children's mental health. In A. J. Pumariega & N. C. Winters (Eds.), *The handbook of child and adolescent systems of care: The new community psychiatry* (pp. 82–104). San Francisco: Jossey-Bass.

Pumariega, A. J. (2005). Community-based treatment. In B. J. Sadock & V. A. Sadock (Eds.), *Kaplan & Sadock's comprehensive textbook of psychiatry* (Vol. II, pp. 3390–3394). Philadelphia: Lippincott Williams & Wilkins.

Quay, H. C. (1986). Classification. In H. C. Quay & J. S. Werry (Eds.), *Psychopathological disorders of childhood* (3rd ed., pp. 1–34). New York: Wiley.

Quay, H. C., Morse, W. C., & Cutler, R. L. (1966). Personality patterns of pupils in special classes for the emotionally disturbed. *Exceptional Children, 32,* 297–301.

Quay, H. C., & Peterson, D. R. (1996). *Revised Behavior Problem Checklist, PAR Edition: Professional manual.* Odessa, FL: Psychological Assessment Resources.

Quinn, M. M. & Poirer, J. M. (2004). Linking prevention research with policy: Examining the costs and outcomes of the failure to prevent emotional and behavioral disorders. In R. B. Rutherford Jr., M. M. Quinn, & S. Mathur (Eds.), *Handbook of research in behavioral disorders* (pp. 78–97). New York: Guilford.

Quintar, B., Lane, R. C., & Goeltz, W. B. (1998). Psychoanalytic theories of personality. In D. F. Barone, M. Hersen, & V. B. Van Hasselt (Eds.), *Advanced personality* (pp. 27–55). New York, NY: Plenum.

Randall, J., & Henggeler, S. W. (1999). Multisystemic therapy: Changing the social ecologies of youths presenting serious clinical problems and their families. In S. W. Russ & T. H. Ollendick (Eds.), *Handbook of psychotherapies with children and families* (pp. 405–418). New York: Kluwer Academic/Plenum.

*Random House Webster's College Dictionary.* (1991). New York: Random House.

Rapport, M. D. (2001). Attention-deficit/hyperactivity disorder. In M. Hersen & V. B. Van Hasselt (Eds.), *Advanced abnormal psychology* (2nd ed., pp. 191–208). New York: Kluwer Academic/Plenum.

Raver, S. A. (2004). Monitoring child progress in early childhood special education settings. *Teaching Exceptional Children, 36,* 52–57.

Redl, F. (1959). The concept of the life space interview. *American Journal of Orthopsychiatry, 29,* 1–18.

Redl, F., & Wineman, D. (1951). *Children who hate.* New York: Free Press.

Redl, F., & Wineman, D. (1952). *Controls from within.* New York: Free Press.

Reese, L. E., Vera, E. M., Simon, T. R., & Ikeda, R. M. (2000). The role of families and care givers as risk and protective factors in preventing youth violence. *Clinical Child and Family Psychology Review, 3,* 61–77.

Regan, K. S., Mastropieri, M. A., & Scruggs, T. E. (2005). Promoting expressive writing among students with emotional and behavioral disturbance via dialogue journals. *Behavioral Disorders, 31,* 33–50.

Rehm, L. P., & Adams, J. H. (2003). Self-management. In W. O'Donohue, J. E. Fisher, & S. C. Hayes (Eds.) *Cognitive behavior therapy: Applying empirically supported techniques in your practice* (pp. 354–360). Hoboken, NJ: Wiley.

Reid, J. B., & Eddy, J. M. (2002). Interventions for antisocial behavior: Overview. In J. B. Reid, G. R. Patterson, & J. Snyder (Eds.), *Antisocial behavior in children and adolescents* (pp. 195–202). Washington: American Psychological Association.

Reid, R., Gonzalez, J. E., Nordness, P. D., Trout, A., & Epstein, M. H. (2004). A meta-analysis of the academic status of students with emotional/behavioral disturbance. *Journal of Special Education, 38,* 130–143.

Reid, R., Trout, A. L., & Schartz, M. (2005). Self-regulation interventions for children with attention deficit/hyperactivity disorder. *Exceptional Children, 71,* 361–376.

Reinecke, M. A., Dattilio, F. M., & Freeman, A. (Eds.). (2003). *Cognitive therapy with children and adolescents* (2nd ed.). New York: Guilford.

Reynolds, C. R., & Kamphaus, R. W. (1992). *Behavior Assessment System for Children.* Circle Pines, MN: American Guidance Service.

Reynolds, C. R., & Kamphaus, R. W. (2002). *The clinician's guide to The Behavior Assessment System for Children.* New York: Guilford.

Reynolds, C. R., & Richmond, B. O. (1985). *Revised Children's Manifest Anxiety Scale.* Los Angeles: Western Psychological Services.

Reynolds, C. R., Livingston, R., & Wilson, V. (2006). *Measurement and assessment in education.* Boston: Allyn and Bacon.

Rhee, S. H., & Waldman, I. D. (2002). Genetic and environmental influences on antisocial behavior: A meta-analysis of twin and adoption studies. *Psychological Bulletin, 128,* 490–529.

Rhoads, S. E. (2004). *Taking sex differences seriously.* San Francisco: Encounter Books.

Rhodes, W. C. (1967). The disturbed child: A problem of ecological management. *Exceptional Children, 33,* 449–455.

Rhodes, W. C. (1970). A community participation analysis of emotional disturbance. *Exceptional Children, 36,* 309–314.

Richards, P. S., Rector, J. M., & Tjeltveit, A. C. (1999). Values, spirituality, and psychotherapy. In W. R. Miller (Eds.), *Integrating spirituality into treatment: Resources for practitioners* (pp. 133–160). Washington: American Psychological Association.

Richardson, J. G. (1999). *Common, delinquent, and special: The institutional shape of special education.* New York: Falmer Press.

Rimland, B. (1969). Psychogenesis versus biogenesis: The issues and the evidence. In S. C. Plog & R. B. Edgerton (Eds.), *Changing perspectives in mental illness.* New York: Holt, Rinehart & Winston.

Ripple, C. H., & Luthar, S. S. (2000). Academic risk among inner city adolescents: The role of personal attributes. *Journal of School Psychology, 38,* 277–298.

Robinson, T. R., Smith, S. W., & Miller, M. D. (2002). Effect of a cognitive-behavioral intervention on responses to anger by middle school students with chronic behavior problems. *Behavioral Disorders, 27,* 256–271.

Roccatagliata, G. (1986). *A history of ancient psychiatry.* Westport, CT: Greenwood Press.

Rodkin, P. C., Farmer, T. W., Pearl, R., & Van Acker, R. (2000). Heterogeneity of popular boys: Antisocial and prosocial configurations. *Developmental Psychology, 36,* 14–24.

Rogan, J. (2000). Learning strategies: Recipes for success. *Beyond Behavior, 10,* 18–22.

Rogers, C. R. (1951). *Client-centered therapy.* Boston: Houghton-Mifflin.

Rogers, C. R. (1969). *The freedom to learn.* Columbus, OH: Merrill.

Rogers, S. J. (1998). Empirically supported comprehensive treatments for young children with autism. *Journal of Clinical Child Psychology, 27,* 168–179.

Rogers-Adkinson, D. L., & Hooper, S. R. (2003). The relationship of language and behavior: Introduction to the special issue. *Behavioral Disorders, 29,* 5–9.

Rosenberg, M. S., Wilson, R., Maheady, L., & Sindelar, P. T. (2004). *Educating students with behavior disorders* (3rd ed.). Boston: Allyn and Bacon.

Rosenfeld, A. A., Altman, R., & Kaufman, I. (1997). Foster care. In R. K. Schreter, S. S. Sharfstein, & C. A. Schreter (Eds.), *Managing care, not dollars: The continuum of mental health services* (pp. 125–138). Washington, DC: American Psychiatric Press.

Rosenzweig, M. R., Breedlove, S. M., & Watson, N. V. (2005). *Biological psychology: An introduction to behavioral and cognitive neuroscience.* Sunderland, MA: Sinauer Associates.

Ross, A. O. (1980). *Psychological disorders of children: A behavioral approach to theory, research, and therapy* (2nd ed.). New York: McGraw-Hill.

Rothbart, M. K., & Bates, J. E. (1998). Temperament. In W. Damon (Ed.), *Handbook of child psychology: Vol. 3. Social, emotional and personality development* (5th ed., pp. 105–176). New York: Wiley.

Rounsaville, B. F., Alarcon, R. D., Andrews, G., Jackson, J. S., Kendell, R. E., & Kendler, K. (2002). Basic nomenclature issues for DSM-V. In D. J. Kupfer, M. B. First & D. A. Regier (Eds.), *A research agenda for DSM-V* (pp. 1–29). Washington, DC: American Psychiatric Association.

Rowe, E. W. (2003). The Minnesota Multiphasic Personality Inventory—Adolescent. In C. R. Reynolds & R. W. Kamphaus (Eds.), *Handbook of psychological and educational assessment of children: Personality, behavior, and context* (2nd ed., pp. 368–386). New York: Guilford.

Rowland, M. D., Halliday-Boykins, C. A., Henggeler, S. W., Cunningham, P. B., Lee, T. E., Kruesi, M. J. P., et al. (2005). A randomized trial of multisystemic therapy with Hawaii's felix class youths. *Journal of Emotional and Behavioral Disorders, 13,* 13–24.

Rubenstein, J. L. R., & Puelles, L. (2004). Survey of brain development. In H. Steiner (Ed.), *Handbook of mental health interventions in children and adolescents: An integrated developmental approach* (pp. 98–139). San Francisco: Jossey-Bass.

Rubin, K. H., Burgess, K. B., Kennedy, A. E., & Stewart, S. L. (2003). Social withdrawal in childhood. In E. J. Mash & R. A. Barkley (Eds.), *Child psychopathology* (2nd ed., pp. 372–406). New York: Guilford.

Rubin, K. H., Coplan, R., Chen, X., Buskirk, S., & Wojslawowicz, J. C. (2005). Peer relationships in childhood. In M. Bornstein & M. Lamb (Eds.), *Developmental psychology: An advanced textbook* (5th ed.) (pp. 469–512). Hillsdale, NJ: Erlbaum.

Russell, A. T. (1994). The clinical presentation of childhood-onset schizophrenia. *Schizophrenia Bulletin, 20,* 631–646.

Rutter, M. (2002). Development and psychopathology. In M. Rutter & E. Taylor (Eds.), *Child and adolescent psychiatry* (4th ed., pp. 309–324). Malden, MA: Blackwell.

Rutter, M. (2005a). Autism research: Lessons from the past and prospects for the future. *Journal of Autism and Developmental Disorders, 35,* 241–257.

Rutter, M. (2005b). Environmentally mediated risks for psychopathology: Research strategies and findings. *Journal of the American Academy of Child and Adolescent Psychiatry, 44*, 3–18.

Ryan, N. D. (2003). The pharmacological treatment of child and adolescent bipolar disorder. In B. Geller & M. P. DelBello (Eds.), *Bipolar disorder in childhood and early adolescence* (pp. 255–271). New York: Guilford.

Sabornie, E. J. (2002). Homework and students with emotional and behavioral disorders. In K. L. Lane, F. M. Gresham, & T. E. O'Shaughnessy (Eds.), *Interventions for children with or at risk for emotional and behavioral disorders* (pp. 144–158). Boston: Allyn & Bacon.

Sabornie, E. J., & DeBettencourt, L. U. (2004). *Teaching students with mild and high-incidence disabilities at the secondary level.* Upper Saddle River, N.J., Merrill/Prentice Hall.

Sadock, B. J. (2005). Signs and symptoms in psychiatry. In B. J. Sadock & V. A. Sadock (Eds.), *Kaplan & Sadock's comprehensive textbook of psychiatry* (Vol. I, pp. 847–859). Philadelphia: Lippincott Williams & Wilkins.

Salend, S. J. (2005). *Creating inclusive classrooms: Effective and reflective practices for all students* (5th ed.). Columbus: Merrill Prentice Hall.

Salkind, N. J. (2004). *An introduction to theories of human development.* Thousand Oaks, CA: Sage.

Salvia, J., & Ysseldyke, J. E. (2004). *Assessment in special and inclusive education* (9th ed.): Boston: Houghton Mifflin.

Substance Abuse and Mental Health Services Administration, Office of Applied Studies. (2004). *Results from the 2003 National Survey on Drug Use and Health: National findings* (DHHS Publication No. SMA 04-3964). Rockville, MD: Author.

Sandall, S., Hemmeter, M. L., Smith, B. J., & McLean, M. E. (Eds.). (2004). *DEC recommended practices: A comprehensive guide for practical application in early childhood special education.* Arlington, VA: Council for Exceptional Children.

Sandberg, S., & Rutter, M. (2002). The role of acute life stresses. In M. Rutter & E. Taylor (Eds.), *Child and adolescent psychiatry* (4th ed., pp. 287–298). Malden, MA: Blackwell Science.

Sanson, A., & Prior, M. (1999). Temperament and behavioral precursors to oppositional defiant disorder and conduct disorder. In H. C. Quay & A. E. Hogan (Eds.), *Handbook of disruptive behavior disorders* (pp. 397–417). New York, NY: Kluwer Academic/Plenum.

Sarason, I. G., & Sarason, B. R. (2005). *Abnormal psychology: The problem of maladaptive behavior* (11th ed.). Upper Saddle River, NJ: Prentice Hall.

Sarason, S. B., & Doris, J. (1979). *Educational handicap, public policy, and social history: A broadened perspective on mental retardation.* New York: Free Press.

Sasso, G. M. (2004). Measurement issues in EBD research: What we know and how we know it. *Behavioral Disorders, 30*, 60–71.

Satel, S. E., & Redding, R. E. (2005). Sociopolitical trends in mental health care: The consumer/survivor movement and multiculturalism. In B. J. Sadock & V. A. Sadock (Eds.), *Kaplan & Sadock's comprehensive textbook of psychiatry* (Vol. I, pp. 644–655). Philadelphia: Lippincott Williams & Wilkins.

Scahill, L., & Martin, A. (2002). Pediatric psychopharmacology. II: General principles, specific drug treatments, and clinical practice. In M. Lewis (Ed.), *Child and adolescent psychiatry: A comprehensive textbook* (3rd ed., pp. 951–974). Philadelphia: Lippincott Williams & Wilkins.

Schachar, R., & Tannock, R. (2002). Syndromes of hyperactivity and attention deficit. In M. Rutter & E. Taylor (Eds.), *Child and adolescent psychiatry* (4th ed., pp. 399–418). Malden, MA: Blackwell Science.

Scharrer, E., & Comstock, G. (2003). Entertainment televisual media: Content patterns and themes. In E. L. Palmer & B. M. Young (Eds.), *The faces of televisual media: Teaching, violence, selling to children* (pp. 161–193). Mahwah, NJ: Lawrence Erlbaum Associates.

Scheff, T. J. (1975). *Labeling madness.* Englewood Cliffs, NJ: Prentice-Hall.

Scheuermann, B., & Guetzloe, E. (2002). Top 10 guidelines for talking to legislators. *Beyond Behavior, 12*, 20.

Scheuermann, B., & Johns, B. (2002). Advocacy for students with emotional or behavioral disorders in the 21st century. *Behavioral Disorders, 28*, 57–69.

Schloss, P., & Smith, M. A. (1998). *Applied behavior analysis in the classroom* (2nd ed.). Needham Heights, MA: Allyn & Bacon.

Schloss, P. J., Holt, J., Mulvaney, M., & Green, J. (1988). The Franklin-Jefferson Program: Demonstration of an integrated social learning approach to education services for behaviorally disordered students. *Teaching: Behaviorally Disordered Youth, 4*, 7–15.

Schmid, R. E., & Evans, W. (1998). (Eds.), *Curriculum and instruction practices for students with emotional/behavioral disorders.* Reston, VA: Council for Exceptional Children.

Schoenwald, S. K., Borduin, C. M., & Henggeler, S. W. (1998). Multisystemic therapy: Changing the natural and service ecologies of adolescents and families. In M. H. Epstein, K. Kutash, & A. Duchnowski (Eds.), *Outcomes for children and youth with emotional and behavioral disorders and their families* (pp. 485–511). Austin, TX: PRO-ED.

Schoenwald, S. K., & Henggeler, S. W. (1999). Treatment of Oppositional Defiant Disorder and Conduct Disorder in home and community settings. In H. C. Quay & A. E. Hogan (Eds.), *Handbook of disruptive behavior disorders* (pp. 475–493). New York, NY: Kluwer Academic/Plenum.

Schroeder, C. S., & Gordon, B. N. (2002). *Assessment and treatment of childhood problems: A clinician's guide.* New York: Guilford.

Schultz, D. P., & Schultz, S. E. (2005). *Theories of personality* (8th ed). Belmont, CA: Wadsworth.

Schultz, R., Rosenberg, D., Pugh, K., Pine, D., Peterson, B., Kaufman, J., et al. (2002). Pediatric neuroimaging. In M. Lewis (Ed.), *Child and adolescent psychiatry: A comprehensive textbook* (3rd ed., pp. 132–154). Philadelphia: Lippincott Williams & Wilkins.

Schwartz, J. A. J., Kaslow, N. J., Racusin, G. R., & Carton, E. R. (1998). Interpersonal family therapy for childhood depression. In V. B. Van Hasselt & M. Hersen (Eds.), *Handbook of psychological treatment protocols for children and adolescents* (p. 109–151). Mahwah, NJ: Erlbaum.

Scott, T. M., McIntyre, J., Liaupsin, C., Nelson, C. M., & Conroy, M. (2004). An examination of functional behavior assessment in public school settings: Collaborative teams, experts, and methodology. *Behavioral Disorders, 29*, 384–395.

Scott, W. D., & Cervone, D. (2003). Enhancing perceived self-efficacy: Guided mastery therapy. In W. O'Donohue, J. E. Fisher, & S. C. Hayes (Eds.), *Cognitive behavior therapy: Applying empirically supported techniques in your practice* (pp. 288–293). Hoboken, NJ: Wiley.

Scott, J. R., & Morris, T. L. (2000). Diagnosis and classification. In M. Hersen & R. T. Ammerman (Eds.), *Advanced abnormal child psychology* (2nd ed.) (pp. 15–32). Mahwah, NJ: Erlbaum.

Seidman, L. J., Buka, S. L., Goldstein, J. M., Horton, N. J., Rieder, R. O., & Tsuang, M. T. (2000). The relationship of prenatal and perinatal complications to cognitive functioning at age 7 in the New England cohorts of the National Collaborative Perinatal Project. *Schizophrenia Bulletin, 26*, 309–321.

Segal, D. L., & Coolidge, F. L. (2001). Diagnosis and classification. In M. Hersen & V. B. Van Hasselt (Eds.), *Advanced abnormal psychology* (2nd ed.) (pp. 5–22). New York: Kluwer Academic/Plenum.

Segrin, C. (2003). Social skills training. In W. O'Donohue, J. E. Fisher, & S. C. Hayes (Eds.), *Cognitive behavior therapy: Applying empirically supported techniques in your practice* (pp. 384–390). Hoboken, NJ: Wiley.

Seligman, M. (2000). *Conducting effective conferences with parents of children with disabilities*. New York: Guilford Press.

Sergeant, J., & Taylor, E. (2002). Psychological testing and observation. In M. Rutter & E. Taylor (Eds.), *Child and adolescent psychiatry* (4th ed.) (pp. 87–102). Malden, MA: Blackwell Science.

Serna, L. A., Nielsen, E., Mattern, N., & Forness, S. (2003). Primary prevention in mental health for Head Start classrooms: Partial replication with teachers as intervenors. *Behavioral Disorders, 28*, 124–129.

Severson, H. E., & Walker, H. M. (2002). Proactive approaches for identifying children at risk for sociobehavioral problems. In K. L. Lane, F. M. Gresham, & T. E. O'Shaughnessy (Ed.), *Interventions for children with or at risk for emotional and behavioral disorders* (pp. 33–53). Boston: Allyn & Bacon.

Shaffer, D. (2002). *Developmental psychology: Childhood and adolescence* (6th ed.). Belmont, CA: Wadsworth/Thompson Learning.

Shaffer, D. (2005). Depressive disorders and suicide in children and adolescents. In B. J. Sadock & V. A. Sadock (Eds.), *Kaplan & Sadock's comprehensive textbook of psychiatry* (Vol. II, pp. 3262–3273). Philadelphia: Lippincott Williams & Wilkins.

Shaffer, D., & Craft, L. (1999). Methods of adolescent suicide prevention. *Journal of Clinical Psychiatry, 60* (suppl. 2), 70–74.

Shaffer, D., Fisher, P., Lucas, C. P., Dulcan, M. K., & Schwab-Stone, M. E. (2000). NIMH Diagnostic Interview Schedule for Children Version IV (NIMH DISC IV): Description, differences from previous versions, and reliability of some common diagnoses. *Journal of the American Academy of Child and Adolescent Psychiatry, 39*, 28–38.

Shaffer, D., & Gutstein, J. (2002). Suicide and attempted suicide. In M. Rutter & E. Taylor (Eds.), *Child and adolescent psychiatry* (4th ed., pp. 529–554). Malden, MA: Blackwell Science.

Shapiro, E. S., & Kratochwill, T. R. (2000). *Behavioral assessment in schools* (2nd ed.) New York: Guilford.

Shelton, T. L., Williford, A. P., & Woods, J. E. (2003). Internalizing disorders: Mood and anxiety disorders. In M. J. Breen & C. R. Fiedler (Eds.), *Behavioral approach to assessment of youth with emotional/behavioral disorders* (2nd ed., pp. 337–379). Austin, TX: PRO-ED.

Shepard, J. M. (2005). *Sociology* (9th ed.). Belmont, CA: Wadsworth.

Shippen, M. E., Houchins, D. E., Steventon, C., & Sartor, D. (2005). A comparison of two direct instruction reading programs for urban middle school students. *Remedial and Special Education, 26*, 175–182.

Shippen, M. E., Simpson, R. G., & Crites, S. A. (2003). A practical guide to functional behavioral assessment. *Teaching Exceptional Children, 35*, 36–45.

Shirk, S., Burwell, R., & Harter, S. (2003). Strategies to modify low self-esteem in adolescents. In M. A. Reinecke, F. M. Dattilio, & A. Freeman (Eds.), *Cognitive therapy with children and adolescents* (2nd ed., pp. 189–213). New York: Guilford.

Shure, M. B. (1992). *I can problem solve (ICPS): An interpersonal cognitive problem solving program*. Champaign, IL: Research Press.

Shure, M. B. (1999, April). Preventing violence the problem-solving way. *OJJDP Bulletin* (NCJ 172847), 1–11.

Sickmund, M. (2002). *Juvenile residential facility census, 2000: Selected findings*. Washington, DC: U.S. Department of Justice.

Silk, J. S., Nath, S. R., Siegel, L. R., & Kendall, P. C. (2000). Conceptualizing mental disorders in children: Where have we been and where are we going? *Development and Psychopathology, 12,* 713–735.

Silver, A. A., & Hagin, R. A. (2002). *Disorders of learning in childhood* (2nd ed.). New York: Wiley.

Simkin, D. H. (2005). Adolescent substance abuse. In B. J. Sadock & V. A. Sadock (Eds.), *Kaplan & Sadock's comprehensive textbook of psychiatry* (Vol. II, pp. 3470–3489). Philadelphia: Lippincott Williams & Wilkins.

Simpson, R. L. (2004). Inclusion of students with behavior disorders in general education settings: Research and measurement issues. *Behavioral Disorders, 30,* 19–31.

Simpson, R., & Myles, B. (2003). *Asperger syndrome: A guide for educators and parents.* Austin, TX: PRO-ED.

Sinclair, M. F., Christenson, S. L., & Thurlow, M. L. (2005). Promoting school completion of urban secondary youth with emotional or behavioral disabilities. *Exceptional Children, 71,* 465–482.

Singh, N. N. (1998). Cultural diversity: A challenge for evaluating systems of care. In M. H. Epstein, K. Kutash, & A. Duchnowski (Eds.), *Outcomes for children and youth with emotional and behavioral disorders and their families* (pp. 425–454). Austin, TX: PRO-ED.

Sitlington, P. L., & Neubert, D. A. (2004). Preparing youths with emotional or behavioral disorders for transition to adult life: Can it be done within the standards-based reform movement? *Behavioral Disorders, 29,* 279–288.

Skinner, B. F. (1953). *Science and human behavior.* New York: Free Press.

Skinner, B. F. (1957). *Verbal behavior.* New York: Appleton-Century-Crofts.

Skinner, B. F. (1968). *The technology of teaching.* New York: Knopf.

Skinner, B. F. (1969). *Contingencies of reinforcement: A theoretical analysis.* New York: Appleton-Century-Crofts.

Skuse, D. H., & Kuntsi, J. (2002). Molecular genetic and chromosomal anomalies: Cognitive and behavioral consequences. In M. Rutter & E. Taylor (Eds.), *Child and adolescent psychiatry* (4th ed., pp. 205–240). Malden, MA: Blackwell Science.

Smith, D. K. (2004). Risk, reinforcement, retention in treatment, and reoffending for boys and girls in multidimensional treatment foster care. *Journal of Emotional and Behavioral Disorders, 12,* 38–48.

Smith, C. R., & Katsiyannis, A. (2004). Behavior, discipline, and students with emotional or behavioral disorders: Promises to keep . . . miles to go. *Behavioral Disorders, 29,* 289–299.

Smith, C. R., & Wood, F. H. (1986). *Education of behaviorally disordered students: Accomplishments, problems, and prospects.* Reston, VA: Council for Children with Behavior Disorders, Council for Exceptional Children.

Smith, C., & Denton, M. L. (2005). *Soul searching: The religious and spiritual lives of American teenagers.* New York: Oxford University Press.

Smith, D. K. (2004). Risk, reinforcement, retention in treatment, and reoffending for boys and girls in multidimensional treatment foster care. *Journal of Emotional and Behavioral Disorders, 12,* 38–48.

Smith, J. D., Schneider, B. H., Smith, P. K., & Ananiadou, K. (2004). The effectiveness of whole-school antibullying programs: A synthesis of evaluation research. *School Psychology Review, 33,* 547–560.

Smith, S., Lochman, J. E., & Daunic, A. P. (2005). Managing aggression using cognitive-behavioral interventions: State of the practice and future directions. *Behavioral Disorders, 30,* 227–240.

Smith, T., Polloway, E., Patton, J., & Dowdy, C. (2006). *Teaching students with special needs in inclusive settings* (4th ed.). Boston: Allyn and Bacon.

Smith-Boydston, J. M. (2005). Providing a range of services to fit the needs of youth in community mental health centers. In R. G. Steele & M. C. Roberts (Eds.), *Handbook of mental health services for children, adolescents, and families* (pp. 103–116). New York: Kluwer Academic/Plenum.

Snyder, H. N. (2005). *Juvenile arrests 2003. OJJDP Bullletin* (NCJ 209735). Washington, DC: Office of Juvenile Justice and Delinquency Prevention.

Snyder, H. N., & Sickmund, M. (1999). *Juvenile offenders and victims: 1999 National Report* (NCJ 178257). Washington, DC: Office of Juvenile Justice and Delinquency Prevention.

Snyder, J. (2002). Reinforcement and coercion mechanisms in the development of antisocial behavior: Peer relationships. In J. B. Reid, G. R. Patterson, & J. Snyder (Eds.), *Antisocial behavior in children and adolescents* (pp. 101–122). Washington: American Psychological Association.

Solhkhah, R., & Armentano, M. (2002). Adolescent substance abuse and psychiatric comorbidity. In D. T. Marsh & M. A. Fristad (Eds.), *Handbook of serious emotional disturbances in children and adolescents* (pp. 304–322). New York: Wiley.

Spencer, E. K., & Campbell, M. (1994). Children with schizophrenia: Diagnosis, phenomenology, and pharmacotherapy. *Schizophrenia Bulletin, 20,* 713–725.

Spies, R. A., & Plake, B. S. (2005). *The sixteenth mental measurements yearbook.* Lincoln, NE: University of Nebraska Press.

Spivack, G., & Shure, M. B. (1974). *Social adjustment of young children: A cognitive approach to solving real-life problems.* San Francisco: Jossey-Bass.

Steele, R. G., & Roberts, M. C. (2005). Mental health services for children, adolescents, and families: Trends, models, and current status. In R. G. Steele & M. C. Roberts (Eds.), *Handbook of mental health services for children, adolescents, and families* (pp. 1–14). New York: Kluwer Academic/Plenum.

Steinberg, Z., & Knitzer, J. (1992). Classrooms for emotionally and behaviorally disturbed students: Facing the challenge. *Behavioral Disorders, 17*, 145–156.

Steiner, H., & Karnik, N. (2005). Child or adolescent antisocial behavior. In B. J. Sadock & V. A. Sadock (Eds.), *Kaplan & Sadock's comprehensive textbook of psychiatry* (Vol. II, pp. 3441–3448). Philadelphia: Lippincott Williams & Wilkins.

Steinhauer, P. D., & Rae-Grant, Q. (Eds.). (1977). *Psychological problems of the child and his family.* Toronto: Macmillan of Canada.

Sterba, M., & Dowd, T. (1998). *Treating youth with DSM-IV disorders.* Boys Town, NE: Boys Town Press.

Stewart, A. J., Steiman, M., Cauce, A. M., Cochran, B. N., Whitebeck, L. B., & Hoyt, D. R. (2004). Victimization and posttraumatic stress disorder among homeless adolescents. *Journal of the American Academy of Child and Adolescent Psychiatry, 43*, 325–331.

Stichter, J. P., & Conroy, M. A. (2004). A critical analysis of the role of measurement on the validity of emotional and behavioral disorders (EBD) research. *Behavioral Disorders, 30*, 7–18.

Stormont, M., Lewis, T. J., & Beckner, R. (2005). Positive behavior support systems: Applying key features in preschool settings. *Teaching Exceptional Children, 37*, 42–49.

Stormshak, E., & Dishion, T. (2002). An ecological approach to child and family clinical and counseling psychology. *Clinical Child and Family Psychology Review, 5*, 197–215.

Strain, P. S., & Timm, M. A. (2001). Remediation and prevention of aggression: An evaluation of the Regional Intervention Program ove a quarter century. *Behavioral Disorders, 26*, 297–313.

Straus, M. A., & Stewart, J. H. (1999). Corporal punishment by American parents: National data on prevalence, chronicity, severity, and duration, in relation to child and family characteristics. *Clinical Child and Family Psychology Review, 2*, 55–70.

Strober, M. A. (1996). Outcome studies of mania in children and adolescents. In K. I. Shulman, M. Tohen, & S. P. Kutcher (Eds.), *Mood disorders across the life span* (pp. 149–158). New York: Wiley.

Stroul, B. A. (2003). Systems of care: A framework for children's mental health care. In A. J. Pumariega & N. C. Winters (Eds.), *The handbook of child and adolescent systems of care: The new community psychiatry* (pp. 17–34). San Francisco: Jossey-Bass.

Stroul, B. A., & Friedman, R. M. (1986). *A system of care for seriously emotionally disturbed children and youth.* Washington, DC: CASSP Technical Assistance Center, Georgetown University Child Development Center.

Strout, M. (2005). Positive behavioral support at the classroom level: Considerations and strategies. *Beyond Behavior, 14*, 3–8.

Sugai, G., Horner, R. H., Dunlap, G., Hieneman, M., Lewis, J. J., Nelson, C. M., et al. (2000). Applying positive behavior support and functional behavioral assessment in schools. *Journal of Positive Behavior Interventions, 2*, 131–143.

Sugai, G., Horner, R. H., & Gresham, F. (2002). Behaviorally effective school environments. In M. R. Shinn, G. Stoner, & H. M. Walker (Eds.), *Interventions for academic and behavior problems: Preventive and remedial approaches* (pp. 315–350). Silver Spring, MD: National Association of School Psychologists.

Sugai, G., Sprague, J. R., Horner, R. H., & Walker, H. M. (2000). Preventing school violence: The use of office discipline referrals to assess and monitor school-wide discipline interventions. *Journal of Emotional and Behavioral Disorders, 8*, 94–101.

Sussman, N. (2005). General principles of psychopharmacology. In B. J. Sadock & V. A. Sadock (Eds.), *Kaplan & Sadock's comprehensive textbook of psychiatry* (Vol. II, pp. 2676–2698). Philadelphia: Lippincott Williams & Wilkins.

Sutherland, K. S., Alder, N., & Gunter, P. L. (2003). The effect of varying rates of opportunities to respond to academic requests on the classroom behavior of students with EBD. *Journal of Emotional and Behavioral Disorders, 114*, 239–248.

Swanson, T. C. (2005). Provide structure for children with learning and behavior problems. *Intervention in School and Clinic, 40*, 182–187.

Sweeney, D. P., & Hoffman, C. D. (2004). Research issues in autism spectrum disorders. In R. B. Rutherford Jr., M. M. Quinn, & S. Mathur (Eds.), *Handbook of research in behavioral disorders* (pp. 302–317). New York: Guilford.

Szasz, T. S. (1960) The myth of mental illness. *American Psychologist, 15*, 113–118.

Szasz, T. S. (1970). *The manufacture of madness.* New York: Dell.

Taieb, O., Cohen, D., Mazet, P., & Flament, M. (2000). Adolescents' experiences with ECT. *Journal of the American Academy of Child and Adolescent Psychiatry, 39*, 943–944.

Tanguay, P. E. (2000). Pervasive developmental disorders: A 10 year review. *Journal of the American Academy of Child and Adolescent Psychiatry, 39*, 1079–1095.

Tankersley, M., Landrum, T. J., & Cook, B. G. (2004). How research informs practice in the field of emotional and behavioral disorders. In R. B. Rutherford Jr., M. M. Quinn, & S. Mathur (Eds.), *Handbook of research in behavioral disorders* (pp. 98–113). New York: Guilford.

Tarbox, J., & Hayes, L. J. (2003). Differential reinforcement of low-rate behavior. In W. O'Donohue, J. E. Fisher, & S. C. Hayes (Eds.), *Cognitive behavior therapy: Applying empirically supported techniques in your practice* (pp. 129–135). Hoboken, NJ: Wiley.

Tarnowski, K. J., Brown, R. T., & Simonian, S. J. (1999). Social class. In W. K. Silverman & T. H. Ollendick (Eds.), *Developmental issues in the clinical treatment of children* (pp. 213–230). Needham Heights, MA: Allyn & Bacon.

Taylor, E., & Rutter, M. (2002). Classification: Conceptual issues and substantive findings. In M. Rutter & E. Taylor (Eds.), *Child and adolescent psychiatry* (4th ed., pp. 3–17). Malden, MA: Blackwell Science.

Taylor, H. (2003, February 26). The religious and other beliefs of Americans, 2003. *The Harris Poll,* #11.

Taylor, R. L. (2006). *Assessment of exceptional students: Educational and psychological procedures* (7th ed.). Needham Heights, MA: Allyn and Bacon.

Teplin, L. A., Abram, K. M., McClelland, G. M., Dulcan, M., K., & Mericle, A., A. (2002). Psychiatric disorders in youth in juvenile detention. *Archives of General Psychiatry, 59,* 1133–1143.

Thienemann, M. L. (2005). Group psychotherapy. In B. J. Sadock & V. A. Sadock (Eds.), *Kaplan & Sadock's comprehensive textbook of psychiatry* (Vol. II, pp. 3342–3351). Philadelphia: Lippincott Williams & Wilkins.

Thomas, A., Chess, S., & Birch, H. (1968). *Temperament and behavior disorders in children.* New York: New York University Press.

Thomas, C. R. (2005). Disruptive behavior disorders. In B. J. Sadock & V. A. Sadock (Eds.), *Kaplan & Sadock's comprehensive textbook of psychiatry* (Vol. II, pp. 3205–3216). Philadelphia: Lippincott Williams & Wilkins.

Thornberry, T. P., Huizinga, D., & Loeber, R. (2004). The causes and correlates studies: Findings and policy implications. *Juvenile Justice, IX,* 3–19.

Thornburgh, D., & Lin, H. S. (Eds.). (2002). *Youth, pornography, and the Internet.* Washington: National Academy Press.

Tindal, G., & Crawford, L. (2002). Teaching writing to students with behavior disorders: Metaphor and medium. In K. L. Lane, F. M. Gresham, & T. E. O'Shaughnessy (Eds.), *Interventions for children with or at risk for emotional and behavioral disorders* (pp. 104–124). Boston: Allyn & Bacon.

Tobin, T., & Sprague, J. (2000). Alternative education strategies: Reducing violence in school and the community. *Journal of Emotional and Behavioral Disorders, 8,* 177–186.

Todd, A. W., Horner, R. H., & Sugai, G. (1999). Self-monitoring and self-recruited praise: Effects on problem behavior, academic engagement, and work completion in a typical classroom. *Journal of Positive Behavior Interventions, 1,* 66–76, 122.

Tonigan, J. S., Toscova, R. T., & Connors, G. J. (1999). Spirituality and the 12-step programs: A guide for clinicians. In W. R. Miller (Eds.), *Integrating spirituality into treatment: Resources for practitioners* (pp. 111–132). Washington, DC: American Psychological Association.

Toppelberg, C. O., & Shapiro, T. (2000). Language disorders: A 10 year research update review. *Journal of the American Academy of Child and Adolescent Psychiatry, 39,* 143–152.

Torres-Valasquez, D. (2000). Sociocultural theory: Standing at the crossroads. *Remedial and Special Education, 21,* 66–69.

Trickett, K., Kurtz, D. A., & Noll, J. G. (2005). The consequences of child sexual abuse for female development. In D. J. Bell, S. L. Foster, & E. J. Mash (Eds.), *Handbook of behavioral and emotional problems in girls* (pp. 357–380). New York: Kluwer Academic/Plenum.

Trout, A. L., Epstein, M. H., Mickelson, W. T., Nelson, J. R., & Lewis, L. M. (2003). Effects of reading intervention for kindergarten students at risk for emotional disturbance and reading deficits. *Behavioral Disorders, 28,* 313–326.

Trout, A. L., Nordness, P. D., Pierce, C. D., & Epstein, M. H. (2003). Research on the academic status of children with emotional and behavioral disorders: A review of the literature from 1961 to 2000. *Journal of Emotional and Behavioral Disorders, 11,* 198–210.

Trudeau, L., Spoth, R., Lillehoj, C., Redmond, C., & Wickrama, K. (2003). Effects of a preventive intervention on adolescent substance use initiation, expectancies, and refusal intentions. *Prevention Science, 4,* 109–122.

Truscott, S. D., Cohen, C. E., Sams, D. P., Sanborn, K. J., & Frank, A. J. (2005). The current state(s) of prereferrel intervention teams: A report from two national surveys. *Remedial and Special Education, 26,* 130–140.

Tryon, W. W. (2001). Behavioral model. In M. Hersen & V. B. Van Hasselt (Eds.), *Advanced abnormal psychology* (2nd ed., pp. 93–123). New York: Kluwer Academic/Plenum.

Turnbull, H. R., Huerta, N., & Stowe, M. (2006). *Explanation of IDEA Improvement Act of 2004.* Columbus: Merrill Prentice Hall.

U.S. Department of Education. (1994). *Sixteenth annual report to Congress on the implementation of the Individuals with Disabilities Education Act.* Washington, DC: Author.

U.S. Department of Education. (1995). *Seventeenth annual report to Congress on the implementation of the individuals with Disabilities Education Act.* Washington, DC: Author.

U.S. Department of Education. (1998). *Twentieth annual report to Congress on the implementation of the Individuals with Disabilities Education Act.* Washington, DC: Author.

U.S. Department of Education. (1999). *Twenty-first annual report to Congress on the implementation of the Individuals with Disabilities Education Act.* Washington, DC: Author.

U.S. Department of Education. (2000). *Twenty-second annual report to Congress on the implementation of the Individuals with Disabilities Education Act.* Washington, DC: Author.

U.S. Department of Education. (2002). *Twenty-fourth annual report to Congress on the implementation of the Individuals with Disabilities Education Act.* Washington, DC: Author.

U.S. Department of Education. (2005). *25th annual (2003) report to Congress on the implementation of the Individuals with Disabilities Education Act* (Vols. I and II). Washington, DC: Author.

U.S. Department of Health and Human Services (1999). *Mental health: A report of the Surgeon General.* Rockville, MD: U.S. Department of Health and Human Services, Substance Abuse and Mental Health Services Administration, Center for Mental Health Services, National Institutes of Health, National Institute of Mental Health.

Unruh, D., & Bullis, M. (2005). Female and male juvenile offenders with disabilities: Differences in the barriers to their transition to the community. *Behavioral Disorders, 30,* 105–117.

Valsiner, J. (2000). *Culture and human development.* Thousand Oaks, CA: Sage.

Van Acker, R. (2002). *Establishing and monitoring a school and classroom climate that promotes desired behavior and academic achievement.* Arlington, VA: Council for Exceptional Children.

Van Acker, R., Yell, M. L., Bradley, R., & Drasgow, E. (2004). Experimental research designs in the study of children and youth with emotional and behavioral disorders. In R. B. Rutherford Jr., M. M. Quinn, & S. Mathur (Eds.), *Handbook of research in behavioral disorders* (pp. 546–566). New York: Guilford.

Vanderbilt, A. A. (2005). Designed for teachers: How to implement self-monitoring in the classroom. *Beyond Behavior, 15*(1), 21–24.

Vargas, L. A., & Brambila, A. D. D. (2005). Inpatient treatment models. In R. G. Steele & M. C. Roberts (Eds.), *Handbook of mental health services for children, adolescents, and families* (pp. 133–149). New York: Kluwer Academic/Plenum.

Verhulst, F. C. (2001). Community and epidemiological aspects of anxiety disorders in children. In W. K. Silverman & P. D. A. Treffers (Eds.), *Anxiety disorders in children and adolescents: Research, assessment, and intervention* (pp. 293–312). New York: Cambridge University Press.

Verhulst, F. C., & Van der Ende, J. (2002). Rating scales. In M. Rutter & E. Taylor (Eds.), *Child and adolescent psychiatry* (4th ed., pp. 70–86). Malden, MA: Blackwell Science.

Vickers, B. (2002). Case study: The treatment of auditory hallucinations in children with emotional disorders. *Child and Adolescent Mental Health, 7,* 25–30.

Villa, R. A., Thousand, J. S., & Nevin, A. I. (2004). *A guide to co-teaching.* Thousand Oaks, CA: Corwin.

Vitulano, L. A., & Tebes, J. K. (2002). Child and adolescent behavior therapy. In M. Lewis (Ed.), *Child and adolescent psychiatry: A comprehensive textbook* (3rd ed., pp. 998–1015). Philadelphia: Lippincott Williams & Wilkins.

Volkmar, F. R., Klin, A., & Schultz, A. R. (2005). Pervasive developmental disorders. In B. J. Sadock & V. A. Sadock (Eds.), *Kaplan & Sadock's comprehensive textbook of psychiatry* (Vol. II, pp. 3164–3182). Philadelphia: Lippincott Williams & Wilkins.

Volkmar, F. R., Lord, C., Bailey, A., Schultz, R. T., & Klin, A. (2004). Autism and pervasive developmental disorders. *Journal of Child Psychology and Psychiatry, 45,* 135–170.

Volkmar, F. R., Lord, C., Klin, A., & Cook, E. (2002). Autism and the pervasive developmental disorders. In M. Lewis (Ed.), *Child and adolescent psychiatry: A comprehensive textbook* (3rd ed., pp. 587–597). Philadelphia: Lippincott Williams & Wilkins.

Volkmar, F. R., & Tsatsanis, K. D. (2002). Childhood schizophrenia. In M. Lewis (Ed.), *Child and adolescent psychiatry: A comprehensive textbook* (3rd ed., pp. 746–754). Philadelphia: Lippincott Williams & Wilkins.

Wacker, D. P., Harding, J., Berg, W., Cooper-Brown, L. J., & Barretto, A. (2003). Punishment. In W. O'Donohue, J. E. Fisher, & S. C. Hayes (Eds.), *Cognitive behavior therapy: Applying empirically supported techniques in your practice* (pp. 307–313). Hoboken, NJ: Wiley.

Wagner, H., & Silber, K. (2004). *Physiological psychology.* New York: BIOS Scientific Publishers/Taylor & Francis.

Wagner, M. M. (1995). Outcomes for youths with serious emotional disturbance in secondary school and early adulthood. *The Future of Children, 5,* 90–112.

Wagner, M., Kutash, K., Duchnowski, A. J., Epstein, M. H., & Sumi, W. C. (2005). The children and youth we serve: A national picture of the characteristics of students with emotional disturbances receiving special education. *Journal of Emotional and Behavioral Disorders, 13,* 79–96.

Walberg, H., & Wynne, E. (1989). Character education: Toward a preliminary consensus. In L. Nucci (Ed.), *Moral development and character education: A dialogue* (pp. 19–36). Berkley, CA: McCutchan.

Walker, H., Severson, H., & Feil, E. (1995). *Early screening project: A proven child-find process.* Longmont, CO: Sopris West.

Walker, H. M., Hops, H., & Greenwood, C. R. (1984). The CORBEH research and development model: Programmatic issues and strategies. In S. C. Paine, T. C. Bellamy, & B. Wilcox (Eds.), *Human services that work* (pp. 51–77). Baltimore: Paul H. Brookes.

Walker, H. M., Kavanagh, K., Stiller, B., Golly, A., Severson, H., & Feil, E. (1997). *First Step to Success: An early intervention program for antisocial kindergartners.* Longmont, CO: Sopris West.

Walker, H. M., Block-Pedigo, A., Todis, B., & Severson, H. (1991). *School archival records search (SARS): User's guide and technical manual.* Longmont, CO: Sopris West.

Walker, H. M., Ramsey, E., Gresham, F. M. (2004). *Antisocial behavior in schools: Evidence-based practices* (2nd ed.). Belmont, CA: Wadsworth.

Walker, H. M., & Severson, H. H. (1992). *Systematic screening for behavior disorders (SSBD): User's guide and administration manual* (2nd ed.). Longmont, CO: Sopris West.

Walker, H. M., & Severson, H. H. (2002). Developmental prevention of at-risk outcomes for vulnerable antisocial children and youth. In K. L. Lane, F. M. Gresham, & T. E. O'Shaughnessy (Eds.), *Interventions for children with or at risk for emotional and behavioral disorders* (pp. 175–194). Boston: Allyn & Bacon.

Walker, J. S., & Schutte, K. M. (2004). Practice and process in wraparound teamwork. *Journal of Emotional and Behavioral Disorders, 12,* 182–191.

Wallace, M. D., & Robles, A. C. (2003). Differential reinforcement of other behavior and differential reinforcement of alternative behavior. In W. O'Donohue, J. E. Fisher, & S. C. Hayes (Eds.), *Cognitive behavior therapy: Applying empirically supported techniques in your practice* (pp. 136–143). Hoboken, NJ: Wiley.

Wallace, R. A., & Wolf, A. (2006). *Contemporary sociological theory: Expanding the classical tradition* (6th ed.). Upper Saddle River, NJ: Prentice Hall.

Warren, C. S., & Messer, S. B. (1999). Brief psychodynamic therapy with anxious children. In S. W. Russ & T. H. Ollendick (Eds.), *Handbook of psychotherapies with children and families* (pp. 219–237). New York: Kluwer Academic/Plenum.

Wasserman, G. A., McReynolds, L., Lucas, C., Fisher, P., W., & Santos, L. (2002). The Voice DISC-IV with incarcerated male youth: Prevalence of disorder. *Journal of the American Academy of Child and Adolescent Psychiatry, 41,* 314–321.

Watson, G. S., & Gross, A. M. (2000). Familial determinants. In M. Hersen & R. T. Ammerman (Eds.), *Advanced abnormal child psychology* (2nd ed.) (pp. 81–99). Hillsdale, NJ: Lawrence Erlbaum.

Watson, J. B. (1913). Psychology as the behaviorist views it. *Psychological Review, 20,* 158–177.

Watson, J. C., & Greenberg, L. S. (1998). Humanistic and experiential theories of personality. In D. F. Barone, M. Hersen, & V. B. Van Hasselt (Eds.), *Advanced personality* (pp. 81–102). New York, NY: Plenum.

Webb, M. B., & Harden, B. J. (2003). Beyond child protection: Promoting mental health for children and families in the child welfare system. *Journal of Emotional and Behavioral Disorders, 11,* 49–59.

Webb-Johnson, G. (2003). Behaving while black: A hazardous reality for African American learners? *Beyond Behavior, 12,* 3–7.

Webster, R. E., & Hall, C. W. (2004). School-based responses to children who have been sexually assaulted. *Education and Treatment of Children, 27,* 64–81.

Webster-Stratton, C., & Reid, M. J. (2003). Treating conduct problems and strengthening social and emotional competence in young children: The Dina Dinosaur treatment program. *Journal of Emotional and Behavioral Disorders, 11,* 130–143.

Weinberger, D. R., & Marenco, S. (2003). Schizophrenia as a neurodevelopmental disorder. In S. R. Hirsch & D. R. Weinberger (Eds.), *Schizophrenia* (2nd ed., pp. 326–348). Malden, MA: Blackwell.

Weinberg, W. A., Harper, C. R., & Brumback, R. A. (2002). Substance use and abuse: Epidemiology, phamacological considerations, identification and suggestions towards management. In M. Rutter & E. Taylor (Eds.), *Child and adolescent psychiatry* (4th ed., pp. 437–454). Malden, MA: Blackwell Science.

Weiss, M., & Weiss, G. (2002). Attention deficit hyperactivity disorder. In M. Lewis (Ed.), *Child and adolescent psychiatry: A comprehensive textbook* (3rd ed., pp. 645–670). Philadelphia: Lippincott Williams & Wilkins.

Weist, M. D. (1997). Expanded school mental health services: A national movement in progress. In T. H. Ollendick & R. J. Prinz (Eds.), *Advances in clinical child psychology* (Vol. 19, pp. 319–352). New York: Plenum.

Weitoft, G., Hjern, A., Haglund, B., & Rosen, M. (2003). Mortality, severe morbidity, and injury in children living with single parents in Sweden: A population-based study. *The Lancet, 361,* 289–295.

Wekerle, C., & Wolfe, D. A. (2003). Child maltreatment. In E. J. Mash & R. A. Barkley (Eds.), *Child psychopathology* (2nd ed., pp. 632–684). New York: Guilford.

Weller, E. B., Weller, R. A., Rowan, A. B., & Svadjian, H. (2002b). Depressive disorders in children and adolescents. In M. Lewis (Ed.), *Child and adolescent psychiatry: A comprehensive textbook* (3rd ed., pp. 767–781). Philadelphia: Lippincott Williams & Wilkins.

Weller, E. B., Weller, R. A., & Sanchez, L. E. (2002a). Bipolar disorder in children and adolescents. In M. Lewis (Ed.), *Child and adolescent psychiatry: A comprehensive textbook* (3rd ed., pp. 782–791). Philadelphia: Lippincott Williams & Wilkins.

Wells, M. G. (1999). Religion. In W. K. Silverman & T. H. Ollendick (Eds.), *Developmental issues in the clinical treatment of children* (pp. 199–212). Needham Heights, MA: Allyn and Bacon.

Werry, J. S. (1996). Childhood schizophrenia. In F. R. Volkmar (Ed.), *Psychoses and pervasive developmental disorders in childhood and adolescence* (pp. 1–48). Washington, DC: American Psychiatric Press.

Werry, J. S., Zametkin, A., & Ernst, M. (2002). Brain and behavior. In M. Lewis (Ed.), *Child and adolescent psychiatry: A comprehensive textbook* (3rd ed., pp. 120–132). Philadelphia: Lippincott Williams & Wilkins.

Whelan, R. J., & Kauffman, J. M. (1999). *Educating students with emotional and behavioral disorders: Historical perspective and future directions*. Reston, VA: Council for Children with Behavioral Disorders.

Whitaker, A. H., Birmaher, B., & Williams, D. (2002). Traumatic and infectious brain injury in children. In M. Lewis (Ed.), *Child and adolescent psychiatry: A comprehensive textbook* (3rd ed., pp. 431–447). Philadelphia: Lippincott Williams & Wilkins.

Wicks-Nelson, R., & Israel, A. C. (2006). *Behavior disorders of childhood* (6th ed.). Upper Saddle River, NJ: Prentice Hall.

Williams, S. L., & Cervone, D. (1998). Social cognitive theories of personality. In D. F. Barone, M. Hersen, & V. B. Van Hasselt (Eds.), *Advanced personality* (pp. 173–207). New York, NY: Plenum.

Wilmshurst, L. (2005). *Essentials of child psychopathology*. New York: Wiley.

Wilson, J. J. (2004). Sociotherapies for children and adolescents: An overview. In H. Steiner (Eds.), *Handbook of mental health interventions in children and adolescents: An integrated developmental approach* (pp. 804–827). San Francisco: Jossey-Bass.

Windsor, A. P. (2003). Direct behavioral observation for classrooms. In C. R. Reynolds & R. W. Kamphaus (Eds.), *Handbook of psychological and educational assessment of children: Personality, behavior, and context* (2nd ed., pp. 248–258). New York: Guilford.

Wing, J. K., & Agrawal, N. (2003). Concepts and classification of schizophrenia. In S. R. Hirsch & D. R. Weinberger (Eds.), *Schizophrenia* (2nd ed., pp. 3–14). Malden, MA: Blackwell.

Winters, N. C., & Terrell, E. (2003). Case management: The linchpin of community-based systems of care. In A. J. Pumariega & N. C. Winters (Eds.), *The handbook of child and adolescent systems of care: The new community psychiatry* (pp. 171–200). San Francisco: Jossey-Bass.

Witt, J. C., VanDerHeyden, A. M., & Gilbertson, D. (2004). Instruction and classroom management: Prevention and intervention research. In R. B. Rutherford Jr., M. M. Quinn, & S. Mathur (Eds.), *Handbook of research in behavioral disorders* (pp. 426–445). New York: Guilford.

Wolf, M. M., Risely, T. R., & Mees, H. (1964). Application of operant conditioning techniques to the behavior problems of an autistic child. *Behavior Research and Therapy, 3,* 305–312.

Wolfe, D. A. (1999). *Child abuse: Implications for child development and psychopathology* (2nd ed.). Thousand Oaks, CA: Sage.

Wolfe, D. A., Crooks, C. V., Lee, V. McIntyre-Smith, A., & Jaffe, P. G. (2003). The effects of children's exposure to domestic violence: A meta-analysis and critique. *Clinical Child and Family Psychology Review, 6,* 171–187.

Wolfgang, C. H. (2005). *Solving discipline and classroom management problems: Methods and models for today's teachers* (6th ed.). New York: Wiley.

Wolraich, M., Wilson, D. B., & White, J. W. (1995). The effect of sugar on behavior or cognition in children. *Journal of the American Medical Association, 274,* 1617–1621.

Wood, F. H. (1999). CCBD: A record of accomplishment. *Behavioral Disorders, 24,* 273–283.

Wood, M. M., Brendtro, L. K., Fecser, F. A., & Nichols, P. (1999). *Psychoeducation: An idea whose time has come*. Reston, VA: Council for Exceptional Children.

Wood, M. M., Davis, K. R., Swindle, F. L., & Quirk, C. (1996). *Developmental therapy—developmental teaching* (3rd ed.). Austin, TX: PRO-ED.

Woodruff, D. W., Osher, D., Hoffman, C. C., Gruner, A., King, M. A., Snow, S.T., et al. (1999). *Systems of care: Promising practices in children's mental health, 1998 series. Volume III: The role of education in a system of care: Effectively serving children with emotional or behavioral disorders*. Washington, DC: Center for Effective Collaboration and Practice, American Institutes for Research.

Woodward, L. J., & Fergusson, D. M. (1999). Childhood peer relationship problems and psychosocial adjustment in late adolescence. *Journal of Abnormal Child Psychology, 27,* 87–104.

Wright, G., & Phillips-Smith, E. (1998). Home, school, and community partnerships: Integrating issues of race, culture, and social class. *Clinical Child and Family Psychology Review, 1,* 145–162.

Zimmerman, M., & Spitzer, R. L. (2005). Psychiatric classification. In B. J. Sadock & V. A. Sadock (Eds.), *Kaplan & Sadock's comprehensive textbook of psychiatry, Volume I* (pp. 1003–1033). Philadelphia: Lippincott Williams & Wilkins

Wyrick, P. A., & Howell, J. C. (2004). Strategic risk-based response to youth gangs. *Juvenile Justice, IX,* 20–29.

Yampolskaya, S., Brown, E. C., & Greenbaum, P. E. (2002). Early pregnancy among adolescent females with serious emotional disturbances: Risk factors and outcomes. *Journal of Emotional and Behavioral Disorders, 10,* 108–115.

Yell, M. (2006). *The law and special education* (2nd ed.). Upper Saddle River, NJ: Merrill Prentice Hall.

Yoshikawa, H., & Knitzer, J. (1997). *Lessons from the field: Head Start mental health strategies to meet changing needs*. New York: National Center for Children in Poverty.

Ysseldyke, J. E., & Christenson, S. L. (2002). *Functional assessment of academic behavior: Creating successful learning environments*. Longmont, CO: Sopris West.

Yule, W. (2002). Post-traumatic stress disorders. In M. Rutter & E. Taylor (Eds.), *Child and adolescent psychiatry* (4th ed., pp. 520–528). Malden, MA: Blackwell Science.

Zahn-Wexler, C., Race, E., & Duggal, S. (2005). Mood disorders and symptoms in girls. In D. J. Bell, S. L. Foster, & E. J. Mash (Eds.), *Handbook of behavioral and emotional problems in girls* (pp. 25–78). New York: Kluwer Academic/Plenum.

Zhang, D., Katsiyannis, A., & Herbst, M. (2004). Disciplinary exclusions in special education: A 4-year analysis. *Behavioral Disorders, 29,* 337–347.

Zigler, E. F., Finn-Stevenson, M., & Tanner, E. M. (2002). National policies for children, adolescents, and families. In M. Lewis (Ed.), *Child and adolescent psychiatry: A comprehensive textbook* (3rd ed., pp. 1340–1352). Philadelphia: Lippincott Williams & Wilkins.

Ziboorg, G., & Henry, G. W. (1941). *A history of medical psychology.* New York: Norton.

Zimet, D., & Jacob, T. (2001). Influences of marital conflict on child adjustment: Review of theory and research. *Clinical Child and Family Psychology Review, 4,* 319–335.

Zimmerman, M., & Spitzer, R. L. (2005). Psychiatric classification. In B. J. Sadock & V. A. Sadock (Eds.), *Kaplan & Sadock's comprehensive textbook of psychiatry* (Vol. I, pp. 1003–1033). Philadelphia: Lippincott Williams & Wilkins

Zionts, L. T., & Callicott, K. (2002). The many faces of children's advocacy *Beyond Behavior, 11,* 33–34.

Zionts, P. (1996). *Teaching disturbed and disturbing students* (2nd ed). Austin, TX: PRO-ED.

Zionts, P., & Fox, R.W. (1998). Facilitating group classroom meetings: Practical guidelines. *Beyond Behavior, 9,* 8–13.

# Name Index

AACAP. *See* American Academy of Child and Adolescent Psychiatry
Aarons, G. A., 136, 140, 443, 451
Ablon, J. S., 333
Abram, K. M., 26, 136, 476
Abramson, L. Y., 329, 437
Achenbach, Thomas M., 36, 39, 42, 44, 71, 71, 72, 78, 79, 94, 97, 98, 99, 100, 102, 127, 187, 443, 463
Achilles, G., 306, 448
Adams, H. E., 91, 94, 95, 97, 100, 101, 102, 108, 437
Adams, J. H., 333, 469
Adams, R. L., 73, 437
Addy, C. L., 187, 445
Adler, N., 475
Adnopoz, J., 437
Agras, W. S., 262, 437
Agrawal, N., 150, 151, 165, 480
Aichhorn, August, 53, 437
Akiskal, H. S., 150, 153, 437
Al Otaiba, S., 401, 438
Alarcon, R. D., 97, 470
Albano, A. M., 116, 117, 118, 119, 306, 317, 329, 333, 443, 443
Alberg, J., 294, 437
Albert, L., 229, 437
Alberto, P. A., 58, 68, 74, 266, 271, 272, 274, 277, 279, 280, 287, 356, 437
Albrow, M., 341, 437
Alexandrin, J. R., 382, 438
Algozzine, B., 343, 466
Allen, D. E., 57, 438
Allen, J. C., 74, 438
Allen, J. S., 189, 438
Altman, R., 422, 470
Amann, L. L., 319, 334, 451
American Academy of Child and Adolescent Psychiatry, 163, 164, 169, 170, 171, 177, 438
American Psychiatric Association, 95, 119, 152, 162, 163, 164, 165, 171, 201, 202, 438
Ammerman, R. T., 36, 446
Ananiadou, K., 381, 384, 474
Anastopoulos, A. D., 124, 126, 333, 438
an der Heiden, W., 453
Anderson, E. R., 204, 452
Anderson, G. M., 189, 438
Anderson, J. A., 453, 491
Anderson, R. N., 141, 438
Andreason, N. C., 160, 450

Andrews, G., 97, 470
Andrews, J. A., 140, 438
Aneshensel, C. S., 342, 344, 438
Angold, A., 68, 71, 72, 73, 112, 117, 118, 122, 126, 135, 344, 444, 449, 447
Anthony, J. C., 140, 141, 456
Aoba, A., 171, 464
Arbelaez, C., 158, 440
Archer, R. P., 71, 442
Archwamety, T., 22, 397, 459
Ardila, A., 343, 468
Arias, B. E., 343, 468
Arias, E., 141, 438
Armentano, M., 140, 474
Armsden, G., 423, 438
Arnold, C. R., 56, 439
Arnold, M. E., 397, 438
Artiles, A. J., 21, 342, 343, 344–348, 434, 467
Asarnow, J. R., 152, 163, 165, 169, 177, 438
Asarnow, R. F., 152, 163, 165, 169, 177, 444, 442
Asher, K. N., 383, 453
Asperger, Hans, 148
Attar, B., 410, 453
Auslander, W. F., 423, 463
Austin, N. B., 157, 178, 448
Axelrod, S., 277, 279, 283, 460
Axelson, D., 45, 157, 158, 416, 417, 419, 421, 445, 451
Azrin, N. H., 279, 438

Bachman, J. G., 139, 140, 456
Bacon, S. B., 416, 438
Baer, D. M., 271, 438
Baer, S., 333, 438
Bagnell, A., 393, 440
Bailey, A., 16, 152, 168–176, 463, 478
Baldessarini, R. J., 157, 178, 448
Bambara, L., 399, 458
Bandura, Albert, 307, 308, 309, 310, 439
Barenbaum, E., 118, 122, 466
Barenz, R., 264, 280, 283, 444
Barkley, R. A., 16, 124, 125, 126, 127, 439
Barlow, D. H., 116, 117, 118, 119, 437
Barnhill, G. P., 88, 439
Barretto, A., 280, 478
Barrish, H. H., 279, 439
Barry, T. D., 205, 439
Bartel, N. R., 84, 392, 398, 453

Barth, J. M., 210, 356, 439
Bartollas, C., 425, 439
Barton, C. C., 349, 350, 455
Bates, J. E., 202, 213, 214, 467, 470
Bates, P., 382, 460
Battalio, R., 294, 404, 439
Bazron, B. J., 434, 445, 455
Bear, G. G., 400, 439
Beard, K. Y., 80, 296, 439
Bearden, C. E., 165, 439
Bec, A. T., 307, 317, 329, 330, 445, 446
Becker, D. F., 414, 439
Becker, W. C., 57, 202, 203, 439
Beckner, R., 379, 387, 475
Beebe-Frankenberger, M., 210, 380, 459
Beers, Clifford, 44
Begtrup, W., 167, 168, 466
Beland, K., 383, 453
Bell, S. K., 275, 439
Bellac, A. S., 78, 440
Ben-Porath, Y. S., 71, 442
Benes, F. M., 213, 439
Benjamin, M. P., 434, 455
Benner, G. J., 137, 466
Bennett, K. J., 13, 14, 110, 466
Benoit, D., 202, 462
Benoit, M., 423, 462
Benoit, M. B., 422, 433, 439
Benson, H., 361, 439
Berg, W., 280, 478
Ber, L. E., 42, 185, 200, 202, 307, 440
Berkowitz, Pearl H., 53, 440
Bernat, J. A., 91, 94, 95, 97, 100, 101, 102, 108, 437
Bernet, W., 207, 440
Besalel, V. A., 279, 438
Bhatara, V. S., 420, 456
Bhugra, D., 361, 363, 445, 465
Biederman, J., 155, 157, 440
Bierman, K. L., 128, 131, 321, 327, 334
Biglan, A., 387, 453
Bijou, S. W., 57, 440
Birch, H., 213, 476
Birmaher, B., 45, 158, 160, 199, 201, 416, 417, 419, 421, 445, 461, 479
Birnbrauer, J. S., 57, 440
Blac, C., 387, 453
Blackman, D. R., 124, 454
Blair, J., 387, 453
Blase, K. A., 423, 440
Block-Pedigo, A., 72, 478
Bloomquist, M. L., 333
Boc, M. A., 368, 440

Bockoven, J. S., 39, 440
Bodine, R. J., 384, 385, 444, 445
Boegels, S. M., 311, 440
Boggs, S. R., 275, 439
Boland, R. J., 150, 440
Bolhofner, K., 157, 158, 451
Borduin, C. M., 437, 457, 472
Boris, N. W., 128, 440
Bornstein, M. R., 78, 440
Borstin, D. J., 38, 42, 440
Bos, C. S., 277, 282, 285, 352, 356, 381, 393, 398, 400, 401, 440
Bostic, J. Q., 393, 440
Botvin, G. J., 334, 386, 445, 446, 453
Bower, E. M., 8, 441
Bowlby, J., 202, 441
Boxer, P., 327, 349, 453
Boyum, L. A., 202, 204, 441
Bradley, C., 45, 441
Bradley-Klug, K. L., 285, 334, 403, 441
Bradley, R., 13, 20, 399, 417, 446, 477
Brambila, A. D. D., 414, 434, 477
Bramon, E., 213, 465
Brannan, A. M., 435, 455
Braswell, L., 306, 313, 441
Braukmann, C. J., 423, 441
Bray, M. A., 290, 457
Breedlove, S. M., 189, 192, 193, 198, 470
Breen, M. J., 71, 98, 122, 441
Brems, C., 212, 441
Brendtro, L. K., 54, 55, 242, 249, 318, 355, 361, 363, 363–365, 364, 401, 446, 480
Brent, D., 158, 329, 333, 445, 443
Brewer, R. D., 383, 441
Bridges, M., 204, 454
Brigham, F. J., 14, 16, 101, 395, 457
Broden, M., 286, 441
Brokenleg, M., 363, 364, 365, 366, 441
Brolin, D. E., 403, 441
Brondino, M. J., 437, 455
Bronfenbrenner, U., 186, 441
Brooks-Gunn, J., 208, 460
Brown, D., 393, 441
Brown, E. C., 136, 428, 455, 480
Brown, K. J., 416, 442
Brown, R. T., 209, 416, 419, 476
Brown, S. A., 140, 437
Brown, W. H., 80, 387, 444
Brumbac, R. A., 139, 479
Bruss, J., 189, 438
Bry, B. H., 333, 457
Buc, J., 426, 442

Buell, J. S., 57, 438
Buka, S. L., 472
Bukatko, D., 42, 442
Bullis, M., 23, 188, 295, 403, 447, 448, 477
Bulloc, C., 384, 442
Bulloc, L. M., 47, 442
Bumbarger, B., 376, 410, 452
Bumby, K. M., 211, 410, 457
Burgess, K. B., 68, 128, 128, 208, 470
Burke, L. B., 420, 456
Burns, B. J., 412, 434, 442
Bursuc, W. D., 82, 334, 381, 391, 392, 393, 397, 398, 401, 403, 450
Burwell, R., 334, 473
Buskir, S., 129, 470
Buss, A. H., 213, 442
Busse, R. T., 69, 447
Butcher, J. N., 36, 38, 71, 442
Butts, J., 426, 442

Cai, X., 137, 456
Callicott, A., 358, 481
Cancio, E. J., 286, 442
Cangelosi, J. S., 381, 382, 442
Cannon, T. D., 165, 439
Cantrell, M. J., 349, 351, 353, 356, 415, 442
Cantrell, R. P., 349, 351, 353, 356, 415, 442
Caplan, R., 165, 442
Carey, W. B., 214, 352, 442
Carlson, J. S., 419
Carnine, D. W., 401, 442
Carson, P. M., 71, 447
Carter, D. R., 428, 454
Cartledge, G., 21, 286, 342, 343, 344–348, 434, 462, 467
Carton, E. R., 333, 472
Caspi, A., 186, 213, 214, 458, 464
Cauce, A. M., 207, 447, 475
Cauffman, E., 26, 136, 442
CDC. See Centers for Disease Control and Prevention
Centers for Disease Control and Prevention, 138, 139, 140, 141, 142, 387, 389, 442
Cervone, D., 310, 334, 447, 472, 479
Chafel, J. A., 206, 208, 442
Chamberlain, P., 414, 422, 423, 447, 443
Chan, H. Y. E., 208, 448
Chandler, L. A., 73, 443
Chard, D. J., 403, 447

Charney, D. S., 117, 443
Chase-Lansdale, P. L., 186, 187, 205, 208, 450
Chassin, L., 138, 140, 141, 443
Chen, C., 343, 452
Chen, X., 128, 129, 470
Cheney, D., 23, 137, 403, 448, 466
Chesney-Lind, M., 345, 443
Chess, S., 213, 448, 476
Chivers, R., 397, 449
Chmelka, M. B., 423, 424, 460
Choate, J. S., 402, 443
Chorpita, B. F., 116, 117, 118, 119, 437
Choudhury, M., 313, 458
Christenson, S. L., 80, 352, 388, 448, 472, 480
Chung, H. L., 313, 458
Clar, E., 290, 457
Clarke, G. N., 333, 460
Clemmer, J. T., 69, 128, 448
Cloos, J. M., 161, 165, 468
Coatsworth, J. D., 69, 188, 435, 448, 462
Cochran, B. N., 207, 475
Cockerham, W. C., 101, 342, 343, 344, 345, 346, 443
Cocozza, J. J., 428, 443
Coggeshall, M., 426, 442
Cohen, 52, 120, 155
Cohen, C. E., 392, 477
Cohen, D. J., 189, 220, 444, 464, 475
Cohen, J. A., 443
Cole, B. S., 361, 443
Coleman, M., 401, 440
Coles, R., 361, 443
Colletti, L. A., 333, 457
Colp, R., 36, 37, 38, 39, 44, 200, 443
Colvin, G., 285, 381, 399, 400, 448, 460
Combrinck-Graham, L., 201, 443
Comer, D. M., 421, 454
Compas, B. E., 188, 190, 211, 213, 448, 463
Compton, S. N., 329, 333, 344, 448, 444
Comstoc, G., 210, 211, 471
Conduct Problems Prevention Research Group, 384, 444
Conners, C. K., 71, 200, 444
Connor, D. F., 112, 113, 114, 115, 135, 137, 444
Connor-Smith, J. K., 188, 211, 443
Connors, G. J., 361, 362, 476
Conroy, M. A., 80, 88, 89, 387, 394, 449, 472, 475

Conyers, C., 264, 280, 283, 444
Coo, B. G., 42, 397, 476
Coo, E., 172, 478
Coo, J. A., 414, 444
Cook-Morales, V. J., 431, 444
Cooley, C., 294, 460
Coolidge, F. L., 37, 39, 97, 100, 108, 472
Cooper-Brown, L. J., 280, 478
Cooper, R. G., 185, 186, 200, 202, 307, 446
Coplan, R., 128, 129, 470
Coppolillo, H. P., 228, 444
Cornell, D. G., 112, 463
Corsini, R. J., 52, 53, 226, 444
Costa, P. T., 225, 444
Costello, E. J., 68, 72, 73, 112, 117, 118, 122, 126, 129, 344, 444, 449, 447
Cothern, L., 26, 455
Cotten, S. J., 205, 439
Coupland, K., 414, 464
Coutinho, M. J., 20, 21, 342, 343, 344, 348, 434, 449, 452, 467
Cowen, E. L., 343, 387, 449, 468
Cox, J. L., 361, 444
Craft, L., 388, 473
Craighead, W. E., 334, 468
Crain, W., 186, 444
Craney, J. L., 157, 158, 451
Crawford, D. K., 384, 385, 445, 444
Crawford, L., 401, 476
Cremin, L. A., 40, 444
Crews, S. D., 296, 452
Cric, N. R., 312, 444
Crites, S. A., 266, 473
Crockett, J. B., 396, 444
Crooks, C. V., 205, 480
Cross, T., 363, 434, 449, 445
Crowe, A. H., 141, 445
Crowley, E. P., 400, 401, 456
Cruz, L., 290, 445
Cuffe, S. P., 187, 445
Culbertson, J. L., 73, 437
Cullinan, D., 9, 16, 17, 71, 85, 91, 98, 100, 101, 108, 112, 113, 118, 122, 128, 135, 136, 139, 290, 348, 449, 450, 451
Culver, S. W., 435, 462
Cummings, M. R., 194, 458
Cunningham, P. B., 437, 470
Curry, J. F., 329, 333, 445, 448

Cutler, R. L., 42, 46, 466, 469
Cutting, J., 158, 161, 445
Cutting, P. E., 428, 433, 460

Daehler, M. W., 42, 442
Daly, D. L., 423, 424, 460
Daly, P. M., 286, 445
Damasio, H., 189, 438
D'Amato, R. C., 191, 445
Dane, H., 210, 356, 439
Darch, C. B., 285, 381, 382, 399, 445
Dattilio, F. M., 307, 469
Daunic, A. P., 285, 327, 328, 333, 474
Davidshofer, C. O., 65, 67, 465
Davies, M., 361, 464
Davis, B., 110, 128, 203, 270, 445, 460
Davis, C. A., 352, 399, 445
Davis, J., 401, 445
Davis, J. L., 423, 424, 460
Davis, K. R., 255, 480
Dawson, C. A., 242, 245, 250, 445, 447
Dawson, G. D., 168–176, 458
DeAntonio, M., 414, 445, 446
Deardorf, P. A., 69, 449
DeBettencourt, L. U., 393, 400, 471
DeCicco-Bloom, E., 186, 446
Dedric, R. R., 428, 452
DeGarmo, D. S., 204, 452
DeHart, G. B., 185, 186, 200, 202, 307, 446
DeHay, T., 419
DelBello, M. P., 157, 158, 451
Dembinski, R. J., 254, 446
DeMyer, M. K., 57, 449
Dennis, K., 434, 445, 455
Denny, R. K., 64, 74, 272, 352, 399, 445, 456, 464
Denton, M. L., 361, 474
DeRosa, R. R., 205, 467
DeRubeis, R. J., 330, 446
Deshler, D. D., 403, 460
DesJarlais, D. C., 346, 446
Desjarlais, R., 342, 446
DeVoe, J. F., 24, 26, 134, 135, 139, 140, 141, 142, 210, 446
Diaz, T., 386, 441
Dickstein, L. J., 128, 446
DiGiuseppe, R., 330, 333, 446
Dimsdale, J. E., 211, 446
Dinkmeyer, D., 225
Dishion, T., 355, 475
Dix, Dorothea, 39, 40

Dobson, K. S., 306, 446
Dodge, K. A., 128, 134, 208, 213, 312, 449, 458, 463
Dohrn, E., 210, 290, 352, 356, 391, 393, 399, 456
Dols, M. W., 37, 446
Domalanta, D. D., 136, 446
Domitrovich, C., 376, 410, 452
Dong, Q., 343, 452
Donohue, E., 36, 37, 446
Donovan, C. L., 410, 446
Doris, J., 41, 471
Dorta, K. P., 333, 465
Doucette, A., 100, 446
Doucette-Gates, A., 436, 446
Doukas, G. L., 380, 460
Dowd, T., 361, 401, 450, 475
Dowdy, C., 80, 84, 392, 474
Doyle, M. M., 334, 386, 453
Dozois, D. J. A., 38, 41, 42, 43, 50, 108, 109, 110, 306, 450, 462
Drasgow, E., 13, 477
Dreikurs, Rudolph, 229, 230, 231, 446
Driscoll, A., 235, 450
Dryden, W., 307, 330, 447
Duchnowski, A. J., 23, 26, 294, 342, 435, 452, 478
Duggal, S., 122, 481
Duggan, D., 242, 245, 250, 447
Dulcan, M. K., 26, 72, 136, 472, 476
Duncan, G. E., 171, 464
Dunlap, G., 348, 379, 469, 475
Dunlap, S. T., 205, 210, 356, 439
Dunn, C., 210, 290, 352, 356, 391, 393, 399, 456
DuPaul, G. J., 71, 447
Dusenbury, L., 334, 386, 440
Duval-Harvey, J., 348, 436, 468
Dykens, E. M., 138, 454
D'Zurilla, T. J., 306, 321, 323, 445, 447

Eber, L., 51, 348, 353, 358, 431, 436, 447
Eckert, T. L., 71, 447
Ecton, R. B., 325, 448
Eddy, J. M., 410, 469
Edelbroc, C. S., 99, 437
Edmondson, J. C., 189, 447
Edwards, L. L., 254, 402, 447
Egger, H. L., 117, 447
Egley, A., Jr., 135, 447
Ehrlich, J., 219, 220, 460
Eisenberg, L., 342, 446
Eisler, I., 85, 447

Elkind, D., 361, 443
Elksnin, L. K., 292, 294, 295, 447
Elksnin, N., 292, 294, 295, 447
Eller, S., 294, 437
Elliott, D. J., 432, 433, 447
Elliott, S. N., 69, 71, 451, 452
Ellis, Albert, 8, 307, 330, 447
Embry, D., 279, 447
Emery, R. E., 188, 198, 204, 205, 206, 207, 451, 458, 467
Emmer, E. T., 381, 451, 448
Enwefa, R., 343, 466
Enwefa, S., 343, 466
Eppe, S., 205, 448
Epstein, M. H., 16, 17, 20, 23, 26, 69, 71, 85, 113, 118, 122, 128, 135, 136, 137, 294, 342, 387, 431, 432, 435, 445, 451, 452, 469, 475, 478
Erickson, S. J., 306, 412, 448
Erkanli, A., 112, 117, 129, 444, 447
Ernst, M., 189, 190, 192, 479
Essau, C. A., 121, 122, 155, 158, 460
Etscheidt, S., 412, 448
Evans, C., 113, 118, 122, 128, 136, 445
Evans, G. W., 208, 448
Evans, W., 400, 403, 472
Everson, T. J., 361, 448
Evertson, C. M., 381, 451, 448
Ewen, R. B., 361, 448
Ey, S., 190, 213, 463
Eyberg, S. M., 275, 439

Fabiano, G. L., 282, 448
Faedda, G. L., 157, 158, 159, 178, 448
Fagan, S. A., 247, 252, 448
Falb, M. D., 466
Fallon, T., 428, 454
Fals-Stewart, W., 205, 457
Fannery, D. J., 381, 448
Farmer, T. W., 12, 69, 115, 128, 452, 470
Farrell, D., 414, 444
Farrell, Elizabeth, 46
Farrington, D. P., 204, 270, 410, 411, 461
Farver, J. A. M., 205, 448
Fecser, F. A., 54, 209, 212, 242, 245, 249, 250, 349, 351, 353, 356, 355, 356, 447, 463, 480
Federal Interagency Forum on Child and Family Statistics, 134, 135, 200, 205, 206, 208, 448
Feil, E., 58, 296, 297, 478
Feil, M., 420, 421, 457, 456

Feindler, E. L., 325, 327, 448
Feingold, B. F., 200, 448
Feist, G. J., 219, 361, 448
Feist, J., 219, 361, 448
Fennig, S., 165, 449
Ferguson, K. E., 299, 449
Fergusson, D. M., 134, 480
Fernandez, A., 205, 448
Ferster, C. B., 57, 449
Fiedler, C. R., 84, 449
FIFCFS. See Federal Interagency Forum on Child and Family Statistics
Finch, A. J., 69, 449
Fincham, F. D., 204, 453
Findling, R. L., 160, 459
Fin, A. H., 46, 465
Fin, B. C., 262, 274, 449
Finn-Stevenson, M., 50, 428, 481
Finney, J. W., 280, 450
First, M. B., 97, 459
Fischer, T. A., 88, 449
Fisher-Bloom, E., 414, 464
Fisher, P. H., 72, 136, 333, 453, 473
Fisher, P. W., 478
Fitzgerald, K. D., 192, 449
Fixsen, D. L., 423, 445, 468
Flament, M., 159, 475
Flannery, D. J., 384, 449
Flanzer, J., 414, 415, 468
Fleisch, B., 48, 49, 50, 226, 458
Fletcher-Janzen, E., 191, 445
Fletcher, K. E., 120, 449
Flice, M., 397, 449
Flojo, J. R., 401, 451
Flory, V., 159, 449
Foa, E. B., 333, 450
Fochtmann, L. J., 165, 449
Foegen, A., 384, 442
Fogt, J., 399, 458
Fombonne, E., 110, 175, 176, 449
Fonagy, P., 225, 226, 449
Fonseca, A. C., 116, 118, 449
Forgatch, M. S., 204, 452
Forness, S. R., 9, 10, 14, 16, 45, 56, 159, 271, 333, 348, 387, 395, 417, 419, 421, 453, 459, 461, 472
Foskett, J., 38, 360, 450
Foster, E. M., 115, 116, 137, 456
Foster, S. L., 344, 450
Fox, G., 201, 443
Fox, J. J., 88, 271, 450
Fox, R. W., 332, 481
Fran, A. J., 392, 477

Franklin, M. E., 333, 450
Fraser, M. W., 437, 450
Freeborn, K., 423, 440
Freeman, A., 207, 469
Freeman, J. B., 116, 119, 120, 450
Freiberg, H. J., 234, 235, 236, 255, 450
Freud, Sigmund, 52, 53, 219, 221
Frey, K. S., 88, 383, 450
Fric, P. J., 14, 110, 115, 117, 126, 135, 450
Friedman, H. S., 51, 52, 53, 219, 220, 223, 228, 231, 450
Friedman, R. J., 186, 188, 205, 208, 450
Friedman, Robert, M., 49, 50, 428, 430, 431, 432, 435, 454, 455, 475
Friend, M., 13, 47, 82, 334, 381, 391, 392, 393, 397, 398, 401, 403, 450
Friesen, B. J., 432, 433, 447
Friman, P. C., 280, 422, 423, 448, 450
Fristad, M., 160, 459
Fulford, K. W. M., 361, 450
Fuller, D. L., 237, 238, 240, 450
Fuller, G. B., 237, 238, 240, 450
Fuller, R. L. M., 161, 162, 450
Fulton, B. A., 426, 451
Furer, M., 223, 462
Furlong, M. J., 112, 115, 138, 269, 381, 450

Gable, R. A., 88, 113, 271, 454, 451
Gagnon, J. C., 404, 451
Gallagher, B. J., 342, 343, 344, 345, 346, 451
Gallagher, K., 431, 432, 436, 448
Galloway, A., 332, 452
Gansle, K. A., 401, 466
Garber, J., 121, 155, 451
Garcia, A. M., 116, 118, 119, 450
Garland, A. F., 136, 140, 343, 443, 454, 460
Garland, E. J., 333, 438
Garrison, C. Z., 187, 445
Gartner, A., 395, 461
Gauger, E. S., 401, 445
Gaylin, N. L., 231, 233, 451
Gaynor, S. T., 285, 468
Geller, B., 157, 158, 451
Gerrard, L. M., 333, 438
Gershaw, N. S., 71, 319, 451
Gershon, S., 45, 451
Gersten, R., 401, 451
Gesell, Arnold, 42
Ghezzi, P. M., 290, 451

Gibbs, J. C., 318, 319, 320, 335, 359, 451
Gilbert, G. M., 91, 451
Gilbertson, D., 274, 285, 394, 480
Glaser, D., 207, 451
Glassberg, L., 137, 462
Glasser, William, 237, 239, 451
Glic, B., 318, 320, 335, 359, 451
Glovinsky, I. P., 157, 158, 159, 178, 448
Godwin, T. M., 426, 451
Goeltz, W. B., 219, 220, 222, 469
Goetze, H., 242, 453
Goforth, J. B., 69, 128, 448
Goldfried, M. R., 321, 445
Goldstein, Arnold, P., 313–320, 334, 335, 359, 454, 463
Goldwyn, R., 202, 452
Golly, A. M., 58, 296, 454, 478
Gomez, L. F., 343, 468
Gonzalez, J. E., 23, 332, 455, 469
Good, B., 342, 446
Goodman, J., 307, 463
Goodman, R., 189, 199, 452
Gordon, B. N., 85, 472
Gordon, M. F., 185, 214, 452
Gordon, R. A., 115, 126, 127, 459
Gordon, T., 234, 235, 452
Gossen, D., 238, 452
Graczy, P. A., 115, 205, 410, 455, 462
Granger, R. H., 199, 462
Grant, K., 190, 213, 463
Grebb, J. A., 190, 452
Green, C. D., 36, 452
Green, J., 202, 298, 300, 455, 472
Green, L., 171, 462
Green, R. W., 333
Greenbaum, P. E., 136, 428, 455, 480
Greenberg, L. S., 232, 234, 479
Greenberg, M. T., 376, 384, 410, 455, 456
Greenberger, E., 343, 452
Greene, B., 188, 343, 345, 466
Greene, S. M., 204, 452
Greenwald, S., 361, 464
Greenwood, C. R., 58, 478
Gregg, R. M., 380, 460
Gresham, F. M., 58, 114, 121, 160, 264, 269, 270, 277, 281, 282, 284, 292, 294, 296, 333, 381, 382, 388, 399, 404, 410, 455, 456, 474, 478
Griffin, K. W., 334, 446, 453
Grisso, T., 428
Grob, G. N., 36, 453

Groen, G., 333, 388, 468
Groff, P. R., 36, 452
Gross, A. M., 204, 262, 457, 478
Grossman, D. C., 383, 453
Greenberger, E., 452
Grskovic, J. A., 242, 453
Gruber, C. P., 73, 459
Gruner, A., 436, 480
Grych, J. H., 204, 453
Guerra, N. G., 327, 349, 410, 453
Guetzloe, E., 5, 358, 400, 401, 456, 458, 472
Gunn, B., 387, 453
Gunter, P. L., 64, 74, 272, 352, 399, 445, 456, 465, 475
Guo, S., 384, 449
Guthrie, D., 165, 442
Gutstein, J., 123, 141, 142, 140, 473
Guzzo, B. A., 383, 450
Gwalla-Ogisi, N., 343, 466

Haager, D., 68, 398, 453
Hadley, K. G., 206, 208, 442
Hadley, T., 165, 439
Haffey, W. G., 387, 444
Hafner, H., 170, 453
Hagin, R. A., 137, 473
Haglund, B., 206, 479
Hall, G. Stanley, 42
Hall, R. V., 275, 276, 286, 446, 453
Hallahan, D. P., 376, 395, 453
Halliday-Boykins, C. A., 437, 470
Hallmayer, J., 196, 453
Hammen, C., 121, 122, 123, 155, 157, 158, 159, 161, 205, 313, 453
Hammill, D. D., 84, 392, 398, 453
Hancoc, T. B., 137, 456
Handwer, M. L., 423, 424, 460
Hansen, S. D., 283, 453
Harding, J., 280, 478
Haring, N. G., 58, 453
Harper, C. R., 139, 479
Harrington, R., 121, 155, 160, 453
Harris, T. R., 57, 438
Harrower, J. K., 176, 459
Hart, B. M., 57, 438
Harter, S., 334, 473
Harvey, M. T., 356, 453
Hautzinger, M., 333, 388, 468
Havsy, L. H., 388, 443
Hayes, L. J., 282, 476
Hazel, J. S., 294, 454
Head, L. S., 262, 454
Healy, William, 44

Hechtman, L., 16, 126, 454
Heffron, W. M., 428, 454
Hellander, M., 160, 459
Hemmeter, M. L., 387, 471
Henao, G. D., 343, 468
Henderson, K., 20, 399, 417, 441
Hendrickson, J. M., 113, 387, 394, 449, 451
Henggeler, S. W., 429, 437, 438, 457, 458, 469, 471, 472
Henley, M., 247, 249, 255, 454
Henry, G. W., 36, 37, 38, 39, 40, 481
Herbener, E. S., 157, 467
Herbst, M., 25, 481
Hernandez, M., 45, 435, 457, 462
Hersen, M., 36, 78, 445, 446
Hester, P. P., 387, 394, 444
Heston, J. D., 413, 458
Hetherington, E. M., 203, 204, 455, 454
Heward, W. L., 28, 47, 454
Hewett, Frank M., 57, 58, 298, 454
Heyman, I., 45, 454
Heyne, D., 333, 458
Hibbs, E. D., 412, 454
Hieneman, M., 379, 475
Higgins, A., 336, 359, 468
Hightower, A. D., 387, 444
Hinshaw, S. P., 112, 114, 115, 116, 124, 138, 270, 454
Hippocrates, 36–37
Hirschstein, M. K., 383, 450
Hjern, A., 206, 479
Hoagwood, K., 333, 412, 421, 434, 447, 457, 458, 465
Hobbs, Nicholas, 50, 415, 454
Hodapp, R. M., 138, 454
Hoffman, C. C., 436, 480
Hoffman, C. D., 174, 176, 475
Holden, E. W., 435, 455
Hollifield, J., 73, 438
Hollis, C., 151, 163, 165, 170, 171, 455
Hollister, J. M., 165, 439
Holt, J., 298, 300, 472
Homme, L. E., 307, 455
Hooley, J. M., 36, 38, 442
Hooper, S. R., 137, 458, 464, 470
Hoover, J. J., 400, 403, 455
Hops, H., 58, 110, 128, 203, 270, 296, 333, 445, 458, 462, 478
Horn, A. B., 333, 388, 468
Horner, R. H., 89, 287, 333, 355, 356, 379, 381, 382, 456, 474, 476
Horowitz, J. L., 121, 155, 451

Houchins, D. E., 401, 473
Hough, R. L., 136, 140, 343, 435, 443, 454, 462, 462
Houmanfar, R., 291, 455
Howard, K. A., 349, 350, 455
Howell, J. C., 134, 458, 480
Howell, K. W., 85, 87, 135, 455
Hoyt, D. R., 207, 447, 475
Hsiang-Ching, K., 141, 438
Huberty, T. J., 63, 78, 455
Hudson, C. G., 344, 455
Hudson, S., 273, 382, 399, 461
Huerta, N., 13, 29, 48, 477
Huey, S. J., 437, 455
Huff, C. R., 381, 448
Hughes, J. N., 397, 438
Huizinga, D., 26, 136, 458, 476
Hummel, J., 399, 464
Humphrey, L. A., 191, 456
Hune, J. B., 327, 333, 455
Hurlburt, M. S., 435, 462
Hussey, W., 12, 448
Hyatt, K. J., 85, 87, 455

Ifill-Williams, M., 386, 441
Ikeda, R. M., 410, 469
Insabella, G., 204, 454
Institute of Medicine, 387, 388, 455
IOM. *See* Institute of Medicine
Irwin, M., 211, 446
Isaacs, M., 434, 435, 445, 454
Isaacs-Shockley, M., 434, 455
Israel, A. C., 13, 14, 16, 19, 41, 43, 52, 91, 101, 112, 119, 120, 135, 164, 169, 171, 186, 187, 196, 198, 202, 203, 204, 214, 270, 342, 343, 479
Itard, Jean-Marc-Gaspard, 41

Jablensky, A., 169, 170, 455
Jackson, D., 275, 276, 453
Jackson, J. S., 97, 470
Jackson, M. S., 425, 455
Jacob, R. G., 261, 262, 268, 299, 456
Jacob, T., 205, 481
Jacobs, A. K., 22, 348, 404, 436, 455
Jaeger, D., 423, 440
Jaffe, J. H., 140, 141, 456
Jaffe, P. G., 205, 480
Jaffe, S. L., 139, 140, 456
Jaffee, S. R., 213, 456
Jensen, P. S., 420, 456
Jenson, W. R., 290, 457
Jimerson, S. R., 112, 115, 138, 269, 381, 450

Johns, B., 358, 400, 401, 458, 472
Johnson, Lyndon, 49
Johnson, N., 273, 382, 399, 461
Johnson, S. L., 155, 456
Johnston, L. D., 139, 337, 456
Joint Commission on the Mental Health of Children, 49, 456
Jolivette, K., 89, 285, 379, 382, 461
Jones, J. M., 349, 351, 353, 356, 442
Jones, L. S., 210, 456
Jones, M. R., 211, 410, 457
Jones, V. F., 290, 352, 356, 391, 393, 399, 456
Jonikas, J., 414, 444
Jordan, N. C., 401, 451
Joseph, G., 387, 456
Josephson, A. M., 412, 456
Jura, M. B., 191, 456
Jurgens, M., 264, 280, 283, 444
Justice, L. M., 387, 456
Juvonen, J., 117, 208, 466

Kagan, J., 213, 456
Kaiser, A. P., 137, 456
Kakar, S., 36, 456
Kalat, J. W., 189, 190, 194, 198, 456
Kam, C. M., 384, 456
Kameenui, E. J., 285, 381, 382, 399, 445
Kame'enui, E. J., 399, 442
Kamphaus, R. W., 71, 71, 78, 80, 94, 469
Kamradt, B., 423, 462
Kanfer, F. H., 307, 456
Kanner, Leo, 152, 173, 456
Kaplan, S. J., 205, 467
Karasu, T. B., 219, 220, 456
Karenga, M., 345, 457
Karni, N. S., 112, 201, 209, 342, 459, 474
Karoly, P., 307, 456
Kashani, J. H., 211, 410, 457
Kaslow, N. J., 333, 472
Katsiyannis, A., 22, 25, 355, 358, 397, 399, 459, 461, 473, 481
Kauffman, J. M., 9, 14, 15, 16, 49, 210, 376, 395, 396, 449, 456, 459, 479
Kaufman, C. J., 397, 449
Kaufman, I., 422, 470
Kaufman, J., 85, 191, 192, 472
Kaufman, J. M., 98
Kaufman, P., 23, 24, 26, 134, 135, 139, 140, 141, 142, 210, 446

Kavale, K. A., 9, 14, 128, 271, 292, 294, 296, 333, 348, 395, 404, 453, 457
Kavanagh, K., 58, 296, 478
Kaye, D. L., 226, 457
Kazdin, A. E., 13, 40, 56, 58, 74, 87, 123, 261, 264, 271, 273, 278, 279, 280, 283, 290, 457
Kearney, C. A., 120, 457
Keefe, F. J., 211, 446
Keeler, G., 344, 444
Keenan, S., 51, 348, 353, 358, 431, 436, 451, 468
Kehle, T. J., 290, 457
Kelleher, K. J., 421, 454
Keller, M. B., 150, 440
Kelley, M. L., 205, 278, 457
Kellner, M. H., 333, 457
Kelly, F. D., 228, 230, 458
Kelly, J. B., 205, 458
Kendall, P. C., 35, 36, 41, 137, 306, 313, 317, 327, 333, 446, 460, 461, 473
Kendell, R. E., 97, 470
Kendler, K., 97, 470
Kendziora, K. T., 137, 387, 458
Kennedy, A. E., 68, 128, 208, 470
Kennedy, C. H., 273, 458
Keogh, B., 214, 458
Kern, L., 121, 160, 296, 399, 455, 458
Kerr, M. M., 88, 89, 210, 269, 276, 277, 278, 285, 287, 290, 291, 393, 399, 400, 401, 403, 458
Kessler, R. C., 201, 342, 344, 345, 458
Kidder, J. D., 57, 440
Kim, T. E., 327, 349, 453
Kimball, R., 416, 438
King, K. M., 138, 140, 141, 443
King, M. A., 436, 480
King, N. J., 116, 119, 333, 460, 466
King, R. A., 78, 85, 201, 208, 460
Kirigin, K. A., 423, 458
Kirkpatric, B., 151, 163, 458
Kirschenbaum, H., 359, 458
Kiser, L. J., 413, 458
Kissam, B. R., 403, 460
Kizer, A., 155, 456
Klein, D. N., 157, 158, 460
Klein, P., 319, 451
Klein, R. G., 117, 118, 119, 333, 453, 458
Kleinman, A., 342, 446
Klin, A., 16, 168–176, 478
Klinger, L. G., 168–176, 458

Klingner, J. K., 68, 398, 453
Klug, W. S., 194, 458
Knapp, P., 188, 209, 211, 458
Knepper, P., 425, 455
Knitzer, Jane, 10, 48, 49, 50, 51, 226, 428, 453, 460, 473, 480
Kochane, K. D., 141, 438
Kode, K., 46, 459
Koegel, L. K., 176, 459
Koegel, R. L., 176, 459
Koenig, K., 172, 459
Koepsell, T. D., 383, 453
Kohlberg, L., 336, 359, 468
Komo, S., 165, 442
Konold, K. B., 382, 459
Konold, K. E., 382, 459
Konopase, D. E., 45, 159, 176, 417, 419, 421, 459
Koren, P. E., 432, 433, 447
Koroloff, N. M., 432, 433, 447
Kowatch, R. A., 160, 459
Koziel, M., 414, 444
Krain, A. L., 116, 317, 327, 333, 443, 459
Kratochwill, T. R., 84, 473
Kruesi, M. J. P., 437, 470
Kubiszyn, T., 419
Kuipers, E., 171, 462
Kuntsi, J., 195, 198, 474
Kupfer, D. F., 97, 459
Kurtines, W., 435, 443
Kurtz, D. A., 207, 476
Kurtz, E., 360, 459
Kusche, C. A., 384, 455, 456
Kutash, K., 23, 26, 294, 342, 428, 435, 452, 455, 478
Kutcher, S. P., 159, 461, 467

La Greca, A. M., 208, 459
LaBarbera, J., 167, 168, 466
Lachar, D. L., 73, 459
Lahey, B. B., 115, 126, 127, 212, 459
Laing, R. D., 346, 459
Lamiell, J. T., 100, 459
Landolf, B. M., 26, 412, 459
Landrum, T. J., 9, 22, 36, 42, 47, 397, 459, 461, 476
Landsver, J., 435, 462
Lane, K. L., 137, 210, 294, 352, 380, 399, 401, 445, 461, 460
Lane, R. C., 219, 220, 222, 469
Langer, Marion F., 50
Lanthier, R., 202, 466
Lardieri, S. P., 428, 452

Larson, J., 328, 460
Larson, S. J., 361, 460
Larzelere, R. E., 203, 423, 424, 460
Lau, A. S., 343, 460
Laumann-Billings, L., 206, 207, 447
Lawson, G. W., 361, 362, 460
Leckman, J. F., 194, 461
Lee, D. L., 277, 279, 283, 460
Lee, S. S., 112, 115, 116, 138, 270, 454
Lee, T. E., 437, 470
Lee, V., 205, 480
Leedy, A., 382, 460
Leigh, J. E., 463
Lenz, B. K., 403, 460
Leonard, H. L., 116, 119, 120, 450
Leone, P. E., 26, 136, 137, 404, 428, 433, 454, 462, 465
Lerman, R. I., 206, 460
Lerner, H. D., 219, 220, 460
Lerner, R. M., 349, 350, 455
Leung, M. C., 69, 128, 448
Levendoski, L. S., 286, 460
Leventhal, T., 208, 460
Lewin, L. M., 110, 134, 460
Lewinsohn, P. M., 121, 122, 155, 157, 158, 333, 460
Lewis, C., 360, 461
Lewis, J. J., 379, 475
Lewis, L., 431, 432, 436, 448
Lewis, L. M., 387, 476
Lewis, M., 78, 85, 87, 88, 460
Lewis-Palmer, T., 56, 58, 262, 271, 274, 280, 285, 356, 456, 461
Lewis, R. B., 63, 67, 194, 462, 463
Lewis, T. J., 56, 58, 262, 271, 273, 274, 280, 285, 331, 379, 382, 387, 399, 462, 463, 475
Li, C. E., 333, 446
Liau, A. K., 384, 449
Liaupsin, C. J., 88, 89, 285, 379, 382, 463, 472
Lickona, T., 359, 360, 361, 461
Lieberman, J. A., 171, 464
Lignugaris/Kraft, B., 283, 453
Lillehoj, C., 334, 386, 477
Lin, H. S., 211, 476
Lippman, H. S., 8, 461
Lipsky, D. K., 395, 461
Liu, P., 383, 453
Livingston, R., 63, 78, 88, 469
Lochman, J. E., 205, 210, 306, 327, 328, 329, 333, 337, 356, 445, 462, 463, 464, 468, 474

Loeber, R., 26, 136, 203, 270, 410, 411, 458, 463, 476
Lombardo, E., 321, 466
Lombroso, P. J., 194, 461
Loney, B. R., 115, 450
Long, J. E., 242, 245, 461
Long, Nicholas J., 54, 55, 209, 212, 242, 243, 245, 246, 247, 248, 249, 250, 254, 356, 355, 361, 363, 368, 446, 452, 461
Lord, C., 16, 152, 168–176, 463, 478
Lorion, R. P., 461
Lotspeich, L., 262, 274, 449
Loughran, M. J., 226, 461
Lourie, I. S., 44, 45, 428, 429, 462, 463
Lovaas, O. I., 57, 462
Lovejoy, M. C., 205, 462
Lovitt, T. C., 286, 462
Loyd, R. J., 403, 441
Luby, J., 157, 158, 451
Lucas, C. P., 72, 136, 472, 478
Lu, E. S. L., 159, 449
Lund, D., 275, 276, 453
Luscher, K. A., 91, 94, 95, 97, 100, 101, 102, 108, 437
Luthar, S. S., 210, 470
Lyons, J. S., 423, 462
Lyons-Ruth, K., 202, 462

Maag, J. W., 68, 74, 333, 462
MacAleese, K. R., 290, 451
Madsen, C. H., 57, 439
Maglieri, K. A., 291, 455
Maheady, L., 210, 290, 470
Maher, S., 316, 465
Mahler, M. S., 223, 462
Major, A. K., 135, 447
Maki, A., 264, 280, 283, 444
Malhi, G. S., 157, 464
Mandel, F. S., 205, 467
Manteuffel, B. A., 435, 455
Marans, S., 52, 220, 462
March, J. S., 329, 333, 448, 450
Marchand-Martella, N. E., 210, 266, 277, 279, 280, 283, 285, 286, 382, 399, 401, 462
Marciano, P. L., 123, 457
Marenco, S., 193, 479
Maroney, S. A., 381, 462
Martella, R. C., 210, 266, 277, 279, 280, 283, 285, 286, 382, 399, 401, 462
Martin, A., 45, 416, 471
Martin, B., 203, 454

Martin, G., 271, 273, 274, 282, 285, 462
Martindale, B. V., 171, 462
Marton, P., 159, 459
Marx, Karl, 344
Marx, L., 423, 462
Mash, E. J., 38, 41, 42, 43, 50, 100, 108, 109, 110, 462
Masia-Warner, C., 333, 449
Masten, A. S., 69, 188, 462
Mastropieri, M. A., 401, 469
Mathur, S. R., 128, 292, 294, 296, 404, 457
Mattern, N., 387, 472
Mattison, R. M., 135, 137, 462
Maultsby, L. T., 412, 434, 442
Mayer, M., 306, 337, 462
Mayes, L. C., 199, 462
Mazet, P., 159, 475
McCabe, K. M., 136, 140, 343, 435, 454, 462, 462
McCarney, S. B., 71, 85, 463
McClellan, J. M., 164, 165, 463
McClelland, G. M., 26, 136, 476
McConaughy, S. H., 68, 71, 72, 79, 98, 99, 100, 118, 122, 443, 463
McConville, D. W., 112, 463
McFadyen-Ketchum, S. A., 128, 134, 208, 212, 463
McGinnis, E., 319, 320, 454, 463
McGuffin, P., 196, 198, 463
McHale, S. M., 334, 468
McInerney, M., 331, 453
McIntyre, J., 88, 472
McIntyre-Smith, A., 205, 480
McIntyre, T., 348, 463
McKee, J. E., 231, 233, 234, 359, 464
McKeown, R. E., 187, 445
McLean, M. E., 387, 471
McLeer, S. V., 420, 463
McLoughlin, J. A., 63, 67, 87, 88, 463
McLoyd, V. C., 209, 463
McMahon, S., 190, 213, 463
McMillen, J. C., 423, 462
McRae, R. R., 223, 444
McReynolds, L., 136, 478
Meadows, N. B., 283, 294, 383, 463
Medved, D., 211, 463
Medved, M., 211, 463
Meese, R. L., 84, 401, 463
Meichenbaum, D., 307, 463
Meissner, W. W., 52, 219, 222, 223, 225, 463
Mendez, V., 361, 443
Menendez, A. L., 47, 442

Menninger, K., 100, 463
Menninger, W. W., 415, 463
Menzies, H. M., 380, 460
Mercer, A. R., 393, 401, 403, 463
Mercer, C. D., 393, 401, 403, 463
Mericle, A. A., 26, 136, 476
Merikangas, K. R., 118, 119, 463
Merrell, K. W., 69, 78, 317, 323, 324, 327, 333, 464
Merydith, S. P., 225, 228, 464
Messer, S. B., 226, 478
Meteyer, K., 199, 462
Meyer, Adolph, 54
Mezzich, J. E., 110, 464
Mickelson, W. T., 387, 476
Milin, R., 414, 464
Miller, A. K., 23, 24, 26, 134, 135, 139, 140, 141, 142, 210, 446
Miller, C., 382, 467
Miller, K. A., 399, 464
Miller, L., 361, 464
Miller, L. K., 264, 464
Miller, M. D., 333, 470
Miller, S. J., 425, 439
Miller, S. P., 382, 459
Miller, T. L., 115, 126, 127, 459
Miller, W. B., 26, 135, 136, 464
Miller, W. R., 360, 361, 464
Miltenberger, R. G., 261, 264, 268, 272, 274, 278, 279, 280, 281, 283, 286, 287, 291, 449, 464
Mineka, S., 36, 38, 442
Mitchell, M., 363, 401, 441
Mitchell, P. B., 157, 464
Mitchell, W., 167, 168, 466
Mitts, B., 286, 441
Miyamoto, S., 171, 464
Moc, D. R., 14, 16, 101, 395, 457
Moffitt, T. E., 186, 213, 214, 458, 464
Molina, B. S. G., 125, 127, 467
Monfore, D. A., 20, 399, 417, 441
Montgomery, L. E., 69, 449
Mooney, P., 399, 464
Moore, H. B., 231, 233, 234, 359, 464
Moore, R. B., 436, 465
Morris, P. A., 186, 441
Morris, R. J., 128, 464
Morris, T. L., 91, 95, 97, 100, 101, 472
Morris, Y. P., 128, 464
Morrison, G. M., 112, 115, 138, 269, 381, 450
Morse, W. C., 42, 46, 54, 55, 242, 244, 245, 246, 249, 253, 356, 398, 463, 465, 466, 469

Moscicki, E. K., 141, 465
Moss, N. E., 73, 465
Mostert, M. P., 128, 292, 294, 296, 404, 457
Mraze, D., 377, 378, 388, 410, 465
Mraze, P., 377, 378, 388, 410, 465
Mueser, K. T., 171, 462
Mufson, L. H., 333, 465
Mulvaney, M., 298, 300, 472
Munger, R. L., 351, 352, 353, 356, 356, 410, 465
Munson, M. R., 423, 463
Munton, S. M., 380, 460
Muris, P., 116, 119, 466
Murphy, K. R., 65, 67, 465
Murphy, S. L., 141, 438
Murray, J. P., 211, 213, 465
Murthy, N. V., 161, 165, 468
Muscott, H. S., 360, 465
Musto, D. F., 41, 42, 44, 465
Myers, L. J., 345, 465
Myles, B. S., 153, 175, 397, 466, 473

Nastasi, B. K., 436, 465
Nath, S. R., 35, 36, 41, 473
National Center for Education Statistics, 14, 19, 22, 23, 25, 134, 140, 210, 465
Naugle, A. E., 316, 465
Nayani, T., 361, 465
NCES. *See* National Center for Education Statistics
Neckerman, H. J., 383, 453
Nelson, C. M., 26, 88, 89, 136, 137, 210, 269, 276, 277, 278, 285, 287, 290, 291, 327, 333, 379, 393, 399, 400, 401, 403, 452, 458, 460, 466, 472, 475
Nelson, C. S., 401, 445
Nelson, J. R., 210, 266, 277, 279, 280, 283, 285, 286, 332, 382, 387, 399, 401, 431, 432, 436, 452, 455, 464, 467, 476
Nelson, K. E., 437, 450
Ness, A., 363, 401, 441
Neubert, D. A., 355, 399, 473
Neuman, G., 205, 462
Neve, M., 151, 466
Nevid, J. S., 188, 343, 345, 466
Nevin, A. I., 397, 477
Newcomb, M. D., 134, 466
Newcomer, 56, 58, 118, 120
Newcomer, L., 55, 57, 262, 271, 274, 280, 285, 356, 461

Newcomer, P. L., 118, 122, 466
Newman, C. F., 307, 317, 329, 439
Newman, R. G., 247, 248, 461
Nezu, A. M., 48, 321, 323, 445, 451, 466
Nezu, C. M., 321, 466
Ng, D., 361, 443
Nichols, P., 54, 242, 245, 249, 355, 480
Nichols, T. R., 334, 386, 453
Nickman, S. L., 422, 433, 439
Nielsen, E., 387, 472
Nishina, A., 117, 208, 466
Noell, G. H., 401, 466
Noll, J. G., 207, 476
Noonan, M., 23, 446
Nordness, P. D., 20, 23, 137, 431, 432, 436, 452, 469, 476
Nucci, L., 359, 466
Nurcomb, B., 167, 168, 466
Nyre, J. E., 22, 348, 404, 436, 455

Obiakor, F., 343, 466
O'Brien, S. T., 360, 465
O'Connell, D. F., 467
O'Connor, T. G., 116, 128, 466
Office of Juvenile Justice and Delinquency Prevention, 168, 206, 466
Offord, D. R., 13, 14, 110, 466
O'Hare, E., 205, 462
OJJDP. *See* Office of Juvenile Justice and Delinquency Prevention
Olfson, M., 333, 409, 466
Olive, M. A., 381, 466
Ollendic, T. H., 116, 119, 333, 460, 466
Ollie, M. T., 423, 463
Olsen, C., 397, 449
Olson, S. L., 202, 466
Oltmanns, T. F., 188, 198, 205, 466
O'Malley, P. M., 139, 140, 456
Osborne, S., 113, 445
Osgood, R. L., 41, 466
Osher, D., 21, 342, 343, 344–348, 434, 436, 468, 480
Osofsky, J. D., 205, 467
Ost, L.-G., 119, 467
Oswald, D. P., 20, 21, 342, 343, 344–348, 429, 434, 449, 467
O'Toole, B., 254, 447

Palmer, L. L., 412, 448
Papatheodorou, G., 155, 467
Paradise, M., 207, 442
Pardini, D. A., 328, 468, 323

Parese, S. B., 249, 467
Pargament, K. I., 361, 443
Parke, R. D., 202, 204, 441
Parrinder, G., 36, 360, 467
Patterson, G. R., 57, 115, 270, 410, 467
Patton, J. R., 80, 84, 334, 352, 356, 381, 392, 397, 400, 401, 403, 458, 469, 474
Paul, J. L., 346, 446
Pavuluri, M. N., 157, 467
Payne, V. H., 423, 438
Peacock Hill Working Group, 49, 51, 467
Pear, J., 271, 273, 274, 282, 285, 462
Pearce, J. M. S., 152, 467
Pearl, R., 115, 470
Pearson, G. T., 348, 436, 468
Pearson, N., 85, 118, 122, 451, 466
Pecora, P. J., 423, 438
Pedro-Carroll, J. P., 387, 444
Pelcovitz, D., 205, 467
Pelham, W. E., 125, 127, 261, 262, 268, 299, 456
Pelham, W. E., Jr., 27, 448
Peris, T. S., 205, 467
Perrin, S., 116, 118, 449
Peter, K., 23, 24, 26, 134, 135, 139, 140, 141, 142, 210, 446
Peterson, B., 85, 191, 192, 472
Peterson, D. R., 42, 469
Peterson, L. D., 287, 467
Peterson, M. H., 287, 467
Peterson, R. L., 382, 467
Petry, C., 294, 437
Pfeffer, C. R., 111, 141, 142, 140, 387, 467
Pfefferbaum, B., 120, 468
Phelan, J. C., 342, 344, 438
Phillips, E. A., 424, 468
Phillips, E. L., 58, 424, 456, 468
Phillips-Smith, E., 435, 480
Pianta, R. C., 202, 468
Pickens, P., 352, 399, 445
Pickrel, S. G., 437, 455
Pierce, C. D., 20, 23, 137, 476
Piers, D. R., 71, 468
Pigott, R. L., 343, 468
Pine, D. S., 85, 117, 118, 119, 191, 192, 460, 472
Pineda, D. A., 343, 468
Pinel, Philippe, 39, 41
Plake, B. S., 65, 474
Planty, M., 23, 24, 26, 134, 135, 139, 140, 141, 142, 210, 446

Poe, M., 137, 455
Pogloff, S. M., 358, 468
Poirer, J. M., 376, 469
Poling, A., 285, 468
Polloway, E. A., 80, 84, 334, 352, 356, 381, 392, 397, 400, 401, 469, 474
Polsgrove, L., 285, 286, 452, 468
Pope, A. W., 334, 468
Porter, G. K., 348, 436, 468
Possel, P., 333, 388, 468
Potter, G. B., 318, 319, 451
Powell, D., 348, 468
Powell, K. E., 384, 449
Power, C., 336, 359, 468
Presbury, J. H., 231, 233, 234, 359, 464
Pringle, B., 414, 415, 468
Prinstein, M. J., 208, 459
Prior, M., 213, 471
Prudic, J., 159, 468
Pruitt, D. B., 413, 458
Pruitt, J., 167, 168, 466
Pryzwansky, W. B., 393, 441
Puelles, L., 189, 470
Pugh, A. M., 428, 452
Pugh, K., 85, 191, 192, 472
Pull, C. B., 161, 165, 468
Pumariega, A. J., 346, 348, 353, 428, 430, 434, 457, 468

Quay, H. C., 42, 91, 94, 469
Quinn, K., 448
Quinn, M. M., 12, 333, 376, 452, 456, 469
Quintar, B., 219, 220, 222, 469
Quir, C., 255, 480

Race, E., 122, 481
Racusin, G. R., 73, 333, 466, 472
Rae-Grant, Q., 224, 475
Ramsey, E., 58, 114, 264, 269, 270, 277, 281, 282, 284, 292, 296, 381, 388, 399, 410, 478
Ranalli, P., 286, 445
Randall, C., 22, 348, 404, 436, 455
Randall, J., 437, 438, 469
*Random House Webster's College Dictionary*, 360, 469
Rapport, M. D., 124, 126, 469
Rathus, S. A., 188, 343, 466
Raver, S. A., 387, 469
Reagles, K. W., 318, 334, 451
Rector, J. M., 361, 470
Redding, R. E., 343, 471
Redl, Fritz, 53, 54, 249, 469

Redmond, C., 334, 386, 477
Reese, L. E., 410, 469
Regan, K. S., 401, 469
Regier, D. A., 97, 345, 459
Rehm, L. P., 333, 469
Reid, J. B., 285, 410, 469
Reid, M. J., 387, 479
Reid, M. S., 383, 441
Reid, R., 23, 469
Reinecke, M. A., 307, 333, 445, 469
Renner, P., 168–176, 458
Rescorla, L. A., 42, 71, 78, 79, 98, 99, 100, 127, 437
Reynolds, C. R., 63, 71, 78, 80, 88, 94, 191, 445, 469
Rhee, S. H., 198, 469
Rhine, B. G., 383, 441
Rhoads, S. E., 190, 205, 469
Rhodes, W. C., 8, 349, 351, 353, 355, 356, 470
Richards, P. S., 361, 470
Richardson, J. G., 41, 470
Richardson, M. A., 134, 466
Richmond, B. O., 71, 469
Richter, M., 273, 382, 399, 461
Riggs, N., 384, 452
Riley, A. W., 115, 126, 127, 459
Rimland, B., 8, 470
Ripple, C. H., 210, 470
Risley, T. R., 57, 271, 438
Risser, J. M. H., 136, 446
Risser, W. L., 136, 446
Ritter, J., 138, 140, 141, 443
Rivard, J. C., 437, 450
Rivera, M. O., 401, 438
Roberts, J. E., 348, 436, 455
Roberts, M. C., 22, 404, 410, 458, 474
Roberts, R. E., 136, 137, 446
Robin, J. A., 313, 458
Robinson, T. R., 333, 470
Robles, A. C., 283, 478
Roccatagliata, G., 35, 36, 37, 470
Rodkin, P. C., 115, 470
Rogan, J., 403, 470
Rogers-Adkinson, D. L., 137, 470
Rogers, C. R., 232, 233, 234, 359, 471, 997
Rogers, L., 423, 462
Rogers, S. J., 174, 470
Rohde, P., 333, 460
Roman, H. R., 291, 455
Rosen, M., 206, 479
Rosenberg, D., 85, 191, 192, 472
Rosenberg, D. R., 192, 449

Rosenberg, M. S., 210, 290, 470
Rosenfeld, A. A., 422, 433, 445, 470
Rosenzweig, M. R., 189, 192, 193, 198, 470
Ross, A. O., 8, 470
Rosselli, M., 343, 468
Rosso, I. M., 165, 439
Rothbart, M. K., 213, 214, 470
Rothman, Esther P., 53, 440
Rounsaville, B. F., 97, 470
Rowan, A. B., 121, 122, 155, 158, 159, 160, 479
Rowe, E. W., 73, 470
Rowland, M. D., 437, 470
Rubenstein, J. L. R., 189, 470
Rubin, K. H., 68, 128, 129,134, 135, 208, 470
Ruddy, S. A., 23, 24, 26, 134, 135, 139, 140, 141, 142, 210, 446
Rudolph, K. D., 121, 122, 123, 155, 157, 158, 159, 161, 205, 313, 453
Rush, Benjamin, 39
Russell, A. T., 161, 165, 471
Rutherford, 26, 136, 137, 465
Rutter, M., 43, 100, 102, 174, 186, 187, 190, 194, 196, 198, 209, 211, 212, 213, 214, 458, 464, 465, 471, 476
Ryan, N. D., 159, 471
Rynn, M., 333, 450
Ryser, G., 85, 113, 118, 122, 128, 136, 445, 447

Sabornie, E. J., 113, 118, 122, 128, 136, 393, 400, 403, 445, 471
Sadoc, B. J., 95, 471
Safran, S. P., 382, 460
Sailer, A., 264, 280, 283, 444
Salend, S. J., 283, 356, 397, 400, 471
Salkind, N. J., 188, 471
Saltzman, H., 188, 208, 211, 448, 448
Salvia, J., 65, 67, 87, 471
Salzinger, S., 205, 467
SAMHSA. *See* Substance Abuse and Mental Health Services Administration
Sams, D. P., 392, 477
Sanborn, K. J., 392, 477
Sanchez, L. E., 157, 158, 165, 445, 479
Sandall, S., 387, 471
Sandberg, S., 190, 211, 471
Sandy, J. M., 202, 466
Sanson, A., 213, 471
Santiago, R. L., 435, 455
Santisteban, D. A., 435, 443

Santos, A. B., 429, 454
Santos, L., 136, 478
Santosh, P., 45, 454
Sarason, B. R., 35, 36, 188, 344, 345, 471
Sarason, I. G., 35, 36, 188, 344, 345, 471
Sarason, S. B., 41, 471
Sartor, D., 401, 473
Sasso, G. M., 89, 471
Satel, S. E., 343, 471
Saunders, M., 279, 439
Scahill, L., 45, 416, 471
Schachar, R., 124, 126, 471
Schaps, E., 360, 461
Scharrer, E., 210, 211, 471
Schartz, M., 285, 469
Scheff, T. J., 346, 472
Scheuermann, B., 358, 472
Schloss, P. J., 287, 298, 300, 472
Schmid, R. E., 400, 403, 472
Schneider, B. H., 381, 384, 474
Schoenwald, S. K., 437, 457, 472
Schrepf, S., 431, 432, 436, 448
Schroeder, C. S., 85, 472
Schulenberg, J. E., 139, 140, 456
Schulte, A. B., 393, 441
Schultz, A. R., 169–175, 478
Schultz, D. P., 52, 53, 219, 220, 222, 261, 472
Schultz, R., 85, 191, 192, 472
Schultz, R. T., 16, 168–176, 478
Schultz, S. E., 52, 53, 219, 220, 222, 261, 472
Schultz, S. K., 161, 162, 450
Schumaker, J. B., 294, 454
Schustac, M. W., 49, 52, 53, 213, 221, 226, 229, 450
Schutte, K. M., 432, 478
Schwab-Stone, M. E., 72, 473
Schwartz, D., 205, 448
Schwartz, J. A. J., 333, 472
Scott, J. R., 472
Scott, L. D., 423, 463
Scott, T. M., 88, 89, 285, 379, 382, 463, 472
Scott, W. D., 334, 472
Scruggs, T. E., 401, 469
Sealander, K., 113, 451
Seeley, J. R., 157, 158, 333, 460
Segal, D. L., 37, 39, 41, 97, 100, 108, 472
Segrin, C., 317, 472
Seidman, L. J., 472

Seligman, M., 358, 472
Seligman, M. E. P., 329, 437
Sensky, T., 171, 462
Sergeant, J., 78, 472
Serna, L. A., 334, 352, 356, 381, 387, 397, 400, 401, 403, 469, 472
Severson, H. E., 270, 296, 297, 472, 478
Shaffer, D., 42, 72, 123, 141, 142, 140, 141, 155, 158, 387, 388, 389, 473
Shah, K., 128, 464
Shahbazian, M., 363, 441
Shapiro, E. L., 285, 334, 403, 441
Shapiro, E. S., 84, 473
Shapiro, T., 137, 476
Sheeber, L., 203, 270, 445
Shelden, R. G., 443
Sheldon, J., 294, 345, 454
Shelton, C., 117, 361, 443
Shelton, T. L., 124, 126, 444, 473
Shepard, J. M., 341, 342, 473
Sherman, J. A., 294, 454
Shippen, M. E., 266, 401, 473
Shir, S., 334, 473
Shure, M. B., 321, 323, 472, 474
Shwery, C. S., 332, 452
Sickmund, M., 23, 26, 425, 426, 427, 472, 474
Siegel, L. R., 35, 36, 473
Silber, K., 189, 190, 198, 478
Silbert, J., 401, 442
Sil, J. S., 35, 36, 41, 473
Silver, A. A., 137, 473
Silverthorn, P., 14, 110, 115, 117, 126, 135, 450
Simkin, D. H., 138, 140, 473
Simkin, D. R., 139, 140, 456
Simon, T. R., 410, 469
Simonian, S. J., 209, 476
Simpson, R., 175, 473
Simpson, R. G., 266, 473
Simpson, R. L., 397, 473
Sinclair, M. F., 388, 473
Sindelar, P. T., 210, 290, 470
Singh, N. N., 429, 434, 468, 473
Sitlington, P. L., 355, 399, 473
Skiba, R. J., 382, 467
Skinner, B. F., 55, 56, 261, 262, 268, 474
Skowyra, K., 428, 443
Skuse, D. H., 195, 198, 474
Smith, B. J., 387, 471
Smith-Boydston, J. M., 348, 412, 432, 474

Smith, C. R., 46, 58, 358, 361, 474
Smith, D. K., 211, 474
Smith, J. D., 285, 381, 384, 474
Smith, L. W., 231, 233, 234, 359, 464
Smith, M. A., 287, 472
Smith, P. K., 381, 384, 474
Smith, S., 327, 328, 333, 474
Smith, S. W., 186, 285, 333, 469, 470
Smith, T., 80, 84, 392, 474
Smolkowski, K., 387, 453
Snow, S. T., 436, 480
Snyder, H. N., 23, 26, 425, 426, 427, 474
Snyder, J., 270, 474
Snyder, T. D., 23, 446
Soler, R., 435, 455
Solhkhah, R., 140, 474
Solomon, M. L., 414, 444
Sondell, M., 186, 446
Spence, S. H., 410, 446
Spies, R. A., 65, 474
Spitzer, R. L., 94, 95, 97, 100, 108, 481
Spivac, G., 321, 474
Spoth, R., 334, 386, 477
Sprafkin, R. P., 319, 451
Sprague, J. R., 89, 296, 355, 381, 404, 447, 474, 476
Sroufe, L. A., 185, 186, 200, 202, 307, 446
Steele, R. G., 410, 474
Steiman, M., 474, 2201
Stein, M. B., 211, 446
Steinberg, Z., 48, 49, 50, 51, 226, 460, 474
Steiner, H., 112, 474
Steinhart, D. J., 426, 451
Steinhauer, P. D., 224, 475
Stephens, J. T., 294, 404, 439
Stephens, R. L., 435, 455
Sterba, M., 401, 475
Stevens, D. J., 254, 448
Stevens, K. B., 283, 294, 383, 463
Steventon, C., 401, 473
Stewart, A., 207, 442
Stewart, A. J., 475
Stewart, J. H., 203, 475
Stewart, S. L., 68, 128, 128, 208, 470
Stichter, J. P., 56, 58, 89, 262, 271, 274, 280, 285, 356, 463, 475
Stiller, B., 58, 296, 454, 478
Stormont, M., 379, 387, 475
Stormsha, E., 355, 475
Stouthamer-Loeber, M., 204, 270, 410, 411, 461

Stowe, M., 13, 29, 48, 477
Strain, P. S., 387, 458, 475
Straus, M. A., 203, 475
Strober, M. A., 158, 159, 475
Stroul, Beth A., 49, 51, 348, 353, 429, 430, 431, 432, 435, 475
Stroup, T. S., 171, 464
Strout, M., 381, 475
Substance Abuse and Mental Health Services Administration, 139, 140, 412, 471
Sugai, G., 80, 89, 285, 287, 296, 333, 355, 356, 379, 381, 382, 445, 456, 462, 474, 476
Sumi, W. C., 23, 26, 294, 342, 478
Suveg, C., 333
Sussman, N., 416, 419, 475
Sutherland, K. S., 21, 342, 343, 344–348, 352, 399, 434, 445, 468, 475
Svadjian, H., 121, 122, 155, 158, 159, 160, 479
Swanson, T. C., 381, 475
Swearer, S. M., 333, 462
Sweeney, D. P., 174, 176, 475
Sweeney, J. A., 157, 467
Swindle, F. L., 255, 480
Szapoczni, J., 435, 443
Szasz, T. S., 100, 101, 346, 475
Szatkiewicz, J. P., 423, 444, 443

Taieb, O., 159, 475
Tally, S. R., 343, 452
Tang, B., 165, 442
Tang, T. Z., 330, 446
Tanguay, P. E., 174, 175, 475
Tankersley, M., 9, 42, 397, 476
Tanner, E. M., 50, 428, 481
Tannoc, R., 124, 126, 471
Tarbox, J., 282, 476
Tarbox, R. S. F., 290, 451
Tarnowski, K. J., 209, 476
Tarver, S., 401, 442
Taylor, A., 213, 456
Taylor, E., 78, 100, 102, 472, 476
Taylor, F. D., 58, 454
Taylor, H., 360, 476
Taylor, R. L., 63, 65, 85, 476
Teasdale, J., 329, 437
Tebes, J. K., 261, 477
Te, C., 151, 163, 458
Tellegen, A., 71, 442
Teplin, L. A., 26, 136, 476
Terman, Lewis, 42

Terrell, E., 430, 436, 480
Theodore, L. A., 290, 457
Thienemann, M. L., 226, 475, 506
Thomas, A., 213, 448, 476
Thomas, C. R., 57, 112, 476
Thomas, D. R., 56, 439
Thomas, L. A., 211, 440, 459
Thompson, J. H., 69, 128, 448
Thomsen, A. H., 188, 211, 443
Thoresen, C. E., 360, 361, 464
Thornberry, T. P., 26, 136, 458, 476
Thornburgh, D., 211, 476
Thousand, J. S., 297, 477
Thurlow, M. L., 343, 388, 467, 473
Thurm, A., 190, 213, 463
Timm, M. A., 387, 475
Tindal, G., 401, 476
Tjeltveit, A. C., 361, 470
Tobin, T., 404, 476
Todd, A. W., 287, 476
Todis, B., 72, 478
Tolan, P. A., 115, 410, 452
Tonigan, J. S., 361, 362, 476
Toppelberg, C. O., 137, 476
Torres-Valasquez, D., 343, 476
Toscova, R. T., 361, 362, 476
Tramontana, M., 167, 168, 466
Treffers, P. D. A., 119, 467
Trickett, K., 207, 476
Trim, R. S., 138, 140, 141, 443
Trout, A. L., 20, 23, 137, 285, 387, 469, 476
Troutman, A. C., 58, 68, 74, 266, 271, 272, 274, 277, 279, 280, 287, 356, 437
Trudeau, L., 334, 386, 477
Truscott, S. D., 392, 477
Tryon, W. W., 55, 261, 262, 275, 477
Tsatsanis, K. D., 163, 165, 169, 168, 461, 478
Tuke, William, 39
Turnbull, H. R., 12, 29, 48, 477
Turner, T., 151, 466

United States Department of Education, 7, 9, 14, 15, 16, 19, 20, 21, 22, 23, 25, 26, 29, 47, 50, 137, 342, 379, 380, 414, 477
United States Department of Health and Human Services, 13, 26, 49, 128, 138, 140, 158, 159, 165, 170, 185, 186, 187, 193, 197, 201, 207, 208, 209, 211, 226, 342, 343, 346, 348, 375, 409, 414, 422, 434, 437, 477

Unruh, D., 188, 477
USD Education. *See* United States Department of Education
USDE. *See* United States Department of Education
USDHHS. *See* United States Department of Health and Human Services
Ustun, T. B., 110, 464

Valdez-Menchaca, M., 176, 459
Valore, T. G., 349, 351, 353, 356, 442
Valsiner, J., 342, 344, 477
Van Acker, R., 13, 115, 306, 337, 381, 382, 401, 464, 471, 477
Van Bockern, S., 363, 364, 366, 368, 365, 441
Van der Ende, J., 69, 126, 477
Van Kammen, W. B., 204, 270, 410, 411, 461
Vance, A. L. A., 159, 449
Vanderbilt, A. A., 286, 477
VanDerHeyden, A. M., 274, 285, 394, 480
Vargas, L. A., 414, 434, 477
Varjas, K. M., 436, 465
Vaughn, S., 277, 282, 285, 352, 356, 381, 393, 398, 400, 401, 440
Vazonyi, A. T., 384, 449
Venn, M. L., 399, 464
Vera, E. M., 410, 469
Verhulst, F. C., 6, 119, 122, 126, 477
Vernberg, E. M., 22, 348, 404, 436, 455
Vesterdal, W., 384, 449
Vickers, B., 161, 477
Villa, R. A., 397, 477
Virleson, P., 159, 449
Vitiello, B., 420, 456
Vitulano, L. A., 261, 477
Volkmar, F. R., 16, 163, 165, 168–176, 169, 478

Wacker, D. P., 280, 478
Wadsworth, M. E., 188, 211, 443
Wagner, H., 189, 190, 198, 342, 478
Wagner, K. D., 160, 459
Wagner, M. M., 23, 26, 294, 428, 478
Walberg, H., 359, 478
Waldman, I. D., 198, 469
Walker, H. M., 68, 72, 78, 80, 84, 89, 112
Walker, Hill M., 58, 264, 269, 270, 271, 277, 281, 282, 284, 292, 296, 297, 333, 355, 381, 388, 399, 410, 447, 454, 458, 459, 472, 474, 478

Walker, J. S., 432, 478
Walker, S., 414, 464
Wallace, M. D., 283, 478
Wallace, R. A., 341, 342, 345, 478
Walsh, M. E., 349, 350, 455
Warfield-Coppoc, N., 361, 443
Warren, C. S., 226, 478
Wasserman, G. A., 136, 478
Watson, G. S., 204, 478
Watson, J. C., 232, 234, 479
Watson, John B., 55, 479
Watson, N. V., 189, 192, 193, 198, 470
Webb-Johnson, G., 21, 479
Webster, R. E., 479
Webster-Stratton, C., 387, 479
Wedding, D., 52, 53, 226, 444
Weersing, V. R., 329, 333, 443
Wehby, J. H., 288, 292, 350, 378, 397, 445, 460
Weinberg, W. A., 139, 479
Weinberger, D. R., 193, 479
Weiss, G., 124, 127, 479
Weiss, M., 124, 127, 479
Weissberg, R. P., 410, 453
Weissman, M. M., 333, 465
Weist, M. D., 436, 479
Weitoft, G., 206, 479
Wekerle, C., 206, 207, 208, 479
Weller, E. B., 121, 122, 155, 157, 158, 159, 160, 479
Weller, R. A., 121, 122, 155, 157, 158, 159, 160, 479
Wells, K., 71, 444
Wells, K. C., 205, 210, 328, 356, 445, 461
Wells, M. G., 361, 479
Wells, N. M., 208, 448
Werry, J. S., 151, 152, 162, 169, 189, 190, 192, 479
West, R. P., 286, 287, 447, 467
Whelan, R. J., 35, 479
Whitaker, A. H., 199, 201, 479
Whitbec, L. B., 207, 442
White, J. W., 201, 480
White, K. J., 328, 461
Whitebec, L. B., 475
Wickrama, K., 334, 386, 477
Wicks-Nelson, R., 13, 14, 16, 19, 41, 43, 52, 91, 101, 112, 119, 120, 135, 164, 169, 171, 186, 187, 196, 198, 202, 203, 204, 214, 270, 342, 343, 479
Wilcox, B., 478
Wiley, L. P., 399, 464
Wilhite, K., 88, 450

Williams, C. L., 71, 442
Williams, D., 199, 201, 310, 479
Williford, A. P., 117, 473
Wills, C., 420, 463
Wilmshurst, L., 186, 209, 479
Wilson, D. B., 201, 480
Wilson, G. R., 290, 451
Wilson, G. T., 262, 437
Wilson, J. J., 348, 480
Wilson, R., 210, 290, 470
Wilson, V., 78, 88, 469
Windsor, A. P., 74, 480
Wineman, David, 53, 54, 469
Wing, J. K., 150, 151, 165, 480
Winters, N. C., 430, 436, 480
Witkow, M. R., 117, 208, 466
Witt, J. C., 274, 285, 394, 480
Wojslawowicz, J. C., 129, 470
Wolf, A., 341, 342, 345, 478
Wolf, M. M., 57, 271, 279, 423, 424, 444, 445, 446, 460, 469, 480
Wolfe, D. A., 100, 205, 206, 207, 208, 464, 480
Wolfgang, C. H., 229, 230, 231, 235, 238, 240, 381, 480
Wolraich, M., 201, 480
Wood, F. H., 46, 47, 58, 473, 480
Wood, M. M., 54, 209, 212, 242, 245, 249, 250, 255, 355, 356, 463, 480
Wood, P. A., 136, 140, 343, 443, 454, 460
Woodruff, D. W., 436, 480
Woods, J. E., 117, 473
Woodward, L. J., 134, 480
Wor, W. C., 387, 444
Worsham, M. E., 381, 451, 448
Wright, G., 435, 480
Wyman, P. A., 387, 444
Wynne, E., 359, 478
Wyric, P. A., 134, 136, 480

Xu, Y., 205, 448

Yampolskaya, S., 136, 480
Yeh, M., 136, 140, 343, 435, 454, 462
Yell, M. L., 13, 25, 28, 48, 84, 87, 355, 395, 397, 399, 459, 478, 480
Yoerger, K., 115, 270, 410, 467
Yoshikawa, H., 48, 480
Young, K. R., 286, 287, 447, 467
Ysseldyke, J. E., 65, 67, 80, 87, 352, 471, 480
Yule, W., 120, 480

Zahn-Wexler, C., 122, 481
Zametkin, A., 189, 190, 192, 479
Zeanah, C. H., 128, 202, 445, 462
Zeisel, S. A., 137, 455
Zhang, D., 25, 481
Zigler, E. F., 50, 428, 481
Zigterman, D., 311, 440
Zima, B. T., 423, 463
Zimet, D., 205, 481
Zimmerman, M., 94, 95, 97, 100, 108, 481
Zionts, L. T., 358, 481
Zionts, P., 332, 481

# Subject Index

A-B-C contingency in behavioral theory, 263
A-B-C framework in Rational-Emotive Therapy, 330
AACP. *See* Adolescent Anger Control Program
ABAB research design, 269–270
Abrupt cognitive deterioration, 188
Accepting-Rejecting continuum in parental discipline styles, 202–203
Achenbach System of Empirically Based Assessment (ASEBA), 70, 78–79, 97–99
    Aggression pattern and, 112
    Anxiety pattern and, 116
    cooccurrence, 174
    Depression pattern and, 122
    Impulsiveness pattern, 124
    Mood Disorders and, 157
    patterns of E&B disorders, 112
    Psychotic Disorders, 173
    Relationship Problem pattern, 129
Acquisition versus performance, 308–309
Active phase in schizophrenia, 163
Actual functioning measurement, 67, 74–77
Actualizing tendency, 229
Acute onset, 160
Adaptive versus maladaptive behavior in aggression pattern, 115
ADHD. *See* Attention Deficit/Hyperactivity Disorder
Administrative definitions of E&B disorders, 7–10
    federal definition, 7–9
Adolescent Anger Control Program (AACP), 325–327, 333, 335
Adolescent Coping with Depression Course, 329
Adoption comparisons, 192–193
Adult versus child manifestations in extreme E&B disorders, 148
Adventure experiences, 412
Advocacy organizations, 45, 47, 433–434
African Americans, 341, 345
Aftercare (parole) supervision, 423
Aggression management, 299, 300
Aggression pattern, 112–116
    adaptive versus maladaptive, 115
    cognitive interventions for, 333
    course of, 115
    description, 112

Law-Breaking Behavior, 115
    measurement of, 112–114
    other considerations, 114–115
    relation to classification and definition, 112–113, 114
    relational aggression, 115
    subcategories of, 116
    target behavior definitions in, 268
Aggression Replacement Training (ART), 335–336
Aggressive drives, 216, 217
Alcohol use, 23, 135
    *see also* Substance Misuse
Anal stage, 217, 218
Anger control in Aggression Replacement Training (ART), 335–336
Anger Coping program, 328–329, 333
Anger management lessons, 379
Anoxia, 196
Antecedent control of behavior, 284–289
Antecedent self-control, 286
Antecedents in behavioral theory, 262, 266
Antianxiety medications, 412, 415, 416
Anticonvulsants, 416
Antidepressants, 412, 413, 414
Antimanics, 412, 415, 416
Antipsychotics, 412, 414, 415
Anxiety pattern, 114–118
    cognitive interventions for, 333
    course of, 117
    description of, 114–115
    measurement of, 116–117
    other considerations, 117–118
    Posttraumatic Stress Disorder (PTSD), 118, 120
    prevalence of, 119
    relation to classification and definition, 112, 117–118
    and school attendance, 120
    target behavior definitions in, 268
    terms used in defining, 117–118
Applied behavior analysis, 271–274
ART. *See* Aggression Replacement Training
ASEBA. *See* Achenbach System of Empirically Based Assessment
Asian/Pacific Islanders, 341
Asperger's Disorder, 167, 171
Asphyxia, 196
Assessment, 62–89

    appropriate, 26
    defined, 63
    in determining services, 85–86
    in ecological perspective, 333–359
    in eligibility for ED under IDEA 2004, 86
    functional behavioral assessment, 88–89
    in monitoring outcomes, 87–89
    for program evaluation and research, 91
    in the psychodynamic model, 228
    in the psychoeducational approach, 244–245
    purposes of, 81–89
    for referral of students, 81–83
    screening, 84
    in sociological perspective, 346–347
    in special education and the IEP, 63, 82
    student progress, 88
    *see also* Classification; Measurement concepts; Measurement methods
Asylums, 38
*At the Schoolhouse Door* (Knitzer et al.), 50
Attachment in family socialization, 202
Attention Deficit/Hyperactivity Disorder (ADHD), 123, 124, 125
    and Mood Disorders, 161
    self-instruction for, 329
    and stimulants, 413
Attention seeking, 225
Atypical autism, 171
Atypical PDD, 171
Atypical Psychotic Disorder, 164
Authoritative definitions of E&B disorder, 7, 8
Autism spectrum disorders, 148–149, 168
Autistic disorder, 148, 167, 168, 169–170
Aversive punishment, 279
Axes in *DSM-IV-TR*, 94–96

BASC. *See* Behavior Assessment System for Children
Baseline data, 268–269
Behavior and emotional variables, 85
Behavior Assessment System for Children (BASC), 70, 71, 77, 80

Behavior chains in behavioral theory, 267–268
Behavior classes in behavioral theory, 266
Behavior Evaluation Scale, 70
Behavior factors in reciprocal determinism, 309–310
Behavior generalizations, 262
Behavior maintenance, 283
Behavior management in the separate classroom, 396
Behavior modification, 56–58, 271, 274–289
Behavior modification programs, 296–300
   in regular classes, 296–298
      Contingencies for Learning Academic and Social Skills (CLASS), 296–298
      First Step to Success, 296–298
   in separate classes, 298–230
      the Engineered Classroom, 298
      the Franklin-Jefferson Program, 298–300
Behavior problem management plan, 387–388
Behavior-products recording, 76
Behavior rating scales, 68–71
*Behavioral and Emotional Rating Scale—Revised*, 428
Behavioral contracting, 289–290, 292
Behavioral interventions, 271–296
   applied behavior analysis, 271–274
   behavior modification, 275, 279–293
   behavioral contracting, 289–290, 292
   package interventions, 290
   social skills training, 292–296
   token economies, 288–289
Behavioral model, 55–58, 258–302
   behavior modification programs, 298–302
   for ED students, 58
   interventions, 273–298
   operant conditioning, 55–56
   in schools, 56–57
   scientific evaluation of, 58
   summary of, 251–262
   theory of, 263–273
Behavioral perspective of E&B disorders, 8, 10–11
Behavioral theory, 261–271
   A-B-C contingency, 263
   antecedents, 262, 266
   behavior chains, 267
   behavior classes, 266
   complex behavior, 268
   conditioned and primary reinforcers, 267
   conditioned punishers, 267
   consequences, 262
   discrimination, 268
   extinction, 264
   generalized reinforcers, 268
   negative reinforcement, 263
   negative reinforcement via coercion-compliance, 270–271
   operant conditioning and E&B disorders, 268–271
   operant conditioning (Skinner), 261–266
   operants, 261, 262
   positive reinforcement, 263, 275
   positive reinforcement via misallocated attention, 269–270
   punishment, 264, 279
   reinforcement, 262
   respondents, 251–262
   schedules, 264–266
   stimulus generalization, 268
   verbal and covert behavior, 268
Bellevue Hospital school, 53
Belonging as basic human need, 360, 362, 363
Bicêtre Hospital, 38, 39
Biological and psychosocial influences, 184–217
   biological influences, 182, 188–201
   interaction of, 182, 188, 208–210
   psychosocial influences, 182, 201–212
   research on, 43, 210–211
   variables in, 181, 183
   *see also* Biological influences; Child development; Psychosocial influences
Biological influences, 182, 188–201
   the brain, 189–190
      neurotransmitters, 189, 195, 196
      systems in, 190
   brain disorders, 189, 190–201
      causes of, 193–201
      E&B disorders related to, 193
      incomplete knowledge of the brain, 190–191
      measurement problems, 191–193
   hereditary influences, 194–198
      direct gene research, 194–196
      findings on, 198
      indirect study of groups, 196–198
   physical influences, 198–201
      before conception, 199
      perinatal period, 200
      postnatal risks, 200–201
      prenatal period, 199–200
   temperament, 213–214
   *see also* Biological and psychosocial influences
Biological perspective of E&B disorders, 8, 110
Bipolar disorders in children and adolescents, 157
Bipolar I Disorder, 155
Bipolar II Disorder, 155
Bipolar Mood Disorder, 120, 125
Brain, 189–190
Brain disorders, 189, 190–201
*Brown v. Board of Education*, 47

Career education, 399
Catharsis, 224
CASSP. *See* Child and Adolescent Service System Program
CAT. *See* Computed axial tomography
Categorical resource programs, 394
Categories in classification, 100
Causes of E&B disorders, 110, 222
CCBD. *See* Council for Children with Behavioral disorders
CCM. *See* Combined Classroom Model
CEC. *See* Council for Exceptional Children
Character education, 359, 360
Check & Connect, 388–391
Checklists, 68
Child advocacy, 346, 355
Child-aides, 383
Child and Adolescent Service System Program (CASSP), 50, 425
Child and family welfare system, 405, 422–425
Child Behavior Checklist in ASEBA, 99
Child development, 181–184
   defined, 181
   developmental pathways, 186–187
   developmental psychopathology, 186–187

## Subject Index

maturation, 186–186
protective factors, 188, 210
psychosocial variables, 187
risk factors, 187–188, 210
*see also* Biological and psychosocial influences
Child guidance clinics, 44
Child maltreatment, 206–208
Child mental health, 44–45
Child-rearing disruptions, 200
Child service systems, 50
Child versus adult manifestations in extreme E&B disorders, 148
Childhood Disintegrative Disorder, 167, 171
Children
helping, 18
and the psychodynamic model, 52–55
*see also* Students
Christian church, 37–38
Chromosomes, 190, 194
Circle of courage spiritual values program, 362–368
basic needs and related behaviors, 364–365
intervention, 367–368
theory, 365–366
Citizenship, 113
Civil rights, 47
CLASS. *See* Contingencies for Learning Academic and Social Skills
Classical Greek era, 36–37
Classification, 89–101
Achenbach System of Empirically Based Assessment (ASEBA), 78–79, 97–99
*Diagnostic and Statistical Manual of Mental Disorders (DSM-IV-TR)*, 94–96
dimensional (empirical) classification, 96–99, 101
evaluating, 99–101
in extreme emotional and behavior disorders, 173
and labeling people, 100–101
nosological classification (disease-oriented or clinical), 92–96, 101
purposes of, 91–92
sample emotional and behavior problems, 90
*see also* Assessment
Classroom management, 377–378

managing surface behavior, 243–244
person-centered approach in, 234–235
prevention in, 232
psychoeducational approach in, 242–252
reality therapy approach in, 237–241
social discipline approach in, 228–231
Clients, 222
Clinical classification, 93–97, 101
Clinical exploitation of life events in Life Space Crisis Intervention (LSCI), 249–251
Clinical psychology, 146
Club drugs, 136
*see also* Substance Misuse
Co-occurrence in dimensional classification, 97, 110
Cognitive deficits/distortions, 309–312
interventions for cognition distortions, 323–328
interventions for cognitive deficits, 316–327
Cognitive model, 304–339
in E&B disorders, 311–316, 337
cognitive deficits/distortions, 313–316
social information processing (SIP), 312–313
intervention, 316–337
Aggression Replacement Training (ART), 335–336
for cognitive deficits, 316–327
for cognitive distortions, 327–332
modeling, 316
for particular E&B disorders, 3232–335
Rational-Emotive (R-E) Therapy (Ellis), 331–332
modeling and social cognitive theory (Bandura), 310–320
acquisition versus performance, 308–309
E/B/P factors in reciprocal determinism, 309–310
and E&B disorder, 310–311
modeling, 307–309
summary of, 305–306

Cognitive perspective of E&B disorders, 8, 10–11
Cognitive restructuring in Rational-Emotive Therapy, 327
Collaboration
in indicated prevention, 393
in the regular classroom, 393
Combined Classroom Model (CCM), 393
Communication and classification, 91
Community, 208–209
Comorbidity, 110, 132
Complex behavior in behavioral theory, 268
Compulsory schooling, 40
Computed axial tomography (CT or CAT), 188
Conclusions in classification measures, 100–101
Concurrent comorbidity, 132–133
Conditioned and primary reinforcers in behavioral theory, 267
Conditioned punishers in behavioral theory, 267
Conduct Disorder, 110
Conflict Cycle (Long), 54, 238–240
Conflict resolution, 384–386
Conflict theory, 343–344
Conners-Wells Adolescent Self-Report Scale, 71
Consequence sharing, 280
Consequences in behavioral theory, 262
*Consistency Management and Cooperative Discipline* (Freiberg), 231–232, 251
Consultation
in indicated prevention, 392–393
in the regular classroom, 393
Contingencies for Learning Academic and Social Skills (CLASS), 292–294, 384
Contingency contracting, 287–288, 289
Continuous schedule, 261
Continuum of education environments for students with ED, 20, 21, 22, 24, 249, 373, 392
Cooccurrence, 174
Council for Children with Behavioral Disorders (CCBD), 46, 355
Counseling, 408
*see also* Intervention in other systems
Covert behavior, 264
Crime, 25
Crisis/Helping Teacher, 252–253

Crisis-intervention techniques, 208
Cross-categorical resource programs, 394
Cross-cultural situations, 430
Cross-informant syndromes in ASEBA, 94, 98
CT or CAT. See Computed axial tomography
Culture, 197
Cycles in Mood Disorders, 153
Cyclothymic Disorder, 151

Day treatment in mental health system, 413–414
Decreasing target behaviors, 274–279
DEFENDS strategy, 399
Defense mechanisms, 222–224
Delinquencies, 421
　and E&B disorder, 424
　see also Juvenile justice system
Delirium, 146
Delusions, 192
Dementia, 146
Dementia praecox, 147
Democratic class meetings, 231
Deoxyribonucleic acid (DNA), 190
Dependent group contingency, 280
Depression pattern, 121–124
　cognitive interventions for, 333
　course of, 123
　description of, 121
　early recognition and intervention, 123
　measurement of, 122
　other considerations, 123–124
　prevalence of, 121–123
　relation to classification and definition, 112, 122
　screening programs, 124
　target behavior definitions in, 268
　see also Mood Disorders
Depressive disorders
　in children and adolescents, 155, 158
　norepinephrine and serotonin, 185
Detention, 405, 423
Detrimental effects in classification, 100
*Developing Understanding of Self and Others* (Dinkmeyer & Dinkmeyer), 251
Developmental Delay, 19
Developmental pathways, 186–187
　see also Child development

Developmental psychopathology, 43, 182–183
Developmental stages, risk factors by, 406, 407
*Developmental Therapy* (Wood, Davis, Swindle, & Quirk), 251
Deviance defined, 340–341
Deviations from standards, 11
*Diagnostic and Statistical Manual of Mental Disorders (DSM-IV-TR)*, 94–96, 413
　Aggression pattern and, 110
　Anxiety pattern and, 117–118
　Depression pattern and, 124
　Impulsiveness pattern and, 125
　Mood Disorders, 110, 121, 122, 123, 153–161
　patterns of E&B disorders and, 114
　Pervasive Developmental Disorders, 108, 171–176
　Psychotic Disorders, 108, 161–171
　Relationship Problem pattern and, 129
Diathesis-stress, 212–213
　see also Stress
Differential reinforcement, 271
　of incompatible behavior (DRI), 283
　of low rates of behavior (DRL), 282–283
　of other behavior (DRO), 279
Dimensional (empirical) classification, 97–100, 101
Disabilities, students with, 47
Discipline styles, 202–203
Discrimination in behavioral theory, 268
Discriminative stimulus for reinforcement, 262
Disease-oriented or clinical classification, 94–96, 101
Disengagement, 226
Displacement, 219
Disputing irrational beliefs in Rational-Emotive Therapy, 331
Distal risk factors, 187
Distorted attributions and beliefs, 329–332
Distorted information processing, 327–329
Diversion in juvenile justice system, 426–427
Diversity, 430–431
Dizygotic (MA) twins, 193

DNA. See Deoxyribonucleic acid
Dopamine, 185
Double depression, 155
Dream interpretation, 37, 216
DRI. See Differential reinforcement of incompatible behavior
Drives (needs) in psychoanalytic theory, 216, 217, 221
DRL. See Differential reinforcement of low rates of behavior
DRO. See Differential reinforcement of other behavior
Drug prevention education, 386
Drugs, 135–136
　treatment for E&B disorders, 44–45
　see also Psychotropic drug therapy; Substance Misuse
*DSM-IV-TR*. See *Diagnostic and Statistical Manual of Mental Disorders*
Due process, 27
Dyspedagogia, 134
Dysthymic Disorder, 153, 155

E/B/P factors in reciprocal determinism, 309–310
E&B disorders. See Emotional and behavior disorders
Early intervention, 383
Early-onset of extreme emotional and behavior disorders, 152
Early Western Civilization viewpoints of E&B disorders, 36–37
Echolalia, 169
Ecological perspective, 351–357, 411
　assessment and intervention, 351–357
　and E&B disorders, 351
　ecosystems, 397–351
　Multisystemic Therapy (MST), 437, 438
　summary of, 344–345
　theory, 353–355
Ecological perspective of E&B disorders, 8
Ecosystems, 347–349, 433
ECT. See Electroconvulsive therapy
ED. See Emotional disturbance
Education
　alternative practices, 401
　compulsory schooling, 40, 45
　and extreme emotional and behavior disorders, 152–153, 173–174

Subject Index **499**

growth of, 40–41
person-centered approach
  (Rogers) to, 231–232
special education profession,
  45–46
for special groups, 40–41
special teaching techniques, 41
Education environments for students
  with ED, 20, 21, 22, 24, 373, 392
Education for All Handicapped
  Children Act, 28, 47, 48
Educational concerns, 18–24
  behavior problems at school,
    23–24
  completing school, 23
  continuum of education
    environments for students with
    ED, 20, 21, 22, 249, 373, 392
  education expenditures, 25
  Individual with Disabilities
    Education Improvement Act of
    2004 (IDEA), 27–28, 48, 63
  lawful obligations, 29
  learning performance, 21–22
  personal and schooling
    demographics, 19–22
  placement of students, 249
  regular class education
    environment, 20–21, 292–294
  removal from school, 24–25
  separate classes, 294–296
  teacher supply, 25
  *see also* Schools; Students
EEG. *See* Electroencephalograph
Ego, 216, 217, 221
Electroconvulsive therapy (ECT), 159
Electroencephalograph (EEG), 188
Emotional first aid, 245, 246
Emotional and behavior disorders, 2–31
  brain disorders related to, 189
  characteristics of, 16
  and cognitive model, 311–316, 337
  defining, 3, 6–12
  and delinquency, 424
  and ecological perspective, 351
  methods for serving students with,
    28–29
  modeling and social cognitive
    theory (Bandura), 310–311
  multiple problems, 15–17
  prevalence of, 13–17
  professionals serving students
    with, 28
  questions about, 5–6

reasons for serving students with,
  17–29
samples of students with, 4
and teachers, 5–6
*see also* Extreme emotional and
  behavior disorders; Historical
  perspectives; Patterns of
  emotional and behavior
  disorders
Emotional disturbance (ED), 7–9, 10
  patterns of E&B disorders, 112
Empathy, 230
Empathy lessons, 379
Empirical (dimensional) classification,
  42, 97–100, 101
  *see also* Achenbach System of
    Empirically Based Assessment
    (ASEBA)
Engineered Classroom, 56–57, 294
  *see also* Schools; Teachers
Environmental factors in reciprocal
  determinism, 309–310
Environmental measurement,
  79–81
Enzymes, 190
Episodes in Mood Disorders, 153, 154
Erogeneous, 217
Existential approaches, 227
Experimental evaluation in applied
  behavior analysis, 273–274
Expressive therapies, 224
Externalizing syndromes in ASEBA, 98
Extinction in behavioral theory, 264
Extinction schedule, 261
Extreme emotional and behavior
  disorders, 148–181
  adult versus child manifestations,
    152
  autism spectrum disorders,
    152–153
  background, 150–153
  childhood schizophrenia, 152
  in children, 152
  classification uncertainties, 173
  defined, 149–150
  early-onset, 152
  and education, 152–153, 173–174
  key information, 153
  Mood Disorders, 153–161
  one-disorder perspectives, 151
  Pervasive Developmental
    Disorders (PDD)s, 148, 171
  prognosis, 179
  Psychotic Disorders, 148, 161–171

terms used in the past, 146–147
two-disorder perspectives, 151

Family socialization, 201–208
Fast Track, 406–408
Fear, 117, 118
Federal definition of emotional
  disturbance (ED), 7–9
  Aggression pattern and, 110–111,
    112
  Anxiety pattern and, 118
  Depression pattern and, 124
  and extreme E&B disorders,
    148–149
  Impulsiveness pattern, 128
  and Learning Difficulty, 137
  measurement linked to, 84–85
  Mood Disorders and, 153
  and patterns of E&B disorders,
    109, 112
  Psychotic Disorders, 169
  Relationship Problem pattern, 129
Federal financial support for special
  education, 47
Federal Interagency Forum on Child
  and Family Statistics
  (FIFCFS),131
Federation of Families for Children's
  Mental Health, 433–434
FIFCFS. *See* Federal Interagency
  Forum on Child and Family
  Statistics
Firearms, 23
FIRST-Letter strategy, 399
First Step to Success,
  292–294,384
Fixed-interval schedule, 261
Fixed-rate schedule, 261
Forfeiture punishment, 280
Foster homes, 409, 422, 423
Foster placements, 423
Franklin-Jefferson Program,
  294–296
Free appropriate public education, 26
Freedom needs in reality therapy
  approach, 237
Full continuum versus full inclusion,
  395–396
Functional analysis, 267
Functional behavior class, 262
Functional behavioral assessment,
  88–89, 262
Functional MRI (fMRI), 188
Functionalism theory, 344

Fundamental academics in the separate classroom, 401–402
Future adjustment, 108

Gangs, 23, 134–136
Gene research, 190–192
Generalizations, 109
Generalized Anxiety Disorder, 118
Generalized reinforcers in behavioral theory, 268
Genes, 190–192
Genital stage, 217, 218
Goodness-of-fit, 347
Grading and evaluation, 378
Group contingencies in behavior modification, 281–284
Group expectations, 197
Group homes, 405, 418

Hallucinations, 192
Helplessness, 226
Hereditary influences, 194–198
Heritability, 194
Hispanics, 341
Historical perspectives, 34–59
  early Western Civilization, 36–37
  late 18th and 19th centuries, 39–41
  Middle Ages, 37–38
  prehistoric viewpoints, 36
  Renaissance, 38
  *see also* Emotional and behavior disorders; Twentieth century perspectives
Home-based services, 433
Homebound settings, 400
Homosexual adolescents, suicide in, 140
Hospital settings, 400
House-Tree-Person drawings, 74
Human culture, 197
Human Genome Project, 195
Humanistic approaches, 227
Humors, 37
Hyperactive behavior, 187
Hyperarousal, 118
Hypnosis, 216
Hypomanic episodes, 151–152

I-messages, 235
Id, 216, 217, 221
IDEA. *See* Individual with Disabilities Education Improvement Act of 2004
IEP. *See* Individualized Education Program

Illegal drug use, 23
Immigrants, 48
Impairment in functioning, 11–12
Impulsiveness pattern, 124–127
  cognitive interventions for, 333
  course of, 126–127
  description of, 124–125
  measurement of, 126
  other considerations, 127
  prevalence of, 126
  relation to classification and definition, 112, 125–126
  target behavior definitions in, 268
Incongruence, 229
Increasing target behaviors, 271
Independence as basic human need, 360, 362, 364
Indicated prevention, 378–395, 388–394
  behavior problem management plan, 391–392
  Check & Connect, 388–391
  collaboration, 393
  consultation, 392–393
  Contingencies for Learning Academic and Social Skills (CLASS), 388
  First Step, 388
  prereferral intervention, 392
Individual with Disabilities Education Improvement Act of 2004 (IDEA), 27–28, 48, 63, 355
  assessment for eligibility, 84–86
  disciplinary exclusion from school, 394
  and psychotherapy, 408
Individualized Education Program (IEP), 27, 63, 394
  assessment in, 63, 82
Individually tailored rating scale (ITRS), 68, 69
Inquisition, 37
Insidious onset, 160
Insight, 223
Institute of Medicine (IOM), 373
Interdependent group contingency, 279
Internalizing syndromes in ASEBA, 98
Intervention in other systems, 408–441
  child and family welfare system, 409, 422–425
    foster placements, 423
    Teaching-Family (T-F) Model of intervention, 423–425
    home-based services, 437

juvenile justice system, 409, 425–428
  delinquency and E&B disorder, 428
  diversion, 426–427
  juvenile justice process, 425–426
  residential placement, 427
  teen court, 426–427
mental health system, 409, 412–422
  day treatment, 413–414
  outdoor challenges, 416
  outpatient treatment, 412–413
  psychodynamic model, 222–224
  residential settings, 414–416
  prevention, 410–412
    Fast Track, 410–412
    risk factors by developmental stages, 410, 411
  psychotropic drug therapy, 413, 414, 416–422
    background and definitions, 416–417
    classification and examples of, 417–420
    concerns about, 420–421
    teacher's role, 421–422
  reforms in service to children with E&B disorder, 428–438
  support organizations, 437–438
  *see also* Intervention in the education system; System of care
Intervention in the education system, 374–407
  full continuum versus full inclusion, 395–396
  least restrictive environment, 375–376
  more restrictive education settings, 404–405
  prevention, 232, 376–395
    drawbacks and costs of, 378
    preventing prevention, 394–395
    primary/secondary/tertiary, 377–378, 380
    refinements needed, 394
    universal/selective/indicated, 378–395
  regular class, 397
    consultation or collaboration, 397
    modified regular class, 397
  resource room, 398

separate classroom, 398–404
  behavior management, 400
  fundamental academics,
    401–402
  individual educational needs,
    400
  physical aspects, 400
  scheduling, 400
  social competence, 404
  structured environment,
    399–400
  study skills, 403
  subject content, 402–403
  survival-and-success behaviors,
    400, 401
  teachers in, 401
  transition skills, 403–404
  six education environments for,
    377, 396
  see also Indicated prevention;
    Intervention in other systems;
    Noneducational interventions;
    Selective prevention; Universal
    prevention
Intervention selection and
  classification, 93
Interviews, 71–74, 116, 120
IOM. See Institute of Medicine
IQ scores, 134
Irrational beliefs in Rational-Emotive
  Therapy, 330–331
ITRS. See Individually tailored rating
  scale

Juvenile justice system, 50, 405,
  425–428

Labeling people, 100–101,
  344–345
Late 18th and 19th centuries
  viewpoints of E&B disorders, 39–41
Latency stage, 217, 218
Law-Breaking Behavior, 113, 133–137
  cognitive interventions for, 334
  connections to E&B disorder, 133
  description, 131
  gangs, 134–136
  other considerations, 134
  prevalence, 131
  victimization in school, 134
Lawful obligations in educating all
  children, 29
Learning Difficulty, 137–138
  cognitive interventions for, 334

connections to E&B disorder,
  137–138
  description, 137
  other considerations, 138
  prevalence, 137
Learning performance, 22–23
Learning principles, 257
Learning strategies, 399
Least restrictive environment, 26,
  375–376, 407
Legal developments, twentieth
  century, 46–48
Legal services, 405
Lesch-Nyhan syndrome,
  191–192
Lethality of suicide acts, 138, 141
Levels system, 284–285, 286–287,
  294–300, 400, 420–421
Life skills education, 399
Life Skills Training (LST), 330, 382
Life Space Assessment Interview,
  240–241
Life Space Crisis Intervention,
  249–252, 365, 410
Life space interviews, 53
Life trajectory, 4404
Limbic system, 186
Litigation-legislation-litigation cycle, 48
Logical consequences, 227
Love needs in reality therapy
  approach, 237
LSD, 192
Lunacy, 146

Magnetic resonance imaging (MRI), 188
Major Depressive Disorder, 149, 151
Major depressive episodes, 150
Mania, 146–147
Manic depression, 151
Manic episodes, 150
Marijuana use, 23, 135
  see also Substance Misuse
Mass electronic media, 210–211
Mastery as basic human need, 360,
  362, 364
Matching in self-management, 287
Maturation, 181–182, 196
Measurement concepts, 64–66
  defined, 63, 64
  norms, 66
  operational definitions, 64–65
  percentiles, 66
  reliability, 65
  and special education, 66

validity, 65
variables, 64, 66, 85, 87, 100
see also Assessment; Measurement
  methods
Measurement in brain disorders,
  191–193
  history of development, 191
  neurological examination, 191
  neuropsychological testing,
    191–192
  physiological assessment, 192–193
Measurement methods, 66–81
  actual functioning, 67, 74–77
    in a simulated situation, 76–77
    behavior-products recording, 76
    target-behavior recording,
      74–76
  in applied behavior analysis,
    271–273
  environmental measurement,
    79–81
  multifaceted measurement systems,
    77–79
    Achenbach System of
      Empirically Based
      Assessment (ASEBA), 70,
      78–79
    Behavior Assessment System
      for Children (BASC), 70, 80
    Systematic Screening For
      Behavior Disorders (SSBD),
      67, 80
  reported functioning, 67–74
    interviews, 71–74
    peer nomination (referral), 68
    personality measurement,
      73–74
    ratings by others, 68–69
    ratings by self, 71
    teacher nomination (referral),
      68
  see also Assessment; Measurement
    concepts
Measurement reliability, 65
Measurement systems, 77–79
Media, 210–211
Medical/health services, 405
Medical, social, and learning variables,
  85
Medication. See Psychotropic drug
  therapy
Melancholia, 37, 147
Mental disorders, 10
  prevalence of, 13–14

Mental health system, 405, 412–422
Mental hygiene movement, 44
Mental retardation, 189, 191, 192
Metabolism, 190
Middle Ages viewpoint of E&B disorders, 37–38
Milieu therapy, 409–410
*A Mind That Found Itself* (Beers), 44
Minerals, 196
Minnesota Multiphasic Personality Inventory-Adolescent, 71
Minorities, 430
　*see also* Race-ethnic culture
Mixed episodes, 150
Modeling, 303–305, 312
Modeling and social cognitive theory (Bandura), 307–316
Modified regular classroom environment, 393
Monozygotic (MA) twins, 193
Mood Disorders, 108, 119, 120, 121, 153–161
　bipolar disorders in children and adolescents, 157
　Bipolar I Disorder, 155
　Bipolar II Disorder, 155
　and brain disorders, 189
　course of, 158–159
　cycles in, 153
　Cyclothymic Disorder, 155
　depressive disorders in children and adolescents, 155, 157
　description, 153–158
　double depression, 159
　Dysthymic Disorder, 153, 155
　electroconvulsive therapy (ECT), 159
　episodes of, 153, 154
　interventions, 159–161
　Major Depressive Disorder, 153, 155
　prevalence, 157
　relation to classification and definition, 157
　*see also* Depression pattern
Moral education in Aggression Replacement Training (ART), 332
Moral reasoning, 358
Moral treatment, 39
Morbid, 129
MRI. *See* Magnetic resonance imaging
MST. *See* Multisystemic Therapy
Multidisciplinary teams, 44

Multifaceted measurement systems, 77–79
Multiple ecosystems, 354
Multiracial members, 341
Multisystemic Therapy (MST), 437, 438

NAMI (National Alliance for the Mentally Ill), 434
National Agenda, 51
National Alliance for the Mentally Ill (NAMI), 434
National Association for the Mentally Ill, 355
National Committee for Mental Hygiene, 44, 48
National Institute of Mental Health, 44
National Mental Health and Special Education Coalition, 9–10
National Mental Health Association, 44, 434
Native Americans, 341, 361
Natural or logical consequences, 227
NCLB. *See* No Child Left Behind
Needs in reality therapy approach, 237
Negative cognitive triad, 326
Negative psychotic symptoms in schizophrenia, 167–168
Negative reinforcement, 259
　via coercion-compliance, 266–267
Neuroimaging, 188
Neurological examination, 187
Neurons, 190, 191
Neuropsychological testing, 187–188
Neurotic anxiety, 217, 218
Neurotransmitters, 189, 195, 196
Niacin, 196
No Child Left Behind (NCLB), 395
Noncategorical resource programs, 394
Noneducational interventions, *see also* Intervention in the education system
Nonphysical maltreatment in child maltreatment, 206
Nonverbal variations of therapy, 224
Nonviolent victimitzation of students, 23
Norepinephrine, 185
Norms, 66
Nosological classification (disease-oriented or clinical), 94–97, 101
Nutrition, 196

Observational learning, 308
　of appropriate behavior, 311
　of maladaptive behavior, 310–311
Obsessive-Compulsive Disorder, 116, 117
Oedipus complex, 221
Office of Special Education Programs, United States Department of Education, 46–47
One-disorder perspectives, 151
Operant conditioning, 55, 257–262
　and E&B disorders, 264–267
Operants, 257, 258
Operational definitions, 64–65
Oppositional Defiant Disorder, 110, 127
Oral stage, 217, 218
Organization and classification, 91–92
Other Health Impairments (OHI) education disability, 15–16, 124, 148
Outdoor challenges, 412
Outpatient treatment in mental health system, 412–413
Outward Bound, 416

Package behavioral interventions, 290
Panic Disorder, 116
Paraphrasing, 399
Parasuicides, 141
Parent training, 408
Parents
　advocacy of, 45, 47
　single, 48
Parole, 423
Partial hospitalization, 409–410
PATHS. *See* Promoting Alternative Thinking Strategies (PATHS) prevention program, 380
Patterns of emotional and behavior disorders, 106–146
　cognitive interventions for, 332–334
　connected problems, 130–141
　　Law-Breaking Behavior, 113, 133–137
　　Learning Difficulty, 137–138
　　Substance Misuse, 138–141
　　Suicidality, 141–144
　defining, 109–108
　drug treatments for, 417
　intervention for particular E&B disorders, 328–331
　key information, 109–110
　　1) description, 109
　　2) relation to classification and definition, 109

3) measurement, 108
4) prevalence, 108–109
5) course, 109
6) other considerations, 110
linkages between and among patterns, 131–133
patterns, 110–129
    Aggression, 112–116
    Anxiety, 114, 116–120
    Depression, 112, 121–124
    Impulsiveness, 112, 126–128
    Relationship Problem, 112, 128–131
target behavior definitions in, 268
PBS. *See* Positive behavior support
PDD-NOS. *See* Pervasive Developmental Disorder not otherwise specified
Pedigree analysis, 192
Peer court, 422–423
Peer influences, 182, 204
Peer nomination (referral), 68
Peer support in suicide, 3382
Pellagra, 196
*Pennsylvania Association for Retarded Children v. Commonwealth of Pennsylvania*, 47
Percentiles, 66
Performance versus acquisition, 304–305
Perinatal period, 196
Permitting-Controlling continuum in parental discipline styles, 202–203
Person-centered approach (Rogers), 231–236
Personal and schooling demographics, 18–21
Personal factors in reciprocal determinism, 309–310
Personality development stages in the psychodynamic model, 216–218
Personality measurement, 73–74
Personality structure in the psychodynamic model, 216, 223–225
Pervasive Developmental Disorders (PPDs), 108, 127, 171–176
    Asperger's Disorder, 171, 175
    autism spectrum disorders, 172
    Autistic Disorder, 171, 173–174
    Childhood Disintegrative Disorder, 171, 175
    description, 171–176

not otherwise specified (PDD-NOS), 171, 175
    prevalence issues, 175–176
    Rett's Disorder, 171, 175
    treatment issues, 176
    types of, 171
PET. *See* Positron emission tomography
Phallic stage, 217, 218, 221
Phases of schizophrenia, 163–164
Phenomenological approaches, 227
Philosophical issues in classification, 101
Philosophies, 17
Phobia, 117, 118
Physical abuse in child maltreatment, 206
Physical influences, 194–197
Physical neglect in child maltreatment, 206
Physical punishment, 199, 200
Physical trauma, 196, 197
Physiological assessment, 188–189
Physiological responses, 116–117
Piers-Harris Children's Self-Concept Scale, 71
Pioneer House, 53
Play therapy, 224
Pleasure needs in reality therapy approach, 237
PMHP. *See* Primary Mental Health Project
Points-and-levels system, 284–285, 286–287, 295–296, 400, 420–421
Positive approach to decreasing behavior, 282–283
Positive behavior support (PBS), 89
Positive practice interventions, 275–276
Positive psychotic symptoms in schizophrenia, 167
Positive regard, 229
Positive reinforcement, 259, 271
    via misallocated attention, 265–266
Positron emission tomography (PET), 188
Possession by spirits, 36, 37
Post-suicide crisis intervention, 384, 385
Postnatal risks, 196–197
Posttraumatic Stress Disorder (PTSD), 118, 118
Poverty, 24, 48, 105
Power needs, 225
    in reality therapy approach, 237

Precorrection, 281
Predictive validity, 65
Preferred activities, 273
Prehistoric viewpoints of E&B disorders, 36
Premack Principle, 273
Prenatal period, 195–196
Prereferral intervention, 82, 84, 388
Prevalence
    of E&B disorders, 14–17
    of mental disorders, 14
Preventing prevention, 390–391
Prevention, 232, 372–391, 406–408
    in classroom management, 232
Primary Mental Health Project (PMHP), 383
Primary prevention, 373–374, 376
Primary reinforcers in behavioral theory, 267
Probation, 405, 422
Prodrome phase in schizophrenia, 163
Professional journals (periodicals), 43
Professionals serving students with E&B disorders, 28
Prognosis, 109
    in extreme emotional and behavior disorders, 175
Program evaluation, assessment for, 91
Project Re-ED, 415
Projection, 219, 220
Projective personality assessment, 73–74
Promoting Alternative Thinking Strategies (PATHS) prevention program, 380, 408
Prosocial competencies, 383–384
Protective factors in child development, 188, 210
Proximal risk factors, 188
Psychiatric hospitalization, 405
Psychiatry, 146
Psychoanalysis, 52, 219–225
Psychodynamic model, 52–55, 218–297
    and children, 52–54
    intervention in, 227–230
        assessment, 228
        nonverbal variations, 230
        therapy, 228–230
    person-centered approach (Rogers), 233–236
    programs and curricula, 255–257
    psychoanalysis, 219–225
        causes of E&B disorder in, 222–225

Psychodynamic model (*cont'd*)
  conflict resolution, 224
  defense mechanisms, 222–224
  personality development
    stages, 220–222
  personality structure, 220,
    223–226
  summary of, 227
  theory (Freud), 52, 219–220
psychodynamic theories, 221–222
psychoeducational approach,
    242–252
  assessment, 244–245
  background and theory,
    242–244
  Conflict Cycle (Long), 242–244
  daily teaching and
    management, 247–249
  Life Space Crisis Intervention,
    249–252
  long-term goals of discipline,
    246
  scope of intervention, 245
  summary of, 253
  teacher characteristics, 245–246
  reality therapy approach (Glasser),
    237–241
  social discipline approach (Adler),
    224–227, 228
Psychodynamic perspective of E&B
  disorders, 8, 218–221
Psychodynamic theories, 52, 215–216,
  221–222
Psychoeducational approach, 53,
  242–252
Psychological models, 51–57
  behavioral model, 55–58
  psychodynamic model, 52–55
Psychosis, 220
Psychosocial influences, 110, 201–212
  community, 208–209
  family socialization, 201–208
    attachment, 202
    child maltreatment, 206–208
    discipline styles, 202–204
    disruptions to child-rearing, 204
    single parenting, 205–206
  media, 210–211
  peer influences, 182, 208
  schools, 209–210
  stress, 215–216
  *see also* Biological and
    psychosocial influences
Psychosocial intervention, 408

  *see also* Intervention in other
    systems
Psychosocial variables, 183
Psychotherapy, 408
  *see also* Intervention in other
    systems
Psychotic Disorders, 121, 161–171
  in children and adolescents,
    157–158, 161–164
  course, 165
  description, 157–164
  interventions, 167
  prevalence, 165
  psychoses and other mental
    disorders with psychotic
    symptoms, 165–168
  psychotic symptoms, 161–162
  relation to classification and
    definition, 169
  schizophrenia, 162–165, 166
Psychotic symptoms, 161–162, 192
  in schizophrenia, 163–164
Psychotropic drug therapy, 45, 405,
  408, 412–418
Public mental hospitals, 39–40
Public schools, separate, 400, 401
Punishment
  aversive, 279
  in behavioral theory, 264, 281
  forfeiture, 280
  physical, 199, 200

Questionable logic in classification, 101
Questionnaire, 68

Race-ethnic culture, 341–343
  classification of race-ethnic
    groups, 341
  cultural competence for a system
    of care, 430–431
  disorders vary across cultures and
    subcultures, 342
  normality is relative, 342
Ratings
  of multiple characteristics, 70,
    111, 124
  by others, 68–69
  by self, 71
Rational-Emotive Education (R-E
  Education), 332
Rational-Emotive (R-E) Therapy (Ellis),
  330–332
Reality therapy approach (Glasser),
  237–241

Reciprocal determinism, 300–310
Recreation services, 405
Referral by peers, 67–68
Referral by teachers, 67
Reflecting client's expressed
  feelings/thoughts/values, 230
Reforms in service to children with
  E&B disorder, 428–438
Regular class education environment,
  22, 393
Reinforcement in behavioral theory, 262
Relational aggression, 115
Relationship Problem pattern, 128–131
  cognitive interventions for, 334
  course of, 130–131
  description of, 128–129
  measurement of, 130
  other considerations, 131
  prevalence of, 130
  relation to classification and
    definition, 112, 129–130
  target behavior definitions in, 268
Relaxation, 299
Reliability, 65
  in applied behavior analysis, 273
Religion, 359–362
Religious beliefs, 431
Religious expression in public
  schools, 361
Renaissance viewpoint of E&B
  disorders, 38
Reported functioning measurement,
  67–74
Research, 7, 109
  in applied behavior analysis,
    273–274
  biological and psychosocial, 43
  scientific study of children, 41–43,
    303
Residential settings, 400, 401
  in juvenile system, 423
  in mental health system, 412,
    414–416, 422
  for people with disabilities, 45
  placements in, 406
Residual phase in schizophrenia, 163
Resilient children, 184
Resource room, 394
Respite care, 405, 418
Respondents in behavioral theory,
  261–262
Response cost, 276
Restitution, 405
  in reality therapy approach, 238

## Subject Index

Restrictive education settings, 400–401
Rett's Disorder, 167, 168, 171
Revenge goals, 229
Revised Children's Manifest Anxiety Scale, 71
Risk factors
  in child development, 183–184, 210
  by developmental stages, 406, 407
Roman era, 37
Rorschach Inkblot, 73–74
Routines in classroom management, 377
Rule of one-third, 16
Rules in classroom management, 377

SAED. *See* Scale for Assessing Emotional Disturbance
Salicytic acids, 196
SASS. *See* Skills for Academic and Social Success
Scale for Assessing Emotional Disturbance (SAED), 70, 84–85
Schedules in behavioral theory, 264–266
Scheduling in classroom management, 378
Schizoaffective Disorder, 161
Schizophrenia, 147, 162–165, 166
  and brain disorders, 189
  in children and adolescents, 148, 164–166
  diagnostic criteria for, 162–1563, 164
  diathesis-stress in, 208–209
  dopamine in, 185
  drug treatment for, 415
  genetic relationships, 193
  insidious and acute onset, 164
  phases of, 163
  positive and negative psychotic symptoms, 167–164
School gatekeeping programs for suicide, 384
Schools
  attendance and Anxiety pattern, 120
  behavior problems at, 23–24
  behavioral model in, 55–58
  continuum of education environments for students with ED, 21, 22, 24, 249, 373, 392
  discipline policy, 378
  the Engineered Classroom, 56–57
  lawful obligations in educating all children, 29
  liaison with, 408
  personal and schooling demographics, 18–21
  as psychosocial influence, 205–206
  removal from school (suspension), 24–25
  safety considerations, 378
  special education, 35, 41
  students with E&B disorders, 3–4, 17
  victimization in, 131–132
  *see also* Educational concerns; Special education
Science, 38
*Science and Human Behavior* (Skinner), 55
Scientific methods, 257
Scientific study of children, 41–43, 303
Scorer reliability, 65
Screening assessment, 84
Screening programs for Depression pattern, 124
Second Step prevention program, 379
Secondary prevention, 373–374, 376
Seizures, 188, 416
Selective prevention, 374–391, 386–394
  early intervention, 387
  Primary Mental Health Project (PMHP), 383
  suicide prevention, 387–388
Self-awareness of teachers, 241–242
Self-concept, 229
Self-Control Behavior Inventory, 250
Self-Control Curriculum (S-CC), 254, 255
Self-directed learning in reality therapy approach, 239
Self-efficacy, 307
Self-esteem building program, 330–331
Self-fulfilling prophecies, 100
Self-instruction, 317, 329
Self-management in behavior modification, 285–287
Self-monitoring, 286–287
Self-mutilation, 192
Self-rating scales, 116, 120
Self-reinforcement, 287
Self-reliance, 113
Self-report measurement methods, 116
Self-Report of Personality (SRP), 71, 79
Semistructured Clinical Interview for Children and Adolescents (SCICA) in ASEBA, 72
Separate classroom environment, 394–400
Separate public schools, 400, 401
Separation Anxiety Disorder, 117
Serotonin, 185
Service systems, 355
SES. *See* Socioeconomic status
Setting generalization, 283
Sexual abuse in child maltreatment, 202
Sexual drives, 216, 217
Shelter care settings, 405, 418
Simulated situations, 76–77
Single parenting, 48, 201–202
Single photon emission computed tomography (SPECT), 188
SIP. *See* Social information processing
Skills for Academic and Social Success (SASS), 329
Skillstreaming, 317–321, 333, 335
Skinner, B.F., 257
  *Science and Human Behavior*, 55
Social attention, 271–273
Social causation, 343–345
Social cognitive theory. *See* Modeling and social cognitive theory (Bandura)
Social context, 197
  *see also* Psychosocial influences
Social discipline approach (Adler), 224–227, 228
Social drift, 343, 345
Social information processing (SIP), 308–309
Social Phobia, 116, 127
Social problem-solving, 317–321, 379
Social skills, 126
Social skills training, 292–296
Social stress, 344
Social validity in applied behavior analysis, 273
Socialization, 197
Socially disadvantaged communities, 205
Societal concerns, 25–29
  poverty, 25–26
  in serving students with E&B disorders, 18–25
  treatment for E&B disorders, 26
  violence and crime, 26
Socioeconomic disadvantage, 205

Socioeconomic status (SES), 341, 342–343, 345, 431
Sociological perspective, 341–349
  assessment, 346–347
  intervention, 345–347
  race-ethnic culture, 341–343
  social causation, 344–346
    conflict theory, 344–346
    functionalism theory, 345
    labeling, 345–346
  social drift, 344
  socioeconomic status (SES), 342, 343–344, 346, 431
  summary of, 347
  theory, 341–346
Sociometric procedures, 68, 128
Special courts, 405
Special education, 35, 41
  and assessment in the IEP, 63, 82
  federal financial support for, 47
  and measurement concepts, 66
  service process as related to measurement, 82
  see also Schools
Special education profession, 45–46
Specific Phobia, 116
SPECT. See Single photon emission computed tomography
Spiritual beliefs, 431
Spirituality, 359–362
SRP. See Self-Report of Personality
SSBD. See Systematic Screening for Behavior Disorders
Stability reliability, 65
Stages in psychoanalytic theory, 216–218
Standardized measurement procedures, 65
Standardized tests, 67
Standards, deviations from, 11
Status offenses, 422
  see also Juvenile justice system
Stimulants, 412, 413, 414, 416
Stimulus generalization in behavioral theory, 268
Stress, 211–212
  diathesis-stress, 212–213
  social, 344
Stress (Conflict) Cycle, 238–240
Structured environment in the separate classroom, 395–396
Structured learning in Aggression Replacement Training (ART), 331

Students
  with disabilities, 47
  grading and evaluation of, 378
  IQ scores of, 134
  learning performance, 21–22
  numbers by age-groups with ED, 19
  percentage by race-ethnic groups with ED, 20
  placement of students, 249
  progress assessment of, 86–87
  referral assessment of, 81–83
  and school completion, 22
  see also Children; Educational concerns; Schools
Study skills in the separate classroom, 399
Subcultural differences, 431
Subcultures, 341, 342
Sublimation, 217
Substance Misuse, 23, 138–141
  cognitive interventions for, 334
  connections to E&B disorder, 137
  description of, 135–136
  other considerations, 138
  prevalence of, 136–137
  tolerance, 137
  types of, 135–136
Suicidality, 121, 141–144
  cognitive interventions for, 334
  connections to E&B disorder, 139
  description of, 141
  in homosexual adolescents, 143
  lethality of suicide acts, 141, 144
  misconceptions, 143–144
  other considerations, 142–144
  parasuicides, 143
  peer support, 384
  post-suicide crisis intervention, 384, 385
  precipitating risk factors, 143, 144
  predictors of, 143
  prevalence of, 141–142
  prevention of suicide, 383–384
  rates of, 142, 143
  school gatekeeping programs, 384
Superego, 216, 217, 221
Supernatural explanations, 36
Support organizations, 433–434
Survival-and-success behaviors in the separate classroom, 396, 397
Suspension from school, 23–24
Symptoms and signs, 93–94
System of care, 50, 406, 429–437
  core values, 431–435

  child-centered and family-focused, 431–433
  community based, 433–434
  culturally competent, 434–435
  definition and philosophy, 430
  development of, 435–436
  education in, 436
  service functions and representative services, 430
  see also Intervention in other systems
Systematic Screening for Behavior Disorders (SSBD), 67, 77, 80

Target-behavior recording, 74–76, 116, 120, 124, 128
Teacher effectiveness approach, 230
Teacher nomination (referral), 67
Teacher Report Form (TRF) in ASEBA, 70, 84, 99
Teachers
  attention from, 265
  as child advocates, 355
  Crisis/Helping, 249–250
  dyspedagogia, 134
  in psychoeducational approach, 241–242
  self-awareness of, 241–242
  in the separate classroom, 397
  of students with E&B disorders, 5–6
  supply of, 25
Teaching-Family (T-F) Model of intervention, 419–421
*Teaching Self-Control: A Curriculum for Responsible Behavior* (Henley), 251
Teaching techniques, 41, 291–292
Technical issues in classification, 101–102
Teen court, 422–423
Temperament, 213–214
Tertiary prevention, 373–374, 376
Tests, standardized, 67
Therapeutic foster care, 419
Therapeutic group homes, 419
Therapeutic milieu, 54, 409–410
Therapies
  nonverbal, 224
  in the psychodynamic model, 226–228
Thomas and Chess theory of temperament, 213–214
Timeout from reinforcement, 280, 281

Token economies, 288–289
  *see also* Points-and-levels systems
Tokens, 278
Tolerance in Substance Misuse, 140
Toxic substances, 196, 197
Transition skills in the separate classroom, 399–400
Trephining, 36
TRF. *See* Teacher's Report Form
Triggers, anger-provoking, 326
Twelve-step programs, 358–359
Twentieth century perspectives, 41–51
  child mental health, 44–45
  criticism of society's response to children with E&B disorder, 48–51
  developmental psychopathology, 43
  drug treatment, 45
  legal developments, 46–48
  litigation-legislation-litigation cycle, 48
  mental hygiene movement, 44
  National Agenda, 50–51
  professional journals (periodicals), 43
  scientific study of children, 41–43
  special education profession, 45–46
  *see also* Historical perspectives
Twin comparisons, 193–194
Two-disorder perspectives, 151

*Unclaimed Children* (Knitzer), 49, 424–425
Unconditional care, 428
Unconditionality, 229
Unconscious, 216, 221, 222
United States Constitution, due process, 27
United States Department of Education
  Office of Special Education Programs, 46–47
  religious expression in public schools, 361
Universal prevention, 374, 376–382
  classroom management, 377–378
    grading and evaluation, 378
    opportunities to respond, 378
    routines, 377
    rules, 377
    scheduling, 378
  conflict resolution, 380–382
  drug prevention education, 382
  prosocial competencies, 379–380
  school management, 378
    discipline policy, 378
    safety considerations, 378
Usability of classification measures, 101–102

Validity, 65
  in applied behavior analysis, 273
Values and spiritual perspective, 357–368
  character education, 359, 360
  circle of courage program, 362–367
  moral reasoning, 358
  religion, 359–362
  religious expression in public schools, 363
  spirituality and intervention, 359–362
  summary of, 341–342
  twelve-step programs, 360–361
Variable-interval schedule, 261
Variable-ratio schedule, 261
Verbal and covert behavior, 264
Vicarious effects, 304–305
Vicarious emotional arousal, 307
Victimization in school, 134
Victor ("wild boy"), 41
Violence and crime, 25
Violent behavior, 23
Vitamins, 196
Vocational education, 399
Vocational services, 405

Weapons, 23
Whites, 341
Wilderness experiences, 412
World War II, 45
Wraparound, 428

York Retreat, 39
Youth court, 422–423
Youth Self-Report in ASEBA, 71, 99